Sophistication & Simplicity

The Life and Times of the Apple II Computer

Steven Weyhrich

VARIANT
PRESS

VARIANT PRESS
3404 Parkin Avenue
Winnipeg, Manitoba
R3R 2G1

Copyright (C) 2013 by Variant Press
All rights reserved, including the right of
reproduction in whole or in part in any form.

Designed by Hayden Sundmark

Manufactured in Canada

Apple, Apple II, and Macintosh are trademarks of Apple
Incorporated. Apple does not sponsor, authorize,
or endorse this book.

Library and Archives Canada Cataloguing in Publication

Weyhrich, Steven, 1956-, author
Sophistication & simplicity :
the life and times of the Apple II computer / Steven Weyhrich.

Includes bibliographical references and index.
ISBN 978-0-9868322-7-7 (bound)

1. Apple II (Computer)–History. 2. Apple Computer, Inc.–
History. I. Title. II. Title: Sophistication & simplicity.

TK7889.A66W39 2013   621.39'16   C2013-903803-5

Acknowledgements

A project of this magnitude did not happen without a significant amount of help from many, many people. All of them are owed a great debt of thanks, but I want to mention some of the most important here.

First of all, thanks to my wonderful wife, Kim, who has had to deal with an Apple II fanatic as long as she has known me. She has had to put up with my focus on this project, both now and over twenty years ago when I first began to create it. You are the best!

Secondly, another large group for whom applause is due are those many, many people who worked so hard over the years to bring about all of the things that made the Apple II what it was. This includes the people who worked on the Apple II at Apple Computer, especially when it was not popular at the company. It also includes the companies who made hardware and software that made this computer so amazing and versatile. Each of those companies was born out of a passion to bring something special to the platform, and each of them made a difference.

Also, I want to thank two people from the Department of Pharmacy at University Hospital, of the University of Nebraska Medical Center in Omaha. To Wayne Young, who submitted a purchase order to obtain a "calculator" called an Apple II Plus back in 1981 (because only the University computer department was allowed to purchase a computer), and who later allowed me, a medical student, to explore and learn about this "calculator" when it was not being used for something else. Thanks also to his successor, James Dubé, who allowed me ongoing access to the Apple IIe in the Drug Information Center (along with its 300-baud acoustic modem), and who hired me while I was in my residency in 1983 to revise and update an Apple II program that was used to print labels for IV meds used in the pharmacy. His trust and generosity brought my funds to the point where I could purchase my own Apple IIc.

Thanks also to:

Al Tommervik and Margot Comstock for creating the amazing magazine, *Softalk*. What fun that was, from start to end!

Tom Weishaar, whose "DOSTalk" column in *Softalk* led me to his great newsletter, *Open-Apple*. His clear style of explaining complex topics in simple language taught me more about the Apple II than almost any other publication.

John Ranney and Steve Corlett of the Metro Apple Computer Hobbyists (MACH) in Omaha, who allowed me to participate in the group newsletter, and gave me a chance to try my hand at writing.

The GEnie A2 Roundtable, the staff and members whose incredible brain trust provided me with the access to knowledge about the Apple II and its story, and made this history possible in the first place.

Tom Hoover, whose *GEnie Master* offline reader made it possible for me to really participate in the A2 Roundtable, keep up with all of the conversations that it carried, and archive the important information.

Doug Cuff, the editor of *GenieLamp A2*, who was responsible for helping me polish my words in the early versions of this history.

Erik Kloeppel and Jawaid Bazyar, who started Hypermall.com in 1995, and thought a three-year-old history of the Apple II might make a cool web site, back when I didn't even know what a web site was.

Everyone associated with KansasFest, Syndicomm, and *Juiced.GS*, from their respective beginnings to the present. All of you are the real torchbearers who maintained an organized presence for the Apple II when much of the rest of the world had abandoned it.

Ken Gagne, who made me realize that there actually might be a place for a printed version of this history, and who with Andy Molloy and many, many others have put up with my incessant questions and requests for review.

All of you are the ones who made this book possible, and you all are owed my deepest gratitude.

Oh, and thanks also to Steve Wozniak. It was your foresight in creating a computer that was eminently hackable and expandible that made this all possible in the first place.

Table of Contents

Acknowledgements III
Table of Contents V
Introduction VII
Chapter 1 - Igniting the Flame 1
Chapter 2 - A Company Built From a Circuit Board 13
Chapter 3 - II is Better than 1 27
Chapter 4 - The BASICs 47
Chapter 5 - Concentric Circles of Magnetic Data 55
Chapter 6 - Spinning Chaos into Order 63
Chapter 7 - Homebrew Community in Print 77
Chapter 8 - Connections and Video 89
Chapter 9 - Accessing the World 95
Chapter 10 - Online Origins 101
Chapter 11 - More than a Plus 115
Chapter 12 - Pascal Proliferation 125
Chapter 13 - DOS Developments 133
Chapter 14 - Boosting Performance 141
Chapter 15 - The Apple II Abroad 145
Chapter 16 - Der Apfel II in der Presse 151
Chapter 17 - Some Assembly Required 159
Chapter 18 - Music and Speech 169
Chapter 19 - Second Wave 173
Chapter 20 - E for Enhanced 193
Chapter 21 - DOS Gets Professional 205
Chapter 22 - "Will Someone Please Tell Me What an Apple Can Do?" . . . 215
Chapter 23 - Bits to Ink 231
Chapter 24 - Compact and Powerful 239

Chapter 25 - The Tower of Babel	253
Chapter 26 - Improving Your Memory	265
Chapter 27 - The Juggernaut of Integration	271
Chapter 28 - Online Boom and Bust	287
Chapter 29 - Input Devices	305
Chapter 30 - Send in the Clones	317
Chapter 31 - Robots and Clocks	331
Chapter 32 - The Next Generation	339
Chapter 33 - Expanding Storage	353
Chapter 34 - DOS Gets Sophisticated	365
Chapter 35 - Hyperactivity	377
Chapter 36 - Magazines on the Newsstand	381
Chapter 37 - Black Hat Contagions	389
Chapter 38 - BASIC Evolves	401
Chapter 39 - Hardware for the Next Generation	409
Chapter 40 - Ahead of their Time: Digital Magazines	419
Chapter 41 - Latter Day Languages	441
Chapter 42 - Small Publisher Magazines	447
Chapter 43 - New Horizons for AppleWorks	465
Chapter 44 - Falling Out of Favor	475
Chapter 45 - Online Assimilation	493
Chapter 46 - Reunions	507
Chapter 47 - The History of this History	517
Appendix A - Software Hits	521
Appendix B - Apple II Timeline	533
Index	551

Introduction

The story of Apple, Inc. has been covered extensively in the years since the Apple-1 was assembled in Jobs' family garage in Los Altos, California. Decades later, the company and its products enjoyed a resurgence of popularity and profit that pushed it past other computer companies into the lead. Previously, Apple had been stuck with an exceedingly low market share ever since the IBM PC, powered by Microsoft's early operating system, legitimized the use of computers at the desks of office workers around the world. With the inroads Apple made into the consumer electronics arena with the iPod, and its re-invention (again) of the personal computer with the touch-enabled iPhone and iPad, Apple helped make computer technology so simple that two-year-olds and 102-year-olds could use them.

But Apple would never have survived were it not for the amazing popularity of its original hit product, the Apple II. Though it went through revisions and modifications, the Apple IIe that was discontinued in November 1993 was esssentially the same computer that Steve Wozniak created as an upgrade from the Apple-1. The Apple II was a major and sustained success, fueled by its flexibility and expandability, and its profits set Apple on the course to enter the Fortune 500 by 1983—faster than any previous company in history. It also financed the research and development that allowed Apple to misstep its way through the Apple III and Lisa projects, and to keep the Macintosh and its revisions going for several years until it became self-sustaining.

Every other historical look at Apple and its successes during its years of operation has focused on the company as a whole, usually emphasizing the drama involving its charismatic co-founder, Steve Jobs. Both Jobs and Wozniak have had more than one biography published, and the various eras of Apple corporate history have been detailed in articles and books. In all of these stories, the Apple II appears, but only as a supporting character, and only for a brief time on the stage.

One of the first advertisements for the Apple II stated, "Simplicity is the ultimate sophistication." Though not attributed in that ad, this was a quote by Leonardo da Vinci. It certainly applied to what the Apple II brought to the personal computing landscape when it was released. It displayed simplicity in that it required little to set up and use; all the user had to do was to attach a monitor and cassette player for storage, and it was ready to go. But underneath that simplicity was the sophistication of a computer that could be fully expanded to 48K of RAM.

The narrative told in these pages focuses on the Apple II computer as the main character, in its various models and revisions, and branches out into the supporting industry that grew up around it—from hardware and software products, to publications and online services that connected users to each other. Though Apple as a company also plays a significant role, the Apple II itself is the central figure on the stage. This book also tells the story of what happened with the Apple II and its community after the computer was finally removed from active production in 1993, as fans old and young continued to find new things to do with Steve Wozniak's most famous invention.

Apple came up with a phrase that they used as a marketing gimmick when the Apple IIc was introduced. The Apple II community co-opted the phrase as a rallying cry during the years when Apple ignored their platform. It was still in use nearly 30 years later among enthusiasts of what has become a vintage and valued piece of hardware.

That phrase? *Apple II Forever.*

> The information presented in this book is both historical and technical. When you see this symbol, it means this section may only interest collectors or programmers.
>
> Those who enjoy this level of detail will note this area as a place to read more closely. If such technical information does not interest the reader, feel free to skip it.

CHAPTER 1

Igniting the Flame

The Santa Clara Valley south of the San Francisco Bay in California was for many years known primarily for its many fruit orchards. During the 1960s, however, the towns in the valley became home to technology corporations. They began to make use of semiconductor chips (made with silicon) that were increasingly being used in electronics devices. The massive growth of these businesses resulted in the area being dubbed "Silicon Valley".

Its importance in the development of the microcomputer is significant, not because of a lack of activity elsewhere in the world, but due to the concentration of similar businesses in the same limited geographic area. A company called Shockley Semiconductor Laboratory began to manufacture transisitors there in the 1950s. Another called Fairchild Semiconductor continued development of the integrated circuit (a single component that had many smaller electronics parts within it). Intel started in 1968 and furthered the research that had preceded it. Other related businesses were created, and they fed off each other's innovations and developments.

In this environment, the engineers who worked at these companies also put down roots and raised families. If a young man or woman (though men seemed to predominate in the industry) wanted to learn about this aspect of technology, it was available no further away than the dinner table or a next-door neighbor.

WOZ

The son of an engineer, Steve Wozniak grew up in Sunnyvale, California, in the Santa Clara Valley. Like many other children who lived there in the 1960s, his father exposed him to electronics and how things worked. Young Steve was an avid reader, and learned about electronics through books and technical journals that his father obtained for him. His reading soon branched into the growing field of computers, and he taught himself about flow charts and programming logic.

In the sixth grade he began to participate in science fairs, eventually coming up with a computer project to enter in the fair. It was not sophisticated—merely a device that used a transistor circuit to add or subtract numbers—but it won the top award for electronics that year in the entire bay area. Wozniak was fascinated with what computers could do, though he rarely had the opportunity to get his hands on a real computer. He read books about how computers were built, and designed several of his own on paper. Since he did not have the resources to build these more sophisticated computer projects, he occupied himself by refining his layout on paper, looking for ways to do the same thing with fewer parts.

When he started college at the University of Colorado in 1968, Wozniak had the opportunity to take his first computer class. He immersed himself in learning all the details of FORTRAN, the computer language being taught in most computer departments at the time, and ran multiple programs of his own. He personally used so much computer time that he single-handedly ran his class five times over its budget for the year. The result was that he was put on probation for computer abuse.

The next school year, Wozniak stayed back home in California and attended De Anza Community College in Cupertino. He continued designing and re-designing computers on paper, based on the technical manuals for computers made by Hewlett-Packard, Digital Equipment, and others. His focus was still in finding ways to make them work with fewer parts, which would make them less expensive. However, just as before college, he did not have an opportunity to actually use these computers.

Having no hardware didn't stop him from also learning how to create software. Like his hardware designs, he simply did it on paper. Not only did he write software in the machine code unique to that computer, but he went a step further and wrote his own FORTRAN compiler for his non-existant computer, since that would make it even easier to use.

Wozniak and his friend Allen Baum were soon employed writing programs in FORTRAN at a local company. The association ultimately resulted in Woz (as he was known to his friends) being able to obtain free samples of parts to build his first real computer. Reluctant to ask for large numbers of parts, he used his talent in minimalist design to create it with the few available to him. Though it only had 256 bytes (characters) of memory, he was thrilled to have finally built a computer.

Another of Woz's friends who was still in high school, Bill Fernandez, helped assemble the computer. Cragmont cream soda was their beverage of choice while they worked, and this resulted in it being dubbed the "Cream Soda Computer". It was not much more sophisticated than a calculator, and required entry of data via switches, with the results displayed in binary in lights. It resulted in a little writeup in the local newspaper, althought it started smoking when the reporter stepped on wire and caused it to short out.

Not only did he have an interest in electronics and computers, Wozniak was well known by his friends for his sense of humor and enjoyment of practical jokes. While a senior in high school he had built a ticking box, made it look like an actual bomb, and put it in another student's locker. At the University of Colorado he built a hand-held jammer that would interfere with television reception in his dorm and in the lecture rooms, changing their picture to static. Fernandez knew of these and other exploits, and told Woz he knew someone at school with a similar penchant for pulling pranks. Like Woz, this person was also interested in building electronics devices. Hernandez arranged for this friend to meet Wozniak. The friend's name was Steve Jobs.

JOBS

Jobs attended the same high school from which Woz had graduated. However, since he was four and a half years younger, they had never crossed paths before. Unlike Wozniak, whose father was an engineer, Jobs' adopted father was a machinist who had a hobby of repairing automobiles. They lived in Mountain View, California, also in the Santa Clara Valley. The tract home in which they lived had been designed by a real estate developer who made simple homes affordable by most anyone. The design had an open floor plan and lots of glass (including floor-to-ceiling glass walls).

Though his father did not know much about electronics, the growth of the electronics industry in the valley provided neighbors who did. They even provided him with parts to build simple projects. Eventually he and his father obtained several Heathkits—electronics projects in a kit—and built them together.

One of his neighbors enrolled him into the Hewlett-Packard Explorers Club. In that club, Jobs decided to build a frequency counter. To obtain the parts, he called up HP CEO Bill Hewlett who agreed to give him the parts, along with a job in the plant that made the frequency counters sold by HP. Jobs also visited flea markets filled with electronics leftovers, learning to haggle for electronics parts the way his father had done for automotive parts.

As a senior, Jobs had the opportunity to take a popular class in electronics. He tended to work on his own projects, rather than going along with the rest of the class, and infuriated the teacher with his independent methods. When he needed a part that he didn't have, he called a manufacturer called Burroughs in Detroit, Michigan (collect), and asked for the part as a sample for a new product he was designing. It arrived by airfreight. Jobs justified this by stating that the company could afford both the part and the phone call, and he could not.

During his last year and a half of high school, Jobs also followed the crowd of his generation, trying to expand his mind by experimenting with drugs—first with marijuana and later trying out LSD, and even strange diets.

THE DUO

When Jobs and Wozniak met in 1971, they hit it off right away due to a shared interest in pranks and electronics. They also found they were both fans of the same kind of music, and together spent time looking for bootleg tapes of Bob Dylan concerts. Woz impressed Jobs, because he was the first person who understood more about electronics than he did.

Though they had some similarities, there were clearly differences between the two. Jobs was more outgoing, where Woz was almost painfully shy. Unlike Jobs, who wouldn't necessarily worry about the truth if it got him what he wanted, Wozniak strictly followed one of his father's rules about never telling a lie. Also, he did not feel the need to take the path of experimenting with drugs or unusual diets. Despite these differences, the two got along, and even worked together on some pranks at Jobs' high school.

Their first real financial collaboration happened that same year, before Wozniak started his third year of college. He had come across a magazine article about "blue boxes", electronic devices that generated tones that could take control of a toll-free telephone number and use it to dial any other number for free. Wozniak told Jobs about it, and they began to research what was needed to simulate the touch-tone system used by the telephone company.

Armed with this information, the two Steves bought the parts necessary to build tone generators of the proper frequencies needed to match the requirements of the telephone switching system. Woz was able to build a box that worked as was described in the magazine, and Jobs used a frequency counter that he had built to help calibrate it. They were ecstatic when they found that it actually worked. Jobs suggested that they build a number of the blue boxes and sell them, and for a time the pair was in business together. All told, they built and sold about one hundred of the boxes, building them for $40 and selling them for $150.

Steve Wozniak's blue box, at the Computer History Museum – Photo credit: Charles T. Lau

After that school year, Wozniak was unable to return to college. An accident had totaled his car, and he had to go to work to earn money to buy a new one. Through the help of his friend Allen Baum, who was working as an intern at Hewlett-Packard, Woz was able to get a job at the same company. He began there in January 1973, designing scientific calculators. He loved the environment, loved working with the engineers, and decided he wanted to do this kind of work for the rest of his life. He certainly did not want to get involved in management, and his time at HP solidified this view.

While working at Hewlett-Packard, his interests drifted away from computers as he focused on the electronics needed to build calculators and make them work. He did not think of computers again for over a year, until he came across the game *Pong* at a local bowling alley. He was fascinated by the game. It involved a white square bouncing left and right on a television screen, with a knob on each side used by players to control a vertical bar that moved up and down. The player had to maneuver the vertical bar to cause the square to bounce back to the other side. If one player missed, the other player scored a point.

As Wozniak played the game a few times, he realized that he could build something just like it. His past interests in electronics had included television, and he knew how a digital circuit could create a picture on a television screen. Using this knowledge, he created his own home version of Pong, adding the feature of displaying letters on the screen.

During this time, Steve Jobs was on his own journey. After his graduation from high school in 1972, he had started college, but was not enjoying it. When Woz came for a visit, Jobs complained to him about the classes he had to take that he didn't care about. Jobs decided to drop out of college, but didn't leave. Instead of taking those boring required classes, he began to audit classes that interested him, including a course on calligraphy and typefaces. He managed to talk the dean into allowing him to stay in an empty dorm room, and went to a local Hare Krishna temple for weekly free meals. A consequence of these visits was an increased interest in Eastern philosophy and Zen Buddhism.

In early 1974, Jobs returned to his parent's home and started looking for work. He saw an ad for Atari, Inc., a company founded in 1972 by engineer Nolan Bushnell. He crashed Atari headquarters and told them he would not leave until they gave him a job. Rather than calling the police, he was hired. Jobs threw himself into the work. Sometimes he stayed up all night on a project, and could be found the next morning sleeping under a desk.[1] He was able to come up with designs for graphics in some of their games, and appreciated the simplicity and focus of those games.

One of the draftsmen Jobs met while at Atari was Ron Wayne. Wayne had previously been involved in funding some businesses, and Jobs tried to convince him to join him in a business together to build and market a slot machine. Wayne declined the offer, but was impressed with the energy and insight of Jobs.

---

1 Sumra, Husain, "Atari Founder Nolan Bushnell on Steve Jobs at Atari and Finding the Next Jobs", *MacRumors*, February 1, 2013 <http://www.macrumors.com/2013/02/01/atari-founder-nolan-bushnell-on-steve-jobs-at-atari-and-finding-the-next-jobs/>, retrieved August 4, 2013.

Jobs' interest in Eastern religion blossomed, and in mid-1974 Jobs decided he wanted to go to India to visit a guru. He managed to talk an Atari executive into sending him to Europe to help implement a fix for their games there (they were not functioning properly on the European voltage standards), and from there he would find his way to India. Jobs took a friend from college, Dan Kottke, on the trip, and spent seven months searching for enlightenment. Upon his return he continued his search for himself, but eventually made his way back to his former positional at Atari.

The Pong game that had so interested Wozniak was created at Atari. After the success of that game, the company had continued work on other games. In 1975, Nolan Bushnell devised a successor to Pong that could be played by a single player. He envisioned having the moveable paddle at the bottom of the screen, with the ball bouncing up and down against rows of horizontal blocks. Each hit on a block would knock it out, and send the ball back down to the player's paddle. The goal was to clear away all of the blocks, and, like Pong, not miss the ball when it bounced back. The game was to be called *Breakout*.

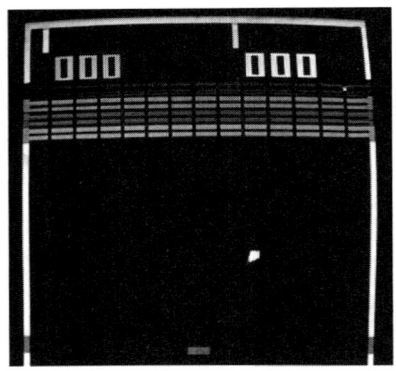

Atari *Breakout* screen shot. The colored bars were actually just colored transparancies placed on the screen, to simulate color; on the screen it was only monochrome – Photo credit: The Dot Eaters <www.thedoteaters.com>

Wozniak had previously visited Jobs at Atari and showed his Pong knock-off. It impressed the other engineers there, including Bushnell and Breakout project manager Al Alcorn. Bushnell asked Jobs to work on Breakout, in particular wanting to reduce the number of components used in the game. Bushnell knew that Jobs would get Wozniak involved in the project, since part reduction was his passion. He offered Jobs a bonus for getting it made with fewer than fifty chips in the final design.

Wozniak threw himself into the project and worked around the clock to get it done. He designed the circuitry and Jobs put the components on the circuit board. They finished it in only four days, and the final design had only 45 chips. However, what Woz had come up with was something that Atari could not easily manufacture; in fact, the other engineers there had problems understanding how it worked. Alcorn ultimately had to have one of his other engineers redesign the game so that it could be built in large quantities. That version had over one hundred chips on it.[2]

---

2 Kent, Steven L, "Breakout", *ArcadeHistory* <www.arcade-history.com/?n=breakout&page=detail&id=3397>, retrieved August 7, 2013.

EARLY MICROCOMPUTERS

Outside of the world of the two Steves, there were others who were fascinated with the potential of computers, and just like Wozniak, they wanted one of their own. Most systems available to use were like the one Woz used at the University of Colorado: a mainframe computer that required a user to present a stack of punched cards to a technician who actually operated the machine, who would then deliver back to the user a printout of the results. Sometimes a smaller computer system would allow a user to actually sit at the console and interactively run a program, fix the bugs, and then run it again, bypassing the intrusive requirement of submitting the program to a trained computer operator. This improved the immediacy of using the computer, but even these smaller computers (such as Digital Equipment Corporation's PDP series) were far too large and expensive for anyone to actually have in their homes as a "personal" computer.

Despite these hurdles, there was still a desire for a computer that was small enough and inexpensive enough to actually own. The change that made it possible to create one of these small machines was the development by Intel in 1971 of the first programmable microprocessor chip, the 4004. This chip could manage only four bits of data at a time, and was originally designed for the Japanese company Busicom to be used in a desktop calculator, the Busicom 141-PF. In an attempt to recover some of the development costs, Intel decided to advertise the chip for general use in the fall of 1971 in *Electronics News*. Meanwhile, some Intel engineers had begun work on an 8-bit version of the 4004, the 8008, which was twice as powerful and would actually approach the ability to function as an adequate central processing unit (CPU) for a stand-alone computer.[3]

By 1972, the Intel 8008 was available for purchase and experimentation. It was somewhat difficult to work with, and could address only 16K of memory, but there were several small computers that were designed around it. The first computer that made use of the 8008 was the Micral N, designed by François Gernelle. Running at a clock speed of 500 kHz (0.5 MHz), it was sold in 1973 by the French company R2E for $1,750, fully assembled, but did not have any impact in the U.S. In 1974, SCELBI Computer Consulting (SCELBI stood for "SCientific, ELectronic, and BIological") began to sell a microcomputer called the SCELBI-8H. It was available as a kit for $565, and could also be purchased fully assembled. The first advertisement for the SCELBI-8H appeared in the March 1974 issue of the amateur radio magazine, QST.[4,5] However, it had

---

3   Freiberger, Paul and Michael Swaine, *Fire In The Valley* (Berkley, Osborne/McGraw-Hill, 1984), 14.
4   Manes, Stephen and Paul Andrews, *Gates* (New York, Doubleday, 1993), 65.
5   Veit, Stan, *Stan Veit's History Of The Personal Computer* (Asheville, North Carolina, WorldComm, 1993), 11.

limited distribution, did not make a profit for the company, and due to the designer's health problems it didn't go very far.

Another 8008 computer available the same year was the Mark-8. This computer appeared on the cover of the July 1974 issue of *Radio-Electronics*, and was available as a kit. To build it, a hobbyist had to send in $5 for the plans to the kit. Also available were the printed circuit boards used in assembling the kit, and the 8008 processor from Intel, which cost only $120 by that time. Although it was a difficult kit to complete, about 10,000 manuals were sold and about 2,000 circuit board sets were completed, and newsletters and small user groups appeared around the country.[6]

SCELBI-8H Computer – Photo credit: Curtis

In addition to the above machines, other enterprising engineers began to look at ways the 8008 could be used. In Redmond, Washington, Paul Allen convinced a hacker friend, Bill Gates, to join him in writing a BASIC interpreter for this new processor to use in a simple computer circuit that he had designed. They formed their first business venture, a company called Traf-O-Data, to process traffic information using his computer.[7] Although not a success, the effort was a foundation for the role they would play in the future development of the home computer.

Mark 8 Minicomputer – Photo credit: Bryan Blackburn

BREAKTHROUGH

In 1974 Intel released the 8080, an enhanced 8-bit processor that at a speed of 2 MHz was ten times faster than the 8008. The 8080 addressed some of the shortcomings of the 8008, increased to 64K the memory it was capable of addressing, and generally made it more capable of acting as a CPU for a small computer. It was Intel's expectation that these integrated circuits might be usable for calculators, or possibly for use in controlling traffic lights or other automated machinery. As with the 4004 and 8008, they didn't particularly expect that anyone would actually try to create a computer using these chips. But there was a strong desire for a computer to use at home, free of

---

6   Manes, Stephen and Paul Andrews. *Gates* (New York, Doubleday), 65.
7   Freiberger, Paul and Michael Swaine, *Fire In The Valley* (Berkley, Osborne/McGraw-Hill, 1984), 22-23.

the restrictions of the punched-card mainframe environment, and talented engineers began to find ways to make use of Intel's new invention.

During the latter part of 1974, a company called MITS (Micro Instrumentation Telemetry Systems) was in dire straits due to, of all things, one of its most successful products. Ed Roberts started the company in 1969, and he originally sold control electronics for model rocketry. With the new availability of sophisticated electronics in the early 1970s, MITS grew in size and was doing a very profitable business selling electronic calculators, both as kits and pre-built. However, in 1972 Texas Instruments decided to not only produce the integrated circuit chips but also build the calculators that used those chips, at a substantial discount from what it cost their commercial customers, like MITS. Roberts saw his calculator inventory become less and less valuable, and finally he found it difficult to sell them even below the cost of making them. This put his formerly successful business deeply in debt. He desperately needed a new product to help him recover from these losses.

At the same time that MITS was looking for something to revive the company, *Popular Electronics* magazine was looking for a computer construction article that would exceed the Mark-8 computer project that had appeared on the July 1974 *Radio-Electronics* cover. Roberts began to design a computer that would use Intel's new microprocessor, and with a special deal he was able to make with Intel he would be able to supply the computer as a kit, along with the 8080, for only a little more than the cost of the chip by itself.

This project appeared on the cover of the January 1975 issue of *Popular Electronics* magazine. Roberts and the editor, Les Solomon, decided to call the computer the

First announcement of the Altair 8000
– Photo credit: Popular Electronics, January 1975

"Altair 8800". It measured 18-inches deep by 17 inches wide by 7 inches high, and it came standard with all of 256 bytes of memory. Called the "World's First Minicomputer Kit to Rival Commercial Models", the Altair 8800 sold for $395 (or $498 fully assembled).

MITS hoped that they would get about four hundred orders for the computer, trickling in over the two months that the two-part article would be printed. This would supply the money MITS needed in order to buy the parts to send to people ordering the kits (this was a common method used in those days "bootstrapping" a small electronics business). This "trickle" of orders would also give MITS time to establish a proper assembly line for packaging the kits. However, they misjudged the burning desire of *Popular Electronics'* readers to build and operate their own computer. MITS received four hundred orders—in a single afternoon—and in three weeks it had taken in $250,000, eliminating the company's debt.[8]

The *Popular Electronics* article was a bit exuberant in the way the Altair 8800 was described. They called it "a full-blown computer that can hold its own against sophisticated minicomputers now on the market… The Altair 8800 is not a 'demonstrator' or souped-up calculator… [it] is a complete system." The article had an inset that listed some possible applications for the computer, stating, "the Altair 8800 is so powerful, in fact, that many of these applications can be performed simultaneously." Among the possible uses listed were an automated control for a ham station, a digital clock with time zone conversion, an autopilot for planes and boats, a navigation computer, a brain for a robot, a pattern-recognition device, and a printed matter-to-Braille converter for the blind.[9] Many of these features would begin to be possible by the end of the twentieth century, but in 1975 they were excessively optimistic expectations, just like the claim that it would be possible to carry out these tasks simultaneously. The exaggeration by the authors of the *Popular Electronics* article can perhaps be excused due to their excitement in being able to offer a computer that *anyone* could own and use. All this was promised from a computer that came "complete" with 256 bytes of memory (expandable if you could afford it) and no keyboard, display monitor, or storage device.

The success of the Altair overwhelmed MITS in many ways. The hunger for the personal computer made people do crazy things. One person was so anxious to get his Altair working that he couldn't wait for phone help; he drove out to Albuquerque, New Mexico (the home of MITS) and parked his RV right next to the building, running in for help when he needed it. Another enthusiastic person sent MITS a check for $4000, ordering one of everything in their catalog, only to have much of it refunded with an apologetic note that most of these projects had not yet been designed.

All of this excitement was somewhat tempered by the fact that when the Altair 8800 was completed, in its base form it could not do much. One could enter a tiny program a single byte at a time, in binary, through tiny toggle switches on the front panel, and read the output, again in binary, from the lights on the front panel. This novelty wore out quickly. So, to do something useful with the Altair it was essential to add plug-in boards to expand it.

---

8 Levy, Steven, *Hackers: Heroes Of The Computer Revolution* (New York, Dell Publishing Co., Inc, 1984), 187-192.
9 Roberts, H. Edward and William Yates, "Altair 8800 Minicomputer, Part 1", *Popular Electronics* (Jan 1975), 33, 38. The article is interesting also in some of the terminology that is used. The Altair is described as having "256 eight-bit words" of RAM. Apparently, the term "byte" was either not yet in common use, or the authors were not familiar with proper terminology.

MITS could not reliably meet the demand for these boards (their 4K RAM board had problems), and so an entire industry grew up to help make hardware (and software) for the Altair. Examples of these additions included a paper-tape reader (useful for loading and saving programs), a Teletype (which worked as a keyboard, printer, and paper-tape read/write unit all in one), a keyboard, and a video display (often called a "TV Typewriter", after a 1973 *Radio-Electronics* article of the same name). Eventually it became common to use a cassette tape for both loading and saving programs, since it was inexpensive and cassette recorders were easily available.

The difficulty MITS had in supplying the demand for its computers also led to the creation of other similar computers that used the 8080.[10] These usually used Altair's 100-pin hardware bus (a protocol for circuit boards to communicate with the microprocessor, later known popularly as the S-100 bus) and so were compatible with most of the Altair boards.

The IMSAI 8080 was marketed to businesses and was built as a sturdier alternative to the Altair. Polymorphic Systems sold the Poly-88, also based on the Intel 8080. Processor Technology's Sol-20 computer came out in 1977 and did one better than many of these, by putting the keyboard and video display card in the same case, as well as using the Altair-style S-100 bus for add-on boards. Other computers released in 1975 that enjoyed limited success were some based on the Motorola 6800 processor, such as the Altair 680 (also from MITS), the M6800 (Southwest Technical Products), and the Sphere 1, which came complete with keyboard and monitor. One company, Microcomputer Associates, sold a kit called the Jupiter II, based on a new processor called the 6502 from MOS Technology.[11, 12]

At this time, in the mid-1970s, the market for microcomputers was populated by hobbyists—those who didn't mind getting out a soldering iron to wire something together to make the computer work. After the computer was actually operational, it was still necessary to either create a program in assembly language or enter a program written by someone else. Those who were fortunate enough to have enough memory to run a programming language known as BASIC ("Beginner's All-purpose Symbolic Instruction Code") had a little easier time creating and using programs. It was also helpful to have a device to simplify input of the program, either a keyboard or a paper-tape reader. It was an era of having tools that were good enough for the home experimenter, but completely unuseable by the average person.

---

10 Smarte, Gene and Andrew Reinhardt, "15 Years of Bits, Bytes, and Other Great Moments", *BYTE* (Sep 1990), 370-371.
11 Manes, Stephen and Paul Andrews, *Gates*, (New York, Doubleday, 1993), 65.
12 Freiberger, Paul and Michael Swaine, *Fire In The Valley*, (Berkley, Osborne/McGraw-Hill, 1984), 128-129

TIMELINE

Wozniak charged with "computer abuse" – *1969*

Cream Soda Computer – *1970*

Wozniak and Jobs meet – *1971*

Intel 4004 – *November 1971*

Woz & Jobs selling blue boxes – *1972*

Intel 8008 – *August 1972*

Atari Pong released – *September 1972*

Wozniak starts at Hewlett-Packard – *January 1973*

Micral N – *February 1973*

SCELBI-8H – *March 1974*

Intel 8080 – *April 1974*

Mark-8 – *July 1974*

Wozniak & Jobs complete Breakout – *late 1974*

Altair 8800 – *January 1975*

Sphere 1 – *July 1975*

Altair 680 – *November 1975*

IMASI 8080 – *December 1975*

Polymorphic Poly-88 – *1976*

Atari Breakout released – *April 1976*

Processor Technology Sol-20 – *1977*

CHAPTER 2

A Company Built From a Circuit Board

The Homebrew Computer Club was started in Menlo Park, California in the San Francisco area as a meeting place for electronics enthusiasts and hobbyists, with a focus on computers. The announcement of the Altair 8800 in January 1975 motivated the group to get together to discuss the new machine, and to offer help to those wanting to build one. The first meeting was held in March 1975 in a garage owned by Gordon French, one of the two who had suggested starting the group.

Steve Woniak's friend Allen Baum, who also worked at Hewlett-Packard, had heard about the planned first meeting. Baum told Wozniak about the meeting, explaining that it was for people who were interested in building video terminals—something that Woz had already done by this time. To get onto the ARPANET dialup computer network, he had built a terminal that connected to his home television, simulated a Teletype system, and used an inexpensive $60 typewriter keyboard. This was not a computer, but more of a "dumb" terminal, one that simply allowed him to enter commands and see the output. Woz realized that it would be a great way to share information with others who had done the same thing.

Wozniak was immersed in designing and building calculators at HP, and had not been aware of the release of Intel's microprocessor chips over the previous four years. He also missed hearing of the January 1975 announcement of the Altair. Had he known that the Homebrew meeting was more about computers than video terminals, he likely would not have bothered attending, feeling that he would have nothing to offer. However, once there, he decided to stay through the entire event. He listened to what was being discussed, much of it about the new Altair that had been received by one of those attending. It was interesting, but Woz had not been involved with computers for a while and felt very much out of his element.

Initially, he was not inclined to come back. However, what ensured his future attendance was a data sheet being passed out at the end of the meeting. After he returned home Wozniak studied the information on the sheet, which was for a clone of the Intel 8008 microprocessor. He realized that this was just like the Cream Soda Computer he had built several years earlier while he was in college. The primary difference was that most of the computer circuitry was all on a single chip—the microprocessor. All an engineer had to do was to connect this to memory chips and the result was a computer.

Once he grasped this concept, he could see that his previous work designing computers on paper, writing FORTRAN compilers for them, building a video terminal, displaying dots and text on a television screen, and connecting memory had all led to this point. The availability of the microprocessor gave him the power to finally build a computer of his own.

That evening, Wozniak sat down and sketched out the basic design for his vision of a personal computer. He wanted to show people at the Homebrew club that with the right design, a computer could be built with just a few chips, which would make it far less costly. Furthermore, Woz's computer would be easy to use right away. With his video terminal, the user could enter a program with a keyboard, and see the results on a television screen, eliminating the need to find and connect a used Teletype. The calculators he had been designing did not require entry of any special program code to get them started; owners just turned them on and started entering numbers. Similarly, his computer would include a built-in program in ROM (read-only memory—permanent memory that could only be written one time), which would be much simpler than entering a start-up program with those switches on the front panel of the Altair.

Woz called this program a "monitor", since its job was to monitor the keyboard and pay attention to any keys pressed. In addition to this, it also had commands that allowed the user to enter data bytes, examine a range of memory, and run a machine language program at a specific address. This by itself already surpassed what the Altair could do out of the box.

Cost was an issue, however, as the Intel 8080 microprocessor was still too expensive for Wozniak's purposes. Through his friends at work, he found that as an HP employee he could buy the Motorola 6800 microprocessor for only $40, which made it somewhat more affordable for him. However, the regular price of the 6800 was $175, which he felt was still too high. He began to study the technical manual for the 6800 to learn how it worked, and how it could be incorporated into his design.

Over the next several months after work, Wozniak would return to his cubicle at HP after hours and work on his design. He took his video terminal and modified it to include the 6800 microprocessor chip and static RAM chips for memory. (Static RAM, or SRAM chips could be written to any time and maintained data even when the power was turned off.) He designed it to work with 4K of RAM, sixteen times as much as what the basic Altair offered. With only about 40 chips used in the project, it met his requirement of being less expensive to build.

Most of the other Homebrew members were fixated on the Altair, its processor and its design as the only and best way to build a computer. Despite potential advantages of the instruction set of the Motorola 6800, a decision to not use the 8080 was considered foolhardy.

> That summer at the Homebrew Club, the Intel 8080 formed the center of the universe. The Altair was built around the 8080 and its early popularity spawned a cottage industry of small companies that either made machines that would run programs written for the Altair or made attachments that would plug into the computer. The private peculiarities of microprocessors meant that a program or device designed for one would not work on another. The junction of these peripheral devices for the Altair was known as the S-100 bus because it used one hundred signal lines. Disciples of the 8080 formed religious attachments to the 8080 and S-100 even though they readily admitted that the latter was poorly designed. The people who wrote programs or built peripherals for 8080 computers thought that later, competing microprocessors were doomed. The sheer weight of the programs and the choice of peripherals, so the argument went, would make it more useful to more users and more profitable for more companies. The 8080, they liked to say, had critical mass which was sufficient to consign anything else to oblivion.[1]

Despite these attitudes, Woz had what he felt was a better design. However, he was still bothered by the cost of the 6800. Although he had the advantage of his HP employee discount, anyone else trying to build it would have to pay its full price. But a significant event happened at the end of that summer that influenced his project and the rest of the new computer industry for years to come. Ironically, this event happened because of the Motorola 6800.

Chuck Peddle was an engineer who worked at Motorola, and was involved in the development of the 6800 and creation of support chips for it. He saw its potential in lower cost electronics devices, and tried to convince executives at Motorola to reduce its price or to create a less expensive version. He was specifically told that they had no plans to move in that direction. This attitude led Peddle and seven of his coworkers from engineering and marketing to leave Mototola and find a way to make a low cost processor.[2]

MOS Technology, Inc. had been started in 1969 to produce and supply chips and semiconductor parts for calculators. One of its major competitors was Texas Instruments. When TI began to build and sell its own line of cheap calculators, other calculator manufacturers began to falter and MOS began losing its customers. MOS managed to stay afloat for several years, even pro-

---

1 Moritz, Michael, *The Little Kingdom*, (New York, William Morrow and Company, Inc, 1984), 123.
2 Bagnall, Brian, *Commodore: A Company on the Edge* (Winnipeg, Variant Press, 2010), 8-11.

viding Atari with a Pong system on a single chip. In 1974, the company saw the arrival of Peddle and his exiles, who began work on their vision of a less costly version of the 6800. Having the advantage of their previous experience, they made it faster and simpler in design. They also managed to fabricate the new chips in such a way as to have better yields, allowing the company to sell it for a cost much lower than its competitors.[3]

Peddle's team created two versions of the chip. The 6501 would function in a 6800 socket, though its programming was completely different. The 6502 had the same function and instruction set as the 6501, but the pin configuration was different. In mid-1975 the company announced its new microprocessors, and promised that they would be released at the annual WESCON trade show scheduled for September. The advertisement in the August 7, 1975 issue of Electronics promised that the 6501 would be available for only $20 at the show, and the 6502 for $25.

Wozniak heard about the 6502, and attended the WESCON show. As he read the data sheet for this microprocessor, he saw that its similarity to the 6800 would make it simple to modify his design to use the 6502 instead. Furthermore, at $25 per chip, it was just over half the cost of an HP-discounted 6800. Woz knew this was the affordable chip he had been waiting for.

FURTHER DESIGN DECISIONS

Modifying his design to accommodate the 6502, Woz showed off his progress at more Homebrew meetings. He was shy and unable to promote his work; instead he sat in a corner of the room with his computer on a table, answering questions. Steve Jobs had accompanied him several times, and immediately developed an interest in what could be done with the computer. Jobs also had some big ideas about how to improve it.

While Woz had been working on his design, a new kind of RAM chip had become available. Dynamic RAM (DRAM) was actually constructed more simply than static RAM, requiring fewer internal components to store each on/off bit. However, it required a periodic electrical refresh to maintain its contents. Because of its simpler design, 4K of DRAM could be built with only four chips, while it took thirty-two of the SRAM chips to make the same 4K of memory. This change required adjustment of the timing of the video signal to help with the refresh process, but Wozniak used these new chips to simplify his design. Thanks to fast-talking Jobs, Woz was able get some Intel DRAM chips at a low cost, and he incorporated these into the computer, ultimately taking the storage up to a total of 8K.

---

3   Phone conversation with Bill Mensch, incorporated into "MOS Technology" article on *Wikipedia*, <en.wikipedia.org/wiki/MOS_Technology>, retrieved August 8, 2013.

The video output on his 6502 computer was directly derived from the video terminal that he had previously designed. With the high cost of RAM, Woz decided against using that type of memory for the video. Instead, he used shift registers, a less expensive type of memory. At 24 lines by 40 columns, he needed 960 bytes of storage for the characters of the screen display. His shift register could hold 1,024 (1K) bytes, just a little more than was necessary.

As a character was sent from the computer to the shift register, it would be put in a queue along with other characters waiting to be sent to the screen, something like a line of cars going through a toll booth, with a pause as each driver pays the toll. If the line was empty, the character would be displayed immediately. If an entire line of characters was to be displayed, each character had to wait nearly 17 milliseconds for its turn to go to the screen. Consequently, his video terminal displayed characters at a maximum speed of about 60 characters per second—one character sent from the shift register per scan of the TV screen. It was slow compared to computer displays as appearing merely two years later, but was a clear advancement over a Teletype that could only print 10 characters per second.

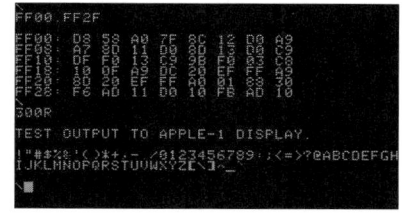

Sample output from Apple-1 – Photo credit: personal

A COMPANY BORN

Steve Jobs had noticed on his visits to Homebrew with Woz that although people picked up the free schematics he distributed for his 6502, he felt it was unlikely that many of them had the time to create the circuit board and actually build one of them. He suggested to Woz that they should go into business together to make the circuit boards and sell them to Homebrew members (or anyone else interested). Those who bought the boards then had only to gather the parts and solder them in.

Wozniak was skeptical that there would be enough people at the club who would want to buy this, as many of them were already fans of the Altair design. Jobs argued that this might be the one time they could look back and say that they had been in business together—that they'd had a company. Wozniak was eventually convinced to give it a try.

To carry out Jobs' plans, there were two expenses that had to be overcome. First, it was necessary to translate Wozniak's hand-drawn printed circuit board layout into a form that could be used by a professional PC board service to make large numbers of the boards. Jobs had a friend at Atari who, for $600, could do this for them. Once the layout was submitted, it would cost $1,000 to produce fifty boards. Jobs hoped to sell these boards for $40 (double the cost of producing them).

But neither Steve had much money available to front this initial investment. They eventually raised some of the needed cash by selling some personal possessions: Woz's HP 65 calculator for $500, and Jobs' Volkswagon bus for another $1,500. (However, Woz's buyer only paid him half the cost, and Jobs' buyer came back complaining that the engine had broken down, making it necessary for Jobs to refund half of the sale price.) Together with what little savings the pair had, they came up with $1,300, which was enough to get started.

A couple of weeks after agreeing to sell Woz's boards, the pair decided their company needed a name. Wozniak originally favored a technical name, and proposed calling it the Matrix Computer Company.[4] But Jobs offered an unusual choice. He had been working at a commune called the All One Farm, south of Portland, Oregon. The farm featured an organic apple orchard, and Jobs proposed they name the company after the fruit grown there. "He thought of the apple as the perfect fruit—it has a high nutritional content, it comes in a nice package, it doesn't damage easily—and he wanted Apple to be the perfect company. Besides, they couldn't come up with a better name."[5]

With the company name settled on "Apple", Jobs began pulling together the necessary resources to make it function, while Wozniak continued to work at Hewlett-Packard. Woz soon realized he needed to ensure that HP would not claim ownership of his design, since he had used company resources for some of the design work. On more than one occasion, he talked with management people at the company about his computer. Although there were several who were interested, they simply did not feel that it was a product that HP would want to handle, and they freely released it to Wozniak and Jobs.

At one of the Homebrew Computer Club meetings in March 1976, Wozniak and Jobs had demonstrated the Apple computer. Apparently it still did not impress very many there (nearly all of the articles from the club's newsletter during that year focus on the Intel 8080, and rarely ever mentioned the 6502). However, one attendee did come up and talk with Steve Jobs after the meeting was over.

Paul Terrell had started a store to sell computer kits and parts in December 1975. He named it "The Byte Shop", and employed a couple of technicians who could assemble Altair kits for interested customers who wanted the computer but didn't want the trouble of building it. The Apple-1 interested him, and he gave Jobs his card and said he should stay in touch. Jobs showed up at his store the following day. The result of their conversation was that Terrell agreed to buy fifty Apple computers, but he insisted that they had to be fully assembled.

Jobs excitedly told Wozniak about this large order. Instead of circuit boards to sell for $40, Terrell would purchase fifty fully assembled Apple-1 computers for $500 each. What this would require, however, was that they had to buy all of the parts to attach to the circuit boards to turn them into full

---

4 Kottke, Daniel, keynote speech, Vintage Computer Festival Southeast 1.0, April 20, 2013.
5 Rose, Frank, *West Of Eden: The End Of Innocence At Apple Computer*, (New York, Penguin Books, 1989), 33.

working computers. Jobs tried several places before he found a company who would sell them the parts on credit for "net 30 days" (30 days interest free).

The parts company would not approve the transaction until they were able to get in touch with Terrell and confirm that he had indeed placed this large order with Apple. This deal was worth $15,000 for the parts they were getting, and Jobs borrowed another $5,000 in cash from Allen Baum's father. All told, this suddenly put Apple in debt for $20,000. However, if they could build all fifty computers and deliver them to Terrell, it would make them $25,000.

CRUNCH TIME

Now that they had a large order from Terrell, they had to get all fifty boards completed before the thirty-day deadline came due on paying for the parts.

Assembly of the Apple-1 started at the company that was making the boards. They had some of the parts Jobs had ordered on credit, and when the boards were etched (the circuit pattern was printed on the board), the parts that required soldering were put in place and that entire side of the board was soldered at once (a process called wave soldering).

About ten or twenty of these boards were delivered to Jobs at a time. It was then necessary to plug chips into the sockets on each board and test them. In addition to Wozniak, Jobs recruited help from his sister and from Dan Kottke, the friend who had accompanied him to India, paying them one dollar for each completed board. The work was initially performed in a spare bedroom in Jobs' home, on their kitchen table, and in the garage. Later, Jobs' father made the entire garage available for the work.

Wozniak would take the completed boards and plug them into a television and keyboard to see if they worked. If they did, he set them aside in a box. If the board did not work, he would check to see what had not been plugged in correctly, or look for a short circuit on the board. After this, the boards were plugged into a burn-in box, where they would run for over a day and then be rechecked after that to be sure that they still worked.

After burn-in, Dan Kottke had another task to perform. He had to plug in a cassette board, load BASIC, and type a one-line program in BASIC to make sure it would run. If it worked successfully, it was considered a good board.[6] When around a dozen Apple-1 boards had been completed, Jobs would drive them down to The Byte Shop, where he was paid for that part of the order.

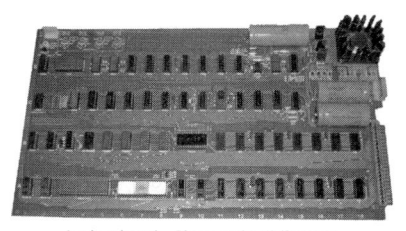

Apple-1 board – Photo credit: Cliff Huston

---

6   Interview with Dan Kottke in Luthor, Robert, J., *The First Apple* (Alexandria, Virginia, MassMobi.mobi Press, 2013), 153-154.

At Jobs' first delivery of the Apple-1, Paul Terrell was a little surprised. He knew the circuit board was not very large, only 16 by 12 inches in size (most hobby computers of the time required at least two boards). However, he had expected it to be somewhat more completed; these boards still required the buyer to supply a keyboard (which had to be wired into a 16-pin connector), a monitor or television, and a power supply that provided 5 volts and 12 volts DC. However Jobs convinced him that he had delivered on the promised product, and so Terrell paid him in cash for the part of the order that he had supplied. Jobs would then return home for the process to start over again.

As for a suggested retail price for the computer, Jobs took the $500 wholesale price offered by Terrell and added a 33% markup. Wozniak had just wanted to sell it for cost, but when he heard that this retail price would come to $666.66, he decided to go along with it because he liked repeating digits.

INCORPORATION

As they were working on The Byte Shop order, Jobs had become concerned about Wozniak's attitude about the computer and the technology he had incorporated into it. Woz seemed to want to keep control over these things and continue to share it freely with others. Jobs argued that he should not give away this intellectual property, as it was what differentiated the Apple computer from others. Jobs appealed to Ron Wayne, his friend from Atari, to intervene. During discussions the three had together, Wayne finally got through to Woz that it was necessary to understand that what he had created was critical to the future of Apple, and he had to keep it separate from other things he was doing.

Wayne had some experience with legal documents and had already advised the pair on starting their business. Due to his success getting through to Woz, Jobs suggested that the three form a partnership, with Wayne having the ability to handle disagreements between the other two. On April 1, 1976 at Wayne's home, he typed up the documents that officially formed the Apple Computer Company. Jobs and Wozniak would each own 45% of the company, and Wayne would own 10%.

Wayne filed the necessary legal documents with the county registrar, and the company was born. However, he was back at the registrar's office twelve days later with an amendment removing him from the partnership. He had developed reservations about the business relationship, especially Jobs' apparent lack of concern about putting the company in debt to achieve a goal. Although the deal with The Byte Shop had worked out, he did not believe he could handle the stress.

He ... fretted that The Byte Shop — one of the first retail computer stores — "had a terrible reputation for not paying its bills." Jobs and Wozniak were essentially penniless, which meant that creditors would eventually come looking for Wayne.

"I just wasn't ready for the kind of whirlwind that Jobs and Wozniak represented ... I felt certain the company was going to be successful; that wasn't the question. But how much of a roller coaster was it going to be? I didn't know that I could tolerate that kind of situation again. I thought if I stayed with Apple I was going to wind up the richest man in the cemetery."[7]

Wayne continued to work with Apple in an informal manner, but he was happier being part of a non-financial arrangement.

SOFTWARE

For a high-level language, Wozniak had originally planned on FORTRAN. However, books and magazines being printed at the time featured listings of games and other programs in BASIC. The language was currently popular at the Homebrew club, spurred by its availability (on paper tape) from Micro-Soft, the company formed by Bill Gates and Paul Allen specifically to be the first to give the new Altair a usable language. Additionally, for a low memory computer, BASIC would be easier to implement than FORTRAN. Since there was at that time no BASIC interpreter for the new 6502 processor, Wozniak decided he would write one for his computer, which would make it easier to use. However, he found it to be a long and complex project.

A friend over at Hewlett-Packard programmed a computer to simulate the function of the 6502, and Wozniak used it to test some of his early routines. He did not have an assembler for creating his BASIC interpreter, so he assembled code by hand, writing the 6502 opcodes (machine language commands) next to the commands, with an address in memory for each command. It took about four months to create the original version of BASIC, and because it took so long, he decided to leave out the ability to handle decimal numbers, focusing instead on integers (whole numbers, positive or negative).

The final version of his language was about 4,000 bytes in size. To be able to use it required entering all of the bytes by hand from the keyboard. He got to know the code so well that he could do it quickly, but even so it took him about forty minutes to key it in. Once it was in and running, he could then enter programs in BASIC and successfully run them.

---

7   Newman, Bruce, "Apple's lost founder: Jobs, Woz and Wayne", *San Jose Mercury News* (June 2, 2010), retrieved from <www.mercurynews.com/bay-area-news/ci_15214122> on August 8, 2013.

What he did not know while he was creating his BASIC was that there were different dialects of the language that were in use on the various mainframe and minicomputers. He had taken advantage of what was available to him—manuals for HP BASIC—and had used that as the model for his version. What he later discovered was that the BASIC used on the Altair, the one created and sold by Bill Gates, was derived from the language as it was used on Digital Electronics PDP computers. The differences were not major, but it required modifications in order for programs from books or magazines to work on the Apple-1.

To broaden the appeal of the Apple-1 (and at the insistence of Paul Terrell), Wozniak designed a cassette interface. It was mounted on a small two-inch-high printed circuit board and plugged into the single slot on the motherboard. The card sold for $75 and a cassette tape of Woz's BASIC was included with it. The advertisement Apple included with the card stated, "Our philosophy is to provide software for our machines free or at minimal cost." The interface worked, but the nature of using cassettes for data was that it could be tricky to get the volume and tone on the cassette player properly adjusted to result in a successful load. It transferred data at 1500 baud (approximately 1500 bits per second) and was more consistently successful at getting a good load into memory when compared to other computers of the day (which operated at 300 baud).

To further enhance sales, The Byte Shop stores found a local cabinet-maker that made some koa-wood cases for the Apple computer (so it was no longer just a naked circuit board).[8, 9]

MARKETING

Apple Computer Company logo
– Photo credit: unknown

The fifty Apple-1 computers sold to The Byte Shop helped Apple to purchase even more boards. They sold about fifty more to friends and those at Homebrew who now expressed an interest. Though Ron Wayne was no longer a partner, he helped the company out by creating a logo, a wood-cut depiction of Isaac Newton sitting under a tree. He also wrote the manual for the computer.

To make it look more like a big company, Jobs arranged for a mailing address that sounded like one that wasn't from a residential area. He found a mail-drop address in Palo Alto, California, and hired an answering service to take calls for them.

---

8 Moritz, Michael, *The Little Kingdom*, (New York, William Morrow and Company, Inc, 1984), 148-149
9 Veit, Stan, *Stan Veit's History Of The Personal Computer*, (Asheville, North Carolina, Worldcom, 1993), 89-98

CHAPTER 2 | *A Company Built From a Circuit Board*

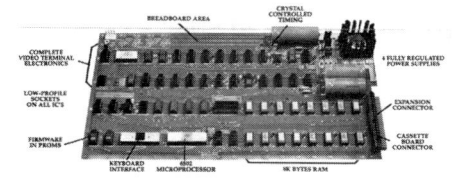

Although most of the design and construction action in the micro world was going on in Silicon Valley, news of the Apple-1 made its way east. In 1976, Stan Veit opened The Computer Mart in New York City, the east coast's first computer store. Operating initially out of a part of Polk's Hobby Department Store in midtown Manhattan, and moving later to a larger store on Madison Avenue, he sold the IMSAI 8080, the Sphere and Southwest Technical Products M6800 (both Motorola 6800-based computers), and others. Paul Terrell of The Byte Shop referred Steve Jobs to Veit, and after a phone call with fast-talking Jobs on the phone, a $500 C.O.D. package appeared on the doorstep of The Computer Mart. Veit showed it to one of his techs, who didn't believe that something that small (16 by 12 inches) could be a computer. Nevertheless, after attaching a power supply and keyboard (they had to call Jobs about the keyboard, and he gladly sent one out, also C.O.D.) they had a working computer that was more compact and used fewer chips on the motherboard than every other microcomputer they had yet seen. Along with the keyboard, Jobs had included their cassette interface, and a tape of the program, *Game of Life*.

Impressed with this compact computer, Veit had his techs install the Apple-1 in an attaché case, and along with a 9-inch monitor and keyboard, he and his wife attended a dinner meeting of the New York Chapter of the Association for Computing Machinery. Most of those attending were involved with large computers (mainframes or minicomputers), but the ACM had invited computer dealers in the area to attend and show their products. Veit set up the Apple-1 and started the Game of Life, so that during the meeting it was visible to the speaker at the podium. When the speaker interrupted himself to ask Veit what was running on the monitor, he did not believe that there could actually be a computer in that briefcase. Some of those attending were sure that the machine was just a portable terminal, attached by a hidden phone line to a mainframe somewhere.[10] Later, during the product demonstration part of the meeting, the Apple-1 caused quite a lot of excitement amongst the other dealers present.

Apple-1 Advertisement – Photo credit: personal

---

10 Chien, Philip, "Apple's First Decade: A Look Back", *The Apple II Review* (Fall/Winter 1986), 12.

Veit later traveled to California and met Jobs and Wozniak in their garage operation. Wozniak demonstrated a prototype of the Apple II with his color *Breakout* game running, and Veit felt that it clearly had better graphics than the Cromemco Dazzler (a popular add-on for the S-100 bus on the Altair and IMSAI computers). Jobs told him that they were dropping the Apple-1 in favor of the better Apple II, but Veit strongly urged him to fulfill the commitment they had made to their customers (and the dealers who purchased Apple-1 boards to sell) in delivering a finished BASIC. He felt that this would be vital to their reputation and any future success the company might have.

They were offered space at PC '76, a national computer show to be held in Atlantic City, New Jersey on August 28, 1976, and so the two Steves packed up demonstration models of the Apple-1 and flew out to join Stan Veit's display booth. Using the hotel television, Wozniak put the finishing touches on his Apple BASIC interpreter to make it ready for its official introduction. With several Apple-1 computers in operation at the show, the small size and speed of its cassette interface caught the attention of attendees, in spite of the fact that there were two other 6502-based computers on display at the show (the KIM-1 and the Baby computer). By the end of the show, Jobs had taken twenty orders from dealers for the Apple-1.[11, 12]

> Computers speak the language of binary, using on (1) or off (0) states. Combinations of these binary digits are used to store data or give instructions to the computer to carry out a task. But since only two digits are used, displaying large numbers can take up a lot of space. For example, the decimal number 21 is "00010101" in binary.
>
> To simplify this, programmers can use a base 16, or hexadecimal method of counting. numbers 10 through 15 are represented by the hex digits "A" through "F". The decimal number 16 is "10" in hex, and the number 21 is "15" in hex. Furthermore, for the 6502 it is customary to identify a hex number by preceding it with a dollar sign. So, $15 represents that hex number.
>
> In the hexadecimal system, two digit numbers range from $00 to $FF (0 to 255 in decimal). The full 64K of memory that the 6502 could address is expressed as four-digit hex numbers, and range from $0000 to $FFFF (0 through 65,535).

The Apple-1 motherboard was designed in such a way as to make it possible for the hobbyist to remove the 6502 processor and use a Motorola 6800 as the CPU instead. This was not a trivial operation, as the 6502 and the 6800 were not pin-compatible (the earlier 6501 was pin-compatible, but was withdrawn after Motorola sued MOS Technology). However, other hardware would need to be added, and the software needed to operate it would be completely different.

---

11 Veit, Stan, *Stan Veit's History Of The Personal Computer*, (Asheville, North Carolina, Worldcom, 1993), 89-98.
12 Green, Wayne, "Remarks From The Publisher . . . Wayne Green", *inCider* (January 1983), 6. Note that this comment about twenty orders differs from the story published by Stan Veit in his book.

> The least expensive Apple-1 motherboard was sold with 4K of RAM. This was only one sixteenth of the total memory space that the 6502 processor could address, but RAM chips in 1976 were very expensive. To use Wozniak's BASIC, it was necessary to have 8K of memory, and a hardware modification was necessary to map the second 4K to a higher address (which was where BASIC was designed to operate).
>
> Unless the Apple-1 owner was entering the 4,000 bytes of hex code from the keyboard (as Woz was able to do), it would be loaded from the cassette interface. To start this up, it was necessary to jump to a memory location designated for that card ($C100 in memory), and then type the command that would load the code for BASIC starting at $E000.
>
> Since about 6K of that 8K Apple-1 system was used by the processor and by BASIC, that left only 2K of space for a user's program.

EXPERIENCES OF USERS

One of the pioneers who took a chance, bought one of the original Apple-1 boards, and dealt with the trials and tribulations of making it a workable computer was Joe Torzewski. He purchased his Apple-1 system in August 1977 for $430, shortly after the release of the Apple II. The motherboard itself was sold to him for only $200, truly a bargain over the original asking price of $666; this probably represented the wishes of the seller to clear out his inventory of a computer that just was not selling well. For his $430, Torzewski received the Apple-1 board with a full 8K of RAM, plus a keyboard, two power transformers (one for needed each voltage), and the cassette interface. And just as many computer buyers today have discovered, soon after he bought his Apple-1 he received notice from Apple Computer about the newer and better model that had come out (the Apple II), and that they were dropping support for his Apple-1. He did not view this as an obstacle; instead, he decided to start an Apple-1 user group, and (at his request) Apple eventually forwarded nearly all of the support requests that they received to his group.

Torzewski and five other Apple-1 owners formed the core of this user group. He later wrote, "We developed hardware and software which included such things as interfacing a graphic board, memory expansion, and writing a chess game. We converted the Focal language for the Apple-1 computer and had it in use. We were also working on the expansion slot hoping to put in a better monitor and other various programs."[13] All this they accomplished with a more primitive ROM than was supplied later with the Apple II, and with only 4K or 8K of RAM (although some users found a way to increase this to as much as 20K).

In April 1977, two months before the Apple II came out, Apple Computer had reduced the official list price of the Apple-1 from $666 to $475 for a computer with

---

13 Apple-1 Owner's Club web site, <www.applefritter.com/apple1>, accessed June 20, 2001.

4K of RAM, or $575 for 8K. There were also several program cassettes available to purchase. These included Wozniak's BASIC (which took about 30 seconds to load), a disassembler, an extended monitor, and games such as *Star Trek* (mini and 16K versions), *Mastermind, Lunar Lander, Blackjack,* and *Hamurabi,* all selling for $5.00, and some of which appeared later in revised forms to run on the Apple II.

> One of the other members of the Apple-1 club, Larry Nelson, used his Apple-1 for a simple payroll and accounts payable program that he wrote in BASIC for his business. He also spent some time with Apple's *DisAssembler* program and examined the BASIC interpreter to see how it worked. Interestingly, he found keywords for graphics commands that did nothing on the Apple-1—commands that later found their way to functionality on the Applew II. He found that he could include a statement such as "COLOR=12" in a line of a BASIC program, and although it would not generate an error, it also did not do anything on the Apple-1. Nelson modified a KIM-1[14] 6502 chess-playing program to run on his Apple-1, and then used that computer to challenge the *Microchess* program on his Radio Shack TRS-80. (As he recalls, the contest was a draw.)[15]

The Apple-1 club also disseminated information to its members about hardware enhancements, such as a monochrome graphics board (recall that the Apple-1 was built as a text-only computer), how to interface a 40-column printer (the SWTPC PR-40), and how to connect a Teletype.

As time passed, some of the users of the Apple-1 group faded away as they graduated to newer and more powerful machines. However, Torzewski's Apple-1 user group never completely disbanded. As of 2013 it was still in existence, run via the Apple-1 Owner's Club web site.

TIMELINE

Important dates for the start of Apple and the Apple-1:

Altair 8800 – *January 1975*
Homebrew Computer Club – *March 1975*
WESCON 75, first 6502 chips available – *September 1975*
Homebrew Computer Club demo of Apple-1 – *March 1976*
Apple Computer Company formed – *April 1, 1976*
Apple-1 – *April 1976 – May 1977*

---

14 MOS Technology, the company that created the 6502, also developed the KIM-1 single-board computer as a way to allow hobbyists to become familiar with and use this new microprocessor.
15 Nelson, Larry, e-mail message to author, October 25, 2001.

CHAPTER 3
II is Better than 1

The Apple-1 had established Apple, and by the beginning of 1977 it had sold about 150 units. These were sold through The Byte Shop, Stan Veit's Computer Mart in New York, and directly to a few members of the Homebrew Computer Club. Both Jobs and Wozniak also made direct contact with stores in California, asking them to carry the computer. But these sales were minor compared to other microcomputers that were available at the time. The Altair 8800 had sold 5,000 units in its first six months, and the other computers that used the same S-100 bus were riding on the same wave of excitement.

Once Wozniak had the design of the Apple-1 locked down, he began to envision changes to the computer that would make it better—the type of computer that he would want to own. He had figured out a clever way to display graphics on the screen in sixteen colors by manipulating the video signal. Color was something that most other computers of the era did not offer, except as an add-on board. He also discovered a way to avoid the slow screen output from the shift registers he previously used by putting the video into main memory. That allowed instant screen updates. To make it more convenient to use, he put his BASIC into ROM, allowing it to be usable immediately after the computer was turned on.

When he began work on his new project in the spring of 1976, he realized that these improvements would take more than just an update to the Apple-1 design. That computer had itself primarily been a modification of his previous video terminal. He needed to start from scratch.

As the designer, Woz did not have a committee or marketing group to tell him what his computer should do. He didn't necessarily worry about what would make it more attractive for a customer to purchase. Wozniak stated:

> *A lot of features of the Apple II went in because I had designed Breakout for Atari. I had designed it in hardware. I wanted to write it in software now. So that was the reason that color was added in first – so that games could be programmed. I sat down one night and tried to put it into BASIC. Fortunately, I had written the BASIC myself, so I just burned some new ROMs with line drawing commands, color*

changing commands, and various BASIC commands that would plot in color. I got this ball bouncing around, and I said, "Well, it needs sound," and I had to add a speaker to the Apple II. It wasn't planned, it was just accidental... Obviously you need paddles, so I had to scratch my head and design a simple minimum-chip paddle circuit, and put on some paddles. So, a lot of these features that really made the Apple II stand out in its day came from a game, and the fun features that were built in were only to do one pet project, which was to program a BASIC version of Breakout and show it off at the club.[1]

The next phase of Apple's development required investment. Although the company was mildly profitable with the Apple-1 during the summer of 1976, it was not making enough to adequately fund the next model. Where their first computer had sold in the low hundreds of units, Jobs and Wozniak felt the new one could easily sell in the thousands or more.

Jobs tried to obtain loans from banks, but his barefoot hippie-like appearance did not engender enough trust for anyone to agree to fund a crazy venture of building computers for the home. He reached out to Chuck Peddle, the primary designer of the 6502 processor. Commodore had purchased MOS Technology, and now Peddle worked for Commodore. He seemed interested in acquiring the design, but when Jobs wanted a large sum of money for Commodore to buy Apple, plus guaranteed positions for himself and Wozniak, Commodore's CEO turned down the offer.

He began to look elsewhere, and eventually arrived at Regis McKenna, Inc., a marketing firm that had done work for Intel in its early years. McKenna took Jobs seriously enough to refer him to famed venture capitalist Don Valentine. Jobs did not make a good impression on Valentine, and he declined any involvement, but instead passed the proposal on to Mike Markkula.

Markkula had worked as a marketing manager at Fairchild Semiconductor and Intel, and made enough money that he was able to retire in 1974 at the age of only 32. Markkula could see the potential of Wozniak's new computer. He agreed to not only fund the company with $250,000 of his own money, but also joined the company as an employee. Through Markkula's help, Apple was able to obtain further funding to move the company to this next phase of its development. He set it onto a true business footing, and helped hire management in the form of Apple's first president and CEO, Mike Scott.

One of the difficult tasks that Markkula had to take on was to convince Wozniak to leave his comfortable, predictable job at Hewlett-Packard and work at Apple full time. Woz initially turned down the idea; he had planned

---

1 Connick, Jack, "...And Then There Was Apple", *Call-A.P.P.L.E.*, (Oct 1986), 24.

to stay at HP for the rest of his life. Jobs, however, would have none of this. He recruited Woz's friends and family to call and urge him to leave HP and work at Apple. He was finally convinced when he was told that he could continue to be an engineer and would not have to become a manager.

RAM

Wozniak added other features that he felt were important for a computer that was useful, one that he would want to own. Since the 6502 processor could address a total of 64K of memory, he designed the computer with the ability to use either 4K RAM chips, or the newer (and more expensive) 16K RAM chips. The first available Apple II computers came standard with 4K of memory, and more could be added, to a maximum of 12K (if using 4K chips) or 48K (if using 16K chips). Since 16K RAM chips cost about $500 when Wozniak designed the Apple II, not many users could afford them. Whereas the Commodore PET and the Radio Shack TRS-80 could not easily be expanded beyond the 4K or 8K they came with, the Apple II from the beginning was designed with expansion in mind.[2]

> The Apple II could be configured with a range of memory from 4K to 48K. To help the system and programs running on it know how much was present and how it was to be used, three memory select blocks were plugged into the motherboard near the RAM chips. The wiring on these blocks provided this information to the computer. The only place in memory that every Apple II had to have was the lowest 4K. The lower half of that space was used by the 6502 processor and the screen display. Like the Apple-1 before it, this left 2K of space for a program.

EXPANSION

The row of eight expansion slots was another feature of the Apple II that Wozniak particularly wanted. Unlike the TRS-80 or PET, you could easily expand the Apple II by simply plugging a card into one of these slots. This degree of expandability made it more expensive to build, however. During the design process, Steve Jobs had pushed for inclusion of only two slots. He felt that no one would ever need more than that, one for a printer and one possibly for a modem. Wozniak knew from his experience at Hewlett-Packard

---

2 Golding ,Val J, "Applesoft From Bottom To Top", *Call-A.P.P.L.E. In Depth #1*, (Seattle, Washington, 1981), 8.

that computer users would always find something to fill those extra slots, and insisted that they keep the number at eight.[3]

MONITOR ROM

The built-in monitor program in ROM that Wozniak included with the Apple-1 made it easier to use out of the box than other first generation microcomputers. He wanted to increase this functionality, and provided additional commands to manage bytes at specific memory locations.

Wozniak's friend Allen Baum helped code additional enhancements to his built-in ROM routines. This included code to handle screen text display, as well as the ability to create and handle different sized text windows (that is, make one or more user-defined text spaces within the standard 24 by 40 text screen, which scrolled text only within that space). The Monitor also incorporated the cassette input/output routines, since the hardware supporting that was included in the Apple II.

Baum and Wozniak had previously published code for a 6502 disassembler in the September 1976 issue of *Interface Age*. This made it easier to examine and debug code, and was itself an outgrowth of the philosophy of the Homebrew Club of making all computer knowledge available to everybody. The published article was part of Apple's culture of supplying software "free or at minimal charge". An improved version of this disassembler was included in the Apple II Monitor. It became one of the most important and unique features of the Apple II, and a significant part of its open design; it allowed anyone to view the 6502 code that any program used.[4] The increased functionality of the final code for the Monitor increased its size from 256 bytes (in the Apple-1) to 2,048 bytes (2K).

KEYBOARD

On the Apple-1, it was necessary for the owner to supply a keyboard. A specific keyboard that Apple recommended to its customers was one made by Datanetics, a company based in Fountain Valley, California. They had been in business since 1964, making keyboards for cash registers and adding machines. The computer keyboard sold by Datanetics had shaped key caps simi-

---

3   Moritz, Michael, *The Little Kingdom*, (New York, William Morrow and Company, Inc, 1984), 157.
4   Wozniak, Steve and Allen Baum, "A 6502 Disassembler From Apple", *Dr. Dobb's Journal of Computer Calisthenics & Orthodontia*, (September 1976), 22-25.

lar in feel to the popular IBM Selectric typewriter. As for keyboard layout, it was modeled after the keyboard on the classic Teletype model ASR-33.[5]

> The Datanetics keyboard was uppercase only. The version used on the Apple-1 and Apple II were very similar, with the exception of the position of the RESET and REPT (repeat) keys. Also, the Apple-1 keyboard had many of the common Teletype Control-key names stamped on the keys; the only named key that made it onto the Apple II version was "BELL" printed on the G key.

Steve Jobs asked Datanetics to make keyboards for the Apple II, and the company worked during the spring of 1977 to have enough available for the release of this new computer that summer. The shape and printing on the key caps was almost identical to the earlier Datanetics keyboard used on the Apple-1 with some small exceptions. A key for RESET was added, the arrow keys were added just above the right shift key, and the RETURN key was widened. All of the Teletype remnant control code names were removed, with the exception of BELL on the G key. An unmarked special character was the right square bracket, "]", accessed by pressing SHIFT-M.

Teletype 35ASR keyboard – Photo credit: Marc Francisco

Apple II keyboard – Photo credit: David Schmidt

---

5 The Teletype was a particular brand of an electromechanical typewriter, designed in the early 20th century to work as a printing telegraph system. The technology was acquired by AT&T in 1930. The ASR-33 came out in 1963, designed to use the ASCII standard character set and built to communicate with mainframe computers.

Although the Teletype standard allowed entry of the left square bracket character, the backslash, and the underscore character ("[", "\", and "_") from the keyboard, the Apple II did not offer a way to directly type those three characters.

BASIC

Having an expanded Monitor program in ROM and color graphics were not the only new features of the Apple II. Wozniak included an updated version of his Apple BASIC (known as Integer BASIC) in ROM. This was available immediately when the power was turned on, allowing non-hackers to easily write programs that used color graphics.

Apple never had an assembly source code listing for Wozniak's Integer BASIC. As mentioned before, he had written it directly in machine language, assembling it by hand on paper:

> *I had no assembler; that was another thing. To use an assembler, they figured that somebody was going to buy this processor [the 6502] to use for a company, and their company can pay a few thousand dollars in time-sharing charges to use an assembler that was available in time-share. I didn't have any money like that, so a friend taught me that you just sort of look at each instruction, you write your instructions on the right side of the page, you write the addresses over on the left side, and you then look up the hex data for each instruction – you could assemble it yourself. So I would just sit there and assemble it myself. The [Integer] BASIC, which we shipped with the first Apple II's, was never assembled – ever. There was one handwritten copy, all handwritten, all hand-assembled. So we were in an era that we could not afford tools.*[6]

Despite Wozniak's hand assembly work, there were few errors in the Integer BASIC interpreter. One error involved just a single byte. If a line was entered that had too many parentheses, the "TOO LONG" error message was displayed instead of the "TOO MANY PARENS" message.[7] Another error involved a FOR/NEXT loop too deeply nested (that is, having a FOR/NEXT loop within another FOR/NEXT loop). If the program repeatedly entered the beginning of the loop without hitting the NEXT statement, it would eventually cause a crash.[8]

---

6 Connick, Jack, "...And Then There Was Apple", *Call-A.P.P.L.E.*, (October 1986), 23.
7 Volpe, Christopher, "Beep: A Tale of (T)ERROR", *Call-A.P.P.L.E.*, (March 1983), 114.
8 Aaronson, Tim, e-mail message to author, November 8, 1999.

> Wozniak devised the memory layout for the Apple II by using the Apple-1 as a template. Just as the cassette interface card on the Apple-1 started at $C100, on the Apple II the first slot used memory starting at the same location. Slot 2 started at $C200, and so on.
>
> The memory locations from $C000 to $C0FF were assigned to handle other aspects of input and output, including the game paddles, cassette port, and annunciators (simple on/off signals used to control attached devices). Some of these memory locations were soft-switches. Storing to or reading from these addresses changed something in the computer, such as clicking the speaker, or turning a graphics mode on or off.
>
> The 4K of memory space from $D000 to $DFFF was empty on all early Apple II models. It was reserved for two 2K ROM chips that allowed the user to have special assembly language programs always available there. The first of these two chips was most often used for a chip sold by Apple, known as "Programmer's Aid #1". It contained various utilities for Integer BASIC, code to help produce musical notes through the speaker, and subroutines to plot graphics on the hi-res graphics screen.
>
> The second of these two ROM sockets never had a similar product released by Apple, but various third-party vendors sold ROM chips for use there, including code to help break copy protection on floppy disks.
>
> As on the Apple-1, Integer BASIC on the Apple II started at $E000 in memory, and covered most of the space left until the Monitor program started at $F800. Some of the space below the Monitor was also used for other utilities useful to assembly language programmers.

OTHER DESIGN FEATURES

Since Steve Wozniak was the designer of the Apple-1 and II, exactly what contribution did Steve Jobs make to the effort? Some hardware designers would not put much thought into the appearance of the box in which a computer circuit board was mounted, as long as it that worked properly. Jobs, however, had an eye for the finished product. He wanted the Apple II to be a product that people outside the Homebrew Computer Club would want to own:

> Jobs thought the cigar boxes [housing the home-made computers] that sat on the … desktops during Homebrew meetings were as elegant as flytraps. The angular, blue and black sheet-metal case that housed Processor Technology's Sol struck him as clumsy and industrial … A plastic case was generally considered a needless expense compared to the cheaper and more pliable sheet metal. Hobbyists, so the arguments went, didn't care as much for appearance as they did for substance. Jobs wanted to model the case for the Apple after those Hewlett-Pack-

ard used for its calculators. He admired their sleek, fresh lines, their hardy finish, and the way they looked at home on a table or desk.[9]

Originally, Jobs had asked Ron Wayne (the former draftsman from Atari) to design a case for the Apple II. Wayne came up with an inexpensive sheet-metal case that had a plastic lid and a roll-top cover to go over the keyboard. Jobs rejected this, as he didn't feel that it would make the Apple II stand out sufficiently amongst its competition. Jobs then turned to Jerry Manock, whom he had met at the Homebrew Computer Club. Manock asked for $1800 to design a case of the Apple II, which Jobs agreed to pay. He wanted it to look good on a desk, and that it should blend in with other items in a home or business. After a few weeks, Manock brought him a foam-molded plastic case, in just the right shape, size and color (beige, specifically Pantone 453) that he wanted. Jobs also had wanted to avoid the need for a cooling fan, but did not plan on any vents in the case initially.[10, 11, 12]

Apple II name plate – Photo credit: Howie Shen

The final case design made the Apple II look quite different from most of their competition. The other computers looked like they had been assembled at home (and many of them were). The Apple had no visible screws or bolts (the ten screws holding the motherboard in place attached at the bottom). It had the appearance of some variation of a typewriter, but still looked futuristic enough to be a computer. The friendliness of the design even extended to the lid, which popped off easily to allow access to the expansion slots, almost inviting the user to look inside (unlike most electronic devices that held the warning "CAUTION! NO USER SERVICEABLE PARTS INSIDE").[13]

He also hired an engineer who was good with analog circuitry (not Wozniak's area of interest) to design a reliable, lightweight power supply that would stay cool. The engineer, Rod Holt, was working for Atari at the time, but was convinced to help Jobs and Wozniak. He developed a new approach (for microcomputers) by taking household current and switching it on and off rapidly, producing a steady current that was safe for the expensive memory chips. The final design of this switching power supply was smaller than a quart carton of milk and was quite reliable. Holt also helped design the RF television interface for the Apple II.[14]

---

9 Moritz, Michael, *The Little Kingdom*, (New York, William Morrow and Company, Inc, 1984), 186.
10 Isaacson, Walter, *Steve Jobs*, (New York, Simon & Schuster, 2011), 73-74.
11 Routly, Paula, "iWitness", *Seven Days: Vermont's Independent Voice*, January 1, 2012.
12 French, Gordon, e-mail message to author, April 13, 2002.
13 Levy, Steven, *Hackers: Heroes of the Computer Revolution* (New York, Dell Publishing Co., Inc, 1984), 263-264.
14 Moritz, Michael, *The Little Kingdom*, (New York, William Morrow and Company, Inc, 1984), 189.

One of the most significant contributions Holt brought to the Apple II involved the final design of the main logic board. Although Wozniak's prototype worked perfectly, when his design was translated into a layout for a printed circuit board, it did not work when the three-row array of RAM chips were fully populated with 48K of memory. Holt added the necessary circuitry to the board that resolved this problem.[15]

Another problem popped up late in the design process. The US Federal Communications Commission was responsible for managing the broadcast airwaves. Not only did it regulate radio stations, but also signal interference between stations or other devices that interfered with broadcast or reception. With the proliferation of microcomputers, people began to report noise on their radios or televisions while computers were turned on in the vicinity. During 1975, the FCC had released new regulations on radio-frequency interference, dealing with a wide variety of electrical devices, including computers.

In order to sell the Apple II, Apple had to receive FCC approval under those new regulations. To allow the option of connecting the computer to a standard television (rather than requiring an expensive computer monitor), Wozniak had put two pins on the motherboard to allow the user to attach an RF (radio frequency) modulator. The modulator attached to the antenna connector on a television, and translated the video to output a signal on VHF channel 3 or 4. However, the RF modulator produced too much interference, and it was probable that the FCC would not approve it.

Apple II with cassette and television for monitor – Photo credit: Carl Knoblock and Phil Pfeiffer

Rather than delay the release of the Apple II for re-engineering of the RF modulator, Apple gave the specifications for the RF modulator to several companies, including M&R Electronics, run by Marty Spergel. That company specialized in hard-to-find parts that hardware hackers wanted for their projects. Their agreement allowed M&R to produce and sell the RF modulators, while Apple could concentrate on the Apple II. Dealers could sell an Apple II with a "Sup'R'Mod" (for about $30) if the buyer wanted to see the graphics on their color TV. Jobs assured Spergel that the item would sell well, maybe as many as fifty units a month. Years later Spergel estimated that he had sold about four hundred thousand Sup'R'Mods.[16]

---

15 Kottke, Dan, keynote speech at the Vintage Computer Festival Southeast 1.0, Roswell, Georgia, April 21, 2013.
16 Levy, Steven, *Hackers: Heroes of the Computer Revolution* (New York, Dell Publishing Co., Inc, 1984), 260-261.

PRODUCT INTRODUCTION

Following in the footsteps of the PC '76 computer show held in Atlantic City the previous August, Homebrew Computer Club member Jim Warren decided to hold a similar show on the other side of the country. They called it the West Coast Computer Faire, and intended it to be an event to allow the new companies creating microcomputers and supporting hardware and software to show their products to the public. This first Faire was scheduled for April 16-17, 1977, and Apple Computer was racing to have the Apple II ready to show. Some last minute bugs had to be eliminated; because of a static electricity problem affecting a sensitive chip, the keyboards went dead every twenty minutes.

Chris Espinosa and Randy Wigginton were Apple's youngest employees—still in high school at the time. Wigginton became involved due to his friendship with Wozniak. Despite his young age, he began to attend meetings at the Homebrew Computer Club not long after starting at Apple. Because he lacked a driver's license, Woz offered to drive him to the meetings. It turned out that the two lived only three blocks apart.

Because of the time he spent with Woz, Wiggington was one of the first to see the work he'd done on the Apple-1, even before Steve Jobs. He subsequently became involved at Apple as a technician, plugging chips into the Apple-1 in the Jobs' living room and later in the garage, writing software for the Apple-1, and now writing it for the Apple II. Together with Mike Markkula, Wigginton had written a checkbook program for the new computer.[17]

Espinosa was also a high school student who worked at Apple from the early days in the garage, writing some of the information that ended up in the Apple-1 manual. Together they helped prepare Apple II software for the West Coast Computer Faire—the checkbook program, Wozniak's Breakout game, and demo software.

Others at Apple were fixing blemishes in the computer cases that had returned from the plastics molding company. The name for the computer was also finalized as "Apple II", following the example of Digital Equipment Corporation, who had given each newer version of its PDP series a higher number (PDP-1, PDP-6, etc.). They stylized the "II" in the product name by using right and left brackets, and displaying it on the case as "][". The final product bore the mark of each person at Apple:

> The computer that appeared at the West Coast Computer Faire was not one person's machine. It was the product of collaboration and blended contributions in digital logic design, analog engineering, and aesthetic appeal. The color, the slots, the way in which the memory

---

17 Luther, Robert J., *The First Apple* (Alexandria, Virginia, MassMedia.mobi Press, 2013), 67.

> *could be expanded from 4K to 48K bytes, the control of the keyboard and hookup to the cassette recorder, and the BASIC that was stored in the ROM chip – in effect the motherboard – was Wozniak's contribution. Holt had contributed the extremely significant power supply, and Jerry Manock the case. The engineering advances were officially recognized when, some months later, Wozniak was awarded U.S. Patent #4,136,359 for a microcomputer for use with video display, and Holt was given Patent #4,130,862 for a direct current power supply. But behind them all Jobs was poking, prodding, and pushing and it was he, with his seemingly inexhaustible supply of energy, who became the chief arbiter and rejector... [Finally,] the combination of [Mike] Markkula [Apple's first president], Jobs, and the McKenna Agency turned Apple's public bow [at the West Coast Computer Faire] into a coup.*[18]

As they prepared for the display at the first West Coast Computer Faire, Jobs and Markkula decided the company needed a new corporate logo. Ron Wayne's original logo was a complex woodcut of Isaac Newton sitting under an apple tree, with a phrase from Wordsworth: "Newton...A Mind Forever Voyaging Through Strange Seas of Thought...Alone". Jobs had been concerned that the logo had been part of the reason for the slow sales of the Apple-1, and the Regis McKenna Agency was hired to help design a new one.

> *Rob Janoff, a young art director, was assigned to the Apple account and set about designing a corporate logo. Armed with the idea that the computers would be sold to consumers and that their machine was one of the few to offer color, Janoff set about drawing still lifes from a bowl of apples ... He gouged a rounded chunk from one side of the Apple, seeing this as a playful comment on the world of bits and bytes but also as a novel design. To Janoff the missing portion "prevented the apple from looking like a cherry tomato." He ran six colorful stripes across the Apple, starting with a jaunty sprig of green, and the mixture had a slightly psychedelic tint. The overall result was enticing and warm ...*
> *[Steve] Jobs was meticulous about the style and appearance of the logo ... When Janoff suggested that the six colors be separated by thin strips to make the reproduction easier, Jobs refused.*[19]

The origin of the multi-colored Apple logo has been the subject of some controversy over the years. One persistent rumor was that it had been designed

---

18 Moritz, Michael, *The Little Kingdom*, (New York, William Morrow and Company, Inc, 1984), 190-191.
19 Moritz, Michael, *The Little Kingdom*, (New York, William Morrow and Company, Inc, 1984), 188.

in honor of Alan Turing, an English mathematician who helped break German war codes during World War II. Because homosexuality was a criminal offense in the 1950s in Britain, he was forcibly treated in 1952 with estrogen as an alternative to imprisonment. In 1954 he committed suicide by eating a cyanide-laced apple. Therefore, since the gay-rights movement had appropriated the use of rainbow colors during the 1970s, and because Turing's death was associated with the apple as a fruit, it made sense to some to connect Turing with the colored Apple Computer logo. However, not only did Rob Janoff give the true story of the logo origin years later, but Steve Jobs also later confirmed that no relation to Turing was originally intended.[20, 21]

Apple Computer corporate logo, 1976 – 1998 – Photo credit: unknown

For the Faire, Markkula had ordered a smoky, backlit, illuminated Plexiglas sign with the new logo. Although Apple had a smaller booth than other companies, and some of the other microcomputer makers (Processor Technology, IMSAI, and Cromemco) had been in business longer, Apple's booth looked far more professional, thanks to Markkula's sign. Some of the other participants, companies larger than Apple, had done no more than use card tables with signs written in black markers.

Because they had been one of the first to commit to displaying at the Faire, Apple's booth was near the entrance and was visible to everybody entering the convention center. They demonstrated the graphics capabilities of the Apple II using a kaleidoscopic video graphics program (possibly an early version of a hi-res graphics display program later distributed with the Apple II called *BRIAN'S THEME*) on a huge display monitor, catching everybody's attention. At the show, they sold a few available Apple II motherboards, and took pre-orders for Apple II computers with a case.

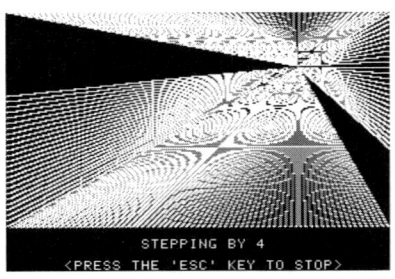

BRIAN'S THEME screen shot – Photo credit: personal

However, Faire organizer Jim Warren didn't think that Apple was a strong exhibitor. *BYTE* magazine, in its report of the show, failed to even mention Apple. Despite these early unimpressed opinions by influential people, over the next few months Apple received about three hundred orders for the Apple II, over a hundred more than the total number of Apple-1 computers sold.[22]

---

20 Hodges, Andrew, *Alan Turing: the enigma*, (London: Burnett Books, 1983).
21 Isaacson, Walter, "Introduction". *Steve Jobs*. New York: Simon & Schuster, 2011, xviii
22 Moritz, Michael, *The Little Kingdom*, (New York, William Morrow and Company, Inc, 1984), 192-193.

The first motherboard-only Apple II computers were shipped to customers on May 10, 1977, for those who wanted to add their own case, keyboard, and power supply (or wanted to update their Apple-1 system with the latest and greatest). A month later, on June 10, 1977, Apple began shipping full Apple II systems. The motherboard-only option didn't last for very long; if a customer did not connect a proper power supply, it could damage the board, and several were returned for that very reason.[23]

COST

Not only was Apple rushed to get a consumer-friendly computer to market during 1977, but two formidable competitors would appear during 1977: Commodore and Tandy Radio Shack.

The Commodore PET 2001 was first introduced at the Consumer Electronics Show in January 1977. It used the same 6502 processor as the Apple II (Commodore had purchased MOS Technology, the company that designed the 6502). The PET came in a metal case with an integrated 25 line by 40-character monochrome monitor, and a built-in cassette drive. It did not offer graphics capabilities, but could accept custom character sets that allowed the user to move beyond ASCII text. It was first offered as a 4K computer, but when taking pre-orders for it at the National Computer Conference in June, Commodore realized that 4K was simply not enough memory to create useful programs. It was redesigned as an 8K computer, and sold for $795 when it was finally available in October.

Tandy announced the Radio Shack TRS-80 in August. It used a Z-80 processor, which was compatible with the Intel 8080 processor (used by the Altair and other similar computers). Although not integrated together in one unit, as with the PET, the TRS-80 also came with a monochrome monitor that displayed 16 lines of 64-characters, and included block graphics. A cassette tape recorder was also included for data and program storage. The only memory size offered was 4K, and it sold for $599.95 when it became available for purchase in November 1977.

Like the other two competitors, the base RAM in the first Apple II computers was quite low, primarily because of the high cost of memory at the time. Apple sold the base 4K system for $1298, significantly more than either the PET or the TRS-80, and it lacked the monitor and storage cassette recorder they both included. A fully populated Apple II with 48K of RAM cost a whopping $2638. Despite its advantages of full memory expansion and color graphics, sales of the Apple II trailed behind Commodore and Tandy during 1977 and into 1978.

---

23 Wigginton, Randy, personal email to author, August 11, 2013.

These three computers, dubbed the 1977 Trinity by *BYTE* magazine in 1994, did not stand still. The following year Radio Shack offered an expansion interface that expanded the memory to 16K and offered other options (such as the ability to attach a printer). It took Commodore until 1979 to address the PET's problems of small memory and its tiny keyboard.

Other than accessories and software enhancements, the primary enhancement the Apple II initially needed was more memory. By June 1978, RAM prices had dropped to the point where the 4K Apple II was only $970, and a 48K Apple II had dropped to $1795. A year later, the 48K system was down to $1495, and $1395 by 1980.

EXPERIENCES OF EARLY USERS

The first Apple II computers sold were literally rough around the edges. The plastic cases were made with a different process from what was used later, and after returning from the company that molded them, they had to be painted the correct beige color, and some areas had to be sanded smooth. They had a toggle switch for power (instead of the rocker switch used later).

The molding process used in making the early cases caused another difficulty for Apple. They had contracted with a local company, paying them $10,000 to create the molds for the cases. However, as the number of orders for cases increased, problems developed with molding process. The case material was sticking to the wood mold, and part of the case would pull off when the mold was removed. It began to significantly constrict the number of computers Apple could sell. Since the company making the cases did not appear to be very interested in fixing the problem, Steve Jobs and a few other Apple employees went down to where the cases were being made. While some of the people from Apple kept the person at the molding company busy, the other Apple employees quietly picked up the molds and left with them.[24]

The first two hundred or so Apple II computers that came off the assembly line had cases without vents in the sides. However, the company soon found out that the chips on the circuit board and the power supply could build up enough heat to soften the lid and cause the case to sag. Jobs arranged to have the cases revised (to his satisfaction) to include vents in the sides of the case. (Recall that Jobs had insisted on no internal fans that would make noise.) Some customers requested replacement of the heat-sagged cases with the new vented cases.

Documentation for the Apple II was initially very limited. Steve Wozniak had some handwritten notes from the summer and fall of 1977 that were assembled into a document that later became known as the *Woz Wonderbook*, used internally as a reference by Apple employees. To provide something for custom-

---

24 ----, "Apple's Steven P. Jobs talks to IW", *InfoWorld* (March 8, 1982), 12.

ers, Apple's president, Mike Scott, had gone through desk drawers at night to find anything that looked like technical information about the computer, whether typed or handwritten. These notes, about thirty pages in all (some of which were included in the *Woz Wonderbook*) were photocopied, three-hole punched, and assembled in clear binders. This mini-manual was dropped in the box with each of the earliest Apple II computers that were sold. The cover was a reproduction of one of Apple's earliest advertisements for the Apple II. It stated, "Simplicity is the ultimate sophistication: introducing Apple][, the personal computer".

In early 1978 these original photocopied manuals were replaced with the new *Apple II Reference Manual* (also known as the Red Book), and copies were mailed to previous customers. However, the material was essentially the same as the mini-manual, except with a red cover. Jobs realized that people often viewed the quality of a product by the quality of its documentation, and so he wanted Apple to have manuals that were easy to read and had a professional appearance.[25]

Jef Raskin had inspected the Apple II at the West Coast Computer Faire, and there he had met Jobs and Wozniak. He was a professor at the University of California at San Diego, teaching computer science and music. At the time of the Faire, Raskin had a consulting firm, and he offered to create better documentation for Apple's products. Apple contracted his services in January of 1978 to write a manual for Apple BASIC (Integer BASIC), and the results were sufficiently impressive that Raskin was hired to start Apple's internal publications group.

Apple II Reference Manual, January 1978 (the "Red Book")
– Photo credit: personal

The Reference Manual was also a target for improvement, and Raskin contacted Chris Espinosa to revise the Red Book. During his fall semester at Berkley in 1978 Espinosa wrote the new manual, and then used a typesetting program on the Berkley UNIX system to produce it.[26]

Setting up the Apple II was fairly simple. The lid popped off easily, and one of the first things usually added was the RF modulator, to allow the computer to display text and color graphics on a standard television. This was

---

25 Chien, Philip, "The First Ten Years: A Look Back", *The Apple II Review*, (Fall/Winter 1986), 12.
26 Pang, Alex Soojung-Kim, "Chris Espinosa on Rewriting the Apple II Manual", *Making The Macintosh: Technology And Culture In Silicon Valley*, last updated June 13, 2000, <www-sul.stanford.edu/mac/primary/interviews/espinosa/apple2.html>, accessed December 27, 2011

attached to two pins sticking up from the rear of the motherboard, near the video output jack. Those who bought a proper NTSC computer monitor did not need to bother with the RF modulator.

The earliest game paddles included with the computer had a lever that could be moved back and forth, with a button to press. Later versions of the game paddles were small black boxes, with a knob to turn and a tiny black button on the side (which would be painful on the finger if being used in a game that required repeated pressing of the button). These boxes were attached via a narrow cable to a plug that looked (and was) fragile; this plug went into a small socket in the motherboard.

After turning on the Apple II, the first thing to greet the user was a screen full of random alphabetic characters and symbols, and possibly some colored blocks (lo-res graphics mode might be turned on.) At this point it was necessary to press the RESET key in the upper right hand side of the keyboard, which would cause the speaker to make a "beep!" sound, and an asterisk would appear in the bottom left-hand corner of the screen. (If the lo-res graphics mode had been on, it would now be off.) The asterisk was a prompt for the Monitor, and next to it was a flashing box, the cursor. To get into BASIC, it was necessary to press the "Ctrl" key and the "B" key simultaneously, then press RETURN. Now the prompt would change to ">", indicating that Integer BASIC was active. Functionally, here was one of the first ways in which the Apple II had the advantage over the Apple-1—BASIC was resident in ROM, rather than requiring the language to be loaded from cassette.

At this point, the new Apple II owner could either begin entering a BASIC program, or try to load one from cassette. The cassette recorder was attached to the input and output jacks on the back of the computer. To load from cassette was not always easy; it took time to get the right volume and tone settings on the tape player in order to avoid getting the "ERR" or "*** SYNTAX ERR" message. (And if the Apple II didn't have much memory, the "*** MEM FULL ERR" message might appear.) When the program loaded properly, it was usually necessary to type "RUN" to get it started.[27]

The cassette interface used in the Apple-1 was incorporated into the Apple II with virtually no changes. At the time Wozniak designed it, there was a wide range of brands and grades of cassette tape on the market, ranging from expensive tapes that were appropriate for quality music recording and playback, down to inexpensive tape that were most suitable for speech, such as making recordings of lectures. Knowing that the typical hobbyist storing or loading programs with cassette tapes would go for a cheap recorder, Woz wrote his data-reading algorithm to be tolerant of sound that would be muddy and possibly have hiss (common with cassettes). As a result, it was possible to consistently get a good load from a number of different brands of cassette

---

27 -----. *Apple II BASIC Programming Manual*, (Cupertino, CA, Apple Computer, Inc., 1978, 1979, 1980, 1981), 1-19.

tape and cassette hardware (once the volume and tone controls were adjusted appropriately). However, once the Apple II was in the hands of enough customers the company began to get complaints from some users that they could save and load only very small programs. Larger programs simply would not load at all. When they investigated the problem, Apple found that the problem was with high-quality cassette decks, those that would give excellent results with the recording and playback of music. Those types of cassette recorders gave poor results when used for data storage, possibly because they reproduced the sound too sharply, or due to the inclusion of noise-reduction circuitry (which would muffle data sounds as "noise").[28]

In the first few years that the Apple II was sold, there were three primary sources of software available to the new user. The user could write his own programs (BASIC or assembly language); he could enter programs from listings found in magazines or books; or he could purchase software. The purchased software came on cassette tapes, usually with sparse documentation, and packaged in zip-lock bags. Some of these were programs that had simply been saved to tape, either with the SAVE command in Integer BASIC, or with the command to write bytes to tape from the Monitor. An early method of copy protection was used at times, by having the tape load to a memory location that could not simply be saved to another tape. (Copying from one tape to another would often introduce hiss and signal degradation, and would make the copy unusable.)

The cassette era for the Apple II lasted from 1977 through 1982. By that year, the number of Apple II owners who could afford to purchase the Disk II drive had increased to such a significant level that sales of commercial software on cassettes dropped to the point where it was no longer a viable medium.[29, 30]

An oddity of Wozniak's Integer BASIC was that it could handle numbers only in the range from -32767 to +32767. However, it was necessary at times to use the CALL statement to make use of some of the assembly language routines in the Monitor ROM. These addresses were well above 32767, and could not be directly entered. To get around this limitation, Wozniak designed his BASIC to allow entry of addresses above that upper limit as a negative number.

For example the address of the ROM code to clear the text screen was at $FC58, which was 64600 in decimal. Since CALL 64600 could not be used in Integer BASIC, the programmer had to translate it to 64600 minus 65536, or -936. So, to clear the text screen in a BASIC program, the command CALL-936 was used.

The most used of these negative addresses was the one that allowed entry to the Monitor program, CALL-151.

---

28 Wigginton, Randy, e-mail to author, September 1, 2013.
29 Vignau, Antoine, "Apple Cassette Tapes", *Brutal Deluxe Software*, accessed December 28, 2011, <www.brutaldeluxe.fr/projects/cassettes/>
30 McFadden, Andy, "Early Copy Protection", *Tech Writings*, accessed October 20, 2012, <fadden.com/techmisc/cassette-protect.htm>

ENHANCEMENTS

The first Apple II motherboards were later identified as Revision 0 boards. As simple enhancements or fixes were created, motherboards on later releases were called Revision 1. Some of the changes built into these Revision 1 boards could be implemented on the older Revision 0 boards. These included a change to add two more colors to the hi-res graphics mode (adding red and blue to the already existing green and violet), hardware to automatically do a RESET when the computer was powered up (the earliest versions required the user to press the RESET key manually), and an attempt to include circuitry to display video in the European PAL or SECAM television standards (although it turned out that this did not work, regardless of what the early reference manual stated).[31, 32, 33, 34]

EARLY HARDWARE ADD-ONS

Most new Apple II owners simply purchased the M&R Sup'R'Mod to display video on their color TV. However, some other enterprising hackers designed their own versions of modulators. One used by an early member of the Apple Pugetsound Program Library Exchange (A.P.P.L.E.) was somewhat better shielded than the Sup'R'Mod. It had its own power supply and plugged into the video output jack on the back of the Apple. However, the Sup'R'Mod was by far the biggest seller.[35]

At first, there were no interface cards for any of Woz's eight slots. With the limited funds that computer purchasers had then (and now) there was not much they could afford after spending anywhere from $1200 to $1800 just to get their own Apple II. But they were innovative, and like many other hardware hackers of the day managed to make do with old or surplus parts. Some people, for instance, obtained used Teletype printers, such as the ASR-33 (often called "battleships" because they were so rugged and heavy). Since there weren't any printer interface cards to plug into the slots to allow the computer to communicate with the Teletype, they used a trick they learned from Woz himself. The Apple II had four single-bit output pins on the game controller socket that could be used for various purposes. A schematic floated through the various user groups that showed how to connect the Teletype to one of

---

31 Willegal, Mike, Scanned image of *Contact #6*, page 6, *Mike's Hobby Page*, accessed October 20, 2012, <www.willegal.net/appleii/images/contact-newsletter005.jpg>

32 Watson, Allen, "More Colors For Your Apple", *BYTE*, (June 1979), 60-68.

33 ----, "Revision 0 / Revision 1 Board", *Apple II Reference Manual*, (Cupertino, CA, Apple Computer, Inc., 1979, 1981), 26.

34 Willegal, Mike, "Apple II Rev 0 Motherboard Project", *Mike's Hobby Page*, <www.willegal.net/appleii/appleii-first_page.htm>

35 ----, "A.P.P.L.E. Co-op Celebrates A Decade of Service", *Call-A.P.P.L.E.*, (Feb 1988), 12-27.

these annunciator pins; along with it was a machine language program that re-directed output from the screen to that one-bit port, and on to the printer.[36]

MARKETING THE APPLE II

By early 1979, the price lists Apple distributed included system bundles to attract customers that had specific needs.

- Beginner's System – 16 K Apple II and tape recorder (no monitor or television) - $1235
- Student's System – 32K Apple II, disk drive and controller, and Applesoft (floating point BASIC) on a plug-in card - $2140
- Scientist's System – 48K Apple II, disk and Applesoft card, communications card and modem, 9-inch monochrome monitor, a Centronics printer and parallel card, and a clock/calendar card - $3814
- Businessman's System – everything in the Scientist's System, plus a second disk drive and a better Centronics printer

These bundles were not offered at any discount; they were the base price of all parts, but put together for simplicity of dealer sales.

APPLE-1 UPGRADES

Nearly all products need customer support. The more complex a product, the greater is the need for support. The Apple-1 was a marvel of compact design compared to other first generation microcomputers, but it still needed a fair amount of handholding for those who owned it when something didn't seem to be working. This created somewhat of a problem for Apple in managing technical support for the Apple-1. Although only 200 to 250 were sold, most questions about it had to be handled directly by Steve Wozniak. Everyone in engineering handled tech support calls for the Apple II when it was released; sometimes even the production line technicians handled those calls. But an Apple-1 call still had to be handed over to Wozniak. It was decided at Apple that the most effective way to handle long-term tech support was to convert Apple-1 owners into Apple II owners. This was further enforced by the forward-thinking attitude of Steve Jobs, who now considered the Apple-1 to be yesterday's news, and insisted that any intelligent person would obviously want to upgrade to an Apple II.

Because of Apple's push to get Apple-1 owners to upgrade, they began to offer attractive deals to them. Initially they were offered a discount on an

---

36 Golding, Val J, "Applesoft From Bottom To Top", *Call-A.P.P.L.E. In Depth #1*, (Seattle, Washington, 1981), 8.

Apple II, then a straight trade-in to get an Apple II in exchange for the old Apple-1. This escalated to offer an Apple II with a full 48K of memory, then a 48K Apple II with a disk drive, and in one case they even threw in several peripheral cards and a monitor. It is this aggressive drive by Apple that has contributed to the dearth of Apple-1 computers that survived to later years.[37, 38]

TIMELINE

The start and end dates for the Apple-1 & Apple II:

Apple-1 – *April 1976 - May 1977*

Wozniak begins work on the Apple II – *May 1976*

West Coast Computer Faire – *April 16-17, 1977*

Apple II – *May 1977 - May 1979*

---

[37] Huston, Cliff, and Huston, Dick, notes on web site setup up to sell early Apple memorabilia, <homep-age.mac.com/cliff_huston/.public/Offering/Early_Apple.html>, accessed March 24, 2010 (inactive October 20, 2012).

[38] James, *RetroMacCast*, "The Huston Brothers", #153, released March 20, 2010, <itunes.apple.com/us/podcast/episode-153-huston-brothers/id209514700?i=81692205>

CHAPTER 4
The BASICs

INTEGER BASIC

The first high-level language available for general use on the Apple II was Integer BASIC. It was a quick, compact language that Steve Wozniak referred to as "Game BASIC". Its disadvantage was the lack of easy access to floating point operations (for numbers that included decimal point, 3.14 instead of just 3), and it lacked some string handling functions.

Despite its limitations, Integer BASIC had a loyal following. For those thousands who purchased an Apple II from June 1977 to June 1979, this was the only programming language available, and it took on a status similar to that of a beloved first-born child. Games, utilities, and even simple business apps were written using Wozniak's hand-assembled masterpiece, and those who followed the pages of *Call-A.P.P.L.E.* magazine learned much about the internals of the language.

With the disassembler built into the Monitor, people tore Integer BASIC apart to learn how it worked, and to make it work better. Val Golding, the editor of *Call-A.P.P.L.E.*, even wrote a series of columns in 1979 entitled "So Who Needs Applesoft?" These articles showed how to simulate some of the more advanced features of Applesoft in this older BASIC.

A.P.P.L.E. even sold (under license agreement with Apple Computer) *Integer BASIC Plus*, a relocatable RAM version of the original ROM BASIC. For those who had purchased an Apple II Plus without an Integer BASIC firmware card, this program allowed them to load, edit, and run programs written for the original Apple II BASIC. It had all the features of the original language, plus a USER command (to allow the user to create custom commands for the language), the ability to easily scroll in four directions on text and lo-res screens, simpler printing of ASCII characters, and improved error handling.[1, 2]

---

1 -----, (ad), *PEEKing At Call-A.P.P.L.E.* (Seattle, Washington, Vol 2, 1979), 62.
2 McBride, Hitchens, *Integer Basic + Manual*, (A.P.P.L.E., Seattle, Washington, 1979), 3-5.

Apple never released a comprehensive reference manual for Integer BASIC. The only manual available for it was a book produced by Jef Raskin at the request of Steve Jobs—primarily a tutorial and a general introduction to using a computer. This *Apple II BASIC Programming Manual* didn't even call it Integer BASIC, but referred to the language as Apple BASIC. It gave most of its programming examples in the form of segments of a graphics and sound demo that created a lo-res ball bouncing off the sides of the screen.[3]

APPLESOFT I

Apple II users, especially those who wanted to produce business applications, wanted something more powerful than Integer BASIC. This product eventually arrived in the form of Applesoft. Back in 1975 and 1976, Microsoft was producing BASIC interpreters for nearly every microprocessor in existence, hoping to license or sell their BASIC to companies who built a computer around that chip. In mid-1976, Microsoft's first employee, Marc McDonald, developed a version of BASIC to run on the then-new 6502 microprocessor, even though there were not yet any computers that used that processor.

They became aware of Steve Wozniak's work on designing his 6502 computer (the Apple-1), and one of Microsoft's programmers called Steve Jobs to see if he would be interested in a BASIC language for this computer. Jobs told him that they already had a BASIC, and if they needed a better one, they could "do it themselves over the weekend."

Even without a potential customer, McDonald worked on 6502 BASIC, using a modified 6800 microprocessor simulator (recall that the 6800 had a similar instruction set to the 6502). For several months, Microsoft's 6502 BASIC sat on a shelf, unwanted and unused.

By October 1976 they finally had a contract to put this interpreter into the new PET computer—under development by 6502 designer Chuck Peddle at Commodore. This would ultimately become the first time that BASIC was included with a computer built into the ROM, rather than being loaded from a paper tape, disk, or cassette.

However, the contract Microsoft had with Commodore was no good to them at that time, as far as income was concerned; it stipulated that they would not be paid until some time in 1977, when the computer was ready to ship. With income and cash reserves running dangerously low, Microsoft was given a reprieve by none other than Apple Computer.[4]

---

3 -----, *Apple II BASIC Programming Manual*, (Apple Computer, Inc., Cupertino, California, 1978, 1979, 1980, 1981).
4 Manes, Stephen, and Paul Andrews, *Gates* (New York: Doubleday 1993), 99-100.

Apple was bombarded by increasing numbers of requests by users of the Apple II for a floating point BASIC. Integer BASIC worked well for many purposes, and a skilled programmer could even make use of the floating-point routines that were included in the Integer BASIC ROM. However, the average Apple II user was not satisfied with Integer BASIC, especially as it made them unable to easily implement business software (where the number to the right of the decimal point is as important as the one to left).

During the fall of 1977, Wozniak tried to make modifications to his Integer BASIC to make use of the floating-point routines, but his other responsibilities at Apple interfered with this project, and his efforts creating a floating point BASIC fell further and further behind. Consequently, Apple's management decided to go back to Microsoft and license the 6502 floating point BASIC that had been offered to them in 1976.

In August 1977, Apple made a $10,500 payment to Microsoft for the first half of a flat-fee license that they had negotiated. Typically, Microsoft licensed its BASIC on a royalty basis, in which they received a set fee for every copy of BASIC that went out the door. For a BASIC in ROM, this meant Microsoft would receive a payment with every computer that was sold. The fact that Microsoft was willing to concede and let Apple license its 6502 BASIC on a flat-fee basis is a reflection of the financial straits that Microsoft was under.[5] The version Apple licensed was almost identical to the MITS extended BASIC that Microsoft had previously written for the Altair 8800.[6,7]

At Apple, Randy Wigginton was assigned the job of incorporating the lo-res graphics commands that were unique to the Apple II into Microsoft's BASIC, working part-time on it after school.

At the same time that Wigginton was working on Applesoft, two new engineers at Apple became involved in the project. Cliff and Dick Huston were brothers who taught themselves digital engineering. Through an acquaintance, they contacted Rod Holt at Apple in the fall of 1977. Holt was looking for engineers to help with hardware and software design for the Apple II, and scheduled the brothers for an interview. They were hired in November 1977 to work on peripheral cards for the computer.

Cliff and Dick had previously built an IMSAI 8080-based computer, and had invested about four thousand dollars into it, including additional memory, a paper tape reader, and a disk drive. They had attended the West Coast Computer Faire, seen the Apple II demonstration, and were surprised that it did so much with so little hardware. However, with all the money they had sunk into their IMSAI, they were reluctant to drop it and move over to the Apple II.

---

5 Manes, Stephen, and Paul Andrews, *Gates* (New York: Doubleday 1993), 111-112.
6 Chien, Philip, "The First Ten Years: A Look Back", *The Apple II Review*, (Fall/Winter 1986), 12.
7 Golding, Val J, "Applesoft From Bottom To Top", *Call-A.P.P.L.E. In Depth* (Seattle, Washington, 1981), 8.

Wigginton was somewhat suspicious of Cliff Huston coming around and looking at his work on Applesoft, particularly because of his IMSAI computer. As they got to know one another, however, Wigginton let him know that the source code that had been obtained from Microsoft was "a mess", and needed considerable bug fixes, over and above the incorporation of the lo-res and hi-res graphics commands.

One problem Wigginton grappled with was a lack of tools. Since there was (at the time) no assembler to use on the Apple II, he used a Teletype and a 110-baud modem, connected through a dial-up connection to a company named Call Computer. On the other end of the phone line, he used a cross-compiler (a program that created machine language code for a computer other than the one on which the compiler ran). Wigginton's work was tedious because of the slow speed of the connection. Not only that, but the cross-assembler being used to compile 6502 code was itself written in BASIC. This resulted in a compile time of over two hours. Printing the source code was out of the question; it would have taken *days*.[8]

By late November 1977, Wigginton hit a crisis. Call Computer had developed a technical problem that became a disaster. The current workspace for its clients had become damaged, and so Call tried to restore from a tape of the previous month—and that tape didn't work. The same happened with the backup from the month before that. It turned out that the backup tapes were being erased by a faulty tape drive, and so all of the backups were destroyed. The effect on Wigginton was that he lost weeks of work on Applesoft. It was gone, save only the handwritten notes on his single source code printout. He had intended to have the finished version of Applesoft ready by January 1978.

At this point, Cliff Huston came to the aid of Wigginton. When he started work at Apple, Huston had brought his IMSAI to work, because at the time it was all he had available. At Apple, he programmed on his IMSAI, using the attached paper tape reader. Wigginton and others had previously criticized him for using this foreign, inferior piece of equipment.

Now, using the paper tape reader, Huston was able to input the original BASIC source code from Microsoft, break it up into multiple segments (he had only a single floppy disk drive), and let Wigginton resume work on fixing the source code, using an IMSAI-based 6502 cross-assembler. Because it required several floppy disks to hold the entire source, it was necessary to swap disks during the compile process, but it took only six minutes (rather than the two hours required for Call Computer's cross-assembler written in BASIC).

Mike Scott, the president of Apple, bought a Centronics printer to use with the IMSAI, and with that Wigginton was able to obtain a full printout of the source code in only 35 minutes. In the end, Scott leased the IMSAI

---

8 James, *RetroMacCast*, "The Huston Brothers", #153, released March 20, 2010, <https://itunes.apple.com/us/podcast/episode-153-huston-brothers/id209514700?i=81692205>.

from Cliff Huston for development at Apple, and did so for nearly two years after this.

With this last-minute help from Huston's "inferior" IMSAI, Wigginton completed Applesoft BASIC in early December 1977. The cassette release in January 1978 contained a 10K program that looked to the computer just like an Integer BASIC program, though only a small part of it really was. To make it easy to load and start from cassette, the Applesoft interpreter was attached to the end of a short Integer BASIC program. When the Integer program started, it poked some values into memory and jumped to the start of the machine language section, which relocated the Applesoft interpreter to the lower part of memory.

Using this version of Applesoft (which later became known as Applesoft I) was an exercise in frustration. It took several minutes to load from the cassette tape, and it was not dependable. If the wrong key was pressed while entering or running an Applesoft program, the program that was being run could be wiped out, and the Applesoft interpreter itself would have to be reloaded from cassette. However, few users knew how to make use of the floating-point routines that Wozniak had written into the Integer ROM, so this unreliable Applesoft BASIC became the only practical means of programming with floating-point math on the Apple II.

Aside from the reliability issue, another problem with this early version of Applesoft involved hi-resolution graphics. Although the Apple II was capable of displaying these graphics, the Applesoft interpreter extended up into the memory used by the hi-res screen, and so prevented its use. Furthermore, like Integer BASIC, this first version of Applesoft did not include any commands to manage hi-res graphics.[9]

Applesoft I came with a manual printed on letter sized paper (8½ by 11 inches), sporting a blue cover.[10] This came to be known as the Blue Book (recall that the Apple II reference book was known as the Red Book). There were actually two versions of the Applesoft Reference Manual.[11] The first edition was dated November 1977 (the manual was completed two months before Applesoft I was available for release), and the second edition came out nine months later, in August 1978.

---

9 Golding, Val J. "Applesoft From Bottom To Top", *Call-A.P.P.L.E. In Depth #1*, (Seattle, Washington, 1981), 8.
10 Bernsten, Jeff, A2 Roundtable, Category 2, Topic 16, *GEnie*, accessed April 1991.
11 Backenköhler, Dirk, post on comp.sys.apple2, April 9, 2011, and confirmed in e-mail message to author.

This early Applesoft had some important differences when compared with the later, more widely used version. One involved requiring the user to answer a question about how much memory was present (common with BASIC interpreters of the day). Another change was a different choice of command names for hi-res graphics (turning graphics on and off, setting colors, and plotting points and lines). There were also some bugs in this early version, and user groups distributed patches to overcome some of the most common ones.

Applesoft I startup screen – Photo credit: personal

APPLESOFT II

In spring 1978, Wigginton and others at Apple made some needed revisions to Applesoft. This time they used a cross-assembler running on a North Star Horizon (Z-80) microcomputer (modified from Dick Huston's IMSAI compiler), and fixed the known bugs and added other commands to control additional features unique to the Apple II. These included commands to draw and manipulate hi-res graphics. The hi-res graphics code he used was the same code that Woz had previously written and had included in the Integer BASIC ROM. Those routines had always been usable from an Integer BASIC program, but required some significant programming knowledge to make them work. Also, the lo-res graphics commands were renamed to be more consistent with the equivalent commands in Integer BASIC (for example, GR, HLIN, and VLIN). Wigginton also put a bit of himself into the code, including his initials in the last three bytes of the Applesoft code.

This version was called Applesoft II, and eventually it was available in five forms: Cassette RAM and Diskette RAM (which loaded to the same memory locations that interfered with hi-res graphics as did Applesoft I), Firmware card ROM, Language card RAM, and finally main board ROM (in the Apple II Plus, released in mid-1979).

When Applesoft II was started up from cassette or diskette versions, the display screen now showed a copyright date of 1978 by Apple Computer, Inc., and 1976 by Microsoft (which may be either their copyright date for the original Microsoft BASIC, or possibly for Microsoft's first 6502 version).[12]

---

12 Bernsten, Jeff, A2 Roundtable, Category 2, Topic 16, *GEnie*, accessed April 1991.

> One of the ways that Microsoft used to identify its various versions of BASIC was to embed the company name within the code. The encoding hid it such that simply looking at the raw code as ASCII text would not reveal it. This "Easter egg" was present in all 6502 versions of BASIC, including Applesoft.
>
> On early versions of Microsoft's 6502 BASIC in ROM on the Commodore PET, a command could be typed from the keyboard to display the message. On the Apple II the encoded text was present, but there was no secret method to invoke it; Randy Wigginton had removed that code when he modified it for the Apple II.17 Using the Monitor, the bytes for this secret message can be found from $F094 to $F09C, just after the definitions for powers of pi. The bytes at those addresses are:
>
> ```
> F094:A6 D3 C1 C8 D4 C8 D5 C4 CE CA
> ```
>
> If printed as ASCII, it reads as "&SAHTHUDNJ". Applying an exclusive-or function with $87 on each byte changes this to "!TFOSORCIM", which is "MICROSOFT!" backwards.[13,14]

Wigginton was also responsible for the addition of a special statement, the "&" command. In the original source code listing for Applesoft, this ampersand command had a comment that read "DOS hooks", as Woz and Wigginton had early on considered this as a means of incorporating commands for a disk operating system.

What this ampersand command became famous for was a means for programmers to add custom commands to Applesoft. Those who were knowledgeable about the internal workings of Applesoft could use the code within Applesoft to parse the information following the ampersand, and act on that to create functions that would be difficult or impossible from BASIC.

TIMELINE

Integer BASIC – *June 1977*

Applesoft I – *January 1978*

Applesoft II – *June 1978*

---

13 Stell, Michael, "Bill Gates' Personal Easter Eggs in 8 Bit BASIC", *pagetable.com*, <http://www.pagetable.com/?p=43>, accessed October 20, 2012.

14 Sander-Cederlof, Bob, "S-C DocuMentor — Applesoft - S.EFEA", <http://www.txbobsc.com/scsc/scdocumentor/EFEA.html>, accessed October 20, 2012.

CHAPTER 5
Concentric Circles of Magnetic Data

By December 1977, the Apple II had been available for six months. Most customers used their television as an inexpensive color monitor, and a cassette recorder to store and retrieve their programs and data. However, sales of the Apple II were significantly lower than those of the other two members of the 1977 Trinity. The PET was outselling the Apple II at a ratio of six to one, and the TRS-80, which benefited from the large network of Radio Shack stores, outsold it by one hundred sixty-six to one.[1]

In early 1978, Apple had introduced some enhancements to the II, including their first version of a floating point BASIC (Applesoft) on cassette, and a printer interface card to plug into one of the slots on the motherboard. But the Apple II still needed something to make it more attractive to buyers, to stand out above the TRS-80 and the PET. One area that needed improvement was its program and data storage and retrieval system on cassette; it was a continued source of frustration for many users. The TRS-80 cassette system, though slower, was more sophisticated than that of the Apple II, allowing named files and easier storage of files and data on the same tape. The PET could actually control the cassette drive from a BASIC program. On the Apple II it took *very* careful adjustment of the volume and tone controls on the cassette recorder for programs or data to successfully load. Users of the Apple cassette system also needed to pay careful attention to the location on the tape where a program was stored, and was no more accurate than the number on the recorder's mechanical tape counter (if it had one).

FLOPPY DRIVES

IBM engineers had invented the 8-inch floppy disk in 1971, and over the next two years made enhancements that increased its capacity from 80K to nearly 240K. Alan Shugart, an IBM manager, left that company and formed his own in 1973.

---

[1] Actual sales figures are difficult to determine, as these companies did not always release hard numbers. However Jeremy Reimer in 2012 compiled data from a number of historical sources, and created a spreadsheet with estimated sales, staring from 1975 and moving forwards. These statistics are based on his data. "Total Share: Personal Computer Market Share 1975-2010", *Jeremy's Blog*, <jeremyreimer.com/m-item.lsp?i=137>

An engineer from Shugart Associates was challenged in 1976 by a company making an S-100 computer (similar to an Altair 8800) to make a smaller size floppy disk, more appropriate to the size of microcomputers. The disk size suggested was about the same as a table napkin, 5 1/4 inches. It was small enough to be a convenient size, but large enough to prevent users from putting it in a pocket (and therefore at risk of bending).[2, 3]

The company went on to design and market the SA400 "minifloppy" drive that same year, with a formatted capacity of 90K.[4] These devices became popular with users of the various microcomputers marketed and sold in the mid 1970s. Though much more expensive than cassette tape storage, diskettes offered dramatically greater convenience and flexibility.

Apple president Mike Markkula was one Apple II user who was dissatisfied with cassette tape storage. He had a favorite checkbook program, but it took two minutes to read in the program from the tape, and another two minutes to read in the check files.[5] Consequently, at the executive board meeting held in December 1977 he made a list of company goals. At the top of the list was "floppy disk". Although Wozniak didn't know much about how floppy disk drives worked, he had once looked through the Shugart manual.

> As an experiment Woz had [earlier] conceived a circuit that would do much of what the Shugart manual said was needed to control a disk drive. Woz didn't know how computers actually controlled drives, but his method had seemed to him particularly simple and clever. When Markkula challenged him to put a disk drive on the Apple, he recalled that circuit and began considering its feasibility. He looked at the way other computer companies – including IBM –controlled drives. He also began to examine disk drives – particularly North Star's. After reading the North Star manual, Woz knew that his circuit would do what theirs did and more. He knew he really had a clever design.[6]

Other issues that Wozniak had to deal with involved a way to properly time the reading and writing of information to the disk. IBM used a complex hardware-based circuit to achieve this synchronization. Wozniak, after studying IBM's drive, realized that if the data was written to the disk in a different fashion, all that circuitry was unneeded. Many floppy disks sold at that time were "hard sectored", meaning that they had a hole punched in the disk near

---

2 Sollman, George, "Evolution of the Minifloppy Product Family", *IEEE Transactions on Magnetics* (July 1978, Vol Mag-14, No. 4) .
3 Porter, Jim (interviewer), "Oral History Panel on 5.25 and 3.5 inch Floppy Drives", Computer History Museum, recorded January 3, 2005.
4 -----, "Shugart Associates SA400 minifloppy Disk Drive", company datasheet, August 1976.
5 Williams, Gregg, and Rob Moore, "The Apple Story, Part 2: More History And The Apple III", *BYTE* (January 1985), 167-168.
6 Freiberger, Paul and Michael Swaine, *Fire In The Valley, Second Edition*, (Berkley, Osborne/McGraw-Hill, 2000), 284-287.

the center ring. This hole was used by the disk drive hardware to identify what section of the disk was passing under the read/write head at any particular time. Wozniak's technique would allow the drive to do self-synchronization, which was called "soft sectoring". This ignored the little timing hole, and saved on hardware.

Steve Jobs had been visiting Shugart offices regularly, insisting that he needed a cheap $100 disk drive. After Wozniak figured out the details of how to control a disk drive, Jobs came back and said that not only did he want a cheap disk drive, he wanted just the mechanism; no read/write electronics, no head load solenoid, no track zero sensor and no index hole sensor. Shugart engineers were puzzled by the request, but agreed to give Jobs the drives he wanted. Identifying these stripped down drives with the product name SA390 (being less than a standard SA400), they provided Apple with twenty-five of them to test.

During the design of his disk interface card, Wozniak first worked with an SA400 drive using the standard controlling electronics included with it. To make it work on the Apple II required two different steps. One was to modify the analog electronics board on the disk drive itself, and the other was to create a new interface card to connect the computer to the drive. Wozniak possessed strong skills in digital electronics, but he was weak in analog electroncs. Converesly, Rod Holt (who had created the switching power supply for the Apple II) was strong in analog, but weak in digital. (Analog electronics involved a continuously variable signal, whereas digital electronics deals with two levels only.)[7]

Shugart's analog board for the disk drive used about 18 chips. Holt was able to obtain a new Motorola chip that consolidated the function of several of the existing chips. With the help of Cliff Huston, he was able to produce a final design that reduced the count to only four chips.

Woznkiak redesigned the disk controller card, resulting in a chip reduction from 40 on Shugart's S-100 board to only eight.

After the design work was done, they began to test some of the Shugart SA390 drives. What they found was that most of them worked, though several required adjustments. Some of the drives simply didn't work at all. Huston solved this problem by optimizing the analog electronics and creating a series of procedures to make it possible to make adjustments to the drives on a production line.

When representatives from Apple returned to Shugart to place orders for more of the SA390 drives to sell under the Apple brand, one of Shugart's engineers admitted to a deception. The prototype drives that had been provided to Apple had actually come from a pile of bad SA400 drives. They had expected that Apple's engineers would be unable to make the drives work, and

---

7   Sander, Wendell, e-mail message to author, August 11, 2013.

out of frustration would have come back and purchased the more expensive SA400 drives.

Another problem with the Disk II was resolved by Wendell Sander. He held a PhD in engineering and had been working at Fairchild Research & Development on dynamic RAM chips. Sander first saw the Apple-1 at one of the Byte Shops, noted that it used DRAM chips, and purchased it. One of his first projects was to use Apple BASIC to program a new version of the *Star Trek* game that was popular on mini and microcomputers at the time. He showed his Apple-1 game to Steve Jobs, and when the Apple II was nearing its shipping date, Jobs hired Sander to port his game for the new computer.

When the Disk II project came along, Sander became a tester of the new drives. He found a timing error, and suggested a change in the controller code to resolve it. His solution made it possible for a wider tolerance of drive hardware to function properly.[8]

As the Disk II drives began to roll off the assembly line, the first drive was given to Cliff Huston in recognition of his work in making the SA390 drives work. The second drive was given to Wendell Sander, for his correction of the timing error.[9,10]

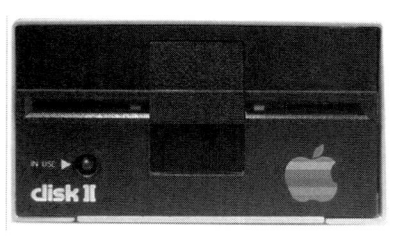

Disk II drive – Photo credit: personal

SOFTWARE AND HARDWARE

Wozniak asked Randy Wigginton for help in writing the software to control the disk drive. Woz created the most timing-sensitive parts of the controller routines, and Wigginton built on his work, designing the remainder of the interface code that would ultimately be used by the disk system.[11]

During their week of Christmas vacation in 1977 the two worked day and night creating a rudimentary disk operating system, aiming to have the drive ready to demonstrate at the Consumer Electronics Show in the first week of 1978. Their system was to allow entry of single letter commands to read files from fixed locations on the disk. However, even this simple system was not working when Wozniak and Wigginton left for the show.

When they arrived in Las Vegas they helped to set up the booth, and then returned to working on the disk drive. The two stayed up all night, making

---

8 Sander, Wendell, e-mail message to author, August 11, 2013.
9 Huston, Cliff, e-mail message to author, March 25, 2010.
10 Sollman, George, and Massaro, Don, interviewed by Jim Porter, "Oral History Panel on 5.25 and 3.5 inch Floppy Drives", *Computer History Museum*, 15-17, <archive.computerhistory.org/resources/text/Oral_History/5.25_3.5_Floppy_Drive/5.25_and_3.5_Floppy_Panel.oral_history.2005.102657925.pdf>, accessed October, 20, 2012
11 Woznkia, Steve, telephone interview with author, August 9, 2013.

incremental changes to the demo system, and by six in the morning they had a functioning demonstration disk. They had been making incremental backups at various times during the night, and Wigginton suggested making a copy of the latest version of their disk, so they would have a backup if something went wrong. Track by track, they copied the disk. When it was done, they found that this time they had, unfortunately, copied the blank disk on top of their working demo. However, Wozniak remembered the changes they had previously made, and he managed to recreate the latest changes by patching them to the demo disk. By 10 am they were able to display the new disk drive at the show.[12, 13, 14]

Following the Consumer Electronics Show, Wozniak set out to complete the design of the Disk II controller card. It was at this time that he reduced Shugart's 40 chips to a smaller number. In his redesign, he decided to use a single 8-bit ROM for tracking and reacting to the changing states of the disk controller as it decoded the bit stream. This concept eliminated more than a dozen of the chips used on the standard SA400 controller. Beyond that, he made additional design changes that reduced the total chip count to only nine. Eventually he reduced this further to eight, since two 555 timers were replaced by a single 556 timer.

On the disk drive itself, Wozniak made modifications to the way in which data was recorded on the diskette. He was able to increase the FM (frequency modulation) encoding from 10 sectors per track to 11, which increased the disk capacity from 87.5K to 96.3K. Then, after coming up with a completely different technique, he abandoned the FM encoding in favor of a group code recording (GCR) method. This further increased the storage density without increasing the number of bits actually written to the disk, and allowed him to increase the number of sectors per track to 13, giving a disk capacity of 113.8K. To make this work, it was necessary to create a lookup table and use some clever programming techniques, but Wozniak had often done this in the past to reduce chip count (for example, the odd text and graphic video screen addressing system of the Apple II).

For two weeks, he worked late each night to make a satisfactory design. When he was finished, he found that if he moved a connector he could cut down on feedthroughs (places where a trace had to go through the board from one side to the other), making the board more reliable. To make that move, however, he had to start his printed circuit board (PCB) layout all over again. This time it only took twenty hours. He then saw another feedthrough that could be eliminated, and again started his design over. As stated by Freiberger and Swain in *Fire In The Valley*, "The final design was generally recognized by computer engineers as brilliant and was by engineering aesthetics beautiful. Woz later said, 'It's some-

---

12 Williams, Gregg, and Rob Moore, "The Apple Story, Part 2: More History And The Apple III", *BYTE* (January 1985), 167-168.
13 Freiberger, Paul and Michael Swaine, *Fire In The Valley, Second Edition*, (Berkley, Osborne/McGraw-Hill, 2000), 286-287.
14 Wigginton, Randy, personal interview, July 25, 2013.

thing you can only do if you're the engineer and the PC board layout person yourself. That was an artistic layout. The board has virtually no feedthroughs.'"[15]

Additionally, Wozniak made his disk drive quieter by modifying the low level code that controlled the drive head. Shugart drives ordinarily made a quiet click as it stepped from one track to the other. Woz fine-tuned this action by adding code for acceleration and deceleration of the head, which eliminated the click and replaced it with a quieter swish.

COST

The Disk II was released in July 1978 with the first full version of DOS. It had an introductory price of $495 (including the controller card) if an order was placed before Apple had them in stock; otherwise, the price would be $595. Even at that price, however, it was the least expensive floppy disk drive yet sold by a computer company. Only two people at Apple handled the early production, and they could assemble about thirty drives a day.[16, 17] Because of the custom hardware and software Apple created to manage and access the disks, they had a formatted capacity of 113K—23K more than what was offered by Shugart.

The drives originally sold with Woz's disk controller were from Shugart. To further cut costs, within a couple of years of the introduction of the Disk II, they approached Alps Electric Company of Japan and asked them to design a less expensive clone. According to Frank Rose, in his book *West Of Eden*:

> *The resulting product, the Disk II, was almost obscenely profitable: For about $140 in parts ($80 after the shift to Alps) [not counting labor costs], Apple could package a disk drive and a disk controller in a single box that sold at retail for upwards of $495. Better yet was the impact the Disk II had on computer sales, for it suddenly transformed the Apple II from a gadget only hard-core hobbyists would want to something all sorts of people could use. Few outsiders realized it, but in strategic terms, Woz's invention of the disk controller was as important to the company as his invention of the computer itself.*[18]

The high entry price of purchasing an Apple II was itself a barrier to sales. However, the Disk II not only made it significantly easier to use, it also accelerated the growth of the platform.[19] Sales of the Apple II increased from 2400

---

15 Freiberger, Paul and Michael Swaine, *Fire In The Valley, Second Edition*, (Berkley, Osborne/McGraw-Hill, 2000), 286-287.
16 -----, "A.P.P.L.E. Co-op Celebrates A Decade of Service", *Call-A.P.P.L.E.* (February 1988), 12-27.
17 -----, "Apple and Apple II History", *The Apple II Guide* (Cupertino, CA, Apple Computer, Inc., Fall 1990), 9-16.
18 Rose, Frank, *West Of Eden: The End Of Innocence At Apple Computer*, (New York, Penguin Books, 1989), 62.
19 Reimer, Jeremy, "Total Share: Personal Computer Market Share 1975-2010", *Jeremy's Blog*, <jeremyreimer.com/m-item.lsp?i=137

units in 1977 (a half year of sales) to 7,600 in 1978, and was up to 35,000 computers in 1979.[20] Within nine months of the release of the Disk II, the other two members of the 1977 Trinity also had a floppy disk drive available. Although they both still outsold the Apple II in absolute unit sales, their growth was less.

TIMELINE

Shugart SA400 – *1976*
Apple II – *May 1977 - May 1979*
Disk II – *July 1978*

---

20 Reimer's estimates are based on reported dollar sales for each year, and the number of units sold was calculated from that number. Unfortunately, it is not clear whether or not these estimates of units sold are at all precise. In many cases, companies were not necessarily willing to share specifics about their sales, especially if those sales were below their announced targets. Despite this, the general concept of sales per company is correct. According to information obtained from Randy Wigginton on July 25, 2013, the Apple II had sold 200 units by August 1977, the company had paid back the money it had borrowed to get the Apple II launched, and was profitable. Wigginton stated that they were selling twenty to thirty per day (not counting weekends), with sales gradually ramping up through the end of the year. With this in mind, starting at August 1, 1977, there were 22 remaining weeks in the year; take away a few days for holidays, and that would place the estimate of units sold for 1977 from June through the end of December to be around 2400.

CHAPTER 6

Spinning Chaos into Order

Wozniak's hardware design for the Disk II had tremendous potential to enhance the success of the Apple II computer. Although the computer had performed well and was profitable, it was still a very small player in the 1977 landscape. He had a clever disk drive design that used only a few chips and offered higher storage capacity than Shugart's original product, but it lacked one important feature: a disk operating system.

Woz and Randy Wigginton had come up with enough of an operating system to demonstrate the Disk II at the January 1978 Consumer Electronics Show. However, their rudimentary control program was neither flexible enough nor user friendly for consumers.

DISK SYSTEM DESIGN

To move beyond these raw basics to something that a customer for the Apple II and Disk II would be able to manage in a BASIC program, there was a lot of work left to do after Wozniak and Wigginton returned from the CES. They needed to fully flesh out a proper control program for the disk drive that would be both simple to use and yet powerful enough for advanced file manipulation. All Apple had at that time was Woz's interface code to control the disk drive, and the ROM code Dick Huston had written for the disk controller card. A useable disk system needed to interface with the BASIC in ROM, and it needed to be easier to use than the cassette system. The work Woz, Wigginton and Huston had done made it possible to transfer disk data, but could only be used from 6502 assembly language and required a deep understanding on how the disk drive worked.

Designing a disk operating system from scratch was no trivial matter. On one side were the RAM chips in the Apple II, waiting patiently for a program to load into memory. On the other side of the interface card and connecting cable was the floppy disk and disk drive hardware itself. The control program that Woz wrote could be compared to a narrow rope bridge crossing a chasm; it worked, but it was not possible to carry much, and it was easy to slip and fall (lose data). A complete DOS was more like a concrete and steel bridge, capable of safely carrying autos and trucks in both directions. Woz's "rope bridge" was a foundation, but there was much work yet to do.

The most common means in which computers started up from a floppy disk was to put fixed code in ROM that was dedicated to load a small amount of code from the disk into memory. This code was then executed, and it would then load the actual disk operating system code from the disk, ultimately transferring control to that system once it was fully in memory. Because of limited storage on these early disks, some early home computer systems (Commodore, for example) put the disk operating system in ROM, which made it unnecessary to use space on the disk for that code. While this method maximized available disk storage, the disadvantage was that it made it very difficult to update or improve the operating system. Having an operating system residing on the floppy disk made it a trivial matter to replace it with an enhanced version. Wozniak followed this standard method in directing the design of his disk system.

Mechanically, a floppy disk drive consisted of a recording head on an arm, which was moved back and forth across the surface of the floppy disk, tracing the radius of the disk from the center to the edge and back. The disk itself spun under the recording head. The process was not unlike the stylus on an audio turntable playing records. Unlike the turntable stylus, which had to play the record from start to finish, the head on a disk drive could be given a command to move to a different track on the spinning disk, in any desired order. Also unlike the turntable, which was essentially a read-only device, the head on the disk drive could either reads bits off or write bits onto the disk.

Inside the Disk II drive; seen here is the felt-pressure pad (above), which holds the disk in place against the read/write head (below) as the disk spins across it – Photo credit: personal

To find where data was stored on a disk, it had to be formatted into a known configuration. A blank disk could be compared to empty land that will be filled with new houses, but currently had no streets, street signs, or house numbers. The initial formatting (called hard formatting) of a blank disk was, then, like building the streets and assigning lots for future construction. The second part of disk formatting (called soft formatting), involved naming the streets and designating addresses.

In the case of Apple's Disk II, it was designed with 35 concentric circles ("streets") called tracks. Each track was subdivided into 13 (and later on, 16) segments ("lots") called sectors. Each sector could hold 256 bytes of information. In the hardware system that Wozniak designed, the timing hole near the center of the floppy disk was not used by the hardware to keep track of which sector was passing the head at any particular time. Because of that, it was necessary for the software to identify in a different way where one sector ended and the next sector began. He used a complicated method of specially encoding each of the 256 bytes so they had a standard, recognizable appearance to a program that was controlling the disk drive, plus some other specialized bytes that identified the start and end of a sector. Although it slightly decreased the storage capacity of the disk, the cost savings due to less complicated hardware compensated for it.

APPLE DOS - STRUCTURE & FUNCTION WITH BASIC

The purpose of an operating system is to insulate the user from the complexity of directly controlling the hardware. Although Apple never publicly released details about the underlying code that made DOS work, Don Worth and Pieter Lechner in their 1981 book, *Beneath Apple DOS*, described a logical division of DOS into four parts according to function and location in memory. They called these parts RWTS (the term that Apple used in its early manuals, an abbreviation for Read/Write Track/Sector), the File Manager, the Main DOS Routines, and the DOS File Buffers (areas in memory dedicated as a temporary holding place for disk data). Consider these four parts of DOS as layers; the closer to the bottom layer, the closer the user is to the hardware (the raw data on the disk and direct control of the disk drive). The disadvantage of that lowest layer is that it greatly increases the difficulty of managing the disk. The farther up in layers, the simpler it is to manage, but that comes at the cost of less direct control of the disk data and hardware.[1, 2] When Wozniak and Huston wrote the disk controller (driver) routines that were included in the Disk II controller ROM, they were working at a layer that was deeper still, directly manipulating the disk hardware and raw data. This involved complex timing and error checking. This layer was used by RWTS to handle erasing and formatting a disk (creating sectors and their addresses).[3]

It was Randy Wigginton who wrote most of the code for RWTS.[4] Besides the command to FORMAT a disk, it offered three other commands to assembly language programmers: SEEK (to move the disk arm to the desired track), READ (load a sector from disk into memory), and WRITE (save a sector to disk from memory).[5] But that still only provided rudimentary control of the

---

1 Deatherage, Matt, "The Operating System", *The Apple II Guide* (Cupertino, CA, Apple Computer, Inc., Fall 1990), 117-125.
2 Wozniak, Stephen, telephone interview with author, September 5, 1991.
3 Don Worth and Pieter Lechner, *Beneath Apple DOS* (Quality Software, Reseda, CA, 1981), 5.1-5.3, 6.4-6.8, 8.1-8.42.
4 Wozniak, Steve, telephone interview, August 9, 2013.
5 Don Worth and Pieter Lechner, *Beneath Apple DOS* (Quality Software, Reseda, CA, 1981), 5.1-5.3, 6.4-6.8, 8.1-8.42.

disk, and was far short of a proper disk system. To complete the task, Apple ultimately reached outside of the company for help.

They had previously contracted with an outside consultant firm, Shepardson Microsystems, to write a BASIC interpreter for a computer that was being designed as a possible successor to the Apple II. Wozniak had prior experience with Shepardson, having performed some work for the firm prior to starting Apple.[6] Paul Laughton was a programmer for Shepardson who was assigned to that project. In the process of working with Steve Wozniak on interfacing a paper tape reader to an Apple II for development and testing purposes (this was needed to load into an Apple II the code for the BASIC interpreter from their development system), he learned about the Disk II project. According to Laughton, Wozniak expressed concern about completing both the hardware and the disk operating system in time to meet the schedule that Apple had assigned him. Laughton had a background in IBM systems programming and hardware, including work with operating systems. He had in his mind the basic design for a disk operating system that would work with this much simpler system. Laughton offered to write the operating system for him, and Woz gladly accepted.

Apple and Shepardson negotiated the arrangements, with Wozniak sharing detailed written explanations about how the disk controller worked. On April 10, 1978, the work contract was signed, paying Shepardson $5,200 immediately, and promising another $7,800 on delivery. After securing this arrangement between Apple and Shepardson Microsystems, Laughton began work on the project.[7, 8]

Laughton took Wigginton's handwritten object code for RWTS and entered it into his 6502 cross-assembler (on punch cards), adding comments to explain how RWTS worked. Next, he decided on how to allow programs written in BASIC to access the Disk II. Laughton commented on this next step in the process:

> *The real genius behind the user interface specifications was Randy Wigginton (who was 19 at the time). Randy was the guy who had adapted Microsoft's BASIC to the Apple II. It was Randy who decided that the way to interface to the DOS was to do it from BASIC – rather than via a command line thing like CP/M. It was also Randy who figured out how to make it work – intercepting the BASIC input stream, the various flags that would show if BASIC was running, etc. With these details provided by Randy, I designed the next layer of DOS – the User Interface. (It turns out this layer was much bigger than we*

---

6 Wozniak, Steve, telephone interview, August 9, 2013.
7 Laughton, Paul, "Apple Computer The Early Days A Personal Perspective", <www.laughton.com/Apple/Apple.html>, accessed October 20, 2012.
8 Weyhrich, Steven, "A Tale of the Disk II", *Apple2history.org*, <apple2history.org/2013/04/12/a-tale-of-the-disk-ii/>, accessed April 12, 2013.

had anticipated. *This led to the first extension (of many) contracts between Shepardson and Apple for the DOS.)* [9]

Those extensions brought the full cost to Apple for Laughton's work to $22,500. Although Apple programmers Dick Huston and Rick Auricchio later made a few modifications, Laughton designed and wrote the rest of DOS, specifically the two layers that *Beneath Apple DOS* called the File Manager and the Main DOS Routines.[10, 11, 12]

Laughton stated that it was not really a complicated project:

> *When looking at the task of writing the DOS, I knew the structure of the sub components needed and the magnitude of each of the sub components. I had, if you will, the Blueprint, in my head from day one. Actually, Apple DOS was not a major project when compared to some of the other tasks I had been assigned at IBM. It was a very simple system.*[13]

The File Manager was responsible for handling files at the disk level and formatting disks. However, it did not know anything about BASIC. It was the responsibility of the Main DOS Routines to allow BASIC programs to interact with the disk drive. It was here that the interface that Wigginton designed came into play.

When DOS was active, it watched all output from a running BASIC program for a Ctrl-M character (a RETURN character) followed by a Ctrl-D. If that sequence was detected, DOS interpreted the text following it as a disk command. The beauty of the system that Wigginton proposed and Laughton designed was that it required no changes to the ROM code for either Integer BASIC or Applesoft. Even though neither version of the language knew *anything* about how handle disk files or a floppy disk, the method they used simply hooked DOS into BASIC in a way that was transparent to the ROM code. Its importance was that it saved money for Apple in having to create updated ROMs, and to the end customers in having to buy a new ROM.

One odd thing about Apple DOS was the version number of the first release. Instead of identifying it as DOS 1.0, the earliest shipping version was called DOS 3. Paul Laughton explains:

---

9   Laughton, Paul, e-mail message to author, February 1996.
10 Little, Gary, *Exploring Apple GS/OS And ProDOS 8* (Addison-Wesley Publishing Company, Inc, Reading, MA, 1988), 2-4.
11 Little, Gary, *Inside The Apple //c* (Brady Communications Co, Bowie, MD, 1985), 1-7.
12 Auricchio, Rick, telephone interview with author, September 4, 1991.
13 Laughton, Paul, e-mail message to author, April 10, 2013.

> *Every time I recompiled the code, I incremented a revision counter. The counter started at Rev 0.1. Whenever I got to (n).9, I would roll the counter over to (n+1).0. The first listing I gave Apple was Rev 2.8. They (I forget who) decided they could not call it DOS 2.8, so they changed it to DOS 3.0. Apple did the beta testing with this version (2.8 renamed 3.0). When Apple shipped the DOS for review, they incremented it to 3.1 to indicate that the code had changed from the beta version. As a final note, when I transferred the source code to Apple in October, 1978 the Rev number was up to 6.3.*[14]

However, contrary to Laughton's note, some of the very earliest Disk II drives shipped with DOS 3.0 (identified in the accompanying photocopied manual as "DOS 3") and within a month was revised to DOS 3.1 to correct some significant bugs. It is this version that had the greatest initial distribution.

DOS 3.1 – MANUAL

The preliminary manual distributed with the new Disk II drive in 1978 contained sparse information—only the basics. Much like the informal reference manual for the Apple II itself that preceded the Red Book, the material documenting DOS 3 was a packet of thirty-three pages stapled together. It used six of those pages to introduce the reader to the concept of floppy disks and their capabilities, and then provided detailed instructions on installation and how to insert the floppy disks. The write-protect feature was illustrated with a poorly hand-drawn picture of a floppy disk, and an arrow pointing to the notch that had to be covered.

The rest of the pages of the included documentation dealt primarily with file management (how to load, save, and delete files). Disk formatting was mentioned in just a single paragraph, and the text file commands were covered in only three pages, with no examples.

DOS 3.1 was released a month after the release of the Disk II, correcting some important bugs. Accompanying it was a five-page supplement that highlighted known problems that still existed, and a more firmly worded precaution against incorrectly attaching the cable to the controller card.

The limited information provided with the Disk II and Apple DOS was a consequence of Apple's engineers working feverishly to produce enough working drives to begin shipping. When a manual for DOS and the Disk II came out late in 1978, it was not much more than a dressed-up revision of the original photocopied pages. With the unwieldy title, *Disk II Floppy Disk Subsystem Installation and Operating Manual*, and subtitled *Apple Intelli-*

---

14 Laughton, Paul, "Apple Computer The Early Days A Personal Perspective", <www.laughton.com/Apple/Apple.html>, accessed October 20, 2012.

gent Subsystems (part #030-0011-00), it was all of 38 pages long, still with insufficient instruction of how to READ and WRITE text files, and no programming examples. The manual also talked about "*3D0G". What it didn't say was that the user was supposed to type "3D0G" from the Monitor prompt (to allow a return to the active BASIC with DOS connected through the command parser).[15, 16]

The lack of proper documentation for Apple DOS resulted in major complaints from customers. One angry letter written to Apple president Mike Markkula bluntly stated, "You [expletive deleted]. I bought an Apple with floppy and nobody, I mean nobody, in L.A. or San Diego knows how to use the [thing] for random access files. I really feel 'ripped off.' Everybody talks about this great manual in the sky that is coming out soon??? ... [more expletives]! I need this computer now in my business not next year. [Expletive]. I hope your dog dies."[17]

DOS 3.1 - FEATURES

Each Apple DOS disk could be identified with a volume number, though the feature was not frequently used. The disk catalog displayed a single letter to identify the file type (I for Integer BASIC, A for Applesoft, B for binary, and T for text). The filenames could be up to 30 characters in length, and could include any ASCII character, even control characters that did not display on the screen.

A catalog of the DOS 3.1 System Master disk produced a listing of eight files.

Notice this file listing starts with a volume number to specifically identify this disk. If no number was specified when initializing a disk, the default number was 254.

Below this, each file on the disk was listed on a separate line, and each line contained important information about the file. An entry that started with an asterisk identified a file that was locked. When locked, it could not be renamed, deleted, or opened.

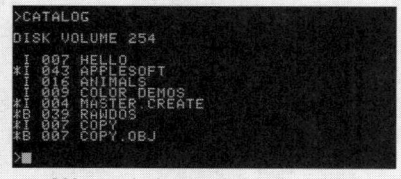

DOS 3.1 catalog listing – Photo credit: personal

The character next in position was a single letter that identified the file type. This catalog listing showed two types: I for an Integer BASIC program file, and B for a binary file (typically an executable machine language file). Two other file types were used: T for text files, and A for Applesoft BASIC files. Integer and Applesoft BASIC program files were stored in a compact form, with a single byte used to represent language-specific keywords (PRINT, IF, FOR, etc.)

---

15 Don Worth and Pieter Lechner, *Beneath Apple DOS* (Quality Software, Reseda, CA, 1981), 1.2.
16 Bragner, Bob, "Open Discussion", *Softalk*, (November 1983), 51-52.
17 Moritz, Michael, *The Little Kingdom* (William Morrow and Company, Inc, New York, 1984), 211.

After the file type, there was a three digit number that indicated how many 256-byte sectors were used by the file.

Following this was the filename, which could be thirty characters long, and could contain any ASCII character, including characters that did not display on the screen (a method used at times by programmers who did not want a disk easily examined by the casual user).

HELLO was the startup file, an Integer BASIC program that executed after the disk booted. On the master DOS disk, the only function of the HELLO program was to display version and copyright information, then quit, leaving the user at an Integer BASIC prompt. The primary purpose of the HELLO program was to allow the disk to automatically start a program when it was booted. On user disks, the HELLO program could be any Integer BASIC program the user wanted it to be. To make it automatically start, it was simply necessary to save the program with that name. It was also possible to make the startup program have any name desired, but this had to be assigned when the disk was initialized.

DOS 3.1 startup screen – Photo credit: personal

Though it required a minimum amount of RAM, Apple DOS was usable with any memory size from 16K to the full 48K. Because multiple memory sizes could be found in the early models of the Apple II, DOS was designed to have the ability to relocate itself to whatever happened to be the highest available address in the available space. The catch was that there were two types of DOS startup disks, a master disk and a slave disk.

A master disk contained the type of DOS that could relocate itself; a slave disk was intended to load DOS to a specific location in RAM. Although the startup process was slightly faster for a slave disk (the relocation code was not executed, and indeed was not even included in the DOS image on that disk), the slave disk put DOS in the same location in memory as the version of DOS that initialized the slave disk. This meant that on a 16K Apple II, loading DOS left 6K of available space for a program to run. If that same slave disk was booted on a 32K Apple, there would still be only 6K of program space; the extra 16K was ignored.

The *MASTER CREATE* program on the DOS 3.1 was used to initialize a master disk. Utilizing the binary file *RAWDOS*, it executed the DOS INIT command, then put a version of DOS on the newly formatted disk that was relocatable.[18]

---

18 Vanderpool, Tom, A2 Roundtable, Category 2, Topic 16, *GEnie*, March & August 1991.

CHAPTER 6 | *Spinning Chaos into Order*   71

    ANIMALS was an Integer program that gave an example of the use of text files, and *COLOR DEMOS* was a disk version of an earlier cassette program that demonstrated the lo-res graphics capabilities of the Apple II.

    The Integer BASIC program *APPLESOFT* was used to start up Apple's floating point BASIC, the version known as Disk Applesoft. It was a 43-sector file that appeared in a catalog as an Integer BASIC program (with the "I" filetype code).

> If the file was loaded, listing lines 10 through 80 showed BASIC statements that produced the following text:
>
> ```
> ****************************************
> *    APPLESOFT ][ FLOATING POINT BASIC  *
> *              APRIL 1978               *
> ****************************************
> COPYRIGHT 1978 APPLE COMPUTER, INC.
> COPYRIGHT 1976 BY MICROSOFT
> ALL RIGHTS RESERVED
> ]▮
> ```
>
> There were also lines in the listing that poked values into memory, and then jumped to a machine language routine that relocated Applesoft into RAM starting at $800 (the same place where Cassette Applesoft loaded). If the entire APPLESOFT program was listed, the lines after line 80 would display as a jumble of Integer BASIC commands. This is because a majority of the file was actually the Applesoft BASIC interpreter that had been appended to the end of the short Integer BASIC program that displayed the copyright information (shown above).
>
> On viewing this DOS 3.1 catalog listing, one would assume that starting Applesoft BASIC was simply a matter of running this APPLESOFT file. However, that was actually the *wrong* way to do it. Running this program would display the copyright information, and then leave the cursor next to the Applesoft bracket prompt. However, doing it this way disconnected DOS, leaving the user with a version that worked much like Cassette Applesoft. The correct way to start Applesoft with this version of DOS was to type "FP" from the Integer BASIC prompt. DOS then loaded the APPLESOFT file and initialized the interpreter, leaving DOS enabled.

    Disk Applesoft still contained a few bugs, and was made obsolete by the Applesoft Firmware card and the Apple II Plus.[19]

    Error messages produced by DOS 3.1 were designed to look similar to those displayed by Integer BASIC. For example, this is what happened if an attempt was made to load a type "B" (binary) file with the LOAD command:

---

19 Bragner, Bob, "Open Discussion", *Softalk*, (November 1983), 51-52.

Integer BASIC had error messages that looked like "*** SYNTAX ERR" (with a space following the asterisks). DOS error messages lacked the space following the asterisks. The possible error messages in this version of DOS that were different from later versions were:

```
>LOAD COPY.OBJ
***DISK: NOT BASIC PROGRAM ERROR
>
```

***DISK: SYS ERROR
***DISK: CMD SYNTAX ERROR
***DISK: NO FILE BUFFS AVAIL ERROR
***DISK: NOT BASIC PROGRAM ERROR
***DISK: NOT BINARY FILE ERROR

DOS 3.1 - USER EXPERIENCES

Early users of the Disk II could encounter a problem connecting the drive to the controller card if the pins were not correctly lined up. The controller had two connectors, one for each Disk II drive that could be connected. The connector on the card was simply a series of pins pointing upward, to which the end of the disk ribbon cable was plugged. The problem with this design was that the pins had to be properly aligned for the drive to function. It a user tried to attach the drive cable in such a way that the pins were accidentally shifted over by one, it would burn out the motor on the disk drive, requiring a trip for repairs to the local Apple dealer. This "fried disk drive" problem was, obviously, a source of much frustration to early Apple disk drive owners, and was apparently a common enough problem that it was addressed in the July 1978 application note sent to early Disk II owners.

Outside of that hardware problem, there were quirks in the software that plagued users at the time of the first releases of DOS 3.1. This included one in which locking a file sometimes mysteriously caused the length of the first file in the catalog to change. Apple told people not to worry about that; in fact, they told people not to pay attention to the sector counts in the catalog at all, as there was a bug in that part of the catalog routine. Another problem in early versions of DOS 3.1 was an inability to execute READ or WRITE statements in an Applesoft program if they occurred in program lines numbered higher than 256. It also wouldn't allow more than one DOS command on the same line of a program, so a program like this was not possible:

```
20 PRINT D$;"VERIFY FILE": PRINT
   D$;"OPEN FILE": PRINT D$;"RE
   AD FILE"
```

Other bugs in early versions of DOS 3.1 included an inability to initialize disks with *MASTER CREATE* unless the disk controller was moved to slot 7. Apple's earliest plans for the disk controller card was to reserve slot 7 for it. Engineers decided just before the product release to make slot 6 the standard location for the card, and leave slot 7 for video cards.

> The A.P.P.L.E. user group (and later Apple itself) released patches for *MASTER CREATE* and *RAWDOS* to fix the slot 7 INIT bug, and the >255 line number bug in Applesoft. Apple later released a modified version of DOS 3.1 that fixed these bugs (without changing the version number).

DOS 3.2 - ENHANCEMENTS

> As mentioned previously, DOS 3.1 had a few problems. When Apple released the Apple II Plus with the Autostart ROM, which would allow a disk to automatically boot when the computer was powered up, DOS required an update to handle the changes.
>
> DOS 3.2, released in June 1979, contained several modifications, but retained 90 percent of the basic structure of DOS 3.1. One change made to plan for the future was a doubling of the number of possible filetypes. In addition to the I, A, B, and T filetypes, DOS 3.2 include types S, R, another A, and another B. Of those four types, only R was ever officially designated by Apple, and that for relocatable assembler object files.
>
> Start screen from a later revision of DOS 3.2 that did not change the version number - Photo credit: personal

The update to Apple DOS finally included a proper reference manual. This was far superior than the booklet provided with DOS 3.1. It was spiral-bound and formatted in the same fashion as other manuals that were produced through the company's new internal publication division. The revised manual included a full chapter about the function of EXEC files, and a chapter each on the use of sequential and random-access text files. For assembly language programmers, info was provided on the use of the low-level RWTS routines. Finally, the book included a table of contents and an index, making it easier to find information.

DOS 3.2 - FEATURES

There were at least two versions of DOS 3.2 System Master disks. The first appeared to be a non-Applesoft version of system. A catalog of this disk produced a listing of files:

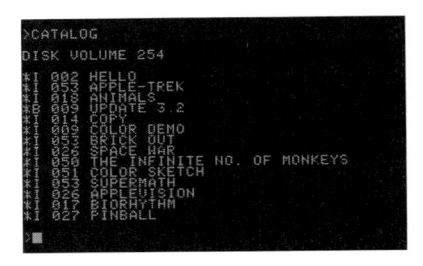

The file RAWDOS that was on the DOS 3.1 disk was no longer needed, as its function was included in the UPDATE 3.2 program. Some of the files from the DOS 3.1 master disk were retained, but some others were added.

Demo programs included with DOS 3.2 included APPLE-TREK, a port of the ubiquitous mainframe and microcomputer Star Trek game, and Wozniak's software-based Breakout game, under the name BRICK OUT.

A later update to the DOS 3.2 master disk included Applesoft versions of some of these programs, and demos that showed how to do random access text files.

One of the limitations of text files on the Apple II under DOS was a lack of specific data types. A program that opened a text file and then wrote text to that file resulted in a data stream that was not much more sophisticated than what would appear on a printer. Similarly, reading data back from a text file was done using the standard INPUT statement from BASIC. Even if the INPUT statement read data into a variable, the data stream being read was just text, the same as if it had been entered from the keyboard. A text file on the disk was text-only; there was no floating point or integer encoding as was used with these variables in memory. It was not a major limitation, but some other microcomputer disk systems had more sophisticated data types that could be used in disk data file storage (TRSDOS for the Radio Shack TRS-80, for example).

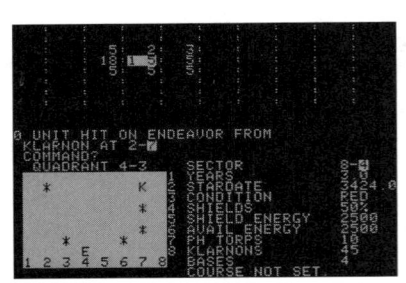

APPLE-TREK screen shot – Photo credit: personal

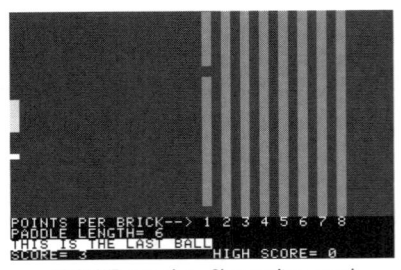

BRICK OUT screen shot – Photo credit: personal

CHAPTER 6 | *Spinning Chaos into Order*

🔧 DOS 3.2.1

In late July 1979, Apple released DOS 3.2.1. This was merely a minor upgrade to make some patches to RWTS and correct a timing problem that caused the utility *COPY* to fail when copying disks with two disk drives. It also began a software revision numbering system at Apple that persisted for many years, that of adding a third digit to indicate a minor upgrade.[20]

This disk contained the new COPY program, and a program called *UPDATE 3.2.1*, which worked just as UPDATE 3.2 and MASTER CREATE had previously. The update program modified existing DOS 3.2 disks to the 3.2.1 version. As a bonus, Apple added some programs to this Master disk that were on the first DOS 3.2 disk. The included games and graphics demonstrations included APPLE-TREK, THE INFINITE NO. OF MONKEYS, BRIAN'S THEME, and BRICK OUT.

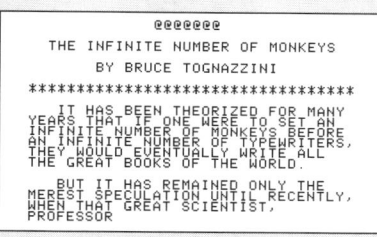

```
           @@@@@@@
    THE INFINITE NUMBER OF MONKEYS
          BY BRUCE TOGNAZZINI
************************************
       IT HAS BEEN THEORIZED FOR MANY
  YEARS THAT IF ONE WERE TO SET AN
  INFINITE NUMBER OF MONKEYS BEFORE
  AN INFINITE NUMBER OF TYPEWRITERS,
  THEY WOULD EVENTUALLY WRITE ALL
  THE GREAT BOOKS OF THE WORLD.
       BUT IT HAS REMAINED ONLY THE
  MEREST SPECULATION UNTIL RECENTLY,
  WHEN THAT GREAT SCIENTIST,
  PROFESSOR
```

THE INFINITE NO. OF MONKEYS screen shot
— Photo credit: personal

TIMELINE

Apple II – *May 1977 - May 1979*

DOS 3.0 – *June 1978*

Disk II – *July 1978*

DOS 3.1 – *July 1978*

DOS 3.2 – *June 1979*

DOS 3.2.1 – *July 1979 - August 1980*

---

20 Don Worth and Pieter Lechner, *Beneath Apple DOS* (Quality Software, Reseda, CA, 1981), 2.1-2.3.

CHAPTER 7
Homebrew Community in Print

Back in the early days of the personal computer, there were three major sources of information: a computer store (if one existed nearby), a local user group, or advertising and reviews in print magazines. Print was the primary static source of news, reviews, commentary, and advertising. And this printed matter not only provided information, but also the flavor of the era.

With the newness of personal computers, it fell on the local computer store to provide service and support. It was common for new customers to come back to the store to talk with the salesman and to each other. These informal talks frequently led to the start of meetings, which led to the formation of user groups. To document their shared knowledge, these groups wrote and distributed newsletters. One group, the Apple Pugetsound Program Library Exchange in Seattle, went national with their newsletter. Another publication came out of the International Apple Core, which was a collaboration Apple Computer encouraged between Apple user groups.

Outside of these user groups, there were several print magazines such as *BYTE* that covered all microcomputers, serving the community in general. These publications began to run regular columns and special articles that dealt with the Apple II, while other magazines formed with the purpose of exclusively serving the Apple II community. This chapter will take a look at the earliest homebrew publications that were in print during the first years of the Apple II.

INTERFACE AGE (Jul 1976 – Dec 1985)

One of the first national microcomputer magazines, *Interface Age* started out as *SCCS Interface*, the club newsletter for the Southern California Computer Society (SCCS). After several issues, Bob Jones, of the advertising agency McPheters, Wolfe, and Jones, offered to transform the newsletter into a magazine that was on par with professionally produced magazines. He made a profit-sharing deal with SCCS, in which that group would provide the majority of the content, and Jones would manage the publishing and marketing. The magazine was released in August 1976 with the new title *Interface*, and began its numbering with Volume 1, Issue 9 (due to the earlier eight issues released under the *SCCS Interface* title). By the following year, the title had been enlarged to Interface Age, with which it remained through the rest of its run. One of the columnists for Interface Age was Adam Osborne, who later became famous for his Osborne 1 computer.

As for the agreement between McPheters, Wolfe, and Jones and the SCCS, the final outcome of this arrangement is unclear. A former member of the SCCS claims that Jones' company took over the magazine when it became profitable from its advertising revenue. The contrary view is that the SCCS did not provide sufficient content and Jones on his own had to find his writers for the columns in the magazine. Ultimately, the agreement with SCCS was terminated, and the magazine continued under the Interface Age title.[1]

SCCS Interface, July 1976 – Photo credit: Vectronics Apple World

The July 1976 issue of SCCS Interface is of particular interest because it ran one of the first advertisements for the new Apple-1 computer. It also had an article, "Comparing Apples and Oranges", which featured the Apple-1. This article identified Wozniak as the Director of Engineering and Steve Jobs as the Director of Marketing. One of Jobs' best quotes in that article was about computer clubs:

> You know, most of the real creative and innovative ideas come about by communicating with these people. If we can rap about their needs, feelings and motivations, we can respond appropriately giving them what they want. Most of the companies that started in this market are now responding to industrial needs and the hobbyist now has to yell louder than before. This hobby market may still only be a baby, but it's going to grow up fast like the CB [radio] market did and we plan to grow with it. We're here for the hobbyist to give him the best performance system that makes sense economically.

The September 1976 issue had an article by Allen Baum and Steve Wozniak, printing the source code for a 6502 disassembler. In October 1976, Steve Jobs wrote about how to interface the Apple-1 to a Southwest Technical Prod-

---

1   Garrett, Roger, and Kaye, Bert, "Interface Age Magazine" forum, *Vintage Computer.com*, accessed January 6, 2005 and May 31, 2007.

ucts Corporation PR-40 printer (using a toggle switch to switch output from the video screen to the printer), and in May 1977 Bob Bishop offered the source code listing for *Apple Star Trek* for the Apple-1. Wozniak also had two articles in the November 1976 issue, one about building a simple analog to digital converter, and another discussing floating point routines for the 6502.[2]

One unusual innovation that was pioneered by Interface Age was a novel way to distribute software with the magazine. Although it had published source code listings for the reader to type in from its beginning, the May 1977 issue included a flexible recording disc that was included in the binding of the magazine. (This was not a digital floppy disk; this was an audio disc, about the size of a 45-RPM record, which played on a turntable.) This technology had been used sporadically for years as a way to distribute inexpensive audio records of music in magazines and other media (including records attached to the back of breakfast cereal boxes). Interface Age decided to use this technology to distribute a version of BASIC for the 6800 processor. It was recorded at 33-1/3 RPM onto the disc using the Kansas City Cassette interface standard used on some early microcomputers. To load the program data from this "floppy ROM", it was necessary to attach the audio-out signal from a turntable to the audio-in connector on a microcomputer, set the program to load (just as if it was coming from a cassette), and then play the record.

Interface Age, Automated Dress Pattern program on Floppy ROM – Photo credit: William Smith

Compared to Wozniak's cassette interface for the Apple-1 and Apple II, the Kansas City standard was much slower (at 300 baud) and was less reliable. Wozniak had designed his Apple-1 cassette interface to work at about 1500 baud, and also made it possible to successfully load the data even when there were minor variations in speed and tape quality (often a problem with the inexpensive cassette recorders of the 1970s).[3]

Although Interface Age focused on microcomputers other than the Apple-1 and Apple II, it published a few programs that worked on these computers. The May 1977 issue included *Apple Star-Trek* (as mentioned above) and a program for logic circuit analysis for the Apple-1. The August 1978 issue had a listing for a television pattern generator for the Apple II, and the September 1978 issue had an Apple II program on floppy ROM.[4]

---

2 "1976-1977 Apple I," *Vectronics Apple World*, <www.vectronicsappleworld.com/ads/ads/applei/ia776.html>, accessed October 20, 2012.
3 -----, "Interface Age Magazine," *Atari Age*, <www.atariage.com/forums/topic/179619-interface-age-magazine>, accessed October 20, 2012.
4 Schreier, Jim, "Appendix A: General Software Index," *Best Of Interface Age, Volume 1* (dilithium Press, Beaverton, Oregon, 1979), 302.

This program, *Automated Dress Pattern*, was written in Integer BASIC by William V.R. Smith III (of the software distributors Softape and Artsci), and was also distributed in that issue as a printed source listing. The program took a specific dress pattern from the McCall's Dress Pattern Company and (with permission of McCall's) printed the pattern outline on a 132-column grid on paper. Though it was not on the vellum-thin paper on which most sewing patterns were sold, it was a unique use of a microcomputer delivered on a unique medium.[5]

Later issues of the magazine did not feature content about the Apple-1 or Apple II products.

MICRO (Oct 1977 – Oct 1984)

Robert M. Tripp started using computers in 1960 as an undergraduate in an unrelated field. He found computer programming so interesting that he became a programmer in 1969, and started using the 6502 microprocessor in 1976, initially with the KIM-1 trainer sold by MOS Technology. He started a business, "The COMPUTERIST", and sold the KIM-1 computer, as well as software and accessories for it.

Soon he started a magazine under the umbrella of his business, and named it *Micro*. It began publication in October of 1977, and was released on a bimonthly basis before going monthly in February of 1979. The first three issues were printed using his KIM-1 and he did the layout for the magazine (using scissors and paste) on his kitchen table. He later began to use a local publishing company to create the magazine. By early 1980 he had changed his publishing name to MICRO-INK, Inc.

The magazine covered the 6502 microprocessor (and later the 6809) and all the various computers that used it, including the KIM-1, the AIM-65, the C1P, the Commodore PET, the Ohio Scientific, the Atari 800, and, of course, the Apple II. The magazine was an excellent source for machine level code for the 6502, eventually including more and more articles that applied specifically to the Apple II. Typically, about half of the articles in these later issues dealt with the Apple II.

Many general-purpose machine language articles appeared in its pages, such as "Improved nth Precision" (code optimization for the 6502), "Precision Programming", and "Computer Assisted Translation of Programs from 6502 to 6809". They also carried do-it-yourself hardware articles, such as "C1P to Epson MX-80 Printer Interface", "PET/CBM IEEE 448 to Parallel Printer Interface", and "Apple II Digital Storage Oscilloscope".

Micro tended to focus each issue on a particular theme, starting out with articles that concentrated on a particular brand of computer per issue, and

---

5 Smith, William, "Automated Dress Pattern," *Artsci*, <www.artsci.net/bill/interface-age>, accessed October 20, 2012.

later expanding to topics that applied to several computers (such as printers, games, and languages). The articles presented were usually technical in nature but useful for the advanced Apple programmer.[6]

At its peak, Micro had a circulation of about 40,000, with half going to subscribers and half being shipped directly to computer dealers to sell in their stores.

Beginning with the first issue in October 1977, a unique column had been included called the "Micro 6502 Bibliography," which presented a reference to articles in different computer publications that were important to programming the 6502.

The cover changed in June 1980, showing a picture that made it look like it was a view from inside a computer monitor out into the room beyond, with text on the screen backwards. If there were graphics on the screen they were reversed, since the computer had the point of view.

By December 1980 the logo underwent a change to a more stylized appearance that continued throughout the run of the magazine, until the last issue in October 1984, after which the magazine disappeared from newsstands.

An important contribution to the Apple II community from Micro-INK came out of an article that appeared in the August 1979 issue.

Micro, July 1982 – Photo credit: personal

William F. Lubbert, who was a professor at Dartmouth, had written an eight-page article called "What's Where in the Apple II" that became popular as a programming reference. Tripp repeatedly urged him to expand the article so it could be published as a book. It took three years to get the Atlas (a detailed list of Apple II memory locations and their functions) and Gazetteer (an alphabetical listing of the named locations in the Atlas) completed, which Tripp published as a spiral-bound book. It took another three years publish the additional Guide—this was provided as a separate booklet for those who had purchased the previous book. Tripp chose to print all three parts as a perfect-bound book (spiral-bound cost much more). Micro-INK ended up selling about 40,000 copies of *What's Where in the Apple* in the early 1980s.[7]

---

6 Peterson, Craig, A2 Roundtable, Category 2, Topic 16, *GEnie*, accessed March 1992.
7 In 2012 Tripp created an iBooks version for Apple's iPad, taking the original information and reformatting it for that modern display.

CALL-A.P.P.L.E. (Feb 1978 – Jan 1990)

In February 1978 a newsletter appeared for a newly formed Apple II user group in Seattle, Washington. This group, which called itself the Apple Pugetsound Program Library Exchange (A.P.P.L.E.), began a newsletter, *Call-A.P.P.L.E.* Under the leadership of its founder and editor, Val J. Golding, it grew to become a full magazine by 1979, and its boundaries spread well beyond the Seattle area.

As pioneers in the era of Apple II exploration, the group discovered and published hints, tips, and programming techniques necessary to the early Apple II community. Its major thrust came from helping members to get their systems working. This covered anything from establishing communication between a computer and the newest low-cost printer, to the nuts and bolts of adding memory chips to achieve a full 48K of RAM.

Call-A.P.P.L.E. also provided reviews of new software and programming languages, and entertained readers with short Integer BASIC and Applesoft programs that did strange or unexpected things (in a recurring feature entitled, "So What Did You Expect?"). It also served its members by scheduling guest speakers for group meetings, and printing a summary of meetings in the magazine. Early speakers included notables such as Apple president Mike Scott), Randy Wigginton, and Steve Wozniak.

By 1980, *Call-A.P.P.L.E.* had become a full magazine published on glossy paper, and it carried advertising by new software and hardware companies. Its articles became more complex, dealing with topics such as "Loading DOS 3.3 on the Language Card", and "Applesoft Internal Structure", as well as various hardware or construction articles.

The year 1984 saw many changes for *Call-A.P.P.L.E.* The front cover had previously been white, with the title logo at the top, followed by a list of major articles. Beginning with the January issue, the cover was graced with color artwork, and a subtitle was included under the logo, "The World's Largest Apple User Group". In April, Val Golding stepped down as editor, handing the position to Kathryn Halgrimson Suther. She had been working with him on production of the magazine since he hired her back in 1980. Then in September 1984 the membership voted to change their organization to a co-operative, officially named A.P.P.L.E. Co-op, to help improve efficiency and allow them, under Washington state law, to continue expanding services inexpensively. Previously selling software written primarily by members, they now began to carry outside software and hardware items considered useful to their members.

A.P.P.L.E. also advanced the cause of providing useful technical information to Apple II (and Lisa and Macintosh) programmers by helping with the formation of APDA (Apple Programmers and Developers Association) in September 1987. Through a membership in this Apple-sponsored group, programmers could obtain up-to-date tech notes and preliminary material directly from

CHAPTER 7 | *Homebrew Community in Print*

Apple, to aid in the refinement of his project. (Apple later took APDA back under its own control in December 1988.)

Another change for the magazine occurred in June 1988. The cover artwork was toned down, and the thrust of *Call-A.P.P.L.E.* changed, as it become more of a technical journal than the "hints and tips" magazine it had originally been. Again the cover listed the major features for that issue, but in a smaller typeface than in the old days.

Even more significant in 1988 was the change in the name of the sponsoring group. In her monthly editorial in December of that year, Kathryn Suther wrote, "Sorry, Val, but the Co-op is undergoing a name change. Apple Computer, Inc., doesn't seem to appreciate the word Apple in our name with or without the periods. Rather than having to license the name back from them, we opted to change the name of the co-op to TechAlliance, a computer cooperative."[8] (Fortunately, they were not required by Apple to change the title of the magazine.) The members felt that this name more accurately reflected what the organization was doing; support, technical journals, and access to products and information. They also laid plans for a journal aimed at Macintosh programmers, called *MacTech Quarterly*.

With declining Apple II sales in the late 1980s, it was becoming harder for TechAlliance to put out the type of magazine they wanted as a monthly publication. Part way through 1989, the decision was made to switch to a quarterly printing

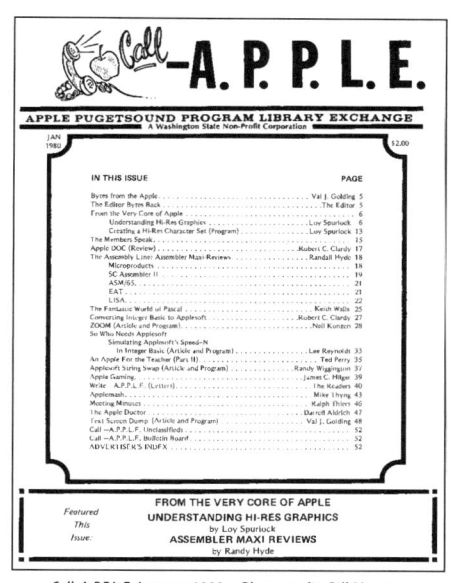

Call-A.P.P.L.E. January 1980 – Photo credit: Bill Martens

Call-A.P.P.L.E. May 1984 – Photo credit: Bill Martens

---

8 Suther, Kathryn Halgrimson, "The Inside Track," *Call-A.P.P.L.E.* (October 1984), 34.

schedule to allow it to stay in print. However, with the ninth issue of that year they had to announce that they were ceasing publication. With the passing of Call-A.P.P.L.E. came the passing of an era. Founder Val Golding wrote to Tom Weishaar, editor of the A2-Central newsletter, saying, "The 12-year illumination of Call-A.P.P.L.E.'s guiding light is about to be extinguished. The next issue will be the last. 'Call' was my baby and I loved it very much, even these last several years when I didn't play a direct role. It is, after all, like a death in the family." He went on to mention that he believed that their research into Applesoft internals and the use of its ampersand command made it possible for the appearance of more advanced programs earlier than would have been possible otherwise. He included a copy of his guest editorial from that final issue, reprinted in the pages of A2-Central in January 1990:

The Editor Bytes Back

Val J. Golding, editor emeritus

Full Circle

Perhaps I've lived in a private dream world all this time, where visions of ampersand faeries were real and 16K of RAM sufficed. My 1978 world where, still wrapped in swaddling clothes, the infant Call-A.P.P.L.E., with wise men guiding, exploded upon the technological night sky – its contagious fountain of knowledge spreading like a Washington wildfire, a depth and rugged determination to share never before and never again to be seen.

Volume 13, Number 1; there will be no Number 2. Words I thought would never be written blur my vision and scar the moist paper with ugly burn marks. "Our last issue." A doorway to another dimension has closed after 12 years.

It would take pages to list our accomplishments and firsts, more still for our failures. But we stood proud while others perished. And so it will be in the future, the Alliance remains to serve its members.

None of it would have been possible without those brilliant pioneering researchers and authors, far too numerous to even consider thanking individually. Virtually every Apple author writing today appeared first in these pages. It isn't fair, however, to leave without at least expressing my gratitude to and admiration for Kathryn Halgrimson Suther, without whom we would not have survived thus far. I love you, Ms. K.

Still everything is O.K. I wouldn't have missed it for anything. "The moving finger, having writ, moves on..."[9]

---

9 Golding, Val, "The Editor Bytes Back," *Call-A.P.P.L.E.* (Winter 1990), 3.

CONTACT (May 1978 – Oct 1979)

The origin of the Apple-1 and Apple II computers came out of Steve Wozniak's involvement in the Homebrew Computer Club, one of the earliest representations of a microcomputer user group. It is not surprising, then, that Apple continued to maintain contact with user groups that were focused on the Apple II. One of the ways Apple did this was by creating its own newsletter, *Contact*. Each of the six issues that were released over 18 months listed user groups across the United States that focused on the Apple II Computer (the first issue also listed Joe Torzewski's Apple-1 user group, based in Granger, Indiana). These newsletters also had announcements from the company about new or upcoming products. For example:

- Issue 1 – New BASIC programming manual, the Apple II Communications card, and planned release of the Apple II Serial card.
- Issue 2 – Disk II and Applesoft II announced
- Issue 3 – Apple Software Bank (for contributed programs)
- Issue 4 – Apple II Serial Interface Card released
- Issue 5 – Apple Hot Line phone number
- Issue 6 – Apple Graphics Tablet, and non-Apple products (Corvus 10 megabyte hard drive, SuperTalker card, lowercase adapter, and Selectric typewriter interface

Apple also used *Contact* to release patches for Cassette Applesoft, offer suggestions for hardware setup (the first issue recommended developers reserve slot 7 for the first disk controller, slot 6 for the second disk controller, and slot 0 for the Applesoft BASIC ROM card), and include listings of short programs and utilities (saving Applesoft strings to cassette, converting Applesoft I to Applesoft II). To help developers, *Contact* listed entry points for important Monitor routines (in issue 5), and tips on how to use the Disk II appeared in Issue 4.

Issue 4 in December 1978 also was interesting as apologies were made to customers who had ordered products (Apple II computers and peripheral cards) but had not yet

Contact #6 cover page – Photo credit: personal

received them. Even in 1978 Apple was experiencing problems in meeting customer demand.

Best of Contact '78 was released in early 1979, and it reprinted useful information from the earlier newsletters, as well as a list of available software for the Apple II.

Around the time of the release of Issue 6 of *Contact*, plans were being made on a different way to get information into the hands of Apple's customers—*Apple Orchard* (see chapter 19).

SOFTSIDE
(Oct 1978 – Aug 1984)

SoftSide was a magazine about software for the Radio Shack TRS-80 Model I, begun in October 1978 by Roger Robitaille. It had a format similar to the early issues of a later Apple-only magazine, *Nibble*, with articles and program listings, some submitted by readers. Beginning in January 1980, SoftSide Publications started a companion magazine called *AppleSeed* for Apple II users. Apparently Apple Computer frowned on this use of the company name in a publication (one of the earliest examples of what within a few years became a broader practice), and the name was changed to *SoftSide: Apple Edition*, while the original magazine became *Softside: S-80 Edition*. The Apple edition was edited by Mark Pelczarski, who was also an Apple II game author and publisher.

With the August 1980 edition, SoftSide Publications decided to combine the Apple and TRS-80 editions, as well as a separate programmer's magazine for the TRS-80, back into a single magazine with the original title. The format of the magazine was changed from a smaller-sized digest up to a standard magazine size. This new version of SoftSide also carried content for the Atari 400 and 800 computers. After a few issues, each platform's articles were identified in the table of contents separately: TRS-80 Side, Apple Side, and Atari Side. Starting in January 1982, the magazine added an IBM-PC Side, as well as beginning each issue with feature articles that might or might not be platform-specific. By November 1983, a Commodore Side was also added, to address Commodore 64 users. With the expansion of these other platforms, the magazine drifted away from its origins, and by February 1984 there was no TRS-80 content at all.[10, 11]

One problem some readers had with SoftSide during the years it was published in the smaller digest format was with its program listings, which were a copy of the printout from a dot matrix printer. The dot matrix printers

---

10 Goldklang, Ira, "SoftSide Magazine / PROG-80 Magzine." *Ira Goldklang's TRS-80 Revived Site*, <www.trs-80.com/wordpress/magazine-softside-and-prog-80>, accessed October 20, 2012.
11 Reed, Matthew, "SoftSide," *TRS-80.org* <www.trs-80.org/softside>, accessed Octobe 20, 2012.

of the time were not as legible as they later became; by the time it was photographed and printed in the magazine, it had become almost illegible. One reader commented, "After a short while of typing, you felt like you needed some of the 'coke bottle bottom' eye glasses!"[12]

Like many computer publications in the mid-eighties, SoftSide fell on hard times because of financial pressures and competition. This came during its attempt in 1983 to increase distribution and reach a larger audience of readers. As a result, Robitaille tried to reorganize the publication into a new magazine called *SoftSide 2.0* (directed towards the computer user), and *Code* (for the programmer), with disk versions of both to be made available. Unfortunately, he was never able to get either concept fully established, and SoftSide disappeared from view.[13]

Softside February 1980
– Photo credit: Underground //e <boutillon.free.fr>

TIMELINE

The start and end dates for homebrew Apple II and related computer magazines:

Interface Age – *July 1976 - December 1985*

Micro – *October 1977 - October 1984*

Call-A.P.P.L.E. – *February 1978 - January 1990*

Contact – *May 1978 - October 1979*

Softside – *October 1978 - August 1984*

---

12 Vanderpool, Tom, A2 Roundtable, Category 2, Topic 16, *GEnie*, accessed October 1991.
13 Barr, Mike, A2 Roundtable, Category 2, Topic 16, *GEnie*, accessed October 1992.

CHAPTER 8
Connections and Video

Personal computing was a notoriously expensive hobby in the seventies, and the cost of computing didn't end with the purchase of a full system like the Apple II. Roger Wagner, a well known programmer and publisher of software starting from the days of cassette distribution, recalled his start in the business:

> I had $700 in my pocket, and was ready to buy [a computer]. I had thought about this for a year, and I thought: Okay, I can get a stereo, I can get a motorcycle, or I can get a computer. And I thought about it, and [decided] that if I get a stereo or a motorcycle, I'll have to keep spending money on it. If I get a computer, all I need is electricity! This will be a really cheap hobby.[1]

Wagner was making fun of the tendency of computers to require the purchase of additional items to make them more useful. It might be a printer, a modem, or other products in an ever-growing family of hardware items to expand its functionality. It was not a cheap hobby.

This chapter examines some of the earliest and most essential add-ons for the Apple II platform, focusing on interface cards to allow other devices to connect to the Apple II, and on video expansion cards.

EARLY PERIPHERALS

The first Apple II offered an advantage over the computers that had preceded it. Two important peripherals were built-in: a keyboard, and the circuitry to allow easy connection of a TV monitor (both of which were lacking on the early 8080-based computers). It had, of course, the slots for inserting expansion cards (none were available), a game port (for attaching the included game paddles), a pin used to connect an RF modulator (so a standard television could be used instead of a computer monitor), and a cassette in-

---
1 Wagner, Roger, *Old-Timers*, A2-Central Summer Conference, 1992.

terface. Since there were no cards available to plug into the slots, one would imagine that the Apple II couldn't make use of any other hardware. However, those early users who had a need usually found a way around these limits.

Printing a program listing, for example, was no trivial matter. First, there were very few printers available. Though not simple to use, some users were able to obtain used Teletypes salvaged from mainframe computers. These noisy, massive clunkers often had no lowercase letters (not a big problem, since the Apple II didn't have lowercase either), and printed at a speed of only 10 characters per second. To use these printers when there were yet no printer interface cards, Apple II owners used a Teletype driver written by Wozniak and distributed in the original *Apple II Reference Manual*. This driver sent characters to the printer through a connection to the game paddle port. One part of being a hacker was improvising with what was available.[2]

Another of the earliest third-party devices designed for the Apple II came from the Apple Pugetsound Program Library Exchange (A.P.P.L.E.). It was involved with distributing Integer BASIC programs on cassette to members of the group. To make it easier to send those programs to the person responsible for duplicating the cassette, one of the club members designed a means of sending the programs over telephone lines. There were no modems available at the time, so his "Apple Box" (as he called it) was attached to the phone line with alligator clips and then plugged into the cassette port on the Apple II. To send a program, he first called up the person who was to receive the file and connected the computers on each end to the Apple Box. He then used the SAVE command in BASIC to tell the computer to save a program to tape. In actuality, the program was being sent through the cassette out port to the Apple Box, and then through the phone line connected. At the other end of that phone line, the data went into the other Apple Box, which was connected to the cassette in port on the other Apple II. The person receiving the file typed the LOAD command in BASIC to load the program from the Apple Box. A.P.P.L.E. sold about twenty of these Apple Boxes at $10 apiece.

INTERFACE CARDS

Not surprisingly, it was Apple who released the first interface cards for the Apple II. The Apple II Parallel Printer Interface Card came out in 1977 and sold for $180.[3]

Originally a division of Wang Laboratories, Centronics Data Computer Corporation was spun off as a separate company at the start of the 1970s. It released the first dot-matrix printer in 1970, the Centronics Model 101. The

---

2 -----. "A.P.P.L.E. Co-op Celebrates A Decade of Service", *Call-A.P.P.L.E.* (February 1988), 12-27.
3 Peterson, Craig. The Computer Store, Santa Monica, CA, *Store Information And Prices*, (August 10, 1979), 1.

CHAPTER 8 | *Connections and Video*

company designed a specific socket for connection and a protocol for sending data to the printer, and these were widely copied over the next decade by other companies who produced printers. Apple released the Apple Centronics Printer Card in 1978. Selling for $225, it was specifically designed to work with Centronics (or compatible) printers.[4] It was similar to the Apple II Parallel Printer Interface Card, but had fewer control codes. The Centronics standard used seven data bits and three handshaking bits, and would automatically send certain control codes (such as a change in line width) to the printer when a program sent the proper command.[5]

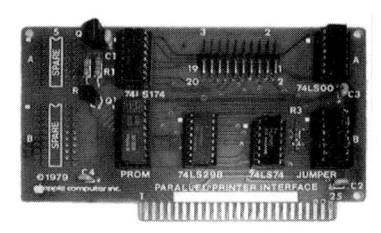

Apple II Parallel Printer Interface Card
– Photo credit: Dave Touvell <apple2info.net>

In 1981, Apple released an updated parallel card that replaced both of these cards. The Apple II Parallel Interface Card had the firmware for both the Apple II Parallel Printer Interface Card and the Apple Centronics Printer card, selectable via dipswitches on the card. Also, a program could directly control the card if needed. It was also compatible with the Pascal 1.1 Firmware protocol, so would be automatically recognized and used by the Pascal System.

Apple II Parallel Interface Card
– Photo credit: Dave Touvell <apple2info.net>

In April 1978, Apple released the Apple II Communications Interface Card, selling for $225. It was intended for use with a modem, and provided full-duplex serial communications at speeds of 110 or 300 baud. It could also drive a serial printer, but the slow speed and lack of handshaking limited its usefulness for that purpose.[6] These low speeds conformed to the Bell 103A dataset standard published by AT&T back in 1962. Although it was possible to use a modem to communicate at speeds greater than 300 baud, this equipment was initially more expensive and not as readily available.

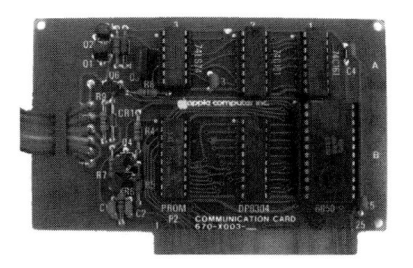

Apple II Communications Card – Photo credit: <Grinnell.edu>

---

4   Peterson, Craig. The Computer Store, Santa Monica, CA, *Store Information And Prices*, (August 10, 1979), 1.
5   Wright, Loren, "On Buying A Printer", *Micro* (August 1981), 33-35.
6   Mazur, Jeffrey, "Hardtalk", *Softalk* (March 1982), 118.

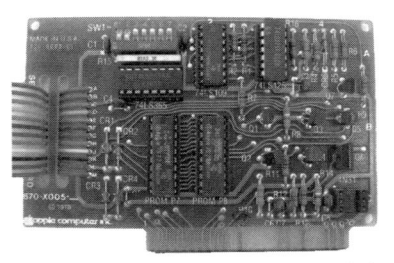

Apple released the Apple II Serial Interface Card ($195) in August of 1978. Serial devices required fewer data transmission lines, and so could work with more compact cables. Instead of sending each byte as eight simultaneous bits as was done in parallel devices, serial interfaces send each byte as a series of eight bits, which only required two wires; one to send and one to receive data. Like the parallel cards, there were a couple of other wires to control handshaking. Also, serial cards required a means of informing the devices when a byte began and ended (specifically, a start bit, a stop bit, and a parity bit if only a seven-bit character was sent). The speed of transmission had to be pre-determined by the sending and receiving devices.

Apple II Serial Interface Card – Photo credit: <Grinnell.edu>

> The original version of the Serial Interface Card had a ROM referred to the P8 ROM. It contained the on-card program that allowed a user to print or otherwise communicate with the card without having to know much on the hardware level. The P8 ROM didn't support handshaking that used two ASCII control characters named ETX (Control-C) and ACK (Control-F), so a later revision called the P8A ROM was released. This worked better with some printers, but unfortunately the P8A ROM was not compatible with some serial printers that had worked with the earlier P8 ROM.

The Apple Super Serial Card firmware was finished in January 1981. It was called "super" because it replaced both the older Serial Interface Card and the Communications Card. To change from one type of mode to another, however, called for switching a block (identified with a triangle) on the card from one position to another (from printer position to modem position). The Super Serial Card was also able to emulate both the P8 and P8A Serial Cards, making it compatible with older software written specifically for those cards.[7]

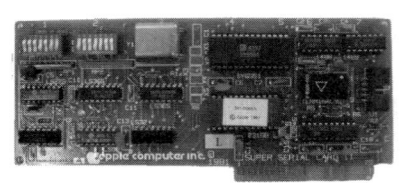

Apple II Super Serial Card – Photo credit: Mike Loewen

VIDEO CARDS

After obtaining a printer interface card (and printer), the next most popular card for the Apple II was a card that displayed 80 columns of text (which was

---

7 Weishaar, Tom. "Control-I(nterface) S(tandards)", *Open-Apple*, (October 1987), 3.65.

rapidly becoming a standard outside the Apple II world). An early entry into this market was the Sup'R'Terminal card made by M&R Enterprises, the same company that made the Sup'R'Mod RF modulator for the Apple II. One of the most popular of the 80-column cards was the Videx Videoterm. Videx even went so far as to make the Ultraterm, a card for the Apple II that displayed 132 columns on a monitor, but it never made much headway in the computer world (being supplanted by bit-mapped graphics displays, as on the Macintosh).[8]

Many other companies made 80-column cards, but for the most part they were not very compatible with each other. One problem was deciding on a method to place the characters on the 80-column screen. With the standard Apple 40-column display, you could use either the standard routines in the Monitor, or directly "POKE" characters to the screen from BASIC. With a third party 80-column card, it was common to use a protocol from the non-Apple world—using special character sequences to indicate a screen position or other functions. For example, to put a character at row 12, column 2, a program sent an ESC character, followed by a letter, followed by 12 and 02. Similar ESC sequences cleared the screen, scrolled it up or down, or performed other functions that Apple's built-in screen routines could do.

Synetix, Inc., released three unique video products in 1983 to enhance the graphics capabilities of the Apple II. The Synetix Systems Sprite I card ($149) offered graphics only; the Synetix Systems Sprite II card ($249) had graphics and sound, and the Synetix SuperSprite ($349), which had the additional capabilities of sound and speech production. These cards plugged into slot 7 (which had access to some video signals not available on other slots), and they were promoted as a graphics enhancement system. They produced their effects by overlaying the hi-res screen with animated "sprite" graphics (programmable characters that moved independently on any screen background). Since each sprite was on its own plane on the screen, they didn't interfere with each other. Also, it didn't take extra effort by the 6502 microprocessor to manipulate the sprites; once the programmer placed the sprite on the screen and started it moving, it would continue until the card received an instruction to change it. This was much easier than trying to program a hi-res game using standard Apple graphics.

Synetix SuperSprite board
– Photo credit: *Softalk* magazine, September 1983

These cards would have made it possible to create arcade-quality graphics and sound for games on the Apple II. Unfortunately, the prices of the

---

8 -----. "A.P.P.L.E. Co-op Celebrates A Decade of Service", *Call-A.P.P.L.E.* (February 1988), 12-27.

cards were high enough to virtually guarantee that it would never sell enough to justify developers to write programs for only the few users who owned the card. In 1984, software company Avant-Garde released three programs, *StarSprite I*, *StarSprite II*, and *StarSprite III* to help programmers develop for the Synetix boards. But even this combination did not make the cards sell sufficiently to make an impact on the Apple II market.[9]

TIMELINE

Apple II Parallel Printer Interface Card – *October 1977*

Apple Centronics Printer Card – *1978*

Apple II Communications Interface Card – *April 1978*

Apple II Serial Interface Card – *August 1978*

Videx Videoterm – *March 1980*

Sup'R'Terminal card – *May 1980*

Apple II Parallel Interface Card – *1981*

Apple Super Serial Card – *January 1981*

Synetix Systems Sprite I, Sprite II, and SuperSprite – *September 1983*

Videx Ultraterm – *September 1984*

---

[9] Neubauer, Peter, "Where are the sprites in my Apple?" *Bluer White* (August 29, 2012), <www.bluerwhite.org/2012/08/sprite-boards/> retrieved May 19, 2013.

CHAPTER 9

Accessing the World

In its earliest days, home computing was a solitary adventure. The computers were not very portable, and sharing software with others required physical transfer of media (cassette tapes or floppy disks) from one computer to another. However, technology inherited from the older mainframe environment made it inevitable that data and program sharing via a phone line would come to these new computers. It happened because of a device known as a modem.

The term "modem" was derived from modulator-demodulator, referring to its function in converting digital information to an analog format for transmission elsewhere, and back to digital on the receiving end. In its simplest form, a printer interface was a one-way device that sent data to the printer, which it then translated into ink on paper. A modem typically involved two-way communication, transferring information back and forth between two computers.

Mainframe computer modems originated from a need to transfer information between them. Use of the existing telephone network was an obvious solution, and in 1958 Bell Telephone published standards on transmission of computer data on standard (non high-speed) telephone lines. That first publication defined the Bell 101 dataset, which allowed for speeds of 110 baud (approximately 110 bits per second). By 1962 this had been updated to the Bell 103 dataset, which increased the speed to 300 baud. Both 101 and 103 datasets allowed for simultaneous two-way data transfer.

The next improvement in data transmission took place in the 1970s, when Bell created the 202 standard, which allowed 1200 baud as half-duplex (one computer at a time sending information). The later Bell 212 standard allowed 1200 baud full-duplex operation (computers on both ends transmitting simultaneously). From the standpoint of the user connected, a half-duplex connection did not echo key presses back to the user. For example, in half-duplex when "A" was typed, the user did not see "A" on the screen, unless the software was set to "local echo" (that is, the terminal software automatically displayed all characters typed). In full-duplex mode, the local echo was not necessary, since the character typed was sent back to the originating computer.

On home computers, modems were available either as internal or external. Internal modems had all the functions on a plug-in card, and attached to that card was either a line to an acoustic coupler (see the photo below of the Apple Modem IIB), or the phone line itself was attached to the card. External modems were, naturally, external to the computer case. They attached to the computer's serial port, usually on a serial interface card that was itself plugged into the motherboard. The modem plugged into the serial card, and then the phone line plugged into the external modem.

The primary problem with internal modem cards was that every different computer required a different card for its own unique card architecture. The advantage of an external modem (from the point of view of the manufacturer) was that it was possible to build one style that worked on many computers, as long as they had a compatible serial port connector on the computer.

D.C. Hayes was one of the first companies to create a modem affordable to the home or hobby computer user. Its first product was made for the S-100 bus on Altair or similar computers. The success of this first product led to the creation of the Hayes Micromodem 100 (for S-100 computers) and the Hayes Micromodem II (for the Apple II). Both products were released in 1979 and sold for $379, operating at transmission speeds compatible with the Bell 103 standards (110 and 300 baud). Although the Micromodem II was a card that plugged into (usually) slot 2 on the Apple II, it had an external box, the "Microcoupler", to which the phone line was attached.

Hayes Micromodem II, 1980 – Photo credit: *Softalk*, November 1980

Another company that sold modem hardware for early microcomputers was Novation. Novation had been in business as far back as 1970, selling an acoustic coupler that could be added onto Model 33 Teletypes.[1] In the late 1970s, they created the Novation CAT, a Bell 103 compatible 300-baud external modem that used an acoustic coupler. This was improved in 1981 with the introduction of the Novation Apple-Cat II. Using a direct connection instead of the acoustic coupler, this modem used the Bell 202 protocol, could achieve speeds of 1200 baud (at half-duplex).

The Apple-Cat II offered other features beyond its functions as a modem. With the optional Expansion module, which attached to the back of the computer, other devices could be connected. These included:

- A standard telephone handset could be plugged into the module mounted on the back of the computer, and it included a cradle that inserted into the ventilation slots on the side of the Apple II. This made the computer look like a very large telephone, but it really worked as a standard phone if desired. Dialing was performed from

---

1 Novation advertisement, *Computerworld* (Vol IV, No. 20, May 20, 1970), 17.

the keyboard, using the included software. Third-party programmers added software that distorted the user's voice on the telephone.
- An RS-232 (serial) port for connection of a printer, or even a second modem (external).
- Plugs to interface a cassette recorder (to allow it to act as an answering machine).
- Also, like many of the cards for the Apple II that had clock and calendar functions, Novation added BSR X-10 support to the Apple-Cat II, also connected to the Expansion module.

Finally, the Apple-Cat had a built-in tone generator (for tone dialing), which was used by some programmers to create music software. Unfortunately, Novation did little promotion of this feature of the Apple-Cat, or it might have been used by games to provide better sound effects. The hacker community made use of it to simulate many telephone network features, such as the sound of a dime, nickel, or quarter being dropped into a pay phone, or the ring sound on an American or UK telephone line.

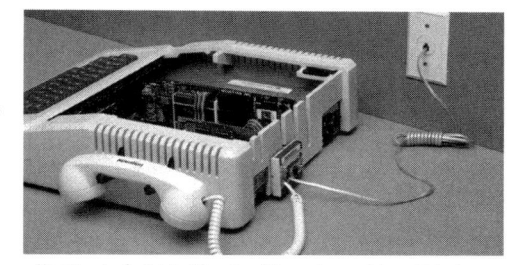

Novation Apple-Cat II with optional Expansion module and telephone cradle – Photo credit: Product brochure

Novation later offered full-duplex 1200-baud (Bell 212) performance. This was accomplished through a second expansion board plugged into a free slot on the Apple II, with a ribbon cable connecting the two boards. If there were no free slots available for the expansion board, it was possible to remove a chip from the second board, connect it with the same ribbon cable, and lie that board horizontally on top of the Apple II power supply (with double-sided tape to hold it in place, and to electrically isolate the board from the metal power supply).[2, 3, 4]

In 1979, Micromate Electronics offered the Micronet Modem, ranging from an acoustic modem at $179 to a direct connect modem that did not require an interface card, for $289. In place of the interface card, this modem connected to the game paddle port.[5]

As a follow-up to the Micromodem II, Hayes began to design external modems for connection to an RS-232 serial interface card. To implement this, the company had to create a set of commands that could be sent from

---

2 Abendschan, James, "The Novation Apple-Cat][", <www.jammed.com/~jwa/Machines/cat/>, accessed October 20, 2012.
3 Brochure, Novation, "Introducing Novation Apple-Cat II", (1981).
4 Brochure, Novation, "Apple-Cat II 212 Upgrade Card – Installation and Operating Manual", (1981).
5 Micromate Electronics ad, *Softalk* (March 1981), 33.

the computer to control functions (dialing, hanging up, etc.), and the modem had to be able to distinguish these commands from the data being sent from the serial port. This led to the creation of what became known as the Hayes command set—instructions for control of the modem. These were in such widespread use, that "Hayes compatibility" became a selling feature for other modems that connected to a serial port.

Following these protocols, Hayes released the Smartmodem in April 1981, a 300-baud external modem that set the standard for others that followed. This was succeeded by the Smartmodem 1200 in 1982 ($699), and the Smartmodem 2400 in 1985 ($549).

Many other companies created modems that were compatible with the Hayes standard, usually selling them for lower prices than Hayes. By the late 1980s, Applied Engineering began selling two modems for the Apple II expansion slots, the DataLink 1200 and the DataLink 2400.

The first modem Apple sold with its logo was a re-branded Novation CAT 300-baud acoustic modem (Novation actually sold this modem for several home computers of the day, branded for each company). It was first advertised in June 1978 as the Modem IIA (later name-changed to Modem IIB), and sold bundled with the Apple Communications Card for $390 ($199.95 for the modem alone). Beyond its labeling, no other changes were made to the modem to make it a uniquely Apple product.

In 1984, Apple released a pair of modems designed specifically for its own computers. The Apple Modem 300 ($225) and Apple Modem 1200 ($495) were released in platinum and white versions, and connected via serial cables to the Macintosh or to any Apple II with a Super Serial Card or similar interface.

Hayes Smartmodem 1200 – Photo credit: 50 Best Technology Products, <www.zhaoniupai.com/blog/archives/687.html>

Apple Modem IIB acoustic modem. The earpiece of the phone would go on the left, and the mouthpiece would go on the right side – Photo credit: Brian Wiser

Apple Modem 1200, beige and white – Photo credit: François Michaud

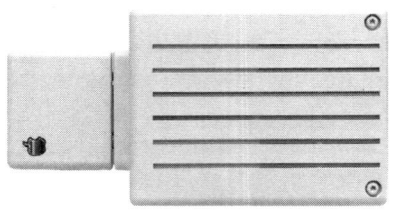

Apple Personal Modem 300/1200 – Photo credit: Apple II Catalog, 1986

The following year the company introduced the Apple Personal Modem for $399, which worked at 300 or 1200 baud, but was more expensive than similar products of the time. By the late 1980s it was no longer in production, as the company had moved on to internal modems that were Macintosh-specific.

Over the following years, as standards were developed to handle it, modem speeds continued to increase, jumping to 4800 baud, then 9600, then 14,400 (or 14.4K), 28.8K, 33.6K, and then finally hitting the maximum possible on phone lines, 56K.

TIMELINE

Novation CAT – *April 1978*

Apple Modem IIA / IIB – *June 1978*

Hayes Micromodem II – *October 1979*

Micronet Modem – *December 1979*

Hayes Smartmodem – *April 1981*

Novation Apple-CAT II – *June 1981*

Hayes Smartmodem 1200 – *June 1982*

Apple Modem 300 – *March 1984*

Apple Modem 1200 – *March 1984*

Hayes Smartmodem 2400 – *May 1985*

Apple Personal Modem 300/1200 – *September 1985*

AE Datalink 1200 – *November 1987*

AE Datalink 2400 – *November 1987*

CHAPTER 10
Online Origins

From the earliest days of the Apple II, there were users who found ways to connect to other Apple II computers over the phone. Although some inexpensive and imaginative methods were employed (such as A.P.P.L.E.'s "Apple Box" which used the cassette port to send and receive programs via the phone line), it was the release of the DC Hayes Micromodem II for the Apple II in 1979 that made it possible for a new type of computing. Although some used their Apple II merely as a home terminal to access a school or business timesharing system, many users created their own self-contained dial-up message systems. Before discussing this, it is necessary to look back a bit farther, to some of the technological innovations that made it possible for modems to work over phone lines.

ARPANET (1972 – 1990)

When the Soviet Union launched the first Sputnik satellite in 1957 it took the United States government by surprise. To ensure that in the future the US government would have better knowledge of technological advancements taking place around the world, President Dwight Eisenhower authorized the formation of a research agency within the Pentagon. The Advanced Research Projects Agency (ARPA) had the mission of enabling communication between intelligence sources and the various branches of the military, as well as with the president and the secretary of defense.

While managing the rapid interchange of information between various government agencies, they discovered an important bottleneck between the different mainframe computer systems used by those agencies. There was no easy means for data on one system to travel to another except by printing the data and re-entering it on the destination computer—a slow process that could introduce errors. The director of the ARPA Information Processing Techniques Office had a room next to his office, which contained three different types of computer terminals, each made by different companies, and each directly connected to mainframe computers at different sites. They operated under their own, unique operating system and had different login procedures.[1]

---

1 Hafner, Katie & Matthew Lyon, *Where Wizards Stay Up Late: The Origins Of The Internet* (New York, Simon & Schuster, 1996), 13-14.

As ARPA began to research ways in which to make it possible for computer installations in widely separated parts of the country to become connected to each other, national security was still foremost in their minds. One essential goal they had was for the network as a whole to still function even if part of it was destroyed in a nuclear attack. The telephone network built by AT&T had central switching points, where a single location served a large number of customers. If the central switching office was not working, none of the customers received telephone service. While this was an inconvenience, it was not acceptable for a computer network on which the defense of the United States would depend. So ARPA researchers devised a distributed network, with each node connected to other nodes, allowing a built-in redundancy that would allow the majority of it to continue to function even if parts of it were offline (or even destroyed).

Not only was the network designed with decentralized pieces of hardware, but also the message traffic on the network was transmitted in pieces. These pieces (data packets) could take different paths through the network, but when they all arrived at their destination, the computer there reassembled the packets in their correct order to create a copy of the original message. This packet approach also allowed the computers handling message traffic for the network to make use of nodes that were idle and bypass those that were either busy or not functioning.[2]

During the 1960's the details were mapped out, the hardware was built to handle the traffic between the nodes across the country, and the network was tested. The entire project was a learning process, from the implementation of the data packet concept (how big and in what format should a packet be sent), to the design of the software (to direct routing of the traffic across the network), and the hardware to carry the traffic. The first public demonstration of this network was ready in time for the first International Conference on Computer Communication, held in Washington, DC in October 1972. It required a tremendous effort on the part of those who were finalizing the design and implementation of the components that made up the network, but they managed to make it all work together just in time for the occasion. It was an incredible event, with most of the country's networking researchers in attendance at the same time. At the conference site they demonstrated how this network could send data packets from many diverse types of hardware to the remote locations to which they were connected.[3]

The success of the ARPANET project resulted in requests from university research groups wanting a connection to the network for all kinds of traffic, not just Department of Defense work. The dominant use of the network was something for which its designers had not foreseen: electronic mail. Between

---

2   Hafner, Katie & Matthew Lyon, *Where Wizards Stay Up Late: The Origins Of The Internet* (New York, Simon & Schuster, 1996), 57-67.
3   Hafner, Katie & Matthew Lyon, *Where Wizards Stay Up Late: The Origins Of The Internet* (New York, Simon & Schuster, 1996), 176-186.

1972 and the early 1980s, network mail (also called electronic mail and eventually e-mail) was discovered by thousands of users who had occasion to use the network. As the message traffic due to e-mail increased, it was necessary to expand the network to handle it.

> E-mail was to the ARPANET what the Louisiana Purchase was to the young United States. Things only got better as the network grew and technology converged with the human tendency to talk. Electronic mail would become the long-playing record of cyberspace. Just as the LP was invented for connoisseurs and audiophiles but spawned an entire industry, electronic mail grew first among the elite community of computer scientists on the ARPANET, then later bloomed like plankton across the Internet.[4]

In 1972, the name ARPA was changed to DARPA (*Defense* Advanced Research Projects Agency), to stress the role the organization had played from the start—to help with the defense of the United States. With the ARPANET concept functioning and flourishing, DARPA decided to find a different group within the government to take over management of the network, and the Defense Communications Agency (DCA) was given that task in the summer of 1975. (When the DCA had first been approached to manage ARPANET in the mid-1960's, when it was still just a concept, leaders in the agency had declined, believing that a decentralized, packet-sending network had no advantage over the communications methods that were already in place.) With ARPANET being managed elsewhere, DARPA was free to move its research money into other experimental areas.[5]

By this time, other computer networks had come into being that were not under the jurisdiction or control of DARPA. With other implementations of networks came alternate methods of interconnecting the computers within those networks—methods that differed (sometimes significantly) with those chosen by the DARPA researchers. In Hawaii, where land connections to link the islands were not possible, there was a network called ALOHANet that used radio transmitters to send signals between computers on a network. DARPA also looked at the use of satellite (SATNet) transmission of network packets to exchange data between computers. Other countries also came up with their own unique computer networking protocols.

The presence of these different networks brought about similar problems as those faced by ARPA in the 1960's, when it first tried to make individual mainframe computers communicate with each other. How was it possible to make dif-

---

4 Hafner, Katie & Matthew Lyon, *Where Wizards Stay Up Late: The Origins Of The Internet* (New York, Simon & Schuster, 1996), 189.
5 Hafner, Katie & Matthew Lyon, *Where Wizards Stay Up Late: The Origins Of The Internet* (New York, Simon & Schuster, 1996), 219, 235.

ferent networks able to exchange data between each other, when they often used different connection methods, packet sizes, transmission rates, and error-checking protocols? DARPA then decided it needed to address ways to overcome this problem, and in May 1974 a paper was published that proposed a transmission-control protocol (TCP) to manage data exchange between different networks.

> The new scheme worked in much the same way that shipping containers are used to transfer goods. The boxes have a standard size and shape. They can be filled with anything from televisions to underwear to automobiles – content doesn't matter. They move by ship, rail, or truck. A typical container of freight travels by all three modes at various stages to reach its destination. The only thing necessary to ensure cross-compatibility is the specialized equipment used to transfer the containers from one mode of transport to the next. The cargo itself doesn't leave the container until it reaches its destination.

As further work was done on finding ways to implement TCP, an additional Internet Protocol (IP) was created to handle routing of the data packages the TCP handled. By 1978, the full protocol was referred to as TCP/IP.[6]

Meanwhile, universities that were not part of ARPANET wanted network access, but a connection to the Department of Defense system cost $100,000 per year. The National Science Foundation was interested in aiding computer sciences departments in universities, and so helped design CSNET (Computer Science Research Network), a less expensive system. It would not be as fast as ARPANET and did not contain the redundancy ARPANET required, but it made the computer networking connections more affordable. It made use of TELENET, a commercial packet-switching service that started in 1973.

Other networks soon began to appear. BITNET (Because It's Time Network) interconnected IBM systems. UUCP was created at Bell Laboratories to handle file transfers and remote command execution. USENET began in 1980 to handle communication between two universities, and developed into a distributed news network. All of these diverse networks had the ability to communicate with each other due to the TCP/IP protocol.[7] By 1982, the term Internet was used for the first time to describe this collection of networks. The continued addition of networks began to blur the distinction between the parts of the Internet that were sponsored by the US government and those that simply connected to the network.

One change that became necessary was the way in which e-mail was handled. From its earliest days, e-mail had been transmitted using the original file transfer protocol, which worked nicely for files, but was awkward for

---

6 Hafner, Katie & Matthew Lyon, *Where Wizards Stay Up Late: The Origins Of The Internet* (New York, Simon & Schuster, 1996), 236-237.
7 Hafner, Katie & Matthew Lyon, *Where Wizards Stay Up Late: The Origins Of The Internet* (New York, Simon & Schuster, 1996), 243-244.

mail. In August 1982, the simple mail transfer protocol (SMTP) was devised to replace the older system. As part of this new protocol, new names were devised to distinguish between different networks on the Internet. The committee working on this problem decided upon seven domains that could be used for various types of networks: "edu" for educational, "com" for a company, "gov" for government, "mil" for military, "org" for a non-profit organization, "net" for a network service provider, and "int" for an international treaty entity. These domain names also allowed for automatic translation of names into the numeric addresses that the computers routing the information actually used, with the help of a domain name server (DNS).

As useful as ARPANET and the Internet had become, the speed of communication became a problem as more and more nodes were added on to it. In 1985, the National Science Foundation began creation of NSFNET, a backbone to connect supercomputer centers from several places in the United States. The power, speed, and capacity of this new network exceeded that of ARPANET, and eventually made it obsolete. In 1990 it was decided to shut down ARPANET and allow the computers accessing it to instead connect to the faster NSFNET.

THE BBS (1978 – Present)

While government research agencies were laying the groundwork for the Internet, another phenomenon happened. The hobbyist computer revolution started in 1975 with the appearance of the Altair 8800, followed by rapid developments, enhancements, and competing systems appearing over the period of just a few years. Historically, Bell Telephone had devised protocols for the connection of a computer to the phone system as far back as 1962 (using only AT&T equipment leased from the phone company). In the late 1960s, a court decision resulted in legal permission for companies other than AT&T to produce equipment that could acoustically connect to the phone system. Furthermore, third-party companies were also allowed to create equipment that could directly connect to phone lines, provided they passed a stringent set of rules created by AT&T. Although initially expensive (because of the need to pass those tests), direct connect modems outside of AT&T began to appear in the early 1970s.[8]

One of the concerns held by Bell Telephone about the use of modems on phone lines had to do with whether or not their use would affect the network. The problem they envisioned had less to do with the type of information (voice versus data) being sent on the phone lines, but rather the amount of time these phones would be in use. In most cases, a telephone call from person to person lasted only a few minutes and then the line was free again. A computer on the phone line could conceivably run continually for several

---

8 ------, "Historical Modem Protocols", *The Linux Documentation Project*, <tldp.org/HOWTO/Modem-HOWTO-29.html>, accessed October 20, 2012.

hours. It was an issue of whether or not the telephone system could handle the load of computers using up available phone connections.

Early hobbyists soon learned how to make use of acoustic modems. The first recorded use of a home computer as a repository of messages for others to dial into was the Computer Bulletin Board System (CBBS) in Chicago, which ran on a Vector 1 computer (an Altair clone). Ward Christensen and Randy Suess designed it for their microcomputer user group, the Chicago Area Computer Hobbyist Exchange (CACHE). The CBBS began in February 1978, and at first was no more than a computerized version of the club's paper-and-thumbtack message board. With time it evolved into a more sophisticated system, allowing other features, including the exchange of files.[9] Although not run on an Apple II, the event is significant because it was the start of a phenomenon that expanded to include nearly all models of personal computers, and ran strong for over fifteen years, finally waning in popularity due to the rise of the Internet.

A typical BBS consisted of a single computer that was always turned on, waiting to answer the phone. When it rang, the computer answered the phone and established two-way communication via the modem. A program running on the host computer would then allow the calling computer to take various actions, such as reading messages left by other users and posting replies for others to read. As with the original CBBS system, the software used for running Apple II BBSes became more complex over time, allowing file uploads and downloads (to and from the host computer), online games (primarily text-based), and participation in online surveys. The system operator (sysop) who owned the computer and paid for the phone line was responsible for maintaining the message databases, usually leaving this dedicated computer available for callers 24 hours a day.

After a user grasped the concept of what was going on when using a modem with a computer, more and more uses for the technology became apparent. Just as email was the driving force behind the growth of the Internet in its early days, so also message boards became the initial primary use for these BBS systems. Close behind the use of a BBS for messages was the use of these boards for games, and files for art, music, programs and other data.

BBS Uses – *Messages and Games*

The era of the BBS was unique not only to Apple II history but also to all of computer history. Even though these were typically single user systems (systems connecting with multiple phone lines eventually appeared), they provided something that had previously been unavailable to the general public. The systems offered the ability to interact with unseen people who had interests and ideas in common, and gave them the opportunity to make friendships that could not have occurred without computers.

---

9 Derfler. Jr., Frank L, "Dial Up Directory", *Kilobaud Microcomputing Magazine* (April 1980), 80-82. (reproduced on *PortCommodore.com*, <www.portcommodore.com/dokuwiki/doku.php?id=larry:comp:bbs:about_cbbs> accessed October 20, 2012.

A BBS allowed the sysop the opportunity to create his or her own unique world, limited only by the sophistication of the software on which it ran. Whether the BBS was a commercial package or was written entirely by the sysop, there was room for customization. By the early 1990s there were several popular packages that could be purchased to run on an Apple II, including *ProLine*, *Warp Six*, and *AppleNet*.

The name and theme of a BBS was a reflection of what the sysop wanted to share with the world. It could be used exclusively for message boards and email, usually focusing on a particular theme or aspect of computers (or life in general). BBSes were places to share and learn information about a specific computer platform; they might be a meeting place to hammer out views on politics, religion, and philosophy; it could cover medical topics, such as substance abuse, mental illness, cancer, diabetes, and many more; or they might be the focal point for debates about social issues like race, war, pro-abortion or pro-life, homelessness, urban problems, and the like.

Regardless of the purpose of the board, for the sysop it was a chance to be the master of a small kingdom for which he or she had the final word. If profanity was not allowed, the sysop had the freedom to exclude those who chose to use such language. If the BBS was a place for Democrats to vent their feelings about Republicans, the sysop could censor any Republican who chose to make contrary statements. For some sysops, it was power that they did not have in their daily life; sometimes it was virtually the only thing over which that person could be The Boss. This was one reason that the prospect of running a BBS was very attractive.

It was common for a BBS to have other things that users could do while they were connected, beyond access to email and the message boards. A popular feature was to host an online game. These were very different from the later massively multiplayer online role-playing games, where a particular game could have thousands of people participating at the same time. The games on a BBS could be as simple as an online version of a board game, to an adventure similar to *Zork* (in which the user typed commands to move a player through a world described entirely in prose), to a multitude of other possible games. Some of the games actually did involve several users interacting with each other, but not at the same time. The reality of the BBS was that one person at a time could login, enter a game, play one or more turns, and then have to wait a specified period of time (usually at least a day) before coming back to see what other players had done.

BBS Uses – Art and Music

Another experience unique to the BBS was the emergence of using it as a place to share and view computer art. This covered numerous types:

- ASCII art (pictures created with text), which had been present since the days of the mainframe computer

- Rudimentary six color hi-res (or sixteen color lo-res) pictures that could be created and viewed on an Apple II
- Art created with the ANSI (American National Standards Institute) character set available on the IBM PC
- More sophisticated art possible on later computer models with better graphics capabilities

Some BBSes focused exclusively on the artscene. With members as passionate about the abilities of computers as classic artists have been about oil versus watercolor painting, for some people this became a competition to see who could create the best and most amazing pictures displayable on their computer.[10]

Music was not left out of the creative files posted on BBSes. Although it was not typical for an Apple II connecting to a BBS to be able to play music while connected, some of these boards made sound and music files available, composed and programmed by those who were talented in those areas. It might be nothing more than a program that played a simple one-voice tune, or as sophisticated as a music file for *Electric Duet* (a program that allowed an Apple II to play two-voice music on its simple one-bit speaker), or music that originated from MODs created on the Commodore Amiga (and playable on an Apple IIGS with programs like *MODZap, soniqTracker, NoiseTracker*, or Apple's *synthLAB*).

Artscene and music even joined forces for what became known as the Demoscene. This was a combination of animated graphics and music to create something amazing that did not necessarily do anything, but was nonetheless fascinating to watch. For the IIGS, some of the best examples of this came from the Free Tools Association (FTA) and Brutal Deluxe, both from France.

BBS Uses – The Underground

A less well-publicized use of BBSes was to share information that was not necessarily legal. The simplest versions came from those who broke copy protection on commercial software (usually games) and shared them with others. These hackers often gave themselves credit for what they did by changing the original startup screen for the program into an advertisement for the cracker's name and BBS. It started with simple text screens, but as games and their graphics became more sophisticated, these crack screens also increased in complexity, sometimes incorporating animation. This in itself became an extension of the Artscene, and some of the hackers found the creation of crack screens more interesting than the games that were being cracked, which led to the development of the Demoscene.

Closely connected to hacking and cracking software came activities that were more clearly illegal. Information available on a BBS might include how

---

10 Scott, Jason, BBS: *The Documentary* (DVD) (Boston, MA: Bovine Ignition Systems), 2005.

to break into corporate or government computer systems, or even how to build a bomb. Boards of this type were not widely advertised; they had a small core group whose members gained a reputation amongst themselves by proving the depths to which they could hack. This could involve breaking into a forbidden site, using information about the telephone system to be able to make free phone calls (echoes of the blue boxes sold by Wozniak and Jobs years earlier), or other similar activities. These members, who all used aliases (often their preferred login name), had to keep their true identities quiet. In some cases, one or more of their members were actively sought by law enforcement for their actions. As with graphics, music and demos, the status of a member was determined by who mastered the skill of the board's focus—in this case, who had performed the most risky or notorious actions with their computers.

BBS Uses – Files

An important use of a BBS that made it popular was as a file repository, a place where users could share software they had written. The ability to transfer files from one Apple II to another evolved over time. In its simplest form, an Applesoft or Integer BASIC program might be downloaded (sent from the BBS to the calling computer) by simply doing a "LIST" of it into the memory of the calling computer (and then saving it to disk). That was fine, unless the program contained machine language. Then, the bytes of that assembly code had to be precisely transmitted as hex digit pairs (for example, 20 00 BF 65 10 03 04), since anything shared between the computers had to be in printable ASCII codes.

Apple II BBSes were not the only ones that had to deal with file transfer problems. At least on an Apple II, a text file containing the statements for a BASIC program could be loaded using the EXEC command in Apple DOS, and the resulting BASIC or machine language program could be saved (or BSAVEd if a binary file) to a disk. But on the S-100 computer series, a file transfer was even more difficult to translate from text to machine code. For this reason, Ward Christensen of the Chicago CBBS developed a method to transfer files reliably. His method used error checking to ensure accuracy and his XModem protocol became available in 1979. Christensen made it public domain, and it began to appear for other platforms beyond the original Intel-based computers, including Apple II BBS and terminal programs.

As Apple software became more sophisticated, it was necessary to also design more sophisticated methods of transferring files between Apple II computers. A file under both Apple DOS and ProDOS did not contain any information that identified the filetype, creation and modification dates, file size, and other information about the file. All of that information was stored in the file's disk directory entry. If the raw data of the file was transferred, it would be difficult to know on the receiving end whether it was a BASIC program, a ProDOS system file, a hi-res picture, or something else. One way of dealing with this was to upload an entire disk, which included all of the directory entries and filetype information. A number of homebrew utilities appeared from the early 1980s onward that allowed an entire disk to be converted into a file suitable for modem transfer. It was not until the major online services began to look for a unifying method to accomplish this that standards finally appeared.

Gary Little was a founding member of the Apples British Columbia Computer Society, and popular author of several Apple II books. He had written a telecommunications program called *Modem MGR* (later called *Modem Magician*, and then *Point-to-Point* when it was sold through Pinpoint Publishing) and wanted a means of transferring both a file and its attributes between Apple II computers. On the Macintosh, a protocol called MacBinary had been created in 1985 to accomplish some of these goals. The problem was somewhat more complex on the Mac, because its file system supported files with both data and resource forks (data forks held the main info in the file; a resource fork held information about the icon to display with the file on a graphic desktop, or other connected info about the file). Little used MacBinary as inspiration to create Binary II for the Apple II. He designed it to make it possible to also encode the source system for a file being transferred (ProDOS, DOS 3.3, Pascal, CP/M, and even MS-DOS). Furthermore, he added a means for the telecommunications program sending the Binary II data to package several files together into a single archive that would then be decoded on the receiving end back to its several source files. Apple later formally adopted his Binary II protocol after Little began to work at the company as a senior software marketing manager.

By the late 1980s, increased file size and complexity called for a better solution for file transfer. Andy Nicholas was a college student who had an interest in the techniques of combining multiple files into a single file for file transfer. He was also familiar with data compression, particularly the Unix "compress" program that could make a file smaller (and therefore faster to transmit on a dialup connection).

He worked with others online and came up with the NuFX (NuFile eXchange) standard in 1988. It was designed as a more robust method of combining multiple files within an archive, as well as adding a more efficient file compression algorithm. He implemented NuFX in his own freeware programs ShrinkIt and later GS-ShrinkIt for the Apple IIgs.

As with Binary II, Apple officially approved the NuFX protocol as a standard for handling file archives for transmission on the Apple II. After graduation from college, Nicholas went to work at Apple.

The Decline of the BBS

As the 1990s progressed, the popularity of BBSes began to wane. This was due primarily to the increased availability of Internet access, and the wealth of information available through that source.

Compared to the Internet, one of the important differences offered by a BBS was that it tended to be a small community of people with shared interests. They often came to know each other quite well, even if they never physically met. Although the web offered dramatically more than BBSes ever did, the depth of participation on the web tended to be considerably shallower. The ease of jumping from one web site to another resulted in a much shorter attention span of potential members. It was significantly more difficult to attract and maintain web site members, and to even have a handle on how many people actually were regular visitors. In the days of the dial-up BBS, it was much easier to keep track of how many callers connected, and how long they stayed on.

The era of the BBS set the stage for expectations that people had for what could be done with a modem online. Access to larger groups than the single-user BBS became possible in the early to mid 1980s.

USENET NEWSGROUPS (1979 – Present)

In 1979, two Duke University graduate students came up with the idea of a method of reading and posting messages that were organized into categories. Their system ran under UUCP (the Unix to Unix Copy Protocol), and the different categories were called newsgroups. It worked like a bulletin board system but on a much larger scale, since it ran on a mainframe that handled many users simultaneously. The system they developed became known as Usenet, and ultimately it ran under a specific protocol that was called Network News Transfer Protocol (NNTP).

NNTP had a specific set of commands to retrieve and post messages for the various different newsgroups that existed and were shared through the computers that made up the Internet. Because many of the systems and their file servers accessing the Internet at that time were not online constantly, it was common for them to use the concept of "store and forward"; they stored message traffic until the computer was connected to the larger network, at which time it sent and retrieved messages, and then disconnected.

By the mid-1980s the newsgroup management board created a new method of organizing newsgroups. These groups were designed to cover multiple topics, and those topics that dealt with computers started with "comp", with sub topics appended to that main category. So, "comp.sys" dealt with specific computer systems, and "comp.sys.apple" was created to deal with conversations about the Apple II. In 1990 a proposal was made and approved to change the newsgroup name to comp.sys.apple2, since Macintosh users were posting on this newsgroup instead of on comp.sys.mac.

College students at institutions that offered Internet access as a paid part of their tuition were the primary early users of the Usenet newsgroups. These groups were a means of sharing and obtaining information on many topics (not just about computers), and did not require an hourly or monthly charge as did the commercial services like CompuServe. Beyond students, education professionals at these institutions also had access to newsgroups.

> Apple II users who dialed into BBSes that ran *ProLine* could also access UUCP traffic. (ProLine was a simplified version of UNIX for the Apple II that worked within the constraints of 48K of RAM. Each different ProLine BBS was a separate node, or dial-up access point to the Internet, and some were directly connected via a serial cable to a second computer that was itself running Unix and connected to the Internet.) ProLine used a timed script to automatically dial into a Unix shell account, send outgoing messages, check for and retrieve incoming messages, and then hang up. These messages were then distributed to the appropriate ProLine users.[11]
>
> Even though it happened late in the lifespan of the Apple II, several related newsgroups for the platform appeared soon after the change to comp.sys.apple2 occurred. Discussions about *GNO/ME* (a Unix environment for the Apple IIgs) were held on comp.sys.apple2.gno; comp.sys.apple2.comm dealt with communications; comp.sys.apple2.marketplace was used to buy, sell and trade anything related to the Apple II; comp.sys.apple2.programmer was for programming; and comp.sys.apple2.usergroups dealt with user groups. Other groups that were related to the Apple II included comp.binaries.apple2 (a source for downloads of freeware or shareware software) and comp.sources.apple2 (software source code files). Due to low traffic, these latter two groups were disbanded in 2005.

Unlike the commercial online services, the Usenet newsgroups typically were not moderated; no one was responsible for making sure that all posters behaved or were civil with each other. More or less, the group members managed issues themselves. Because the number of people accessing these groups was not large, a person posting messages either cooperated with the others in the newsgroup, or learned to stay away when their behavior was not tolerated. Each September, there was an influx of new students who had to learn the net etiquette (netiquette) of how to play nice. During that month the normal activity was somewhat disrupted with new users (newbies). Typical newbie behavior included posting to the wrong groups, disrupting conversations, or purposely trying to annoy group members.

However, in September of 1993 a major influx of new users hit the newsgroups, as America Online, CompuServe, and Demon Internet (a British Internet services provider) made Usenet access available to their users. The near-constant influx of newbies led to what has been called "Eternal September".[12, 13]

---

11 Davis, Morgan, "Apple: II: ProLine", BBS Documentary, An Overview of BBS Programs, <software.bbsdocumentary.com/APPLE/II/PROLINE/>, accessed October 20, 2012.

12 Raymond, Eric, "September That Never Ended", *The Jagon File*, < www.catb.org/jargon/html/S/September-that-never-ended.html>, accessed October 20, 2012.

13 ----, "Usenet History", The Network Administrators' Guide, <tldp.org/LDP/nag/node256.html>, accessed October 20, 2012.

Activity on comp.sys.apple2 (also known as csa2) was busy throughout the 1990s, and for those who didn't want to pay for access to the major commercial online services, it was ideal. They could talk about the Apple II, and as long as they had access to the Internet from school or from a work account, it was all free. Topics appeared about virtually anything regarding the Apple II, including how to break copy protection on commercial software (conversations that were not allowed on the big online services).

It was the activity of some who took a more lenient view of software ownership that provoked some of the greatest controversy on csa2, starting in the mid 1990s. Some users were not just looking to make it easy to copy and share software, they were actually taking work done by others, making a small change, and releasing it as their own work. This led to a few years of heated conflict between three groups: those who felt that no commercially available software should be distributed via csa2; those who felt that only currently selling software should be prohibited from distribution (and anything that was no longer available for purchase was fair game for sharing); and those who felt that anything and everything should be shared. The conflict ultimately led to some leaving the community, but most who preferred csa2 for their Apple II conversations stayed around.

One of the common documents produced by newsgroups was a document of Frequently Asked Questions (FAQ). With no such thing as Wikipedia at the time, the FAQ was the closest thing available to a group-created collection of knowledge on that topic. The comp.sys.apple2 FAQ was maintained and updated for years, although after the turn of the century, it had become more common to find copies of it on web sites.

The comp.sys.apple2 and related newsgroups continued to function well into the 21st century and were still busy, even in the era of individual, focused web sites. It remained the single largest Apple II community available online anywhere, and continued to have the advantage of being an un-moderated and freely available discussion site.

TIMELINE

ARPANET – *1972 - 1990*

The BBS – *1978 - 1996 (end of common usage)*

Usenet – *1979 - ongoing*

CHAPTER 11
More than a Plus

In the first year of the Apple II's release, Apple received feedback from its customers. Because of the popularity and demand for floating point BASIC, Applesoft underwent revisions during 1978 to improve its abilities. For those customers who were clamoring for an Applesoft in ROM, Apple released the Applesoft Firmware Card mid-year. This card, which plugged into slot 0, made it possible for original owners of the Apple II to have some of the benefits of the new BASIC. Even with that card, however, one could not use features of one BASIC while the other was active, and switching from one BASIC to the other erased any program that was being used at the time. The two BASICs could be told apart by the prompt they used; Integer BASIC used the ">" character, where Applesoft used the "]" character.

The success of the Applesoft Firmware Card helped Apple decide to create an update that became the Apple II Plus.[1] The main attraction of this newer Apple would be Applesoft in ROM, available immediately without having to load it from cassette or disk (or requiring purchase of the Firmware Card). Having it in ROM moved it out of the part of memory where the RAM-based Applesoft interpreter conflicted with addresses used by the hi-res graphics modes. This evolutionary enhancement to the Apple II was ready for release in June 1979, two years after the release of the original Apple II.

Apple II Plus and Monitor /// - Photo credit: Dave Dunfield, Dave's Old Computers, <www.classiccmp.org/dunfield/apple2/index.htm>

With the decision made to upgrade the Apple II, other changes were made to make it more attractive to new computer buyers. The cost of RAM chips had dropped considerably, so most new II Plus systems came standard with a full 48K of RAM (although 16K and 32K versions were also available

---
1 Wigginton, Randy, e-mail addressed to author, March 18, 2013.

early in its production run). Since the disk operating system consumed about 10K of memory, having the full complement of available RAM made it easier to use the Disk II with either version of BASIC. Less expensive memory meant that users would not need to add the smaller 4K memory chips, and so they removed the memory configuration blocks that allowed mixed use of 4K and 16K RAM chips on the original Apple II.

Other changes included in the Apple II Plus motherboard included those that had previously been made between Revision 0 and Revision 1 boards.

At $1,195, The 16K Apple II Plus sold for over $100 less than the original 4K Apple II, although it came with more memory and had Applesoft (previously an added expense item) in ROM. It cost only $300 more to get the full 48K of RAM in a new II Plus.

Apple II Plus nameplate – Photo credit: John Stammler

FIRMWARE DESIGN

John Arkley was a systems programmer who began working at Control Data Systems in Palo Alto in 1969, later moving to a bank in San Francisco and working on their IBM 370 mainframe. When the Apple II first came out in 1977, he was one of the customers who opted to purchase the bare motherboard. He built a pine case for his new computer, dubbing it the PineApple. From the beginning he was not satisfied with the uppercase only keyboard support on a stock Apple II, and wired in a keyboard that supported the full lower and uppercase character set. However, he also had to make changes in the Monitor ROM so his PineApple would accept the lowercase entries and display them on the screen properly.

To make these changes required Arkley to learn 6502 assembly language, so he could understand how the Monitor handled input and display. He created a 6502 assembler that ran on his IBM 370 at work, and using the Red Book with its ROM source code listing, he was able to make his changes and make a new ROM to implement them.

Arkley had an opportunity to show his computer to Wozniak, and was offered a job at Apple. He started working there in August 1978, and by November he was assigned the job of making some updates in the Monitor code.

Although the Monitor significantly simplified use of the computer (compared to older competitors like the Altair 8800), there were still customer complaints about some of its idosyncracies. The need to press the RESET key after powering on the computer, and the fact that pressing RESET sometimes caused a loss of the program in memory were particularly annoying. Steve Jobs insisted that the revised computer be more user-friendly, and that it had to be fixed in software (that is, it should not require significant hardware changes to make it happen).

Arkley began making changes to the original Monitor ROM in early 1979, including a clever way for the computer to identify when it had just been powered on (versus a warm start via the RESET key).[2] This became important as an early means to implement software copy protection. However, Arkley's revision hit a small barrier. The source code for the original Monitor no longer existed.

As previously mentioned, the Call Computer dial-up service that Randy Wigginton had been using to make modifications to the 6502 BASIC source code licensed from Microsoft had also been used to store the source code for the Monitor ROM. As a result of the tape-backup problem at Call Computer, not only was Wigginton's Applesoft source code lost, but also the work previously done on the Monitor. Making the problem even worse was the fact that there were no disk or cassette copies of the source code for the original Monitor ROM back at Apple.

The loss of the source code made it necessary for Arkley to re-enter the original source code, working from the source listing in the Red Book. He did the work on a cross-assembler running on a North Star Horizon (8080-based) computer, and then used that source file to create his Autostart ROM source file. That reconstructed listing appeared in the 1981 edition of the *Apple II Reference Manual*. What the new listing did not spell out was the purpose of some of the bytes associated with the disassembler in the Monitor, though the code could be viewed in the old Monitor listing that was printed in the same manual, or in the older Red Book.[3,4]

FIRMWARE FEATURES

The changes made by Arkley met Steve Jobs' requirements to be more user-friendly, and also had a beneficial effect for the new floppy disk. On a hard reset, it cleared the screen (bypassing the need for the user to press Ctrl-B to enter BASIC), and then checked for a floppy disk. If found, it transferred control to the disk controller and loaded code from that disk. This "Autostart ROM", as it was called, made it possible to have a system that automatically booted up a floppy disk and started a program with little action needed by the user.

The new ROM also automatically reconnected DOS when the RESET key was pressed. Screen editing was improved, utilizing more intuitive cursor

---

2 Arkley maintains that Wozniak cut some corners in his desire for a low chip count, and should have designed the RESET hardware differently from the start. Had he done so, some of the problems that required the Autostart ROM changes would have been unnecessary.
3 Arkley, John, personal email to author, September 9, 1991.
4 Arkley, John, personal email to author, June 2, 2013.

moves with "I" (up), "M" (down), "J" (left), and "K" (right), instead of the older "D", "C", "B", and "A" keys in the old Monitor ROM. Programmers appreciated the new feature of using Ctrl-S to pause the screen display of a long program. Most importantly, Applesoft was included in ROM, replacing Steve Wozniak's hand-assembled Integer BASIC.[5,6]

BELL & HOWELL

Apple made a marketing deal in 1979 with Bell & Howell to sell the Apple II and II Plus with a Bell & Howell nameplate on it for use in schools. Bell & Howell had long been associated with education institutions through their sturdy movie projectors and other audio-visual equipment, which were used extensively by schools throughout the United States. The Apple II computers sold through Bell & Howell were black colored (instead of the standard beige), earning them the nickname among computer hobbyists as the "Darth Vader" Apple II (reminiscent of the black colors worn by the villain of *Star Wars*). These computers came with screws on the back to keep the lids on, specifically to comply with UL certification, a requirement for equipment sold to schools. A typical Apple II Plus could not be certified as such, since it was designed to function with the lid off, which provided access to the internal components and, theoretically, electric shock.

One model of the Bell & Howell Apple II Plus, Model A2S1048B, had an optional "backpack" at-

Bell & Howell Apple II Plus – Photo credit: personal

Bell & Howell Apple II plus nameplate – Photo credit: personal

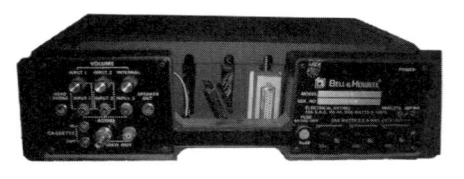

Bell & Howell Apple II Plus, rear panel – Photo credit: David Hodge

---

5 -----, "Apple and Apple II History," *The Apple II Guide*, (Cupertino, CA, Apple Computer, Inc., Fall 1990), 9-16.
6 -----, *Apple II Reference Manual*, (Cupertino, CA, Apple Computer, Inc., 1979, 1981), 25-27, 34-36.

tached to the rear of the computer. This backpack provided support for a coaxial cable to be attached for video output to the monitor (as well as the standard RCA phono jack for video), three 110 volt power outlets for peripherals, a carrying handle, three audio-in jacks, an audio-out jack, a standard 1/4 inch headphone jack, as well as the standard cassette input/output jacks. The power cord was much longer than on a standard Apple II, enough to allow it to sit on a cart in a classroom and still reach a power outlet. Another model, A2S1032B, did not come with the backpack option.[7, 8] These computers also came with the "shift-key mod" (see below) already applied.

Bell & Howell Apple II Plus, audio/visual rear panel – Photo credit: personal

This version of the Apple II Plus could be purchased with Disk II drives that were colored the same black as the computer. Bell & Howell also sold a printer called the P-100, which was actually a renamed Micro Peripherals MPI model 99G with a Centronics-compatible parallel interface cable and a parallel printer card.[9]

An additional enhancement provided in the Bell & Howell version of the Apple II was a means of attaching game paddles externally. DIN sockets on the right side of the computer (as viewed from the front) made it possible to easily plug in and remove the game paddles without risking the delicate pins used for the original paddles supplied by Apple. There would be no similar improvement offered by Apple until the release of the Apple IIe in 1983.

Bell & Howell Apple II Plus, power block rear panel – Photo credit: personal

Through their association with Bell & Howell, Apple had the means of gaining a stong foothold in the school environment.[10, 11]

Bell & Howell also had electronics correspondence courses, and used the black Apple II

Bell & Howell paddle connector – Photo credit: personal

---

7   Additional Bell & Howell info from J Mayrand's Computer Museum (offline)
8   Villados, Brian, "Apple II Plus – Bell & Howell Model," *The World According To... The Mac Geek*, <www.macgeek.org/museum/bhapple2plus/index.html>, accessed December 13, 2002.
9   Villados, Brian, "Apple II Plus – Bell & Howell Model," *The World According To... The Mac Geek*, <www.macgeek.org/museum/bhapple2plus/index.html>, accessed December 13, 2002.
10 Regan, Joe, A2 Roundtable, *GEnie*, Category 2, Topic 16, accessed April 1991.
11 Paymar, Dan, "Curing A Shiftless Apple," *Call-A.P.P.L.E.* (May 1982), 63-64.

UNBOXING THE APPLE II PLUS

Plus for one of their courses. They offered a one-year warranty, instead of the ninety-day warranty offered by Apple.[12, 13, 14]

Not all users were pleased with the modifications made in the new Autostart ROMs. Some of the writers at the magazine *Call-A.P.P.L.E.* referred to the new computer as the "Apple II Minus", since Arkley had to remove some of their beloved routines from the ROMs to make room for the new features. Missing from the Apple II Plus ROMs were Integer BASIC, the Mini-assembler, and Woz's SWEET16 interpreter, that entire space now being used by Applesoft. Also missing from the Monitor were the assembly language STEP and TRACE features, and a set of sixteen-bit multiply and divide routines.[15]

The packing list included with the original Apple II Plus read as follows:

```
                        APPLE II PLUS
                        PACKING LIST

           This package should contain the following items:

  item no.  part no.   description
  --------  --------   -----------
  1    1    600-2023   cassette tape: LITTLE BRICKOUT, COLOR DEMOSOFT
  2    1    600-2024   cassette tape: RENUMBER/APPEND, ALIGNMENT TEST TONE
  3    1    600-2025   cassette tape: FINANCE I, PENNY ARCADE
  4    1    600-2026   cassette tape: LEMONADE, HOPALONG CASSIDY
  5    1    600-2027   cassette tape: BRIAN'S THEME, PHONE LIST
  6    1    030-2057   manual: Introductory Programs for the Apple II Plus
  7    1    030-0044   manual: The Applesoft Tutorial
  8    1    030-0013   manual: Applesoft II BASIC Programming Reference Manual
  9    1    030-0004   manual: Apple II Reference Manual
  10   1    030-0035   publication: Apple Magazine
  11   1    600-0033   1 pair of game controls
  12   1    590-0002   cable: to hook up a cassette recorder
  13   1    590-0003   cable: power cord for the Apple II Plus
  14   1    030-0001   Apple Warranty Card
  15   1    600-0816   Apple II Plus System 16K
                          or
            600-8032   Apple II Plus System 32K
                          or
            600-0848   Apple II Plus System 48K
```

LITTLE BRICKOUT was an abbreviated Applesoft version of Woz's Integer BASIC *Breakout* game BRICKOUT (the reason he designed the Apple II in the first place). BRIAN'S THEME was a hi-res graphics program that drew lines on the screen in various patterns.

---

12 Vanderpool, Tom, A2 Roundtable, Category 2, Topic 16, *GEnie*, accessed March and August 1991.
13 Zuchowski, Tom, A2 Roundtable, Category 2, Topic 16, *GEnie*, accessed March 1991.
14 Hirsch, Steve, Tom, A2 Roundtable, Category 2, Topic 16, *GEnie*, accessed March 1991.
15 -----, *Apple II Reference Manual*, (Cupertino, CA, Apple Computer, Inc., 1979, 1981), 25-27, 34-36.

HOPALONG CASSIDY was a "guess who" program that also used the hi-res screen).[16, 17]

Also included in the Apple II Plus box was an instruction sheet:

> **TAPE LOADING INSTRUCTIONS**
>
> 1) If problems are encountered in LOADing tape programs, it may be necessary to "queue" [sic] the tape before LOADing. To queue a tape, use the following procedure:
> 2) Rewind the tape.
> 3) Disconnect the cable from the tape recorder (so you can hear what's on the tape).
> 4) Start the tape recorder in PLAY mode.
> 5) When a steady tone is heard, STOP the tape recorder.
> 6) Connect the cable to the tape recorder and adjust the volume and tone controls on the tape recorder to the recommended levels.
> 7) Make sure your computer is in BASIC.
> 8) Type LOAD.
> 9) START the tape playing.
> 10) Press RETURN. The program should LOAD properly. If an error message occurs, repeat the procedure, but try readjusting the tone and volume controls on the tape recorder.

Cassette users often found that it could take a number of tries to get a program to load properly from tape.

MORE HARDWARE ADD-ONS

Lower-case was still not supported on the new Apple II Plus, though it was a popular user-modification. The thriving industry for Apple II peripherals made up for this shortcoming, with various vendors supplying small plug-in circuit boards that fit under the keyboard, allowing display of lower-case on the screen (and sometimes direct entry of lower-case from the keyboard). By 1981, when the Revision 7 motherboard was released for the Apple II Plus, a different method of character generation was used, which reduced radio-frequency interference. For Revision 7 boards, lower-case characters could be displayed on the screen with the addition of only a single chip. However, unless a user changed the keyboard encoder with a third-party product, typing was still limited to upper-case characters.[18]

The keyboard itself underwent some changes, both by users and by Apple. The original RESET key was in the upper right-hand corner of the keyboard. The problem with that key was that it had the same feel as the keys around it, making it possible to accidentally hit RESET and lose the entire program that was being so carefully entered. One user modification was to pop off the RESET keycap and put a rubber washer under it, making it necessary to apply more pressure than usual to do a RESET. Apple fixed this twice, once by replacing the spring under the keycap with a stiffer one, and fi-

---

16 Ulm, Dennis, A2 Roundtable, Category 2, Topic 16, *GEnie*, accessed April 1991.
17 Felty, Wes, A2 Roundtable, Category 2, Topic 16, *GEnie*, accessed April 1991.
18 Field, Bruce. "A.P.P.L.E. Doctor," *Call-A.P.P.L.E.* (January 1984), 74-75.

nally by making it necessary to press the CTRL key and the RESET together to make a RESET cycle happen. The keyboards that had the CTRL-RESET feature made it user selectable via a small slide switch just inside the case (some people didn't want to have to press the CTRL key to do a RESET).

Another keyboard limitation was addressed through a modification that became known as the "shift-key mod." This was such a widely used trick that Apple ended up supporting it in hardware when they designed later models of the Apple II. Since the II and II Plus keyboards could not directly generate lower-case characters, early word processing programs had to find some way to make up for that deficiency. This modification allowed one to use the shift key already present on the keyboard. It was installed by attaching a wire to the contact under the shift key, and running it to the game port where the input for push-button 2 was found. (This push-button was for one of an optional second pair of game paddles that third-party hardware companies supplied for the Apple II). A program the utilized the shift-key mod assumed that all letters being typed were in lower-case, unless the shift key (attached now to paddle button PB2) was also being pressed; in that case the letter would be entered as upper case. Since the PB2 button was not often used for a second pair of game paddles, it was unlikely that this modification would be accidentally triggered by pressing one of the game paddle buttons.

SUCCESS

The Apple II and II Plus was an unusual success story in the early days of the personal computer. Wozniak designed it with considerable flexibility and expandibility at its heart. And it was that strength that caused the Apple II Plus to not only survive during the three and one half years in which it received no significant upgrades, but also to thrive.

The hardware and software ecosystem that exploded during the first few years in which the Apple II platform was in existence contributed greatly to its continued growth in sales. This growth happened despite being ignored by Apple, and despite the release of competing home computers with more impressive features. During 1982, sales of the Apple II (279,000 units) actually exceeded those of the new and more powerful IBM PC (240,000 units).

The profitability of the Apple II platform enabled Apple to invest in the research and development that led to the company's ultimate survival and successes. With time it became clear that the future of personal computing was, indeed, that of the graphic display and user interface that would be popularized by the release of the Lisa in 1983 and the Macintosh in 1984. However, it would be several years before the power needed to properly run a graphic interface would be sufficient *and* affordable enough to surpass text-based computing.

TIMELINE

The start and end dates for each model of the Apple-1, Apple II and II Plus:

Apple-1 – *April 1976 - May 1977*
Apple II – *May 1977 - May 1979*
Apple II Plus – *June 1979 - December 1982*

CHAPTER 12

Pascal Proliferation

Assembly language was ideal for programs that needed to control all aspects of the computer. However, it could be tedious for large-scale projects, and required manual control of all data types (integer numbers, floating-point numbers, character strings, and so on). BASIC could much more easily handle those data types, but did not offer the degree of deep hardware control, and a program could easily run out of available memory, requiring segmentation that made the program more difficult to manage.

It was necessary to introduce programming languages that were more flexible than assembly language and more powerful than BASIC. One of the most popular alternative languages on the Apple II was Pascal.

TO BETTER TEACH PROGRAMMING

In the late 1960s, Swiss computer scientist Niklaus Wirth created a language designed to teach structured programming and good programming techniques. He named the language "Pascal", after the French mathematician Blaise Pascal. Early implementations of Pascal were created in such a way as to make it possible for programs written in the language to be independent of the peculiarities of specific hardware. This allowed a Pascal program written on one computer to compile with little to no changes on another computer. It was accomplished through the creation of what was known as a p-code interpreter for each computer. The Pascal compiler created a p-code (pseudo-code) representation of the Pascal program that was actually executed. The speed and quality of the p-code interpreter determined how well Pascal programs ran on a particular computer.

At the University of California in San Diego, the Institute for Information Systems developed in 1978 what became known as the UCSD p-System, based on a specific version of Wirth's compiler. The p-System not only created p-code, but also provided a standardized programming environment and operating system for file management. The pseudocode created by the p-System was for an ideal 16-bit processor, modeled after the campus DEC PDP-11, but adapted to run even on 8-bit computers that were just becoming available. Both Pascal and FORTRAN compilers were written to run under the UCSD p-System. As per Wirth's original design, these compilers created p-code, and the p-System then executed that p-code optimized for the computer on which it was running.

IMPLEMENTATION

One student familiar with the p-System was Bill Atkinson, who had studied at UCSD under Jef Raskin. While he was studying neuroscience, Steve Jobs lured him to work at Apple with the promise to "make a dent in the universe." His position at Apple was given the odd name Application Software Department, and his initial task was to collect user-contributed software for the Apple II and make free cassette tapes of this software available to user groups.

After he started at Apple, Atkinson found himself sitting in a meeting about improvements for the Apple II.[1] He had previously proposed to his boss that he wanted to port UCSD Pascal to the Apple II, being aware that a version of the p-System had been created for the 6502 processor. That request had been turned down, but Atkinson brought it up again in this meeting. He argued for its inclusion, stating that its connection to education and its additional power would increase the value of the Apple II to potential customers.

> *I explained to Steve [Jobs] that the Pascal system would let us build cumulative libraries of software. This was hard to do in BASIC, which had no local variables, and the variable names were only significant to two characters. Jobs felt that Apple users had all they needed with BASIC and 6502 assembly language, but because I was so passionate, he would give a week to show him otherwise. Within hours I was on a plane to San Diego.*[2]

Steve Wozniak recalled the meeting:

> *Bill Atkinson thought it was a mistake to pass it up [the implementation of Pascal]. Those of us who were programmers and in software engineering, we loved the idea of a nice, new language that, because of the p-System, could be put on any processor ... Bill turned to me and said, "Why don't we show Apple it could work?" I knew enough how to insert the disk routines, and Bill could insert graphics routines.*

---

1 "Bill Atkinson", *Designing Interactions*, <www.designinginteractions.com/interviews/BillAtkinson> retrieved August 12, 2013.
2 Atkinson, Bill, e-mail to author, August 24, 2013.

> We hopped on a plane that night, and spent all night with those kids in San Diego, re-doing paper tape versions, getting our code put in. We came back to Apple with it not quite working, but within a week we had it working ... Apple changed its mind and said that yes, we would put out the Pascal System.[3]

One of the challenges of making the UCSD system work on the Apple II was its requirement for a minimum of 64K of RAM. The path towards creation of a 64K Apple II was paved by the engineers at Apple who had created the Applesoft Firmware Card for the original Integer BASIC Apple II computer. Since they were able to use this process to substitute one ROM for another, they reasoned that the same method could be used to replace the motherboard ROM with RAM, and that opened up the Apple II for other languages besides BASIC.

To adapt the p-System to the Apple II, Atkinson created the BIOS (Basic Input/Output System) that duplicated some of the Monitor ROM routines necessary for keyboard input and screen output on the Apple II. He also created the module to manage the graphical display.

Being itself a complete operating system, the UCSD software could not run under the current Apple DOS 3.2, but required a more complex solution. In order to store the files necessary to make a minimal p-System work on the Apple II, a bit more space was needed than the 113K that the Disk II currently offered.

Around this time, Wozniak had found that by changing the method used for encoding data bytes on the disk it was possible to fit more sectors into each of the 35 tracks on the disk, raising the total to 16 sectors per track. This resulted in a disk that could now hold a maximum of 140K of data, minus the overhead for the disk directory. This was just enough extra space to create a single-disk drive solution that could run Pascal. The remarkable thing about this upgrade was that the disk drives themselves required no mechanical change to make this happen.

Ultimately, the greater power of Pascal resulted in increased popularity amongst programmers at Apple, which led to the development of the operating system for the Apple III computer (Apple's attempt to capture the business market), and was later used to create the operating system for the more sophisticated Apple Lisa computer.[4,5]

---

3 Wozniak, Steve, telephone call, August 9, 2013.
4 Booch, Grady (interviewer), "Oral History Of Andy Hertzfeld and Bill Atkinson", transcript of audio recording, Computer History Museum, 2004, <http://archive.computerhistory.org/resources/access/text/Oral_History/102658007.05.01.acc.pdf>, accessed October 20, 2012.
5 Maher, Jimmy, "Pascal and the P-Machine", *The Digital Antiquarian*, <http://www.filfre.net/2012/03/pascal-and-the-p-machine/>, accessed October 20, 2012.

PASCAL DISK SYSTEM

In August 1979, soon after the Apple II Plus became available, Apple released a new product they called the Apple Language System. It included the Language Card (a 16K RAM card to plug into slot 0), and a copy of UCSD Pascal for the Apple II, with associated manuals. It also required a ROM update on the Disk II controller card, to handle the revised data encoding that made the larger storage capacity possible. The language was named Apple Pascal, and the operating system it ran under was referred to as the *Apple Pascal* System. At $495 for the full system, it was an investment that cost as much as another Disk II drive.

> For those who purchased the Language System and upgraded the code on the disk controller card, what was lost was the ability to directly start up older 13-sector DOS 3.2 disks. To accommodate those who already had a library of Integer or Applesoft programs and still wanted access, Apple provided a disk called BASICS. This was a disk formatted in the Pascal file system, and which contained three files: FPBAS.DATA, INTBAS.DATA, and BOOTSIM.DATA.[6] A standard Pascal disk, when booted, loaded code from block 0 that would look for and run a file called SYSTEM.APPLE. Block 0 of the BASICS disk, however, contained code that loaded the Language Card with whichever version of BASIC that was not on the motherboard, and then displayed a message to prompt the user to insert a DOS 3.2 or 3.1 disk. The code then would startup Apple DOS on that disk, which worked from that point onward the same as it did when booting with the old disk controller ROM code.

Storing files under the Pascal System was quite different from DOS. Instead of the 256-byte sectors used by DOS, the Pascal System used 512-byte blocks—two sectors per block. This offered a bit more speed because it loaded larger chunks of information at a time than DOS. Unlike the eight different file types (A, I, B, T, and the other four infrequently used ones) in DOS, the Pascal System offered only three: Code, Text, and Data. Also, its method of file naming was more limited. Instead of names that could be as long as 30 characters and could contain any ASCII character (as was the case with DOS), Pascal System filenames were limited to 15 characters, and could contain only letters, numbers, or a period.

The file information also had space for a date to indicate when the file was created or updated. DOS could not do this without being modified to use part of the 30-character filename for the date, and even then it required the presence of a third-party clock card in one of the slots.

---

6 Nickolas, Steve, posting on comp.sys.apple2, Feb 26, 2013.

With the Pascal System, if no clock card was installed, the date could be set at startup, and would be used until it was next started and set.[7, 8]

Pascal disks differed also in being able to have a name to designate each disk. A DOS catalog could display volume numbers, but this feature was seldom used and did not allow disks to be very unique. The Pascal disk name could be up to 7 characters in length, and had the same limits of character choice as did file names.

Another feature of the Pascal disks that differed from the older DOS disks was how space was allocated for a particular file. Under DOS, a catalog map identified the used and free sectors. When a new file was created or an existing file was enlarged, DOS consulted this track/sector list to find where free space could be found, and the list was updated when a new sector was used. The advantage was that all space on the disk could be used as it was needed, but the disadvantage was that a file could be fragmented, with the sectors that made up that file scattered throughout the disk.

Pascal disks did not have any map of free blocks. Instead, a Pascal file used only consecutive blocks on a disk, and a new file started immediately after the end of the last file on the disk. The advantage of this system was faster access to disk files, since they were all on one continuous section of the disk. The disadvantage was that if a file was deleted, the newly freed space could not be used unless Pascal's "Krunch" utility was used to move all files forward over the unused space.

UCSD Pascal was designed to identify anything connected to it, whether an input device, output device, or storage disk, as a "volume". That meant that a printer was a volume, a modem was a volume, and even the screen was a volume. Being platform independent, UCSD Pascal had a standard designation for all of its volumes, giving each a unit ID number and a name. The standard volumes used in Pascal were:

Unit No.	Volume ID	Description
1	CONSOLE:	Screen and keyboard with echo
2	SYSTERM:	Screen and keyboard, no echo
3	GRAPHIC:	The graphic screen
4	<volume name>:	System disk
5	<volume name>:	Alternate disk
6	PRINTER:	Line printer
7	REMIN:	Serial line input
8	REMOUT:	Serial line output
9-12	<volume name>:	Additional disk drives

---

7 Little, Gary, *Exploring Apple GS/OS And ProDOS 8* (Addison-Wesley Publishing Company, Inc, Reading, MA, 1988), 2-4.
8 Hunter, Skillman, "Road Maps To Apple II Disks: DOS 3.3, CP/M, Pascal, and ProDOS", *Call-A.P.P.L.E.* (February 1985), 10-21.

The Pascal System also included additional built-in disk utilities, a 6502 assembler (which many preferred over the available assemblers that ran under DOS), and a compiler. As part of this system one could also purchase from Apple a compiler for FORTRAN programs and a few other computer languages.[9,10]

PASCAL LANGUAGE

Applesoft was easy to use because it was interactive. After entering a command or a short program, it could be immediately executed. The disadvantage was a lack of more powerful commands, and it was difficult to create large and complex programs.

The release of Apple Pascal and the Language System in 1979 helped address some of these concerns. Since it was a compiled language, an Apple Pascal program could conceivably run a little faster than an Applesoft program, but not as fast as assembly language. The extra power it offered made it an attractive choice for some programmers.

The earliest version of Apple Pascal received complaints from users because it would not support lowercase (for those who had modified their Apple to display lowercase), and the files required to support it took up so much space on a disk that it was difficult to use by those who owned only one disk drive.

Since the original UCSD Pascal language was designed to work with a full 80-column text screen, this was somewhat of a problem on a 40-column Apple II. For those who did not own an 80-column card, Apple Pascal displayed half of the screen at a time. In the Pascal Editor, entry of a line longer than 40 columns caused the screen to scroll to the left (producing a moving 40 by 24 window of program code).[11]

For developers, one significant limitation of Apple Pascal was the requirement of the Language Card (or a third-party 16K RAM card), and the fact that it was incompatible with the library of Apple DOS 3.2 programs and files that were already available. This limited the potential market for software written in Pascal to those who already owned Pascal (and had paid its $495 entry fee).

However, it was possible to create an end-user Pascal application that ran on a standard 48K Apple II or II Plus. This run-time version only supported execution of the Pascal application; there was no included assembler, compiler, editor, filer, or linker. The program had to handle everything, including

---

9   "1.2 File Handler", UCSD Pascal System II.0 User Manual Reconstruction, <http://miller.emu.id.au/pmiller/ucsd-psystem-um/reconstruct/01-02-file-handler.html>, accessed October 20, 2012.
10 Hunter, Skillman, "Road Maps To Apple II Disks: DOS 3.3, CP/M, Pascal, and ProDOS", *Call-A.P.P.L.E.* (February 1985), 10-21.
11 Walls, Keith S, "The Fantastic New World Of Apple Pascal", *PEEKing At Call-A.P.P.L.E.* (Seattle, Washington, Vol. 3, 1980), 237.

file or disk copying, and it had to assume that the user didn't know anything about how to use Pascal. Due to its memory limitations, a 48K run-time Pascal application could only store data to a Disk II, and that only in slot 6.[12]

There was another significant limitation with Apple Pascal 1.0—it was designed to only support the four peripheral cards that Apple then sold, specifically the Disk II controller card, the Apple II Communications Card, the Apple II Parallel Printer Interface card, and the Apple II Serial Interface card. As more and more cards became available from Apple and from third-party sources, it was necessary to update the language and system to support those cards.

Apple Pascal 1.1 came out in 1980, and was designed with a new firmware card protocol, which required defined entry points on a card that made it easier for Pascal to use the card without special drivers. Each card that complied with the new protocol had to have specific signature bytes in a specific location.

Under its new firmware card protocol, Apple created definitions to support printers, serial or parallel cards, joysticks, modems, speech or sound devices, clock cards, mass storage devices, 80-column cards, or network cards. Furthermore, this new 1.1 system made it easier to create custom drivers to add to the Pascal System for those devices that needed extra control beyond the generic drivers in the BIOS.[13]

Aside from bug fixes and small language enhancements, Apple Pascal 1.1 also supported the ability to handle upper and lowercase display on a standard 40-column Apple II, using the same method as did the original version of *Apple Writer* (lowercase was displayed as normal video, uppercase was in inverse video).[14]

TIMELINE

Apple II – *May 1977 - May 1979*
DOS 3.0 – *June 1978*
Disk II – *July 1978*
DOS 3.1 – *July 1978*
DOS 3.2 – *June 1979*

DOS 3.2.1 – *July 1979 - August 1980*
Apple Pascal – *August 1979*
Apple Pascal 1.1 – *1980*

---

12 Ewey, Cheryl, "Pascal #10: Configuration and Use of the Apple II Pascal Run-Time Systems", *Apple II Technical Notes*, Developer Technical Support (November 1988).
13 Haynes, Barry, "ATTACH-BIOS Document for Apple Pascal 1.1", Apple Computer (January 12, 1980).
14 "Apple Pascal Update", (Apple Computer, Cupertino, California, 1980).

CHAPTER 13
DOS Developments

The open architecture of the Apple II platform made it an ideal environment for modifications to take it beyond what Steve Wozniak originally envisioned. And computer users continued to demand expanded capabilities for the Apple II. One of those enhancements was to find a way to bring the larger 16-sector disk format pioneered by the Pascal System to Apple DOS. But before that came about, another innovation came that literally made the Apple II into another computer capable of running software under the earliest microcomputer disk operating system: CP/M.

CP/M

Back in 1972, the Intel 4004 microprocessor caught the attention of Gary Kildall. At the time he was teaching computer science at a naval post-graduate school. He purchased one of the chips to experiment with, and although there were virtually no computers built around it, he was interested enough in it to start working for Intel one day per week as a consultant to create a programming language for the 4004. He created PL/M (Programming Language for Microcomputers) on an IBM 360 mainframe. The object code for a program created under PL/M was then put into a ROM chip in a system using the 4004.

Kildall's work for Intel gave him early access to the Intel 8008 and a development system that used it, and he adapted PL/M for the 8008. This was later updated to use the 8080 while it was under development, and Kildall added a paper tape reader, display monitor, and eventually an early Shugart floppy disk drive. He could see the disk drive as a significant enhancement to his small computer, but there was no operating system to manage a disk. So, just as Wozniak and others did years later on the Apple II, Kildall wrote his own. He used his PL/M programming language and in 1974 created what he called CP/M, which stood for Control Program for Microcomputers, one year before the original Altair 8800 appeared, and four years before the Apple II had a disk drive.

Kildall tried to interest Intel in CP/M, but they decided they didn't need a disk operating system. Instead, Kildall and his wife formed their own company in 1976, calling it Intergalactic Digital Research (the "Digital Research" name was already in use by another company at the time, though Kildall's company was later able to use that shorter and less cosmic name). When Altair and IMSAI computers and their descendants began to use the new 5.25-inch floppy disks, CP/M was readily available to license as a system to handle not only disk management, but also other aspects of microcomputers, making them easier to use.

With all of the 8080 and Z-80-based computers that came to market in the mid-1970s, demand for a disk operating system significantly increased, and CP/M was able to meet that demand. However, Kildall had to make changes to CP/M in order to make it more adaptable for use on different computer systems. He created what he called the Basic Input/Output System, or BIOS, to handle the tasks that were unique to each machine, and then used this as the interface between the hardware and the operating system. CP/M didn't have to know the details about how this keyboard or that monitor worked; the BIOS took care of that, translating this low-level communication to and from CP/M.[1]

Since CP/M was designed to work exclusively with 8080 or Z-80 microprocessors, it could not be directly used on a standard Apple II, which ran on the very different 6502. That limitation was resolved when Microsoft got into the hardware business.

Microsoft had built its original business on selling BASIC and other computer languages for the early 8080 and Z-80 based microcomputers that exploded into the marketplace in the mid-to-late 1970s. The company had created a subdivision, Microsoft Consumer Products, to sell consumer games and utilities for microcomputers, but had no major hit product beyond its core languages.

Seeing the large user base in the Apple II, Microsoft faced a dilemma. It wanted to be able to sell to Apple's customers, but Microsoft's products were coded for the incompatible Intel processor. To modify them to run under the 6502 would be a significant investment in time and money for an uncertain payoff.

Paul Allen, one of the company's founders, provided the solution. He came up with the idea of putting a Z-80 processor into an Apple II. If the computer could be modified to work just like the market that Microsoft served, it would be possible to sell their products to this subset of Apple II users.

Microsoft turned to Tim Paterson of Seattle Computer Products for the initial design of a hardware card for the Apple II that would contain a Z-80, and use the rest of the Apple II as a host for input, output, and memory for the Z-80 environment. Bill Gates and another engineer at Microsoft also worked on the product. They licensed CP/M from Digital Research, and brought the prototype to the fourth West Coast Computer Faire in March 1980. (Paterson would later become even more important to Microsoft when they came to him for a disk system for the IBM PC.)

---

1 Libe, Sol, "The Gary Kildall Legacy", <http://www.cadigital.com/kildall.htm>, retrieved Feb 22, 2013.

There had been concern about whether or not there would be sufficient demand for a hardware product like this amongst Apple II users. Gates and Allen thought that if they could sell 5,000 of the cards, it would pay for itself. What took Microsoft by surprise was the response of over one thousand potential buyers who expressed interest in the product after seeing it demonstrated at the Faire. Over the first three months that the SoftCard was available, the company sold its 5,000-unit target goal, and continued to sell well for years afterwards. In fact, during 1980, the Microsoft SoftCard product brought in the highest amount of revenue for the company.[2, 3, 4]

Soon after its release, Microsoft had to change the name of the product to Microsoft SoftCard, since Zilog (maker of the Z-80 processor used in the SoftCard) threatened a lawsuit over the use of their trademarked Z-80 name.

Microsoft's success with SoftCard was surprising in two ways: First, it was a hardware product sold by a software company; and second, the software that ran on the card, particularly the CP/M operating system, was written primarily by one of Microsoft's competitors. Nevertheless, Microsoft put considerable marketing muscle behind the SoftCard, to the extent of selling it in colorful boxes and creating documentation that looked professional, much different from many products selling at that time for the Apple II. Their success ultimately made CP/M on the Apple II the most popular platform on which CP/M was available.[5] With time, other companies made similar peripheral cards to support running CP/M on an Apple II.

Turn your Apple into the world's most versatile personal computer.

MICROSOFT CONSUMER PRODUCTS

Microsoft SoftCard – Photo credit: *BYTE*, October 1981

One reason that there was a demand for CP/M on the Apple II was the wealth of significant software available for it. Ashton-Tate's *dBase* database program and Micropro's *Wordstar* word processing program were in particular demand, due to the large user base commanded by those programs. Being able to run a CP/M program as well as standard Apple II software significantly increased the functionality of the computer to some users. Since this

---

2 InfoWorld Staff, "Seminar Spills Negotiating Secrets", *InfoWorld*, November 24, 1980, 24.
3 Freiberger, Paul, and Swaine, Michael, *Fire In The Valley*, (Osborn/McGraw Hill, Berkley, California, 1984), 269.
4 "At our foundation, Bill Gates and Paul Allen made a bet . . . on software. At the same time, it was always clear that our unique view of what software could do would require us to push hardware. . . . In fact, our number one revenue product . . . the year I joined Microsoft, 1980, was a hardware product, something known as the SoftCard." Steve Balmer, Microsoft Surface Keynote, June 18, 2012
5 Manes, Stephen and Paul Andrews, *Gates* (New York, Doubleday, 1993), 200-201.

software expected an 80-column screen size, the SoftCard was designed to be compatible with 80-column cards that were currently on the market.[6,7]

Making a hardware environment able to run CP/M software was only part of the challenge in making the SoftCard into a usable product. CP/M had been designed as an operating system to allow use of floppy disks, and the way it was designed to organize and store files was very different from that designed for the Disk II drive. In fact, much of the early available software to use with CP/M was recorded on 8-inch floppy disks, which was standardized amongst all manufacturers using them.

Since the various companies that had made use of the 5.25-inch disk format all made their own modifications, there was no similarity even between disk drives made to run with similar microprocessors. For example, a 5.25-inch CP/M disk for the IMSAI could not be directly used on a NorthStar Horizon computer. And certainly the Disk II drive for the Apple II was incompatible, since it used a different recording method than the other computer companies. Apple DOS could not be modified to work with the format expected by CP/M, and so Microsoft had to create a CP/M compatible environment on a disk formatted to work with the Disk II drive.

CP/M disks on the Apple II were organized to use four 256-byte sectors as one block (twice as large as a Pascal System block). Like Apple DOS, the first three tracks on the disk were used to store the CP/M code that was loaded into memory when booting the disk. Like Pascal, the CP/M directory was found at the start of the disk, instead of in the middle as DOS was designed.

Apple II CP/M disks followed the standard CP/M file naming system. A file name consisted of 8 characters, followed by a period, and then a three-character extension. One unusual feature of CP/M files was that if a file was larger than 16 CP/M blocks (64 DOS sectors), it created a new directory entry with the same file name. This entry included a special byte that showed this was a continuation of a previous file, instead of a new, separate file.

Apple II CP/M disk directory – Photo credit: personal

By 1981, when the IBM PC was introduced, CP/M was in lower favor at Microsoft, as much of its energy and efforts were being put into Microsoft's own MS-DOS for the new PC. As the IBM PC began dominating, so too did MS-DOS, and CP/M slowly lost its relevance. Kaypro corporation, one of the last companies using CP/M, discontinued use of the operating system in 1986.

---

6 -----. "A.P.P.L.E. Co-op Celebrates A Decade of Service", Call-A.P.P.L.E., (February 1988), 12-27.
7 -----. (ads), *Call-A.P.P.L.E. In Depth #1*, (Seattle, Washington, 1981), 106.

IMPROVING APPLE DOS

In August of 1980, a year after the introduction of the Language System, an update to Apple DOS was finally released. Those who had purchased the Language System but still wanted to run programs in the older Integer and Applesoft languages had to take the extra step of using the BASICS disk to boot DOS 3.2. Those who had not invested in the expensive new system wanted the extra 27K of storage available to Pascal users.

For a cost of $60, the DOS 3.3 upgrade came with the same new chips for the disk controller card and the BASICS disk that had come with the Language System, plus an updated and expanded version of the DOS manual, and a new Master disk. The computer owner could change out the chips on the disk controller card if comfortable with that, but many decided to let the dealer do it for them.[8]

DOS 3.3 – FEATURES

One of the first changes users of DOS 3.3 noticed on the new system master disk was the method used to load the alternate BASIC. There were two groups of users Apple needed to serve with its disk operating system, owners of the original Apple II with Integer BASIC in ROM, and those who had the Apple II Plus and Applesoft in ROM. The Language Card (or third-party 16K RAM cards) provided a flexible opportunity to make both languages available (more so than the Firmware card, which was still ROM and could not be changed).

Like the BASICS disk released with Apple Pascal, the HELLO program on the DOS 3.3 Master disk would detect on which type of Apple II it was booting. On the Apple II Plus it loaded the file *INTBASIC* into the upper 16K of RAM, and on the older Apple II, it loaded *FPBASIC* (Applesoft) into that high memory. It was then a matter of simply using the FP command in DOS to switch to Applesoft, or the INT comment to switch to Integer BASIC.

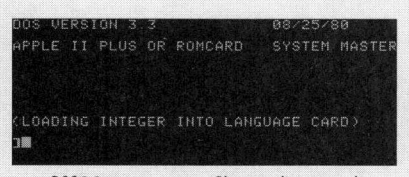

DOS 3.3 startup screen – Photo credit: personal

After starting up the new disk, the screen displayed the version number and its date, information about what model was being started (Apple II standard or II Plus), and that the other language had been loaded onto the Language Card:

The DOS 3.3 System Master disk included several of the demo programs that had been previously released on the DOS 3.2 Master. A few new ones were also included. *COPY* (used to copy entire disks) was translated to Applesoft as *COPYA* for those Apple II Plus users who didn't have access to Integer BASIC.

---

8 Don Worth and Pieter Lechner, *Beneath Apple DOS* (Quality Software, Reseda, CA, 1981), 2.1-2.9.

The updated COPY and COPYA program also worked properly on single drive systems (previously, it only worked properly with two disk drives). In addition to the BASICS pre-boot disk, a binary program called *BOOT13* could be executed to start up older 13-sector DOS 3.2 disks.

Because of the changes in the ROM controller, it was not easy to read files from disks formatted under DOS 3.2 directly from DOS 3.3. It could have been incorporated into DOS 3.3, but it would have made DOS larger than the earlier versions. Instead, Rich Williams, an Apple programmer who worked on a number of Apple II-related projects during his time with the company, wrote a conversion program called *MUFFIN*, (Move Utility For Files In NewDOS), which could be used to move files from 13-sector to 16-sector disks. The utility was included on the DOS 3.3 System Master disk.

Enterprising programmers in the Apple II world made modifications to MUFFIN and created *DE-MUFFIN,* a DOS 3.2 utility to move the files back to the 13-sector disks.[9] In the same vein, *Call-A.P.P.L.E.* magazine eventually published the source code for utilities called *HUFFIN* to allow files to be moved from Pascal System disks to DOS 3.3, and *PUFFIN* to move from DOS 3.3 to Pascal.

MUFFIN screen shot – Photo credit: personal

The System Master disk also contained a new utility called *FID* (which, inexplicably, started at version "M", rather than version "A"). *FID*, written entirely in assembly language, allowed users to easily copy files between disks, particularly helpful for text and binary files that couldn't simply be loaded and saved from one disk to another as could Applesoft and Integer programs.

The name FID was odd, however. The Apple manuals said it stood for FIle Developer, but Rich Williams (who had also written the utility) said that the original name of the program was *FISHEAD* (which stood for FIle Shower, HElper, And Duplicator). Apple Marketing said he couldn't name a program FISHEAD, so he changed it to FID, which they said was okay. It really stood for Fishead In Disguise (or Fishead In Drag by some within Apple).[10, 11, 12, 13]

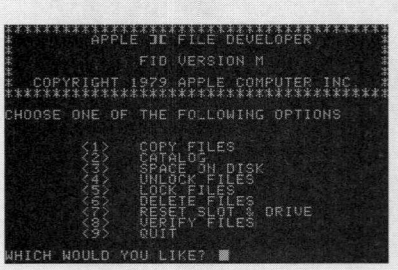

FID screen shot – Photo credit: personal

Some Apple II users didn't want to have to use utility programs to manage their collections of disks in both the 13 and 16 sector formats. One method that was used to overcome this inconvenience was to piggyback the old and the new disk controller ROMs and use a switch to toggle between systems.

---

9   Don Worth and Peiter Lechner. *Beneath Apple DOS* (Quality Software, Reseda, CA, 1984) pp. 2.1-2.9.
10 -----. (ads), *Call-A.P.P.L.E. In Depth #1*, (Seattle, Washington, 1981), 106.
11 Auricchio, Rick, telephone interview with author, Sepember 4, 1991.
12 Wozniak, Stephen, telephone interview with author, September 5, 1991.
13 Weishaar, Tom, "Ask (or Tell) Uncle DOS", *Open-Apple* (February 1987), 3.1.

A more elegant solution was a ROM chip that plugged into a special card (the ROMPlus sold by Mountain Hardware, or the ROMBoard by Andromeda). A call to a memory location switched between DOS 3.2 and 3.3, making file conversions easy.

Soft Ctrl Systems, the company that sold the Dual DOS ROM used in these cards, also sold ROMs that gave instant access to an Applesoft renumber and merge program, an Applesoft editor, and a specialized disk command menu and disk map.[14]

Like the preceding versions of Apple DOS, the major problem with DOS 3.3 was its exclusive support of the Disk II drive. Hard disks, RAM disks, and the larger capacity 3.5-inch disks could not be used with DOS 3.3 without a patch that would likely be incompatible with other patches.[15]

TIMELINE

The start dates for Apple DOS, Pascal, and CP/M:

DOS 3.0 – *June 1978*
Disk II – *July 1978*
DOS 3.1 – *July 1978*
DOS 3.2 – *June 1979*
Apple II Plus – *July 1979*

DOS 3.2.1 – *July 1979*
Apple Pascal – *August 1979*
Apple CP/M – *March 1980*
DOS 3.3 – *August 1980*

---

14 -----. (ads), *Call-A.P.P.L.E. In Depth #1*, (Seattle, Washington, 1981), 106.
15 Deatherage, Matt, "The Operating System", *The Apple II Guide* (Cupertino, CA, Apple Computer, Inc., Fall 1990), 117-125.

CHAPTER 14
Boosting Performance

COPROCESSORS

The success of the Microsoft SoftCard introduced the broad library of CP/M software to Apple II users. When the IBM PC was introduced in 1981 and gained wide acceptance, some Apple II users were interested in a similar co-processor that would allow access to IBM PC software. Rana Systems of Chatsworth, California, which had produced third-party disk drives for the Apple II for several years, released the Rana 8086/2 sometime in 1984. This was a system that plugged into slots on a II Plus or IIe, and allowed the user to run programs written for the IBM PC. It also read disks formatted for that computer (which used the MFM recording system, rather than the GCR method used by the Apple II).

Unfortunately, the product had problems. One Rana owner wrote of his experience with it: "We also have one of the Rana 8086/2 boxes, with two [Rana] Elite II compatible drives and a more-or-less (mostly less) IBM-PC compatible computer inside it. Nice idea. Terrible execution. The drives are half-high instead of the full height drives used in the normal Elite II, and are very unreliable for reading or writing in either the Apple or IBM format ... And this product again shows that Rana has no knowledgeable technical folks (or they lock them up very well). We have identified several fatal incompatibilities with IBM programs, such as the system crashing totally if any attempt to generate any sound (even a beep) occurs in a program, or if inverse characters are sent to the display ... The response from Rana has been no response at all, except that we can return the system if we want to. Curious attitude for a company, isn't it?"[1]

Rana Systems disk drives – Photo credit: Tony Diaz

---

1 Russ, John, "Ask Uncle DOS," *Open-Apple* (April 1985), 1.32.

The problems with this system were apparently related to the 65c02 processor in the newer enhanced Apple IIe computers. Despite investments by outside companies (including $900,000 by Apple itself, who hoped to have a workable IBM compatibility mode for the Apple II), the company shut down operations in July 1985, and the product was never upgraded or fixed.[2]

Also in 1984, ALF Products, Inc. of Denver, Colorado released the ALF 8088 co-processor for the Apple II, selling for $345. It was designed to work with either the CP/M-86 operating system or with MS-DOS v1.1 (either operating system costing an additional $100 above the price of the card). The company offered an add-on memory board, either 64K or 128K ($295 without any memory installed, and $75 for each 64K installed), and this memory could be used under DOS 3.3 or Apple Pascal as a RAM disk when the co-processor was not being used.

For those who wanted to simply use the ALF 8088 co-processor to speed up normal Apple II operations, software was included to access the card. Under DOS 3.3 (ProDOS was not supported), it could speed up computations in a program. Under Apple Pascal, it transferred time-consuming p-code operations to the card.

> To emulate an IBM PC with the ALF 8088, it was necessary to install the card in slot 2, which interfered with the typical location for an Apple II modem or serial card. Since the disk formats were incompatible, it was necessary to transfer software from an IBM PC to the Apple II via a serial cable. The ALF did not include other software or hardware to simplify execution of IBM PC-specific programs, so it was up to the user to find a way to make it work.[3]

Even the Motorola 68000 processor used in the Macintosh was offered as a co-processor for the Apple II. The Gnome Card worked on the II Plus and IIe, but like other 68000 cards for the II, it didn't have a major impact, with the exception of programmers doing cross development (creating programs for a computer using a microprocessor other than the one being used).

ACCELERATORS

Computer users often find that, after they become accustomed to their computer, they want it to run faster. It took about five years for technology to appear that could accelerate the speed of the Apple II. Once these devices became available, several companies jumped in with their own solutions.

---

2 Bannister, Hank, "Rana Quietly Goes Under", *InfoWorld* (July 1, 1985), 22.
3 Davidson, Keith, "The ALF 8088 Co-Processor," *Call-A.P.P.L.E.* (February 1984), 54.

CHAPTER 14 | *Boosting Performance*

Frequently, these cards used RAM memory dedicated to a cache—memory which stored frequently accessed bits of the main computer's memory, using faster RAM than that on the Apple II board. Accessing data from the RAM cache was faster than accessing it from the stock Apple II RAM, resulting in programs running more quickly. The one small limitation of this trick was that it could not be used on the ROM code on some of the cards plugged into slots, particularly if they were timing-sensitive (such as the Disk II drive).

Number Nine Computer Corporation appeared on the scene briefly in 1982 with what may be the earliest accelerator for the Apple II and II Plus. The Number Nine Apple Booster card, which sold for $598, increased the speed from the stock 1 MHz to 3.58 MHz. It used 64K of RAM on the card, basically running the Apple II on the RAM on this card, using the actual Apple II for input and output.

Microcomputer Technologies (M-c-T) released the SpeedDemon by 1983, selling it for $295. It used a 65c02 processor running at 3.58 MHz, and both static and dynamic RAM (recall from an earlier discussion that static RAM retained the contents of data stored in it when power was removed, whereas dynamic RAM required power to keep its data active). When accessing peripheral cards, it was possible to configure the SpeedDemon to slow down for slots 4, 5, and 6 if those slots held cards with disk controllers.

M-c-T SpeedDemon – Photo credit: Tony Diaz

The Apple Pugetsound Program Library Exchange later sold the Speed-Demon card under the name "Mach 3.5," with a price reduction to $199.[4]

In 1983, Number Nine Corporation's accelerator was back on the market. The company had changed its name to Saturn Systems, and its improved product was called the Accelerator II. Like the Apple Booster card, it had 64K of RAM and it ran programs on the fast RAM on the card. If a slot on the Apple II held a RAM expansion card, the Accelerator II could be configured to run the RAM on that card at accelerated or normal speeds.

Although the Accelerator II worked on the Apple II and II Plus, it gave inconsistent results on an Apple IIe. The company released an updated product, the Accelerator IIe, in 1984. By that time it again found it necessary to rename itself, this time to Titan Technologies. Its former name (Saturn Systems) was found to be in conflict with another business.

Saturn Systems Accelerator II – Photo credit: *Softalk*, April 1983

---

4 Sander-Cederlof, Bob. "Review of M-c-T SpeedDemon," *Apple Assembly Lines* (V5N10, July 1995).

The new card used the 65c02 processor, and added another 16K of RAM to which the Apple IIe ROM code was copied, for faster execution. However, the card did not accelerate the additional 64K of auxiliary RAM from the extended 80-column card on the IIe.

TIMELINE

Microsoft SoftCard – *March 1980*

Number Nine Apple Booster – *1982*

M-c-T SpeedDemon – *1983*

Accelerator II – *1983*

Accelerator IIe – *1984*

Rana 8086/2 – *1984*

ALF 8088 coprocessor – *1984*

Gnome card – *circa 1984*

CHAPTER 15
The Apple II Abroad

Andre Sousan was a former vice-president of engineering and board member of Commodore Electronics, Inc. In the summer of 1976 he had accompanied Chuck Peddle to visit Jobs and Wozniak in the garage at Jobs' house, when the company was looking for outside financing to fund the development and production of the original Apple II. As previously mentioned, when they finished demonstrating the prototype computer, Jobs made an offer to sell the Apple II to Commodore. Ultimately, Commodore turned the offer down, feeling that Jobs was asking too high a price for their unproven computer. Souson, however, remained impressed.

In April 1977, soon after the visit and two months before the release of the Apple II, Sousan began negotiations with Apple to start a company named Eurapple, Inc., with the mission of setting up European operations as a distributor for the Apple II outside of the US, as well as to make the necessary changes to the product for it to function in those parts of the world.[1] Eventually, Eurapple also took on sales to other parts of the world.

Souson had to handle not only language differences, but also variances in standards for electricity and television video. Many other countries used 220 volts AC at 50 Hz, instead of the 110–120 volts, 60 Hz AC standard in the United States.

As for video standards, the United States adhered to NTSC (National Television System Committee), which was devised in 1953 for broadcast television. While there were many countries in the world that followed this standard (including Japan and Canada), many chose to follow the path developed in Europe. SECAM (Séquentiel couleur à mémoire, "Sequential Color With Memory") was created in France in 1956, improving on some limitations of NTSC. While a number of countries in the world adopted it, many others (such as the UK) chose to go with a different standard, called PAL (Phase Alternation by Line), which was adapted from both NTSC and SECAM. Each of these methods had their own peculiarities that required adjustments to produce screen output from a computer.[2]

---

1 -----, *Preliminary Confidential Offering Memorandum*, Apple Computer, Inc., c. 1977. This document discussed Apple's early business, in anticipation of a public stock offering, and discussed the formation of Eurapple, Inc., amongst other topics about its early business plans.

2 Geiken, Cordelia Baron, and Tony Baylis, "Video Standards," *NCSA Media Technology Resources User Guide*, <archive.ncsa.uiuc.edu/SCMS/training/general/details/video_standards.html>, accessed February 20, 2012.

Eurapple was tasked with promoting the Apple II in foreign markets, creating a distributor network, and selecting companies to sell the Apple II. It purchased computers from Apple and used its own engineers to make the necessary changes to accommodate regional differences in voltage and video. By September 1977, it had sold about twenty units in Europe and had orders for fifty more. One distributor who wanted to sell the computer to Arab countries had plans for the necessary changes in the character generator ROM and keyboard to handle the Arabic alphabet.

During that year, Eurapple was in talks with distributors in England and Germany. The result of one of its agreements was the first legal clone of the Apple II.

ITT 2020

Selling the Apple II in Europe was difficult in the beginning, primarily because of the effort needed to make it work properly with the video and power differences. Although some sales were happening during the latter part of 1977, the first widely available Apple II computer marketed in Europe came from a separate company and was not made by Apple.

International Telephone & Telegraph was founded in 1920 and grew through acquisitions of various national telephone companies, first in Central America and then Spain and further into Europe. The company continued to grow through the addition of businesses outside of the telephone industry, including German aircraft and radar manufacturing. After World War II, ITT expanded into many other types of business, ultimately including consumer electronics. It was the ITT Consumer Products division that obtained a license from Apple to create an authorized version (what would in later years be considered a legal clone) of the Apple II.

This computer was sold under the name ITT 2020, and the finished product was advertised as early as October 1978. Sales in the UK and France began in January 1979. The first version of the ITT 2020 used the very same case design as the Apple II, but colored silver instead of beige.

ITT 2020 – Photo credit: Yves de Ryckel

ITT Consumer Products built their Apple II in ways that differed more than just in how it handled the different voltage and video standards. One change they made involved the hi-res graphics. Unlike the standard 192 lines of 280 dots each, the engineers that created the ITT 2020 had hacked in a *ninth* bit (in an extra 4K of RAM on the motherboard) to create 192 lines by 360 dots each in the hi-res graphics display. It did not create any additional colors, but allowed slightly better graphics, and made it more compatible with the PAL video signal that was in use in the UK and other parts of Europe. However, this different hi-res graphics arrangement caused compatibility problems with Apple II software from America that used the hi-res screen; specifically, it resulted in the appearance of blank "tram lines" (as users called them) on the screen where the extra bits were unused by the standard software.[3]

The first versions of the ITT 2020 were much the same as the original Apple II, using the original Monitor ROM and Integer BASIC. After the Apple II Plus became available in the US in July 1979, an updated version of the ITT 2020 was produced that also included floating point BASIC. The update came with a modified case that was no longer the same exact shape as that on the Apple II from the US.

ITT 2020, later revision – Photo credit: unknown

The version of Applesoft on the newer ITT 2020 was called "Palsoft," and included modifications to handle the different hi-res graphics modes. Other changes in Palsoft included correcting known bugs in Applesoft. One bug involved a command, ONERR, which was used to trap errors in a running program. Apple had an official patch, a short machine language program, that they recommended programmers use to work around this bug. However, since Palsoft had already corrected the bug, an Applesoft program that used Apple's patch would crash when running on an ITT 2020, since it was trying to fix an already fixed bug.

Another cause of crashes came from programs that made calls directly into the Applesoft code space. Since Palsoft had been modified and recompiled, the entry points were not the same, which

ITT COLOUR DEMO cassette – Photo credit: Philip Lord

made machine language access to Palsoft much more difficult. To avoid these software problems, it was not uncommon for an ITT 2020 user to perform a ROM transplant, and put genuine Apple II Plus ROMs into the computer, making it a true Applesoft/Autostart Monitor computer.[4]

---

3   Marcel, comp.sys.apple2.marketplace, posted March 30, 2002.
4   Gasperschitz, Michael, comp.sys.apple2, posted July 9, 1995.

On the hardware side, there were timing differences on the ITT 2020 motherboard, due to the 50 Hz frequency used with the 220 VAC power standards in the UK and Europe. Because of this, certain peripheral cards (especially disk drives) had problems. To avoid problems with disks, there was an ITT-specific disk controller and disk drive sold for the computer, one that did *not* have the timing problem. However, this disk controller worked only with the older 13-sector DOS 3.2, and the chips were the wrong size to allow the DOS 3.3 conversion package to work when it became available. Attaching an ITT disk drive to an Apple-brand disk controller card would work with some drives, and with others it was necessary to make a timing adjustment on the drive. Many users chose to make more modifications to the motherboard to fix the timing problems and to allow them to use more standard Apple II peripherals.[5]

ITT included a copy of the *2020 Reference Manual* with the ITT 2020. This book, with a bronze colored cover, was simply a copy of the Red Book reference manual, edited (not too cleanly) to remove the name "Apple" and replace it with "ITT" when possible. The typeface was different than in the original, and not all references were caught and changed when this book was produced.[6]

Microsense Computers Limited was the company officially authorized to distribute the ITT 2020 and other Apple products in the United Kingdom. In 1981, Apple Computer acquired Microsense Computers Limited for $3.5 million, forming Apple Computer UK from this acquisition. Further sales of the The ITT 2020 were then formally discontinued with this transaction.

APPLE II EUROMOD AND EUROPLUS

The availability of the ITT 2020 in Britain caught the attention of Sonotec, a company based in France. It wanted to be the first to get Apple computers approved by the Ministry of Education. ITT Consumer Products was also trying to get approval for its computer with the Ministry. Requirements to make a computer work in France were the same as the ITT 2020, regarding voltage and line frequency. However, the television video standard in France was SECAM, not PAL.

Sonotec tried to do what ITT did: obtain permission from Apple to produce a clone for the French market. However, Apple turned down the request, apparently realizing that allowing yet another company to make a clone of the Apple II would dilute the impact of its own official European Apple computer. Sonotec then became involved in the project to create this

---

5   Siggins, Mike, "Apple - ITT 2020 Compatibility," *Hardcore - The Journal Of The British Apple Systems User Group* (February 1984).
6   Beesley, Phil, "ITT 2020 (Europlus clone)," *VintageMacWorld.com*, <www.vintagemacworld.com/itt2020.html>, accessed October 14, 2008.

modified Apple II, and even supplied an adviser to Apple to help with the video signal issues. SECAM would have required additional hardware and added to the cost, so like ITT before them, Apple went with PAL for video.

The resulting computer was called the Apple II Euromod. It was an Integer BASIC Apple II, offered with 16K, 32K, or 48K of RAM, and the original Monitor ROM. On the outside, the case and nameplate were identical to the US version, which made it difficult to immediately notice any differences. It was marketed through Eurapple, and became available not long after the ITT 2020 came to market. The primary problem with the Euromod, however, was that the video did not work as planned. It only produced a monochrome signal, and monitors and videocassette recorders made in France could not display (or record) the video. To output proper color video from the Euromod, it was necessary to use a third-party PAL video card in slot 7.[7]

Soon after the Apple II Plus was released in the US, Apple also created a version to complement the Euromod, called the Apple II Europlus. It produced a better video signal, but still had problems producing color. On this updated version, a special nameplate was added, specifically identifying it as a Europlus.[8, 9]

Apple II Europlus nameplate – Photo credit: Hans Franke

The primary reason that video was a challenge for the non-US computers was because in his original design Wozniak had used a trick with the NTSC signal to make color work on the Apple II. This trick did not work with PAL (or SECAM) video, and so even with a circuit adjustment on the motherboard, output from the built-in video output connector could only produce a monochrome PAL signal. To get color, it was still necessary to use a card in slot 7 to produce proper PAL-compatible color video. In fact, slot 7 was the only slot in which this PAL video card worked.

As with American users who wanted lowercase display, it was necessary to add an after-market character generator ROM to handle special characters for those European languages that had characters requiring accents or diacritical marks, such as è, ä, or ü.[10]

In August 1980, Apple purchased the Eurapple, Inc. subsidiary, and took over management of international distribution of its computer products, including the Apple II Euromod and Europlus. The Europlus was produced until 1983, when the Apple IIe was released.

---

7 In the *Apple II Reference Manual* published in 1979 and 1981, there were instructions on making a motherboard modification that was supposed to make PAL output work. However, this method did not work, and Apple specifically published a note that stated this.
8 -----, *Apple: The Personal Computer Magazine & Catalog* (Vol 1, No 2, 1979), C-4.
9 Because of the greater demand for the version with floating point BASIC, far more Europlus models were sold than the Euromod, and so consequently fewer of the Euromods survived to become collectable in the 21st century.
10 Franke, Hans, e-mail message to author, March 2013.

APPLE II J-PLUS

Apple II j-Plus nameplate – Photo credit: Philip Lord

Apple II j-Plus keyboard. Notice that with only one exception, the keys that had two characters on them on the American keyboard (shifted and unshifted) also have two katakana characters on them. The one exception is the letter "M", which also has two katakana characters. – Photo credit:Philip Lord

Apple II j-Plus screen shot demonstrating katakana character entry and display – Photo credit: personal

In July 1980, Apple released a version of the Apple II Plus specifically for the Japanese market. Called the Apple II j-Plus, this model presented different challenges for Apple engineers. In Japan, power is supplied as 100 volts AC, and regions of Japan use different frequencies (60 Hz in the west, 50 Hz in the east). As with the Europlus, a change was necessary to accommodate these voltage and frequency options.

Engineers also added the ability to display the Japanese katakana character set, with some less commonly used memory soft-switches. With appropriate use of the POKE command from BASIC and the Ctrl-T key from the keyboard, a program could display both Roman and katakana characters.

When the Japanese characters were activated, all subsequent output used those characters, until it was turned off again (in the screenshot below, pressing Ctrl-T caused the system to print the phrase "SYNTAX ERROR" in Roman characters after it had displayed the same phrase in katakana).

TIMELINE

Apple II Euromod – *circa 1978*
ITT 2020 – *January 1979*
Apple II Europlus – *August 1979*
Apple II j-Plus – *July 1980*

CHAPTER 16
Der Apfel II in der Presse

When the microcomputers that made up the 1977 Trinity originally hit the market, the focus was primarily in the United States. Outside of the country, however, there was a delay in availability for at least a short time, as none of the three companies were set up for large-scale production in their early months. Radio Shack had the greatest storefront presence in the US and also had its Tandy stores in Europe. Commodore was ready to sell the PET in Europe as early as 1978. For Apple, the first Apple II Euromod was available in Europe some time in 1978, but they were not available in great volume. The ITT 2020 licensed clone appeared early in 1979, but it was not until late 1979 before the Apple II Europlus was ready to sell. Consequently, the Apple II did not have an established foothold outside of the US before its competitors. This resulted in a delay of Apple II publications becoming available for several years.

FRANCE – POM'S (Sep 1981 – Oct 1990)

In the early 1980s, Apple II computers were scarce in France, but interested buyers could import them from Great Britain. The manuals for these computers were, of course, in English, which posed a problem for many of the new owners who were exclusively French-speaking. Hervé Thiriez decided to solve this problem by starting a magazine for Apple II users in France, and named the new publication *pom's*.

His magazine started in September 1981, and featured an Apple on the cover that was similar to the Apple logo, but without the missing bite on the side. It was printed quarterly until March 1984, at which time it changed to a bi-monthly schedule. The cover also showed a list of article titles.

The magazine contained articles with type-in listings of programs, not unlike the content of Nibble magazine in the United States. It was also possible to buy a disk of software with each issue of pom's. The publisher gathered authors who were well-known in the French Apple world for articles about software development, reviews, and (when it was available after 1984) AppleWorks.

Minitel was a widely used national computer system available in France, with terminals provided free to telephone subscribers. The service provided telephone directory service, as well as the ability to purchase airline and train tickets, connect to and make purchases from mail-order retail companies, and access national databases and message boards. This was available in the early 1980s, long before the Internet was available outside of universities or the military. Unlike online services that had a presence in the US, charging by the hour for access, Minitel was "free" (paid for by taxation). It was not surprising that those citizens who owned an Apple II with a modem would want to use it to connect to Minitel, and so a popular topic in pom's was finding ways to make that happen.

By 1987, the Apple image disappeared from the cover of pom's (likely at the request of Apple Computer). At that time, pom's coverage included the Macintosh line of computers, but it still ran articles about the Apple II. That issue even had an article entitled "Apple // forever". By the final issue, there were sections of the magazine that covered the Apple II, the Apple IIGS, and the Macintosh. It included a massive type-in program that ran eleven pages of Applesoft code, and a multi-page UltraMacros script for an AppleWorks spreadsheet application. Disks associated with the last seven issues contained demos by the French software programming group, the Free Tools Association (FTA).

pom's #42, May-June 1989; the sentence at the top of the cover translates as, "The French-speaking magazine/review for Apple users". – Photo credit: Antoine Vignau

The end of the magazine in 1990 was not due to the declining market. Rather, a burglary at the publisher's offices resulted in the loss of all of their equipment as well as its archives. The publisher never recovered from this theft, and the magazine was discontinued.[1, 2]

---

1 "La revue francophone indépendante pour les utilisateurs d'Apple", <sbm.ordinotheque.free.fr/apple/poms/>, accessed October 20, 2012.
2 Vignau, Antoine, e-mail message to author, May 11, 2012.

FRANCE – TREMPLIN MICRO (Mar 1985 - Jan 1989)

Printed on approximately a quarterly schedule, *Tremplin Micro* ("Springboard Micro") was programmer-focused French magazine for the Apple II computer. It came with a disk of software for Apple II computers. Starting with the first issue, it was 64 pages nearly completely filled with program listings to type in. By the final issue, Number 22, there were still program listings (including assembly code), but content also included a review of "Apple Expo 88," an Apple-sponsored trade show held in Paris in July, 1988.[3]

Tremplin Micro, Premier issue, Mar 1985 – Photo credit: Antoine Vignau

UNITED KINGDOM – HARD CORE / APPLE2000 (Jan 1981 – Nov 1992)

In Great Britain in 1980, early owners of the Apple II or ITT 2020 met in St. Albans, UK. They created a new user group, and named it the British Apple Systems User Group, or BASUG. They soon became affiliated with the International Apple Core (which will be discussed later in the book). Starting in January 1981 the first publication by this group was created and distributed. Named *hard core: The Journal of the British Apple Systems User Group*, its appearance and content was initially reminiscent of the early years of Call-A.P.P.L.E. BASUG published the magazine six times a year

Hardcore, Dec 1981 – Photo credit: Ewen Wannop

---

3 "Revue Tremplin Micro", <www.apple-iigs.info/doc/doctremplin.htm>, accessed October 20, 2012.

and included technical information for programmers, program listings for utilities and other programming topics. It also dealt with 6502 assembly code and Pascal programming.

In August 1986, hard core (and the user group) was renamed to *Apple2000*, and included color covers and content that included the Macintosh. One of the writers for the magazine (and a leader of the user group) was Ewen Wannop, who later wrote the popular telecommunications program *Spectrum* for the Apple IIGS.

The user group Apple2000 also distributed a bimonthly newsletter called *Apple Slices*, an 8-page update of events going on between releases of the larger magazine.

As the club moved into the 1990s, membership began to fall as owners of Apple computers were discovering other sources of information. One of the most popular sources of information was a bulletin board system called TABBS (which had originally been part of the Apple2000 group) and another was the Liverpool UK Bulletin Board. Wannop (who was at this time chairman of the group) described the problem in the Chairman's Corner column of the November 1992 issue of Apple2000, citing the costs involved with production of a color magazine and the declining availability of members to help produce it. Even so, in this last issue of the magazine, one of the articles was entitled "Beginner's Guide to the Apple II".

Apple2000, Aug 1986 – Photo credit: Ewen Wannop

The last Apple Slices included an article written by Wannop, entitled, "Epilogue: Apple2000 1980-1993". It discussed the final meeting of the club on January 16, 1993, and the decision to close down the organization. The members were advised to make use of GEnie or CompuServe for ongoing support of their computers, and they were also directed to existing publications and national bulletin board systems.[4]

---

4   Wannop, Ewen, "BASUG/Apple2000", <www.wannop.info/Apple2000/Home_Page.html>, accessed October 20, 2012.

UNITED KINGDOM – WINDFALL (Jul 1981 – Dec 1983) / APPLE USER (Jan 1984 – May 1988)

Derek Meakin managed a UK magazine and newspaper publishing company called Database Publications (later renamed to Europress). After seeing a news item about the first meeting of a North West Apple User Group to be held at Manchester University, he decided to attend. He did not yet own one of the new microcomputers that were in the news, and he was curious about them. At the end of the meeting, the chairman of the group commented that they should have their own newsletter. As a publisher, Meakin volunteered and launched the first commercial Apple computer magazine in Britain. He named the magazine *Windfall*, which was a pun of sorts; in the UK, the word "windfall" is used to refer to apples that get blown off of trees.

Windfall was later renamed *Apple User* beginning with the January 1984 issue, and ran through early 1988. The target audience for the publication was the hobbyist and small business market, and it provided product and software news and reviews. Meakin also encouraged reader involvement by accepting submissions of useful hints and tips.

Toward the end of its run, the publisher of Apple User wanted to create a new magazine that was focused on the growing Macintosh market. It was clear existing readers did not want to see content about the Macintosh water down Apple II content in Apple User, and the

Windfall, Nov 1979 – Photo Credit: Cliff McKnight

Apple User, Nov 1984 – Photo credit: Ewen Wannop

publisher guessed that Macintosh users would not want to be bothered with stories that were about the Apple II. A fresh start was attempted with a magazine called *Mac User*, but Apple Computer UK put its advertising behind a competitor that took on that same name. The advertising money that Apple Computer put into that other magazine made it hard for Apple User to compete for customers, and the magazine was discontinued in May 1988.[5]

AUSTRALIA – AUSTRALIAN APPLE REVIEW (Oct 1983 – Aug 1987)

Gareth Powell was a publisher of numerous magazines in Australia, as far back as the 1960s. In 1983 he started a magazine for Apple computers, the *Australian Apple Review*, which ran for four years. (He also published for other platforms, including the *Australian Business PC Report* and the *Australian Commodore Review*.) The decision to publish was galvanized by Apple's decision to open a division in Australia that same year. The premiere issue included a detailed article that looked at Apple II clones, and lack of quality control in their production that potentially made them a bad long-term investment regardless of the low cost of the initial purchase. The issue also discussed the new release of ProDOS, the production of the one millionth Apple II, a review of the Olympia ES-100 typewriter/printer and the Vision-128 RAM card (which was produced in Australia), comments on how to repair damaged disks and disk drives, a review and overview of two Australian-produced word processors, *Sandy's Word Processor* and *Spellbinder*, with comparisons to *Zardax* and *WordStar*. The first issue also provided a significant service to its readers by including a long listing of what may well have been every dealer of Apple computers on the continent. Taking the precedent from *Softalk*, there was also a Top 5 list for entertainment and business software for Australians.

Australian Apple Review v1n6, July 1984
– Photo credit: aar.applearchives.com

---

5   McKnight, Cliff, e-mail message to author, May 16, 2012.

Later issues included a contest for the best program submitted by readers, providing long listings for the reader to type in. And after the Macintosh became available, they integrated coverage of it as well.

GERMANY – PEEKER (Sep 1984 – Mar 1987)

Peeker was a magazine for German Apple II users, produced by Hüthig-Verlag Publishing. Subtitled, "Magazin Für Apple-Computer" ("Magazine for Apple Computers"), it was published monthly for most of its run of 28 issues, and focused on programming. Like Nibble in the U.S., it contained listings of programs that could be entered and run on an Apple II. Other articles gave information about how to write programs and how to make use of the computer hardware. Also like Nibble, the programs for each issue were available on floppy disk.[6]

Peeker 01, Jan 1984 – Photo credit: Ulrich Stiehl

TIMELINE

The start and end dates for foreign Apple II magazines:

hard core / Apple2000
– January 1981 - November 1992

Windfall
– July 1981 - December 1983

Pom's *– September 1981 - October 1990*

Apple User
– January 1984 - May 1988

The Australian Apple Review
– October 1983 - August 1987

Peeker *– Sep 1984 - March 1987*

Tremplin Micro
– March 1985 - January 1989

---

6 Stiehl, Ulrich, "Apple II Plus Nostalgia", <www.sanskritweb.net/apple/index.html>, accessed October 20, 2012.

CHAPTER 17

Some Assembly Required

If an application is so useful that it motivates someone to purchase the hardware on which it runs just to get that application, it is referred to as a killer app.

For the first generation of microcomputers, the killer app was the BASIC language. The hobbyists who spent the money on a piece of hardware wanted to do something with it, and creating and writing software was one of the easiest ways to "do something" on a computer. BASIC and the other programming languages and tools that came later made it possible to create applications (some of them good enough to fit into that killer app category), as programmers grew their skills from rudimentary to sophisticated.

An example of programming evolution on the Apple II was presented during the A2-Central Summer Conference (KansasFest) in July of 1991. Most Apple II users were familiar with APPLEVISION, the program released on cassette in 1978 and later included on the DOS 3.2.1 System Master disk in 1979. It was a fun little display that showed off the use of hi-res graphics.

It began by creating a simple line drawing of a room, with a picture on the wall (containing the words "HOME SWEET HOME") and a television set. On the screen of the TV appeared a man who danced to the tune of *Turkey in the Straw*, which sounded on the built-in speaker. It ran repeatedly, until the user interrupted the program. It was fascinating at the time, since there was nothing in the program code that showed off exactly how the hi-res effects were accomplished. Though a very simple program compared to later offerings, it came out at a time when hi-res graphics were still mysterious and secret, and few knew how to use it.

With the passage of time, the sophistication of software also increased. Roger Wagner's keynote at KansasFest in 1991 demonstrated this increasing sophistication:

> Roger Wagner's keynote address featured a history of hypermedia, which Roger set into action and left to run as he wandered offstage. The history began with Bob Bishop's classic APPLEVISION, done in black and white on the original Apple II. Progressive screens enhanced the APPLEVISION image using subsequent incarnations of Apple

II graphics (single hi-resolution, double hi-resolution, and the IIGS's Super Hi-Resolution modes). Finally, thanks to a laserdisc player under HyperStudio's control and a video overlay card, Roger's image appeared within the [super high-resolution] television's screen and spoke to the audience, completing the introduction before turning the presentation back to Roger (returning from offstage).[1]

It took time for the user community to master programming skills (and time for hardware improvements to appear) to the point where these degrees of programming advancements could come about. In its earliest days, sophistication was no more than what Bishop's APPLEVISION could create. Although he used BASIC to program the demo, and that was the language most commonly used by new Apple II owners, it was assembly language that made BASIC possible. This chapter will look at that most rudimentary language.

🛠 FUNDAMENTALS OF PROGRAMMING

A programming language contains a collection of rules needed to translate "what I want" into commands that the computer understands. To do so, it must take a subset of human language and convert it into the binary dialect of the computer on which it is executed.

Computer languages usually come in one of two different types: interpreted and compiled. An interpreted language translates the program code at the time of execution into commands the computer can understand. A compiled program, on the other hand, has already had the program text translated into executable code before it is run, and often includes some extra code needed to carry out necessary functions of input, output, and calculations.

As such, an interpreted program usually runs more slowly, but has the advantage of being easier to modify and re-run without the delay of recompiling. A compiled program will ordinarily run faster, but depending on the language may use more memory than an equivalent interpreted program.

Languages are called high-level or low-level, depending on how close they are to the base language of the computer on which they run. The lowest level of computer programming is at the level of the bytes understood as commands by the microprocessor. Known as machine language, it is not very understandable to humans.

Another low-level language more often used by programmers is assembly language. It uses commands somewhat more understandable ("LDA $24" means "load the accumulator with the contents of memory location $24"), which are then assembled (actually compiled) into machine-readable code. Assembly language is very powerful, since it

---

1 Doms, Dennis, "KansasFest 1991", *A2-Central* (September 1991), 7.57.

> works on the byte level of the computer. However, as a low-level language it can be very complicated and requires an intimate understanding of the function of the computer.
>
> As a language becomes more high-level, it is easier for humans to read, but requires more effort from its interpreter or compiler to translate it into the native language of the computer.

CODING AT THE BYTE LEVEL

In the era when mainframe computers ruled the world, they were restricted by the same hardware limitations as were the early generations of microcomputers. Memory was very small, and this made some aspects of programming tedious. On a mainframe, editing a program typically meant reviewing the printout of the program, finding the errors, then going through the stack of cards to find those lines, typing new cards to replace them, then re-loading, re-compiling, and re-running the program.

On a home computer, the process was similarly difficult. The programmer there had to load the program source code into the program editor, make the changes, save them, leave the editor, load the compiler and re-compile (if it was a compiled language), and then try again. All of this because there was not enough space for both the editor and compiler to reside in memory at the same time, particularly when one was running with only 16K or less of memory.

BASIC on a microcomputer was able to avoid the compilation step, since it was an interpreted language. Assemblers and most other languages, however, demanded this type of workflow, until larger memory sizes became affordable.

Since there were no assemblers available to run on the Apple II when it was released, Wozniak included what he called the Mini-assembler. It made it possible to enter simple 6502 source code, and have it immediately entered in memory, without the need to look up the individual byte codes for each command. What the Mini-assembler did not offer was a way to easily insert, delete, or rearrange lines of code, or include comments about how code worked. This required a standalone program that offered more features.

The first available assemblers for the Apple II did not run on the Apple II. Instead, a cross-assembler—one that created 6502 code—ran on a different computer. The resulting machine language code was then transferred to the Apple II for execution. It was not long before efforts were made to create assemblers that ran directly on the Apple II.

TED/ASM

Developed at Apple and smuggled out the doors around May 1978, the TED/ASM assembler had memory conflicts with DOS, so they couldn't be used together. Randy Wigginton wrote the text editor module, and Gary Shannon wrote the assembler. (Shannon was an early employee at Apple who later ported the chess game *Sargon* to the Apple II for Hayden Software.) In the early days, it was the only assembler they had available for the Apple II.[2]

RANDY'S WEEKEND ASSEMBLER

Also written by Wigginton, *Randy's Weekend Assembler* slipped out of Apple in September 1978. The text editor was written mostly in SWEET16 (Wozniak's 16-bit emulator in the Integer BASIC ROM), and was therefore slow. Unfortunately, it had its own set of bugs.

MICROPRODUCTS/APPLE II ASSEMBLER

Microproducts of Redondo Beach, California, was the first to market with a native assembler for the Apple II. The *Microproducts/Apple II Assembler* was released in early 1978, about a year after the release of the computer. It was a four-character assembler, meaning that labels (a designation identifying a line or variable) were limited to four characters. To save on the size of the assembler, it made heavy use of ROM routines in the original Apple II.

A year later, Microproducts added a disassembler, which was capable of creating a source code text file of any machine language code in memory. That file could then be loaded into the Microproducts Assembler and edited, which allowed a programmer to learn how a 6502 program functioned. About that same time, they also updated the assembler to use six-character labels.

Both products were provided on cassette. The assembler sold for $34.95 on cassette, and later for $38.95 for a floppy disk version, with the disassembler priced at $29.95.[3]

By January 1980, six months after the Apple II Plus came out, a revised version of the Microproducts/Apple II Assembler was released, removing its dependency on the older ROM code. The company rounded out its programming tools the following month with *AppleBug*, a debugging and testing tool.[4]

S-C ASSEMBLER II

Bob Sander-Cederlof worked in the computer industry for years before he bought his first Apple II. One of his first such jobs was working for Interna-

---

2   Hertzfeld, Andy, "A Consumer's Guide To Apple II Assemblers", *PEEKing At Call-A.P.P.L.E.* (Seattle, Washington, Vol. 2, 1979), 164-166.
3   Colsher, William, "Apples Get Disassembler", *InfoWorld* (June 11, 1979), 86.
4   "Software Briefs", *InfoWorld* (February 18, 1980), 15.

tional Timesharing, selling computer time via telephone lines. This allowed customers to write programs in BASIC or FORTRAN, paying by the minute. While at that company, he created FORTRAN II and FORTRAN IV compilers and a database program for the dial-up users to access. Later, working for Texas Instruments, he wrote software to control robotic arms used on the calculator assembly lines, and also wrote a text editor and debugger for the TI-960, TI-980, and TI-990 minicomputers.

In September 1977, Sander-Cederlof purchased one of the earliest available Apple II computers (serial number 219) with 8K of RAM. With his programming background, he wanted to do assembly language programming on his new computer. He purchased the Microproducts/Apple II Assembler (on cassette) and began to use it. However, its limitations frustrated him, and so he decided to use the Microproducts assembler to write his own assembler, starting in April 1978. Like that earlier product, Sander-Cederlof also used as many of the built-in ROM routines as possible, including code from Integer BASIC and the SWEET16 pseudo-16-bit package Wozniak had included in the ROM. This made the final product very compact, working in just 16K of RAM, but the dependence on SWEET16 had an effect on the speed of the compiler.

He named the final product *S-C Assembler II*, and released it on cassette in August 1978—likely the second commercially available assembler for the Apple II. A 20-page manual for the program was also included, which he created on a typewriter and had duplicated. For the cassettes, he saved his code to each cassette manually, one at a time, and then used the same typewriter to create cassette labels. Sander-Cederlof was able to sell a number of copies at the Dallas Apple Corps user group. He was also able to sell it at local computer stores and through ads in *Micro* magazine.

After the release of the Disk II drive, Sander-Cederlof modified his assembler to work from a floppy disk. Like the Microproducts assembler, the release of the Apple II Plus made it necessary to do further revisions to the S-C Assembler to be independent of the Integer BASIC and old Monitor ROM. His disk version came out in July 1979, and in less than a year, sales had increased to the point where he was able to quit his job at Texas Instruments and work full time on the SC-Assembler II and other projects. That same year he started the *Apple Assembly Lines* newsletter, to both support his product and to be an information center for 6502 assembly language tips and techniques.

Sander-Cederlof saw the macro capabilities (a single line of code creating a number of pre-defined lines of code) of the *Big Mac* assembler sold by A.P.P.L.E., and added this capability to his product, changing the name in February 1982 to the *S-C Macro Assembler*. He already offered the ability for it to act as a cross-assembler for the Motorola 6800, 6801, and 6802, and in time expanded the selections to include the 6809, and 68000 processors, the

8048, 8051, and Z-80 processors, as well as the Digital Equipment Corporation PDP-11 minicomputer, the RCA 1802, and a custom version of the 6502 made by Mitsubishi. When the Western Design Center released the 65c02, 65802 and 65816 processors, he added these capabilities to his assembler.

The S-C Assembler continued to be sold until 1988, when the market for it had shrunk to the point where it was no longer financially viable to continue to produce it. That same year he also closed down his newsletter, and went to work for Applied Engineering, still using his assembler to write software and firmware for their products.[5]

LISA

Randy Hyde was a prolific programmer during the Apple II era. Under his company name, Lazerware Microsystems, Hyde produced *Lazerware's Interactive Symbolic Assembler*, or *LISA* (pronounced "liza"). Like other assemblers of the day, it could handle code for SWEET16, included a disassembler, and included custom hi-res graphics routines. It was unique amongst other assemblers because it would immediately report syntax errors as the program was being entered in the editor. Its other unique feature was its speed of assembly. By version 2.6, it could assemble over 30,000 lines of code per minute.

Programma International, a company that sold software products for many early microcomputers (including the Apple II) published LISA in 1979, and continued to do so until Hayden Software bought the company in 1980. At that point, On-Line Systems (later known as Sierra OnLine) took over sales of LISA. In 1983, Sierra decided to drop the product, and Hyde took back his program to sell directly through his own company.

UCSD PASCAL ASSEMBLER

Part of the Apple Pascal package released in 1979, *UCSD Pascal Assembler* was popular because it had macro capability, could do conditional assembly and create relocatable code, and had a good text editor. However, programs created with it could not run on a standard (non-Language Card) Apple, because at the time there was no utility to transfer the files to DOS 3.2. (Later, A.P.P.L.E. published transfer utilities called *HUFFIN* and *PUFFIN* for movement to and from DOS, named after Apple's *MUFFIN* utility for DOS 3.2 to 3.3 file transfers).

APPLE EDASM

Apple released the *Applesoft Tool Kit* in 1980. It included some programming tools for Applesoft, including a high-res character generator to allow

---

5 Sander-Cederlof, Bob, personal e-mail to author, March 19, 2013.

text in custom bitmapped fonts to be displayed on the hi-res screen. Also included with it was an assembler that was officially called *Editor/Assembler II*, but programmers always called it by its name on the disk, *EDASM*. Written by John Arkley, it was Apple's official assembler for the II Plus and later 8-bit Apple II computers.

Shortly after the introduction of ProDOS in 1983, Apple included a new version of EDASM as part of an Apple II programmer package called the Workbench Series. Arkley also wrote this ProDOS version of EDASM, and included a 65c02 debugging program called *Bugbyter*.

Applesoft Tool Kit, 1980 – Photo credit: personal

BIG MAC/MERLIN

Glen Bredon began teaching mathematics at Rutgers University in New Jersey back in 1967. He bought his first Apple II in 1979, but was initially disappointed in his new computer because of a lack of available software. Bredon taught himself 6502 assembly language by using the Monitor mini-assembler and disassembler. Further self-education came from taking apart some of the early programs he was able to obtain and fixing bugs in them.

From A.P.P.L.E. Bredon obtained a public domain assembler, an update of the TED/ASM program called TED TWO. He saw problems with it and took that program apart also, creating a new assembler that worked far better, and offered more features. One useful feature added was the ability for it to use macros, which were custom commands that would produce a pre-defined block of code every time the assembler came across it while assembling a program. Bredon contacted A.P.P.L.E. and offered the program back to them, which they released in July 1981 as *Big Mac* (highlighting its macro capabilities).

Merlin ad – Photo credit: Softalk, December 1981

In addition to its assembler and editor, Bredon had included his own custom disassembler, which he called *Sourceror*. This could create an assembly source code listing from a block of binary program code, either from ROM code or from a binary file on disk. He also included various sample source code files and utilities, including a file that made the mini-assembler and step and trace commands in the Monitor available to Apple II Plus owners (these files were unique to Integer BASIC and old Monitor ROM).

Val Golding, the editor of the club's magazine, *Call-A.P.P.L.E.*, felt Big Mac was good enough to become a commercial program. He put Bredon in touch with Roger Wagner's Southwestern Data Systems, and that company released it in 1982 as *Merlin*.[6]

ORCA/M

ORCA/M was another early commercial assembler for the Apple II series. Mike Westerfield created it in 1979, after he'd purchased an Apple II Plus. He wanted to code a large project (a chess game in 6502 assembly code), and none of the assemblers then available could handle a project of that size. He was also more comfortable with the style of the assembler on the IBM 360 mainframe on which he had been trained on his first assignment out of the Air Force Academy.

ORCA/M ad – Photo credit: Softalk, March 1983

To that point, no Apple II assembler had been written to work like an IBM 360 assembler. Westerfield ultimately had to write his own on one of the less capable assemblers he could get his hands on. He created it in three pieces, two of them at memory locations the old assembler could handle, and the third piece hand-assembled by entering the bytes into the appropriate memory location using the Monitor.

After putting these three parts together manually, he then used this new assembler to make modifications to itself, ultimately creating an assembler, linker, libraries, and the ability to create macros (shortcuts for longer bits of code).

With the program brought up to a level where others could use it, Westerfield sought out a publisher, and settled on Hayden Software. Hayden product manager David Eyes suggested the name ORCA/M, an acronym for Object Relocatable Code Assembler for Microcomputers; however, it was also MACRO spelled backwards. It was released in 1982, running under DOS 3.3. Westerfield eventually hired another programmer to help with improvements in the product.

---

6 Bredon, Glen, interview by Charles Turley, February 1, 1996, <www.apple2.org.za/gswv/USA2WUG/Glen.Bredon.In.Memoriam/Interview.1996.html>

TIMELINE

Mini-assembler – *June 1977*
Microproducts/Apple II Assembler – *March 1978*
TED/ASM – *May 1978*
S-C Assembler II – *August 1978*
Randy's Weekend Assembler – *September 1978*
LISA – *1979*
ORCA/M – *1979*

UCSD Pascal Assembler – *July 1979*
Apple EDASM – *1980*
Big Mac – *July 1981*
Merlin – *1982*
S-C Macro Assembler – *February 1982*
Apple EDASM (ProDOS) – *1983*

CHAPTER 18

Music and Speech

Apple II computers have been involved in sound from the beginning, with Wozniak's decision to include a speaker so his Apple II version of *Breakout* could produce sound effects. As simple as it was, enterprising programmers managed to make this single-voice speaker sound like two and even three different voices (tones) simultaneously (Paul Lutus' *Electric Duet* is an example of such a program). But that was not enough for those who wanted quality music production, and so production of synthesizer cards was in full swing by the early 1980s.

ALF Products, Inc. created one of the first music products for home computers in the mid-1970s, specifically for S-100 systems. With the release of the Apple II in 1977, the company began to make a version of their card for that computer. It was first to be called ALF's Apple Music Synthesizer, but Apple later decided they wanted the name changed so it was clear that it was not their product. Renamed as the ALF Music Card MC16, it was released in June 1979, with included software to assist music production. They released a second card later that year, using some increased new Texas Instruments chips that had advanced sound production features. The new card, called ALF's Apple Music II (and changed to Music Card MC1), was capable of producing nine simultaneous voices, a feat that would have required three MC16 cards.

The Mountain Music System (Mountain Computer, Inc.) was a more advanced sixteen oscillator (voice) digital synthesizer, consisting of two peripheral cards and software to control it. It was capable of playing eight stereo voices simultaneously. The included software made use of a hardware light pen to allow placement of notes on a graphic musical staff on the hi-res screen.

The alphaSyntauri was a significant music product for the Apple II. It was released early on, in 1980. For $1,500, it duplicated some of the features of contemporary digital synthesizers that cost as much as $40,000. The system included a keyboard, foot pedals to control some of the sounds, game paddles to control other effects, a card to plug into the Apple II, and the Mountain Music

alphaSyntauri – Photo credit: Bill Cone <www.synthony.com>

System cards. It could play 16 notes at the same time, and could have even more capabilities depending on the type of musical keyboard that was attached. The software was written in a combination of 6502 assembly language and BASIC, which made it possible to customize some functions. Some well-known musicians, such as Herbie Hancock and Emerson, Lake & Palmer keyboard performer Keith Emerson used the alphaSyntauri system in their performances.[1,2]

Soundchaser System (Passport Designs, Inc.) was a package that included the Mountain Music System (using slots 4 and 5), plus the Soundchaser, which was a piano-style keyboard for music input, and whose card went in slot 7. It allowed four track recording and sound manipulation, using the Apple II primarily as a controller. This was one of the most advanced music hardware system available in the days before MIDI.

The Drum-Key (made by PVI) was specifically a percussion synthesizer. It required an external amplifier and used included software to produce a wide variety of drum and other percussion sounds. The engineers who created the Drum-Key founded the Ensoniq Corporation.[3]

Beginning in the early 1980s several speech synthesizers became available for the Apple and other home computers. One made by Mountain Hardware in 1981 was the $279 Supertalker. Street Electronics came out with the Echo II card for the Apple II in 1982, and the Cricket (for the modem port on the Apple IIc) in 1984. Street's TextTalker software gave these devices the ability to produce a robotic voice, a female voice, sound effects, and stereo music.

Some games released at the time produced enhanced sound output when they detected one of these two devices. For speech reproduction, they used a method of accepting ASCII text from the computer in specific combinations to describe and produce voice through a built-in speaker. They used this approach because words have a variety of pronunciation depending on their context. Properly programmed, the voice synthesizers could pronounce the word "root" to rhyme with either "boot" or "foot".

Street Electronics Cricket synthesizer
– Photo credit: *Softalk*, May 1984

Sweet Micro Systems produced one of the most popular sound cards for the Apple II. Their original products appeared on the market in 1981, and were called the Sound series. These cards utilized music and sound microchips that were significantly advanced over the one-bit sound that had been

---

1 "About The alphaSyntauri" *proximaSyntauri*, <www.purplenote.com/syntauri/>, accessed October 20, 2012.
2 "Apple II Sound & Music Software", *8-Bit Sound And Fury*, <eightbitsoundandfury.ld8.org/hardware.html>
3 -----, "Reviews: Music Systems For The Apple II", *Call-A.P.P.L.E.* (June 1984), 17-31.

designed into the Apple II. These cards came in four different versions: Sound I, which could produce sound effects and music; Speech I, for speech using phonemes, as well as some sound effects; Sound II, which had two audio outputs, each of which produced music and sound effects; and Sound/Speech I, also with two audio outputs, one for music and one for speech.

After the early success of Sweet Micro Systems' Sound series, in 1985 they redesigned the card, named it Mockingboard, and sold a new set of sound cards for the Apple II. There were initially three versions, models A, C, and D. The Mockingboard A sold for $99, had two audio outputs (which made stereo sound possible), and featured a better music and sound synthesizer. The card also had two empty sockets that made it possible to add speech synthesis to either or both outputs. With these chips and the right program, it was possible for the card to sing in two voices, in harmony.

The Mockingboard B, for $89, was actually not a board. Rather, it was the product name for the speech synthesizer chip to add to the Mockingboard A. The Mockingboard C, for $179, was simply a Mockingboard A with a Mockingboard B chip upgrade already installed.

Mockingboard C – Photo credit: <www.apple2world.jp>

The Mockingboard D, which sold for $195, was a version of the Mockingboard C designed as an external device for the Apple IIc. It connected via one of the serial ports, and offered stereo music, speech synthesis, and sound effects.

A software company, Mindscape, released a music program called *Bank Street Music Writer* in 1986. It was released for the Commodore 64 and Atari 800 (using the sound capabilities built into those computers), while the IBM PC and Apple II versions required add-on sound hardware. They contracted with Sweet Micro Systems to bundle another version of their sound card, called the Mockingboard M, with *Bank Street Music Writer* on the Apple II version. This card featured two music generator chips and an open spot for the optional speech chip. Sound was played through a headphone jack, and a modification to the board allowed sound output through the Apple II speaker.

(In 2005, Henry Courbis of ReactiveMicro.com produced a fully functioning modern clone of the Mockingboard C, called the Mockingboard v1, selling it for $60. Since he was not equipped for large-scale production and had delays in meeting demand for it, another enterprising hacker, Tom Arnold, produced a clone of this clone in 2010, and sold it through the ReactiveMicro web site as the Mockingboard v1a.)

Entertainment companies produced over fifty programs to take advantage of the additional sound capabilities of the Mockingboard. The game making the most elaborate use of this feature was *Ultima V*, which supported two Mockinboards, utilizing eight out of twelve possible voices (sound channels).[4,5]

In the 1980s, Applied Engineering began to offer audio cards. Their first card in 1984 was simply called Music Synthesizer, offered sixteen voices, and could play music designed for the ALF system cards. The Phasor card was released in 1986, and offered 12 music and sound effect channels, as well as speech synthesis. Both cards also offered compatibility with software for the Mockingboard cards.

TIMELINE

ALF Music Card MC16 – *June 1979*

ALF Music Card MC1 – *October 1979*

Mountain Music System – *August 1980*

alphSyntauri – *1980*

Mountain Hardware Supertalker – *1981*

Street Electronics Sound I, Sound II, Speech I – *1981*

Soundchaser System – *1982*

Street Electronics Echo II – *1982*

AE Music Synthesizer – *1984*

Street Electronics Cricket – *May 1984*

Drum-Key – *August 1984*

Mockingboard – *August 1985*

Mockingboard M – *1986*

AE Phasor – *1986*

Mockingboard v1 – *August 2005*

Mockingboard v1a – *July 2010*

---

4 Hurlburt, Jeff, "Mockingboard Mini-Manual", *8-Bit Sound & Fury* <eightbitsoundandfury.ld8.org/docs/MockingBoardMiniManual.html>, accessed October 20, 2012.

5 "Mockingboard v1a", *Reactivemicro.com*, <www.reactivemicro.com/product_info.php?products_id=152>, accessed October 20, 2012.

CHAPTER 19
Second Wave

Most of the earliest computer magazines dealt with more than one microcomputer platform, due to the small size of the market. Pioneers such as *Interface Age* (discussed earlier), *Creative Computing* (October 1974 – December 1985), *BYTE* (September 1975 – July 1998), and *Kilobaud Microcomputing* (January 1977 – December 1982) began to provide service to the era of those who were building their own computers, and gradually expanded to deal with the microcomputer community in general. As the various platforms became established, entrepreneurs saw a market for publications that dealt with a single computer in greater detail. Although *Call-A.P.P.L.E.* pioneered this style, a second wave of magazines began in 1980 that also chose to exclusively spotlight the Apple II computer.

NIBBLE (Jan 1980 – Jul 1992)

Begun in his living room in January 1980 by Mike Harvey, Nibble survived longer than many Apple II magazines. His original advertisement for the magazine explained his goals for it:

> **NIBBLE**
>
> NIBBLE is an unusual new Newsletter for Apple II Owners. Each Issue will follow a major theme... such as:
>
> * DATA BASE MANAGEMENT
> * PROGRAMS FOR THE HOME
> * TEXT PROCESSING
> * COMPUTING FOR KIDS
> * SMALL BUSINESS JOBS
> * GAMES AND GRAPHICS
> * PRACTICAL PASCAL
> * etc.
>
> Significant programs will be in each issue, surrounded by articles which show how to USE the programming ideas in your OWN programs.
>
> Examples of Upcoming Articles...
>
> * Building A Numeric Keypad
> * Home Credit Card Management
> * LORES Shape Writing
> * Designing Games that Last
> * Arcade Shooting Gallery
> * Random #'s in Assy. Lang.
> * HIRES Weaving Design
>
> And many many more. NIBBLE will literally "Nibble Away" at the mysteries of the Apple II to help Beginning and Advanced Programmers, Small Businessmen, and the Whole Family enjoy and USE the Apple MORE!
>
> It costs a paltry $15.00 for 8 Issues! It will invite and publish user ideas and programs. DON'T WAIT! Send your check or money order right now, to receive the January issue! Mail to:
>
> S.P.A.R.C.
> P.O. Box
> Lincoln, Mass. 01773
>
> Software Publishing And Research Co.

Nibble announcement – Photo credit: Mike Harvey

Harvey worked carefully to avoid the pressure of bank loans and investors, instead using his own savings to finance the magazine, running the company on a "pay as you go" basis. He printed enough of the first issue, 42 pages long in black and white, to mail to the few who responded to his ad, and the rest were sent free of charge to Apple dealers to make them aware of *Nibble's* existence. His initial schedule was for eight issues per year, which was what he could afford to produce. By mid 1981 the magazine had grown to the point where Harvey could quit his regular job (president of a subsidiary of Exxon Enterprises) and work full-time as publisher of *Nibble*.[1]

His editorials over the years covered topics that were helpful to small businesses, offering advice to help them survive in good times and bad. He certainly took his own advice; although *Nibble* expanded to the point where it went to a monthly schedule (around 1984) and was printed as a square-bound magazine, it had to reduce its size by 1990 back to a center-stapled format with fewer pages. With his careful financial oversight, *Nibble* lasted longer than most other magazines that started at the same time.

Nibble's articles covered a wide array of topics, from simple Applesoft and Integer BASIC programs, to complex assembly language applications, BASIC extensions, and games. In its prime it also included a popular series called "Disassembly Lines", by contributing editor Sandy Mossberg, M.D. In his series, Mossberg taught tricks and techniques of assembly language by taking parts of DOS 3.3, and later the BASIC.SYSTEM and PRODOS files, and disassembling them into readable assembly source code. This provided insight into why Apple's system programs worked the way they did, and made it possible to either modify them to fix bugs, or to incorporate the programming techniques in other projects.

Nibble was a valuable resource to learn how to write programs. Its published listings were well commented, and the tricks described by programmers were available for all to see and learn. Along with the various utilities were games (some were very complicated with long tables of hex bytes to en-

Nibble March 1983 – Photo credit: Mike Harvey

---

1 Harvey, Mike, "Time Flies When You're Havin' Fun!" *Nibble* (January 1985), 5.

ter). It also included in later issues reviews of commercial software products, and the publisher offered disks containing all of the programs from a single issue of the magazine.

In April 1985 a section was added to the magazine called *Nibble Mac*, to cover topics of interest to Macintosh users. Later in 1985 this was spun-off into a short-lived publication with the same title.

Nibble also helped establish the concept of copyright protection on program listings printed in magazines. This was important to *Nibble*, as they sold disks of their old programs to save readers the trouble of typing in the long listings.

With decreasing sales, a decision was made in 1991 to no longer supply *Nibble* to newsstand vendors and continue the magazine on a subscription-only basis. The market for Apple II programming-oriented magazines continued to decline, and the July 1992 issue announced itself as the last one. Subscribers received issues of *A2-Central* to complete the balance of their subscription.[2]

APPLE ORCHARD (Mar 1980 – Sep 1984)

In September 1979, several Apple user group leaders began to hold phone conversations about the possibility of coordination between existing groups, and ways to help new groups get started. These leaders included Val Golding of A.P.P.L.E, Randy Hyde (author of the LISA assembler) from the Original Apple Corps, representatives of the San Francisco Apple Core and others. Eventually they discussed a larger magazine to be prepared in time for the fifth West Coast Computer Faire in March 1980 (the March 1980 faire was the fifth such event because there had been two held in 1978). The following month, these

Apple Orchard, March 1980 – Photo credit: personal

and several other user group representatives met at Apple corporate offices. The meeting resulted in the formation of the International Apple Core, com-

---

2 Starting in October 2005, Nibble editor Mike Harvey made available the entire run of Nibble on either CD-ROM or DVD. This, as well as scans of Nibble Mac, could be found at his web site at www.nibblemagazine.net.

mittees to help run it, and the *Apple Orchard* magazine to be the voice of the organization.

The first issue was a collection of articles contributed by each of the founding clubs, to make up just over one hundred pages of material. Also, Apple chose to contribute material to this inaugural issue that was to have been published in issue seven of *Contact*, Apple's user group publication. Apple's John Crossley had compiled a detailed list of internal entry points and zero page usage for Applesoft BASIC. That material first appeared in this inaugural issue.

The initially subscription rate was $10 per year. The second issue appeared in the fall of 1980, and contained several additional articles submitted by *Contact* from Apple, focusing on the new Apple III and other topics. This issue also focused on hi-res graphics on the Apple II, and it contained a listing three and a half pages long of the user groups affiliated with the International Apple Core.

Apple Orchard, January 1984 – Photo credit: personal

With further issues, the *Apple Orchard* grew and matured. By December 1981 it started publishing quarterly; by July 1982 it became bimonthly; then nine issues per year starting June 1983; and ten issues per year by August 1983. As with a number of Apple II publications, however, it was hit by the downturn in the computer market during 1984, and the last issue came out in September 1984.

PEELINGS II (May 1980 – Feb 1984)

The National Aeronautics and Space Administration (NASA) has been responsible for a large number of spin-off products and industries since it was created in 1958. One of the least well-known was an Apple II magazine called *Peelings II*. [3]

John Martellaro was a physics graduate student working on his Ph.D at New Mexico State University in Las Cruces. He had the opportunity to participate in the NASA Summer Intern program in Houston during the sum-

---

3   Golding, Val J, "Call-A.P.P.L.E. Book Review", *PEEKing At Call-A.P.P.L.E.* (Seattle, Washington, Vol. 3, 1980), 249.

mer of 1977. The job he was asked to do was to survey all of the various simulators in use by NASA Houston. They wanted a comprehensive list of the capabilities of these simulators, and in the case of an emergency during an orbital mission, help pinpoint quickly which simulator would be best suited to help resolve the emergency.

One of the several available devices used for training pilots was the the Shuttle Mission Simulator (SMS)—a full mockup of a cockpit sitting on top of pistons that simulated banking and descent maneuvers. Prior to Martellaro's internship, one of the methods used to simulate the view outside of the cockpit was to show a landscape on television monitors outside the windows. The cockpit controls moved a TV camera over a hand-made miniature terrain, which looked much like a sophisticated model railroad set. The newer technology introduced that summer replaced the camera views of miniatures with computer-generated images of the landscape. As part of his assignment to understand the capabilities of the simulators, Martellaro was given a ride during one of the practice missions on the SMS. He watched and experienced a descent from 100,000 feet, including the approach and landing. He saw the ways that a shuttle was controlled, and experienced what it was like to actually fly in the craft.

Peelings II, Vol 4, No 3, 1983 – Photo credit: personal

His enthusiasm continued as he returned to graduate school the next fall, and he decided that he wanted to write a computer program that would recreate the Shuttle Mission Simulator experience in software. In early 1978 he purchased an Apple II with cassette storage, and wrote a simulator in Applesoft BASIC, using assembly language routines to display his images using hi-res graphics. To sell his Space Shuttle Landing program, Martellaro formed a company called Harvey's Space Ship Repair. Listed for $15, he sold about 1,000 copies of his program, first on cassette and later on floppy disk.

After buying his Apple II, Martellaro began to subscribe to computer magazines, learning all he could about the Apple II. He also contributed several articles, including one in *Microcomputing* about assembly language use of the Apple II hi-res graphics routines, and another in *BYTE* that reviewed the chess game, *Sargon*. He noticed that with the array of available publications for the Apple II, there were none that spent much time on product reviews. This gave him the idea to start his own magazine that would prominently feature reviews of software and hardware for the Apple II, much like *Consumer Reports*.

In the spring of 1980, while still in his graduate program, Martellaro began the process of making his vision a reality. He knew that he would need help in order to launch his magazine and proceeded to recruit the help of four members of the Las Cruces Computer Club who were also knowledgeable about the Apple II. All four were eager to participate in his venture, and became co-founders of the magazine.

The first issue debuted in May-June 1980. With no available word processor yet, Martellaro and his friends typed the articles on typewriters. These were cut up and laid out on waxboards and then sent to a printer. By the second bi-monthly issue they had obtained a copy of *Apple Writer*, which considerably simplified the process, and one of the four cofounders obtained a 9-pin printer they could now use to create the early issues of the magazine. The reviews of Apple II word processors they published in their fourth issue in Nov-Dec 1980 showed them a better program, *P.I.E.* published by Programma (later called *PIE Writer* after the company was acquired by Hayden Software), which they used through the rest of the run of the magazine.

They were able to rent a small office in town to house their small staff, but none of the partners ever quit their regular jobs, writing for the magazine in the evenings.

Many issues had reviews based on a theme, and compared several products in the same category (such as word processors, assemblers, and the like), and rated the products based on performance, ease of use, and other criteria.

In the April 1982 issue, Martellaro played an April Fool prank on readers by writing a review for a fictional product called The Scintillator from the "Rama Corporation". This was supposed to be a plug-in card for the Apple II utilizing a 68000 CPU. The software to be used with The Scintillator was described as accepting text from a written script and translating it into a video showing the scene the script described. He described a demo in which he had created a partial script for the hit CBS television show, *M*A*S*H*, and the card produced a video scene (in which one character shot another) that he stated was indistinguishable from what was created on film for the real TV show. The article resulted in considerable excitement, with the magazine's office overwhelmed with calls about the product, and one college professor who was ready to teach a film-making course with it.

Overall, *Peelings II* was successful for a homebrew magazine. It reached a peak of 20,000 subscribers, including a number from outside of the United States. Martellaro hired a professional to improve the cover art, and received additional help to handle subscriptions and distribute the magazine onto newsstands. However, they learned that newsstand sales did not financially work well for *Peelings II*, and the outside person they had hired to sell advertising did not have the enthusiasm that someone working on the magazine itself would have. Those issues, combined with the major publishing houses entering the computer magazine business for the Apple II (and IBM PC), advertising revenue began to fall, and the magazine was shut down after the February 1984 issue.[4]

SOFTALK (Sep 1980 – Aug 1984)

Of all the magazines that have dealt with the Apple II since its release in 1977, none have been quite like *Softalk*. The first issue in September 1980 was 32 pages, including the cover that featured Darth Vader with the title, "Apple Helps the Empire Strike Back". That first issue opened with the following introductory remark describing its hopes and goals:

> Welcome to *Softalk*. Whether you're a hobbyist or a businessperson, a programmer or a nonprogrammer, *Softalk* is designed for you, because each of you has chosen Apple for your computer; and so did we.
>
> *Softalk* is a feature magazine, intended to pique the curiosity and intrigue the intellect of everyone who owns an Apple. In *Softalk*, you'll find articles about people who own and use Apples, some of them famous, some merely ingenious. You'll find articles about issues--those most pertinent within the microcomputer industry, such as piracy, and those the microcomputer is helping to solve, such as unemployment among the handicapped.
>
> *Softalk*'s regular columns will strive to keep you up with what's new in software and hardware and what's new in the companies that make software and hardware. We'll also try to keep you informed of how the computer is making news, both in the United States and abroad, both seriously and lightly.
>
> *Softalk* is not a programming magazine. Beginning in October, our programming columns will be intended as tutorials, offering running courses on how to program. Although we believe that those of you who are seriously involved in programming will enjoy *Softalk*, for your programming applications we recommend that you seek out the excellent programming articles and tips in such magazines as Apple Orchard, Micro, Call-A.P.P.L.E., Creative Computing, and the many other fine magazines that address themselves to this aspect of computing.

---

4   Martellaro, John, e-mail message to author, March 16, 2013

Fun is another feature of Softalk. There will be puzzles, games, contests. The prizes won't be huge, but they will be fun. This month, you'll find a contest on page 2; later in the magazine lurks another puzzler.

We encourage you to patronize our advertisers. Those advertisers make it possible for you to receive Softalk. And, further, we hope you'll support your local computer store. A healthy retail sector is crucial to our industry on every level; it is to all our benefits to help our retailers prosper.

I hope you share my enthusiasm for Apple and for the remarkable microcomputer industry, because, when you share it, you'll find yourself looking forward to the fast-coming future with excitement and optimistic anticipation. If Softalk serves only to instill such a positive enthusiasm in you, it will be well worthwhile.[5]

Oddly enough, Softalk owed its beginning to a television game show. Margot Tommervik was a contestant on *Password*, and with part of her winnings in late 1979 she purchased an Apple II computer. She was fascinated with the machine and what it allowed her to do. When a local computer store offered a prize for the first person to solve On-Line's *Mystery House* adventure, she dove into it headlong and had it solved in twenty-four hours.

Back in 1977, not long after the release of the Apple II, William V.R. Smith (who had created the dress pattern program distributed on "floppy ROM" in *Interface Age*) banded together with programmers William Depew and Gary Koffler. Together they started a company named Softape to sell Apple II software on cassette. Along with their printed catalog, the company distributed three issues of a newsletter called *Softalk*. When Margot discovered that this software company was located close by, she came to visit.

Softalk, September 1980 promo flyer

Out of the conversations she had with Smith and Depew, an arrangement was reached for Margot and her husband Al to turn the *Softalk* newsletter into a glossy magazine. Contributing money from the remainder of her Password winnings, Margot and her husband agreed to produce the maga-

---

5   Tommervik, Margot Comstock, "Straightalk", *Softalk* (September 1980), 3.

zine if they were allowed to determine its course and retain management control. It would be as much a magazine for Apple II enthusiasts to enjoy as a platform for software publishers to display their wares.

Although it had the modest beginning of only 32 pages printed on newsprint stock, within a year there were over one hundred advertising pages in each issue. It was an ideal arrangement: the readers received a magazine specifically about their computer, and the software and hardware companies could showcase their products to those readers.[6]

Softalk carved its niche among the other Apple II magazines of the time by providing a variety of articles not available anywhere else. Whereas *Nibble* was best known for its games and utilities, *Call-A.P.P.L.E.* for its technical information, and *Apple Orchard* for its focus on beginners and Apple user groups, *Softalk* concentrated on the Apple computer industry. This included information about Apple Computer, Inc., as well as the many companies that provided software or hardware for the Apple II. A monthly series called "Exec" (taken after the Apple DOS disk command), profiled a company that made hardware or software for the Apple II, and provided background about how the company got started, the people who worked there, and its products. It carried reviews of new releases each month, and news about the companies making those products. It also developed a monthly best-seller list for Apple II and III software, and used not the sales figures provided by the companies who marketed the programs, but rather the actual figures provided by the software and computer stores that sold them. Their reason for doing it this way was to get a more accurate picture of what was selling, not just what was shipping.

Part of the uniqueness of *Softalk* was due to the way it did business. Although it was available by mail or in computer stores (as were other computer magazines of the day), this one offered every Apple II owner a free six-month subscription as a trial, after which a regular subscription would be needed to continue to receive it. One only had to provide the computer's serial number and you were in the club. And it felt like a club—almost a family—of fellow Apple II (and later, Apple III, Lisa, and Macintosh) enthusiasts. This unusual marketing method lasted even until the final issue.

As time went by, *Softalk* expanded its coverage to include programming, but chose to do so in a tutorial fashion, as they promised in their introduction article. They were written by luminaries in the Apple world, including:

- Roger Wagner, founder and president of Southwestern Data Systems, started a column in October 1980 called "Assembly Lines". He taught 6502 assembly language, explaining a few opcodes per column, and how to use them in a program. He later revealed that

---

6 Levy, Steven, *Hackers: Heroes of the Computer Revolution* (New York, Dell Publishing Co., Inc, 1984), 308-310.

what he knew about 6502 assembly was only about one month ahead of what the readers were learning.[7]
- Doug Carlston, co-founder of software publisher Brøderbund, instructed users in the art of BASIC programming in "All About Applesoft".
- Mark Pelczarski, founder of software publisher Penguin Software, had started the company with his program, *Complete Graphics System*. He used this knowledge to expound on hi-res graphics techniques in the column "Graphically Speaking".
- Taylor Pohlman was a product-marketing manager at Apple for the Apple II and III. He was very involved in the Apple III, and wrote "The Third Basic" to educate readers about Business Basic on the Apple III.
- Jim Merritt, a programmer at Apple, championed Pascal in "The Pascal Path".
- Bert Kersey, founder of Beagle Bros, and later Tom Weishaar, who wrote software for Beagle Bros, deciphered DOS 3.3 and ProDOS in "DOSTalk".
- Greg Tibbetts, employed by Microsoft as manager of technical support, wrote "SoftCard Symposium" to explain the use of CP/M on the Microsoft SoftCard.

Other regular features included "Fastalk" (an annotated listing and description of current and classic software), "Marketalk News" (product release announcements), "Marketalk Reviews" (detailed product reviews), "Tradetalk" (Apple industry news), "Hardtalk" (hardware projects or information), "Storytalk" (fiction, primarily computer related), and eventually a column called "Backtalk", which was a look back at older issues of *Softalk* itself (this began on the third anniversary of the magazine).

One unusual column, called "Open Discussion", was similar to Internet forums. The magazine printed letters from readers that ranged from comments on previous articles to questions such as "How do I get Apple Writer to work with my printer?" Rather than directly answering each question, *Softalk* often left it to readers to send in replies with help. (Needless to say, this two month delay was much slower than exchanging emails.) In its final year, *Softalk* began a column called "If Then Maybe", which took some of those technical questions and actually used its consulting writers (the "Softalk Sages") to answer them.

Each month there was a new contest, often involving a puzzle that might require the use of a computer to help solve it. The winners of the previous month's contests were awarded a credit towards $100 worth of products advertised in *Softalk*. The puzzles were creative and unique. One issue asked to have various shapes in a later part of the magazine identified (some that were obvious, such as a computer monitor, some less so, such as a hand phaser

---

7 Bird, Alan, & Weishaar, Tom. "Old Timers: Two Survivors", *1991 A2-Central Summer Conference* (tapes), (July 1992).

from Star Trek). Another contest had lists of five-character scrambled words — no clues, no instructions, no direction. One month had a crossword puzzle with *very* obtuse clues. One issue featured tiny "hi-res" turkeys scattered throughout the magazine; the goal was to count them all.

Some of the contests even allowed those entering to be creative. One asked entrants to write a short paragraph that might illustrate the use of an Apple computer by a fictional or non-fictional historical figure (for example, Emperor Nero playing an adventure game in which he is trying to figure out the correct commands to burn down Rome).

By 1984, Softalk Publishing offered three other periodicals besides the magazine, *Softalk*. In cooperation with Apple II game publisher On-Line Systems (which later renamed itself Sierra On-Line), *Softline* began in September 1981. It was a bi-monthly magazine that focused on computer gaming, not only on the Apple II but also on other home computers. Its March 1984 issue was produced with a new name, *St.Game*, but its advertisers were getting insufficient return on their ads, and the May issue was cancelled. It also printed *Softalk* PC from June 1982 through August 1984, focusing on the IBM PC and its surrounding hardware and software industry. The new Macintosh got its own magazine, *St. Mac* starting in February 1984, and published monthly through August of that year.

Softalk Publishing also printed several books of material produced by *Softalk* columnists. Roger Wager's column became *Assembly Lines: The Book - A Beginner's Guide to 6502 Programming on the Apple II*, and Mark Pelczarski released a book titled *Graphically Speaking*.

At its peak, *Softalk* had a readership of 150,000, *St. Mac* had 30,000, and *Softalk PC* had 55,000 subscribers. Despite these healthy numbers, *Softalk* sud-

Hi-res turkeys! In the places where these appeared in the magazine, they were very tiny, about 3 mm wide by 5 mm tall – Photo credit: *Softalk*, November 1982

Softalk, final issue from August 1984 – Photo credit: personal

denly disappeared after the August 1984 issue. There was nothing that had indicated this was going to happen, and with its disappearance the Golden Age of the Apple II also passed. This ending could have been predicted by the way in which the magazine had shrunk in size over the previous few months, but its ending was still a shock to readers. One wrote later in the inaugural issue of Tom Weishaar's *Open-Apple* that had he known the magazine was in trouble, he would have taken up a collection for it. This sentiment was an example of the strong connection readers felt with the magazine.

According to an article in *InfoWorld*, Softalk Publishing had filed for Chapter 7 bankruptcy on August 22, which resulted in the liquidation of the company's assets. The attorney for the company stated they had attempted to find other sources of financing, but it had not worked out. A quote in *InfoWorld* given by Al Tommervik later that year indicated that management problems were more at fault in the failure of the magazine than were market factors. However, that same article discussed the difficulties that faced single-platform magazines in remaining profitable.[8,9]

What led to the bankruptcy of *Softalk*? Several factors played a role. One was the explosion in the number of new computer magazines between 1981 and 1983. Each magazine was yet another venue for a vendor to consider putting advertising dollars, and for small companies it was simply not affordable to put ads in all of them. Another factor was the introduction of the IBM PC, and the sudden need for software companies to produce versions of their programs for that computer. When the recession of 1982-84 arrived, the computer market began to lose steam, and small single-product companies either had to associate with larger ones or go out of business. Lower consumer spending on computer hardware and software hurt the market further, and advertising dollars were simply not available. *Softalk* became, unfortunately, one of the casualties.[10]

Another factor that contributed to the demise of *Softalk* was that it did not have a large publishing company backing it up; it was owned and operated by the Tommerviks and a few others in partnership, and they didn't have cash reserves that would allow them to cover expenses during periods of low advertising revenue.[11] Perhaps if a major publisher had taken an interest, *Softalk* would have been around for longer than its four short but eventful years.

At its height in December 1983, *Softalk* was over 400 pages long, but by its final issue in August 1984 it had shrunk down to only 128 pages. Although a next issue was in the works (according to the previews section in the table of contents), it never made it to the printer. Remaining subscriptions were filled out by *inCider* magazine, but sadly, the magic was gone.

---

8 Bartimo, Jim & Bergheim, Kim, "Softalk Files For Bankruptcy", *InfoWorld* (September 17, 1984), 12.
9 Bartimo, Jim, "Magazines Woo Users", *InfoWorld* (December 10, 1984), 35-36.
10 Golding, Val J, "The Magazine That Dared To Sing", *Call-A.P.P.L.E.* (October 1984), 34.
11 Statt, Paul, & Weishaar, Tom, "Old Timers: Apple II Magazines", *1991 A2-Central Summer Conference* (tapes) (July 1992).

APPLE ASSEMBLY LINE (Oct 1980 – May 1988)

Apple Assembly Line was something more than a newsletter, but not quite a magazine. It was initially produced by Bob Sander-Cederlof as a newsletter in support of his product, the *S-C Assembler II* and *S-C Macro Assembler*. Naturally, his initial focus was on the 6502 processor, but when the earliest 65c02 chips became available in the summer of 1983, he began to include coding examples that demonstrated the new opcodes. In October of 1984 the new 65802 and 65816 processors received a similar treatment in the pages of *Apple Assembly Line*.

The publication included information about how to write assembly language routines, and one of Sander-Cederlof's favorite pastimes was finding ways to squeeze the most code into the fewest bytes possible. Often he would take sections of code from Apple's system software, and later from *AppleWorks*, disassemble it, and explain how it could have been coded more tightly or efficiently. He also included products that he or others had written that were useful for other programmers, including a package of extensions for Applesoft that allowed 18 digit precision math functions.

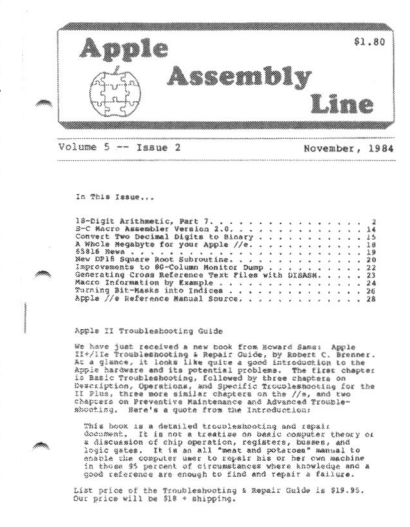

Apple Assembly Line, Nov 1984 – Photo credit: personal

By 1988 the Apple II market had receded to the point where renewals of Apple Assembly Line and sales of the S-C Assembler could no longer generate enough revenue to support Sander-Cederlof, and the May 1988 issue was the last.

COMPUTIST (Jul 1981 – Jul 1993)

By 1981, the Apple II software industry was going strong, and generating millions of dollars of revenue. But the successful companies feared the same scenario faced by Bill Gates when he discovered that the BASIC he had written for the Altair 8800 was being widely copied and given away at computer club meetings. To address this (and sometimes just to preserve programming secrets) software publishers devised a number of methods to make it harder to pirate their products. This was good for the publishers, but generally a nuisance for the honest software-buying public because they could not make legal backups for themselves.

To deal with this problem, some enterprising programmers created and sold software that made it possible to copy these protected disks, ostensibly for the purpose of making an archive copy in case the original went bad. The earliest of these programs were sold by Omega Microware (*Locksmith*), Sensible Software (*Back-It-Up!*), and Central Point Software (*Copy II Plus*). But these companies (particularly Omega Microware) had a problem; they were unable to advertise their products in the primary venue for software sales in the early 1980s—Apple II computer magazines. This was because when the software publishers (whose products might be copied) learned that one of these copy programs was about to run an advertisement in an upcoming issue, they threatened to boycott the magazine. Faced with a significant drop in revenue, and siding with those publishers, most magazines made the decision to refuse advertising for such products.

This action outraged Charles Haight. He stood on the side of those who felt it was their right to be able to copy software—to break the protection and the locks that had been placed on disks. Not only did he feel these programs should be sold just as freely as all others, he considered it a betrayal by the magazines towards their readers, and felt that the relationship between the magazines and the software publishers was just a little too cozy. Haight considered it an insult that he and others like him were categorized as pirates simply because they wanted a backup copy of the software that they had legally purchased. His stance led him to start his own company, Softkey Publishing, in 1981. The expression of his hard-core stance was the title of the magazine produced by that company: *Hardcore Computing*.

Haight made a strong declaration in his editorial in the very first issue of *Hardcore Computing*:

> HARDCORE...
> A *magazine dedicated to the Apple-users*
> ...
> When I acquired my Apple II+, I examined the spectrum of computer magazines that contained information for Apple-users. The list was large, yet none truly met my needs. I was after a magazine that had useful information for a true Apple-user (someone who wanted to get into the "core" of the Apple and all its peripherals). Most seemed to be peddling software, and doing it very uncritically.
>
> Then I became aware of a raging, silent battle between Apple-users and the magazines. The users were accusing the magazines of censorship, of hypocritically announcing their objective to be a magazine for Apple-users while encouraging the suppression of information (in this case, advertising about a program that would permit the user to make legal backups of protected disks). The magazines, on the other hand, were obliquely

accusing the Apple-users of being pirates and thieves. It was then I realized that most of the magazines had to take a stance against consumer "piracy" because those magazines were financially dependent on other software houses. It would be suicide for them to stand up for Apple-users.

This problem became more apparent when "Locksmith", a bit-copier that would make duplicates of many copy-protected diskettes, was censored (the magazines refused to publish the ad, thereby denying their readers the knowledge of the existence of such information.

That was censorship! And the battle was on. They knew that every serious Apple-user had both a need and a right to make back-up copies of protected disks.

Any magazine that took a stance against Apple-users could not be a magazine for me, no matter how large and profitable it was (for now I knew how they came to be so profitable; at the expense of their readership).[12]

Haight stated at the end of that first editorial that he expected it to be difficult to publish his magazine, since he would not be supported by advertising revenue from software publishers whose products his magazine would be trying to unlock. He stated that he expected it to be supported primarily by subscription.

Certainly he faced an uphill battle. Not only was it going to be a challenge to get software companies to advertise in Hardcore Computing (except those who sold products like Locksmith), but also the magazine was unable to advertise itself in other Apple II magazines. Like their ban on advertising products that could be used to circumvent copy protection, these other publications did not want to promote something that would be a source of education on the process of how to break that protection. In the pages of his magazine, Haight discussed the censorship problem, as well as issues involving copyrights and technology. The articles specifically stated that they were not in favor of duplication and distribution of unprotected software in such a way

Hardcore Computing #1 – Photo credit: Mike Maginnis

---

12 Haight, Charles, "What I Need Is A USERS Magazine", *Hardcore Computing* (Vol 1, No 1, 1981), 2.

that deprived sales to the publishers and authors of software; he just felt it was wrong to make it impossible to make a legal copy for the use of the purchaser of the product.

After the first issue of 32 pages, there was an update that Softkey Publishing sent out in September 1981, with info that they wanted to get into the hands of their readers before the next issue could be completed. Issue #2 was released in October 1981. At 64 pages in length, it not only continued to give information about breaking copy protection, but also how to *create* copy protection. And an opposing view editorial was printed in favor of copy protection for some products (an editorial that Haight strongly disagreed with, but was willing to print anyway).

In the third issue of *Hardcore Computing* from February 1982, further debate was held about the pros and cons of protection, and featured an interview with Mike Markkula of Apple Computer regarding comments he had made in favor of the elimination of copy protection at a Boston Computer Society forum in October 1981. Haight also announced that he was splitting his publication into two magazines: *Core*, which was to be a quarterly magazine with each issue focused on a different topic, and *Hardcore Computist*, which would have eight issues per year and continue to focus on methods of breaking software protection. These would all be covered with the same $20 per year subscription price.

By 1983, Softkey Publishing began to hit its stride, and the magazines produced began to take on a much more professional look. Despite Haight's original concerns about having no one willing to buy advertising in his magazine, in the first few years there were a number of companies who placed ads in the magazine, typically vendors who were not directly affected by breaking copy protection. These included hardware ads from Applied Engineering, and other smaller companies, including vendors of floppy disks; software companies selling their own disk copy products or software that they sold unprotected; assemblers (including the S-C Assembler II); and resellers who sold popular products from many different companies (including some whose publishers protected their programs). The quarterly *Core* came out as planned, but only three issues were ever published. Issue #1 appeared in Spring 1983, and focused on graphics. Plans announced in that first issue stated that *Core* #2 would be about utilities, #3 on databases, and #4 was to focus on games. Although the second issue did indeed appear as planned, the third release of *Core* became the games issue, and the story about databases was delayed. Further topics in the "Core" category later appeared as a column in *Hardcore Computist*.

As for *Hardcore Computist*, issue #1 was released in the beginning of 1983, carrying on with the same focus *Hardcore Computing* had delivered from the beginning. "Softkeys" were a list of steps needed to make a copy of a protected disk, and this first issue included Softkeys for Synergist Software's

Data Reporter, Microsoft's *Multiplan*, and Infocom's *Zork*. It also explained how to use parameters in Copy II Plus to copy a number of products. Further issues continued with more information about how disk protection worked, and how to remove it. Letters from readers also became a place to find new Softkeys to explain how to copy a particular product. The magazine also began to educate readers on how to trace the code used to boot a disk, using a specific product as an example. This knowledge assisted users in understanding how the copy protection process worked, and therefore how to better use the available copy products.

For the first four issues, the name "HARDCORE" dominated the title page. Beginning with issue #5, "Hardcore" appeared in smaller type, with "COMPUTIST" taking over a dominating position on the cover. Haight and his small staff of six had not been able to achieve their goal of eight issues per year, and so an advertisement in that issue announced the merger of *Core* with *Hardcore Computist*. Over the following year, the magazine reached its new goal of twelve issues per year. Issue #27 dropped the name "Hardcore" completely from the cover.

Over the next several years, the magazine continued to perform well. Each issue contained Softkey entries for various protected products. A column entitled "Input" contained letters from readers, sometimes with further information on copying disks. Another section called "Readers' Softkey & Copy Exchange" allowed readers to send in their

Computist #27 – Photo credit: Mike Magginnis

Computist #89 – Photo credit: Mike Maginnis

own Softkeys. Other articles contained product reviews or hardware hacking projects.

Like most other Apple II publications, the shrinking Apple II market gradually had an impact on *Computist*. Although it began as a glossy format magazine, this was discontinued with issue #45 in 1987, to reduce printing costs. Editor Haight decided by issue #47 that he would increase the page count back to 48, which he hoped would offset the loss of the stiff cover. An editorial in that issue also stated that he was combining the "Input" and "Readers' Softkey & Copy Exchange" pages into a single page, called "Readers Data Exchange" or RDEX (since the information in the two earlier columns seemed to leak across to each other).

Furthermore, he had decided that it was too time consuming to verify each set of user-submitted Softkeys, and elected to print it as-is, without verification—the readers would notify the magazine if there were errors, as they had in the past. Haight also had to make changes in how writers were paid for their contributions, to keep the magazine going. With that change, the magazine content shrunk to be primarily RDEX submissions and a catalog of back issues to purchase. Additionally, more and more readers were sending in their RDEX info directly on a floppy disk, which simplified putting it into the magazine (it did not have to be retyped and proofread). Eventually, Haight made disk submissions a requirement.

Starting in issue #52, *Computist* had tried to expand its readership by including Softkeys for protected IBM-PC and Macintosh program disks, though this did not continue for very long.

Again, as a cost-savings measure, *Computist* changed into a tabloid format with issue #66 in 1989. Haight discussed the reasoning for this. By this time, the operation had been reduced to Haight as editor, and one other person in charge of circulation. Volunteers who loved *Computist* and wanted to help keep it going handled the rest of the work to develop each issue. Sales of back issues and of disks containing programs featured in those back issues also helped subsidize the *Computist* operation. But even with that help, the magazine was barely hanging on. Due to costs, Haight decided that changing to the tabloid format was the most affordable way to keep the magazine going, continue to put out the same volume of information, and avoid raising subscription fees (to which most readers had strongly objected). He also reduced the print schedule to eight issues per year. And like many other magazines, he felt that this decline was directly related to Apple Computer's lack of clear support of the Apple II line.

By the end of its run, the publishing schedule became irregular, and rather than offering a subscription for 8 issues per year, the subscription was for

8 issues, whenever they could be released. Until the end of its run with issue #89, each new subscription still came with a tutorial on disk de-protection.[13]

As a whole, *Computist* is a historical treasure trove of information. One reason is that with the many products for which deprotection information was printed, these back issues contain one of the most comprehensive lists of Apple II software in existence, short of perusing ads from vendors in old magazines. Another reason is that it is a unique look at one side of the Apple II that no other magazine of the era provided. No one else took the controversial stand that Charles Haight did that it was the right of the owner of a piece of software to be able to make a backup copy of a disk, and no one else took such pains to make sure that this information was freely available to any and all. Without a doubt, the large number of disk images that eventually became available would have been much smaller were it not for this information on how to break copy protection. The knowledge that *Computist* accumulated also made it possible for emulators to run this old software.

TIMELINE

The start and end dates for homebrew Apple II and related computer magazines:

Interface Age
– July 1976 - December 1985

Micro – October 1977 - October 1984

Call-A.P.P.L.E.
– February 1978 - January 1990

Contact
– May 1978 - October 1979

Softside
– October 1978 - August 1984

Nibble – *January 1980 - July 1992*

Apple Orchard
– March 1980 - September 1984

Peelings II
– May 1980 - February 1984

Softalk
– September 1980 - August 1984

Apple Assembly Line
– October 1980 - May 1988

Computist – *July 1981 - July 1993*

---

13 Felty, Wes, A2 Roundtable, Category 2, Topic 16, *GEnie*, accessed October 1991.

CHAPTER 20

E for Enhanced

Between the years 1979 and 1983, although no new versions of the Apple II were released, it enjoyed a broad popularity and annually increasing sales. The open architecture of the computer, with its fully described hardware and firmware via its technical reference manual, made it appealing both to hardware and software hackers. Third-party companies designed cards to plug into the internal slots, and their function varied from making it possible to display and use 80-column text, provide clock and calendar functions, and allowing the Apple II to control a variety of external devices.

During this time there was also an explosion of new software written for this easily expandable machine, from the realm of business (*VisiCalc* and its successors), to utilities, to games of all types. Each month a host of new products arrived for those who wanted to find more things to do with their computer, and the Apple II was finding a place in the home, the classroom, and the office.

At Apple Computer, Inc., however, the Apple II was not viewed with the same degree of loyalty. Although it had continued to be very profitable to the company, there were sentiments within the company as early as September 1979 that it was unlikely the II could continue to be a best seller for more than another year or two. Since Apple Computer was a business, and not just a vehicle for selling the Apple II computer, they enlarged the engineering department and started designing new products.

THE APPLE III PROJECT

The earliest of these new design efforts was in the fall of 1977. According to the company's preliminary public stock offering documentation that year, two products were planned. One, tentatively called the Apple IIA, would have the same six-color hi-res graphics, a floating point BASIC in ROM, and come in a bundle with a color television and a cassette recorder (much like the products already being sold by Commodore and Radio Shack). It was to be sold at at $995 price point, and was to be announced at the January 1978 Consumer Electronics Show. The second, identified as the Apple IIB, was to be much like the IIA but with custom components to reduce cost, a cartridge port (with functionality of the slots on a standard Apple II), ports specifically for a printer and floppy disk, and a redesigned case. This was to be priced at $600 to $700, and would be announced at the June 1978 Consumer Electronics show. These products never made it past the planning stage.[1]

Engineers also began work on a different, more powerful computer that would use several identical microprocessor chips sharing tasks. The main advantage would be speed, and the ability to do high precision calculations. This computer was code-named Lisa, and because it was such a revolutionary design, they knew it would take several years to come to production. Because of the power it was to have, Apple executives felt that Lisa would be the future of the company.[2]

Those executives knew that since the Lisa project would take a long time to complete, and because the Apple II was perceived to have only a short life as a product, engineers began work on a separate computer called the Apple III, one that could be completed and brought to market sooner than Lisa. Instead of building upon the Apple II as a basis for this new computer, the design team decided to start from scratch.

Also, although Wozniak made most of the design decisions for the II, it was a marketing committee at Apple that decided what capabilities the Apple III should have. They decided to make the Apple III a business machine, without the home or arcade-game reputation that the II had. It was to have a full upper/lowercase keyboard and display, 80-column text, and a more comprehensive operating system. Also, since it would be a while before sufficient numbers of application programs would be available for this new computer, the committee decided it should be capable of running existing Apple II software. This actually handicapped the project, since it was then necessary to use the same microprocessor, disk drive hardware, and video display modes as were used in the Apple II.[3]

Apple executives also decided that with the introduction of the Apple III they wanted a clear separation between it and the Apple II with regards to marketing. They did not want any overlap between the two. The III would be an 80-column business machine and was predicted to have ninety percent of the market, while the Apple II would be a 40-column home and school machine and would have ten percent of the market. Apple's executives were confident that after the release of the Apple III, the Apple II would quickly lose its appeal.[4]

Because of this desire for a strong and distinct product separation, the Apple II emulation mode designed into the Apple III was purposely limited. The engineers actually added hardware chips that prevented access to the more advanced features of the Apple III from Apple II emulation mode. Ap-

---

1 -----, *Preliminary Confidential Offering Memorandum*, Apple Computer, Inc., circa October 1977. Of note, the date for first presentation of the Apple IIA was written as January 1977; this is certainly a typographic error, since that date had already passed at the time this document was created.
2 Freiberger, Paul and Michael Swaine, *Fire In The Valley, Second Edition*, (Berkley, Osborne/McGraw-Hill, 2000), 292-295.
3 Rubin, Charles. "The Life & Death & Life Of The Apple II", *Personal Computing*, (Feb 1985), 72.
4 Williams, Gregg, and Rob Moore. "The Apple Story, Part 2: More History And The Apple III", *BYTE*, (January 1985), 177-178.

ple II emulation couldn't use 80 columns, and had access to only 48K memory and none of the improved graphics modes. As a result, it wouldn't run some of the more sophisticated Apple II business software, during a time when there wasn't much business software for the Apple III.

The Apple III engineers were given a one-year target date for completion. The reason for this short cycle for research, development and production was because they knew IBM was working on their own product to enter the personal computer market, and Apple wanted to have a product ready to compete with them *before* IBM released theirs. Apple's engineers had their job complicated further because the marketing team continued to make changes in the specifications for the Apple III, while they were in the process of designing it.[5]

The Apple III was to have been ready for release in the spring of 1980, but there were problems with both design and manufacturing. (It was the first time that Apple as a company tried to come out with a new product; the Apple II had been designed and built by Wozniak when he was the sole member of the engineering department.) The release date was pushed back to September, and it did not begin to show up in quantity until December.[6] Tragically, the first run of Apple III computers was plagued with nearly 100% defects, resulting in a recall for fixes.[7] Despite the efforts that Apple took to fix these problems, even taking the step of repairing all of the defective computers at no charge, they never recovered the momentum they lost with that first mistake. With time, all of the bugs and limitations of the Apple III were overcome, and within Apple it became the computer of choice. However, it did not capture the favor of the market or become even mildly successful.[8]

Apple III and Silentype – Photo credit: Obsolete Technology Website <oldcomputers.net>

However, the company was not exactly sure that do with the Apple II. Despite Apple's neglect of it in the four years since the II Plus was released, it was the continued strong sales of this old computer that kept them in business. In a 1985 interview in *BYTE* magazine, Steve Wozniak stated:

---

5   Bishop, Bob, Keynote Address, KansasFest 2011, July 20, 2011.
6   Mitchell, John H. R., "The Apple III Appears", *InfoWorld* (February 16, 1981), 10-11.
7   An apocryphal story that I have for years included in this history on my web site was that a problem with the Apple III was heat production, which caused chips on the motherboard to come loose, requiring the computer be lifted a few inches and dropped to resolve. However, in an unpublished interview Mike Maginnis conducted with Wendel Sander in 2012, the actual problem was simply the memory board connector. Replacing this connector was the solution to the computer's problems. However, picking up and dropping the computer probably also likely temporarily resolved the memory connector problem.
8   Rubin, Charles. "The Life & Death & Life Of The Apple II", *Personal Computing*, (Feb 1985), 72.

> When we came out with the Apple III, the engineering staff cancelled every Apple II engineering program that was ongoing, in expectation of the Apple III's success. Every single one was cancelled. We really perceived that the Apple II would not last six months. So the company was almost all Apple III people, and we worked for years after that to try and tell the world how good the Apple III was, because we knew [how good it was]... If you looked at our advertising and R&D dollars, everything we did here was done first on the III, if it was business related. Then maybe we'd consider doing a sub-version on the II. To make sure there was a good boundary between the two machines, anything done on the II had to be done at a lower level than on the III. Only now are we discovering that good solutions can be implemented on the II... We made sure the Apple II was not allowed to have a hard disk or more than 128K of memory. At a time when outside companies had very usable schemes for adding up to a megabyte of memory, we came out with a method of adding 64K to the Apple IIe, which was more difficult to use and somewhat limited. We refused to acknowledge any of the good 80-column cards that were in the outside world – only ours, which had a lot of problems.[9]

Wozniak went on in that interview to say that at one time he had written some fast disk routines for the Pascal system on the Apple II, and was criticized by the Apple III engineers. They didn't think that anything on the II should be allowed to run faster than on a III. At that time, that was the mindset of the entire company.

Fans of the Apple II vocally criticized the attention the company gave the Apple III project, while ignoring the Apple II. The company had pegged its chances for the business market in 1980 on the Apple III, disregarding the inroads into business that already had been made by the Apple II. In a different interview, Wozniak stated, "We'd have sold tons of [computers in the business market] if we'd have let the II evolve ... to become a business machine called the III instead of developing a separate, incompatible computer. We could have added the accessories to make it do the business functions that the outside world is going to IBM for."[10]

Part of the problem was the immaturity of the entire microcomputer industry at the time. There had never been a microcomputer that had sold well for more than a couple of years before it was replaced by a more powerful model, often from another company. The Altair 8800 and IMSAI had fallen to the more popular and easier to use 1977 Trinity (Apple II, TRS-80 and Commodore PET), as well as other new machines based on the Intel

---

9 Williams, Gregg, and Rob Moore. "The Apple Story, Part 2: More History And The Apple III", *BYTE*, (January 1985), 177-178.
10 Rubin, Charles. "The Life & Death & Life Of The Apple II", *Personal Computing*, (Feb 1985), 72.

8080 and 8088 processors. It is entirely understandable that Apple's attitude between 1978 and 1980 would be of panic and fear that they wouldn't get a new computer out in time to keep their market share and survive as a company. However, during the period when Apple was working on the III as a computer to carry the company through until Lisa would be ready, the Apple II continued to quietly climb in sales, despite being virtually ignored by the company. It is a credit to both the ingenuity of Wozniak in his original design, and to the users of the Apple II in their resourcefulness at finding new uses for the II, that its value increased and stimulated yet more new sales. The Apple II beat the odds of survival that historically and corporately were against it.

THE APPLE IIE: BEGINNINGS

When Apple saw that the sales on the Apple II were not dwindling away, they finally decided to take another look at it. The first new look at advancing the design of the II was a project called "Diana" in 1980. Diana was intended primarily to be an Apple II that had fewer internal components, and would be less expensive to build. The project was later known as LCA, which stood for "Low Cost Apple". Inside Apple this meant a lower cost of manufacturing, but outsiders who got wind of the project thought it meant a $350 Apple II. Because of that misconception, Apple went into propaganda mode and changed the project code name to "Super II".[11]

HARDWARE

Engineer Walt Broedner had formerly worked at Synertek Systems, a semiconductor manufacturer that had supplied chips for the Apple III project. Broedner had done significant work on creating custom integrated circuits for that computer, and in 1981 he started looking at ways that the same custom work could be extended to the Apple II. Specially designed chips would have the double benefit of reducing the number of components on the Apple II motherboard, as well as making it more difficult to clone.

Broedner pushed to not only make the Apple II less costly to build, but also to add new features. Initially he had planned to give the Apple II an 80-column text display and a full upper/lowercase keyboard. To help maintain compatibility with older 40-column software (which often addressed the screen directly for speed), he decided to make 80-columns work by mirroring the older 40-column text screen onto a parallel 1K memory space, with the even columns in main memory and the odd columns in this new auxiliary memory.

---

11 Tommervik, Al. "Apple IIe: The Difference", *Softalk*, Feb 1983: 118-127, 142.

To display 80-column text would require switching between the two memory banks. Broedner realized that with little extra effort he could do the same for the entire 64K memory space and get 128K of bank-switchable memory. They put this extra memory (the 1K "80-column card" or a 64K "extended 80-column card") in a special slot called the auxiliary slot that replaced slot 0. The previously released 16K Language Card had mirrored the upper memory where BASIC and the Monitor were mapped, allowing other programming languages to be used. That card had made the Apple II into a full 64K computer, and was designed to be used in slot 0. On the Apple IIe, the Language Card RAM would become a built-in feature.

Apple IIe nameplate – Photo credit: personal

The 80-column firmware routines were mapped to slot 3, since that was a location commonly used by people who bought 80-column cards for their Apple II computers, and was also the place where Apple Pascal expected to find an external terminal. The auxiliary RAM slot also supplied some special video signals, and was used during manufacture for the purpose of testing the motherboard.

The engineers who worked on the IIe tried hard to make sure that cards designed for the II and II Plus worked properly in the new computer. They even had to "tune" the timing on the IIe to be slightly off (to act more like the II Plus) because the Microsoft SoftCard refused to function properly with the new hardware.

A socket was included on the motherboard for attaching a numeric keypad, a feature that many business users had been adding (with difficulty) to the II Plus for years. The full 63-key keyboard they designed was similar to the one found on the Apple III. This included an auto-repeat feature, where holding a key down for more than a second caused the character to repeat. This new feature was especially helpful for cursor movements using the arrow keys. For touch typists, they included a raised bump on the D, K, and a cursor key.[12]

Apple IIe power light & Open-Apple key – Photo credit: David Finnigan

The new keyboard also included two unique keys that had first appeared with the III—one with a picture of a hollow apple ("open-apple") and the other with the same apple picture filled in ("solid-apple"). These keys were connected to buttons 0 and 1 on the Apple paddles or joystick. They were available to software designers as modifier keys when pressed with another key; for example, open-apple-H could be programmed to call up a

---

12 Goodman, Danny, "The Apple IIe personal computer; a first hand examination", *Creative Computing* (March 1983), 116-130.

help screen. The newer keyboard electronics also made it easier to manufacture foreign language versions of the Apple IIe.[13]

The RESET key was important to regain control of the computer under certain circumstances. However, its location on the Apple II and II Plus just above the RETURN key made it a frequent accidental target. On the IIe, the RESET key was placed to the right of the keyboard proper and shaped differently.

Broedner created two custom chips for the IIe. The Memory Management Unit (MMU) contained the Applesoft BASIC language, the code for 80 and 40-column support, other ROM code, and the circuitry that handled reading the keyboard. The Input/Output Unit (IOU) controlled the video display, the legacy cassette interface, and speaker. He gave Synertek his design for these chips in June 1981, and by December of that year he had working chips back from them.[14]

Over all, Broedner and Peter Quinn (the design manager for the IIe and later the IIc projects) and their team managed to decrease the number of components on the motherboard from over one hundred to thirty-one, while adding to the capabilities of the computer by the equivalent of another hundred components.

FIRMWARE

Quinn had to beg for someone to help write the firmware revisions to the Monitor and Applesoft for the IIe. He finally got Rick Auricchio, who had been a hacker on the Apple II almost from the beginning. Quinn said in a later interview, "You cannot get someone to write firmware for this machine unless he's been around for three or four years. You have to know how to get through the minefield [of unofficial but commonly used entry points]. He [Rick] was extremely good. He added in all the 80-column and Escape-key stuff."[15, 16]

Changes were made in the ROMs to support the new bank-switching modes made necessary by having two parallel 64K banks of RAM memory. To have enough firmware space for these extra features, the engineers increased the size of the available ROM by making it bank-switched. Auricchio further enhanced the screen editing to allow use of the left and right arrow keys and the new up and down arrow keys. When the 80-column firmware was active, this editing mode was identified by displaying an inverse plus-sign cursor when it was active. The new IIe ROM also included a self-test that was activated by pressing both apple keys, the control key, and RESET simultaneously.[17]

---

13 Williams, Gregg, "'C' Is For Crunch", *BYTE* (Dec 1984), A75-A78, A121.
14 Goodman, Danny, "The Apple IIe personal computer; a first hand examination", *Creative Computing* (March 1983), 116-130.
15 Williams, Gregg, "'C' Is For Crunch", *BYTE* (Dec 1984), A75-A78, A121.
16 Little, Gary, *Inside The Apple //c*, (Bowie, Maryland, Brady Communications Company, Inc., 1985), 1-7.
17 Tommervik, Al. "Apple IIe: The Difference", *Softalk*, Feb 1983: 118-127, 142.

SUCCESS

Apple announced the new IIe at its annual stockholders meeting on January 19, 1983, alongside the more glamorous and powerful Apple Lisa. Though the Lisa was trumpeted as the future of business computers, Apple was smart enough to know where its primary revenue was to be found. The $9,995 Lisa was still in beta testing, and would not be available for purchase until June of 1983. The Apple IIe could be purchased at authorized dealers within a couple of weeks of its announcement, and in its 64K configuration sold for $1,395.

To promote the IIe, Apple ran two-page magazine ads that proclaimed, "It's the same old Apple II. Except for the front, back and inside." The ad pointed out its larger memory, the improved keyboard that allowed input of the full standard ASCII character set (including lowercase), the 80-column display, superior construction and included self-diagnostics. Technically capable users could (and often did) add most of these improvements to the older models through third-party vendors. Now, for a price that was almost the same as the II Plus that it replaced, nearly all of the most popular and desireable features came standard.

Apple IIe system, with Duodisk and monochrome monitor, at Computer History Museum, Moutain View, California – Photo credit: Marcin Wichary

Al Tommervik of *Softalk* wrote about the Apple IIe:

> [Apple's] update to the Apple II is a thoughtful amalgam of hardware changes that honors the software and peripherals industries that have made Apple II the most used and the most useful microcomputer. That homage to the past has been a salient point in each change Apple has made to their II series, and the installed base of Apple owners can take great comfort in knowing that the company has remained steadfast in their dedication to their old constituency. Even the major revisions executed to accomplish the IIe do not disenfranchise owners of older systems, nor do they invalidate most already existing software and peripherals.[18]

BYTE magazine also pointed out Apple's efforts at maintaining compatibility with the past:

---

18 Tommervik, Al. "Apple IIe: The Difference", *Softalk*, Feb 1983: 119-120.

> Rather than start from scratch and design an entirely new machine, Apple Computer Inc. chose to make a very careful series of enhancements and improvements while keeping the flavor and style of the Apple II. Although completely redesigned internally, the Apple IIe is clearly a member of the Apple II family.[19]

The new Apple IIe did very well for Apple. Not only was it more functional than the II Plus for a similar price, but Apple was able to sell it to dealers for about three times what it cost to manufacture. The company had gotten its "Low Cost Apple", and by May of 1983 the Apple IIe was selling sixty to seventy thousand units a month—over twice the average sales of the II Plus.

The Apple IIe had its success in the middle segment of the market, competing with the IBM PC business market. This happened even in the context of lower-end competing home computers being sold for significantly lower prices. Tommervik's comments about the Apple II being "the most used" microcomputer either represented an acceptance of Apple's advertising propaganda, or a lack of knowledge about the market share of the Apple II platform relative to some of its competitors. During the early 1980s, Commodore had captured the low end of the market with its Commodore 64, which initially sold for only $595. Commodore's later price war with the Texas Instruments TI-99/4A ultimately forced that company out of the home computer business by the latter part of 1983. Although not Commodore's direct target in the war, the $899 Atari 800 was also adversely affected by this price war, and gradually lost market share as the Commodore 64 continued to climb in sales. But riding over all of the carnage in the low end, the Apple IIe did well enough to continue to carry the company through its struggles in finding a successful replacement.

> Early Apple IIe motherboards were labeled as "Revision A". Engineers determined soon after its introduction that if the same use of parallel memory was applied to the hi-res graphics display as was done with the text display, they could create higher density graphics. These graphics, which they called "double hi-res", also had the capability of displaying a wider range of colors, similar to those available with the original Apple II lo-res graphics. The IIe motherboards with the necessary modifications to display these double hi-res graphics were labeled "Revision B", and a soft switch was assigned to turn on and off the new graphics mode.[20]

---

19 Moore, Robin, "Apple's Enhanced Computer, the Apple IIe", *BYTE* (February 1983), 68.
20 Weishaar, Tom, "Ask Uncle DOS", *Open-Apple*, (December 1986), 2.86.

THE ENHANCED IIE

The enhanced version of the Apple IIe was introduced in March of 1985. It involved changes to make the IIe more closely compatible with the Apple IIc and II Plus. The upgrade kit (for previous IIe owners) consisted of four chips that were swapped in the motherboard: The 65c02 processor, with more assembly language opcodes, replaced the 6502; two more chips with Applesoft and Monitor ROM changes; and the fourth chip was a character generator ROM that included graphics characters (first introduced on the IIc) called "MouseText".

> The Enhanced IIe ROM changes fixed most of the known problems with the IIe 80-column firmware, and made it possible to enter Applesoft and Monitor commands in lower-case. The older 80-column routines were slower than most software developers wanted; they disabled interrupts for too long a time. Also, there were problems in making Applesoft work properly with the 80-column routines. These problems were solved with the newer ROMs.

Apple IIe Enhanced keyboard and power light
– Photo credit: personal

For those who purchased the Enhanced IIe new, there were modifications to the appearance of the keyboard, including a darker color to the keys, a smaller size of the typeface on the keys, a change to black color for the keycap text, and movement of the character to the upper part of the key. Also, the power light had the word "Enhanced" added to it, to help distinguish it from the original Apple IIe. (This sticker was also included in the upgrade kit).

Monitor changes also included a return of the mini-assembler, absent since the days of Integer BASIC. It was activated by entering a "!" followed by RETURN in the Monitor, instead of a jump to a memory location as in the older Apple II. Other new features included the ability to enter ASCII characters directly into memory, and an "S" command to make it possible to search memory for a byte sequence. Interrupt handling was also improved. However, the "L" command to disassemble 6502 code still did not handle the new 65c02 opcodes as it did with the disassembler in the Apple IIc.

Applesoft was modified in the Enhanced IIe ROMs to let commands such as GET, HTAB, TAB, SPC, and comma tabbing work properly in 80-column mode.

The new MouseText characters caused a problem for some older programs at first, until they were revised; characters previously displayed as inverse upper case would sometimes display as MouseText instead.[21, 22]

With the release of the Enhanced IIe, there was finally an Apple II easily adaptable to the foreign market. The German version was built with an external switch below the keyboard, allowing the user to change between a standard U.S. layout and a German layout. (American versions of the IIe lacked the switch, but had a place on the motherboard that could be modified to select a Dvorak keyboard layout instead of the standard keyboard.)

TIMELINE

The start and end dates for each model of the Apple IIe and Apple III:

Apple III – *September 1980 - November 1983*

Apple IIe – *January 1983 - February 1985*

Apple III Plus – *December 1983 - April 1984*

Apple IIe Enhanced – *March 1985 - December 1986*

---

21 Weishaar, Tom, "A Song Continued", *Open-Apple*, (March 1985), 1.20-1.21.
22 Weishaar, Tom, "Demoralized Apple II Division Announces Enhanced IIe...", *Open-Apple*, (April 1985), 1.25-1.27.

CHAPTER 21
DOS Gets Professional

SOS

The next big innovation for the Apple II was ProDOS, which resulted from the ill-fated Apple III and its custom operating system. The code name for the Apple III was Sara, which came from the name of engineer Wendell Sander's daughter. Since the computer was called Sara, the disk operating system created for it was, then, Sara's Operating System, or SOS. Marketing decided to keep the SOS name, but chose the more professional name of Sophisticated Operating System.

SOS was the first operating system for a microcomputer to use the concept of device drivers—code segments taken from the startup disk and made part of the operating system. These drivers told the computer how to communicate with the various devices that were attached to it, from disk drives to printers and modems to the keyboard and monitor. This gave flexibility to the Apple III to use new technology as it became available.[1]

When Apple's engineers designed the Apple III, they were under constraints of maintaining some compatibility with the Apple II disk format. It was felt necessary to continue to use the same disk controller and the same capacity disks as the Pascal/DOS 3.3 systems: 35 tracks of 16 sectors each. However, they were free to make any changes in the way in which files were stored on the disk. What was created was something that was a hybrid between the Apple DOS and Pascal System methods of file storage.

From Pascal they took three things: the concept of using 512-byte blocks as the basic unit of storage, with a one block system loader program at the start of the disk (this loader would locate a larger system file elsewhere on the disk to actually start the operating system), and a four-block main catalog (which they called a directory). They also brought over the feature of a time-stamp (including both date and time), and the 15-character file name using only letters, numbers, and a period.

---

[1] Deatherage, Matt, "The Operating System", *The Apple II Guide* (Cupertino, CA, Apple Computer, Inc., Fall 1990), 117-125.

From DOS 3.3 they used the concept of disk maps and block lists for each file, allowing parts of files to be stored anywhere on the disk (and eliminating the need for the Pascal "Krunch" function). The SOS filing system also continued the use from DOS 3.3 of a byte to identify different filetypes, but greatly expanded the number of filetypes.

The Apple DOS directory structure provided only a single level of files—one long list that could make it hard to find a particular file if there were many on the disk. Because the Apple III was intended to be a business machine and had to be able to access larger disk devices than were standard for the Apple II, they also added the ability to create and use different levels of file directories—which they called subdirectories (commonly known as folders in modern computer usage). A single four-block directory on an SOS disk had space for 51 files; even if it had been expanded to more than four blocks to allow more files, on a large disk it would soon become difficult to find a file in a list that grew longer than a couple of hundred names. The use of subdirectories made it easier to (and almost enforced the need to) organize files.

> With the subdirectory structure came the concept of pathnames. A legal pathname for SOS started with a slash, followed by the name of the disk, followed by either the name of the desired file, or the name of another subdirectory. There was a practical limit to the depth of subdirectories, because SOS could only handle a pathname up to 65 characters in length (which had to include the slash character). Rarely was this limit a problem, and if it was, the solution was to use shorter directory names.
>
> With this structure, the pathname to a file named AMAZING.STUFF, within a subdirectory named WP, which was itself in a subdirectory named TEXT, on a disk called WORK, would be:
>
> ```
> /WORK/TEXT/WP/AMAZING.STUFF
> ```
>
> This allowed organization of similar files in named subdirectories that identified their function or what they had in common. It made it much easier to find a particular file, if the user chose to spend a little time organizing how files were stored.

The SOS disk file system also allowed a single file as large as 16 MB, and a single disk volume (storage device) could be up to 32 MB in size. In 1981, when Apple had just released the 5 MB Profile hard disk for the Apple III at a cost of $3,499, this limit of 32 MB was considered more than adequate.

XDOS

The original DOS for the Apple II was designed primarily to support BASIC. If a programmer wanted to make use of the disk system from within an assembly language program, he had to make use of undocumented, low level calls to the DOS File Manager, or possibly to some of the Main DOS Routines. This method was clumsy, and often made inefficient use of memory, as DOS expected that any calls made to it were done on behalf of BASIC. Moreover, this tied the hands of programmers at Apple in their ability to enhance DOS, since any changes they might make would most likely change internal addresses, and cause older software to malfunction if used with the revised DOS.

Another problem with DOS was speed. Since each byte read from the disk was copied between memory buffers *three* times, much of the disk access time was spent moving data around in memory. Consequently, as hackers took DOS apart and found better ways to do things, several variations of DOS speed-up programs appeared by 1983, including *Diversi-DOS*, *ProntoDOS*, and *David-DOS*. Each of these programs was mutually incompatible in terms of the low-level calls they made, and had slightly different ways of speeding up DOS.

Other problems with DOS included poor support for interrupt signals generated by various hardware devices, obstacles in designating protected memory areas from being overwritten by DOS, and difficulty customizing DOS for special functions.

Engineers at Apple knew about these problems. One of them in particular, Dick Huston, began to push for an update to DOS 3.3 as early as 1980. In October of that year he wrote up specifications for a new DOS, trying to address all of these limitations. In the next year, he took things a step further in promoting his project by writing a memo called "Why A New DOS". In that memo, he made mention of comments made by Mike Markkula soon after he became CEO in 1981. Markkula had stated that it was expected that the Apple II would continue to sell well through at least 1983, and that although by then the sales would flatten, they would continue to sell at the rate of 25,000 systems per month through at least 1987. In his memo, Huston took these predictions and pointed out that there was at that time (1980) an estimated user base of 200,000 Apple II users. Markkula's forecast, if accurate, meant that there could potentially be 1.5 million new Apple II systems by 1987. This large potential customer base, in addition to the limitations currently in DOS 3.3, were compelling reasons to creation a new operating system that would accommodate the larger storage devices customers would demand for the Apple II.

Huston pointed out problems with several current software programs that made it difficult if not impossible to use disk drives other than the 140K Disk II. *The Controller*, a small business management and accounting program sold by Apple, *EDASM* (Apple's 6502 assembler), *VisiCalc*, and *DB Master* all had custom ways of loading and saving files that were locked to the Disk II. Corvus sold a hard drive that used a modified version of Apple DOS to allow access to its 10 MB of storage, and *FID*, Apple's file management program, could not be used with that hard drive because it was tied to using only slot and driver parameters in identifying a disk. To work on an Apple II, the Corvus was partitioned into multiple 140K volumes, and under Applesoft or Integer BASIC it depended on the little-used "Volume" parameter. FID, however, had not been written to be able to use that feature and could not manage files on Corvus with its patched DOS.

Having identified these problems, Huston outlined the argument for a completely new DOS. Simply updating to a DOS 3.4 would not fix these problems without breaking software that was already making use of direct, undocumented calls to DOS routines. Furthermore, DOS was limited to a fixed number of files per disk, and had no ability to organize them into subdirectories. Since a major change would be needed anyway, he proposed that they make a complete break with the structure of DOS 3.3 and the past, and make use of the file system that had been designed for SOS on the Apple III. That disk system allowed for up to 32 megabytes per disk volume, individual files potentially as large as 16 megabytes in size, and a more robust directory arrangement. It would also have the side advantage of making file sharing between the Apple II and Apple III simpler.

Because the changes Huston proposed were going to change many facets of the disk system, from the way in which files were named to ways programs interacted with it, he proposed it be called XDOS instead of DOS 4.0. This different name would make it clear that it was a significant change from the older system, and was not just an update. In planning for the changes, engineers also had to anticipate what changes would be needed to software that Apple sold to make them work with the new system. These programs include *Apple Writer*, *Apple Plot* (a graphing program), *The Controller*, *Apple PILOT* (a programming language aimed at education), and *Apple Post* (a mailing list program).[2]

Under this more advanced disk operating system, BASIC was just one of many possible applications to interact with a storage device. The part of DOS that worked with BASIC in ROM was separated out from the rest of the disk routines. Early specifications planned support for both Applesoft and Integer BASIC, as well a standardized way for disk access for non-BASIC applications.[3]

---

2 One of the other concerns that engineers at Apple were trying at this time to address was software piracy. The methods that were currently being used for DOS 3.3 could still work, but were specific to the Disk II drive, and did not allow moving a program onto a larger drive. As far back as 1978, Apple had been working on a higher capacity disk drive to ultimately replace the Disk II drive. Engineers had come up with a different design for disks which they called Fileware disks. These disks had two opposing ovals for two read/write heads to access the disk, to allow for greater density storage, and the design was ultimately used in the Lisa. Also, the disks had space for 12 extra bytes per block that could be used as a key to authenticate the disk as valid (that is, not an unauthorized copy). Potentially, this same scheme could allow the program to be legally copied to a hard drive. The disk drives, best known by their code name, "Twiggy", and in service manuals as Apple 871 drives, were developed far enough to have a product name, Unifile and Duofile, for single and dual drive units that were to eventually be sold for the Apple II and III. Due to significant problems with reliability, these were ultimately scrapped in favor of Sony's 3.5-inch drive. Presumably, the plans for program-specific anti-piracy keys also disappeared with these drives.

3 Huston, Dick, Personal notes, 1981-1982.

The XDOS project was stopped and restarted several times, due to politics within Apple. Some years later, at the 1992 A2-Central Developer's Conference, someone asked event organizer Tom Weishaar why Apple made a certain decision about an unrelated issue, and his answer was applicable to the XDOS saga. He responded, "[People] have this vision of Apple as an organism with a brain. And I don't think that's a correct metaphor." He went on to explain that the company was a collection of many different goals and people and egos, and all of those factors led to different outcomes of the many projects going on in the company at any one time.[4] The success of a project usually depended on a champion who pushed hard for a project and worked on it even when it was set aside. For ProDOS, that champion was Dick Huston, who originally anticipated only a few months of work would be needed to bring the XDOS project to completion. During the time that Huston was singlehandedly working on the kernel and the Applesoft interface, his position within the company changed several times. He was moved to work in the Disk Division, coding for the ProFile hard drive (which he named), then moved to the Apple II/III systems group, and later moved to a project working with Steve Jobs on the Macintosh. But no matter what else he worked on, Huston eventually kept coming back to XDOS.

Finally in 1983, soon after the release of the Apple IIe, the XDOS project had been given its final product name "ProDOS" and was in its final stages to prepare for production and distribution, including artwork and design of the manuals. Then, at the last minute, it was again cancelled. There were powerful voices within the company that expressed concern that ProDOS would confuse customers, since it used the same file system as SOS. They argued that since the Apple III was targeted as the direct competitor to the IBM PC, and the Apple II was the company's home and education computer, this would potentially dilute the impact of the Apple III. Furthermore, the Lisa was a significantly better product than the Apple II, and the Macintosh that was coming soon would also be a big player.

The reality of the situation was that the Apple III was barely turning a profit, the Lisa was not doing well, and the Macintosh was still a year away from release, while the Apple II (and the new IIe) was still selling quite well and actually growing in sales. Dick Huston took his concerns directly to Mike Markkula, who allowed him to present it to Apple's board of directors, asking approval for the release of ProDOS.

According to Huston, one of the rumors circulating at the time was that Rupert Lissner, author of */// E-Z Pieces* on the Apple III, had been able in just a week's time to convert it to run under ProDOS in the Apple II. If Apple management killed ProDOS, Lissner was fully prepared to buy it from Apple

---

4   Weishaar, Tom, "Old-Timers: Magazines", audio-tape, *A2-Central Developer's Conference*, 1992.

and distribute it himself, in order to sell his conversion. (Had this come to pass, it most likely would not have been called *AppleWorks*.)[5]

After some deliberation, Apple's board of directors decided that the marketplace should decide how well ProDOS was accepted, and not a committee within the company. They approved the final release of ProDOS, and it was shipped to dealers for sale to customers. Sadly, this victory for the Apple II came at a price. Due to politics, several individuals lost their jobs for having backed Huston's project despite orders from their supervisors, including Huston's marketing partner on the project.

PRODOS

The result of Huston's work was finally released in 1983 as ProDOS, the "Professional Disk Operating System". It addressed all of the weaknesses inherent in Apple DOS. ProDOS could access 5.25-inch disks up to eight times faster than DOS. It supported a standardized protocol for hardware-based devices, allowing reads, writes, status calls, and formatting. This broke free of dependence on the aging Disk II drive, and made it possible to use a variety of disk devices on an Apple II. Support was also included to handle an optional hardware clock, which allowed date and time stamping of files. Hardware interrupts were supported, necessary system calls were placed in a standard location in memory (called a global page), and blocks of memory could be protected from being overwritten by the actions of ProDOS.

The robust file system created for SOS was utilized in the design of ProDOS. The limited single-letter filetypes that DOS had used (I, A, B, T, and so on) were replaced with the SOS concept of single-byte filetype codes, from $00 to $FF. The codes in the lower part of the range were reserved primarily for SOS filetypes or for the disk system itself. Those in the upper range were used for ProDOS-specific files. On the Apple II, the most commonly used ones were:

$04	TXT	text file
$06	BIN	binary file
$0F	DIR	subdirectory file
$F0 - $F8		user defined filetypes
$FC	BAS	Applesoft BASIC source file
$FD	VAR	Applesoft BASIC variables file
$FF	SYS	ProDOS system file

A few of the available filetypes were eventually approved to use with software released for the Apple II. Filetypes in the range from $B0 to $EF that were later used for system

---

5 Huston, Dick, email to author, May 9, 2012.

> files on the Apple IIgs, and with time many of the remaining filetypes were either officially assigned by Apple or appropriated by software authors.

The boot code on ProDOS disks included code to allow such a disk to successfully start up on an Apple III, if the appropriate SOS system files were included. Thus, the same disk could be used to start either type of computer, depending on which system files resided on the disk.

Even after the Apple III had been out of production for years, disks formatted by the Apple II System Utilities still had SOS boot information located on block 1. It was not until several years later that Apple no longer required utilities the formatted a disk to put the SOS boot code on block 1 of the disk.

The PRODOS file contained code that was similar to RWTS and the File Manager in DOS.[6] This code was moved to the 16K bank switched RAM (and so left as much of the main 48K of memory available as was possible). It would then look for the first file in the root (or main) directory with a filetype SYS whose name ended in ".SYSTEM". That file would be loaded into memory and executed. This made it possible for a specialized program (such as a word processor) to not have to compete for space in memory with operating system code that was only used to manage BASIC.

To specifically support Applesoft BASIC, a boot disk would have to include a file named BASIC.SYSTEM. That file included code that worked nearly the same as Main DOS Routines in DOS. In addition, it included further enhancements that had been requested for years by Applesoft programmers. For example, Apple DOS already had the commands BLOAD and BSAVE commands that were used to move binary data to and from the disk from memory, but only could operate on the entire file at once. Under ProDOS, these commands had parameters that offered enough precision to move as little as a single byte to a specific location in a binary file.

HELLO was the name of the standard BASIC startup program used in DOS. Under ProDOS, BASIC.SYSTEM would look in the directory it started from for *any* executable file named STARTUP (usually an Applesoft program, but could be a binary file, system file, or text file with ProDOS or Applesoft commands to execute).

BASIC.SYSTEM was designed so that programs written for Apple DOS would be relatively simple to update. It continued the tradition of watching output from a program for a Ctrl-M follow by a Ctrl-D to signal a disk command to the operating system. It also still used the relatively primitive text-only data storage as had existed since the first version of DOS was released, and

---

6 Wozniak, Stephen, telephone interview with author, September 5, 1991.

did not try to improve that aspect of data file management. The commands used for text file management were almost the same as those used in DOS, although some types (such as the Volume parameter to choose a specific DOS volume) were no longer necessary, whereas others were enhanced.

The only theoretical disadvantage of the new ProDOS was that it did not support Apple's original Integer BASIC, since ProDOS loaded itself into high memory where Integer BASIC was loaded in an Apple II Plus. However, little software development had been done in Integer BASIC since the introduction of Applesoft, so this was felt to be a reasonable trade-off. If Integer BASIC was needed, it could still run under DOS 3.3. Neither Apple nor any other company ever created an INTBASIC.SYSTEM file to allow Integer BASIC programs to run under ProDOS, with the exception of an Integer BASIC compiler (which ran only on the IIGS) distributed by The Byte Works in late 1991 for instructional purposes.[7]

The user experience was improved for those who used ProDOS from Applesoft. While in 40-column mode, the command to display a disk catalog was changed from CATALOG to just CAT. On the list that was displayed, it carried over from Apple DOS the same all-uppercase filenames, preceded by an asterisk character to identify a file that was locked. The filetype column now followed the file name, and showed the three character codes for the most common types encountered on an Apple II. A directory would have the type "DIR", and if an uncommon filetype was stored on the disk, it could be displayed by its hex code (for example, "$0C" instead of "SOS", which was an Apple III SOS system file).

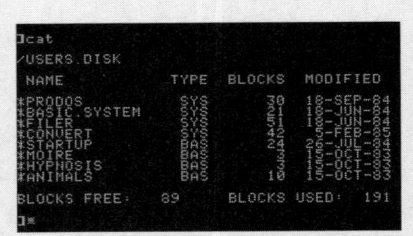

40-column catalog from BASIC.SYSTEM
– Photo credit: personal

Following the filetype code, the file size was displayed in blocks, followed by the date the file was last modified. If there had not been a date set when the file was changed, this entry might read "<NO DATE>". There were utilities available that allowed the user to manually enter a date and time, so that null date would not appear.

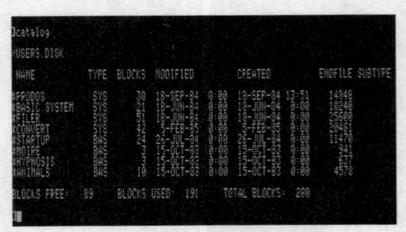

At the bottom of the catalog was a count of available free blocks on the disk, followed by a count of how many blocks were used by files on the disk.

When in 80-column mode, the disk catalog displayed by BASIC.SYSTEM provided additional information. Typing the command CATALOG would produce a detailed listing that spanned the entire screen. It provided

80-column catalog from BASIC.SYSTEM
– Photo credit: personal

---

7   Don Worth and Peiter Lechner, *Beneath Apple DOS* (Quality Software, Reseda, CA, 1984), 2.1-2.9.

the same information as in the 40-column version, but added a field for the time following the date the file was modified, and another pair of columns displayed the date and time the file was originally created.

The two final columns were ENDFILE (which gave the size of the file in bytes), and SUBTYPE, which displayed a little additional information, depending on what kind of file was in the catalog (for example, a binary file, filetype BIN, showed A$=$2000 if the file was designed to load and execute starting at $2000 in memory).

The last line added count of the total number of available blocks on the disk.

The ProDOS Users Disk distributed with the early versions of the new operating system included two important utilities and a few demo programs. FILER replaced the Apple DOS FID program, to allow file copy, disk formatting, and other useful file management functions. CONVERT made it possible to exchange files between a DOS 3.3 disk and a ProDOS disk.

ProDOS also added a feature that made the extra 64K of RAM on a 128K Apple IIe available to the average user for scratch file storage. It automatically created a RAM disk out of that space, giving it the name /RAM, and assigning it to slot 3, drive 2. It offered 127 blocks of storage, just under half of the space on a 5.25-inch disk (which was 280 blocks in size). It was a great place for fast, temporary storage of files, and on a single-drive system it made it easier to move files from one disk to another, using /RAM as an intermediate holding place.

For system programs that were designed to make use of all 128K of RAM, programmers could remove this virtual disk from the list of available drives.

Unlike Apple DOS, which by default used space for a copy of itself on every disk, a ProDOS disk offered the flexibility of allowing a data-only disk that had no operating system on it; all that was necessary was to format a disk and not copy the file PRODOS or any SYSTEM file onto the disk.

Since BASIC.SYSTEM was just one of many different possible system files that ProDOS could run, one could leave Applesoft by entering the command BYE, which displayed a screen that required entry of the pathname of another system file to execute. Later enhancements to this code made it possible to select a SYSTEM program through the use of the arrow and RETURN keys (eliminating the need to type the full pathname).

It is a credit to the Apple III design team that the SOS file system had the power and flexibility that this system, designed in 1978 or 1979, was still completely adequate for Apple II computers into the 1990s and beyond.[8]

---

8 Hunter, Skillman. "Road Maps To Apple II Disks: DOS 3.3, CP/M, Pascal, and ProDOS", *Call-A.P.P.L.E.* (February 1985), 10-21.

TIMELINE

The start dates for Apple DOS, Pascal, CP/M, SOS, and ProDOS:

Apple Pascal – *August 1979*
Apple CP/M – *March 1980*
DOS 3.3 – *August 1980*
Apple III SOS
– *September 1980 – April 1984*
Apple IIe
– *January 1983 – February 1985*

ProDOS 1.0 – *October 1983*
ProDOS 1.0.1 – *January 1984*
ProDOS 1.0.2 – *February 1984*
ProDOS 1.1 – *August 1984*
ProDOS 1.1.1 – *September 1984*

CHAPTER 22

"Will Someone Please Tell Me What an Apple Can Do?"

One of the most important features when considering a computer is, "What can I do with it?" It might be an attractive box, with incredible features and potential, but if it can only run pretty demos, it won't prove very useful.

In the early years of the microcomputer era, most computer owners had to become amateur programmers and write their own software. Commercial software written by professionals was unavailable, except possibly from the company that produced the computer.

Ultimately, some of those amateur programmers turned out programs that others wanted to use and maybe even purchase, especially if those programmers were good at deciphering the secrets on how the computer worked. Unless they taught themselves assembly language and could figure out the internals of that computer (which depended on the willingness of the manufacturer to divulge those secrets), the only programs available were likely written in BASIC. Those who have used the versions of BASIC available at the time are aware of the quirks and limits placed on the programmer by the language and by the small available memory.

The Apple II debuted with few intentional secrets; the primary limitation on information distributed with it was the time Apple required to produce a printed manual. When the first manual finally arrived, it included a commented source code listing for the entire Monitor and all its supporting routines. This openness had a lot to do with the early success of the Apple II.

Other manufacturers, such as Atari (with their models 400 and 800, based on the same 6502 as the Apple II) and Texas Instruments (who made a 16-bit machine called the TI 99/4 and 99/4A), kept almost everything secret and thus tried to maintain some control over software distribution. They *may* have done this to ensure that only high quality programs were released, but more likely they were concerned about controlling who received royalties on sales of the software. Unfortunately for them, it choked the effectiveness of those budding amateur software authors (who may have developed into professional software authors).

An example of this corporate secrecy involves the Atari home computer. One early programmer named John Harris wanted to write games for the Atari, but he could not get the company to release any information on how certain effects were achieved in their commercially released games. He was smart enough to eventually figure out the secrets himself, and created a version of *Pac-Man* for the Atari 800 that was so faithful that it raised the specter of lawyers from Atari. Once he changed the graphics and renamed the game to *Jawbreaker*, it was a hit not only for the Atari, but also later for the Apple II. Harris also created a licensed version of the arcade hit *Frogger* for the Atari 800, which was at the top of software sales charts for months during 1982.[1] Harris eventually became one of the wealthy software stars of the late 1970s and early 1980s.

Many computer makers of the time did not yet grasp the principal of the software/hardware loop—available software stimulates sales of hardware (computers and peripherals), which further enlarges the software market, which sells more computers, and so on. The industry was too new to know how to do much more than make and sell new computers.

A couple of years after the Apple II debut, the company sent a poster to computer dealers, with the title "Will someone please tell me what an Apple can do?" Underneath that title was a large list of the many games, utilities, and productivity programs that were then available to use on an Apple II or II Plus. Apple's point was that if a potential customer was not sure how they could use one of these new home computers, that extensive list of software should make it clear.

Apple advertisement, circa 1983, showing a list of the thousands of programs available for the Apple II – Photo credit: personal

Sofsearch International, a software locator service based in San Antonio, Texas, compiled the list. As of early 1984, the company had made a compari-

---

1 Levy, Steven, *Hackers: Heroes Of The Computer Revolution* (New York, Dell Publishing Co., Inc, 1984), 314-319.

son of the quantity of software available for Apple, Commodore, CP/M-86, CP/M, PC-DOS and MS-DOS, and TRS-80 computers. The Apple II had the largest amount of software for home and education use, with CP/M leading the market for business software. (The amount of 16-bit software for the IBM PC was rapidly growing at this point, and it was predicted to soon eclipse the older 8-bit offerings.)[2]

SOFTWARE ON THE APPLE II

In the Apple II world, the first software titles came from home authors. These people were usually first-time computer buyers who were captivated by the excitement of owning their own computer, and then had to sit down to actually find something useful or fun to do with it. They often brought their first programming efforts to show off at the computer store where they had bought their machine.

Since the storeowners had very little software to offer to potential customers, some of these authors ended up with the opportunity of having their programs duplicated and made available for sale. Ken and Roberta Williams started their company On-Line Systems (later Sierra On-Line) this way with a game called *Mystery House*, one of the first adventure games featuring hi-res graphics.[3]

Other software arrived at the first user groups. These usually developed out of the gatherings that took place at computer stores. Since the people who actually used these computers day in and day out at home had a better grasp of how they worked and what could be done to work around problems, the store owners often ended up referring their new customers to these groups for the detailed help they needed.

Not only were there the older groups (like the Homebrew Computer Club), but many newer, more machine-specific groups developed. Names like A.P.P.L.E. (Apple PugetSound Program Library Exchange) and International Apple Core became known beyond their local region as they began to distribute their newsletters and magazines to a national audience. Later, they became major sources of articles and utilities that were as yet unavailable anywhere else.

Many of the programs sold by A.P.P.L.E. were popular with Apple II owners. A.P.P.L.E. was designed as a club with dues, which paid for the collection of programs—all considered to be public domain, but sold to members at a nominal price to cover the costs of duplication. Members of A.P.P.L.E. also wrote programs and contributed them to the club. Originally collected on cassettes, and later on disks, some of the programs were eventually made available as commercial products. Their authors knew they had something unique that

---

2 Shea, Tom, "News Briefs", *InfoWorld* (February 6, 1984), 20.
3 Levy, Steven, *Hackers: Heroes Of The Computer Revolution* (New York, Dell Publishing Co., Inc, 1984), 298-300.

would be in demand by Apple owners hungry for something to use on their computer. Game programs contributed to A.P.P.L.E. were combined into GamePaks, which contained several games on the same tape.[4]

Understanding that a large variety of available programs would help encourage more sales for the Apple II, Apple took steps to help software authors take their programs to market. In 1980 Apple employee Mike Kane suggested that Apple help distribute promising software titles, but whose authors couldn't get a publisher to distribute them or didn't have access to computer stores that were willing to sell it for them. Kane formed a division within Apple called "Special Delivery Software," and promoted both third party and Apple-sponsored software under that label.

Between 1979 and 1981 a number of different programs were sold through Special Delivery Software, sporting the Apple logo and including standardized packaging and manuals, all listed in a dealer catalog. *Apple Writer* was originally distributed in this fashion, as were other less well-known programs such as *Tax Planner*, *Plan 80*, *Script II* (for Pascal), and *MBA* (a spreadsheet).

Special Delivery Software logo
– Photo credit: personal

Apple also established the Apple Software Bank and used it for special programs through 1980. It was more clearly a set of Apple-sponsored programs than those sold through Special Delivery Software, and some of the programs, such as *Quick File* and *Apple Plot*, achieved strong popularity and were moved into the mainstream of sales.[5, 6]

THE COMMAND LINE INTERFACE

The keyboard interface for the personal computer grew out of the mainframes that preceded it. These typically used a deck of punched cards to deliver their line-by-line commands; one card to execute the program, and one card per line of formatted data to input to the program. The same effect could be achieved by typing at a Teletype, which was essentially a typewriter interfaced with a computer. This provided direct command entry as well as a way to output results on the roll of paper that ran through the typing terminal. Even in the situation where computers had a video display (sometimes called

---

4 -----, "A.P.P.L.E. Co-op Celebrates A Decade of Service", *Call-A.P.P.L.E.* (February 1988), 12-27.
5 Espinosa, Chris, telephone interview with author, February 4, 1992.
6 Pohlman, Taylor, telephone interview with author, February 14, 1992.

a "glass Teletype") instead of a typewriter for printing the commands typed, it still worked on a line-by-line basis.

Working on a computer in this command line environment involved entering a command, waiting for control to return to the terminal, and then typing another command. If a programmer had written a program to load lines of text into a file to print out later, these could be no longer than 80 columns (the typical character width on a punched card), and allowed for no word-wrap. Also, once a line was typed, one could not reverse the roll and make changes in an already entered line. As such, it was only slightly more useful than a typewriter.

Later enhancements in programming for a video display on a mainframe allowed the cursor to be moved to specific locations on the screen, making it more useful than a standard Teletype. Nevertheless, the primary means of interacting with these computers was by giving commands line-by-line.

The interface of the Apple-1 and Apple II followed this long-established standard. The Apple-1 could *only* work on a line-by-line basis; there was no support for direct screen addressing. On the Apple II, though it offered more flexibility with the video screen directly addressable in memory, the rudimentary operating system (the Monitor or BASIC) still required commands typed one line at a time. Once a program was running, text or graphics could be displayed at specific locations on the screen, but between programs it was still a command line environment. Even so, it took time for fledgling Apple II programmers to grasp the concept of handling different parts of the screen.

A more sophisticated operating system that would allow work to be done with any of the lines on a screen was not beyond the ability of the Apple II, but the firmware to support that would have significantly enlarged the size of the Monitor ROM, and would have likewise increased the size and complexity of the BASIC language in ROM. With memory at a premium price, simple would have to do. Thus, the Apple II used the command line interface in both the Monitor and in Integer BASIC. These were the building blocks to create more complicated software, once people figured out how to do it.

The command line interface, though simple to implement in a program, had the disadvantage of requiring the user to know (and correctly type) the commands. For example, a word processing program might use the command "LOAD" to get a text file into memory, the command "EDIT" to begin to make changes to that file, and then the command "SAVE" to put a copy of the completed work back onto tape or disk. With various pieces of modifying information called parameters, "SORT" might be the necessary command to arrange the information in a database file into the desired order. Other commands might be needed to search for a specific word, replace a word, and move lines around.

In fact, early word processors were quite similar to writing a program in BASIC. Each line had its own line number, and inserting new lines often meant having to renumber the lines to make a new line available between two existing ones. If extra text had to be added to a line in the process of editing, making it too long, the end of that line often had to be re-typed into the following line and deleted from the current one.

More sophisticated text editing programs eventually began to appear that took advantage of the fact that the user was not working with a typewriter and paper, but with a video screen. These full-screen editors allowed the use of the arrow keys (or the IJKM "diamond" on the keyboard) to move the cursor around on the entire screen, and it made text entry and editing easier.

As they were further refined, these newer word processors even allowed what had previously been impossible: Text could be typed in the middle of a line, and the text to the right of the cursor was magically pushed to the right (even wrapping around to the next line if needed). Deletions were just as easy.

What was still cumbersome was the need to have specialized commands, often entered as combinations of the Control key and another letter, to carry out some of the functions of search and replace, copy, and so on. Moreover, these command keys were often different from one program to another, with Ctrl-F in one program being used to find text, and in another program as a command to jump to the first line of the file.

As the full-screen method of text editing became more standard, the command-line interface became less commonly used.

MENUS

The command-line method was difficult especially for those who were unfamiliar with computers, and it required the user to have a good memory for the names of the various commands. If the command name was typed incorrectly, or if a specific parameter was omitted or entered in the wrong order, an error message appeared, causing great anxiety and hand-wringing to those who were still trying to overcome their fear of using a computer.

COLOR DEMO menu example – Photo credit: personal

Software developers soon began to address the problem with this method. As an alternative for certain functions in a program, the concept of menus became more popular (these were used as early as the Apple *COLOR DEMO* program that came on cassette with the first Apple II computers). A menu was simply a list of user choices. At this early stage, it still used a command style prompt to enter a choice, but it was easier to use since the user did not have to memorize specific command names.

A further enhancement of the menu was called a magic menu, after a sample program written in BASIC and distributed by Apple. With this type of menu, the user had the option of typing the number of the desired menu entry at the prompt, or he could use the arrow keys to move a large inverse bar up and down the menu to that item. After selecting the item with the arrow key, it was executed by pressing the RETURN key. This came to be known as the "point and shoot" method of command selection.

AppleWorks (which will be discussed in detail later) took the magic menu interface to its highest form, adding the metaphor of file cards. One menu appeared on the screen enclosed in a box, with a tab on the top left of that box. This box resembled a 3x5 file card. When a selection was made from the menu, another file card appeared on top of the previous one, slightly down and to the right, leaving the tab on the lower box still visible. This allowed stacking of menus, with a clear path identifying which previous menu led to the current one. The ESC (escape) key was used to back up one level, erasing the menu card on top and re-drawing the menu card underneath it. Also, prompts were displayed on the top line of the screen that told where ESC would lead and what function was currently being executed.

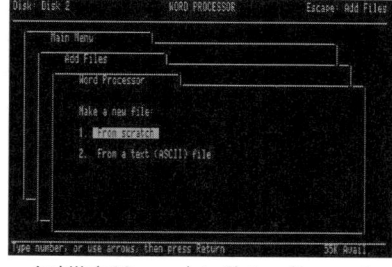

AppleWorks 1.3 screen shot – Photo credit: personal

Part of the success of AppleWorks stemmed from its ease of use in this respect. Not only were there no cryptic commands that had to be remembered and typed, but the use of special command keys was reserved for advanced use of the program. And when such special keys were needed, a standard help screen was available for quick reference. It was possible to do quite a bit in AppleWorks without even opening the instruction manual.

APPLE'S GREATEST HITS[7]

By 1980, the Apple II software market had established itself. Owners of the computer no longer had to write their own programs, but instead could simply purchase and use them. *Softalk* magazine, which began in that year, had started nearly from the beginning with an analysis of top selling software of the day. In its second issue in October 1980, their bestseller list first appeared, with the top thirty software programs ranked based on actual sales information obtained by polling retailers across the country. In that first list the top selling program was VisiCalc.

---

7 It is beyond the scope of this writing to go into much detail about the many programs released over the years, as the sheer volume of them since 1977 is enormous. Even a brief mention of them all could become a book in its own right, but Appendix A contains a listing (in moderate detail) of some of the most popular software released over the years. The remainder of this chapter will examine two programs that were particularly influential in the Apple II world: VisiCalc and Apple Writer. A later chapter will focus exclusively on AppleWorks.

VISICALC

A major part of the answer to the question, "What can I do with this computer?" lies in whether or not a software program is so important that it literally sells the computer. Robert X. Cringely, in his book *Accidental Empires*, put it this way:

> VisiCalc was a compelling application – an application so important that it alone justified the computer purchase. Such an application was the last element required to turn the microcomputer from a hobbyist's toy into a business machine. No matter how powerful and brilliantly designed, no computer can be successful without a compelling application. To the people who bought them, mainframes were really inventory machines or accounting machines, and minicomputers were office automation machines. The Apple II was a VisiCalc machine.[8]

VisiCalc was a way of using a computer that no one had ever thought of before, especially at a time when most computers were mainframes with limited access to the average person. It was written by Dan Bricklin, a programmer who had decided to enter Harvard Business School in the fall of 1977 and learn a second profession. Because of his programming background, he saw ways in which some of his class work could be simplified through the use of computers. He wrote programs in BASIC on the college time-sharing system to do his financial calculations, but found it tedious to have to re-write the program to deal with each new type of problem.

In a class that dealt with business production, Bricklin learned that some companies used long blackboards (sometimes stretching across several rooms) that were divided into a matrix of rows and columns. Each row and column had a specific definition, and calculations were made based on the contents of each cell (the intersection of a row and a column). If the value of one cell changed, the values of any cell that made use of the first cell's value also had to be changed. Because this was all written on a blackboard, the results had to be checked and re-checked to make sure that something hadn't been missed when changes were made during a planning session.

Bricklin conceived of a computerized approach to this production and planning matrix. Even though the computer could not display the entire matrix at once, the video screen could be used as a window on a part of the matrix, and this window could be moved at will to view any part of it. Best of all, the computer could keep track of all the calculations between the various cells, making sure that a change made in one place would be properly reflected in the result of a calculation in another place.

---

8 Cringely, Robert X., *Accidental Empires* (Addison-Wesley, Reading, Massachusetts, 1992), 64.

Over a single weekend he wrote a program in BASIC that demonstrated this concept. This demo program was rather slow and could only display a single screen of cells, but it was enough to illustrate the idea.

Bricklin teamed up with a friend from MIT, Bob Frankston, and together they looked for a publisher for the program. They found Dan Fylstra, who graduated from Harvard Business School a couple of years earlier.

Fylstra was the founding associate editor for *BYTE* magazine when it started in 1975, and by 1978 he and a friend, Peter J. Jennings, had started a small company called Personal Software, which was run out of Fylstra's apartment. Their primary product at the time was a chess program called *Microchess*, written by Jennings for the KIM-1 computer, and they were preparing to release the first commercial version of the adventure game *Zork*.

After hearing what Bricklin and Frankston had in mind, Fylstra and Jennings negotiated a deal to fund further development and eventual publication of VisiCalc. To create a more full-featured (and faster) machine language version of Bricklin's program, Personal Software gave Bricklin and Frankston an advance on royalties to pay for the use of a 6502 cross-compiler on a timesharing computer. Fylstra also loaned them an Apple II on which to test the program.

During 1978 and 1979 they worked together, as time permitted, with Bricklin doing the program design and Frankston writing the code. Jennings helped create a file system to use with VisiCalc. He had previously disassembled Apple DOS, and could offer more efficient file handling than could be done through its BASIC language interface.

One design contribution that was made by Frankston was the idea of using lookup tables. This technique allowed a spreadsheet to access one type of data and return a different type of data. Frankston wanted lookup tables so he could use the program to help calculate his taxes.

By October 1979, the program was ready for release. At first, VisiCalc was not a big hit. When most customers at computer stores were shown what the program could do, they didn't really grasp the concept behind it well enough to appreciate its possibilities. However, when business customers who had some computer knowledge came in and saw the program, they immediately saw that

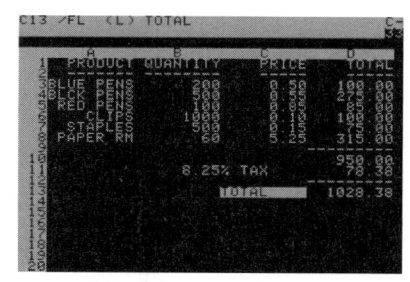

VisiCalc screenshot – Photo credit: personal

it could simplify much of what they did. VisiCalc actually sold the Apple II to these businessmen, who then managed to sneak the new computers onto their desks (despite company policies that discouraged use of anything but the company's mainframe).

The combination of Apple II computers with a full 48K of memory and the new Disk II drive made VisiCalc an ideal program to sell potential users on this three-year-old computer. It also made the Apple II *the* computer on which to run VisiCalc, as it took time to port the program to other personal computers that had adequate RAM and a disk drive for storage.[9]

Although executives at Apple Computer had been shown a pre-release version of VisiCalc, they failed to grasp the potential of the program. Trip Hawkins, the Director of Strategy and Marketing at Apple, understood what it could do, and could see that that this could become a major selling point for penetrating into the business market. He negotiated with Dan Fylstra about the possibility of Apple purchasing all rights to VisiCalc from Personal Software (thus locking up the market in Apple's favor). However, Apple's president, Mike Markkula, felt that the $1 million in Apple stock offered by Hawkins was too expensive and cancelled the deal. If his decision had been otherwise, the future of the microcomputer industry might have been quite different; however, Apple was headlong in their push to create their next product, the Apple III, and a million dollar investment in an untried program for the aging Apple II was not in their agenda at the time.

Bricklin and Frankston had themselves formed a company called Software Arts, and it was this company that had contracted with Fylstra's Personal Software. As part of the arrangement, they were instructed to create versions of VisiCalc for other microcomputers, from the TRS-80 to the Commodore PET and eventually the IBM PC. As sales of VisiCalc grew by leaps and bounds, Personal Software (and Software Arts) became quite wealthy.

To more closely identify his company with his flagship product, Fylstra changed its name from Personal Software to VisiCorp. He also hired other programmers to write companion software to extend the usefulness of VisiCalc. These included *VisiFile* (a database system), *VisiSchedule*, which was capable of creating PERT schedules (Project Evaluation and Review Technique, a statistical tool used in managing complex projects), *VisiCalc Business Forecasting Model* (a set of business templates for VisiCalc), and *VisiTrend/VisiPlot* (graphs, trend forecasting, and descriptive statistics).

Despite these additional products, VisiCalc remained VisiCorp's cash cow. This, ironically, led to the company's biggest problem, centering on a disagreement about money. VisiCorp's contract with Software Arts guaranteed Bricklin and Frankston a hefty 37.5 percent royalty on each copy of the program that VisiCorp sold. VisiCorp was responsible for marketing and distribution of the program, but it was Software Arts who owned the rights to it, and they had no motivation to change their contract to decrease the royalty percent to a number that was more typical for programmers.

The problem escalated when VisiCorp filed a lawsuit seeking damages because Software Arts was supposedly late in providing them upgrades to VisiCalc. Software Arts countersued, and demanded back the rights to distribute

---

9 Jennings, Peter, "VisiCalc – The Early Days", *Benlo Park*, <www.benlo.com/visicalc/index.html>

the product themselves. Further complicating matters was the fact that the name VisiCalc was a copyright of Software Arts, but a trademark of VisiCorp.[10]

By early 1985, things had worn on to the point where Bricklin decided to end the battle by selling the VisiCalc rights—but not to VisiCorp. Instead, Mitch Kapor, who ran the Lotus Development Corporation, purchased the program. Kapor had previously worked for VisiCorp, and had helped write VisiTrend/VisiPlot. After he sold the rights for those programs to VisiCorp, he began design on a spreadsheet program that would run specifically on the IBM PC, with the additional features of limited word processing and the ability to create graphs.

His program, *Lotus* 1-2-3, worked as well on the IBM PC as the original VisiCalc had on the Apple II, and Lotus eventually captured the spreadsheet market on the IBM. In fact, it became a killer app in its own right that helped push that computer platform into prominence. It also ate into sales of VisiCalc, and after Lotus succeeded in purchasing it from Software Arts, VisiCalc quietly disappeared from software store shelves.

APPLE WRITER

Apple Writer was certainly not the first word processor for the Apple II, but during the first few years of the Apple II it was the most popular. While *Softalk* magazine was in print, Apple Writer rarely (if ever) disappeared from its top thirty list of best selling software. When the magazine began to list the word processors in their own group, Apple Writer never was out of that list, from 1980 through 1984.

Though sold by Apple, the program did not originate within the company. Instead it came from the talents of an amateur programmer named Paul Lutus. He did not complete college, but his talents in building electronics devices made him valuable enough to be employed by NASA at the Jet Propulsion Laboratory. While there, he designed the lighting system and other electronic devices used for the space shuttle program. He also created a mathematical model of the solar system used during the Viking Mars missions in 1976. After working on these efforts, he turned his life in a completely different direction, and moved to a cabin in a wilderness area of Oregon, living on the land and without electricity.

Though he was living a lifestyle apart from the rest of the world, he didn't completely isolate himself, and kept up with the latest trends by reading magazines. One night, using a kerosene lantern for light, he came across an advertisement in *Scientific American* promoting the new Apple II computer. Its possibilities intrigued him, and he immediately ordered one.

To power his new computer, Lutus ran an electrical cord 1,200 feet through the trees to reach his cabin. He taught himself how to write software, and created

---

10 Tommervik, Al, "The Double Hi-Res VisiSuit", *Softalk* (April 1984), 28-29.

several programs that he felt were useful. Some of them he sent off to Apple, and the company paid him to include them in their Special Delivery Software division.

His success resulted in earnings that quickly paid for the cost of his new computer, so he turned to a more ambitious project. He had a fair amount of writing experience in the past, and decided he wanted to find a way to use his new computer to do that writing. The result of his efforts was Apple Writer, which he also sent off to Apple. The company was so interested in it that they offered him a flat fee of $7,500 for the rights to sell the program.[11]

Apple released the original version of Apple Writer in 1979, and it quickly became a hit. Version 1.0 had to deal with the limitations of the Apple II in the form of its uppercase-only keyboard and 40-column display. Clearly, a document produced on a computer could be uppercase only, but it was more valuable if it could look more like that produced on a typewriter.

To achieve entry of upper and lowercase characters, Lutus designed Apple Writer to use inverse text to display uppercase, and normal text to display lowercase. When entering text, pressing the ESC key once allowed entry of an uppercase letter. This changed the usual cursor box to an inverse caret (^), and the next letter typed was uppercase (displayed in inverse). If the ESC key were pressed twice in a row, the cursor changed into an inverse plus sign (+), and was now an editing cursor that could be moved through the text.[12]

Below is some sample text, as Apple Writer would display it on the screen. Notice in this example the inverse "^" cursor, ready to start the next sentence as an uppercase letter. Also notice the lack of word-wrap, with the word "expanded" split between the first and second lines.

Apple Writer screen shot – Photo credit: personal

Apple Writer produced the following when the above was printed on paper:

```
The Apple II computer's memory can be expanded
to as much as 48K of RAM.
```

The IJKM diamond on the keyboard was used to move the cursor, just as it was used for moving the cursor for editing lines of BASIC programs. Although the box cursor used in Apple Writer looked just like the flashing box also used in Apple BASIC, this cursor floated through the text instead of sitting on top of a character. If the editing cursor was moved through the word "AND", the inverse "+" box would move through the text, inserting itself between characters:

---

11 Lutus, Paul, "Cottage Computer Programming", *Digital Deli* (Workman Publishing, New York, 1984), reproduced on *AtariArchives.org*.
12 Dubnoff, Jerry, e-mail message to author, August 1992.

This original version of Apple Writer consisted of two separate binary programs: TEDITOR and PRINTER. The first program was used for text editing, and the second one printed the files created by TEDITOR.

> In its first release, Apple Writer had two problems that bothered early users of the program. One was that the files created by the program were Binary files (instead of Text files), apparently as a means to speed saving and loading under Apple DOS. Although it worked fine for Apple Writer, other programs could not use the files.
>
> Another problem had to do with the way in which the Apple II used (or misused) the ASCII character set for screen display, which differed from how most other computers of they day used it. Some translation had to be done to account for the various inverse and flashing characters displayed by the Apple II. This was part of the problem with the Apple Writer files and their incompatibility with other software. However, it resulted in yet another problem.
>
> When some users began plugging different ROM characters chips that could handle lowercase characters into their Apple II Plus computer, they found that Apple Writer wouldn't display text properly. The number "3" appeared as a lowercase "s", and "%" as an "e". It became necessary to patch Apple Writer to intercept its text output to the screen and make the correct translation to display lowercase as lowercase, and numbers and special characters where they were supposed to be.[13]

Apple Writer version 1.0 was distributed on a 13-sector DOS 3.2 disk and the binary files it produced had names that began with the prefix "TEXT". For example, a file named "LETTER" appeared on disk as "TEXT.LETTER". The 1.1 revision of the program appeared in 1980 on the larger capacity 16-sector DOS 3.3 disks. It provided minor bug fixes, and the extra disk space allowed inclusion of a companion spell checker called *Goodspell*.

The program had become so successful that Apple moved it up from the minor leagues of Special Delivery Software to be a front line product. However, after two years on the market, the features of Apple Writer were beginning to fall behind what was offered by some of the other early word processors. Apple wanted to be able to offer a significant update, but programmers at the company were unable to reverse-engineer the work Paul Lutus had done.

Consequently, Apple contacted Lutus, who convinced the company to give him a new contract. Instead of the flat fee that they had previously paid, he would now receive a royalty for each copy sold, and Lutus retained the rights to the program. Over the next several years, the royalties paid to Lutus amounted to a daily total that was as much as Apple had paid him for the first version of Apple Writer.[14]

---

13 Widnall, Sheila, "Lower Case For Apple Writer Using The Paymar Chip", *PEEKing At Call-A.P.P.L.E.* (Seattle, Washington, Vol. 3, 1980), 264-266.
14 Lutus, Paul, "Cottage Computer Programming", *Digital Deli* (Workman Publishing, New York, 1984), reproduced on AtariArchives.org.

Lutus' new version was called *Apple Writer][*, and was released in 1981 on copy-protected disks. This update saved documents as standard Text files instead of the older Binary files, and could properly display 40-column lowercase characters when the character generator ROM was replaced (as was done by some Apple II owners). It also supported 80-column text if a Sup-R-Term card was plugged into slot 3. In 40-column mode, words now wrapped to the next line if they were too long to display on the current line (unlike the older versions of Apple Writer that split the word and continued it on the next line).

Other new features included a glossary and a scripting package called Word Processing Language (WPL). This made it possible to automate nearly everything of which the program was capable. A WPL program could create templates like form letters, or allow for entry of repetitious text (such as a return name and address for correspondence).[15]

Apple Writer IIe, also copy-protected, came next in 1983 with the Apple IIe. This version took advantage of the features of the new IIe (such as the built-in 80-column display and full keyboard). It also included improvements in tabbing, since a TAB key was now available on the keyboard, and it allowed larger text files (these could be larger than the size of memory, by loading just a segment of the file into memory at one time). Other miscellaneous features included "printing" text files to the disk, directly connecting the keyboard to the printer (to use like a typewriter), and improvements in the WPL language. When the Apple IIc came out, users of this version of Apple Writer encountered some problems, as the inverse status line at the top of the screen displayed uppercase characters as MouseText; however, patches quickly appeared to remedy this situation.[16]

The first version to run under the ProDOS operating system was called *Apple Writer 2.0*. It came out in September 1984, was not copy-protected, and it fixed the MouseText problem. It also allowed the user to set right and left screen margins, displaying a closer approximation of the final appearance of the printed text. This version also had the capability of connecting the keyboard directly to the printer or to a modem, allowing it to be used as a rudimentary terminal program. This version had problems printing to certain third-party parallel printer cards (such as the Grappler).[17]

> *Apple Writer 2.1* appeared in late 1985. It contained minor bug fixes, including the above-mentioned problem with some parallel printer cards. The 2.0 version had printed characters as low-ASCII (values $00-$7F), which caused a problem with some kinds of interface cards and printers. Version 2.1 changed this so characters were printed as high-ASCII ($80-$FF),

---

15 Dubnoff, Jerry, e-mail message to author, August 1992.
16 Lancaster, Don, *Apple Writer Cookbook* (Howard W. Sams & Co, 1986), 29-30.
17 Lancaster, Don, *Apple Writer Cookbook* (Howard W. Sams & Co, 1986), 102-103, 111-112.

CHAPTER 22 | "Will Someone Please Tell Me What an Apple Can Do?"

> although files printed to a disk file were saved in the original low-ASCII format.[18] This version also was not copy-protected, making it possible to easily install on a 3.5-inch disk or hard disk.

When AppleWorks appeared on the scene, Apple Writer began to decrease in popularity; however, many Apple Writer veterans did not like AppleWorks as well as Apple Writer, primarily because it put a layer of protection between the user and the program. This made it easier for the computer novice to immediately put the program to use, and less likely to do something that disrupted printer or interface card internal settings. That same protection also made it harder to do specialized jobs.

For example, Apple Writer allowed entry of control characters (which allowed very specific control of printers and their interface cards), but AppleWorks was much more restrictive in this sense, handling more of the details of printer control internally. This openness made it possible for Apple Writer to create documents on Postscript laser printers (as demonstrated by Don Lancaster in his *Computer Shopper* column, "Ask the Guru"), something that many did not think possible on an Apple II.

Where Apple Writer allowed an experienced user to use all features on a printer and interface card to the maximum, AppleWorks was more dependent on internal settings for a particular printer and card. However, the same thing that gave Apple Writer its power also made it harder for less skilled users, who were probably intimidated by its nearly blank screen with no prompts or visible instructions.

For several years, from around 1988 through 1992, Apple Writer was unavailable except as a used program. The exact reason for this is not clear. One reason probably had to do with the more popular AppleWorks, which had the additional features of a spreadsheet and database. But with its Word Processing Language, Apple Writer was still more suitable for certain jobs than was AppleWorks; and yet, Apple simply stopped upgrading, distributing, and supporting it.

This orphaned status changed in the summer of 1992. The online service GEnie had an Apple II group, and one of the leaders of that group, Tim Tobin, was in charge of what became known as The Lost Classics Project. The purpose of this project was to seek out software that had ceased publication (typically because the distributor had gone out of business), and try to obtain permission to make it available again as a free download. Recovering Apple Writer was at the top of their list of abandoned software to re-release, and that summer Tobin was successful in contacting the author. Lutus agreed to make his program available as freeware, which meant that it could be copied freely and given away, but it could not be sold for a profit.

---

18 Weishaar, Tom, "Does Your Mother Love You?", *Open-Apple* (January 1986), 1.97.

This arrangement was quite similar to an earlier program Lutus had written, *FreeWriter*. He had released this program as freeware in 1984, shortly after Apple Writer 2.0 came out. FreeWriter was very much like Apple Writer, except it did not have a built-in ability to print the documents it created, and it did not have WPL. It worked well on the Apple IIe and IIc, but earlier models of the Apple II had problems because they had no lowercase, no DELETE key, and did not have the Open-Apple key (though its actions could be performed, with difficulty, by using the button on paddle 0, if attached). Lutus did include a program written in Applesoft that would read files created by FreeWriter and print them.

This new, free distribution of Apple Writer was possible because although Apple Computer held the copyright on the Apple Writer documentation, Lutus had retained the copyright on the program itself (Apple had held the copyright on versions 1.0 and 1.1 of the program).

The release of FreeWriter inspired an elementary school teacher name Al Rogers. He had worked in the Chula Vista, California school district for over 20 years, and the microcomputer revolution that started in the mid 1970s inspired him to learn programming, and ultimately re-directed him to become a curriculum specialist in the San Diego schools Teacher Education and Computer Center.

Rogers took FreeWriter and made modifications to make it work better for Spanish-language and bilingual classes. He also added menus to simplify the use of the program, prompts to help teachers guide students within a word processing document, and reintroduced a print function. He released his efforts in the spring of 1985 as FrEdWriter (Free Education Writer), distributing it for a nominal fee and encouraging teachers to make as many copies of the program as necessary. It became popular amongst teachers and school districts across the country as a very low cost way to introduce students to writing and word processing concepts.

Rogers later created *FrEdMail*, an Apple IIe-based network that allowing students to share their writing.[19]

TIMELINE

Apple Writer 1.0 – *August 1979*
VisiCalc – *October 1979 - June 1985*
Apple Writer 1.1 – *August 1980*
Apple Writer][– *1981*
Apple Writer //e – *January 1983*

Apple Writer 2.0 – *September 1984*
Freewriter – *October 1984*
FrEdWriter – *1985*
Apple Writer 2.1 – *November 1985*

---

19 Williams, Christopher, "Trendsetrer Al Rogers: Software Earns Him Respect, Not Money" Electronic Learning, (January 1987).

CHAPTER 23

Bits to Ink

By the late 1970s and early 1980s many printers were available for use with home computers. However, the cost was often over $1,000, which limited the number of people who could afford one. Most printers offered 96 characters in the standard ASCII set, including both upper and lowercase characters. The cheaper printers only printed uppercase characters, while some of the more expensive ones were capable of lowercase output, could accept programmable characters, or had built-in graphics characters.

There were two main types of printers available. One type operated like a typewriter by striking a piece of metal type against a ribbon and onto the paper. This type of printer was often called an "impact" or "letter quality" printer. It used either a type ball like IBM's Selectric typewriters, or a wheel with spokes that radiated out from the center, with the type characters at the end of the spokes. This latter type of letter quality printer was also called a "daisy wheel" printer, because the changeable print wheels looked like the petals on a daisy. Businesses used this type of printer more commonly than the dot-matrix variety, because of the quality of output. They were quite expensive, often costing more than $2,000 and were beyond the reach of the average home hobbyist.

The other type of printer in common use was dot matrix. These less expensive printers formed characters with a series of pins in a vertical row that struck the ribbon and produced dots on the paper. As the print head moved across the paper, the dots were printed in patterns that resembled (sometimes vaguely) letters and numbers. The matrix used to form a character was usually referred to as the number of horizontal dots by the number of vertical dots. A 5x7 matrix, for example, used up to five dots across and up to seven dots down. Some printers (like some computers of the time) did not use "descenders" on the lowercase letters that drop below the baseline (g, j, p, q, and y). To print lowercase letters with descenders often required nine or more vertical pins. Over time, print technology improved the appearance of dot matrix printing, first by increasing the vertical printing density to 9 or more dots, which allowed creation of true descenders on those lower case letters, and later by adding additional horizontal printing to get rid of the "dot" appearance.

Example of descenders on dot matrix print
– Photo credit: personal

The Centronics 730, released in 1979, may well have been the first widely used printer for the Apple II (and other microcomputers). Though selling for as much as $700, it was still less costly than other dot matrix printers available at the time. It used a parallel cable whose pin layout became a standard for use with personal computers, and was still in use well into the 1990s.[1] Centronics also produced several other models, including the 737 and 739. Another printer made by Centronics, the 779, used the smaller 5x7 dot matrix characters, and was sold in 1978 by Apple in their "Printer IIA" bundle, but was very pricey at $1,445.

To help with print speed, the printer had a buffer larger enough to hold about one line of text (up to 132 characters). It could print in sizes from 10 to 16.5 cpi (characters per inch), ranging from 60 cps (characters per second) at 10 cpi to 100 cps at 16.5 cpi, although it only had a limited 64 character ASCII character set, all uppercase plus some special characters. As previously mentioned, several personal computers of the time lacked lowercase, so this limitation wasn't necessarily a drawback.

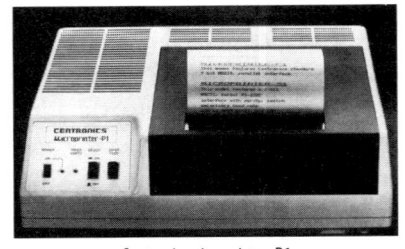

Apple offered another Centronics printer bundle in June 1978. Its "Printer II" bundle included an interface card and a Centronics thermal printer the company called the "µicroprinter" P1. This was somewhat more affordable at $695.

Centronics µicroprinter-P1
– Photo credit: *BYTE*, March 1978

Centronics' high-end printers had a larger matrix and could produce true descenders on lowercase characters.[2,3]

A company named Trendcom released a printer that became important to Apple and the Apple II. It had two models, the 100 and 200. Instead of using mechanical solenoids (tiny electromagnets that drove pins into a print head), these were thermal printers that used heat-sensitive paper. Their operation was very quiet, about as loud as sliding a finger across a piece of paper. They were inexpensive compared to other printers of the day (most of which cost over $1,000), although the printing looked very much like that produced by a dot-matrix printer. The Trendcom Model 100 printed 40 characters per line on paper that was about 4.5 inches wide. The Model 200 could print 80 characters per line on paper 8.5 inches wide. Compared to the first printer offered by Radio Shack for their TRS-80 computer (a thermal printer which used a silver-type of paper), the Trendcom printers were a step above.

The significance of the Trendcom model 200 was that Apple selected it as the first printer it released under the Apple name. It could be programmed

---

1 Zuchowski, Tom, A2 Roundtable, Category 2, Topic 16, *GEnie*, accessed March 1991.
2 Ulm, Dennis, A2 Roundtable, Category 2, Topic 16, *GEnie*, accessed April 1991.
3 Wright, Loren, "On Buying A Printer", *Micro* (August 1981), 33-35.

to control printing of each dot in a column, and so was ideal as an inexpensive means of printing Apple II hi-res graphics. Apple included a special interface card and announced the printer as the Apple Silentype in June 1979. It was not, however, available for purchase until March 1980, selling for $599. It was identical to Trendcom's Model 200 except for the Apple logo in the lower left corner of the front cover.[4] One legend suggests that part of the popularity of this printer at Apple stemmed from the fact that its small size allowed it to fit under the seat of Steve Wozniak's private airplane.[5, 6, 7]

Andy Hertzfeld, who later wrote much of the ROM code for the original Macintosh, wrote the firmware for the Silentype printer.[8]

Anadex, MPI, and Microtek were manufacturers of early printers. However, there were other printers that had much higher market penetration. The Japanese company Epson supplied printers for personal computers early on, and had long-term success in the market. It started in the printer business with the Epson TX-80 and MX-80, one of the first dot matrix printers that sold for under $1,000. The MX-80, released in August 1980, was popular with computer hobbyists of the time, and was capable of printing Apple II hi-res graphics with the optional Graphtrax ROMs. Epson released another version of this printer, the MX-100, in early 1982. The MX-100 was a wide carriage model, and could print hi-res graphics without additional hardware.

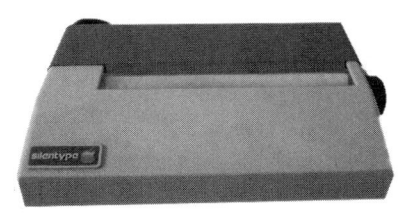

Apple Silentype Printer – Photo credit: François Michaud

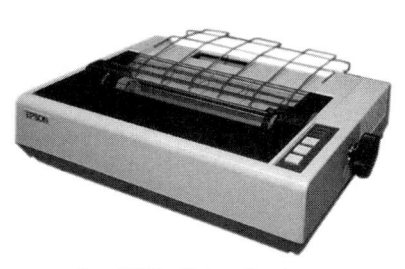

Epson MX-80 – Photo credit: unknown

Epson printers were unique because they had a special feature called a double print mode where a line was printed normally, then the paper was advanced 1/216 of an inch and the same line printed again. This filled in some gaps between dots on individual letters, and made printouts more pleasing to the eye. Another feature used in these printers was print enhancement mode, in which the pins hit the ribbon harder and made it possible to make multiple copies using carbon paper.[9, 10]

---

4 Bernsten, Jeff, A2 Roundtable, Category 2, Topic 16, *GEnie*, accessed April 1991.
5 -----. (ads), *Call-A.P.P.L.E. In Depth #1*, (Seattle, Washington, 1981), 106.
6 -----. "A.P.P.L.E. Co-op Celebrates A Decade of Service". *Call-A.P.P.L.E.* (February 1988), 12-27.
7 Felty, Wes, A2 Roundtable, Category 2, Topic 16, *GEnie*, accessed April 1991.
8 Hertzfeld, Andy, "I'll Be Your Best Friend", *Folklore.org*, <folklore.org/StoryView.py?project=Macintosh&story=I'll_Be_Your_Best_Friend.txt>, accessed October 20, 2012.
9 Wright, Loren, "On Buying A Printer", *Micro* (August 1981), 33-35.
10 Kindall, Jerry, A2 Roundtable, Category 2, Topic 16, *GEnie*, accessed March 1991.

Integral Data Systems was another early manufacturer of printers. It released the IP-125 ($799) and IP-225 ($949) printers in March 1978.[11] These printers used a 7x7 matrix to create characters. The IP-125 used a pressure feed method to hold paper in place (similar to the method used by typewriters), and typically the paper became crooked after more than a couple of pages.

The IP-225 used a tractor feed mechanism, which was more reliable. This second method required special paper with two rows of holes punched along the sides of the paper. The IDS printers had the flexibility of connecting to either parallel or serial interfaces (with serial speeds up to 1200 baud). It could plot dot graphics, and also had an optional built-in graphics character set.[12]

By 1979, Integral Data Systems upgraded its printers, adding more capabilities and marketing them with flashier names. Its Paper Tiger line of printers (models 440 and 460) had an attractive typeface, and used two vertical rows of pins in the print head, slightly offset from each other. This produced overlapping dots to achieve a more solid appearance. Some models could print up to 160 cps, and supported a more complete upper and lowercase character set. These were also capable of reproducing Apple II hi-res graphics (with the appropriate software). IDS later sold a printer called the Prism, which printed in color using a special multicolored ribbon.[13]

Integral Data Systems, Paper Tiger 440
– Photo credit: *BYTE*, September 1979

APPLE'S PRINTERS

After the Silentype printer was released in 1979, Apple looked for another printer that could produce better, more permanent output than could be achieved with a thermal printer. The main problem with thermal paper was that with time the printing faded (especially if cellophane tape was used on the paper). The Apple Dot Matrix Printer was released in October 1982

---

11 *BYTE*, (March 1978).
12 Golding, Val, "Integral Data IP 225 Printer - A Review", *PEEKing At Call-A.P.P.L.E.*, (Seattle, Washington, Vol. 2, 1979), 151.
13 Vanderpool, Tom, A2 Roundtable, Category 2, Topic 16, *GEnie*, March & August 1991.

for $699. Made from a modified C. Itoh printer, it was one of the first few dot-matrix printers that sold for under $1,000. Apple needed this higher-end printer to help promote the Apple III as a business computer. More importantly, Apple chose it because it was capable of heavy-duty graphics reproduction (such as output from the Apple Lisa computer, still in development at the time). Known also as the Apple DMP, it used a custom ROM programmed by Apple to control the printer's features.[14]

Because Apple was looking for as many business solutions for its customers as it could find, it announced a modified Qume brand printer along with the DMP. This printer, a daisy wheel model called the Apple Letter Quality Printer, was expensive at $2,195. It could print at only 40 cps, but produced high quality output. It was released with the Lisa and the Apple IIe in January 1983.[15]

Apple Letter Quality Printer
– Photo credit: Apple III Information Analyst Brochure, 1980

The Apple ImageWriter debuted in December 1983 as the successor to the Apple DMP. Also made by C. Itoh, the ImageWriter had a faster print speed (120 cps), and could print in eight different pitches (character widths). It was a reliable, sturdy printer, and sold originally for $675. Later, Apple released a wide carriage version whose abilities were otherwise identical. The ImageWriter II replaced both in September 1985. While the original Apple DMP

Apple ImageWriter printer
– Photo credit: Vectronic's Apple World

and the ImageWriter I came in the same beige color as the Apple II, II Plus, and IIe, the ImageWriter II was the same platinum color as the newer Macintosh computers. The ImageWriter II could do everything the original ImageWriter could, plus it was capable of printing MouseText characters and color (using a multicolored ribbon).[16]

In 1984, as part of its promotion of the Apple IIc (discussed in the next chapter), Apple released a new printer with impressive features—in theory at least. The Apple Scribe came in the same "Snow White" color as the IIc and cost only $299. It was a thermal *transfer* printer, with a significant advancement over the old Silentype. It could print in four colors on regular paper

---

14 Williams, Gregg, "The Lisa Computer System", BYTE (February 1983), 43.
15 Baum, Peter, "Expanding The Unexpandable IIc", Softalk, (June 1984), 95-97.
16 Vanderpool, Tom, A2 Roundtable, Category 2, Topic 16, GEnie, March & August 1991.

(instead of heat sensitive paper) using a unique heat-transfer method and a wax-impregnated ribbon. It also printed in a "near letter quality" mode (with overlapping dots) at 50 cps, and a draft and graphics mode (80 cps). Its major limitation, however, was a print quality that was inferior to most dot-matrix printers, and a ribbon that was expensive and required frequent replacement. These problems resulted in low sales, and the Scribe did not last for more than a year before it was discontinued.

In 1984 Hewlett-Packard introduced the LaserJet laser printer. This was a significant breakthrough in printer quality, and was capable of producing documents that looked professionally typeset. Apple decided to develop its own laser printer, and in January of 1985 released the LaserWriter. Although it was slow (four pages a minute by the early 1990s), and expensive (over $2,000), it was popular with those who wanted high quality printing.

At Apple, the new LaserWriter was supported only on the Macintosh, but since the printer did its work through a page description language called PostScript, it was usable on Apple II computers. It was only necessary to learn the PostScript language, create a file that gave the necessary commands, and send that file to the printer through a serial interface card. As previously mentioned, Don Lancaster's "Ask the Guru" column in the magazine *Computer Shopper* often discussed how use the PostScript language with a laser printer on an Apple II.

Apple Scribe Printer
- Photo credit: Christian Rehberg <www.classiccomputer.de>

Unfortunately, for many years there was a perception that it was not possible to use a laser printer with an Apple II, something that persisted even with the more advanced IIGS (released in 1986). This was partly because there were few software packages for the Apple II that produced PostScript files that could be interpreted by a laser printer—with the notable exception of *Publish-It!*, which supported the LaserWriter.

For purposes of creating various types of graphs, a printing device called a plotter was introduced. It was ideal for reproducing vector (line-oriented) graphics, and the earliest versions were introduced in the 1960s and 1970s for specialized applications. By the early 1980s, the technology to do this type of printing dropped to the point where they could be released for consumer use with microcomputers.

Apple released its own version of this device in June 1984, called the Apple Color Plotter. It had an advantage over printers, in that it could draw smooth lines and curves. By automatically selecting one of four colored pens in a rotating pen head, the Color Plotter worked by moving the paper up and down to draw vertical lines, and the pen left and right to draw horizontal lines. Control of the plotter was accomplished by sending text commands through a serial card, and consisted of two letter commands (DA = Draw Absolute, DR = Draw

Relative, etc.) followed by other parameters. It could move the pen without drawing, plot points, draw lines, arcs, and circles, and print text at any location, tilt, rotation, or scale. Lines could be drawn as solid or as patterns of dots.d

Presumably this product did not take off because of the limited need for this type of output, and the high $1200 price tag. Because of the continuously improving quality of graphics and printers, plotters soon became unnecessary. The right software could reproduce drawings with a dot matrix or laser printer in as good or better detail than a plotter.[17]

Apple Color Plotter – Photo credit: Brent Benrud

TIMELINE

Centronics 779 – *January 1978*

Centronics µ P1 – *March 1978*

IDS IP-125, IDS IP-225 – *March 1978*

Trendcom 100 – *May 1979*

IDS Paper Tiger 440, 460 – *September 1979*

Trendcom 200 – *September 1979*

Centronics 730 – *December 1979*

Apple Silentype – *March 1980*

Epson MX-80 – *August 1980*

Centronics 737 – *August 1980*

Epson MX-100 – *1982*

Apple Dot Matrix Printer – *October 1982*

Apple Letter Quality Printer – *January 1983*

Apple ImageWriter – *December 1983*

HP LaserJet – *May 1984*

Apple Scribe – *June 1984*

Apple Color Plotter – *June 1984*

Apple LaserWriter – *January 1985*

Apple ImageWriter II – *September 1985*

---

17 Durkee, David, "Marketalk Reviews", *Softalk* (June 1984), 120.

CHAPTER 24

Compact and Powerful

Flush with the profits produced by the immensely successful Apple II and Apple II Plus, executives at Apple began to hire engineers and programmers to begin work on new products that could be successors to the Apple II line. Beyond the Apple III, two other important projects began to take shape in late 1979.

PRELUDE: STEVE JOBS AND MACINTOSH

It was previously discussed that Jef Raskin got his start at Apple writing the manual for Integer BASIC, and later began the company's internal publications group. He spent a year establishing that department, then turned it over to someone else to maintain. In early 1979 he began to work on his own vision of an easy-to-use consumer computer, writing his notes up in a series of essays. Raskin pitched the idea for this to Apple president Mike Markkula in March of that year, and by September 1979 he had been allowed to hire a small number of people to further research the concept. He named the project (and computer) after his favorite variety of apple, the McIntosh, but later changed the name to Macintosh to avoid conflict with the McIntosh Laboratory, a company that produced high-end audio equipment.

Raskin felt that a computer for the typical non-technical consumer should be simple to use, and should not require installation of anything inside the computer; in fact, opening up the computer should not be allowed at all. Furthermore, he had envisioned graphic-based computing as far back as 1967, using it as his thesis for a computerized drawing system (he even called the system Quick-Draw, a name which years later found its way into the Mac and Lisa systems). Raskin was further influenced by what he learned during a sabbatical from UCSD, when he visited and was able to interact with the scientists at the Xerox Palo Alto Research Center (PARC). There he found others who shared his vision for easy-to-use computers and a graphical user interface. After he started work at Apple, Raskin ceased his visits to PARC, to avoid a conflict of interest. But what he learned there he incorporated into his vision for a computer usable by anybody, and during 1979 and 1980 collected his essays about this computer in what became known as "The Book of Macintosh".

Elsewhere at Apple, another team was working on the Lisa project, which had started in 1978. The original design for Lisa involved several microprocessors in parallel, and for a video display it used a traditional black phosphor screen with green characters, similar to most other computers of the day. It had a much larger team and greater financial resources behind it than did Raskin's Macintosh project. Steve Jobs was very involved in the design process for the Lisa, and focused most of his attention on that team.

Raskin was aware of the work being done by the Lisa team, and he tried to interest the team leader in doing something more like the bitmapped graphics display he was designing with the Macintosh. To try to generate interest in this type of technology, he wanted to make it possible for some of the engineers from Apple to visit PARC, and see what the researchers there had been working on. At about that same time, in 1979, Xerox had expressed interest in investing in Apple. In exchange for the right to buy one million dollars worth of Apple stock before its IPO (initial public offering of stock), Xerox granted permission for a team from Apple to visit and be shown the work PARC researchers had been doing with the Xerox Alto, a computer using multiple windows, icons to represent documents, a mouse-driven-pointer, and bitmapped fonts. Furthermore, the deal allowed Apple to create an office computer based on this technology.[1,2]

Twice in 1979, a team from Apple came to the PARC campus to get a demonstration of the Alto technology. Because Steve Jobs had more than once tried to cancel funding for the Macintosh project (which was, at its core, a graphic-based computer), Raskin encouraged Jobs to come on the second visit to PARC. He really wanted to let Jobs see the potential of the graphic user interface.

The response of Jobs and the rest of the team from Apple to the wonders they saw at PARC set the future of the company. Jobs pushed the Lisa team to change its focus to use these revolutionary features, and the project finally took on the distinct personality that made it possible to become the ultra-computer Apple needed. With the technical problems involved in the launch of the Apple III and the effect it had on Apple's reputation, it was clear that the company needed something better and more powerful to take attention away from the IBM PC.

At this point, however, Jobs ran into problems caused by his own abrasive personality. The disasterous launch of the Apple III had resulted in a

---

1 Pang, Alex, "Jef Raskin on PARC and the Macintosh", *Making the Macintosh*, <www-sul.stanford.edu/mac/primary/interviews/raskin/parc.html>
2 This is what actually happened, and is in stark contrast to the often-repeated story that Steve Jobs pushed his way into PARC, saw their work, and stole it to use for the Lisa and Macintosh. Xerox got Apple stock at a bargain price, and Apple got permission to use PARC ideas in a commercial product.

reorganization within the company in the fall of 1980, putting the Apple II and III into one division, and the Lisa into another. Apple's Vice President of Software, John Couch, was put in charge of the Lisa, and Jobs was excluded from involvement in that project.

It was around this time that management had given Raskin's Macintosh project yet another extension to continue its research into his own vision of the graphic user interface. Raskin had previously hired Burrell Smith, a self-taught engineer, to work on hardware design, and Bud Tribble to work on writing the firmware for the computer. Raskin knew Tribble from his years at UCSD, when Tribble was an undergraduate. In early 1980, Smith had created a prototype running on the 8-bit Motorola 6809 processor, driving a 256 by 256 bitmapped display with black text on a white background. With the Lisa team settled on using the more powerful 16-bit Motorola 68000 processor, Tribble convinced Smith to switch his design to also use it. The clever means in which Smith came up with his new prototype caught the attention of Steve Jobs. That attention resulted in the project taking a turn that cemented its future.

For Jobs, perhaps it hearkened back to the smaller team that created the Apple II. Certainly it was a desire to compete with and possible beat the Lisa team at its own game (he ultimately had a bet with John Couch about which would ship first, Macintosh or Lisa). Regardless of his motiviation, Jobs, to the dismay of Jef Raskin, swept in and took over the Macintosh project. He moved Raskin's small group to a building that was larger, but was also further away from the main Apple campus, and hired more people to move the project along. It did not take long for Raskin to become frustrated with Jobs' quirks and attitude; by late February 1981, Jobs forced Raskin to take a mandatory leave of absence.

Over the next two years, development on the Lisa and the Macintosh took place in parallel, with some technical crossover between the two groups, particularly in the way in which the graphic interface was fine-tuned and improved. Jobs took on Raskin's attitude that the Mac should be an appliance, a closed box, unlike the open Apple II. Instead of those messy slots and a lid that popped off (which made the Apple II so popular with the hacker community), he and his team were sold on the idea that all necessary features should simply be built-in and the case sealed. It would be something the customer just plugged in, turned on, and started using. With the Xerox mouse/

Macintosh 128K – Photo credit: Apple product brochure, 1984

icon/window interface it would not only be easy to set up and turn on, but also easy to use.[3, 4, 5, 6]

APPLE IIC: BEGINNINGS

During this same time period, engineers in the Apple II division had begun their efforts to make the Apple II less expensive to manufacture, and the Apple IIe was in its formative stages. In the summer of 1981 someone proposed a portable Apple II, a book-sized computer. It wasn't until Steve Jobs became interested in it as an engineering challenge, well after Macintosh was under way, that anything came of the idea:

> ...one day late in '82, Paul Dali showed him [Jobs] a photograph of a Toshiba portable and they started fooling around with the idea of an Apple II that would look like the Toshiba but come with a built-in disk drive. They took out a IIe circuit board and a disk drive and a keyboard and played with them until they arrived at a promising configuration – keyboard in front, disk drive in back, circuit board in between. What got Jobs excited about this idea was the engineering difficulty of squeezing it all into a package not much bigger than a notebook. And a machine so small wouldn't have the expandability that characterized all the other Apple II models. Like Macintosh, it could be taken out of the box, plugged in, and put to work – no extra parts to buy, no cables to figure out. It was the II reinvented as an appliance.[7]

As with all Apple projects, the IIc went by various code names during its development, for the sake of internal communications and to keep outsiders from knowing what was going on. The various names used included VLC (Very Low Cost), Yoda, ET, IIb (for "Book"), and Teddy (which stood for "Testing Every Day"). Also, following a long standing tradition at Apple, some of the code names assigned to the project at various times were children of employees at Apple: Chels, Jason, Lolly, Sherry, and Zelda. These names persisted in the source code for the IIc firmware as later printed in the technical reference manual; the serial port driver was called a "Lolly" driver.[8]

---

[3] Hertzfeld, Andy, "The Father of the Macintosh", *Folklore.org*, <folklore.org/StoryView.py?project=Macintosh&story=The_Father_of_The_Macintosh.txt>

[4] Raskin, Jef, "Articles from Jef Raskin about the history of the Macintosh", <mxmora.best.vwh.net/JefRaskin.html>

[5] Pang, Alex, "Interview with Jef Raskin", *Making the Macintosh*, <www-sul.stanford.edu/mac/primary/interviews/raskin/trans.html>

[6] Hertzfeld, Andy, "Black Wednesday", *Folklore.org*, <folklore.org/StoryView.py?project=Macintosh&story=Black_Wednesday.txt>

[7] Rose, Frank, *West Of Eden: The End Of Innocence At Apple Computer*, (New York, Penguin Books, 1989), 110-112.

[8] Hogan, Thom, "Apple: The First Ten Years", A+ (January 1987), 45.

CHAPTER 24 | *Compact and Powerful*

During the time the IIc was under development, Apple was working on a change in the look of their products. The Apple II design was over five years old, and the company wanted something that was cleaner and more modern. Jerry Manock, who had designed the case for the Apple II and was at that time working on the case for the Macintosh, and Rob Gemmell, who was head of design in the Apple II devision, decided to invite product designers from around the world to Apple to make a pitch for a new design the company's products.

One of the companies who became involved in this competition was an industrial design group from Germany. Frogdesign had made a distinctive look for Sony's products, and most of those products had gone on to be successful. To prepare for his presentation to Apple, founder Harmut Esslinger met with Steve Jobs in 1982, at at time when he was working out how the Macintosh should look. Esslinger advised Jobs to make design the responsibility of a separate team at Apple, one whose goal would be to create a look that was consistent across all Apple products. The existing Apple II, Apple III, and Lisa each had its own distinctive look, each inconsistent with each other. Esslinger thought the company should create a "design language", which would not only define how something should look, but would help with the creation of future products.

Esslinger's team submitted to Apple what they called the "Snow White" design language. It consisted of several important features, including a case that was as small as possible, with minimal texture on the surface, and few angles. It was to be symmetrical in appearance and have thin grooved lines on the top, sides, and back, with specific measurements. The Apple logo should have a defined, consistent appearance on each product. Furthermore, the character typefaces used on all products should be the same. Frogdesign specifically recommended using the typeface Garamond Condensed Italic for the name, and Univers Condensed for the keycaps. The color to be used for the product case was white, with soft olive gray as a contrast.

Though the Apple IIe was in development at the same time as the Macintosh and the IIc, management made the decision to give it the same form factor and color as the older Apple II and II Plus. The new Snow White design language concept was applied to the Macintosh, but its color was changed to a light gray they called "platinum". The only product released using the original the Snow White language description was the Apple IIc (and its accessories, the Monitor IIc and the Scribe printer released to use with the IIc) and its later revision, the Apple IIc Plus.[9]

---

[9] Esslinger, Harmut, *Design Forward: Creative Strategies for Sustainable Change*, Arnoldsche Verlagsanstalt publishing, as quoted on "From Phones To Tablets: 26 Apple Designs That Never Came To Be", *Co.Design*, <www.fastcodesign.com/1671718/from-phones-to-tablets-26-apple-designs-that-never-came-to-be>, retrieved February 10, 2013.

HARDWARE

When Steve Jobs became involved with the development of the Apple IIc, he felt they should continue with the open IIe as had already been planned, but this compact Apple II should be marketed as a product focused to a specific group of customers, primarily new users. Early on, he envisioned a closed Apple II that had a built-in mouse port, one serial port, and some other features. What they ended up with at that point was just a computer and a keyboard. Walt Broedner, the engineer who campaigned for the production of the Apple IIe, used some of their previous work with custom integrated circuits for the disk controller and combined both projects together to make the IIc.[10]

Although he was initially told it was not possible, Jobs pushed for the mouse in this closed Apple II to be compatible with the Macintosh mouse—and the engineers managed to make it work. Regarding the plans for a single serial port, however, Apple's marketing people pointed out to Jobs that many people were going to want both a printer *and* a modem, so they added a second port to the original design. They decided to use serial ports on the IIc instead of parallel ports for a couple of reasons. First, the socket for a serial port was smaller than a parallel port, and it would fit better onto a small box like the IIc. Also, Apple's general direction at the time was to get consistency in its hardware, and they had decided to use a serial interface in every computer they made.

Work on the Apple IIc began in earnest immediately after the IIe was finished. Because the engineering team was trying to squeeze an Apple IIe with 128K of RAM, 80 column routines, two serial cards, disk controller, and a mouse card into an 11 by 12-inch case, the design challenges were greater than with the IIe (recall that this was what appealed to Steve Jobs). The size of the case was determined by the decision to make it fit into a standard-sized briefcase.[11]

Apple also had the international market in mind when designing the IIc. A special chip containing the keyboard map could easily be changed depending on the country, to make it consistent with regional keyboard differences. The external pushbutton would switch between the two different keyboards—between a UK and German layout, for example. On the British version, the primary difference was substitution of the "£" symbol for the "#" symbol. On French, German, Italian, and Spanish versions there were several different language-specific symbols available with the switch in the down position. The Canadian version of the IIc was the same as the American version with the switch up, and some other special symbols when it was down. This version was unique, as each keycap had the symobols for both switched versions. For example, the "3" keycap had a "3", "#", and "£" on it, making it more crowded than a typical keycap.

---

10 Williams, Gregg, "'C' Is For Crunch", *BYTE* (December 1984), A75–A78, A121.
11 Williams, Gregg, "'C' Is For Crunch", *BYTE* (December 1984), A75–A78, A121.

In the US version of the IIc it switched from a standard Sholes keyboard (also known as "QWERTY") to a Dvorak keyboard (which allowed faster touch typing). The decision for the foreign keyboards came first; the added bonus for American versions of getting Dvorak came as an extra bonus, to save having two different cases (one for US and one for foreign versions).

One problem in creating such a compact computer was dealing with heat production. Apple engineers wanted it to be able to function in environmental temperatures up to 40 degrees Celsius (about 104 degrees Fahrenheit). One article published at the time of its introduction mentioned that the designers wanted to make the IIc tolerant of doing a long disk sort (sorting data in a disk file) while on the beach in Florida in the summer! Their major obstacle was the heat generated by the internal 5.25-inch disk drive. They tried special low power drives (which would have been much more expensive), but these too could not overcome the heat problem. Eventually they tried a complicated venting scheme that involved drilling holes into a case, putting it into an oven, and then measuring the internal temperatures. The engineers were surprised when they found that the normal power disk drive worked and generated less overall heat within the case than the special low power drive did. The only explanation they could come up with was that the normal drive generated enough heat to cause air around it to rise, which in turn pulled cool air in through the vents by convection.

> Since they used the newer 65c02 chip, which ran cooler and had 27 additional commands that could be used by assembly language programs, Apple's programmers could improve the firmware design. Such power was needed to squeeze in all the firmware code for the IIe, plus code for the disk controller, serial cards, mouse card, and 80-column card into 16K of ROM space.

The programmers fixed some known bugs in the IIe ROMs and added 32 graphics characters they called MouseText. To make MouseText fit in the character ROM, they chose to remove the ability to use flashing characters (when in 80 column mode) and replaced those characters with MouseText.

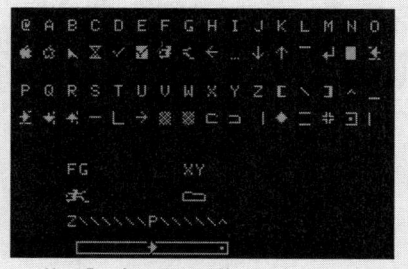

MouseText character set – Photo credit: personal

Changes were made to Applesoft so that commands could be entered in lowercase (and automatically translated into uppercase). They removed the Applesoft commands that were specific to the cassette interface (which was absent in the IIc) and made Applesoft more compatible with 80 columns.[12, 13]

---

12 Williams, Gregg, "'C' Is For Crunch", *BYTE* (December 1984), A75-A78, A121.
13 Weishaar, Tom, "Miscellanea", *Open-Apple*, (August 1985), 1.61.

PRODUCT INTRODUCTION

Under Steve Jobs, Apple was developing a reputation for creating events to introduce new products. In January 1984, Jobs had used just such an event to introduce the Macintosh, raising it as a standard to push back the specter of IBM's potential domination of computers. This was demonstrated in the famous 1984 commercial that had played during the Super Bowl that year.

Apple's introduction of the new IIc came at an event not as dramatic, but no less enthusiastic. It was held at the Moscone Center in downtown San Francisco on April 24th, 1984. The gathering was called "Apple II Forever", and was described in *Softalk* magazine as "part revival meeting, part sermon, part roundtable discussion, part pagan rite, and part county fair." Apple's objectives here were to introduce the Apple IIc, describe how it fit into the company's marketing strategy, show off software that was made to work with the new computer, and emphasize that Apple was still firmly behind the Apple II line of computers. Despite the intended focus on the Apple II, Steve Jobs could not prevent himself from taking some of the time to report on the sales of the Macintosh in its first 100 days.[14]

Apple IIc with Monitor IIc
– Photo credit: Adam Jenkins, Wikipedia

Apple took the further step of contracting with a singer named Jill Colucci (who sounded a lot like pop-star Pat Benatar) to record songs for the company. In January, this singer had done a song for the Macintosh introduction called "We Are Apple (Leading The Way)". For the Apple II Forever event, the song extolled the event's theme. Admittedly, the lyrics were not very profound, but the tune was catchy:

> Remember how we started, not so long ago,
> We dreamed of giving everyone a personal way to grow.
> Our dream became reality, and now we're making
> History!
>
> We took imagination, and let it lead the way
> To a new world of discovery, affecting lives every day
> Bringing smiles to children's faces,
> Opening doors to brand new places

---

14 Durkee, David, "Marketalk", *Softalk* (June 1984), 54-55.

CHAPTER 24 | Compact and Powerful

Apple II forever, making life better and better
Apple II forever and ever, bringing the rainbow to you
Apple II –
Forever!

And as the world keeps changin', we'll be changin' too,
Reaching out with new ideas, bringing them all to you
Our future keeps on growing and growing,
Our colors keep on showing and glowing.

Apple II forever, making life better and better
Apple II forever and ever, bringing the rainbow to you
Apple II –
Forever!

Accompanying the song was a slide show video. It showed the historical development of the company, starting with the Apple-1 built in a garage, to the early days of the Apple II, to photos of people using their Apple II computers. The song was clearly designed to be a feel-good celebration of the Apple II, as well as marketing hype stressing their commitment to the platform for an indefinite length of time. However, the Apple II user and development community took the event and the song as a *promise* that the company would support their favorite platform—what else?—*forever*. Had they all watched the video and listened to the lyrics carefully, the signs were all there. After the picture of early days of the Apple II, it was primarily children (not businessmen or adults) happily using their Apple II computers. When it got to the verse *"as the world keeps changin', we'll be changin' too"*, it showed people with their Apple III, Lisa, and Macintosh computers—and not even an Apple IIc in the bunch. The Apple II took the forefront again briefly at the end of the video, but the coolest people in the video were the ones with the Lisa and the Mac.

For the actual introduction of the IIc, a bit of grandstanding was done for the crowd. Giant video screens were used to show previews of Apple's TV commercials for the IIc, as well as slides and images of the speakers, including Wozniak, Jobs, and Apple's new president, John Sculley. He spoke of "sharing power", and then demonstrated that in a unique way:

> After holding up the tiny IIc for everyone to see and eliciting a response that they'd like to see it better, Sculley ordered the house lights on. As the light burst forth, nearly every fifth person in the audience stood up, waving high a IIc. As startled dealers cheered uproariously, the Apple plants passed the IIc computers to them. Within seconds of

its introduction, more than a thousand Apple dealers had a production line IIc in their hands.[15]

"Apple II Forever" event at the Moscone Center April 24, 1984. The picture shows the Apple employees holding up Apple IIc computers for the computer dealers to examine – Photo credit: *Softalk*, June 1984

When Jobs gave his report on the Mac, he revealed some interesting statistics. He told them that the first industry standard was the Apple II, which sold fifty thousand machines in two and a half years.[16] The second standard was the IBM PC, which sold the same amount in eight months. Macintosh had done sold its fifty thousand machines only 74 days after its introduction. Although actual sales would not be nearly as good, Apple took orders that day for fifty thousand Apple IIc computers in just over seven *hours*.

At the Apple II Forever event, they also had a general software exhibition and a setup called the Apple II Museum. This contained Apple memorabilia, and included Woz's original Apple-1, and a reproduction of Steve Jobs' garage where it was built. Although not on the schedule, Apple II Forever included an early-afternoon earthquake centered south of San Jose that measured 6.2 on the Richter scale.

SUCCESS?

Apple's original goal had been to sell the IIc for $995. Due to production costs, it couldn't hit that price, so compromised with $1,295, balancing the decision with the number of people who were predicted to buy the optional Monitor IIc or an external Disk IIc drive.

The only problem was that although the IIc was a technological breakthrough in miniaturization, customers at that time didn't value smallness.

---

15 Durkee, David, "Marketalk", *Softalk* (June 1984), 54-55.
16 Jobs and Apple have had a penchant for hyperbole and exaggeration since its earliest years. While touting the sales of 50,000 Apple II computers in its first two and a half years, he conveniently ignored the fact that 450,000 Atari 400 and 800 computers, 350,000 TRS-80 computers, and 56,000 Commodore PET sold over the first two and a half years of sales of those computers.

They viewed something that was too small as also being cheap and lacking power. Although the Apple IIc was equivalent to a IIe loaded with extra memory, a disk drive, two serial cards, and a mouse card, most customers seemed to want the more expandable IIe. Apple marketing went to much effort to make the IIc attractive, but it didn't sell as well as the IIe. Just as IBM overestimated the market when producing its PCjr (which eventually failed and was discontinued), so did Apple when producing the IIc (as well as the original Macintosh).[17]

Apple IIc rear panel, showing paddle port, modem serial port, RGB video connector, composite video connector, disk connector, printer serial port, power connector, and power switch – Photo credit: *Setting Up Your Apple IIc*. Cupertino, California, Apple Computer, Inc., 1984

OVERCOMING LIMITATIONS

Although the IIc did not have any slots for plugging in peripheral cards that had traditionally been used in the Apple II, the ports that were built-in had the capability to do much of what the slots had often been used for. The serial ports were compatible with any serial device; this included common ones such as printers and modems, and uncommon ones like security controllers, clocks (to allow date and time calculations in programs and date stamping of files), and speech synthesizers. Some third party companies also supplied serial-to-parallel converters for IIc owners who wanted to use parallel printers made by Epson, Okidata, and C. Itoh that were popular elsewhere in the computer world.

There was, of course, the AppleMouse IIc sold by Apple. It plugged into the game port on the IIc. Also available were two types of touch tablets: The Power Pad (Chalkboard) and Koala Pad (Koala Technologies), though the latter sold best. The Koala pad would appear to a program to be the same as a joystick, but could not emulate the mouse.[18]

The disk port on the original IIc was only designed to control an external 5.25-inch disk drive. Apple sold the Disk IIc for $329, and other companies later sold similar drives for less. Despite this firmware limitation, Quark Engineering released a 10 MB Winchester hard drive called the QC10 that would work with this disk port, and was the first hard disk available for the IIc.

The video port worked with a standard monitor, but had access to all video signals. Included with the original IIc was an RF modulator that allowed it to connect to a standard television (for color games). An RGB adapter box attached to the video port would allow a true RGB monitor to be attached, giving color and sharp, readable 80 column text on the same monitor.

---

17 Durkee, David, "Marketalk", *Softalk* (June 1984), 54-55.
18 Baum, Peter, "Expanding The Unexpandable IIc", *Softalk* (June 1984), 95-97.

Apple also sold a flat-panel liquid crystal display for the IIc that attached to this video port. It was capable of 80 columns by 24 lines, as well as double hi-res graphics. Apple's price was about $600, but it looked somewhat "squashed" vertically, and did not sell well. SVI marketed a somewhat better flat panel liquid crystal display called the C-Vue. It measured 9 inches wide by 3¾ inches high, had less graphic distortion than Apple's screen did, and it's size better accommodated the built-in handle on the IIc.[19] However, either product could be difficult to use, depending on ambient lighting; this was a common problem with LCD displays of any kind.

With a battery attached to the 12V input, and one of these LCD displays, the IIc could be made into a truly portable computer.

After the release of the original Apple IIc, there were several motherboard upgrades offered to customers. The UniDisk 3.5 upgrade was a major one, and this opened the door to attaching large storage devices to the disk port on the back of the IIc. The upgrade also included enhancements to the Monitor, with reinstatement of the Mini-assembler, and assembly step and trace commands.

Apple IIc with LCD display – Photo credit: Dean Nichols

The Memory Expansion revision made it possible to add large internal storage to the IIc, allowing as much as 1 MB of memory as a RAM disk or extra memory for software designed to handle it. It was designed to work even with third-party memory cards. Some minor bugs introduced in that motherboard were addressed by the revised Memory Expansion motherboard, offered during the last year the IIc was in production.

TIMELINE

The start and end dates for each model of the Apple IIc, IIGS, Lisa, and early Macintosh:

Lisa – *January 1983 - December 1983*

Macintosh – *January 1984 - August 1984*

Apple IIc (UniDisk 3.5) – *November 1985 - August 1986*

Macintosh Plus – *January 1986 - March 1987*

---

19 Fields, Cynthia E, "Once Again, An Apple IIc LCD", *InfoWorld*, (June 8, 1985), 52.

Lisa 2 – *January 1984 - December 1984*

Apple IIc – *April 1984 - October 1985*

Macintosh 512 – *September 1984 - December 1985*

Macintosh XL – *January 1985 - April 1985*

Apple IIc (Mem Exp) – *September 1986 - December 1987*

Apple IIGS (all versions) – *September 1986 - December 1992*

Apple IIc (Rev Mem Exp) – *January 1988 - August 1988*

CHAPTER 25
The Tower of Babel

In the era of 8-bit computers, assembly language was ideal for complex programs that could control all aspects of the computer and it would run as fast as the microprocessor could manage. However, it could be tedious for large-scale projects, and required manual control of all data types (integer numbers, floating-point numbers, character strings, and so on). BASIC could much more easily handle those data types, but did not offer the degree of deep hardware control, and a program could easily run out of available memory, requiring segmentation that made the program more difficult to manage.

It was necessary to introduce programming languages that were more flexible than assembly language and more powerful than BASIC. These languages also addressed the need for translation of software from older mainframe programs to use in a microcomputer environment. This chapter looks at several that were available for the Apple II, all of which offered solutions to these difficulties. These include Pascal, C, and several less popular languages, including FORTRAN, COBOL, Forth, PILOT, and Logo.

FORTRAN

FORTRAN was one of the oldest high-level languages for computers, originally developed for IBM mainframe computers in the 1950s. Its name was derived from the first formal proposal for the project to IBM, *The IBM Mathetmatical FORmula TRANslating System*. The advantages it offered to programmers was in creating code that was much easier to read than assembly language. FORTRAN gained popularity amongst scientists and engineers for its power in doing precision floating-point calculations.

Apple FORTRAN was released in July 1980. It ran under the Pascal System, and sold for $200, over and above the $495 cost for the Language System hardware and Pascal System software. Written for Apple by Silicon Valley Software, this version was supposed to be compliant with the FORTRAN 77 standard that had been approved in 1978 by the American National Standards Institute. However, end users found that it acted more like a FORTRAN 66 implementation with additions to try to function like FOR-

TRAN 77, as programs written for that later revision did not always run under Apple FORTRAN.

With these caveats, FORTRAN code written on other computers *in general* ran with little modification under Apple FORTRAN. It compiled to a similar p-code as did Pascal programs, so was not any faster than Pascal. Because it ran under the Pascal System, Apple FORTRAN did offer the ability to use Pascal subroutines from FORTRAN programs, and FORTAN subroutines from Pascal programs.

Apple FORTRAN was supplied on two floppy disks. The first disk, FORT1 was the boot disk, and contained the files to start up the Pascal System. The second disk, FORT2, had the FORTRAN compiler and libraries, and was protected, making it difficult to copy.

Apple's version of FORTRAN contained many bugs, and after its introduction in 1980 it was never upgraded. When Pascal System 1.2 came out in 1983, the Apple FORTRAN compiler would not even run unless it was patched with a Pascal program provided by Apple. By September 1986 it had disappeared from its product catalogs.

Another way for an Apple II user to program in FORTRAN was to buy the Microsoft SoftCard for $345 and *Microsoft FORTRAN* for $200. This version of FORTRAN was more full-featured than Apple's, and offered some advantages in usability. It did not require changing to the 16-sector disk controller ROMs (if the user did not want to upgrade). Also, standard *Microsoft BASIC* (which was more advanced than Applesoft) was included in the SoftCard package.[1]

Apple FORTRAN manual cover – Photo credit: personal

The original UCSD p-System became a commercial product in its own right. In 1979 the University of California transferred further development on it to SofTech Microsystems, a company established specifically to maintain the p-System. The work changed hands twice more before ending up under the control of Pecan Software Systems, Inc., a small company formed by p-System users and enthusiasts. Besides the Pascal compilers they maintained, Pecan also released other languages for multiple different platforms. For the Apple IIGs, Pecan released FORTRAN for the IIGs for $99. It ran under Pro-

---

1   Winston, Alan B, "The Multi Lingual Apple", *PEEKing At Call-A.P.P.L.E.* (Seattle, Washington, Vol. 3, 1980), 222-224.

DOS 16 (GS/OS), but still used the UCSD Pascal System disk format for its FORTRAN by creating a ProDOS file that then acted as a UCSD Volume.[2]

COBOL

Another early computer language was COBOL, developed in the late 1950s soon after FORTRAN. The name was an acronym for COmmon Business Oriented Language, and was intended to allow programming business and finance applications. Just as FORTRAN made programs more readable than offered by assembly language programs, COBOL was even more readable. Most of its commands used English phrasing and fewer abbreviated commands. With its focus on business use extending back to the 1960s, COBOL was a language that continued to be utilized and updated even into the twenty-first century.

On the Apple II, however, the COBOL language had limited availability, and was likely not much in demand. Microsoft sold it for $599 as a language to run under the CP/M system with the Microsoft SoftCard.[3] There were reportedly plans by another company for a 6502 version to run under the Pascal System, but this was never officially released.

FORTH

An advantage of BASIC was that it did not force any particular structure on the program code. The disadvantage of that freedom appeared when a program grew beyond a certain point. The ability to use the GOTO statement to transfer control from one part of a program to another made it easy to create what became known as "spaghetti code", a program so twisted and convoluted that it was nearly impossible to follow. As a response to this unstructured type of programming, languages such as Pascal were designed so the programmer had to organize the code in such a way that it was easy to follow. Another structured programming language that had modest popularity on early microcomputer systems was called Forth. It had been created in the late 1950s, and when it was implemented on the IBM 1130 computer, its name had to be truncated from Fourth (as in "fourth generation software") to Forth, as that operating system was limited to 5 character file names.

Forth was a compact language, and so was well suited to the limited memory space of computers like the IBM 1130, and also on microcomputers in the 1970s and 1980s. It was not only a structured language, but it was also extensible — meaning the programmer could create new commands within

---

2 Geenen, Donald, "FORTRAN-77 Forever!" *Call-A.P.P.L.E.* (March 1989), 20-26.
3 -----, (ads), *Call-A.P.P.L.E. In Depth #1*, (Seattle, Washington, 1981), 106.

the language. In essence, the new command was a type of subroutine that became part of the language, and could then be used in other programs.

The first version of the language available for the Apple II was *Apple Forth*, written by the infamous hacker John Draper[4] (known by his handle, Cap'n Crunch) and sold through his company, Cap'n Software. The initial release in the late 1970s was available only on cassette, since Draper did not yet have a Disk II drive.[5] The language included commands to display lo-res and hi-res graphics.

By the time he released version 1.6, it was available on disk, but it used Draper's own unique operating system that was not compatible with Apple DOS. Draper had created the OS himself to work with the Forth language, and he enjoyed the ability to create whatever commands he needed for either the language or the disk system. He chose to use his own disk system specifically because it was faster than Apple DOS 3.2.

Draper later wrote the first word processor for the Apple II, *EasyWriter*, entirely in his Apple Forth language. The disk system was so speedy that it took only a few seconds to go from startup to the text editor.[6] Draper's work also demonstrated that languages other than BASIC or Pascal could create professional software on the Apple II.

Programma's *AppleFORTH* splash screen – Photo credit: personal

Another version of the language was *AppleFORTH 1.2*, marketed by Programma International in 1979. Programma's Forth was more extensive, but also more complicated. It supported lo-res but not hi-res graphics. The company sold versions of this language not only for the Apple II, but also for the Commodore PET and CP/M-based computers.[7]

GraFORTH was written by Apple Writer author Paul Lutus and published in 1982 by his company, Insoft. It was a very fast compiled implementation of Forth, and ran under DOS 3.3. It was unique to other versions available on the Apple II in that it included the ability to draw on the hi-res screen using Turtle graphics, much in the same way as Logo (which will be discussed). It used integer math only, and could draw fast enough for a program to display animation. It even allowed creation of simple 3D wireframe shapes. Additionally, GraFORTH could

---

4 John Draper was the legendary phone phreaker "Cap'n Crunch" who had taught Wozniak about making blue boxes, and later worked at Apple in its early days. During his time at Apple he had designed one of the first peripheral cards for the Apple II: A telephone controlling device that also just happened to be capable of hacking into long distance telephone switching systems, and was therefore quite illegal.
5 Besher, Alexander, "The Crunching Of America", *InfoWorld*, June 18, 1984, 66-67.
6 Draper, John, "The Creation of EasyWriter", *WebCrunchers*, <http://www.webcrunchers.com/stories/easywriter.html>
7 Winston, Alan B, "The Multi-Lingual Apple: Languages", *PEEKing At Call-A.P.P.L.E.* (Seattle, Washington, Vol. 2, 1979), 183-190.

create sound effects and music, similar to what was possible using the sound routines in the Integer BASIC ROM.

Lutus also wrote a more robust version of the language, called *TransFORTH II*. Released the same year as GraFORTH, Lutus stated in the accompanying manual that he had designed it as "a general purpose scientific and business language" for the Apple II.

TransFORTH II had the advantage of being a structured language that could run in both interpreted and compiled forms (the compiled programs could be executed from DOS 3.3 via the BRUN command). Additionally, the TransFORTH language was compact, included the ability to create lo-res and hi-res graphics, and could make full use of the RAM in a 128K Apple IIe. The second version, *TransFORTH IIB*, could load itself into the Language Card RAM, leaving more memory available for programs. Lutus marketed TransFORTH for scientific and business programming, while GraFORTH was intended for games and educational software, and had a richer set of graphics features. Insoft sold TransFORTH for $125, and GraFORTH for $75.

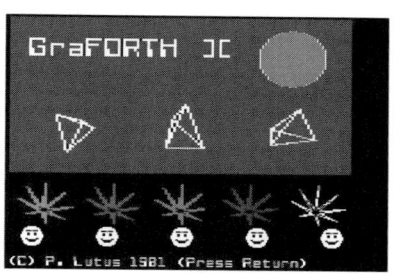

GraFORTH splash screen – Photo credit: personal

PILOT

In the 1960s, Dr. John Starkweather at the University of California designed PILOT as a special-purpose language for educational programming. The name was an acronym for Programmed Inquiry, Learning Or Teaching. He designed it primarily for educators to create tutorial modules for computer-aided instruction.

The language was quite simple, and allowed design of interactive programs to instruct students and test them on their responses during the process. One early version for the Apple II (not produced by Apple) was written in Applesoft and was entirely text-based.

Apple released its own graphics and sound enhanced version called *Apple PILOT* in 1980. Selling for $125, it ran under version 1.0 of the Pascal System, thus requiring the $495 Language System.[8] There were two modes— Author mode, in which the programmer created a lesson, and Lesson mode, in which a student followed a lesson. PILOT required two disk drives to operate in Author mode, and one disk drive to run a Lesson disk.

---

8 Vanderpool, Tom, A2 Roundtable, Category 2, Topic 16, *GEnie*, accessed March & August 1991.

When an Author disk initialized a Lesson disk, it formatted the disk under the Pascal System, and then included the necessary files to allow the disk to boot (much like Apple DOS created bootable disks). After those files were written to the disk, 144 blocks (just over half of the disk space) was available for lesson, graphics, and sound files. To create lessons, Apple PILOT used the hi-res screen to display upper and lowercase characters (not possible on the text screen without extra hardware on an Apple II or II Plus). The sound effects, graphics, and character set editors worked on the hi-res screen, using either the keyboard or the paddles to draw. To create lesson files (using the PILOT programming language), it used the standard 40-column text screen. In this mode, again the Apple Writer method was used, with lowercase characters displayed as standard uppercase ASCII, and uppercase as inverse ASCII characters.

Apple PILOT program screen – Photo credit: personal

The Lesson disks contained enough of the Pascal System files to allow it to boot (still in a 48K environment), and execute the PILOT system file, which then looked for a file HELLO.TEXT. If this was a PILOT lesson file, it executed. The default HELLO.TEXT file was a sample program that asked the user to enter the name of a lesson file to load (not unlike the requirement in Apple DOS to type "RUN PROGRAM").

Apple released *Apple SuperPILOT* in 1982. It ran under Pascal System 1.1 and had increased memory requirements that made it necessary to own a full 64K Apple II. The editing tools were improved and made faster, and the lesson editor was changed to use the hi-res screen just like the other modules (allowing direct display of upper and lowercase characters). The graphics drivers were enhanced, allowing new graphics effects. The language itself was also improved, offering commands to control external devices (such as videodisc and videotape players).

At some point after Pascal System 1.3 was released in 1985, Apple made available an updated version called *Apple SuperPILOT Special Edition*. Because of the enhancements in this 1.3 environment, it was possible to access 3.5-inch disks and hard drives.[9]

---

9 Karasoridis, Stavros, e-mail message to author, October 16, 2012.

LOGO

LISP (the name derived from LISt Processing) was a language developed at MIT by Dr. John McCarthy at the Massachusetts Institute of Technology (MIT) in the late 1950s. The creation of LISP was closely related to his research into artificial intelligence. One of its unique features was allowing the programmer to create custom commands, specifically combinations of existing commands. This was in contrast to FORTRAN and COBOL, which had a fixed set of statements that could not be expanded upon. The problem with LISP was that it had a very confusing syntax, so was not very friendly to learn.

In 1967, with the help of a National Science Foundation grant, Dr. Seymour Papert and a team at Bolt, Beranek and Newman in Cambridge, Massachusetts, worked to create a simpler LISP. Their goal was to make a version suitable to use in education. This new language, which they called Logo, was originally designed specifically to teach math concepts to children. Furthermore, they tried to make it a less complicated language to learn and use.

To aid in this process, Papert's team created simple graphics on a computer screen that could be controlled with Logo commands, and then later expanded on this by making use of a small mechanical device called a turtle. These robot devices had been utilized in computer research as far back as the 1940s. In adapting the older work to the Logo language, they gave these robots a role that had not previously been possible. Commands in the language could move the turtle in different directions, and use it to draw the results on a piece of paper as it moved on the floor. The command-creation feature of Logo allowed a specific type of movement to be designed, and then repeated in a pattern.[10]

Like Forth, it was possible to create custom commands in Logo. To make the turtle on the screen draw a square, it was necessary to execute four times the command to move forward a measured amount, and then turn 90 degrees to the right. Making this into a defined command for the user's workspace required only a line to define its name, and one more to tell when the procedure had ended:

```
TO SQUARE
REPEAT 4 [FORWARD 50 RIGHT 90]
END
```

This new command, SQUARE, could then be used in other programs.[11]

During the 1970s, research was done with elementary school students and how they could make use of Logo for learning, and its advantages made it clear that it could help improve math understanding and reasoning even at

---

10 Mace, Scott, "Where Is Logo Taking Our Kids?", *InfoWorld* (January 23, 1984), 46-51.
11 Abelson, Harold, "A Beginner's Guide To Logo", *BYTE* (August 1982), 88-112.

early ages. This increased the interest in getting computers into schools, and the home computers of the late 1970s were more affordable than getting an account and equipment to use a mainframe remotely. For these reasons, the MIT Logo researchers worked on getting the language onto those computers.

In 1981, MIT initially authorized two companies to produce versions of the language for the Apple II, *Krell Logo* from Krell Software Corporation and *Terrapin Logo* from Terrapin Software.[12] Krell Logo sold for $90 for a very basic version, or $150 with additional disks and manuals, whereas Terrapin Logo offered only a single version for $150. These ran under DOS 3.3, and could run on a 16K Apple II. Terrapin Logo could be purchased also with an actual mechanical turtle that moved on the floor in response to commands on the computer.[13] It's manuals were less comprehensive manuals about the language, and dealt more with operation of the Terrapin Turtle robot. *Krell Logo*, on the other hand, was distributed with two technical manuals, and four disks, including the program disk, a backup disk, a utilities disk, and a computer-assisted tutorial on disk called *Alice In Logoland*.

By 1984 both Krell Software and Terrapin Software also offered peripheral cards (at different price points and capabilities) for the Apple II. These cards extended the computer's graphics abilities for Logo programs, allowing creation and display of sprites. Sprites were small pictures that displayed on different overlapping planes on the graphics screen, and could be programmed to move in a specific direction and speed, until instructed to stop. The hardware that managed this feat was based on a graphic chip designed by Texas Instruments (a chip that was built into the TI 99/4A home computer and was directly accessible to *TI Logo* for that platform).[14]

Apple Logo II splash screen – Photo credit: personal

Logo Computer Systems, Inc. created Apple's first version of Logo, which sold for $175. (The same company also sold *Atari Logo* and *IBM Logo*.) It operated under the Pascal System, and ran on any 64K Apple II with the 16K Language Card. *Apple Logo* was distributed on a copy-protected disk, and included two large reference manuals with tutorials. *Apple Logo II*, released in July 1984 for $100, was modified to run under ProDOS, and required an Apple IIc or Apple IIe with 128K memory.[15]

---

12 Adams III, Roe R, "The New Shell Game", *Softalk* (July 1982), 44.
13 Roth, Richard, "A Comparison Of Logo: Today's Turtle Is No Slowpoke", *Creative Computing* (Vol 10, No. 12, December 1984), 94.
14 Mace, Scott, "Where Is Logo Taking Our Kids?", *InfoWorld* (January 23, 1984), 46-51.
15 -----, *Apple IIc Memory Expansion Card Owner's Guide* (Apple Computer, Inc, Singapore, 1986), 2-4.

C

The C language was created in the early 1970s at Bell Labs, and its development occurred in parallel with the beginnings of the Unix operating system. The language became sufficiently powerful that Unix itself was rewritten in C (previously it had been in assembly language). Like Pascal, it offered structured programming, but like assembly language it offered the ability to do low-level control of the computer. Its later widespread use stemmed from it's the inexpensive licensing fee for universities to use Unix for their computers, and the close connection with C led those programmers to learn C along with Unix.[16]

There were a few versions of the C language that became available for the Apple II. For those with the SoftCard CP/M environment, *BDS C* was an available option. Since it had been created originally in 1979, it was possible to create programs in C as soon as 1980 when the SoftCard was released. However, it was specifically for the 8080 or Z-80 microprocessor, and so was not native for the 6502.

Manx Software Systems of Shrewsbury, New Jersey wrote C compilers for many of the early home computer systems. In 1983 the company released *Aztec C65* for the Apple II, running under DOS 3.3, with later revisions updated to run under ProDOS.

Hyper-C was another such product that operated under ProDOS. It was sold by the WSM Group, but was a subset of C. It ran on any 64K Apple II, included an assembler, and would fit on a single 140K disk. The WSM Group went out of business by the early 1990s, and Hyper-C was released to freeware status.

APPLE PASCAL UPDATES

The release of Apple Pascal 1.2 in 1983 provided bug fixes and made changes to better utilize some of the improved features available on the Apple IIe. This included support for the cursor keys (the Apple IIe had up and down arrows lacking on the older Apple II models), proper support for upper- and lowercase input from the IIe keyboard, and the ability to use the open-apple and solid-apple keys.

On a 128K Apple IIe, Apple Pascal 1.2 could make use of this extra memory; it was done by replacing the SYSTEM.APPLE and SYSTEM.PASCAL files on the startup disk with files on the APPLE3 volume. This larger version of Pascal used the main board RAM for assembly code and data, and the auxiliary RAM for compiled p-code and for the Pascal operating system. Also, this 1.2 version allowed the Pascal compiler to stay entirely in memory dur-

---

16 von Bassewitz, Ullrich, *cc65 – The 6502 C Compiler*, <www.cc65.org>, accessed March 14, 2013.

ing compilation of a Pascal program, which eliminated some disk swapping that was otherwise necessary.

With the proliferation of the 64K Apple IIe and 128K Apple IIc, an adequate platform for Pascal applications had finally become available. However, by the time that occurred, the primary disk system being promoted for the Apple II was ProDOS, and Apple never released a version of their original UCSD Pascal to run under that operating system. (Possibly, since by definition UCSD Pascal was the language *and* the operating system, it would be unnecessarily complex to modify that version of Pascal to run under ProDOS.)

In 1985, Apple Pascal was upgraded to version 1.3, which supported the more advanced features of the Apple IIe and IIc. It could handle access to larger storage devices attached to the Smartport on a IIc, and the run-time environment was enhanced to work with 64K and 128K systems.

However, when the Apple IIGS was released three years later, a problem surfaced. Apple Pascal was not capable of making use of the larger memory on that computer, and still worked as an 8-bit operating system. When third-party Pascal solutions became available (such as *ORCA/Pascal* from The Byte Works), IIGS programmers turned to that or other IIGS-specific Pascal languages, since they were designed take full advantage of that machine in 16-bit mode.

INSTANT PASCAL

Massachusetts-based THINK Technologies originally wrote and published *Instant Pascal* for the Apple II. Then in 1985 Apple bought the rights to sell it as a program for teaching Pascal. It only ran on the Apple IIc or a 128K IIe because it used the double hi-res graphics mode, functioning much like a Macintosh desktop with multiple resizable windows. Though it displayed on the double hi-res *graphics* screen, it was not recommended to try to use it with color monitors, and did not support color text (it was simply unreadable under those circumstances).

It had a mouse-based editor that checked program syntax as each line was entered (much like the older Integer BASIC) and automatically indented lines and boldfaced Pascal reserved words. Since it was intended for teaching, it also had a single-step trace function and the ability to modify the contents of variables while running a program.

Instant Pascal 1.5 screenshot – Photo credit: personal

Though useful for learning the language, it was quite slow because of the overhead needed to display code in graphics, and because it was an interpreted version of Pascal (instead of a compiled version). Not coincidentally, programs written in Instant Pascal on the Apple II ran under Apple's *MacPascal* (which had also been created by THINK Technologies) on the Mac, making the Apple II language no more than a training ground for transitioning to a Mac.

Fans of the original Apple Pascal complained loudly after Apple introduced Instant Pascal, as the company no longer appeared motivated to make any further upgrades to their older Pascal. Instant Pascal worked under ProDOS, but the older Pascal still required the incompatible Pascal disk system.[17]

TIMELINE

Apple Forth 1.6 (Cap'n Software) – *1979*

AppleFORTH 1.2 (Programma) – *1979*

Apple Pascal – *August 1979*

Apple Pascal 1.1 – *1980*

Apple FORTRAN – *July 1980*

Apple PILOT – *1980*

Microsoft COBOL – *1980*

Krell Logo – *1981*

Terrapin Logo – *1981*

GraFORTH – *1982*

TransFORTH II – *1982*

Apple SuperPILOT – *1982*

Apple Logo – *July 1982*

Apple Pascal 1.2 – *1983*

Aztec C65 – *1983*

Apple Logo II – *1984*

Apple SuperPILOT Special Edition – *1985*

Apple Pascal 1.3 – *1985*

Instant Pascal – *1985*

---

[17] Howerton, Christopher, and Purvis, Lee, "The Apple IIgs Pascal Revue", Call-A.P.P.L.E. (April 1988), 12-17.

CHAPTER 26

Improving Your Memory

The first ROM expansion card for the Apple II was the previously discussed Applesoft Firmware Card, released in June 1978. It switched out the Integer BASIC ROM code in upper memory on the motherboard for Applesoft, and made the full version of this floating point language available for owners of the original Apple II. Conversely, Apple II Plus users were later able to purchase an Integer Firmware Card to allow themselves access to the thousands of Integer BASIC programs that were created in the two years before the II Plus was released.

The advantage Apple II Plus users had over the original Apple II was the ability to create a system that would automatically boot a disk when the computer was turned on or when RESET was pressed. The disadvantage (to some) was that the Autostart ROM forced a reboot, even when the user didn't want it to. Game authors made use of this feature as a means of copy protection. Often, this software would not only reboot the disk when RESET was pressed, but would also purposely clear memory before rebooting.

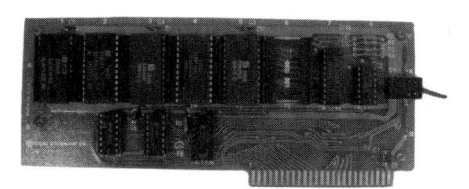

Applesoft Firmware Card – Photo credit: Mike Loewen

The Integer Firmware Card became popular amongst software hackers because it gave them the tools to look at the code in games that forced a reboot. All that was necessary was to start the game with the switch on the card in Applesoft/Autostart ROM mode, and then flip the switch on the card to Integer BASIC/Old Monitor mode. At that point, pressing the RESET key would leave the computer at the Monitor prompt, which allowed examination of the code in memory.

The next card Apple released for slot 0 was the Language Card, released in 1979 with Apple Pascal. Besides providing addition RAM space for the Pascal System, under DOS 3.2 and 3.3 it made it possible to load into RAM the version of BASIC that was not in the motherboard ROM. This was a more flexible alternative to the Firmware Card, and opened the way to other languages beyond BASIC for Apple II users.

The Language Card paved the way for adding additional memory into an Apple II. In late 1979, programmers at Apple were using Apple II computers to program in Pascal for the Lisa project. They had hit the 64K barrier and required more space. Burrell Smith, who later designed the hardware for Jef Raskin's Macintosh project, came up with the idea of adding an additional 16K bank of RAM to the Language Card. This custom 32K Language Card created an 80K Apple II, which the Lisa team used until the Lisa hardware and firmware were developed enough to use the Lisa itself for coding.[1] However, Apple did not see this as a marketable product, and it was years until Apple released its own larger memory expansion options for the Apple II.

At a price of $495, purchasing the Language Card from Apple (which included Apple Pascal) was too expensive for many users. Other companies soon released similar cards that did not require purchasing Pascal, and some of them designed the cards with more banks of memory, allowing 256K or more of extra memory. Saturn Systems was one such early supplier of the large RAM cards. As with Burrell Smith's hack, each 16K bank on the card switched into the same memory space occupied by the Language Card RAM through the use of special software code.[2]

1982 was significant for the release of RAM cards, as a number of them were introduced that year. Many of these cards worked by simulating a floppy disk drive. MPC Peripherals released the MPC BubDisk, using bubble memory technology (which did not lose its data when power was removed). However, at $895 for 128K, it was not very affordable for the home hobbyist.[3]

Entrepreneur Nolan Bushnell started a number of other companies after Warner Communications bought his early big success, Atari. One of them, Axlon, Inc., created a variety of products, including one directed towards business users of the Apple II. The RAMdisk 320 looked to the computer like two floppy drives, but it was fully solid-state. It was significantly more expensive than other solutions at the time, selling for $1,395. The card worked with DOS 3.3, Pascal, or CP/M, and even included battery backup to maintain the stored contents for up the three hours, in case of a power failure.[4]

Synetix Industries of Redmond, Washington also released a solid-state disk emulator, the Synetix 2202 SSD. For $550 it provided 147K (emulating a single disk drive), and for $950 it released a 294K card for dual disk emulation. These were likewise compatible with DOS 3.3, Pascal, and CP/M.[5]

Another release in 1982 came from Legend Industries, Ltd. of Pontiac, Michigan. One of its cards was called the 18SRC, and contained 18K of static RAM that retained its contents when the power was turned off (making

---

1 Hertzfield, Andy, "We'll See About That", *Folklore.org*, <folklore.org/StoryView.py?project=Macintosh&story=Well_See_About_That.txt>, accessed October 20, 2012.
2 Weishaar, Tom, "A Concise Look At Apple II RAM", *Open-Apple* (December 1986), 2.81.
3 Edwards, Benj, "Apple II Bubble Memory – Evolution Of The Solid-State Drive", *PC World.com*, <www.pcworld.com/article/246617/evolution_of_the_solidstate_drive.html>, accessed October 20, 2012.
4 "InfoNews Hardware", *InfoWorld*, (April 26, 1982), 44.
5 "Hardware News", *InfoWorld*, (August 9, 1982), 55.

it a kind of portable memory, similar to modern flash drives). Another of its products was the 128KDE Soft Disk, which offered 128K of additional storage. This slot 0 card had a ribbon cable that connected to the socket for a specific RAM chip on the motherboard, in order to access timing signals. It worked like a Language Card, and the software with the card allowed it to emulate a floppy disk drive.[6, 7]

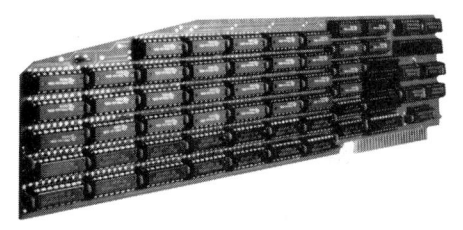

Synetix SSD – Photo credit: *Appalogue*, June-July 1982

When the Apple IIe was released, Apple sold two different kinds of RAM cards for it, although the names were deceiving. The Apple IIe 80-Column Text Card was nothing more than a 1K memory card that plugged into the Auxiliary slot on the IIe motherboard, in line with slot 3. It mirrored the 1K of text screen memory from $400 to $7FF, and with the built-in Apple IIe firmware routines allowed display of 80-columns of text. The more useful Extended 80-Column Text Card duplicated the entire 64K RAM on the IIe motherboard (including the built-in Language Card). Depending on the motherboard version present on the IIe, a jumper on the card might have to be removed in order to support double hi-res graphics.

Extended 80-Column Text Card – Photo credit: François Michaud

Based out of Carrolton, Texas, Applied Engineering (AE) started business in 1979 selling peripheral cards for the Apple II series. The company achieved a reputation for quality construction, excellent customer service and warranties, and was popular among fans of the Apple II series. RAM cards of various sizes, eventually serving all models of the Apple II, were some of its most popular products. The company's earliest offering was a 16K RAM card for slot 0 on the Apple II, distinguished by not requiring the RAM socket cable.

In 1984, AE offered a memory expansion card for the Apple IIe that went one step further than Apple's card. The MemoryMaster IIe card offered expansion in the Apple IIe Auxiliary slot to either 128K (for $169) or 192K of RAM (for $249). Other than the larger size, it worked like Apple's card, and Applied Engineering included utilities to allow CP/M software, VisiCalc, and AppleWorks to utilize the extra memory.

---

6 *128KDE Users Manual* (Legend Industries, Ltd, 1981).
7 Williams, Dave, e-mail message to author, February 6, 2012.

RAMWorks 1985 – Photo credit: Applied Engineering 1986 catalog

The next in AE's line of RAM cards was the RamWorks card, Wreleased in 1985. Also used in the Apple IIe auxiliary slot, it offered expansion to as much as 1 megabyte of RAM, and cost $649. An extra add-on feature was the ability to output RGB video, via the ColorLink RGB daughter card.

In 1986, AE added greater variety to its line of memory cards. The RAMWorks II card expanded memory to as much as 3 megabytes (for $1,599) on a single card, and up to 16 megabytes with additional daughter cards that attached to the main card. Like the original RAMWorks, AE offered an optional RGB video output module for the card. At the same time, the company also sold a card called RAMFactor, intended for use in a standard Apple II slot (which meant it worked on an Apple II or II Plus, as well as a Franklin ACE). The RAMFactor also allowed up to 16 megabytes with additional plug-in cards. A battery backup device called RAMCharger kept the contents of memory active even in the case of a power failure. In 1987 the next version, RAMWorks III, offered the same expansion options, for a slightly lower cost.

By this time AE also sold memory expansion for the Apple IIc. The Z-RAM card offered 256K ($449) or 512K ($549) of additional RAM for this supposedly unexpandable computer. Furthermore, the Z-RAM contained a Z-80 coprocessor, which allowed access to CP/M software. By 1987, AE's product line for the IIc had grown to Z-RAM Ultra 1, Ultra 2, and Ultra 3, with capacity increasing to as much as a full megabyte of RAM, a clock, and the CP/M option (costing $459 for everything).

TIMELINE

Applesoft Firmware Card
– June 1978

Apple Language Card
– August 1979

MPC BubDisk – 1982

Legend 128KDE – 1982

Applesoft Firmware Card
– June 1978

AE MemoryMaster IIe
– October 1983

AE RamWorks – 1985

AE RAMWorks II – 1986

AE RAMFactor – 1986

AE RAMCharger – 1986

AE MemoryMaster IIe
– October 1983

Apple Language Card – *August 1979*

MPC BubDisk – *1982*

Legend 128KDE – *1982*

Axlon RAMdisk 320 – *February 1982*

Synetix 2202 SSD – *August 1982*

Apple IIe 80-Column Card – *January 1983*

Apple IIe Extended 80-Column Card – *January 1983*

AE RamWorks – *1985*

AE RAMWorks II – *1986*

AE RAMFactor – *1986*

AE RAMCharger – *1986*

AE Z-RAM – *1986*

Apple IIGS Memory Expansion Card – *1986*

AE RAMWorks III – *1987*

AE Z-RAM Ultra 1, Ultra 2, Ultra 3 – *1987*

CHAPTER 27

The Juggernaut of Integration

There was one program for the Apple II that showed amazing staying power in a world where this year's software hit was next year's yawn. Not only that, but it went on to spawn a number of software companies and magazines that did nothing else but sell or promote add-on products for it. That program was *AppleWorks*. Originally released in 1984 by Apple Computer, it became in its day one of the best selling computer programs of all time, on any computer. Although few seem to mention the influence it had, it was evident in the number of computer programs that later come out for the IBM and Macintosh that included the "Works" name (*Microsoft Works*, *ClarisWorks*, *Beagle Works*, and others).

"WORKS" WAS HERE FIRST

AppleWorks was one of the first integrated software packages, preceded only by the 1983 releases of *The Incredible Jack* for the Apple II (published by Business Solutions) and by *Lotus 1-2-3* for the PC (although that was more of a spreadsheet with additional features of graphing and simple database features than a true integrated software program).

AppleWorks included modules that performed word processing, database management, and spreadsheet calculations into a single environment, using similar commands in each module. Previous software programs were stand-alone and specialized for each of those jobs and had their own unique keyboard commands that were often very different from each other. Moving from Apple Writer to VisiCalc, or from VisiCalc to DB Master, it was necessary to learn a completely different method of controlling the program. Furthermore, the data files created by those programs were usually not compatible with each other, making it difficult and awkward to move information directly from one program to another. AppleWorks not only created continuity between these modules, but also allowed them to share data with each other via a memory space called a clipboard. This clipboard was part of a larger memory area called a desktop, which could hold data for up to twelve different files at the same time, which made data sharing even more convenient.

Rupert J. Lissner (who later changed his first name to Robert) wrote AppleWorks.[1] Its earliest incarnation was in another program written by Lissner called *QuickFile* and sold by Apple. This was an Apple III database program written in Pascal. It was flexible and easy to use, and Apple agreed to market it for Lissner in 1980. It was later translated into a version for the Apple IIe (also in Pascal) called *QuickFile IIe*. As a database program it was flexible and powerful, but somewhat slow due to the inherent limitations of the UCSD Pascal System under which it ran.

After seeing the Office System on the Lisa computer, Lissner conceived the idea of a single program that would put word processing, database, and spreadsheet capabilities together, and would run on an Apple II. Calling it *Apple Pie*, he began work on it in 1982. Lissner took two years to complete his program, and did it entirely in assembly language to achieve better speed. He wrote versions of the program to work on both the Apple II and Apple III computers, making use of the same filetypes and data structures. Apple Pie files created on an Apple II could be used on an Apple III, and vice-versa.

Apple decided to market the Apple II version themselves, calling it AppleWorks. Lissner was left with the rights to the Apple III version. He sold those rights to Haba Systems, who brought it out under the name */// E-Z Pieces*. That program continued to be compatible with the Apple II version up until AppleWorks was upgraded to version 3.0 in 1989.

A STAR IS BORN

When it was finally released, AppleWorks was recognized as one of the most comprehensive programs ever written for the Apple II. Although none of the three modules were significantly more powerful than other standalone programs, they had enough features to satisfy the average computer user. The memory management system was extremely flexible, eventually being able to handle not only the basic 64K or 128K on a IIe or IIc, but also several different types of memory cards used on those computers and on the IIgs.

Far larger than the memory of the 64K Apple IIe on which it ran (as a minimum memory configuration), the program was smart enough to swap in or out from disk the parts it needed to carry out its various functions. Considering that it ran on a computer whose microprocessor could address only 64K of memory at one time, the power achieved by this program is remarkable. There were few other software packages that could seamlessly treat up to two megabytes of memory on an 8-bit computer as one contiguous space.

AppleWorks' user interface was designed with menu bars, rather than the older command line interface (such as the one used in Applesoft, Integer BA-

---

1 Weishaar, Tom, "Miscellanea", *Open-Apple* (November 1986), 2.74.

SIC, and the Monitor). In its research, Apple's software engineers sat test subjects (often new employees who had not used a computer before) in front of a computer keyboard to learn what was easiest to use. They designed an interface that was based on using arrow keys to move a cursor (actually a highlighted bar) to different choices in a list, and then using the return key to make the selection (the magic menu method previously discussed). They also came up with the concept of the desktop (represented in text rather than in graphics as on the Lisa and Macintosh), and a clipboard for transferring data between files. Apple shared this research with Lissner, and he went on to incorporate it in his program design.[2]

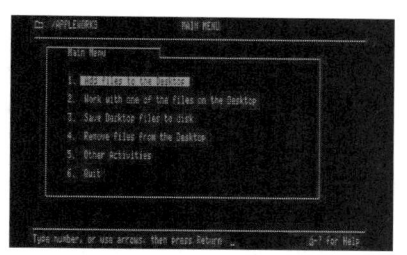

AppleWorks main screen – Photo credit: Ken Gagne

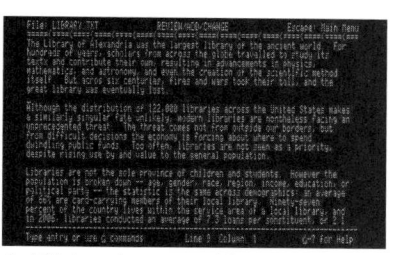

Lissner took the three most common productivity programs and combined them in a format that allowed consistent use of shortcut keyboard commands, as well as the aforementioned copy and paste feature between the modules.

AppleWorks word processor module; under ProDOS it was given the filetype AWP – Photo credit: Ken Gagne

THE DUBIOUS MARKETING OF APPLEWORKS

Apple's so-called promotion of AppleWorks made little sense to outside observers over the years. At the time that AppleWorks was ready for release, Apple was spending a considerable amount of money and time trying to market the Macintosh. Those who had the most influence at Apple were not interested in a simple text-based program, when the Mac and its graphic interface was the cutting edge in technology. They believed that the Mac represented the future of Apple, and were apparently not interested in wasting time or money promoting old Apple II technology.

Another problem Apple marketing had to handle with delicacy was the company's past record of directly selling software. Tom Weishaar of the *Open-Apple* newsletter, made these comments:

> ...Apple was trying very hard to get the big MS-DOS developers to work with the Macintosh. One of the reasons these developers gave for their reluctance to work on the Mac was their fear that Apple itself

---

2 Williams, Warren, and Carlton, Steve, "AppleWorks", *The Apple II Guide* (Cupertino, CA, Apple Computer, Inc., Fall 1990), 36-45.

would compete with them – Apple, obviously, had tremendous advantages in terms of distribution and access to inside information. Apple had a reputation for developing applications software for its machines that would kill the market for similar software – Apple Writer (which was at the top of the Apple II software charts at the time) and a complete set of applications software for the Lisa being major examples. Powerful voices inside Apple wanted the company to get out of the applications software business.[3]

However, despite the concern about Apple selling AppleWorks, the decision to release it was eventually made.

Apple's punishment for its indiscretion was immediate – within six weeks its illegitimate child sat at the top of the Apple II best-seller list. AppleWorks achieved this without the benefits of a mother's love – it succeeded in spite of, not because of, Apple's meager marketing efforts [on] its behalf. Since AppleWorks was released, for example, Apple has run 26 pages of ads in A+. The word 'AppleWorks' appears in those ads exactly zero times. Four of the ads show screen shots of AppleWorks... the Apple IIGS ad in the September 1987 A+ [shows a screen shot of] AppleWorks... in the gutter between the pages and is the only one of the 23 programs shown that isn't mentioned by name. This is typical of the treatment Apple's bastard child gets from its mother. [Del] Yocam, [Apple's Executive Vice-President in 1987], didn't mention it or Lissner in his birthday speech [at the 1987 AppleFest, celebrating the tenth anniversary of the Apple II], and John Sculley, Apple's president, doesn't mention it or Lissner in his... book, Odyssey.[4]

When it first appeared on the market, AppleWorks started at number 2 on *Softalk*'s top thirty list. It moved to the number one spot in Apple sales by the following month, and stayed there through the magazine's final issue in August 1984. In December 1984, AppleWorks had moved into the number one spot in monthly retail software sales for *all* computers, overtaking the MS-DOS best-seller Lotus 1-2-3. (That month, AppleWorks accounted for ten percent of retail software sales, and Lotus 1-2-3 sold only seven present.)[5] Some reports estimate that it was selling thirty to forty thousand copies per month at one time.[6] If VisiCalc had been the killer application that sold the

---

3 Weishaar, Tom, "Reality And Apple's Vision", *Open-Apple* (November 1987), 3.73-3.74.
4 *IBID*
5 Rubin, Charles, "Appleworks: New King Of The Mountain", *InfoWorld* (February 25, 1985), 15-16.
6 Brandt, Randy, "Enhancing AppleWorks", (video tape) (Quality Computers, July 1993).

Apple II Plus, AppleWorks became the killer application that sold the Apple IIe and IIc.

But since it was not their beloved Macintosh that put an Apple program into first place, corporate Apple ignored the milestone. Although it did not retain that top position indefinitely, AppleWorks remained immensely popular, despite an absence of advertising on the part of Apple.

> Versions 1.1 and 1.2 of AppleWorks were minor changes, and were provided free of charge to existing owners of the program. Version 1.3 was released in 1986, required a $20 update fee, and provided support for the new UniDisk 3.5 and the larger 800K disks. It also supported large memory cards that Apple was now selling to use on the Apple IIe, and could expand the desktop to as much as 1,012K.[7]

APPLEWORKS 2.0

Up through the release of AppleWorks 1.3, the only changes that had been made were bug fixes and enhancements to work with new hardware. In September 1986 Apple released version 2.0 of AppleWorks. It now required a minimum of 128K (previous versions worked with 64K, but allowed only a 10K desktop). In exchange for the greater memory requirements, it gave users a built-in ability to do mail merge, added more functions to the spreadsheet, and offered better support for non-Apple memory cards. Furthermore, word processing, database, and spreadsheet files could be larger than in previous versions. Existing users were able to upgrade to v2.0 for $50, which included a completely new manual.[8]

July 1987 saw one change that had an impact on future distribution of AppleWorks. Apple had decided to create a separate company called Claris, whose function would be to handle application software that Apple had previously released. This included Macintosh programs like *MacWrite*, *MacPaint*, and others, and Apple Writer and AppleWorks for the Apple II. As mentioned, products released by Apple had a tendency to be the "kiss of death" for third-party companies trying to market similar programs. After the outstanding success of AppleWorks, virtually no text-based word processors released for the Apple II made much of an impact on the market. Supposedly, having a separate company handling these products would level the playing field for other competing products.

---

7 Weishaar, Tom, "Does Your Mother Love You?", *Open-Apple* (January 1986), 1.97.
8 Weishaar, Tom, "New $999 Apple IIgs Arrives", *Open-Apple* (October 1986), 2.65-2.67.

Considering that AppleWorks had previously received no advertising at all, the ads that Claris used to publicize it were a welcome change. Its first promotion stated that AppleWorks 2.0 had received a very unique upgrade — its own company. This was primarily a plug for Claris,of course. The second ad was rather clever. This one had a white background with a red Porsche up on blocks with its wheels missing. The caption read, "There are still some Apple II users who don't have AppleWorks", suggesting that working without that program was like owning a sports car without wheels.

AppleWorks Claris Porsche – Photo credit: Tony Diaz

Claris released a free AppleWorks update to version 2.1 in September 1988. This provided some bug fixes (some of which had been discovered by Beagle Bros in the process of creating the TimeOut engine).[9] These were intended to make it work better on the IIGS, plus it was supposed to support a desktop as big as eight megabytes, if that much memory was installed. However, because of the way in which desktop memory in AppleWorks was handled, this turned out instead to be a maximum of only two megabytes. No further functionality was added to AppleWorks at that time.

PINPOINT

AppleWorks had such a major influence in the Apple II world that the program itself spawned a number of related products that enhanced or expanded its usability. One of the first customizations that appeared for AppleWorks was from a company calling itself Pinpoint Publishing. They had originally been called Virtual Combinatics, and had sold a program for the Apple II called *Micro Cookbook*. Suddenly in 1985 they burst upon the market with a new name and a significant new product. Their *Pinpoint Desk Accessories* was primarily an enhancement for AppleWorks, though it was also possible to install its features for use under Applesoft, and eventually Apple Writer and *Word Perfect*.

---

9   Brandt, Randy, e-mail message to author, October 10, 2012.

Taking after the popularity of pop-up desktop programs like *Sidekick* for the IBM PC, Pinpoint added some similar features to AppleWorks. These features were available at any time, simply by pressing solid-apple and P (option-P on the IIGS). At this point a small Accessories menu popped up on the screen, drawn using MouseText characters. Like the menus in AppleWorks, the user could then select an option with the arrow keys, and pressing RETURN.

The accessories included:

- Appointment Calendar
- Calculator
- Communications (a small terminal program for use with a modem, which could send AppleWorks word processing files or save incoming text as a word processor file)
- Dialer (highlight a phone number on the screen, and the program dialed it via the modem)
- GraphMerge (which allowed printing a word processing document with all or part of a double hi-res picture included with the text)
- Notepad (a miniature word processor, holding up to 32 lines of text and saving notes in AppleWorks word processor format)
- QuickLabel (take an address off the screen and place it on an envelope template for printing)
- Typewriter (type and print lines one at a time)

Pinpoint desk accessories for AppleWorks
– Photo credit: personal

This was all very exciting at the time, multiplying the abilities of AppleWorks well beyond its original intent. Because of disk-space requirements, these utilities were more convenient to use from a 3.5-inch disk or hard disk, but actually could be used from 5.25-inch disks without much trouble. Eventually a spell checker was also made available to use with Pinpoint.

Additional products sold by Pinpoint to enhance AppleWorks included *Pinpoint InfoMerge* (which handled mail merge and database reporting functions), *Pinpoint KeyPlayer* (scripting functions), and *Pinpoint Spell Checker* (which worked also outside of AppleWorks).

BEAGLE BROS AND COMPANY

Beagle Bros had been created in 1980 by Bert Kersey. He had a degree in graphic arts, but was fascinated by gadgets. When microcomputers came out in the late 1970s, he ultimately bought an Apple II and taught himself BASIC and a little assembly language. The fun he had with it prompted Kersey to enter the mail order software business to sell his programs. He chose "Beagle Bros" as the name (he wanted "Beagle Boys" but knew that Disney had a habit of suing those who used trademarked names for themselves), and placed an ad in *Creative Computing* to sell some of his games. Because of his background in graphic art, Kersey found creating the advertisements was the funnest part of the business, and customers felt these were among the most enjoyable magazine ads. Kersey used woodcut art in his ads, and poked fun at himself, his company, and computer users. He also gathered programmers more talented than himself to increase his stable of offerings to include various types of useful utilities for the Apple II.

Beagle Bros was famous amongst Apple II users for selling its software on un-protected disks. It offered simple but enjoyable games or utilities that allowed users to do things like rename the error messages in Apple DOS. Later it produced more sophisticated offerings.

Beagle Bros company logo
– Photo credit: personal

Kersey's ads were just another facet of his quirky style. His home was full of other examples of his dry sense of humor. One of these included a fake trap door on his front porch, and a sign posted on the door advising visitors to "Ring once for trap door, twice for doorbell." In the upstairs office he had created for his company, he had three clocks on the wall, not unlike those seen on network news broadcasts in the 1960s. But instead of displaying times for San Francisco, Chicago, and New York, his clocks were labeled with San Diego, Los Angeles, and San Francisco—all displaying the same time.

In June 1986, Beagle Bros released an add-on for AppleWorks called MacroWorks.[10] Written by Randy Brandt, this program patched itself into the keyboard-reading routine of AppleWorks and allowed the user to assign certain functions to a specific key on the keyboard.

> The built-in features of AppleWorks were accessed by pressing either the open-apple or solid-apple key (same as the option key on the Apple IIGS keyboard) together with another. For instance, open-apple and "C" (oa-C) together were used to copy data (text

---

10 Weishaar, Tom, "Miscellanea", *Open-Apple* (June 1986), 2.33.

CHAPTER 27 | The Juggernaut of Integration

> in a word processing document, a cell in a spreadsheet, or a database field). Before MacroWorks was patched into the program, either oa-C or sa-C (solid-apple-C) had the same effect. After adding this enhancement, the solid-apple keys were given their own, separate identity, offering more than double the number of functions that could be executed from the keyboard. (Pinpoint was similar, using sa-P for its own purposes.)
>
> A macro was actually a series of keystrokes that could be entered from the keyboard (similar to WPL programs for Apple Writer), but was automated so that a single key press would activate it. For example, typing a return address could be assigned to the sequence sa-A. Or sa-S could be defined to save all the files on the desktop and quit the program. Anything that could be done manually with AppleWorks could be automated with MacroWorks, and it could even do some things that could not be easily done manually.

The idea of automating keystrokes in AppleWorks was not unique to MacroWorks; the same year, Alan Bird of Software Touch released *AutoWorks*, and Pinpoint Publishing got into the act with their product, Pinpoint Keyplayer. Brandt upped the ante later in 1986 with an upgrade called *SuperMacroWorks*, which added a few new features and was made to work specifically with the new version 2.0 of AppleWorks. It didn't take long for the other companies to also release enhanced versions of their programs to work with this update.

The most significant enhancement came in 1987. Beagle Bros had just undergone a change in management, as its founder Bert Kersey retired and sold his company to Mark Simonsen and Alan Bird, owners of Software Touch. They had previously worked at Beagle before leaving to start their own company, but with the purchase of Beagle Bros they elected to take the name of the older, better known company. Aside from AutoWorks, Software Touch had released enhancements for AppleWorks such as *SideSpread* (which allowed a spreadsheet to be printed sideways on a dot matrix printer) and *FontWorks* (which allowed word processor files to be printed using different font styles and sizes, using codes embedded in the text of the word processor document.). As they merged back into the Beagle fold, they brought with them plans for a series of AppleWorks add-ons and enhancements. These would be accomplished via a new core program (or engine, as they referred to it) called *TimeOut*.

Written by Alan Bird, TimeOut installed itself into AppleWorks and interfaced directly with Lissner's remarkable built-in memory manager. A unique feature of TimeOut was that after the engine itself was installed, adding other modules was no more complicated than copying them over to the disk from which AppleWorks started. This addressed one of the problems with all of the other enhancement programs available; if they were not installed in the correct order, the patches would begin to step on each other, and crashes were much more likely. TimeOut provided a clearly defined protocol for adding new features to AppleWorks without this patching hassle.

The first TimeOut modules included *DeskTools*, *FileMaster* (which allowed file copying and more), *Graph* (spreadsheet graphing), *QuickSpell*, *SideSpread* (update of the older Software Touch program), *SuperFonts* (update of FontWorks), and *UltraMacros* (a more powerful version of Randy Brandt's SuperMacroWorks, using ideas from AutoWorks). More followed in subsequent years, including a thesaurus module and a full-featured telecommunications module that worked within AppleWorks.

APPLEWORKS 3.0

In 1988, while Claris was issuing its minor update to AppleWorks, they were planning major improvements to the program. Since they primarily had Macintosh programmers working for them, they first contacted Robert Lissner, the original author. He wasn't interested, since he had already made good money off the program and didn't really have the motivation to make any major changes. Claris then decided to turn to a third-party company to do the work. One company Claris had heard of was Pinpoint Publishing. That company sold an enhancement package for AppleWorks that gave users some features that MS-DOS users had available on their computers (such as pop-up tools), and considered asking Pinpoint to do the update. In their discussions, Pinpoint expressed interest, but planned to make changes only so far as the exact specifications that Claris was requesting.

Claris also kept in touch with user groups, and at meetings when representatives from the company discussed possible enhancements to AppleWorks, most group members told them Beagle Bros was the company to talk to about handling an update to the program. These user groups liked the Beagle extensions to AppleWorks better than those from Pinpoint.

In 1986, Bert Kersey sold the company to Mark Simonsen, who had previously left to start his own company, Software Touch, to create AppleWorks addons. When he returned to take over Beagle Bros, one of the first things released was the TimeOut engine for patching additional features onto AppleWorks. It was likely the user loyalty to Beagle Bros as well as the quality of the TimeOut offerings that led user group members to recommend the company to Claris. After some complicated negotiations that nearly fell through several times, Beagle was finally awarded the contract to update AppleWorks for Claris.

Beagle clearly didn't get the contract because they were well behaved. The previous year, they had tweaked Claris' nose with an ad that responded to the Porsche ad. Beagle also purchased a double-page ad with a white background, with four tires placed in the same location as the blocks in the Claris ad. The Beagle Bros ad read, "There are still some AppleWorks users who don't have TimeOut," suggesting that the Porsche in the Claris ad was AppleWorks, and TimeOut was the wheels for that car.

AppleWorks Beagle Bros Porsche Wheels – Photo credit: Tony Diaz

Beagle programmers Alan Bird, Randy Brandt and Rob Renstrom worked on the AppleWorks 3.0 update for almost a year, in between a few other projects that were going on at the same time. The project, code named "Spike", was created on Macintosh II computers running the MPW (*Macintosh Programmer's Workshop*) cross-assembler, primarily for the sake of speed.[11] As enthusiastic Apple II programmers who also knew AppleWorks inside and out, Beagle's team added features Claris had not planned on in their original specifications. Occasionally they called on Lissner to help explain why certain parts of the code were written as they were, but all of the new code came from the "Beagle Boys."

Viewing it as a labor of love, they went beyond what they were asked to do, and enjoyed making AppleWorks into a program that they wanted to use. Randy Brandt stated, "I think it's safe to say the AppleWorks 3.0 project yielded the worst hourly rate I've ever made in AppleWorks-related programming, but it did give me a lot of insight which came in handy on future projects."[12] Additionally, they fixed over one hundred known bugs in AppleWorks 2.1.[13] Brandt also commented that a number of internal "hooks" were included in the new code, which made it easier for the introduction of future TimeOut add-ons.

In June 1989, Claris announced the AppleWorks 3.0 upgrade at the National Educational Computing Conference in Boston. It presented the new version to the world in its third promotional magazine ad. This one showed an old worn tennis shoe (representing the old version) and a new running shoe (representing the new version).

---

11 Brandt, Randy, "Who's Who In Apple II", *GEnieLamp A2* (January 1994).
12 Brandt, Randy, e-mail message to author, July 1991.
13 Brandt, Randy, A2 Roundtable, Category 13, Topic 16, *GEnie*, accessed June 1992.

The features that were added or improved are too numerous to describe here; in brief, it added nearly all the things users had wanted the program to do, and more. It was easier to use, it took better advantage of extra memory (going beyond the 2 MB limit on the IIGS), and it was easier to customize special printers to work with it. It also included a new feature that was becoming standard in many commercial word processors: a built-in spell checker.

Because of these extra features, the maximum desktop size on a standard 128K Apple II was now reduced to about 40K (down from the original 55K). Also, the program now loaded from two double-sided 5.25-inch disks (or one 3.5-inch disk), instead of the previous one double-sided 5.25-inch disk.

For many years Apple had included registration cards with their products. Unfortunately, although they included those cards with everything they shipped, they performed a less satisfactory job of actually compiling the data from those cards. Consequently, Claris really had no available information about who was a registered owner of AppleWorks. Part of the strategy behind the free update to version 2.1 was an effort to recapture this data and rebuild a customer database and mailing list. However, they were not very successful with that attempt, so it was decided to take a more aggressive stance with the new 3.0 release.[14]

Claris made an initial upgrade offer of $79 for customers who owned any previous version of AppleWorks (from v1.0 to v2.1), and through the *A2-Central* newsletter they even made available a special $99 offer: any *A2-Central* subscriber could get the program from Claris for that price, even if it was not

T-shirt for the Spike project; in the *Peanuts* comic strip, Spike was Snoopy's brother from Needles, California
– Photo credit: Randy Brandt

AppleWorks 3.0 introduction
– Photo credit: *inCider* August 1989

---

14 Brandt, Randy, e-mail message to author, October 10, 2012.

possible to prove previous ownership of AppleWorks.[15] Later, owners of previous versions could still upgrade for $99 if they wanted.

After the release of AppleWorks 3.0, Claris concentrated exclusively on Macintosh products and made no plans for further in-house updates or upgrades to AppleWorks. This was unfortunate, since there were several known bugs in version 3.0 of the program, and Beagle Bros programmer Mark Munz eventually decided to release his own AppleWorks bug-patcher program into the public domain to correct these problems. Rather than take the hint and make a v3.1 release to officially acknowledge and correct these problems, Claris' policy was to simply wait until a customer complained about them and then to direct them to Munz's patcher program.

JEM SOFTWARE

Beagle Bros released many TimeOut enhancements that added to the longevity of AppleWorks. And they did many users a favor by making upgrades available virtually free, through a program they called "Beagle Buddies". To update, it was only necessary to contact a Beagle Buddy representative (usually in a local user group), provide evidence of program ownership, and, for example, UltraMacros could be updated from version 3.0 to 3.1 without charge.

JEM Software logo – Photo credit: Randy Brandt

The down side of this service, however, was that there was no income received by Beagle for updates, making it financially difficult to pay the authors of those updates for their work. For this reason, authors like Randy Brandt (one of the AppleWorks 3.0 revision authors) had decided to start their own private companies for release of other products for AppleWorks. Brandt created a company called JEM Software, and through that company he released *PathFinder*, which made setting the pathname for the "Add Files" menu easier and faster to change.

Brandt did not stop there. With the help of fellow Beagle Bros programmer Dan Verkade, he created *TotalControl*, which added features to the database module to allow specific qualifications for the type of entries that could be made in new or existing records. *DoubleData* changed the database module so AppleWorks could handle twice as many categories per record as it was designed to do. Mr. Invoice provided the ability to produce invoices with AppleWorks, and *DB Pix* added graphic capability to the database, displaying single and double hi-res and *Print Shop* or *Print Shop GS* graphics. Brandt also created an update to UltraMacros 3.1, called *Ultra 4.0*, which added

---

15 Weishaar, Tom, "AppleWorks 3.0 A Blockbuster", *A2-Central* (July 1989), 5.41-5.46.

considerable power to the macro language. All of these add-on programs significantly extended the lifespan and usability of AppleWorks.

> Brandt also came up with the concept of "inits" for AppleWorks. A small patch allowed these inits to be added by searching the AW.INITS subdirectory on the startup disk. Any binary program found there with a name that started with "I." was automatically loaded and patched in at startup time. These inits ranged from one that improved the handling of the screen print function built into AppleWorks, to other much larger applications (TotalControl was added via an init, for instance). The difference between these inits and TimeOut applications was that inits were always working, whereas TimeOut programs had to be specifically activated to work. Brandt used the same concept of simple extensions when he designed Ultra 4.0; more commands (called "dot commands") could be added to the macro language in the same way as other inits.

APPLEWORKS 4

The year 1993, near the end of the commercial lifespan of the Apple II, brought a major surprise: another upgrade for AppleWorks. Two paths converged during that year to bring about this unexpected turn of events. Quality Computers, a mail-order business based in Michigan, had been steadily increasing in size and influence during the previous several years. It had begun by selling software and hardware products for the Apple II available from vendors around the country. One of its earliest enterprises was selling software written by Joe Gleason, the company's founder.

Quality Computers advertised prominently in the Apple II magazines that were still in print; in *inCider*/A+ magazine they always had the first two to four pages of available ad space. During the early 1990s, Quality even began to distribute hardware items of their own (usually produced by another company and rebranded under the Quality name). When Beagle Bros decided to concentrate solely on their upcoming Macintosh product, Quality Computers stepped in and purchased the rights to sell and upgrade the Beagle products, thus expanding its influence in the world of Apple II software.

Although Randy Brandt had added features to AppleWorks 3.0 in 1989 that he himself wanted, he kept devising new ways to enhance it. Through Beagle Bros and later through his own JEM Software, he created add-on tools to allow users to get more out of the program. But in the back of his mind he always wished AppleWorks itself could be enhanced and fixed, to modernize it with features that many of the MS-DOS and Macintosh products on the market had incorporated since Claris released its last version of AppleWorks. Unfortunately, Claris continued to show no interest in doing anything with AppleWorks, such as releasing an update to fix known bugs in the program.

CHAPTER 27 | *The Juggernaut of Integration*

In the spring of 1993, Brandt contacted Joe Gleason at Quality Computers and discussed his interest in a major upgrade to AppleWorks 3.0. Having worked on the "Spike" project to develop 3.0, Brandt knew the program inside and out, and knew exactly how he could enhance the program. The best method would be to incorporate the changes into the program source code and recompile it; but Claris still held the rights to it. Gleason was extremely interested in the proposal, and began holding discussions with Claris to see if they would be willing to license AppleWorks to Quality Computers. This would give Quality the opportunity to upgrade AppleWorks through a re-write, as well as to provide technical support in a way that had not previously been possible.

Brandt and his long-time programming associate, Dan Verkade, began working on the upgrade to AppleWorks (code-named "Quadriga"), while Gleason negotiated with Claris. Although they all hoped that it would be possible to release the finished product as *AppleWorks 4*, they recognized the possibility that Claris would not relinquish its death grip on the program. In that eventuality, it was determined that there would be no choice but to put it out as a large patch program. The proposed product name would be *TheWorks 4.0*, and in order to make use of it a customer would need to already own AppleWorks 3.0. Installing TheWorks would patch into AppleWorks and make use of what code in the program was still useful, but still give access to all the new features they wanted to include.

Many of the features included in the Quadriga project were like a best-of list from TimeOut modules of the past: *Triple Desktop*, which gave access to as many as thirty-six files at a time; UltraMacros, enhanced to the Ultra 4 version that JEM Software had released, but including the ability to playback pre-compiled macros (the compiler would be available separately); Double-Data, to increase the number of available categories in the database module from thirty to sixty; TotalControl, which further enhanced the abilities of the database; support for more printers, including newer style printers such as the Hewlett-Packard DeskJet 500; links between the database and word processor; and links between spreadsheets (similar to the 3-D features that were currently available in MS-DOS programs like Lotus 1-2-3).

While Brandt and Verkade worked on the program code, Gleason was doing his best to convince Claris that it would be in their best interest to sell AppleWorks to Quality. As Quadriga was nearing completion, Gleason showed Claris executives that Quality was prepared to release it as a patch program, even if AppleWorks was not sold to them. Apparently Claris took this as clear evidence that Quality was not only determined to follow through on the project, but also had the ability to pull it off. Negotiations became more serious, and by late August 1993 both parties signed a contract. This contract allowed Quality to purchase (for an unspecified sum) the rights to publish AppleWorks and AppleWorks GS, and to use that product name (which was an Apple trademark licensed to Claris).

With the legalities out of the way, the Quadriga project proceeded at full steam. They had a goal of releasing the program by October 1, but some last minute problems delayed the actual debut of the program until November 1, 1993. As with many programs, some bugs surfaced within a week of the distribution of new revision. However, these were quickly resolved, and shipping of an updated version 4.01 resumed a week later. A version 4.02 update was expected by the end of the year to fix some other less serious problems that had been identified by early users. Compared to four years of inactivity by Claris (failing to fix known problems in version 3.0), this support was significantly improved.[16, 17]

APPLEWORKS 5

The response to Quality Computer's release of AppleWorks 4 was quite positive, and sales were good enough that it inspired Randy Brandt and Dan Verkade to start making plans for yet another update to this productivity program. At the 1994 A2-Central Sumer Conference in Kansas City, Brandt announced his project, which was code-named "Narnia". After several months of beta testing, the product was released as *AppleWorks 5* in November 1994. The following summer, Quality Computers and Brandt released a free 5.1 update to the program, intended to correct bugs that were discovered after the original 5.0 release.

TIMELINE

QuickFile – *1980*
QuickFile IIe – *January 1983*
/// E-Z Pieces – *December 1983*
AppleWorks 1.0 – *April 1984*
AppleWorks 1.1 – *July 1985*
Pinpoint Desk Accessories – *July 1985*
AppleWorks 1.2 – *October 1985*
AppleWorks 1.3 – *February 1986*
MultiScribe – *April 1986*
MacroWorks – *June 1986*
AutoWorks – *August 1986*

AppleWorks 2.0 – *September 1986*
SuperMacroWorks – *November 1986*
TimeOut – *1987*
UltraMacros – *1987*
MultiScribe GS – *April 1987*
AppleWorks 2.1 – *September 1988*
AppleWorks 3.0 – *June 1989*
ClarisWorks 1.0 – *October 1991*
AppleWorks 4.0 – *November 1993*
AppleWorks 5.0 – *November 1994*
AppleWorks 5.1 – *July 1995*

---

16 Selur, Joseph, "Taking Off The Wraps", *II Alive* (July/August 1993), 44-47.
17 -----, "Quadriga To Be AppleWorks 4.0", *II Alive* (September/October 1993), p. 27.

CHAPTER 28
Online Boom and Bust

The introduction of the BBS created a new way for computer users to communicate and share with each other. The small scale allowed by this one-to-one connection demonstrated the promise of bigger things if multiple computers were connected together at the same time. Usenet, FTP (file transfer protocol), and Gopher (a document search protocol) provided a more disseminated means of computer connection, messaging, and file transfer, but they were organized in a fashion that was not profitable. In fact, the cost of maintaining the various small networks that made up the whole was paid for by university and research institutions (and, to some extent, student tuition fees), but they did not typically generate revenue for those organizations.

Science fiction writers in the 1960s and earlier had envisioned the possibility of bringing a library into the home, and a different means of reading and obtaining information. Book-films and film readers were featured in this fiction, and in others there were various devices (sometimes computers) that were used to access encyclopedia articles or to shop from home. In the late 1970s, the advent of large-scale commercial online services made aspects of this vision possible.

One important thing that had to be considered was how to make it financially viable. The homebrew BBSes had a simple model that in the vast majority of situations did not involve any true business. They were built and operated for either the love of the primary topic featured by that BBS, or the ego of the Sysop, or both. A potential profit was usually not considered. Even if profit was a motivating factor, a BBS had to offer content that was a sufficient draw for the audience to come back to again and again, in order to extract a subscription fee. Furthermore, that audience had to be in sufficient volume to make it worthwhile.

A large, multi-user service could offer access from multiple locations that made it valuable to potential customers, far and above the much more limited offerings of a BBS. And to make it pay, these major online services advertised hourly rates that were priced low enough to attract customers, but high enough to pay for the time the mainframe was in use, as well as the cost of the content it hosted, the employees, and a profit. If the user went a little over the hour, the charge typically did not add on the full fee for another hour; instead, like the telephone company, the charges were calculated by the minute.

One other thing about these national online services that differentiated them from BBSes was the concept of prime versus non-prime use. The mainframe computers used for the major online services had business customers that paid a fee for daytime access to the mainframe computer. During the evening, the mainframe was idle, earning no money for its owner. Putting a consumer business (an online service) on that mainframe from, for example, 6 pm to 7 am, helped make it profitable both day and night.

These consumer online services typically operated during these off-hours. This was non-prime, non-business time, and was offered at the lowest hourly rate. Consumers were typically not prohibited from continuing to use that service when prime (business) time rolled around at 7 am. They would, however, have their hourly rate dramatically raised. That higher rate was intended to discourage those who wanted to make extra use of their favorite online service during the time when the company owning the hardware was promising the best access for its more lucrative business clients.

NOTE: *The end dates of the following entries sometimes refer to the end of their service for the Apple II or their classic text access, not necessarily the final end of the service.*

THE SOURCE (1979 – 1989)

Virginia entrepreneur William von Meister had a habit of creating companies based on visionary technology, and then moving on to a new idea. In 1978 one of his ideas was to broadcast data via a side signal on an FM broadcast, which could then be decoded and displayed on a data terminal. This "Infocast" system was successfully marketed to businesses to send information to subsidiaries.

While useful, von Meister envisioned its use as a consumer service. The problem was finding a way to affordably make it work two-way. He realized that by using the existing telephone system with home computers as terminals, he had part of the infrastructure to make this vision a reality. He had to put together the other part—mainframe computers on which to host the service. He formed a company called Telecomputing Corporation of America (TCA), and planned to call his service CompuCom. He leased a mainframe that was used during the day for an email service for the House of Representatives, planning to operate his service during the evening hours when the mainframe was idle.

Email was just one service that CompuCom would provide. He licensed bulletin board software that could run on a mainframe, and negotiated for a network to handle the data traffic. To provide information for his future customers, von Meister made deals with the *New York Times* and Dow Jones, as well as adding wine lists, horoscopes, online shopping guides, and some simple mainframe computer games.

After a name change from CompuCom (a company in Texas was already using the name) to The Source, von Meister announced it by holding a media event on July 9, 1979 at the Plaza Hotel in New York City. Science fiction author Isaac Asimov was in attendance, and stated that the event heralded the beginning of the Information Age. The descriptive term favored by von Meister was to call the new service an "information utility".[1,2]

The new service had a slow start, due to the expense of assembling the needed hardware and software, and also due to its small number of initial subscribers. It was accessible through Telenet or Tymnet nodes; that is, through computers in a locality that acted as gateways to many other online computer services across the country. Often there was an additional fee for using a Telenet or Tymnet node, in addition to the charges for the specific service being accessed.

In a power struggle in 1979, von Meister lost control of the company, and in 1980 a controlling interest in The Source was sold to Reader's Digest Association, for $6 million and an eighty percent stake in the company. The new majority owner had an interest in the ability of The Source service to create online news reports. In 1982 they created a newsroom and subscribers gained access to reports from UPI (United Press International). The connection was so immediate that it only took two and a half minutes after a story was filed before it was available to subscribers.

Finally, a computer breakthrough that really is a breakthrough!

THE SOURCE is here...
the first time-sharing information system devised for home and small business computing!

Advertisement for The Source – Photo credit: BYTE, October 1979

The Source made these reports keyword searchable. Eventually the service offered access to excerpts from thirty major magazines, over twenty financial and business services, several national and international news services, and computer-specific news features. It offered travel services and the ability to retrieve airline schedules and to plan connecting flights. It could also access weather services and offered reviews of restaurants and hotels. An online encyclopedia and shopping were also available, and another service called Information On Demand provided access to more than 150 research-oriented databases.

Some of the most popular features on The Source were electronic mail, bulletin boards, a Mailgram service that guaranteed next-day delivery (by paper), and computer conferencing. There were over sixty text-based online games available, with topics ranging from the Civil War to *Star Trek*. Additionally, access to mainframe computers was also made available, allowing execution on those mainframe computers of programs in FORTRAN or Pascal.

---

1 Smith, Esther, "William von Meister (1942-1995)," *Luyken Family Association*, <www.familie-luyken.de/07Genealogie/urenkel/12Gen/12bk2508E.htm>, accessed October 2012.
2 Banks, Michael, "The Source", *On the Way to the Web: The Secret History of the Internet and Its Founders*, (Apress), 25-38.

One feature unique to The Source was the capability to create scripts that the mainframe kept track of (rather than residing on the user's local disk). These scripts could be used to quickly move to certain areas and perform repetitive functions (such as scanning and reading electronic mail, and checking for new files in the library).

"America's Information Utility" was the initial slogan for The Source; by 1984 it was changed it to "The Information Network".

In its first several years, joining The Source was expensive. For only a 300 baud connection, it cost $100 to gain membership, and then $7.75 per hour, up to as much as $27.75 per hour, depending on the time of day and connection speed. By 1984, after it had expanded to allow access in 400 cities, the access speed was increased to 1200 baud, and the fee to join was dropped to $49.95. This was still pricey, with a $10 per month minimum fee, plus costs of $7.75 per hour at 300 baud and $10.75 per hour at 1200 baud for non-primetime use (and $20.75 and $25.75 respectively for primetime use).

The Source logo from retail package selling the service – Photo credit: Wikipedia

The Apple II had a presence on The Source from its earliest days, with the APPLESIG (special interest group). In 1987, after Reader's Digest Association sold The Source to Welsh, Carson, Anderson & Stower (a New York venture capital firm), many of the SIGs were updated, and Joseph Kohn at the age of 39 became the APPLESIG Chief Sysop.

Kohn was a member of the Gravenstein Apple Users Group in Petaluma, California, and he operated the APPLESIG from May 1987 until The Source closed down.

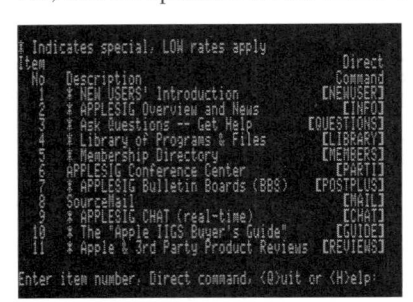

His goal was to make APPLESIG a major information source for Apple II users. He arranged to have it registered with Apple Computer as an official user group, and provided subscribers a large library of articles and software, as well as expert advice. The online charges were lower for APPLESIG than for some other areas on The Source, which also made it attractive for users. The bulletin board section allowed users to have ongoing discussions about pertinent Apple II topics. Kohn also arranged for an area dedicated to *The Apple IIGS Buyer's Guide*, and was allowed to reprint articles from *MicroTimes* and A+.[3]

The Source APPLESIG Main Menu – Photo credit: personal

During its days of ownership by Readers Digest, its membership was 23,000. It finally became profitable by 1986, when subscriber numbers passed 60,000. At its peak, The Source claimed 80,000 members, but by the end of the decade it had declined to only 53,000. The costs of operation had not allowed the infrastructure

---

3 Kohn, Joe, "The Source," *Call-A.P.P.L.E.* (January 1989), 25-28.

to be updated, and lowering customer access costs would have further reduced that ability. According to Kohn, the persistence of a $10 monthly minimum charge was one thing that likely contributed to the decline of the service, long after other national online services had either eliminated or significantly lowered such charges. Another problem that he identified was that their system was not as easy to use as some other services (although some former users felt that The Source's library search protocol was better than any other).

On June 29, 1989, The Source was purchased by CompuServe. Just over a month later, on August 1, 1989, the service was terminated, and remaining subscribers were offered a $20 credit to join CompuServe.[4, 5, 6, 7, 8]

COMPUSERVE (1979 – 1998)

CompuServe began life as Compu-Serv in 1969 as an in-house computer-processing center for Golden United Life Insurance Co. It was started by two graduate students in electrical engineering from the University of Arizona, Dr. John Goltz and Jeffrey Wilkins (son-in-law of the founder of Golden United Life). The pair started the company to support the data processing needs of the insurance company, and also to get involved in the new industry of providing time-sharing computer services during after-hours when the PDP-10 computers were otherwise idle. Goltz was the first CEO, but Wilkins soon took his place.

During the next several years it expanded its time-sharing offerings to business users, and by 1972 Compu-Serv had over four hundred business accounts across the country.

In 1977 the name was officially changed to CompuServe Incorporated and by 1979 it was ready to begin offering service to computer hobbyists in the evenings, during off-peak hours (when businesses were not accessing it). The new service was called MicroNET, and it started on July 1, 1979 after two months of testing with the 1,200 members of the Midwest Affiliation of Computer Clubs. It was initially promoted primarily through Radio Shack stores, and offered bulletin boards, databases, and games.

In 1980, CompuServe merged with H&R Block, and changed its personal computer service name from MicroNET to CompuServe Information Service. It continued to expand its services and capabilities, and also continued offering more access numbers across the country.[9]

---

4 Archibald, Dale, "Apple On The Phone: What Is And What's To Come In Telecommunications, Part II," *Softalk* (March 1983), 100-104.
5 Kohn, Joe, e-mail message to author, February 1992.
6 Utter, Gary, A2 Roundtable, Category 2, Topic 16, *GEnie*, accessed February 1992.
7 Carlson, David, "The Source," *David Carlson's Virtual World*, <iml.jou.ufl.edu/carlson/history/the_source.htm>, accessed October 20, 2012.
8 Howitt, Doran, "The Source Keeps Trying," *InfoWorld* (November 5, 1984), 56-64.
9 Gerber, Carole Houze, "Online Yesterday Today and Tomorrow," *Online Today*, CompuServe Information Service Newsletter (July 1989), 12-19.

Each user on CompuServe was assigned an eight or nine digit octal (digits 0 through 7) ID code, divided into five digits, a comma, and then the other three or four digits. For example, a user's code might be 76543,4321. This was due to requirements of the PDP computer architecture on which the CompuServe system ran. It was not only a customer's user ID but also an address to use in sending that person electronic mail.

The bulletin board and message sections on CompuServe were divided up into Forums, usually dedicated to a specific service. The Apple section covered more than one forum, since the volume of message traffic was too large to manage in a single forum.

Early CompuServe logo – Photo credit: unknown

> Messages within a forum were organized under major subjects, and then under minor subjects. Each message was assigned a number, and the various messages were linked together into threads.
>
> For instance, user #1 could post a question about a brand of modem. User #2 would link an answer to that message and answer the original question. User #3 might join the conversation and also answer the question, but add a comment about terminal programs. User #4 could then pick up on that comment, and add his views about the terminal program that he liked, without mentioning anything about the modem question that user #1 asked. The message thread could continue to expand in this fashion, or stop at any point.
>
> An advantage of this system is that it did not require much management by sysops. However a problem could occur due to the volume of message traffic within a particular forum. The software that CompuServe used assigned a number to each new message, but when the total number of messages exceeded a certain point, the first message was deleted. For example, suppose that a total of 2,000 messages were allowed at one time in a forum. If the range of messages in the forum on Monday ran from 15,000 to 17,000, by Tuesday the messages from 15,000 to 15,500 (the oldest) will have disappeared due to 500 new messages that had been posted, and the message numbers would then range from 15,500 to 17,500. If there were any especially useful conversations, the Sysop for the forum could choose to archive the messages (before they were deleted) into a file in the library for access in the future.

Each forum on CompuServe had the capability of supporting live conferences, where many users were present at the same time to hold live interactive conversations (as opposed to the bulletin board conversations where a user posted a message, and then would have to log on later to see a reply).

There was also a CB Simulator introduced in 1980, given that name to reference the Citizen's Band radio system that was popular at the time. The CB Simulator was simply a chat room, where people could join and leave as they wished, and post messages back and forth to each other, as if they were in the same physical room (or as if they were on a CB radio, talking with each other).

Neil Shapiro was an Apple II user who joined MicroNET in 1979. After spending some time in what ultimately became the CB simulator looking for help for his new computer, he decided to start an Apple special interest group. Shapiro and those who helped him get it started named it MAUG (for MicroNET Apple User Group). It ultimately attracted thousands of Apple II users, and for years was the most popular national place to go for Apple II info and files. Even Apple employees could be found there providing technical information to companies who were producing hardware and software for the Apple II. The MAUG libraries held programs that had been uploaded for years; some from the early part of the 1980s (if one could wait for the file scan to get back that far). There were also new files added daily by the active people on the forum.

In 1984, with the introduction of the Macintosh, Shapiro created separate forums for the Mac under the MAUG umbrella, and turned over management of the Apple II areas to several of its most active and knowledgeable members. By the late 1980s there were four primary areas for the Apple II on CompuServe:

CompuServe ad, Jan 1983 - also taken from *BYTE* magazine; notice the view of the Apple II keyboard – Photo credit: personal

APPUSE: for Apple II users
APPROG: for programmers
APPFUN: for gamers
APPVEN: for hardware and software vendors to provide service and support

As with the other major online systems, there were many other services available besides the MAUG forums, including news, online shopping, games, and much more.[10]

By the late 1980s, MAUG was beginning to feel the pinch of Apple II users who had left for the less costly competing service, GEnie. As noted previously, CompuServe bought out The Source in 1989, and shortly afterwards closed it down. By the early 1990s, CompuServe was itself struggling to adapt to the advances being made in the online world, particularly the burgeoning phenomenon of the Internet. It was not uncommon for members and non-members of the service to refer to it as CompuSpend or Compu$erve, because of its higher hourly

---

10 Apfelstadt, Marc, "All About CompuServe," *Call-A.P.P.L.E.* (November 1988), 44-47.

rates. Competition with those other services and with the Internet made it necessary to adjust the cost of the service, which was dropped from $10 to $1.95 per hour. Furthermore, a portal was added to allow access to the Internet.

By 1997, pricing was changed to offer a flat monthly fee of $24.95, to compete with rates offered by America Online. The company also began to convert its forums from its proprietary format to one compatible with HTML (the language of web pages).

About this same time, CompuServe's owner, H&R Block, decided to sell the online service. It actually consisted of two main divisions, CompuServe Information Services (where the forum and file activity was managed) and CompuServe Network Services (which managed the computer network on which the Information Services was hosted). The Network segment was sold to WorldCom, which also purchased MCI (a telephone long-distance company) and renamed itself MCI WorldCom. Eventually, WorldCom went into bankruptcy and again became just MCI, which was sold in 2006 to Verizon Communications (originally Bell Atlantic, part of the Bell Telephone system). With this change of hands, the original CompuServe Network Services became part of what was in 2012 called Verizon Business.

CompuServe logon message – Photo credit: personal

The CompuServe Information Services division was sold in February 1998 to former competitor America Online. Apple II users who remained members of MAUG realized that this was not good news, as AOL had already excluded direct Apple II access by failing to continue to provide a graphic access program that worked on the Apple II. About the same time, Neil Shapiro announced that MAUG and CompuServe had parted ways. The new managers of CompuServe appointed two veteran members as sysops for the APPUSE area.

Soon after the purchase by America Online, the predicted loss of text-based access came true, when the new owners announced in December 1998 that access to CompuServe would require a front-end program to manage access (available only for the Macintosh and Windows), rather than allow use of any generic text-based telecommunications program. This move accelerated the exodus of Apple II users from the service to competitors (primarily Delphi).

CompuServe logo in its later days – Photo credit: unknown

In 1999, this process moved forward as the mainframe computers on which CompuServe ran were upgraded from the very old 36-bit architecture PDP-10 systems to newer 32-bit computers. The software and operating system changes that accompanied these new systems finally broke access for text-based subscribers. In February 1999 the APPUSER forum for Apple II computers was discontinued because of this change. Space was made available on the MACHW (Mac hardware) forum for Apple II issues. Former APPLESIG Chief Sysop from The Source, Joe Kohn, was one of the first to discover the change, and posted "Apple II Forever!" as the first message there.

For a while, AOL continued to operate CompuServe's dial-up services (called CompuServe Classic), but with the increasing popularity of parent AOL and of the World Wide Web, it became more difficult to compete. By 2007 CompuServe international divisions were closed down, and in 2009 CompuServe Classic was also discontinued.[11]

GENIE (1985 – 1999)

The General Electric corporation was itself a manufacturer of mainframe computers during the 1960s. It sold its hardware operations to Honeywell in 1970, but continued to offer timesharing computer services for a number of years afterwards under the name GEIS (General Electric Information Services). As with other timesharing services, after-hours computing was underutilized. This provided an opportunity to build an alternate consumer online service that could operate during those lonely evening hours.

Bill Louden had been a member of the team that created the original CompuServe consumer service. He and several other CompuServe executives had left the company due to dissatisfaction with management changes that had occurred. Together, they planned to create a new online service that would be an improvement over CompuServe, built with open standards, and meant to serve a local geographic area. They chose Atlanta, Georgia, due its large local telephone dialing area (not requiring long distance charges), and started what was called Georgia Online. They tried to make it work with Internet services available at the time (Usenet groups and FTP), but it didn't sell well. Those who understood what this limited Internet was for could get it for free at a university, and those who didn't understand didn't see a reason for it.

About this time, General Electronic contacted Louden. The company had seen what could be done with time-sharing computers during its non-prime hours, and decided it would be worthwhile to create a consumer service to make use of the otherwise idle computers. Because of his experience with CompuServe, Louden was a natural choice to create the new service. GE budgeted $60,000 for development and marketing costs.

The Honeywell computers that operated GEIS ran with a proprietary operating system known as GCOS (General Comprehensive Operating System). The system was not a simple one on which to build a consumer-friendly service, but Louden's programmers were able to hide the complexity. They came up with a

---

11 Banks, Michael, "The Second Wave", *On the Way to the Web: The Secret History of the Internet and Its Founders*, (Apress), 85-89.

menu system to navigate through the various areas being offered, and shortcuts for those who wanted to skip the menus.

To name the service, Louden tried working with GE's marketing people, but could not find a satisfactory suggestion. He finally sat down with his wife, going through dictionary entries starting with the letter "G." When they hit the name "Genie," she pointed out that it was an ideal choice, and with a little more work came up with an acronym–General Electric Network for Information Exchange.[12]

The newly christened GEnie began operation in October 1985. Unlike CompuServe, which had two different pricing levels for access at different speeds (300 and 1200 baud), GEnie offered both speeds at $6 per hour during non-prime time, which was a significant decrease over the cost of CompuServe. They later offered 2400-baud service for a slightly higher price. During most of its early years in business, GEnie kept its online costs below that of the other systems, to be a more attractive alternative to The Source or CompuServe.

Like other online systems, GEnie offered many different services to its subscribers, including news, an online encyclopedia, online shopping, games, financial information, and areas for users of various brands of computers. GEnie became known for its multiplayer games, popular because of their variety as well as the comparatively lower cost for participation.

CompuServe's sections were called forums, while GEnie called its sections roundtables (or RTs for short). Each RT was divided up into a bulletin board, library, and conference rooms (called Real Time Conferences or RTCs). The bulletin board was divided up into a number of categories, and each category consisted of a number of topics. Each topic then had individual messages that dealt with that topic. Unlike CompuServe, messages did not disappear from a topic until the Sysop decided to delete them (which did not occur until the number of messages either got too large to be manageable, or they became old and outdated). If a topic contained messages that were particularly helpful (such as information about the use of a common computer utility program), the messages were maintained for years. If it became necessary to purge old messages, they were often placed into the library so they were available for future reference.

The advantage of the strict topical system used by GEnie was greater ease in finding concentrated information on a particular subject, without having to sift through unrelated side messages. The disadvantage was the need for a sysop to also function as a "topic cop" and either relocate message threads that strayed

GEnie logo
– Photo credit: *II Alive*, Nov-Dec 1993

---

12 Anthony, Robert S., "It's Over! CompuServe Classic Is Closing," *The Paper PC*, <paperpc.blogspot.com/2009/04/its-over-compuserve-classic-is-closing.html>, accessed October 20, 2012.

from the main subject or post a message reminding people to take that conversation to a different place on the bulletin board.

As for user IDs, GEnie decided to use a combination of letters and other symbols to give each user a unique name, instead of the number system employed by CompuServe. A new user was typically assigned a user name that consisted of their first initial, a period, and their last name. If there was another user with the same user name, a number was added. For instance, Joe Smith was assigned the name J.SMITH; if there were already three Joe Smith's on the system, then this name was changed to J.SMITH4 to differentiate him from the others. A user could ask for a different name (for a price) if the one assigned to him or her was not satisfactory. These tended to be as varied as vanity license plates on automobiles. If J.SMITH4 owned a restaurant, he might ask GEnie to give him a name such as EAT.AT.JOES instead of his original name.

GEnie started supporting the Apple II computer on October 27, 1985, about five days prior to going public. Kent Fillmore had run a successful BBS affiliated with the San Francisco Apple Core user group, and was the first Apple Information Manager. He started the America Apple RoundTable (AART), for the Apple II and III computers, and enlisted the help of two chief sysops to help run the day-to-day activities. Fillmore also started other RTs, including the following:

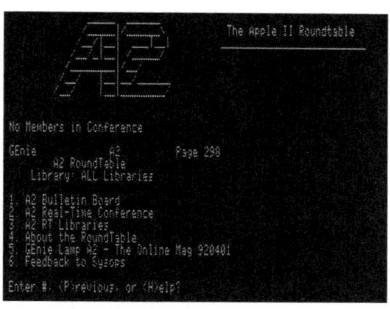

1992 banner message for the A2 Roundtable
– Photo credit: personal

- A2Pro RT for Apple II programmers
- A+ RT, for A+ magazine, hosted by the editor
- Apple/Mac User Group RT
- ProTree RT
- GEnie Sysop's private RT[13]

Fillmore left GEnie in October 1987 to work with a different online service that was then in its formative stages, AppleLink Personal Edition. Fillmore later returned to GEnie in June 1992 to become the Product Manager for Computing RoundTables/ChatLines.[14]

After Fillmore's departure, Tom Weishaar of the *Open-Apple* newsletter took over as manager of some of those RTs. The association with Tom Weishaar was beneficial for both; GEnie's 100,000th member in March 1988 was an Apple II user that joined because of a special offer through *Open-Apple*. Weishaar was also able to use this association to maintain more direct contact with Apple II users,

---

13 E'Sex, Lunatic, A2 Roundtable, Category 2, Topic 16, *GEnie*, accessed February 1992.
14 Fillmore, Kent, A2 Roundtable, Category 2, Topic 16, *GEnie*, accessed September 1991.

both those who worked professionally with the Apple II and with those who were casual users.[15]

Dealing with online services like CompuServe and GEnie meant every minute online cost money. One popular way to access the message boards was with what became known as "offline readers". These consisted of a terminal program that could be scripted (that is, controlled with a text file that automated the commands of what to do and where to go) and a text reader/editor that could create those scripts. One popular system was *GEnie Master*, written by Tom Hoover. This package was compatible with three different terminal programs, *Talk Is Cheap*, *Point-to-Point*, and *ProTERM 3.0*, and made use of AppleWorks with UltraMacros.

To use Hoover's GEnie Master, one would leave the terminal program running, and at a pre-determined time it would dial-up the GEnie access number, connect, and then visit each Roundtable that had been configured, download the new messages, get a list of the new files in the Library, and then log off. The captured content was saved as a text file, the terminal program would then quit, and transfer control to AppleWorks. That program, starting with the UltraMacros script files, would then load the saved text file, and leave it ready to read.

While using AppleWorks to read through the messages in the text file from a GEnie Master session, various UltraMacros commands could be used to reply to a message, start a new topic, copy content to a different file for storage, and download a file from the Library (it even supported file uploads to the Library). The output from that AppleWorks session was saved to a different text file, which could then be used with the next terminal session to automate replies or file transfers, while also downloading new messages that had been posted since the last time the user was on. It was a very efficient way of participating in a Roundtable, and was not limited to just the A2 and A2Pro RTs; it worked with nearly every Roundtable on GEnie. In 1994 GEnie Master was updated to work with AppleWorks 4.

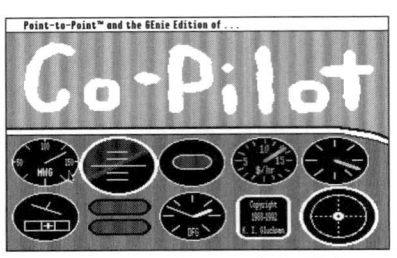

Screenshot of GEnie CoPilot, written by Ken Gluckman – Photo credit: personal

Another offline reader popular in the A2 Roundtable was *GE CoPilot*. It was designed to work specifically with the Apple IIGS, but used the same terminal programs as did GEnie Master.

Besides its popularity with those playing multiplayer games and with the various computer platform Roundtables, another popular RT was the Science Fiction RT (SFRT). It became so large that ultimately it had to be split into four different RTs. J. Michael Straczynski, writer of the television show *Babylon 5*, developed the show while a member of this Roundtable.

---

15 Weishaar, Tom, "All About GEnie: General Electric's Online Information Service," *Call-A.P.P.L.E.* (September 1988), 46-50.

Despite its success, GEnie never achieved the membership numbers of CompuServe. In 1994, its membership was reported at 350,000, while CompuServe had 1.7 million members.[16] Furthermore, General Electric was unwilling to invest in the service to expand its hardware or available access lines; the GEIS executives saw GEnie only as an after-hours revenue source, not as a business valuable enough in which to invest further time or money.

```
                              (-_____o\_
( Delivered by Co-Pilot )-----_____)I
                                       0
```

ASCII art used as signature line with messages sent via Co-Pilot – Photo credit: personal

As it moved into the 1990s, GEnie faced the challenge from the rise of the World Wide Web (as did other services) and from increased popularity of the graphic user interface, particularly from owners of the Macintosh, Windows 3.1, and Windows 95. The GUI was beginning to make the classic text-based services less and less relevant. By the end of 1995, General Electronic Information Services announced that it was looking for a buyer for GEnie.

During 1994, the GEIS engineers and programmers were already planning for a migration to more modern hardware for their networking system. Aside from the need for updates to their old computers, an important consideration was the impending date problem that was ultimately dubbed "Y2K" by the media. This problem involved software written in the days of small memory that used only two digits for the year, and assumed that the first two digits were "19" as they had been for so many years. Computer software and hardware unable to handle those dates would have problems when the calendar changed to January 1, 2000; at that point the internal calendar would read January 1, 1900.

To begin to address this issue, GEIS programmers began what was called Project Toledo. This was a migration to a Unix-based system, which would then be simpler to port to different hardware. The members of the sysop roundtable became aware of this in 1994, and during the following year the software was actually implemented to run the roundtables. By the end of 1995, the transfer of GEnie's menu system to Unix was not yet completed.

IDT Corporation was an Internet and international telephone service provider, based in Hackensack, New Jersey. The company created Yovelle Renaissance Corporation as a so-called "investment vehicle" to acquire GEnie. They envisioned using Genie's digital assets to create a World Wide Web-based service that could compete with America Online.[17] IDT was given the impression that the conversion to the new Unix system was nearly completed, which would make it simple to create this service. In January 1996 it was announced that Yovelle had purchased the service, and was changing its name to Genie (without the uppercase "E" that had linked it to General Electric).

---

16 Lewis, Peter, "A Boom For On-Line Services," *The New York Times* (July 12, 1994), <www.nytimes.com/1994/07/12/business/a-boom-for-on-line-services.html> retrieved July 27, 2013.
17 Staff writer, "GEnie," *Computer Business Review* (January 26, 1996).

However, one of the first steps taken by the new company was to announce a significant hike in the subscription cost, from $8.95 per month to $18.95 per month. Even worse, new subscribers were charged an exorbitant $23.95 per month. The cost for European Genie subscribers was even greater. As one could expect, the initial effect of this change was a high number of subscribers choosing to cancel their accounts.

After the deal was completed, the programmers associated with Yovelle discovered the amount of work still remaining to complete the conversion to the Unix system. Since the service was no longer affiliated with GEIS, those programmers who had done the initial work in converting the roundtables were not available to help finish the work. Although the reasons were never publically announced, it is very possible that the dramatic price hike assessed to its customers was intended to pay for the upgrade costs.

As a token effort to slow the hemorrhage of customers, April 1996 saw an announcement by the new Genie management to offer a service called Genie Lite, which offered five free hours of email per month. Access to the Roundtables was not free, but the cost was only $7.95 per month. As would be expected, a large number of members tried to change from their $18.95 per month charge to the more reasonable $7.95 per month. In response, Genie management cancelled this new program in early May, barely one month after it had been started.

By pricing its customers out of the market, Yovelle/Genie also found it necessary to close down some of the lower traffic Roundtables as a cost-saving measure.

In August 1996, IDT Corp announced it had purchased Genie from Yovelle, which was odd since Yovelle had been set up by IDT for the express purpose of buying Genie from General Electric. (By the time of the sale, Genie's user base had dropped to 20,000 members.) Apparently since the original sale in January, there had been conflict between GE, IDT, and Yovelle about ownership of the over 100 GB of content that made up Genie's Roundtables and libraries.[18] The sale did not, however, bring about any resolution to the problems that the members of Genie had been having since the start of the year.

Tom Weishaar had previously formed a company called Syndicomm, separate from Resource Central that handled his various publications. The purpose of Syndicom was to manage the A2 and A2Pro Roundtables on Genie. He later sold this company to sysops Gary Utter and Dean Esmay. During 1996, it was becoming clear to them that Genie was failing, that Yovelle seemed to have no clear idea of what they were doing, and that it was only a matter of time before the service would be shut down. Syndicomm began to make plans for where to make space for Apple II users when the inevitable happened.

At KansasFest (the annual Apple II conference) in the summer of 1996, Gary Utter gave the keynote speech and pointed out the necessity to diversify online

---

18 Staff writer, "Genie," *Computer Business Review*, (August 20, 1996).

access for the Apple II. He specifically stated that Genie's new direction was not a positive one, and it was necessary to look for at least one additional place to keep the accumulated resources. He later announced that Syndicomm was opening an A2 and A2Pro forum on Delphi, that Syndicomm had started a web site (www.syndicomm.com), and that they were looking at creating a moderated newsgroup for the Apple II (which they felt would be more useful than un-moderated comp.sys.apple2).

Many Apple II members were already beginning to leave for Delphi, and even CompuServe (always a more expensive choice) was beginning to look attractive, though Utter pointed out that text-based access there was also likely to go away. By January 1997, Utter announce his departure from Genie in an emotional post. He expressed his regrets for what Genie had become, but also his hopes that he would see his many Apple II friends again over on Delphi. Unlike other services, Delphi still had text-based access available, compatible with a standard Apple II with a modem.

The ongoing exodus to Delphi resulted in another casualty: A2Pro became another of Genie's low-traffic Roundtables, and was closed in June 1997. On June 26, 1997, the A2 sysops merged all of the content of A2Pro with the A2 RT, which unfortunately resulted in several hundred messages on the A2 Roundtable that were marked as new, even though they had been on A2Pro for several years.

One project that had been in development since 1995 was the production of a GUI interface for Genie to run on the Apple IIGs. Sponsored by Syndicomm and led by Australian programmer Richard Bennett, the program had been code-named Albatross and then later Cassidy[19], but was given the final name *Jasmine*, selected from a poll in the A2Pro RT. It was designed to be a real-time interface for GEnie, and was not an offline reader like GEnie Master and Co-Pilot. In fact, it was not even necessary to have a separate terminal program, as was needed with the other offline readers. It required an Apple IIGS running System 6.0.1, as well as an error-correcting modem, a feature included in many new modems of the day. It was intended to support Zmodem and Ymodem batch file transfers (for downloading files), and could also be used to access the Internet using a text-based interface.

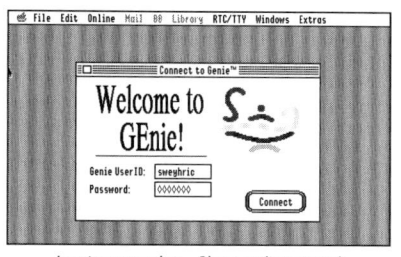

Jasmine screenshot – Photo credit: personal

Jasmine windows – Photo credit: Richard Bennett-Forrest

---

19 Esmay, Dean, e-mail message to author, May 23, 2012.

Bennett had showed a preview of it at KansasFest 1995. The developers had help from several beta-testers, but the progress was slow, and by the time it was released in February 1997 it was provided more as fulfillment of a promise than as the planned final product. The problem by then lay primarily in the changing plans by Genie's management, making it hard to hit a moving target.

Another change happened in the summer of 1997. Genie's management announced in July that the structure of the messages on the remaining Roundtables on Genie would change by September 1st. This would cause problems for all of the offline readers that were being used, since they were dependent on catching known prompts in order to know when a function was ready to start or had completed. The announcement further discouraged use of Genie services. (However, despite these plans, the message structure change did not come to pass.)

By early 1998, traffic on the Delphi Apple II Forum and Genie's A2 Roundtable were about the same. However, major cracks in the Genie infrastructure became apparent. Because there were no longer any of the original programmers or staff engineers working for Yovelle, it was not possible to fix things when they went wrong. By this time, some of the effects of the impending Y2K bug began to manifest. It turned out that beginning in 1998, because the system could not handle dates beyond the end of 1999, it was not even possible to sign up new Genie users, because their credit card expiration dates went past 12/99.

The problems of system maintenance became more apparent by April 1999. For three full weeks it was impossible for either users or staff to access the A2 Roundtable. Email was still available, however, so a group mail was sent out to all A2RT members with the message, "We are sad to note that the A2 RT on Genie seems to have breathed its last. It's been shut down for over a month, and all the Genie people have to say is that they're looking into it. We believe it's gone for good, after ten years of great service to the Apple II community ... Apple II users are welcome to join the Mac RT and talk about the Apple II in several topics there." Although the A2 RT came back for a short time by early summer, another blackout happened soon after, and Apple II users found it necessary to continue to post messages in the Mac Roundtable.

Late in the year, Yovelle announced that after December 27, 1999, all Genie content would have to be accessed via a web browser. This led to conflict between Yovelle management and sysops of some of the Roundtables, as they had not been asked permission for the text-side contend to be mirrored to the web. Some sysops even took a scorched-earth policy, and systematically deleted content from their Roundtable before it could be taken from their control.

Dean Esmay, sysop for the Apple II Roundtable, later recalled looking through the A2 RT near the end of December, but found little to no activity. He went into one of the main chat areas on the last day, looking for anyone who might have shown up, but there was nobody. He typed "goodbye" into chat room

1, and logged off for the last time.[20] Like a family who has moved out of the house they grew up in before it was demolished, the A2 RT was deserted, and held nothing but memories. The family had found a different home, on Delphi.

Users of the Science Fiction Roundtable were more determined to see it out until the end, and held a wake on December 27th, to watch the service's last hours. It continued to be sporadically available for the next three days. On December 30, 1999, members of the SFRT were still gathering, but were having a difficult time doing so. According to the SFRT managing sysop, the official "time of death" was 14:15 PST on 12/30/99. However, even into the latter part of the day, SFRT members were still leaving messages on one of the roundtables they had previously inhabited, but many users reported that they were getting "PAGE NOT FOUND" messages when trying to get there. It appeared that the various roundtables were being deleted one at a time. By late in the day, it was possible to establish a modem connection, but the system would not respond to any typed commands, not unlike a terminally ill person who still has a beating heart but no brain activity.[21]

Beyond that time, further communication with Genie was only possible via the web at www.genie.com. However, Yovelle/IDT was unable to make even that function as planned. Although for much of 2000 and 2001 the webpage displayed the heading "Genie Online Services", it did not contain any useful content. According to Andy Finkenstadt, who had been a sysop on GEnie from the beginning and was principal developer of GEnie's Internet services before Yovelle took over, all email from the old system was completely gone, and other content that survived had been ported "imperfectly and haphazardly" to the web service. Furthermore, what content was there had many broken (non-functioning) links.

To further rub salt into their wounds, some former members of the text-based Genie were even having problems getting IDT to stop billing their credit card accounts for service that they were no longer receiving. One user said the customer service person he called told him that Genie had sent out emails in April 1998 (twenty months before the end) and on December 27, 1999 explaining the changes and the need to obtain a new username and password. The user told the customer support representative that he had tried to contact them by email to ask about the changes before the December 27th cutoff date. The support person responded that they would have to find that email before any refund could be offered. When he finally received an answer from Genie about the time he had been billed for, he was told that since he did not cancel his service before December 27th, they would not issue a refund.

---

20 Esmay, Dean, e-mail message to author, May 23, 2012.
21 For a fascinating read about the subculture of the Science Fiction Roundtable on GEnie, with descriptions that nicely explain not only the behavior of members there but also very reminiscent of the members of the A2 and A2Pro RTs, read Chapter 4 of *Science Fiction Culture* by Camille Bacon-Smith.

By late in 2001, genie.com was redirecting to genie.net, and in 2002 it simply redirected to the IDT Corporation page.

It is unknown outside of IDT exactly what went wrong in its plans to create a competitor to America Online. Was it impossible to do the necessary programming work to complete the conversion to a Unix foundation, which could then be transferred to modern hardware? Was it that the management handling the process was simply grossly incompetent? One of the former A2 sysops truly believed that IDT fully intended to move the service to the World Wide Web, but was unable to do so in a coordinated fashion. He felt that had IDT not purchased GEnie when it did, GEIS would have shut the service down much sooner than its end in December 1999.

TIMELINE

The Source – *July 1979 – August 1989*

CompuServe – *July 1979 – December 1998 (end of Apple II access)*

GEnie – *October 1985 – December 1999*

CHAPTER 29
Input Devices

KEYBOARDS

After the success of the Apple II, Steve Jobs again approached Datanetics, the company that provided their keyboards. He asked them to create a new company focused exclusively on providing keyboards for Apple. The name chosen for this business was The Keyboard Company (also known as TKC), and they not only made keyboards for the Apple II, but also created numeric keypads demanded by business users of the computer, and supplied the Apple III keyboard with its built-in numeric keypad. By 1980, Apple had bought The Keyboard Company and it became Apple's Accessory Parts Division.[1]

When Apple II users began to demand a more complete set of ASCII characters, third-party solutions began to appear. Various expanded keyboards became available for the II and II Plus, bypassing the uppercase-only limit. There was even a keyboard with plug-in modules that redefined specialized function keys to make them specific for different programs. Videx, known for its video cards, sold the Enhancer][in March 1982. It was a set of pressure sensitive pads that attached to the Apple II keyboard above the top row and could be programmed to generate series of key presses (similar to the function keys on modern keyboards).

Videx Enhancer][and keyboard function strip
— Photo credit: *BYTE* August 1982

The original IIe had a socket for the addition of an external numeric keypad, and the IIGS and later versions of the IIe had this keypad built-in. Because of the detached keyboard in the IIGS and its standardized ADB con-

---

1 Muller, Michael, "The Keyboard Company – History", <www.apple1notes.com/old_apple/History_files/The%20Keyboard%20Company.htm>, retrieved April 24, 2013.

nector, it was possible to select between a couple of different versions of keyboards offered by Apple as well as from some third party companies.

By the time the Apple IIe and later models were released, the immense popularity of the IBM-style keyboard (modeled after IBM's famous Selectric typewriter) made it important to put the special characters in the same order as the IBM example, rather than continuing in the tradition of the old Teletypes.

GAME PADDLES

The next most commonly used input device after the keyboard was the set of game paddles included with every Apple II and II Plus from 1977 through 1980. They plugged into the game I/O connector on the motherboard, and the owner had to take care when doing so to avoid bending or snapping the fragile pins on the plug.

Wozniak had designed the game paddles for the *Breakout* game he wanted to run on the Apple II. A paddle functioned by varying voltage from the motherboard through a 150,000-ohm resistor. A BASIC program could read the position of the paddle by using the PDL command, which returned a number from 0 through 255. A specific memory location was assigned to each paddle's pushbutton, and was read using a PEEK to that location. If the value returned was greater than 127, the button was being pressed. Although it was possible to connect as many as four paddles to a custom-wired plug, only three pushbutton (PB) inputs were available.

Game I/O plug, showing its 16 pins
— Photo credit: Jerry Penner

The game paddles supplied with the earliest Apple II models sold were lever controls with a pushbutton labeled "RESET" and the name "Adversary" on them. They were featured in a photo on one of the first two-page Apple II magazine advertisements. Apparently, the company did not have time to create its own branded game controllers, and so purchased a supply of them from an outside source. The source chosen was a *Pong* clone called the Adversary Video Games system, which had been sold by National Semiconductor in 1976. It offered variations on the original Atari game, and was in color, but was not successful enough to last long in the marketplace.[2]

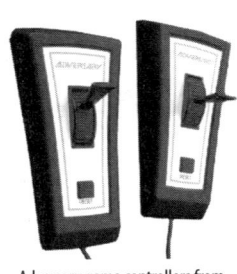

Adversary game controllers from earliest Apple II packages
— Photo credit: Howie Shen

---

2 "Adversary — National Semiconductor", *Chronogamer*, <www.atariage.com/forums/blog/87/entry-540-adversary-national-semiconductor/>, retrieved March 7, 2013.

It was not long before Apple had its own, custom-designed game paddles. Oddly enough, they were still un-branded. They were called the Apple Hand Controllers, used a rotating knob instead of a slider, and had a tiny pushbutton on the side for the PB input. When playing shooting games like SPACE WAR (distributed on cassette and early floppy disks), repeatedly pressing this could result in a painful finger because the button was small.

Later in the product life of the Apple II Plus, these paddles were modified (and finally marked with the Apple logo) and made a bit easier to hold in the hand, but still had that tiny pushbutton.

After the Apple IIe came out, with its foolproof rear panel game controller connector to replace the 16-pin motherboard plug, Apple also released a newer game paddle. It came in the same color as the IIe, and was more ergonomically shaped for the hand. Also, it had replaced the small button with one that could be repeatedly pressed without discomfort.

For those who did not want to use Apple's game paddles or needed to replace them, there were numerous third-party vendors selling compatible versions.

JOYSTICKS

Apple II Hand Controllers, 1977
– Photo credit: Jimmy Maher

Apple II Hand Controllers, 1980
– Photo credit: Jonathan Zufi

Apple Hand Controller IIe, 1984
– Photo credit: Jerry Penner

Some games or drawing programs needed both up/down and left/right movement, and for those it was useful to combine both analog paddles together into a single device. Model airplane enthusiasts had used joysticks for years to control their planes. Apple employee Jef Raskin built and flew model gliders, and had used these controllers. He used this experience soon after the Apple II came to market to create what likely was the first joystick for the Apple II. It used the joystick component from a model airplane, modified so paddle 0 was mapped to horizontal, paddle 1 to vertical. Buttons 0 and 1 were on the side. It also included a couple of trim knobs to fine-tune the settings.

Joystick built by Jef Raskin for Apple II
– Photo credit: Bruce Damer, DigiBarn Computer Museum and Jef Raskin

A joystick provided a different method for games or other input to the computer. Raskin was convinced that a joystick was an ideal pointing device for a computer. He felt so strongly about this that he had a major argument with Steve Jobs, pressing for the use of a joystick instead of a mouse for the original Macintosh. His enforced departure from the project guaranteed the final outcome was in Jobs' favor.

TKC, The Keyboard Company that made keyboards for the early Apple II computers, also made joysticks for the Apple II, often sold through Apple dealers. Apple released its first branded product, the Apple Joystick, in early 1981. That model was designed to work either with the 9-pin plug connector on the Apple III or with the 16-pin plug compatible with the Apple II game I/O socket. A later update released in 1984 worked on the 9-pin socket on the Apple IIe and IIc.

TABLETS & DRAWING PENS

Apple Graphics Tablet

Beyond playing games, some users required more specialized ways to input data. Creating pictures on the hi-res graphics screen was always a challenge. Using the game paddles or a joystick was common, but it was difficult to produce accurate lines and curves. During the 1970s, Summagraphics Corp. of Seymour, Connecticut had been designing and building digitizers and data tablets for computers, used by cartographers and engineers. These often sold for thousands of dollars. In November 1977 they released the Bit Pad, with an eleven by eleven inch working surface, for a cost of only $555. Apple licensed the technology from Summagraphics, added its own firmware and software, and released a larger, thirty by thirty inch version of it as the Apple Graphics Tablet in January 1980, initially for $800.

The surface of the tablet contained an embedded grid of horizontal and vertical copper wires. When activated, these wires created magnetic waves that moved across the surface (waves that were strong enough to damage a diskette or cassette tape if placed on the tablet). The tip of the attached stylus could detect the high frequency field, and through the included ROM firmware it returned to the computer the coordinates of the stylus on the surface.

Sold with the Graphics Tablet was a flexible plastic overlay sheet with a grid and menu labels printed on it. The menu items on the overlay were selected with the stylus, and were intended for use with the software that accompanied the tablet. Whether or not the overlay was used, it was possible to draw free-hand or trace an existing picture on the tablet, with the results showing up on the Apple II hi-res screen.[3]

There were two different releases of the Apple Graphics Tablet. The original one, which came out when the II Plus was the latest machine, was discontinued by FCC order because of radio frequency interference problems. The second version, redesigned to correct that problem, was released after the IIe was in production. It used two nine-pin connectors (DB-9 connectors) to install on the back of the computer, leading to the peripheral card plugged into a slot inside. (These DB-9 connectors were the same type used on the back of the IIc and IIGS for connecting a joystick).[4]

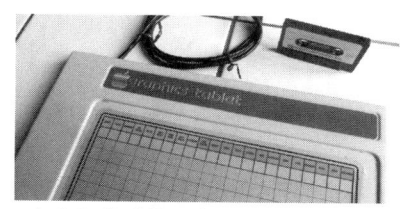

Apple Graphics Tablet – Photo credit: Antoine Vignau

Koala Pad

Dr. David Thornburg was a founding member of Xerox PARC, and researched devices to improve interfaces between computers and humans. After leaving PARC, he co-founded Koala Technologies to market his invention, a touch-sensitive graphics tablet that was inexpensive and also easy for children to use. This tablet, the Koala Pad, was first demonstrated at the summer 1983 Consumer Electronics Show in Chicago. It was available for purchase by October of that year for $125.

The Koala Pad worked with several of the popular home computers of the day, including the Apple II, Atari, Commodore 64, and IBM PC—each version supplying the specific connector for that computer. It consisted of a 4x4 inch drawing space in an 8x6 inch case. On the Apple II, the tablet plugged into the game paddle socket. To the computer, it sent the same electrical signals as did a joystick, and so was compatible with any software that required a joystick. Using a finger or the supplied stylus, a user could draw on the pad and produce pictures on the hi-res screen, using the *KoalaPaint* program included with the pad.

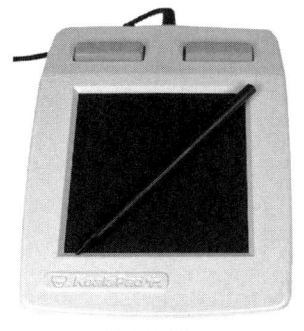

Koala Pad Plus – Photo credit: Vetronics Apple World

Since the Koala Pad did not use a proprietary interface, several other drawing programs could make use of it. One particularly popular one was Brøderbund's *Dazzle Draw*, which could also use the double hi-res graphics

---

3   Wells, Ralph, "The Apple Graphics Tablet", *InfoWorld* (February 18, 1980), 14, 18.
4   Kindall, Jerry, A2 Roundtable, Category 2, Topic 16, *GEnie*, accessed March 1991.

mode on the 128K Apple IIe and IIc. Koala also sold a program called *Graphics Exhibitor* which could take pictures created with the pad and print them in color or grey scale on a number of printers, including Apple's Scribe printer.

Muppet Learning Keys

Another device invented by Dr. Thornburg was Muppet Learning Keys, which Koala Technologies released in November 1984 at a price of $79.95. Also making use of the game paddle socket to connect to the Apple II, this was designed for preschoolers.

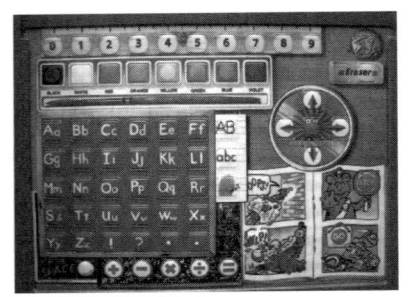

Muppet Learning Keys keyboard
– Photo credit: Antoine Vignau

The software used to interface with this membrane keyboard was designed with the help of Christopher Cerf, who wrote and sang many of the songs used on *Sesame Street*. It was intended to help children ages three and over to learn letters, numbers, and colors, using the Muppets from Sesame Street as a learning aid. The unit used various contact surfaces to send user responses to the computer.[5]

Mechanically, the Muppet keyboard was divided into nine rows and twelve columns, each cell designed to respond to the press of a "key" on the overlay. The response to the computer could be read from the Apple II paddle inputs, in the same fashion as a paddle or joystick (or even the Koala Pad). It was the software that made the interaction with the Muppet keyboard simple enough that even young children could use it.[6]

Gibson Light Pen

At the age of 26, Steve Gibson started his own company with the purpose of creating a pen to manipulate information directly on a computer screen. Gibson Laboratories originally sold the product in 1982 for the Apple II as the LPS II Light Pen System.

The concept of a light pen was not new; it had been used on mainframe computers as far back as the 1950s. However, Gibson's version of the light pen was significantly less expensive than those used on high-end graphics systems. It worked by using a light-sensitive cell on the tip of the pen, which could then pick up the presence or absence of light on the computer screen. The information collected by the sensor was then transmitted back to a custom peripheral card plugged into slot 7 on the Apple II. The software in-

---

5 -----."The Marketplace", *Call-A.P.P.L.E.* (November 1984), 41.
6 Vignau, Antoine, "Muppet Learning Keyboard", *Brutal Deluxe Software*, <www.brutaldeluxe.fr/projects/muppet/index.html>.

cluded with the LPS II allowed the user to manipulate pixels on the hi-res screen, creating the illusion of actually drawing on the screen.

In 1983 Gibson sold his company and its products to the Atari Corporation, just as the home computer market began to be affected by the video game crash. Although he created a version of his light pen for the Atari, management changes at Atari began to occur, and his light pen technology was at risk of being lost in the turmoil. With some effort, Gibson was able to recover rights to his hardware and software. He then updated his LPS II hardware and software under contract to Koala Technologies. They released it for the Apple II in mid-1984 as the Gibson Light Pen System, at a price of $350.

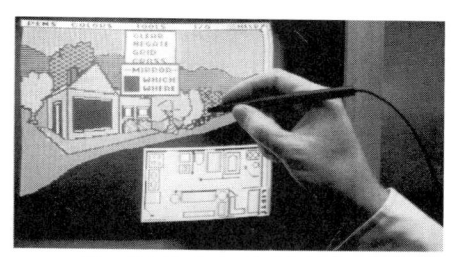

Gibson Light Pen System, Koala Technologies – Photo credit: *inCider*, July 1984

The product included software to draw pictures by moving the pen on the surface of the computer monitor, and even offered the ability to create animation and music. Koala also included a software driver that allowed the user to create programs with Applesoft BASIC to make use of the light pen.

Digital Paintbrush System

Dr. John Osborn was one of four founders in 1982 of a company that they eventually named Computer Colorworks. They initially envisioned a software scheduling program for nurses, but transitioned to something that was easier: a program for creating art on the Apple II. Released in 1984, the program was called *Flying Colors*, and was moderately successful in the market.

The problem the company identified with the program was the awkward way that was required to draw, using a joystick or (less commonly) a trackball. Osborn used some of the profits from Flying Colors to build and market a hardware device called the Digital Paintbrush System. Dacron lines (the same material used is some fishing lines) connected the pen used in digitizing the drawing to two potentiometers within the tablet. These then returned the X-Y coordinates of the pen movements back to the computer. A button on the side of the pen was used to make menu selections.

The device was released in October 1984 for the Apple II Plus and IIe at a price of $299, and later made available for the IBM PC. It could be used to trace over a picture or draw freehand, with the results displayed on the hi-res screen. The included software allowed the cre-

Digital Paintbrush System – Photo credit: *inCider*, September 1984

ation of curves and lines, and used *Fontrix* fonts for lettering. (Fontrix was a program that could produce detailed hi-res graphics pictures, and had numerous fonts available to label those pictures.) A unique feature of the Digital Paintbrush was the ability to connect two computers via a modem and phone line to allow both users to simultaneously draw on the same picture that appeared on both computers.[7]

Computer Colorworks later increased the accuracy of the Digital Paintbrush System, and sold it at a very similar price as a digitizer for scientific measurements. This was significantly more successful, and determined the future direction of the company into the scientific market, and away from the consumer market.[8]

MOUSE

One input device that made inroads in the Apple II world (particularly on the IIGS) was the one that was unique and essential to the Macintosh: the mouse. Burrell Smith, the engineer originally recruited by Jef Raskin to design hardware for the Macintosh, also designed the hardware for the single-button mouse that was used on the Mac. It worked by using a part of the 6522 VIA chip on that computer to generate interrupt signals when the mouse was moved so the software could draw it on the Mac screen. Because the Apple III used the same 6522 chip, Apple engineers Andy Hertzfeld and Dan Kotke developed a way to use a mouse on that computer, and display and move a cursor on its screen.

To create graphics on the Apple III that were appropriate to use with the mouse, they asked for help from a veteran game designer. Bill Budge was an Apple II programmer who had written fast graphics routines for immensely popular games on the Apple II (a hi-res pinball game called *Raster Blaster* in 1981 and later *Pinball Construction Set* in 1982). Together, they were able to create a simple graphic-based word processor on the Apple III, but since that computer was not selling well, they decided they needed to make it work on the Apple II.

It took some clever hardware and software tricks between Smith, Hertzfeld, and Budge to implement it on the Apple II (which did not have easy access to video timing signals as was possible on the Apple III or the Mac). By the summer of 1981 they had the mouse-driven graphical word processor running on the Apple II, even using proportional text. Steve Jobs heard about the project and insisted that he be given a demonstration. After he saw it, Jobs

---

7   Neibauer, Larry. "Reviews: Digital Paintbrush", *Call-A.P.P.L.E.* (November 1984), 36.
8   Mitchell, Dick, "After 100 issues and 14 years - anything new?" *Scientific Computing World*, <www.scientific-computing.com/features/feature.php?feature_id=196>

said that the hardware part of it belonged to Apple, since it was created with company resources. It was turned over to the Apple II division, and they eventually created a card that used quite a few more chips than the original design had required.[9]

Naturally, a mouse for the Apple II did not appear until after the Macintosh was released (it was not allowed to upstage Jobs' special project). In May 1984, five months after the Macintosh debut, and one month after the release of the Apple IIc, Apple announced the AppleMouse II. It came with an interface card for the Apple IIe, or the mouse alone for the Apple IIc (with a plug for the IIc joystick port; the computer already had built-in hardware and firmware to handle the mouse).

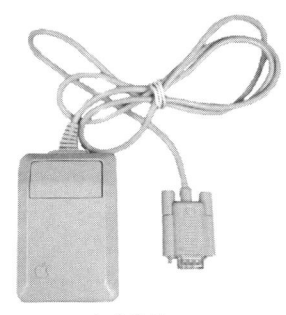

Apple IIc Mouse
– Photo credit: Vectronics Apple World

Bundled with the AppleMouse II was a program called *MousePaint*, written by Budge. This program was not the word processor that had been originally used to demonstrate the mouse, but instead it was a graphics program based on *MacPaint* that came with the original Macintosh. *MousePaint* used the standard hi-res graphics screen and worked only under the ProDOS operating system, but gave Apple II users the ability to do graphics in much the same way as Macintosh users. It also offered a feature the Mac didn't have—color.

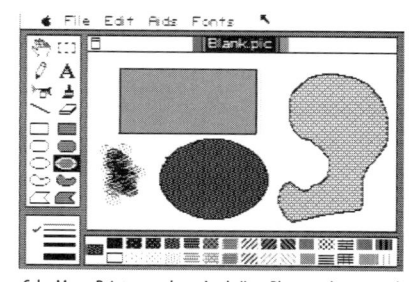

Color MousePaint example on Apple IIe – Photo credit: personal

The AppleMouse II made it possible for programmers to design software that used the mouse as a pointing and input control device. However, many programs using this device on the IIe or IIc were not graphic-based, but rather text-based, and usually made use of the MouseText characters that were built into the Apple IIc and in the Enhanced IIe character ROM.

VIDEO INPUT

Translating video images into hi-res graphics eventually became possible on the Apple II. One of the most popular and easy to use was ComputerEyes, a video acquisition system sold by Digital Vision, Inc. and released in July 1984. The

---

9 Hertzfeld, Andy, "Apple II Mouse Card", *Folklore.org*, <folklore.org/StoryView.py?project=Macintosh&story=Apple_II_Mouse_Card.txt>, accessed October 20, 2012.

product was a black box, 4 by 4 by 1.75 inches in size, which attached to an Apple II on the game paddle socket. Any video source that could output NTSC video or standard non-interlaced video could be used for input to the box. Compatible video sources included video players (VHS or Betamax), videodisc players, or consumer video cameras. That video signal was converted to a pixelated image that could be displayed on the Apple II hi-res screen. The program included with the ComputerEyes hardware could be used to adjust the synchronization of the video source and the computer, capture the images (either normal or grey-scale), and save those images to a disk. With the grey-scale option, eight different versions of the image were created and superimposed on each other. ComputerEyes sold for $129.95 ($349.95 with a video camera).[10,11]

ComputerEyes image
– Photo credit: *The Apple II Review*, Spring 1986

Digital Visions released versions of ComputerEyes that worked on other popular computers in the 1980s and 1990s, including the Commodore 64, Atari, Amiga and IBM PC. (Later, in 1989, they also released a ComputerEyes GS card that ran on the Apple IIGS, though picture scanning was considered too slow.)

SCANNERS

Another way to get pictures into a computer was to scan them. The earliest device able to scan printed images into an Apple II was the ThunderScan from Thunderware. The company released this product in 1984 for both the Apple II and Macintosh. ThunderScan replaced the ribbon cartridge on an ImageWriter printer with an optical scanner. The device (very slowly) scanned a document threaded into the printer, one line at a time, moving back and forth just like a print head. It could take as long as a half hour to scan an 8 by 10 piece of paper.

---

10 -----. "The Marketplace", *Call-A.P.P.L.E.* (July 1984), 61.
11 Anderson, John, and Linzmayer, Owen, "The II Can See And Speak", AppleCart, *Creative Computing* (Vol 10, No. 10, October 1984), 178.

TIMELINE

Datanetics Keyboard – *1976*

National Semiconductor Adversary (paddles) – *1976*

Apple Hand Controllers – *September 1977*

Apple II Hand Controllers – *1980*

Apple Graphics Tablet – *January 1980*

Apple Joystick – *1981*

Videx Enhancer][– *March 1982*

LPS II Light Pen System – *July 1982*

Videx Koala Pad – *October 1983*

Apple Hand Controller IIe – *1984*

Apple Joystick IIe and IIc – *1984*

AppleMouse II – *May 1984*

ComputerEyes – *July 1984*

Gibson Light Pen System – *July 1984*

Digital Paintbrush System – *October 1984*

Muppet Learning Keys – *November 1984*

ThunderScan – *December 1984*

ComputerEyes GS – *1989*

CHAPTER 30
Send in the Clones

The tremendous success of the Apple II in the United States created a demand for the computer elsewhere in the world. Steve Wozniak's hacker ethic and desire to share knowledge resulted in a significant amount of technical information about this computer that was released to the public. In the original *Apple II Reference Manual*, even as far back as the Red Book, it included schematic diagrams of the motherboard, technical information about timing, connector description and voltages, and even a source code listing of the Monitor ROM code. Naturally, the intended purpose of this was to make it easy for programmers to do anything they wanted to do with the Apple II, and for companies or individuals wanting to make peripherals for it to have all the technical information they needed.

Unfortunately, this also put information into the hands of competitors overseas who decided it would be profitable to create and sell their own version of the Apple II at a lower price than Apple. This provided a computer for regional markets that could take advantage of an existing library of software. With American patent and copyright laws extending only to the borders of the United States, there was often little that Apple could do about clone makers (although Apple's lawyers certainly gave it a try).

More than two hundred clones of the Apple II appeared from 1979 onwards, coming from countries all over the world.[1] Only two were created with the permission of Apple (the ITT 2020 and the Bell & Howell Apple II). Many of the illegal clone makers duplicated nearly *every* aspect of the Apple II, changing only the label above the keyboard to include their own product name (which was often fruit-related, such as "Pear" or "Pineapple"), and some even went so far as to use Apple's multicolored logo. Companies made changes to accommodate local languages, or to add other features that the Apple II lacked, such as lowercase text, a numeric keypad, or possibly a detached keyboard. One country, Brazil, had laws that prohibited the import of computer equipment from other countries; in that country, the only way to get a personal computer was for a company to completely design and build a

---

1 *A2Clones.com*, <www.a2clones.com>, accessed January 5, 2011.

new computer, or create a clone. The two most successful clones were those sold as the Franklin ACE and the Laser series.

FRANKLIN COMPUTER

The Franklin Computer Corporation came on the scene in March 1982 with a computer that was the first clone of the Apple II available in the United States. The Franklin ACE 100, which retailed for $1495, made changes so the physical appearance of the computer case differed from the Apple II Plus. The motherboard inside that case was larger than the Apple II Plus, but was laid out much the same. Most importantly, the ACE 100 worked with existing Apple II software because the ROM was an almost exact copy of the Apple II Plus ROM. Like the Apple II Plus, it had 48K of RAM on the motherboard, with a 16K RAM card to function like Apple's Language Card. It had the same eight slots for peripheral cards. An improvement over the Apple II and II Plus was a better keyboard with a numeric keypad and support for full upper and lowercase characters. The ACE 100 had a modified character generator ROM to display these extra characters. Franklin did not include support for cassette storage, and made use of the space used by the cassette input and output routines for code to manage upper and lowercase text entry. The only real incompatibilities with existing Apple II software had to do with programs that did not know how to deal with lowercase characters or used a different method to create lowercase.

Franklin ACE 100 – Photo credit: MaximumPC

At the time Franklin released the ACE 100, there was no state or federal law prohibiting the act of copying computer code that was only available in machine-readable form (either in the ROM or on a floppy disk). Franklin sold their computers on their belief that although Apple had patents on the Apple II hardware, it was not illegal to copyright processes, systems, or functions. In May 1982, just two months after the release of the ACE 100, Apple filed suit against Franklin for copyright violation. Initially, the district court that heard the case found in favor of Franklin.

In June 1982, Franklin updated its Apple II clone and released the Franklin ACE 1000 for the increased price of $1595. As a partial response to Apple's first legal challenges, it removed a chip from the motherboard that allowed color output through the video port. However, for $50 the computer dealer could install the chip that restored color video capability. The ACE 1000 featured a larger power supply (and built-in fan), 64K of RAM on the motherboard, an improved upper and lowercase keyboard, and even special function keys for *VisiCalc*. It booted to the standard 40-column display, but included in hardware the equivalent of an 80-column card.

The next model released was the ACE 1000 Plus, which included a built-in disk controller card, and (oddly enough) added support for color video back to the motherboard. In November 1982, Franklin introduced updates to the 1000 Plus, the ACE 1100, which included a single 5.25-inch Apple-compatible floppy drive, and the 1200, which had dual disk drives. These models actually housed the disk drives in the lid, making them part of the case. The ACE 1200 also offered a built-in 80-column card, an interface card with parallel and serial ports, and a Z-80 coprocessor card to run CP/M software. The primary problem of the disk drives housed in the lid was a tendency to overheat; some users found it necessary to prop their lids open to allow them to run cooler.[2, 3]

Franklin ACE 1000 – Photo credit: <www.1000bit.it>

For an operating system, Franklin included lightly modified copies of Apple DOS, even referring to it as DOS 3.3 in its user manual. For its supporting utilities, Franklin renamed the Applesoft COPYA program to just COPY. Rather than a program called FID to copy files, Franklin's program was called FUD. It also included Apple's CHAIN (to link between programs) and BOOT13 (to allow booting 13 sector DOS 3.2 disks). Other programs on the included master disk ran diagnostics on the computer, something Apple did not include with the Apple II Plus. Franklin's disk also included the INTBASIC and FPBASIC files from Apple's DOS 3.3 master disk.

Franklin ACE 1200 – Photo credit: <vintagecomputer.net>

To circumvent Apple's patents, the ROM in the ACE 1000 series had just enough code to start up the disk, and then load code from the disk into memory. This put the ROM code on a disk instead of in a physical ROM on the motherboard. Likely, this was the main reason for the FPBASIC file on the Franklin DOS disk

After the first court ruled in favor of Franklin, Apple appealed to a higher court. In August 1983, this court found that computer code in ROM and on floppy disk *could* be protected under copyright, and reversed the ruling of the lower court in favor of Apple. Although the company got an injunction that allowed them to continue to sell their computers, the downturn in the tech industry that

---

2 Company Profile: Franklin Computer Corp., *Classic Tech*, <classictech.wordpress.com/tag/franklin-computer>, accessed February 23, 2012.
3 Applegate, Bob, "ACE 1000 Series", *Bob Applegate's Boring Page*, <www.k2ut.org/Franklin/ACE1000/index.html>, accessed March 2, 2012.

happened in 1984 had an adverse effect on their sales, and it became necessary for Franklin Computer Corporation to file for bankruptcy protection that year.[4]

Before Franklin filed for bankruptcy, the company was preparing to release a portable version of the ACE 1000 series, called the Franklin CX. Looking very much like the Osborne-1, the CX had a built-in green phosphor monitor, two half-height disk drives, and a keyboard. When closed up, it looked like a suitcase, and it weighed 25 pounds. The keyboard connected to the main unit with a coiled cable, much like the IBM PC. Included with the Franklin CX was to be the Franklin Office Manager, an integrated software package that offered word processing, graphic design, and a spell checker. There were four models, the CX-1, CX-2, CX-3, and CX-4, each model offering larger amounts of RAM and additional capabilities. They all had a 6502 microprocessor, but the Franklin CX-3 added a Z-80 coprocessor, and the CX-4 an Intel 8086 coprocessor.[5,6]

While reorganizing to get back in business, its engineers did serious work to copy the Apple II without directly copying Apple's code and design. In October 1985 Franklin emerged from bankruptcy and released two new computers, the ACE 2000 series and the ACE 500 (to compete with the Apple IIe and IIc, respectively). To run these legal clones of the Apple II, Franklin wrote its own version of DOS, calling it FDOS.

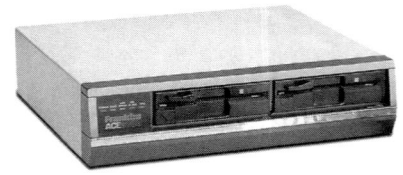

Franklin ACE 2100, upgraded to use two disk drives
– Photo credit: <old-computers.com>

The ACE 2000 had a look that was similar to the popular IBM PC, with disk drives opening on the front of the computer, and a detached keyboard connected with a coiled cable. As with the ACE 1000 series, there were three models in the ACE 2000 series: The ACE 2000 sold at $699 with no disk drives, the ACE 2100 for $799.95 with a single drive, and for $949.99 the ACE 2200 came with two built-in half-height disk drives.[7] The front panel of the computer featured LED lights for disk drive activity, power, diagnostics, double-hires graphics mode, and CPU activity. It used a 65sC02a processor from GTE, which was mostly compatible with software written to use the 65c02 in the Enhanced Apple IIe or IIc, but was different enough that some software would immediately crash. The ACE 2000 series came with 128K of RAM, and an additional 256K on an expansion card (which could be expanded to 1

---

4 Hassett, Rob, "Impact of Apple vs. Franklin", *Interlegal.com* <www.internetlegal.com/impact-of-apple-vs-franklin-decision/>, accessed March 20, 2013.
5 Wallace, Dan, e-mail message to author, December 22, 2002.
6 Polsson, Ken, *Chronology of Personal Computers*, 1984, <pctimeline.info/comp1984apr.htm>, accessed October 20, 2012.
7 Maginnis, Mike, "A Look at the Franklin ACE 2100", *6502 Lane*, <www.6502lane.net/2011/06/03/a-look-at-the-franklin-ace-2100/>, accessed October 20, 2012.

megabyte). This extra RAM could be used by programs like AppleWorks, and with software included with the ACE it was possible to use it as a RAM disk.[8]

On the back panel, the ACE 2000 offered two serial ports, a parallel port, and RGB video. As with the ACE 1000, there was a built-in fan for cooling. Inside, due to space constraints of the altered case design, it did not include all eight slots. Built-in ports offered some of the functionality of slots, and slots that *were* physically present were positioned in unusual ways that made them difficult to use.[9]

The Franklin ACE 500 was built in a similar fashion to the Apple IIc, with a built-in floppy disk drive on the right side. Like the other Franklin ACE models, the ACE 500 included a numeric keypad and programmable function key (which were used by the version of Microsoft BASIC that came with the ACE 500). It had RGB and parallel ports on the back, and came with a standard 256K of RAM, expandable to 512K. A factory-installed option was a clock/calendar chip.[10, 11, 12, 13]

Franklin ACE 500 – Photo credit: VintageMicros, Inc.

Apple continued to put legal pressure on Franklin, and although the company had also released two IBM PC clones between 1986 and 1988, it was finally forced out of the desktop computer business. After 1988, Franklin focused on its handheld computer devices, which the company had initially released in 1986.

LASER

Video Technology, Inc. (later known as VTech) was founded in 1976 in Hong Kong. The company wanted to use new and developing technology to build consumer products. In 1978 they released their first product, a portable electronic game built into a single integrated circuit.[14] The company continued to produce games and educational products, and by the early 1980s was working on home computers. The first one they released was the Laser 100, a Z-80-based clone of Radio Shack's TRS-80 Model I. The ROM used in the Laser 100 was almost identical to that of the Model I, and the Microsoft BASIC used

---

8   Maginnis, Mike, e-mail message to author, January 26, 2012.
9   "Franklin ACE 2000", *Obsolete Technology Website*, <oldcomputers.net/ace2100.html>, accessed October 20, 2012.
10 Wallace, Dan. e-mail message to author, June 1, 2003.
11 "Franklin ACE 2100", *Obsolete Technology Website*, <oldcomputers.net/ace2100.html>, accessed October 20, 2012.
12 Craft, Steve, "REQ: Info on Franklin Ace 2200", *comp.sys.apple2*, posted May 29, 1997.
13 Woodall, John, e-mail message to author, February 7, 2002.
14 "Our History", *VTech*, <www.vtech.com/en/about-vtech/corporate-information/history>, accessed October 20, 2012.

in the machine was modified only slightly from that used in the TRS-80. The graphics chip was the same as the one used in the TRS-80 Color Computer.

By 1983, VTech had set its sights on the Apple II Plus. The company introduced the $499 Laser 3000 that year, and by spring 1984 it was available in the United States. It used a 6502A microprocessor at 2 MHz (twice as fast as a stock Apple II), and came with a full 64K of RAM, expandable to 192K, using the same method as that employed by Saturn Systems (an early third-party source of Apple II memory cards). The version of BASIC in ROM was not Wozniak's Integer BASIC, nor was it Applesoft, but instead was Microsoft's 6502 BASIC. However, use of a plug-in cartridge containing a floating point BASIC made the computer almost identical to an Apple II Plus.

Laser 3000 – Photo credit: Bilgisayarlarim <bilgisayarlarim.com/VTech/Laser_3000>

Video output was standard composite, but also had a port for a better quality RGB signal. The Laser 3000 displayed both standard 40-column text, and via a switch on the bottom of the computer could also display 80-column text. Hi-res graphics were supported, but for some reason lo-res graphics were not. A speaker produced the usual 1-bit sound typical of the Apple II, but also had a 4-channel, 6 octave sound generator.

It supported cassettes and floppy disks. A cartridge that plugged into the back of the computer was an MFM (modified frequency modulation) disk controller that had been modified to also perform GCR (group code recording, the method that Wozniak used in the Disk II controller and drive). Rounding out the features of the Laser 3000 was a built-in Centronics printer interface, a port for connecting a cartridge for an RS-232 port (for modem use), and an optional cartridge with a CP/M co-processor. Software bundled with the computer included *Magic Window II* for word processing, *Magic Memory* for databases, and *MagiCalc* for spreadsheets.[15]

In Australia and New Zealand, Dick Smith Electronics sold a computer called The CAT, which was simply a rebranding of VTech's Laser 3000.[16, 17]

---

15 Kaplan, Andrew, "Laser 3000", *Obsolete Computer Museum*, <www.obsoletecomputermuseum.org/lsr3000/>, accessed October 20, 2012.
16 "Dick Smith's CAT", *AppleLogic*, <www.applelogic.org/TheCAT.html>, accessed October 20, 2012.
17 "Dick Smith CAT", *Old-computers.com*, <http://www.old-computers.com/museum/computer.asp?st=1&c=974>, accessed October 20, 2012.

CHAPTER 30 | Send in the Clones

VTech created clones of other existing computers, including the IBM PC. As the company's engineering abilities improved, it decided to upgrade its Apple II clone, focusing on the Apple IIe. Instead of making Franklin Computer's mistake of copying the ROM directly, they reverse-engineered the ROM, creating a version that had the same major entry points as the IIe ROM, but would not conflict with the ruling from Apple's legal win over Franklin. To achieve Applesoft compatibility, the company directly licensed Microsoft's 6502 BASIC, which was legal since Apple did not have an exclusive license for the language. (Presumably, VTech also reverse-engineered the additional entry points for the Apple II-specific code in that language — specifically the parts for management of hi-res graphics.)

VTech announced the new Laser 128 in 1984, the same year as the Apple IIc, and finally shipped it in 1985. It did not appear in the United States until March of 1986, marketed through Central Point Software (which also sold the popular *Copy II Plus* program for copying protected software). Though it was originally planned with a different form factor, it was redesigned to look more like the Apple IIc. It had a white case, and came with a built-in 5.25-inch floppy disk drive that opened on the right side. The Laser 128 came standard with 128K of RAM, as did the Apple IIc. Because of this abundant memory, the computer was able to duplicate all of the video modes of the IIc, offering 40 and 80-column text, and single and double lo-res and hi-res graphics. Like the IIc, the video port supported a composite monitor, or it could connect to digital video devices, such as the IIc RF Modulator or the IIc LCD screen. The Laser 128 also included support for connection of an analog 15Hz RGB monitor. If RGB output was used, the text font was identical to that of the IBM PC.

Laser 128 – Photo credit: Blake Patterson, The Byte Cellar

Laser 128 with peripheral card plugged into expansion port on side,– Photo credit: *inCider*, December 1986

The MouseText characters were the same as on the Apple IIc, with the exception of open- and solid-triangle characters taking the place of the open-

and solid-apple characters. The full keyboard had keys for those triangle characters, as well as a numeric keypad and ten function keys.

The Laser 128 incorporated other ports compatible with the Apple IIc, including one for the Apple IIc mouse, and serial ports. An expansion port on the left side of the computer made it possible to plug in an actual Apple II peripheral card. Unlike the typical use of one of these cards, plugging one into this external socket was unprotected from debris and dust. This naked card could be assigned to either slot 5 or slot 7 (selected by a switch on the bottom of the computer). In the United States, FCC regulations prohibited using a card directly like this, since it was unshielded and could produce radio frequency interference. Instead, Laser sold an optional metal expansion box, connected to the expansion port via a ribbon cable. Into that box it was possible to plug in two Apple II peripheral cards, one for slot 5 and one for slot 7.[18]

Besides the internal 5.25-inch floppy drive, the Laser 128 had a disk port similar to the one on the Apple IIc. This could be used to connect a second 5.25-inch disk drive or most of the other storage devices made for the IIc. For those who wanted a 3.5-inch drive on the original (white) Laser 128, a controller card was required. There were two ways to make this happen:

- The Laser Universal Disk Controller was introduced after release of the original Laser 128, and was integrated into later models of the Laser 128. This card did not work with the UniDisk 3.5, but worked with AppleDisk 3.5 or similar "non-smart" drives, as well as various Apple-style 5.25 disk drives.
- The Apple II 3.5 inch Disk Controller card (SuperDrive Controller) could be attached to the expansion slot, which then made it possible to use a UniDisk 3.5 on the Laser 128.

To provide additional storage, the Laser 128 had 64K of RAM that could be used as a RAM disk, assigned to slot 5. However, if an expansion card was assigned to slot 5, access to this RAM disk was disabled.

Within a year of the release of the Laser 128, an updated edition was released, this time in a platinum color. The disk port worked more like the Smartport on the Apple IIc, and supported daisy-chaining disks to the disk port (but it still did not work with the UniDisk 3.5).

After release and success of the Laser 128, VTech engineers redesigned the product, making changes to simplify the manufacturing process and to add some features. In 1988 they released the Laser 128EX, at a retail price of $579.95. It used the 65c02 processor, and offered memory expansion to over 1 megabyte without an external RAM card. Using an accelerator similar to Applied Engineering's popular TransWarp, the Laser 128EX ran at three

---

18 "VTech Laser 128 Accessories", *Digital Obscuria*, <www.trhonline.com/obscure/l128a.htm>, accessed October 20, 2012.

speeds, 1 MHz, 2.4 MHz, and 3.6 MHz. It continued to offer serial and parallel ports, connectors for RGB or composite video, and the single expansion slot.[19, 20] Also, the 128EX included built-in functionality of the Laser Universal Disk Controller, allowing several disks to be daisy chained.

Laser 128EX – Photo credit: <www.1000bit.it>

A later revision, the Laser 128EX/2, was released in mid 1988 shortly before the Apple IIc Plus. Selling at $549, it offered all of the features of the Laser 128EX, but like the IIc Plus it had an internal 3.5 inch floppy disk drive. Unlike the IIc Plus, the 128EX/2 included a built-in calendar and clock chip, and populated the internal expansion RAM board with 256K. Additionally, the 128EX/2 had an onboard MIDI controller, which used the Slot 7 space. It used a command set compatible with the MIDI standards defined in the early 1980s by Passport Designs, Inc. It used an 8-pin DIN connector with a Y-connector, to allow connection of MIDI instruments. The addition of the MIDI hardware made it impossible to use an expansion card for slot 7, but by the time the 128EX/2 came out, the Expansion Box was no longer available.[21]

BASIS 108

Basis Microcomputer, GmbH, based in Münster, Germany was created in 1977 to act as a distributor for Apple products in Europe. It identified what it felt were design deficiencies of the Apple II, specifically the lack of lowercase keyboard support. The company had been involved with Apple in developing the Europlus, trying to get Apple address these problems. After Apple started its own sales and distribution operation in Europe, Basis moved forward with plans for its own Apple II clone.[22]

The result was the Basis 108, released in January 1982. Compared to other Apple II clones, the Basis 108 was more expensive; it sold in Germany for 4,345 DM (about $2,950 US). After Basis Microcomputer set up a subsidiary operation in the United States (in Scotts Valley,

Basis 108, - Photo credit: A2Clones.com, <www.a2clones.com/apple_clones_1/basis_108>

---

19 Ferrell, Keith, "Computers Win Big! Report From The Consumer Electronics Show", *Compute!* (Issue 95, April 1988), 6.
20 Laser 128EX Ad, "Laser 128 / Laser 128EX", *1000Bit*, <www.1000bit.it/scheda.asp?id=168>, accessed October 20, 2012.
21 Diaz, Tony, e-mail message to author, January 28, 2012; Info explaining most of the Laser 128 content of this section.
22 Freiberger, Paul, "Basis ships new micro that runs most Apple II software", *InfoWorld* (July 12, 1982), 1, 4-5.

California), the price for the entry-level Basis 108 was $1,949, still well above the price of a genuine Apple II Plus.

Like many clones of the day, the Basis 108 motherboard had both 6502 and Z-80 microprocessors, allowing access to the large library of CP/M software. It came with 64K of RAM, expandable to 128K. The case was made out of beige-painted heavy aluminum, which Basis advertised as a better heat sink than a plastic case and also for minimizing radio frequency interference. Video output was NTSC and composite, but also offered RGB. It produced 40-column and 80-column text (the setting was keyboard selectable), and upper and lowercase display. Following the design model of the IBM PC, it had a detached keyboard with keys appropriate for the German language, a numeric keypad, a better arrangement of cursor controls, and fifteen programmable function keys.

Within the case was space for two front-facing Disk II or compatible drives, with the disk controller built-in. There were six slots for Apple peripherals, and it came with RS-232 and parallel ports.

Basis executives felt that their clone of the Apple II was sufficiently different that it should not result in the same legal pressure from Apple that had affected Franklin Computers. However, Apple's lawyers didn't see things that way. Apple not only once but twice successfully sued the company. In both situations it brought the company to bankruptcy, which made it impossible for them to pay its suppliers.

Basis had contracted with manufacturers in Taiwan to create the motherboards for the Basis 108. When they were unable to pay, the company in Taiwan that made the boards decided to try to recoup its losses by selling its own computers based on that motherboard. This created the odd situation in which not only did the Basis 108 clone itself get cloned, but also it was the successful legal action by Apple that then *resulted* in the production of Apple II clones.[23]

One of the clones made in Australia was called The Medfly, named after the Mediterranean fruit fly that attacked apples (in fact, the logo on the computer showed a fly attacking a multi-colored fruit, though the fruit was not the shape of Apple's logo). According to Basis user group newsletters, the original Medfly was not made very well, so Basis Microcomputer, when it returned to business from bankruptcy, decided to jump in and help the company in Australia make it right, so it would not reflect badly on Basis itself. This also made some licensing money for Basis. The Medfly case was ivory colored, and had a redesigned keyboard.

---

23 Franke, Hans, e-mail to author, March 24, 2013.

TIGER LEARNING COMPUTER

Other Basis clones included the Cal-400, the Lingo, and the Precision Echo Phase II (which was actually a rebranded Basis 108, sold after the company went out of business a second time).[24, 25, 26]

As previously mentioned, the Bell & Howell Apple II sold in the early days of Apple was an officially licensed Apple II, identical to the Apple II, other than the black color of the case and disk drives. The ITT 2020 was also licensed to sell Apple II technology, though it was not entirely compatible. But long after those two computers were on the market, and two years after the Apple IIe ceased production, there was another legal Apple II that nearly made it to market.

In 1995, toy manufacturer Tiger Electronics contacted Apple Computer with the idea of creating a simple, inexpensive Apple II for education. The request went to Apple's vice-president of Apple Learning Strategy, who subsequently contacted Kristi Petters, the Technology Licensing Manager at Apple and asked her to work with Tiger. The function of the licensing group was to find acceptable ways to license Apple technology and bring in additional revenue. Working directly with the co-founders of Tiger Electronics, Petters worked out the details of the device, which they decided should be based on Apple IIe technology. Through a third party, she also negotiated a licensing agreement with Microsoft for the Applesoft BASIC language.

The product that was approved, the Tiger Learning Computer, was essentially an Enhanced Apple IIe, with a 65c02 processor and 128K of RAM, running off a 9-volt external power supply. It looked somewhat like a laptop computer, with a lid that tilted up. However, instead of a screen in that lid, it was just a container to hold program cartridges; it was still necessary to plug the Tiger into a television or composite monitor.

Back side of Tiger Learning Computer retail package – Photo credit: Kristi Petters

On the outside of the lid and at the base of the keyboard was a label that read "Apple Technology", with a single-color Apple logo (this was before Apple's rainbow logo had been retired).

Video output from the Tiger Learning Computer included 40 and 80-column text, and all of the Apple IIe graphics modes (single and double hi-res and

---

24 Ernest (The Collector), "200 apple II clones confirmed", in comp.sys.apple2 posted September 6, 2006; Internet.
25 Basis 108, *A2clones.com*, <www.a2clones.com/apple_clones_1/basis_108/>
26 Company Profile: Basis Microcomputer GmbH, *Classic Tech*, <classictech.wordpress.com/ 2010/02/28/basis-microcomputer-gmbh-muenster-germany/>

lo-res). It also could create a unique "non-Apple mode" of graphics, which was like hi-res mode but in full 16 colors.[27]

The keyboard was not well built, but acceptable for the target audience of elementary age children. There was a row of eleven function keys along the top of the keyboard, and the classic open-apple and solid-apple keys had the words "Player 1" and "Player 2" written on them.

There was a single speaker for standard Apple II sound (no special musical or sound capabilities were added). It had a port for a mouse, but in this case Tiger Electronics borrowed from non-Apple technology and used a PS/2 mouse. It also included a serial port for a modem, a printer port (with default settings for an Epson FX dot matrix), and a joystick port.

On the sides of the Tiger Learning Computer were cartridge slots. A cartridge inserted on the right was mapped to Slot 6, Drive 1, and on the left to Slot 6, Drive 2. Of the software cartridges initially created, some had two programs (or disk images) on them, which could be selected with a small slider switch on the top of the cartridge. Most were educational, such as MECC's *Grammar Gobble* and *Picture Chompers*, and several Weekly Reader Software *Stickybear* titles. There was also a copy of AppleWorks 4.3, but it was crippled somewhat by an inability to save settings to the cartridge; these had to be re-entered each time the program was started. Also, the only program segment included was the word-processing module. The menus still showed database and spreadsheets as possible choices, but trying to create one of these resulted in an error asking for the disk to be inserted. Another reason that AppleWorks was probably not a good choice was its requirement to be used on a screen that could display 80 columns. Since the Tiger Learning Computer was made to plug into a standard television, 80 columns would be unacceptably blurry.[28]

To store data, one of the cartridges included acted as a 128K RAM disk, which could be formatted either as DOS 3.3 or ProDOS. This would have been smaller than a standard 5.25 floppy disk, which held 140K.

On startup, the computer booted from a built-in ROM disk, briefly displayed the ProDOS start screen, and then changed to a graphic icon-based program selector screen. Items on that screen could be selected with the mouse, but after that the mouse was only useful with a program that expected and made use of a mouse; many Apple II programs used a joystick or the keyboard to control them, and were not necessarily mouse-friendly.

The goal for Tiger Electronics was to sell this computer for $149. It was test-marketed in April 1997 in four cities in the United States. About 16,000 units were shipped (though it is unclear how many of these actually sold). However, before the company could do a more widespread rollout, Steve Jobs returned to Apple during that same month. One of the first things he did on his return to the

---

27 Rubywand, Tiger is Loose, AOL News, 1997/02/15.
28 Cavanaugh, Steve, "Tiger Learning Computer Comes To Market", *The Apple Blossom*, March 1997.

company was to cancel the program that allowed licensing the Mac OS. This decision was made in May 1997, and it also included licensing old Apple II technology to outside companies. Tiger Electronics was understandably unhappy that they could not move forward with the project, but due to a loophole Jobs found in the contract, they had no recourse but to kill the Tiger Learning Computer.[29, 30]

TIMELINE

Basis 108 – *January 1982*

Franklin ACE 100 – *March 1982*

Franklin ACE 1000 – *June 1982*

Franklin ACE 1000 Plus – *August 1982*

Franklin ACE 1100, 1200 – *November 1982*

Laser 3000 – *March 1984*

Franklin ACE 2000 – *October 1985*

Franklin ACE 500 – *October 1985*

Laser 128 – *March 1986*

Laser 128EX – *January 1988*

Laser 128EX/2 – *July 1988*

Tiger Learning Computer – *April 1997*

---

29 Molloy, Andy, "The Last Apple II", *Juiced.GS*, Vol 16, Issue 4, December 2011, pp. 8-9.
30 Molloy, Andy, "License To Roar", *Juiced.GS*, Vol 16, Issue 4, December 2011, pp. 10-11.

CHAPTER 31
Robots and Clocks

ROBOTS

Encouraged by the success of the personal computer revolution in the previous decade, the early 1980s saw the start of efforts at creating a market for a home robot. Like the early microcomputers, these robots were more for experimentation and hobbyists than utility. Those limits ultimately determined the fate of these products.

Back when the Logo language was created in the late 1960s, one of its features was to control a real-world device, specifically a small mechanical device called a turtle. Commands from the language caused the turtle to move on the floor in a programmed pattern. Later, the actions of the physical turtle were translated and represented by a picture on a computer screen. In 1979, the Elizabeth Computer Centre in Hobart, Tasmania (Australia) created the first commercially successful mobile robot, or "floor turtle" as they began to be called.

The product was named the Tasman Turtle and it was released in the United States in 1983 by Harvard Associates. It was a little over a foot in diameter, rolled on two rubber wheels, and had two small green lights that looked like eyes, but in actuality did nothing more than blink. Covering it was a clear plastic shell that revealed the circuit board and inner components. The robot

Tasman Turtle robot connected to Apple IIe – Photo credit: Winfield S. Heagy

could draw with a pen on the floor as it traveled, and had touch sensors to allow feedback if it bumped against something. With its built-in speech synthesizer, commands in Logo could be sent to the robot to make it talk. It was popular in schools, where students could learn programming and problem-solving skills, and see the results of their work as the robot traced out a pattern, providing feedback that went far beyond a picture on a computer screen.[1]

Tony Adams, a programmer in Melbourne, Australia, wrote the routines to use with Apple's version of the Logo language to control the Tasman Turtle. It connected to an Apple II via a peripheral card, and was controlled by commands sent to it by the computer. The included software worked under DOS 3.3 from BASIC, but could be managed with any language that sent the proper commands to the robot. Connected to the computer with its cable limited the range of motion of the Tasman Turtle, but it did its job of demonstrating the concepts of robot control.[2, 3]

Terrapin Inc. of Boston, Massachusetts sold a similar floor turtle robot, the Terrapin Turtle, also in 1979. The company sold all of the parts as a kit for $400, fully assembled for $600, and an article complete with circuit board templates and parts list was printed in that year's June issue of *BYTE* magazine.

Terrapin Turtle assembled – Photo credit: *BYTE* magazine June 1979

Though this particular device was produced only for a few years, after its discontinuation the company continued providing its languages, *Terrapin Logo* and a simpler version called *Kinder Logo*, and selling smaller and easier to program robots for use in the classroom. Unlike the earlier Terrapin Turtle, which required a computer to control it, these later educational robots could be programmed entirely on a control pad on the top of the robot.

The first general hobbyist robot to appear on the market was the Heath HERO (Heathkit Educational RObot). The first model, the HERO-1, was released in 1982 at a cost of $1000 in kit form, and as much as $2200 fully assembled. These were self-contained units, and their actions were programmed directly on the robot itself. There were hardware add-ons that provided the ability for the robot to be programmed by a computer, including the Apple II. Heath sold several generations of these, up through the end of the decade.

---

1 Hunder, David, "Robots Come Home", *Softalk* (August 1983), 152-154.
2 Helmers, Carl, "Editorial", *Robotics Age* (May/June 1983).
3 Carter, Peter, "Logo Is 40", *AppleSauce* (November 2007), 14-15.

CHAPTER 31 | Robots and Clocks

Atari founder Nolan Bushnell invested in several other technology-related ventures beyond video games. In 1977 he started Pizza Time Theatre and the first Chuck E. Cheese restaurant and entertainment center. It included animatronics characters playing in a show at the restaurant, including the main character, a mouse with the name Chuck E. Cheese. With the popularity of the chain, Bushnell turned to home-robotics as the next potential area of electronics growth, and in 1982 started Androbot, Inc.

By early 1983, TOPO I was available from Androbot, selling for $495 ($795 for a talking version that used a voice synthesizer). Like Heath's HERO robots, TOPO I was primarily for entertainment and education. Unlike the HERO, the TOPO robot could only be programmed as an extension to a personal computer.

The earliest designed versions of TOPO I could be controlled with a modified 27 MHz radio controller (RC) to move it around, not unlike what could be done with a controller for a toy car. The version that was available for purchase by the general public moved beyond this to allow it to be programmed with an Apple II computer. Androbot made a custom interface card for the TOPO I, which used a timing controller chip to generate radio signals that were the same as those produced by an RC controller. An external box with an RF (radio frequency) transmitter and antenna was plugged into the card, and this sent the controlling signals to the robot.

Androbot's TOPO I robot, standing 36 inches tall – Photo credit: Robert Doerr

To control TOPO I via the custom interface card, Androbot provided assembly language extensions (called TopoBasic) to Applesoft. The company also designed a program that allowed the robot to be moved around in response to movement of a joystick plugged into the computer. Another set of software routines (TopoLogo) were available to add to Apple Logo, and have the robot move in sync with programmed turtle graphics, much as was done with the Tasman and Terrapin Turtles. A series of specific movements could be stored to disk, and then played back to the robot.

With TopoBasic or TopoLogo, the wheels on the robot could be precisely controlled, even to the point of being able to program it to travel in a figure eight, circle, or even to dance. A third language available to use in controlling TOPO was a variety of Forth called TopoForth.[4]

The next model created by Androbot was the TOPO II, released in 1984. Selling for $1,600, it was much more expensive than the first TOPO, but it was also more sophisticated. It added text-to-speech capability, and operated

---

4 . Hunter, David, "Robots Come Home", *Softalk* (August 1983), 146-147.

on two Intel 8031 microprocessors. It was also made to work with additional home computers—not only the Apple II but also Atari, Commodore, and IBM PC computers. Instead of requiring a custom interface card, it connected via a serial port (the Super Serial Card on the Apple II). This version operated with infrared signals instead of the radio connection of TOPO I, and allowed for two-way communication with the robot. The signals sent back from the robot could give feedback on how far TOPO II had moved, and how many of the instructions sent to it had been carried out. TOPO II was programmed via TopoForth and TopoLogo, and it could still be controlled with a joystick attached to the computer.

Despite the unique capabilities of the TOPO robots, the Androbot company did not survive. There were several reasons for this failure. One of the first problems was quality control, as the first few TOPO I units that were shipped did not work. Beyond those problems, sales in general were low, and the company had no investment dollars to carry them through until it became profitable. Furthermore, the planned public stock offering for Androbot, Inc. was adversely affected by the 1983 video game crash. Though that crash had nothing to do with Androbot's products or the public's interest in home robots, it resulted in a broad decline in the tech market that affected many companies during 1983 and 1984.

Finally, Androbot failed because the robots it sold were primarily of use in education, and were not sufficiently sophisticated to offer abilities that would make a robot useful to the consumer. Though the company was working on more advanced robots, by the end of 1984 Androbot was out of business.[5,6]

SENSORS AND CONTROLLERS

An Apple II could control more than educational robots. With A/D (analog/digital) converter cards, it was possible to record information from devices such as a wind speed sensor for weather reports. A computer program could then take this information and send a command signal back to another device (for example, to activate a motor that raised and lowered a cloth deck cover, depending on wind speeds).

In 1975, BSR, Ltd. (Birmingham Sound Reproducers), which built turntables with automatic changers for vinyl records, created a method of using ultrasonic signals to remotely control other devices. This concept was extended to create a line of products that could allow control of anything plugged into an electric socket in a home. BSR began to sell these in 1978, calling the system X-10. Under this protocol, home devices could be controlled or pro-

---

5 . McComb, Gordon, "Personal Robots", *Creative* Computing, (November 1983), 196.
6 Rowland, Rick, "The History of Androbot", *Megadroid.com*, retrieved March 4, 2013.

grammed, with the signals sent through the home wiring system to a device that could sense the commands on the line.

Mountain Hardware of Lomond, California formed in 1977. One of its earliest products was an Introl/X-10 controller for S-100 (Altair style) computers. In 1979, the company released an X-10 interface card for the Apple II, at a price of $279. The commands from the Apple II program were transmitted from the Introl card via an ultrasonic transducer to the BSR/X-10 command console, which was plugged into a power outlet. This in turn sent commands to any or all of the three included remote modules that plugged into wall power sockets elsewhere in the house. Programming X-10 devices allowed them to be turned on or off, or to reduce power so as to dim lights. Included clock features allowed these commands to be executed at predetermined times. Items that could be controlled ranged from security systems to light timers to lawn sprinkler systems.

CLOCKS

While internal, battery-powered clocks are standard in modern computers and are fully supported by modern operating systems, this additional hardware was not part of a typical home computer until the mid-1980s. An internal clock allowed a file to have a date and time associated with it (if the operating system supported that feature), and also made it possible for a program to execute commands at a specific time. Apple Computer did not supply any native clock functionality for the Apple II platform until the release of the Apple IIGS in 1986. There were, however, third-party solutions for those who wanted this clock and calendar functionality.

One of the earliest of these was the Apple Clock, a peripheral card made by Mountain Hardware. Released in 1978, it sold for $199. It contained a battery that was charged by the computer, and then maintained the time when the computer was shut off. The manual recommended the card be installed in slot 4, which became a common place for such cards from that point onward. It did not keep track of the year, only the month, day, and time.

Ad for Apple Clock – Photo credit: *BYTE*, June 1979

The Thunderclock Plus, created by Thunderware, Inc. of Berkley, California in 1980, was such a widely used clock card that ProDOS actually included drivers for it when it was first released. Nearly all clock cards released after this tried to emulate at least the major functions of the Thunderclock.

The Plus part of this product was its ability to control BSR X-10 devices, and included software to allow the computer to manage the various functions possible with those devices. Like the Apple Clock, this card did not manage the year part of the date. When ProDOS was released with native support for the Thunderclock, it had to keep track of the year in a table within the ProDOS code loaded into memory on startup, and that table required updating about every seven years, in order to be produce correct year display in programs requiring that feature.

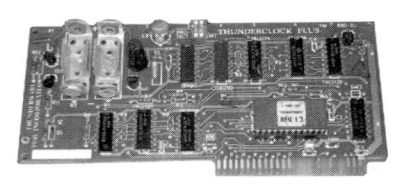

Thunderclock Plus card. Notice the place where two AA batteries were to be installed to keep the time when the computer was powered off – Photo credit Marvin Johnston

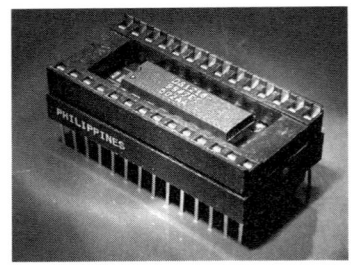

SMT Peripherals of San Marcos, California introduced the No-Slot Clock in 1986. It was a re-branding of the Dallas Semiconductor SmartWatch DS1216 chip. It was unique in that it worked, as advertised, without the need to take up a peripheral slot on the motherboard. It looked somewhat like a 28-pin integrated circuit, with pins below to plug into a chip socket. On top, however, it had a socket for the same pin configuration. It could be used in an Apple IIe, IIc, Franklin 2100, or Laser 128 computers. (In fact, it was also designed to work in IBM PC and compatible computers.) To install the No-Slot Clock, any correctly sized chip had to be removed from the motherboard (it could even be a compatible chip on a peripheral card). The No-Slot Clock chip was installed into that place, and then the original chip was installed into the No-Slot Clock socket. This resulted in that one chip sitting almost three times higher than anything else on the motherboard.

No-Slot Clock – Photo credit: Tony Diaz

The No-Slot Clock contained two tiny lithium batteries, designed to last for at least ten years. These would charge when the computer was powered on, and then took over to continue to keep time when the power was off.

The value that SMT Peripherals brought to the Dallas SmartWatch chip was the included software to make it possible for Apple II programs to access the date and time functions of the chip. There was a driver to install into ProDOS, replacing the clock driver within. Also included were software routines that a programmer could use to set and read the time on the clock chip.[7]

---

7 *No-Slot Clock Users Manual*, 1986.

Applied Engineering, the master of hardware for the Apple II platform, had not ignored this category. Its earliest clock card was the Time II, released in 1980. It was succeeded by the Timemaster II in 1983, and then in 1984 the Timemaster H.O. (for "high output"). Selling for $129, this version of the card was sophisticated enough to emulate the modes of other clock cards. This made it compatible with older software, including programs designed to work with the Thunderclock or even the Mountain Hardware Apple Clock. Further, the Timemaster H.O. kept track of the year, which many other clock cards did not do, and could be used to measure time intervals down to the millisecond. And, like some of the older clock cards, BSR X-10 controls were included.

Even the Apple IIc was included in clock options, thanks to Applied Engineering. The IIc System Clock came out in 1985. Powered by three AA batteries, this external box simply plugged into one of the serial ports on the IIc. Whatever device had been attached to that port was then plugged into the IIc System Clock. (It was designed to work with either the printer or modem port, though Applied Engineering recommended using the modem port.) As far as software accessing that port was concerned, it functioned no differently than if the serial device was still plugged directly into the computer.

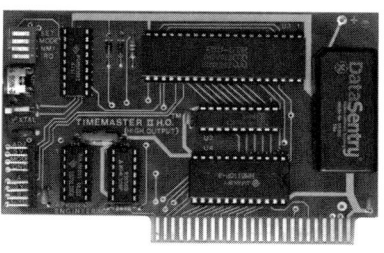

Applied Engineering Timemaster H.O.
– Photo credit: Applied Engineering 1986 catalog

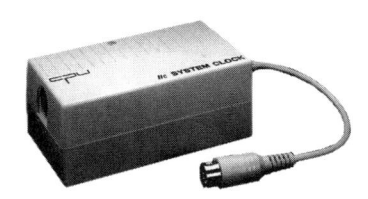

Applied Engineering IIc System Clock
– Photo credit: Applied Engineering brochure

Software included with the IIc System Clock patched ProDOS for date and time stamping files, and patched AppleWorks to display the current date and time in the right lower corner of the screen. Also included was a utility to allow Applesoft programs running under BASIC.SYSTEM to be able to retrieve date and time data from the clock, down to seconds (which ProDOS did not make use of). To use an Applesoft (or Integer BASIC) program running under DOS 3.3 to access the clock would have required custom code. Not included was a patch to support date and time stamping for files under DOS 3.3.

As with most of the other clocks previously mentioned, the IIc System Clock did not manage the year. Programs needing year information depended on the table in ProDOS.

TIMELINE

Mountain Hardware Apple Clock – *May 1979*

Terrapin Turtle – *June 1979*

Tasman Turtle – *August 1979*

Mountain Hardware Introl/X-10 – *November 1979*

AE Time II – *1980*

Thunderclock Plus – *June 1980*

HERO-1 – *1982*

TOPO I – *1983*

AE Timemaster – *May 1983*

TOPO II – *1984*

AE Timemaster II – *April 1984*

AE Timemaster H.O. – *December 1984*

AE IIc System Clock – *1985*

No-Slot Clock – *1986*

CHAPTER 32
The Next Generation

THE APPLE II EVOLVES

With the incremental enhancements to the Apple II line that were introduced between 1977 and 1985, one thing that remained essentially unchanged was the 6502 microprocessor that controlled it. Even though the 65c02 had more commands than the 6502, as an 8-bit processor it was inherently limited to directly addressing no more than 64K of memory at one time. When Wozniak designed it, 64K was considered to be a massive amount of memory, even for some mainframe computers. Most programmers of the time would not have known what to do with four megabytes of memory, even if it had been possible (or affordable) to install that much. Consequently, programs of the day were compact, efficient, and primarily text-based.

The world outside of the Apple II advanced since 1977, and Apple grudgingly gave this computer small improvements. As previously mentioned, at times efforts were made to make a more powerful Apple II, but the lure of other high-end computers always turned the attention of management away from allowing such a project to actually make any progress. First the Apple III, then Lisa, and finally Macintosh swallowed the research and development dollars that Apple's cash cow, the Apple II, continued to produce. The latter two computers were based around the 16-bit Motorola 68000 microprocessor, which had the capability to address far more than 64K of memory. The Apple II could make use of more memory only through complicated switching schemes (switching between separate 64K banks). Although "Mac-envy" hit many Apple II enthusiasts both inside and outside of Apple, causing them to move away from the II, there were still many others who continued to press for more power from the Apple II.

The original 6502 processor was designed by Chuck Peddle and Bill Mensch of MOS Technology and released in 1975. Commodore International purchased MOS soon after the introduction of the 6502, and continued to sell the processor to multiple customers (including Apple). Whereas Chuck Peddle stayed with MOS and Commodore, Mensch left in 1977 to found his own microprocessor company, Western Design Center (WDC).

One of the new company's first products, released in 1978, was the 65c02, which built on the 6502 and included additional assembly opcodes (commands) to allow more sophisticated programming. Apple eventually made use of this in the Apple IIc and enhanced IIe.

In early 1983, WDC revealed plans to produce a new microprocessor called the 65816. This chip would have all of the assembly opcodes of the 65c02 through an emulation mode. However, it would be a true 16-bit processor, with the ability handle 16 bits (two bytes) at a time and to address larger amounts of continuous memory. The address bus was enlarged from 16 to 24 bits, making the 65816 capable of addressing 256 times more memory, or 16 megabytes. The power to make a better Apple II was finally available.

THE RETURN OF WOZNIAK

Back in early 1981, Steve Wozniak had been involved in several projects at Apple. He had helped write some fast math routines for a spreadsheet product written by Randy Wigginton that Apple had planned to release in competition with *VisiCalc*. Apple never released the program, as they feared upsetting VisiCorp. (Instead, they gave it to the Apple Pugetsound Program Library Exchange to distribute at a low cost.) Also, Steve Jobs had managed to convince Wozniak to participate in the early days of his involvement in the Macintosh project. Then, in early February of that year, Wozniak's private plane crashed. He was injured with a concussion that temporarily made it impossible to form new memories. He could not recall that he had an accident; he did not remember playing games with his computer in the hospital; he did not remember who visited him earlier in the day. When he finally recovered from the concussion, he decided it was time to take a leave of absence from Apple.

Wozniak re-married, and returned to college at Berkley under the name "Rocky Clark" (a combination of his dog's name and his wife's maiden name). He decided he wanted to finally graduate, and get his degree in electrical engineering and computer science. When he was done with that, he formed a corporation called UNUSON (which stood for "Unite Us In Song") to produce educational computer materials, wanting to make computers easier for students to use. He also decided to use UNUSON to sponsor rock music events, which he called the "US Festival".[1] Held on Labor Day weekend in 1982 and Memorial Day weekend in 1983, these music and technology extravaganzas were invigorating for Wozniak, but both events were not profitable—in fact, each event lost $12 million. Though nowhere near burning through the value of his Apple Computer stock, he decided that he

---

1 Miller, Jonathan, "The Life And Times Of Rocky Clark," *Softalk* (June 1982), 141-144.

was ready to return to work. In June of 1983, Wozniak entered the building on the Apple campus where the Apple II division was housed and asked for something to do.

THE APPLE IIX

When Wozniak returned, he discovered the latest of the Apple II modernization projects, which was code-named "IIx". When he saw what the 65816 could do, he became excited about the potential of the new Apple II and immediately got involved. It was a tremendous boost in morale for the division to have their founder return to work. However, the IIx project was plagued by several problems. Western Design Center was late in delivering samples of the 65816 processor. First promised for November 1983, they finally arrived in February 1984—and didn't work. The second set that came three weeks later also failed.

The Apple IIx motherboard had the usual eight slots of an Apple IIe, with two auxiliary slots. One of these was lined up with slot 0; the other was closer to the power supply and was called slot "-1". At this point in the design process, the computer had developed code-names of "Brooklyn" and "Golden Gate"; it even displayed "GG" at the top of the screen where "Apple" usually showed up when it was powered on. The thinking was to use the slot "-1" for a co-processor card, which could allow the IIx to easily do what third-party companies had done for the original Apple II with their Z-80 boards (that is, to run CP/M software). Other co-processor cards that were considered included a Motorola 68000 card (the same processor used in the Macintosh), or an Intel 8088 (such as what was used in the IBM PC). With the 68000 processor, the plan was to create a Unix-like operating system, non-GUI, capable of multi-threaded processes.

As with other projects at Apple at this time, there were people who liked designing boxes that would do neat things, but they lacked a unified focus from a leader to pull things together. The marketing department jumped on the concept of a co-processor, and one idea proposed was that with a 68000 co-processor card, the IIx could possibly run Macintosh software. The IIx project got so bogged down in trying to become other computers that they forgot it was supposed to be an advanced Apple II. Politically it also created problems at Apple, because it was being aimed as a high-end business machine, which was where they wanted the Macintosh to go.[2, 3] Wozniak lost interest as progress slowed, and eventually the project was dropped.

---

2 Pinella, Paul, "In The Beginning: An Interview With Harvey Lehtman," *Apple IIGS: Graphics And Sound* (Fall/Winter 1986), 38-44.
3 Duprau, Jeanne, and Tyson, Molly, "The Making Of The Apple IIGS," A+ (November 1986), 57-74.

THE 16-BIT APPLE II RETURNS

When the IIx project was cancelled in March 1984, some of the Apple II engineers were assigned the task of reducing the cost of the Apple II. Engineers Dan Hillman and Jay Rickard managed to put almost the entire Apple II circuitry onto a single chip they called the Mega II. Meanwhile, after the "Apple II Forever" event that introduced the IIc, interest in the Apple II revived and sales improved for both the IIe and IIc. Management saw that the open IIe was more popular than the closed IIc, so they were agreeable to another try at the 16-bit Apple II, possibly utilizing the Mega II chip. By late summer 1984 it was revived with the code name Phoenix (since it was rising from the ashes of the IIx project). Later names for the project included Rambo (at a time when the design team was fighting for final approval of the project from the executive staff), Gumby (from a costume worn by one of the team members at the annual Halloween parade held by Apple employees nearly every year during the 1980s)[4], and, near the end of development, Cortland.[5,6]

GOALS OF THE DEVELOPMENT TEAM

The people involved in the Phoenix project were knowledgeable about the Apple II, from the days of the original Apple II through the Apple IIc. They knew what *they* wanted in a new computer. It should primarily be an Apple II, not just something new that tried to be all things to all people.[7] Dan Hillman, who had also been involved as the engineering manager for the IIx project, stated in an interview:

> Our mission was very simple. First we wanted to preserve the Apple II as it exists today. It had to work with Apple IIe software and Apple IIc software. That was goal number 1. But we recognized that the Apple II was an old computer. It had limitations. The new machine needed to address those limitations, break through those barriers – and the barriers were very obvious: We needed to increase the memory size. We had to make it run faster. We needed better graphics. And we had to have better sound. That was our mission.

---

4 Carlton, Jim, *Apple: The Inside Story of Intrigue, Egomania, and Business Blunders*, (Crown Business, 1997), 30-31.
5 Duprau, Jeanne, and Molly Tyson, "The Making Of The Apple IIGs," *A+* (November 1986), 57-74.
6 Hogan, Thom, "Apple: The First Ten Years," *A+* (January 1987), 45.
7 IBID

Since advanced graphics and sound were what would make this new Apple really shine, the name eventually assigned to the final product was Apple IIGS.

Having learned from their experience in building the Apple IIe and IIc, they knew what would make the new 16-bit Apple II more powerful. The Apple IIc was easy to use because the most commonly needed peripherals were already built-in. The Apple IIe, however, excelled in its ability to be easily expanded (via the slots) to do things that were not commonly needed or built-in. Harvey Lehtman, system software manager for the project, stated, "We ... wanted the Apple IIGS to be easy to set up, like the IIc, and easy to expand, like the IIe."[8]

Apple IIGS "Woz" edition – Photo credit: Tony Diaz

ARCHITECTURE

Steve Wozniak again became interested in the project, once a more clear direction was determined. He was quite involved in designing the general layout of the IIGS. Insisting on keeping it simple, he recommended against a built-in co-processor (as they tried to do with the IIx). He also wanted to keep the 8-bit part of the machine separate from the 16-bit part. To accomplish this, he and the other engineers decided to design it so the memory in the lower 128K of the machine was "slow RAM", which made it possible for it to function just as it did on the older Apple II models. This included the memory allocation for the odd addressing schemes used in the text and graphics modes, which made sense in 1976, but not in 1986. The rest of the available memory space would be fast, and could be expanded to as much as 16 megabytes (though the final design did not support that size). With a faster microprocessor, it would also be possible to run programs more quickly than on the older Apple II models.

GRAPHICS

One area they decided to focus on was bringing the quality of graphics on the new Apple II up to modern standards. Because a change that increased the vertical resolution from 200 dots to 400 dots would make the computer too expensive (it would require a special slow-phosphor monitor), they purposely decided not to go in that direction. Instead, they increased the

---

8 Duprau, Jeanne, and Tyson, Molly, "The Making Of The Apple IIGS," A+ (November 1986), 57-74.

horizontal resolution, and created two new graphics modes (called "super hi-res"); one was 320 x 200 and the other was 640 x 200. This decision also made it easier to keep compatibility with older graphics modes.

The text and graphics addressing on the old Apple II was odd, from a programming standpoint. When Wozniak originally designed the II, he made the memory allocation for text and graphics to be "non-linear", since this saved several chips in the hardware design, making it less expensive to build. This meant that calculating the memory address of a specific dot on the hi-res graphics screen or a character on the text screen was not as simple as most programmers wanted. On the IIGS, the designers wanted linear addressing, which would allow the memory addresses of line 0 to be followed by the addresses for line 1, and so on.

The old hi-res graphics screens used only 2K of memory, and double hi-res only 4K. The new super hi-res graphics were going to have greater resolution and range of available colors, taking up 32K of memory. To manage the memory to handle this, engineers designed a special Video Graphics Controller (VGC).

The new super hi-res graphics modes also gave far more color choices than either the old hi-res mode (which had six unique colors) or even the double hi-res mode (which had sixteen colors). In the 320 x 200 super hi-res mode, each line could have sixteen colors out of a possible pallette of 4,096, and in the 640 x 200 mode, each line could have four colors out of 4,096. This gave graphics power that exceeded even the Macintosh, which at that time was still limited to a black and white screen.

SOUND

The second major area of focus for enhancements over the old Apple II was sound reproduction. The original sound chip that had been proposed for the IIGS would have given it the sound quality of a typical arcade game. However, this was no better than what other computers in 1986 could do. Project manager Rob Moore suggested using a sound chip made by Ensoniq, one that was used in the Mirage music synthesizer. (The Ensoniq Corporation was founded by engineers who had started at MOS Technology, and later worked on the SID sound chip in the Commodore 64.) Moore had to push hard to get this included in the final design, and was finally able to convince management of its importance because he told them it would be "enabling technology" (borrowing a phrase from a Macintosh marketing book). He told them "it would enable people to do things they'd never dreamed of doing."[9]

---

9 Duprau, Jeanne, and Tyson, Molly, "The Making Of The Apple IIgs," A+ (November 1986), 57-74.

The Ensoniq chip was capable of synthesizing fifteen simultaneous musical voices. To help it in doing such complex sound reproduction, they gave the chip a separate 64K block of RAM memory dedicated specifically for that purpose.

The 65816 was designed to address up to 16 MB of memory. The IIGS, however, was built to support only 8 MB of RAM, and up to 1 MB of ROM (in high memory). Memory cards built by third-party companies could potentially add up to 12 MB of RAM, but the memory manager in the IIGS ROM was only aware of the first 8 MB. A special software patch would be needed to allow the system to use memory beyond that point. Such a patch was mentioned in publications back when the IIGS was new, but apparently was not reliable or too expensive to implement, as no large 12 MB RAM card ever appeared. When they became affordable, 4 and 8 MB memory expansion cards were the most common sizes that were sold. Apple never chose to directly support RAM cards with more than 4 MB.[10]

MISCELLANEOUS HARDWARE

Other features Apple engineers added to make the Apple IIGS a next generation computer included a built-in clock, slot space for internal expansion cards, and the electronic equivalents of seven more expansion cards.[11] Taking a cue from their experience with the Apple IIc, they included as built-in features the peripherals that most users would want to use. They allocated serial ports to slots 1 and 2, the classic 80-column firmware to slot 3, the mouse controller to slot 4, a Smartport controller to slot 5, a 5.25-inch disk controller to slot 6, and AppleTalk capability to slot 7. (AppleTalk was the network protocol that Apple had designed originally for use with the Macintosh).

Serial ports had been in common use on computers since the original Apple II was released. Apple had sold peripheral cards to allow serial communications, and its most popular version of it was the Apple II Super Serial Card. The Apple IIc used hardware that worked exactly like one of these cards. On the IIGS, however, the designers wanted the computer capable of connecting to an AppleTalk network. To accomplish this, the serial ports they planned were based on a different communications controller chip than was used in the older 8-bit Apple II computers. Although these new controllers were more capable than the older ones, telecommunications programs written for those older Apples wouldn't work. This was because most terminal programs, for the sake of speed, were written to directly control the Super Serial Card (rather than going through the slower, built-in firmware com-

---

10 Regan, Joe, A2Pro Roundtable, Category 16, Topic 2, *GEnie*, accessed October 1991.
11 Duprau, Jeanne, and Molly Tyson, "The Making Of The Apple IIGS," *A+* (November 1986), 57-74.

mands). The controlling commands necessary to manage the newer chip were very different, and so caused such software to malfunction.[12]

Apple IIe to IIGS conversion – Photo credit: Stavros Karatsoridis

Apple IIGS conversion nameplate – Photo credit: Stavros Karatsoridis

The case and motherboard used in the Apple IIGS was made smaller than that found in the IIe, both in order to make a smaller "footprint" on a desktop, and also to make it easier to make an upgrade available for IIe owners. This original motherboard was released with all the parts necessary to install it into an Apple IIe (the conversion kit included the motherboard, an optional mouse, and a back panel for the IIe).[13] They had wanted to make it possible even for Apple II and II Plus owners to upgrade, but in the end it turned out to be just too expensive and difficult to execute. The Apple IIe-to-IIGS upgrade resulted in a computer that looked like a IIe, but contained the motherboard of a IIGS. A new nameplate on the cover identified the modified computer as a IIGS, even though in all other respects it looked like a IIe.

The Macintosh engineering group was at this time designing a protocol for interfacing standard input devices, such as keyboards, mice, and graphics tablets. This protocol, called the Apple Desktop Bus (ADB), was first implemented on the Apple IIGS. It made possible the interchangeability of hardware devices between the Macintosh and Apple II lines, allowing Apple to sell a common set of peripherals that both computers could use.

FIRMWARE

Recall that firmware is that layer of controlling programs in ROM on a computer that sits between an application program and the hardware it is trying to control. On the IIGS, the firmware was designed after the hardware was finalized. Unlike the older ROM that Wozniak included with the original Apple II, the IIGS software engineers tried to make it more than just a set of addresses to call to carry out a function (such as clearing the screen). Rather, they wanted to make a more comprehensive system, called a "toolbox",

---

12 Pinella, Paul, "In The Beginning: An Interview With Harvey Lehtman," *Apple IIGS: Graphics And Sound* (Fall/Winter 1986), 38-44.
13 Utter, Gary, A2 Roundtable, Category 6, Topic 2, *GEnie*, accessed July 1993.

which could be more flexible for future enhancements of the hardware and firmware. In particular, they didn't want to have the addresses for carrying out certain functions fixed in a single location as on the older Apples. This toolbox would have a single address to call, and a specific command would be passed on through that address. Set up like this, it would allow Apple's firmware programmers to modify the ROM in the future without having to take trouble to make multiple addresses in the ROM line up properly. Additionally, they made it easy to patch the toolbox code in the ROM using code loaded from disk, allowing programmers to fix errors that were later found without having to replace the physical ROM chips.

At first, they were given 64K of space for the ROM, over four times as much as was available on the original Apple II. Later, they had to go back and ask for 128K of ROM, because of the many things that they needed and wanted to do. Of course, Applesoft had to be present in ROM in order to maintain compatibility with the older Apple II software. Additionally, they also put all of the mouse-handling tools into the ROM (unlike the II, II Plus, and IIe, which had to have the mouse firmware on a card in a peripheral slot).[14]

Conflicts between Steve Jobs and Apple's board of directors had led to a crisis in 1985, resulting in Jobs being stripped of any influence at the company. He subsequently left the company, and a reorganization put the Apple II and Macintosh teams in the same division. The result of this change put members of the Macintosh team in the same location on the Apple campus as the IIGS team, which made it possible to collaborate on some aspects of the design of the IIGS.

Bill Atkinson, the programming wizard who wrote *MacPaint* and many of the mouse tools for the Macintosh, helped in the creation of the mouse tools and QuickDraw II for the IIGS. (This was the name given to the ROM tools used to draw on the super hi-res screen, and was borrowed from the older QuickDraw routines on the original Macintosh, itself borrowed from the older-still thesis on the Quick-Draw graphics system written by the originator of the Macintosh, Jef Raskin.)

To allow the user to easily configure certain features of the IIGS to their own tastes, a "control panel" was designed (another idea borrowed from the Macintosh). It was used to set the clock, the system speed (between a "normal" 1 MHz and a "fast" 2.8 MHz), change the default text display between 40 and 80 columns, set colors for the text screen and its border, set sensitivity of the mouse and keyboard, and make the standard settings for the printer and modem ports. These preferences were saved in a special battery-powered RAM that would survive even when the system power was turned off.

Apple continued the practice of making international versions available with the IIGS, but improved on the design by making the various keyboard

---

14 Duprau, Jeanne, and Molly Tyson, "The Making Of The Apple IIGS," *A+* (November 1986), 57–74.

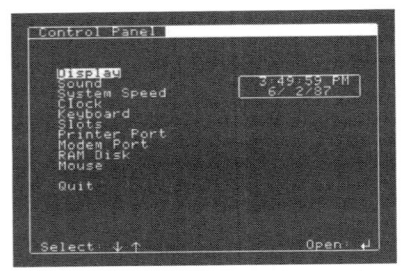

Apple IIGS control panel – Photo credit: personal

layouts all built-in. On the IIGS it was selectable via the control panel, as was the screen display of the special characters for each type of keyboard. The ADB keyboard could then be specifically packaged and sold for each region to allow the correct keycaps for that region.

PRODUCT INTRODUCTION

In September of 1986, Apple introduced the new Apple IIGS, bundled with an Apple 3.5 drive, for $999 (not including a monitor). The Apple II community was excited about the new computer, and *inCider* magazine featured an exuberant Steve Wozniak on the cover of its October 1986 issue with the caption, "It's Amazing!"

Apple, for its part, advertised the new computer in the pages of Apple II publications. However, there was no major push for the new computer, and again it seemed destined to be dwarfed by Apple's preoccupation with the Macintosh.

Though announced in September, the IIGS was not widely available until November. Early production models of the IIGS had some problems; one of the new chips did not work properly, and necessary changes to fix them caused a delay. The upgrade that would turn an Apple IIe into a IIGS was also delayed until early 1987.[15]

inCider cover, October 1986 – Photo credit: personal

The rest of the Apple II tech press was as enthusiastic about the new IIGS as was *inCider* magazine, and most articles written about it touted its new features and backward compatibility. *Call-A.P.P.L.E.* looked at it from a technical and programming aspect, while A+ and *inCider* focused on its consumer and education capabilities. For the Apple II world, this new computer was

---

15 Weishaar, Tom, "Miscellanea," *Open-Apple* (November 1986), 2.74.

seen as a significant advancement and provided new software opportunities for the community.

The general tech press, however, was less enthusiastic (and probably more realistic). BYTE magazine printed two detailed, thoughtful articles dealing with the new computer—first a preview of it, and later a full review. Unlike the Apple II press, BYTE had an audience of readers who were knowledgable about the IBM PC and its clones, and the newer offerings from Atari and Commodore, as well as Apple's other platform, the Macintosh. When compared to this larger world, BYTE viewed the Apple IIGS as a "mixed blessing".

The first article was identified specifically as a preview, rather than a proper product review, as the writers were not able to evaluate a production-line model in time to write the article. They did spend time with the Apple II engineering teams that produced the computer, and were made aware of all of its technical and software features (as of July, two months before it was released). Their conclusion did not pan the product, but neither did it praise it.

> What do you say about such innovative energy that has been directed primarily toward perserving a hardware design that is 10 years old? ... The Apple II GS [sic] affirms several trends in microcomputer design that we should not ignore: improved graphics and sound, larger processor and memory capacity, and the use of a mouse and a desktop/icon/windows interface. The machine also follows a trend but breaks new ground in the Apple II line by including large amounts of system firmware that is as important as the machine's new hardware features ...
>
> ... The Apple II GS, hog-tied by Apple II compatibility, approaches but does not match or exceed current microcomputer capabilities. The 8086-like segmented memory of the 65816 is not as elegant as that of the 68000 used in the Apple Macintosh, the Commodore Amiga, and the Atari 520ST. In addition, the 65c816 lacks the hardware multiply and divide instructions available in both the 8086 and the 68000 processors. The Apple II GS graphics, though now competitive, do not offer any advantages over the Amigs's or the Atari ST's, nor is it price competitive with either. Its only clear superiority is in its sound capabilities, which for many buyers will not outweigh graphics and price.[16]

The full review of the product made these conclusions:

---

16 Williams, Gregg, and Grehan, Richard, "The Apple II GS", BYTE (October 1986), 84-98.

> The Apple IIGS has the potential to be a powerful computer, but it needs a faster microprocessor and the ability to address more memory ... If you are making a choice between the IIGS and other computers such as the Macintosh, Amiga, and Atari ST, the IIGS does not have the programming power of the 68000 microprocessor. However, it can access more memory and is much more expandable.[17]

ENHANCEMENTS

In September 1987, a year after its original release, Apple made an incremental improvement to the IIGS with the release of a new ROM. The ROM 01 revision offered some bug fixes in the code, and minor video display hardware changes. When booting the computer, it now displayed "ROM Version 01" at the bottom of the screen (the original IIGS had no message in this location).[18, 19]

The next change came with the release of the ROM 03 version of the IIGS in August of 1989. (Apparently someone felt that the original ROM was first, ROM 01 was second, and so this ROM should be "03" since it was the third revision.) This new IIGS computer came standard with 1 MB of RAM on the motherboard, and twice as much ROM (256K versus 128K on the older IIGS). This allowed the IIGS to store more of the operating system in ROM, rather than loading it from disk when booting.

The ROM 03 IIGS included enhancements for disabled users. A feature called "sticky keys" made it possible to perform multiple key presses. (To execute an "Option-Control-X" sequence, for example, required pressing three keys at once. This was something that a paralyzed user with a mouth-stick to press keys could not previously do.) Also, more things that had required a mouse now had keyboard equivalents (using the keypad). The new IIGS also had somewhat cleaner sound and graphics. However, because the improvements made were minimal compared to the cost of providing upgrades to previous owners, Apple announced no upgrade program. In any case, many of the new features could be obtained on older IIGS's by upgrading the memory to at least one megabyte and using GS/OS System Software 5.0.2 or greater.[20]

A feature that was added to the ROM 03 firmware that was entirely fun, instead of functional, was accessed by a specific key-sequence. If the computer was booted with no disk in the drive, a message appeared that read "Check

---

17 Chien, Phillip, "The Apple IIgs", *BYTE* (April 1987), 223-230.
18 Platt, Robert, and Bruce Field, "A.P.P.L.E. Doctor," *Call-A.P.P.L.E.* (November 1987), 58.
19 Utter, Gary, A2 Roundtable, Category 6, Topic 2, *GEnie*, accessed July 1993.
20 Doms, Dennis, "Apple upgrades IIgs hardware," *Open-Apple* (September 1989), 5.57.

startup device", with an apple symbol sliding back and forth. At that point, if the user pressed the keys Ctrl, open-apple, Option, and N simultaneously, the digitized voices of the Apple IIGS design team could be heard shouting, "Apple II !" Also, the names of those people would then be displayed on the screen.

If running GS/OS System 5.0 or greater, the user would have to hold down the Option and Shift keys, then pull down the About menu in the Finder. It would then say, "About the System". Using the mouse to click on that title displayed the names and played the audio message.

Long-time Apple employee John Arkley, one of the engineers working on the Apple IIc Plus project, campaigned long and hard to take things a step further. He wanted them to take an Apple IIGS motherboard, remove the slots, change the ROM to support only the internal "slots," and release a IIGS in a IIc case. He felt it would have made a great portable, non-expandable IIGS, but could not generate enough interest in anyone at Apple who would have the authority to approve the project.

TIMELINE

The start and end dates for the Apple IIGS, Apple IIe, and Apple IIc:

Apple IIe (all versions) – *January 1983 - November 1993*

Apple IIc (all versions) – *April 1984 - September 1990*

Apple IIGS – *September 1986 - August 1987*

Apple IIGS ROM 01 – *September 1987 - July 1989*

Apple IIGS ROM 03 – *August 1989 - December 1992*

CHAPTER 33
Expanding Storage

After Steve Wozniak's Disk II floppy drive changed the Apple II from a hobbyist toy to a serious home and business computer in the late 1970s, further progress in disk storage for the Apple II was slow. In 1978, the year the Disk II was released, Mike Scott (Apple's president) and Randy Wigginton were asked at a user group meeting whether they would adopt the larger capacity eight-inch floppy drives (which had been around before the 5.25 floppy drives were invented). They answered that no, the Apple II was not going in that direction, but felt it might get a hard disk by 1979 or 1980, and possibly earlier than that they might offer a double sided, double density 5.25 disk holding 500K per disk.[1]

Of course, this never happened; the Apple III project began to overtake the hearts and minds of Apple executives, and anything newer, bigger, or better was reserved for that machine. As a result, DOS 3.2 and 3.3 remained static—hard-coded to work specifically with the Disk II and its 110K and 140K (respectively) of available storage. DOS was not enhanced to easily access larger capacity drives until late in the life of the Apple IIc (and then, without widespread support across all existing models of the Apple II). In actuality, the way in which the catalog structure for Apple DOS was designed would have made it possible to access a disk with as much as 400K per disk; however, the low-level disk access routines built into DOS were only for the Disk II.

Between 1978 (when Apple released their original Shugart 5.25-inch floppy drive) and 1984, Apple made no improvements to its 5.25-inch disk capacity. Some of the 5.25-inch disk drives sold by these other companies were actually able to handle 40 tracks instead of the standard 35, so a patched DOS could store as much as 160K on a disk. Other patches modified DOS 3.2 (and later DOS 3.3) to work with larger capacity drives, from eight-inch floppy drives to hard disks.

Hard disks, though highly prized, were still not affordable to most Apple II owners. If someone was fortunate enough to be able to add a hard drive to their Apple II, it was still necessary to modify DOS to be able to access it. There were other short-lived innovations, also trying to make it possible

---

1 Thyng, Mike, "Apple Source", *PEEKing At Call-A.P.P.L.E.* (Seattle, Washington, Vol. 1, 1978), 7-8.

to end the "floppy shuffle" (swapping disks to use larger programs); one of the more interesting innovations put five floppy disks into a cartridge, and through software made them appear to the computer as one large disk drive.

Eventually Apple decided that the aging Disk II mechanism needed a face-lift, and they introduced the DuoDisk in May 1984. Sold with a special controller card, the DuoDisk was essentially two Disk II drives in a single cabinet. The drive mechanism was improved to read half-tracks on disks (which some copy-protected software used), and at $795 it was priced to be less expensive than buying two of the older Disk II drives with a controller card.[2] The most important advantage of this new design was an elimination of the "fried disk drive" problem that sometimes happened with the older design. The new DuoDisk design made foolproof the connection of the disk mechanism to the controller.

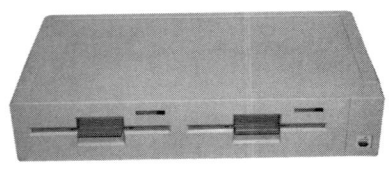

Apple Duodisk drive – Photo credit: Dr. Kenneth Buchholz <www.Apple2Online.com>

With the release of the Apple IIc in April 1984 came an external Disk II drive that was designed to plug into the new disk port in the back of the IIc, and was made with the same color and design as the IIc case. The Disk IIc was specific to the Apple IIc and incompatible with any older version Apple II, since it used a new, unique connector. However, since it was more expensive than a used Disk II drive, many users found out how to make a conversion cable to connect the older drive to the disk port; some even went the other direction and found ways to connect the new drive to the older Disk II controller cards for the II Plus and IIe.

Apple Disk IIc – Photo credit: Vectronics Apple World

The next small evolutionary step in disk storage technology for the Apple II was introduced in June 1985, with the release of the UniDisk 5.25. This drive was designed with the same appearance as the DuoDisk, but was a single 5.25-inch drive. It was also designed to allow one drive to be "daisy-chained" to another (one disk could plug into the back of another, forming a "chain"), instead of the older method of connecting each drive separately to the disk controller card. Its beige color was designed to match the original Apple IIe.[3,4]

---

2 -----. "Tomorrow's Apples Today", *Call-A.P.P.L.E.* (May 1984), 78.
3 -----, "The Marketplace", *Call-A.P.P.L.E.* (July 1985), 49.
4 Baum, Peter and Allen Baum, "Speaking Of Hardware", *Call-A.P.P.L.E.* (October 1987), 30-34, 51.

The last version of the Disk II was called the Apple 5.25 drive. It was identical to the UniDisk 5.25 drive, except for its case, which was designed in the platinum color to match the Apple IIGS and the platinum IIe. The connector also allowed it to connect in a daisy-chain fashion.

Apple 5.25 drive – Photo credit: personal

THE UNIDISK 3.5 AND APPLE 3.5 DRIVE

The first new type of drive that Apple released after the original Disk II was for the Apple Lisa computer in 1983. Code-named "Twiggy" and shipped with the original release of the Lisa, this drive turned out to be too complex and unreliable. The revised Lisa 2 that came out a year later used the Sony-designed 400K single-sided 3.5-inch drive used in the Macintosh, also released that month.

Then, in September 1985 Apple finally released an improved drive for the Apple II series, one that was not simply a cosmetic improvement of the original Disk II drive. The UniDisk 3.5 drive was a double-sided version of the Mac drive, and could hold 800K of data. The only connection that this new drive had with the original 5.25-inch drives was a chip used on its controller card; this IWM chip (for "Integrated Woz Machine") put the function of the original Disk II controller onto a single chip, plus the enhancements needed to operate this higher density drive.[5] Apple's design for the UniDisk 3.5 was unique, in that it used a modification to Sony's design that varied the speed of disk rotation, depending on which concentric track was being accessed. This change made it possible for data to be packed compactly enough in the smaller inner tracks to gain an extra 80K beyond the 720K that was originally possible.

The UniDisk was directly supported by the newer Apple IIc motherboards, but for the older Apple II models a special controller card was required. The UniDisk 3.5 was designed as an intelligent drive, and had a self-contained 65c02 processor and memory to temporarily store (buffer) data read from or written to the disk. This was necessary because of the slow 1 MHz speed of the 6502 processor in the Apple II; it could not keep up with the faster data transfer rates possible with the 3.5-inch disk mechanism, plus the overhead of decoding the raw data. This extra processing cut down the speed in the UniDisk data transfer rate, but compared to the older Disk II drives it was much faster.

With the release of the Apple IIGS in September 1986 came a new version of the 800K 3.5-inch drive. Called the Apple 3.5 drive, it could be used on either a Mac or Apple II, fitting into the trend at Apple at making periph-

---

5 -----. "The Marketplace", *Call-A.P.P.L.E.* (July 1985), 49.

erals compatible between the two computers. The major difference between this drive and the original UniDisk 3.5 was that it had been lobotomized to be a "dumb" drive. Gone was the internal 65c02 processor chip used in the UniDisk 3.5 (which made it an intelligent drive) and the ability of the drive to buffer its own read and write operations. The newer Apple 3.5 drive did away with the extra circuitry, leaving it to the computer to handle direct control of the drive. This could be done in the IIGS because of its faster 65816 microprocessor, which could keep up with the higher rate of data transfer.

Overall, Apple released four versions of 3.5-inch drives between 1984 and 1986. First was the 400K drive used on the original Macintosh, then the 800K UniDisk 3.5 (which wouldn't work on the Mac), then an 800K drive for the Mac (which wouldn't work on the Apple II), and finally the Apple 3.5 drive, which worked on the Apple IIGS and the Mac, but not the IIe and original IIc.

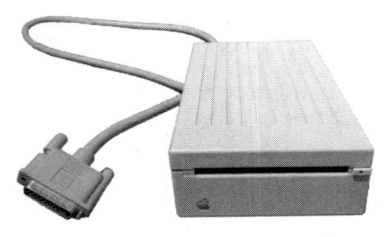

Apple 3.5 drive – Photo credit: personal

MASS STORAGE

After a faster processor and larger amounts of memory, the next improvement many Apple II users wanted was disk storage beyond the 140 offered by the Disk II drive. Although some 8-inch floppy drives briefly appeared on the market, nothing made enough of an impact to gain wide acceptance. The primary barrier was cost. Recall that even the Disk II, as expensive as it was for $495 when it was released in 1978, was still much less expensive than similar drives of the day. When it came to considering fixed disk (hard disk) storage, the technology for building and selling these was initially very expensive, and only a few could afford this convenience.

Back in 1973, IBM had created for its mainframe computers the first hard drive, a sealed unit with heads to read and write data. The drive was referred to as a Winchester drive by the engineer who headed the project at IBM, and for several years the term was applied to other unrelated hard drives (though with time it fell out of common use). Seagate Technology came out in 1980 with its own version of a Winchester-type of sealed hard drive, aimed for the growing microcomputer market. This drive, the 5 megabyte (MB) ST-506, was built to match the size of the increasingly common 5.25-inch floppy drive.

Shugart Associates had previously worked in 1978 to create an interface protocol (set of rules) for communication between a computer and a disk storage device. This interface was originally called SASI (Shugart Associates Systems Interface), and in 1981 Seagate teamed up with NCR to request that this protocol be made into an official ANSI (American National Standards

Institute) standard. Modifications to SASI eventually led to the creation in 1986 of SCSI (Small Computer Systems Interface). Apple's Macintosh Plus, released in 1986, was the first product to include a connector for a SCSI drive.

Other hard drive interfaces were created and sold in the years before the SCSI standard was finalized. The IDE (Intelligent Drive Electronics) interface came about in 1985 from collaboration between Control Data, Compaq, and Western Digital. It was designed for IBM's second-generation personal computer, the IBM PC/AT, and the official ANSI designation was ATA (for "AT Attachment"). The protocol described how to attach numerous disk devices, hard disks and other data storage devices.

Since the Apple II was a strong player in the late 1970s, it was inevitable that hard disk interfaces were built for it. One of the earliest was the Corvus Systems interface card. It was released in 1979, and was designed specifically to attach to the IMI-7710 Winchester hard drive (made by International Memories, Inc. from Cupertino, California). Corvus organized data on the hard drive by dividing it up into 140K volumes, each the size of a standard Apple II floppy disk. Access to each volume involved use of the otherwise ignored Volume parameter in DOS 3.3. (For example, typing the command "CATALOG V20" would list the disk directory for the disk formatted as volume 20). This Corvus interface and drive combo only offered 10 MB of storage, and cost a whopping $5,350.[6]

Apple offered its first branded hard drive in 1981. Called the ProFile, it was a 5 MB drive designed for use with the Apple III, and sold for $3,499. It was not until 1983 that the company began to sell the Apple II ProFile Interface Card to allow it to be used on the Apple II, and then only for ProDOS or Pascal.

At the West Coast Computer Faire in April 1982, the Xebec Corporation of San Jose, California introduced a 5 MB hard drive for Apple II or CP/M systems, connecting via its own SASI interface card.

Percom Data was involved in providing storage solutions to the home computer market as far back as 1976. Although it primarily served the TRS-80 and IBM PC markets, it made a brief foray into the Apple II market in 1984 with a larger drive, selling the 10 MB PHD-10 external hard drive with interface card for $1,220.

With time, prices of hard drives slowly dropped. A new product appeared in late 1985 that was significantly less expensive. Sold by First Class Peripherals of Carson City, Nevada, the new drive was called The Sider, a homophone for cider (as in apple cider), and its position on the desktop, sitting beside the Apple II.

The Sider used the Xebec SASI interface protocol (mentioned above) and a drive mechanism built by MiniScribe of Longmont, Colorado. It had to be partitioned into four sections, one each for DOS 3.3, ProDOS, Pascal, and CP/M. This partitioning was required, even if only a very small partition was made and

---

6 -----, *Apple Orchard*, (Vol. 1, No. 1, March-April 1980)

that operating system was not used. Once the partitions were created, disk volumes from 140K up to 400K in size were created to fill the space in that partition.[7]

First Class Peripherals released two models, the 10 MB Sider for $695, and the 20 MB Sider II for $895. The interface was designed to allow at least two of the drives to be daisy-chained together. The drives could boot into DOS 3.3 or ProDOS, but not into Pascal or CP/M.[8] The following year, the company released a tape cartridge backup unit called the "B-Sider", for $895, which could hold up to 20 MB of data.[9]

By 1989, First Class Peripherals had a range of drives available, from 20 MB to 90 MB, some with an attached tape drive.

In 1988, Chinook Technology of Longmont, Colorado released the CT-20 and CT-30 hard drives (with interface cards) for the Apple II Plus, IIe, and IIGS, and the CT-20c specifically for the Apple IIc. These were 20 and 30 MB SCSI hard drives, and the version for the IIc include an additional internal logic board that converted SmartPort calls on the Apple IIc disk port to the standard SCSI protocol in order to communicate with the drive.[10] Chinook ultimately sold additional model sizes, the CT-30c, CT-40c, and CT-80c. The drive could connect anywhere in the SmartPort chain of devices, as long as any 5.25 drive connected was last in the chain.[11]

Goodbye Floppies, Hello 20 MByte.

New from First Class Peripherals: The Sider II 20 MByte Winchester Hard Disk Storage and Tape Backup Unit for your Apple II+ or IIe

Sider II and B-Sider from First Class Peripherals – Photo credit: *inCider* Feb 1986.

---

7   Bayer, Barry, "The Sider", *Creative Computing* (Vol 11, No. 8, August 1985), 36.
8   Field, Cynthia, "Small Unit With A Big Value", *InfoWorld* (April 29, 1985), 83.
9   "Tape Backup For Apple IIs Announced", *InfoWorld* (May 5, 1986), 55.
10 Weishaar, Tom, "Ask Uncle DOS", *Open-Apple* (December 1988), 4.87.
11 Personal note: The first Apple II that I owned was the IIc, and when this hard drive became available, I purchased the 40 MB version. It was wonderfully simple to have that amount of storage available constantly, after living in a 140K floppy disk world. However, unlike an Apple IIe where a hard drive controller card could be placed in slot 7 so it would boot first, the slot order for devices was unchangeable on the Apple IIc. This meant that when I powered up the system with my power strip, I had to press Control-RESET and then type PR#5 to boot ProDOS from the CT-40c. This minor annoyance inspired me to create my one and only shareware program, *SmartBoot*, which I released sometime in 1989 and updated based on feedback from users. This was an assembly language program saved with the name "PRODOS" on an otherwise empty 5.25 disk, which was to be left in the internal floppy drive. When I powered everything on, this fake PRODOS file would load and execute instead of the real PRODOS. Its job was to repeatedly check the Smartport on slot 5 to see if the Chinook CT-40c was ready. When it was, it then transferred control to slot 5 and booted normally. I announced my product on GEnie and in a letter to *Open-Apple*, and ultimately received about one hundred letters over the space of a couple of years, paying me the five dollars I asked in shareware fees.

INTERFACING MASS STORAGE

In the early years of storage devices for the Apple II, it was necessary to sell both the drive and an interface card at the same time. This happened with the Disk II and the Disk II interface card. Other storage solutions from third-party companies often required the same pairing of drive and card, unless the drive was a clone of the Disk II.

When mass storage hard drives became less expensive and more compatible with IDE, SASI, or SCSI standards, it became more common to purchase an interface card and a hard drive separately. Other computers, such as the Macintosh Plus released in 1986 came with a built-in SCSI interface, making it necessary to only attach a compatible SCSI drive to the port on the back of the computer.

By the time larger hard drives became available for the Apple II, ProDOS was the dominant operating system, and it was capable of accessing a disk volume no larger than 32 MB. This meant that a hard drive larger than 32 MB had to be logically divided (partitioned) into two or more smaller-sized drives, to make all of the storage space available. It was necessary to include information at the start of the hard drive that identified what partitions were on the drive, how large they were, and where each logical partition started and ended on the physical drive. This information was called a partition map.

Apple did not release an Apple II with any included circuitry for a SCSI port, but in 1986 they released the Apple II SCSI Card, which worked on the Apple II Plus, IIe, or IIGS. This card could perform direct memory access (DMA), which meant that data was moved to and from motherboard RAM directly, in large blocks. This bypassed the need for the microprocessor to have to deal with each byte, and improved the speed of disk access. One limitation of this card on the Apple IIGS was its inability to perform DMA beyond the first 4 MB of motherboard RAM. This caused performance problems for IIGS owners who had larger memory cards (6 or 8 MB).[12]

CMS Enhancements of Tustin, California released a SCSI card in 1987 and SCSI hard drives for the Apple IIe and IIGS. The card, however, had some serious limitations. It was designed to work with a CMS SCSI hard drive, and although it was possible to use other hard drives on it, users found that the card could corrupt and (oddly enough) even physically damage the drive. It did not support the full SCSI standard, and did not use the standard Apple partition map. Furthermore, although it was possible to use a 64 MB hard drive (divided into two 32 MB partitions), making use of a larger drive required the user to purchse and install a second CMS SCSI card, with the card set to a different SCSI ID. Technically knowledgeable users ultimately recommended that this card not be used on an Apple IIGS at all.

---

12 Diaz, Tony, A2 SCSI Cards, *Apple2.info*, <apple2.info/wiki/index.php?title=A2_SCSI_Cards>, accessed October 20, 2012.

In March 1990, Apple released a redesigned SCSI card, the Apple II High Speed SCSI card. It supported DMA more efficiently, and this allowed the card to load and save four times faster on the IIGS, and twice as fast on the IIe, compared to the older Apple II SCSI card.

Back in 1985, a company called Ohio Kache Systems of Springboro, Ohio released a $695 card called the Kache Card. Using a Z-80 processor and 256K of RAM, it was intended as a replacement controller card for a hard drive like First Class Peripheral's Sider hard drive. It worked with ProDOS, DOS 3.3, and Pascal. While using the card, the disk operating system sent data to and received data from the hard drive, but the Kache Card kept a copy of the most frequently accessed blocks in its own memory. Since RAM access was much faster than any mechanical drive, this improved disk access speeds.[13]

Ohio Kache later released a product called the Multi-Kache card. It had the caching capabilities of the Kache Card, but included a clock, a serial port and a parallel port. The Multi-Kache had compatibility issues with some large RAM cards on the Apple IIGS as well as other performance problems. It became known by some in the Apple II community as the "multi-crash" card. Also, many potential customers already had printer cards and some had a clock, so the "multi" part of the card was not what they really needed. The card sold for $295 for a 256K version, and $465 for a 1 MB version, and offered a SCSI option for an additional $79.95, plus a disk expander (cache for floppy disks) for $35.[14] The company had planned another product, the Fast-Cache, which only performed disk caching. However, it never appeared on the market, and by 1989 Ohio Kache Systems was out of business.

While a senior in college in 1987, Drew Vogan had worked at Ohio Kache Systems as the firmware engineer on the Multi-Kache card. With another employee who had been his roommate at college, Terry Chlebek, the two began work on a new product that would have the caching abilities of the Ohio Kache products, but was intended to focus on just the SCSI and DMA functions.

They started their own company, CV Technology, the same year Ohio Kache folded, with the help of a loan from Vogan's father. Their product was called the RamFAST SCSI card, and within a year they had made enough profit to repay the loan and earn a modest income.

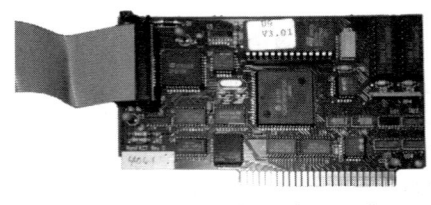

RamFAST SCSI card – Photo credit: personal

---

13 Sander-Cederlof, Bob, "Ohio Systems Kache Card", *Apple Assembly Lines* (Vol 6, Issue 3, December 1985).
14 Finkenstadt, Andy, "Questions And Answers About OKS Products", Real-Time Conference, A2 Roundtable, *GEnie* (October 10, 1989).

Like the Kache Card, it used a Z-80 processor, and included DMA and interrupt controllers. The cards went through three revisions after the first release, the latest being Revision D. The 2.0 ROM update made it possible to control SCSI CD-ROM drives and tape drives. Although the IIGS had problems with DMA beyond 4 MB of RAM, CV Technology found a way to get around that and make its card work on a full 8 MB RAM system (although this trick was not compatible with the Transwarp GS accelerator sold by Applied Engineering).

A publication reviewing the RamFAST at the time of its released showed that booting a hard drive with this card was almost as quick as starting up from a RAM disk.[15]

One useful feature offered on the RamFAST was a ROM disk that included all the configuration files and drivers to add to GS/OS. This made it unnecessary to have a separate installation disk to use (or lose).

As the Apple II market continued to shrink, Vogan and Chlebek decided to sell CV Technology and its products to Sequential Systems of Lafayette, Colorado in 1993. That company sold many more RamFAST cards, primarily because Apple Computer had by that time stopped selling its own Apple II High Speed SCSI card.[16]

Several internal hard drives were marketed for the Apple IIGS in the 1990s. These drives were completely contained within the computer case, where most others had to be attached to the computer with a cable.

Applied Engineering sold the Vulcan, which was not only an internal hard drive but also a replacement power supply for the IIGS. It came in 20, 40, 100 (which cost $1795), and 200 MB sizes, and attached to a proprietary 16-bit AT style controller card that plugged into the motherboard. It worked with GS/OS, ProDOS 8, DOS 3.3, CP/M, and Pascal, and allowed up to sixteen partitions on a disk (though only four were available at one time).

Another internal drive that came with a replacement power supply for the IIGS was the Pegasus 100i, sold by Econ Technologies. This was a SCSI drive, and at $599 was more affordable. It featured a jumper wire that delayed startup of the IIGS until the drive was ready.

Unlike the two previously mentioned internal drives, Zip Technology in 1994 introduced the ZipDrive GS, a hard drive with a proprietary interface, contained completely on a card to plug into a slot on the motherboard. It offered one size, 40 MB, and sold for $579. Following on this same premise in 1995 was the Focus Hard Card, created by Parsons Engineering and sold by Alltech Electronics. This was an IDE drive attached directly to the disk controller on the card. The card was compatible with the Apple IIe or IIGS, and had a 20 MB model that sold for $89, while the 170 MB model sold for $189.[17]

---

15 Doms, Dennis, "Miscellanea", *A2-Central* (Vol 6, No 5, June 1990), 6.54.
16 Vogan, Andrew, e-mail message to author, February 20, 2012.
17 Crotty, Cameron, "Wanted: Hard Drives On The Run", *inCider/A+* (July 1992), 40-42.

MASS STORAGE – REMOVABLE

Beyond internal and external hard drives, several other removable disk methods were tested in the marketplace during the 1980s and 1990s.

The Iomega Corporation released an external disk cartridge system in 1994 called the Zip Drive (not related to the Zip Technology internal hard drive). It was created as a high-capacity replacement for 3.5-inch floppy disks, and came (at least for the Apple II) in 25 and 100 MB capacities. The edition that worked on a SCSI card sold for about $199.[18]

SyQuest Technology, Inc. sold a different type of removable cartridge drive for desktop computers. Though produced for different platforms, they gained brief popularity in the Apple II market by making drives that used the SCSI interface. It was sold with 5.25-inch cartridges that offered 44, 88, and 200 MB capacities, and a 3.5-inch cartridge that could hold 110 and 270 MB.

One other type of storage method was the Insite Peripherals floptical drive. It used a disk that looked like a 3.5-inch floppy disk, but was based on both magnetic and optical storage methods. It used a laser to store 21 MB per disk. The drive had some popularity with Apple II users because it could also read MS-DOS double density and high-density disks under GS/OS System 6.0.1, with the use of the MS-DOS FST. Drives that handled this type of disk were built both by Insite and Iomega, using a SCSI interface. On the Apple II, floptical drives were sold by Tulin Technology and Micro-Peripherals, Inc.[19] Ultimately, the floptical drive was slower and had some reliability issues compared to the Iomega Zip, which sold far better.

Joachim Lange of Stockdorf, Germany started ///SHH Systeme to create hardware for the Apple II, and in June 1994 released the BlueDisk universal floppy disk controller card for the Apple IIe and IIGS. It included MS-DOS tools, a set of disk management utilities that allowed access of files on MS-DOS floppy disks. This card allowed Apple II users to attach MFM (modified frequency modulation) disk drives that had become standard in MS-DOS computers. At the time when the BlueDisk card was released, these disk drives could be purchased for as little as $50 for double density (720K) and high density drives (1.44 MB), and $80 for extra density drives (2.88 meg). The BlueDisk also supported Macintosh 800K and 1.4 MB sizes.

The introduction of CD-ROM drives in 1985 did not exclude the Apple II for long. The Apple CD SC was released in March 1988 for $1,198, for use on both the Macintosh and the Apple II (using revision C of the Apple II SCSI card). When Apple released the Apple CD 150 in 1992, it worked well on the Apple IIGS with either the Apple II High Speed SCSI or the RamFAST SCSI card.

---

18 Cavanaugh, Steve, "Using A ZIP Drive with an Apple IIGS", *The Apple Blossom* (Vol 1, No. 2).
19 Cuff, Doug, "The Floppy Disk Grows Up: Flopitcal Drives and the Apple II", *II Alive* (May/June 1994), 31-34.

CHAPTER 33 | Expanding Storage

The primary limitation of this technology was the small number of CD software titles released for the Apple II platform, compared to those for Macintosh or Windows. Some Apple II software was released which allowed access to encyclopedia CD-ROM titles, and a few educational titles became available for the IIGS in 1992. The discontinuation of the IIGS that same year put a damper on further CD software development. In the remaining years of the decade, CD-ROMs were used primarily to distribute compilations of Apple II shareware titles and graphics, music and sound files.

Two different types of solid-state storage devices ultimately became available for the Apple II platform. SanDisk first introduced compact flash cards in 1994 as a choice for photo storage on digital cameras. Its use on the Apple II became possible when a hardware hacker named Rich Dreher released his first run of the CFFA (Compact Flash For Apple) card in May 2002. He had become frustrated trying to get his old Apple II Plus running, not because of problems with the computer itself, but due to Disk II hardware malfunctions. He then decided he wanted a hard drive, but could not find anything functioning. With the help of a friend, he created a peripheral card for his Apple II that would make use of a Compact flash card for storage, wrote drivers for it to work with ProDOS, and found that he had a saleable product on his hands. By 2011 he had a new version, the CFFA 3000, which had both Compact flash and USB flash connectors on it.

With the CFFA and an appropriate flash memory device, it was possible to create multiple 32 MB partitions to use with ProDOS. The CFFA 3000 included a built-in controller program on the card that allowed the user to select a number of disk images on the flash memory card and assign them to slot and drive numbers that ProDOS could mount. This significantly simplified the process of getting files onto or off of an Apple II. A disk image could be downloaded from the Internet on any Mac or Windows computer, transferred to the Compact flash or USB flash drive plugged into that computer, and then attached to the Apple II using the CFFA. On the Apple II under ProDOS it was then possible to transfer individual files between those disk images and a physical floppy disk or hard drive that worked with the Apple II.

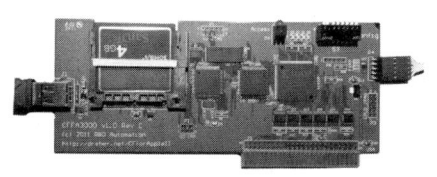

CFFA 3000 card; USB plug is on left, CF card in left on card, and external Disk II switching buttons plug into the right – Photo credit: personal

The availability of this newer technology for the Apple II platform made it possible to continue to use the computer, even if the thirty-plus year old disk hardware had broken and could not be revived.

TIMELINE

Corvus hard drive – *June 1979*

Corvus Systems interface card – *June 1979*

Seagate ST-506 hard drive – *1980*

Apple ProFile hard drive – *September 1981*

Xebec S1410 controller and 5 MB drive – *April 1982*

Apple II ProFile Interface Card – *1983*

Percom PHD-10 hard drive – *1984*

Apple Disk IIc – *April 1984*

Apple DuoDisk – *May 1984*

Ohio Kache Card – *1985*

Apple UniDisk 5.25 – *June 1985*

Apple UniDisk 3.5 – *September 1985*

First Class Peripherals Sider, Sider II – *November 1985*

Multi-Kache Card – *1986*

First Class Peripherals B-Sider – *February 1986*

Apple II SCSI Card – *September 1986*

Apple 3.5 drive – *September 1986*

Apple 5.25 drive – *September 1986*

CMS SCSI card and hard drive – *1987*

Apple CD SC – *March 1988*

Chinook CT-20c – *October 1988*

SyQuest 44 and 100 MB cartridge drives – *October 1988*

AE Vulcan – *July 1989*

Apple II High Speed SCSI Card – *March 1990*

RamFAST SCSI card – *May 1990*

Insite Peripherals Floptical drive – *1991*

Econ Technologies Pegasus 100i – *December 1991*

Apple CD 150 – *1992*

Iomega Zip Drive – *1994*

ZipDrive GS – *1994*

SyQuest 270 MB cartridge drive – *May 1994*

BlueDisk universal floppy disk controller – *June 1994*

Parsons Focus Hard Card – *1995*

SyQuest EZ135 – *August 1995*

CFFA card – *May 2002*

CFFA 3000 card – *July 2011*

CHAPTER 34
DOS Gets Sophisticated

PRODOS 16

When Apple released the IIGS in September 1986 with its considerably greater power, changes were needed in the operating system to better manage that power. This had to be done with another goal—that of maintaining compatibility with the large library of older Apple II software. Apple's engineers decided against creating yet another system of storing files on disks, so the new operating system utilized the same disk structure as ProDOS and SOS before that.

To emphasize the power of the new 16-bit processor in the IIGS, the new operating system was named ProDOS 16, and was part of what Apple called System Software 1.0. The older ProDOS was renamed to ProDOS 8, to indicate that it ran on 8-bit Apple II computers. Even on the IIGS, to run older software it was necessary to temporarily transfer control to ProDOS 8.

ProDOS 16 was only a rudimentary program when the Apple IIGS first shipped. The work on the updated operating system fell behind the work on the hardware, so the new system calls for 16-bit software had to be translated into ProDOS 8 calls to actually carry out disk activities. As such, it was slow and cumbersome.

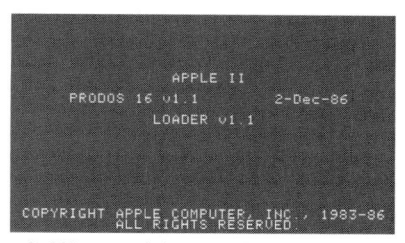

ProDOS 16 v1.1 splash screen – Photo credit: personal

Furthermore, whatever plans the Apple II engineering team originally had for System Software 1.0, those plans were far from complete with this initial release. Consequently, it was decided that the simplest thing to do was to display a program launcher, which at least allowed easy selection and execution of a SYS (8-bit system) or S16 (16-bit system) program file, or navigation down through subdirectories (folders) to find such a program.

The program launcher was displayed on the super hi-res screen, which was built to have an appearance similar to the desktop on the early Macintosh system, though in color and using a different typeface for text. This screen display style laid the groundwork for the IIGS System Software desktop through the rest of the life of the product.

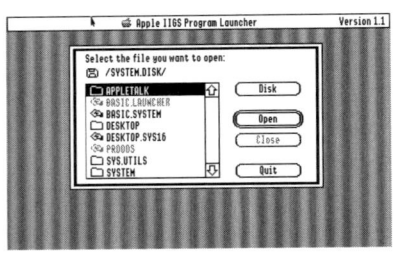

One of the major differences between programs written for a 128K Apple II computer and the Apple IIGS (with up to 8 MB of memory) was the location of the program in memory. On the older computer, a program was most commonly written to run at just one memory location. With such a large memory space to work with on the IIGS, it was not possible to ensure that a specific memory location would always be available.

System Software 1.0 and 2.0 program launcher – Photo credit: personal

To provide portability, part of the information included with each IIGS program was code to allow it to execute in any possible memory location. The Memory Manager Toolbox routine (built into the IIGS ROM code) helped to make space available for a particular program, and the relocation code made it possible to run that code in the allocated memory.[1]

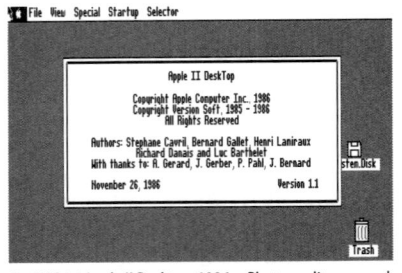

Both the initial System 1.0 and the update System 2.0 (which was released eight months later, in May 1987) provided only a rudimentary Macintosh-like GUI experience. It was possible to start a program called the Apple II Desktop, which looked much more like the Macintosh (even down to being monochromatic like the early Macs). It provided a graphic user interface to manage and launch disk files. This program was a re-branded version of International Solutions' *MouseDesk* program, originally released for the 128K Apple IIe and IIc. International Solutions had created it as a launch vehicle for its *MouseWrite* word processing software.

ProDOS 16 Apple II Desktop, 1986 – Photo credit: personal

The Apple II Desktop was buggy, and actually did not have some of the features found in the latter versions of MouseDesk for the older 8-bit computers. Only a few Desk Accessories (small desktop programs like a calculator and a puzzle) were included, and there were no keyboard shortcuts to help carry out certain functions.[2] The lack of keyboard shortcuts was not necessarily a problem, as the shortcuts that had been created for MouseDesk were too numerous and very difficult to guess.

---

1 Trost, Nate, "Chronos: The Life And Times Of Apple II Operating System, Part II", *II Alive* (September/October 1994), 16-18.
2 Edwards, Jay, "MouseDesk Info", <mirrors.apple2.org.za/ground.icaen.uiowa.edu/MiscInfo/Misc/mousedesk.info>, accessed October 20, 2012.

Because of these limitations, the Apple II System Utilities program from ProDOS 8 was also included with System 1.0 and 2.0, as use of the Apple II Desktop was sometimes just too complicated or didn't work right for certain activities. The 8-bit System Utilities could be used when it was necessary to perform disk and file management more efficiently.[3, 4]

In September 1987, a year after the Apple IIGS first became available, Apple released System Software 3.1 for the IIGS (System 3.0 was never publicly released). This was the first version to include the Apple IIGS Finder, which replaced the Launcher and the Apple II Desktop system program. Following the pattern of the older program launcher, this Finder was in color, which was something that even the Macintosh would not have until the release of the Macintosh II in 1990.

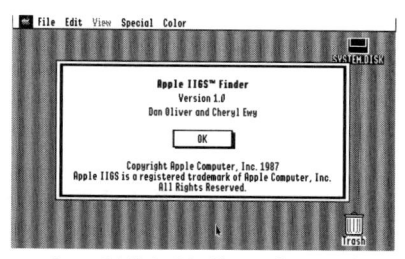

System 3.1, Finder 1.0 – Photo credit: personal

System 3.1 also included version 3.0 of the ProDOS 8 Apple II System Utilities program, which could copy files between ProDOS, DOS 3.2, DOS 3.3, Apple Pascal, and CP/M disks. For the ProDOS 16 environment, there was a folder for Desk Accessories, but it was empty. Unlike Desk Accessories on the Macintosh, which had to be installed with a special utility, the IIGS system allowed the user to simply drop the appropriate files into the right folders and they would work. This simplicity also applied to fonts.

Additionally, System Software 3.1 had a new toolset, the Note Synthesizer, which had been planned for the original release of the Apple IIGS, but had not been ready in time. This tool made it possible for programmers to create music utilizing the power of the Ensoniq chip in the IIGS.[5]

System Software 3.2 for the Apple IIGS was released six months later, in May 1988. It supposedly offered bug fixes for BASIC.SYSTEM (however it turned out that nothing had changed between this and the previous version), improved boot time, and added the MIDI toolset, the Note Sequencer (a companion for the Note Synthesizer), and ACE (audio compression and expansion). Printer drivers were changed—it was now possible to print to an ImageWriter LQ over an AppleTalk network, as well as load the system software over AppleTalk. Finally, the drivers for the ImageWriter and LaserWriter printers were completely rewritten, resulting in faster printer output.[6, 7]

---

3 Kavadias, Tony, "Apple II User Interfaces", *Graphical User Interface Gallery Guidebook*, <www.guidebookgallery.org/articles/apple2userinterfaces>, accessed October 20, 2012.
4 Deatherage, Matt, "The Operating System", *The Apple II Guide*, (Cupertino, CA, Apple Computer, Inc., Fall 1990), 117-125.
5 Trost, Nate, "Chronos: The Life And Times Of Apple II Operating System, Part II", *II Alive* (September/October 1994), 16-18.
6 Weishaar, Tom, "Miscellanea", *Open-Apple*, Vol 4, No 7, August 1988, pp. 4.50-4.51.
7 Sander-Cederlof, Bob, "New Version 1.2 of 3ASIC.SYSTEM", *Apple Assembly Line*, Vol 8, Issue 8, May 1988.

GS/OS

With the experience of SOS, ProDOS, and the Macintosh Operating System to draw from, the engineers and programmers in the Apple II division devised a yet more powerful and flexible disk operating system for the Apple IIGS. It was called GS/OS, and was introduced as Apple IIGS System Software 4.0 in September 1988, at AppleFest.

Written (finally) in full 16-bit code (which allowed faster performance), GS/OS was more than a disk operating system, but a truly comprehensive operating system that also handled keyboard input, video display (text and graphics), mouse input, printers, modems, and more. In these respects it was just as powerful as the older SOS written for the Apple III back in 1980. But they also added a new concept, something that even the Macintosh did not yet have.

Although GS/OS was designed to allow an Apple IIGS to access disks utilizing foreign disk formats, such as those used on the Macintosh or MS-DOS, it still had to know exactly how files were stored on that disk. ProDOS could only handle files stored in the specifically defined ProDOS/SOS format; DOS 3.3 could only handle files stored in that format; and so on. To make this new system as broad-based as possible, Apple programmers built into it the concept of a File System Translator (FST).

With the appropriate FST teamed up with a suitable disk driver, GS/OS could theoretically read any disk formatted by any disk operating system. The FST simply translated the requests made by GS/OS into the language "spoken" by the disk it was trying to read. No disk operating system up to this time had attempted to achieve that feat. Recognizing that the computers used in the real world would never be 100 percent Apple II, Apple used the FST concept to simplify transfer of data between different computer formats.

The concept was first implemented in a limited fashion on the Macintosh, when the Apple File Exchange program was modified to use MS-DOS disks. On GS/OS, it was no more complicated than to drop an appropriate FST file into the proper folder on the GS/OS system disk. FST files included with this first version of GS/OS included PRO.FST (for access to ProDOS-formatted disks), CHAR.FST (to handle character-oriented devices, such as the keyboard, screen, printers, and modems), and HS.FST (to handle access to CD-ROM files in the High Sierra format).

Apple engineers also made 16-bit software running under GS/OS more flexible by removing the older Apple II method of identifying a disk by the disk controller card slot, and removing the limitation of only two disk devices per slot. The limits of maximum file and disk size built into ProDOS 8 were expanded. A GS/OS file or disk volume could be as large as 4 GB (gigabytes), or 4096 MB. However, when GS/OS dealt with ProDOS disk volumes, it still had to stay within the limits of ProDOS (files no bigger than 16 MB, and disk volumes no bigger than 32 MB).[8]

System Software 4.0 included version 1.2 of the Finder. It also had a new program called *Advanced Disk Utility*, for formatting and partitioning disks, and an Installer program to make it easier to update System disks. It was delivered on two 3.5 inch disks, SYSTEM.DISK and SYSTEM.TOOLS, and was made available free to existing users from Apple dealers, user groups, and online services. It required a minimum of 512K of RAM, and at least version 01 of the IIGS ROM.

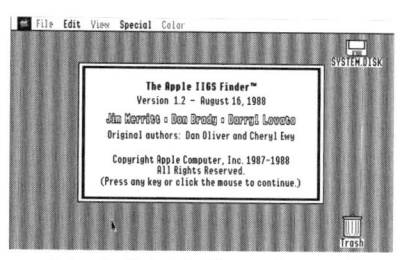

System 4.0, Finder 1.2 – Photo credit: personal

Another simplicity introduced with GS/OS was the method of handling drivers for various devices that attached to the computer. The driver file was simply placed in the DRIVERS folder on the system boot disk, and if GS/OS detected that hardware, it loaded the driver into memory.

System Software 4.0 came with drivers for the ImageWriter, ImageWriter LQ, LaserWriter, and Epson printers. There were also drivers to handle the various IIGS ports, including the printer, modem and AppleTalk ports. Another group of drivers were for disk devices, including 5.25-inch and 3.5-inch disks, and SCSI devices. Finally, there was a driver for the console (keyboard and screen) and for MIDI (Musical Instrument Digital Interface) devices.[9]

Previous versions of IIGS system software showed a boot screen that was nearly identical to the ProDOS boot disk for 8-bit Apple II computers, except that it read "PRODOS 16". Starting with GS/OS, it displayed a deep blue startup screen with a progress bar, much like the Macintosh used.

GS/OS SYSTEM 5

Apple's next enhancement for the Apple IIGS was announced at AppleFest Boston in May 1989, and released in July of that year. System Software 5.0 made it possible for all existing Apple IIGS computers to run faster, whether ROM 01 or ROM 03, doing it all without any changes to the IIGS hardware. It added speed, speed, and more speed to many features of the IIGS, accomplishing this through more efficient software coding.

There were patches to the IIGS ROM Toolbox to improve throughput in many of the built-in capabilities of the machine. A new feature called Expressload was added, making it possible for certain program files to load

---

8   Deatherage, Matt, "The Operating System", *The Apple II Guide*, (Cupertino, CA, Apple Computer, Inc., Fall 1990), 117-125.
9   Weishaar, Tom, "Breaking the incompatibility barrier: An introduction to Apple's GS/OS", *Open-Apple*, (November 1988), 4.75-4.78.

from disk up to eight times faster (and this change could be applied to existing applications).

Also included was a new Apple SCSI Manager, which worked specifically with the Apple II SCSI card. It bypassed the ROM code on that card to accomplish its faster throughput, increasing it from 18K per second to as much as 80K per second.

A new Apple 3.5 driver used a method called "scatter read", sometimes pulling one full track from the disk at a time, temporarily storing it to RAM, and then picking out the blocks it needed.

The performance changes were dramatic for some programs; for example *AppleWorks* GS with the help of ExpressLoad went from taking four minutes to load to as little as one minute. The magic performed by the new Apple 3.5 drivers took this one-minute load time and dropped it further to just 35 seconds.

ProDOS 8 and BASIC.SYSTEM received small updates and bug fixes. One change for Applesoft programmers was the replacement of the non-functioning MON command with MTR. This new command worked exactly like the old CALL-151 command by jumping to the Monitor, but did it with only three characters.

A new feature introduced in System 5.0 was upper and lowercase filenames. To retain compatibility with pre-System 5.0 IIGS computers and older 8-bit Apple II computers, the filename was actually stored as all uppercase, and two bytes in the filename entry were used to indicate which character in a name was lowercase (or a space). These changes were part of the ProDOS file system translator, and were added partly because of the other new translator that allowed access to Macintosh disk volumes over a network. Those Mac files had allowed lowercase filenames from the very beginning of the Mac OS.

The concept of Desk Accessories had been designed into the Apple IIGS from the beginning, and was built into the ROM. These text-based accessories were known as Classic Desk Accessories (CDAs). The user could access CDAs at any time, even from graphic-based programs, by pressing open-apple-control-Escape (as long as interrupts were not disabled). There were a number of third-party CDAs that were released for the Apple IIGS. However, the more interesting types of Desk Accessories were known as New Desk Accessories (NDAs—not to be confused with Non-Disclosure Agreements). These were accessible from the Apple menu in the Finder. In System 4.0, there was only a single NDA present, called Disk Cache, which set aside part of the memory to increase disk access speeds.

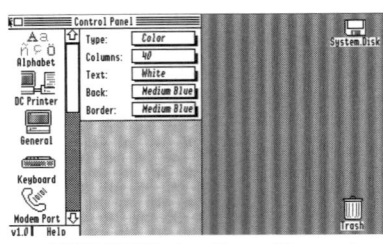

GS/OS 5.0 NDA Display – Photo credit: personal

Apple IIGS System Software 5.0 began to expand on this concept, with a Macintosh-like Control Panel NDA. It performed most of the functions of the text-based Control Panel, though with some small differences. Programmers could add extra functions to the NDA Control Panel by creating their code and putting it into the CDEV (Control Device) folder within the System folder.

Other features introduced in System 5.0 were support for scrolling and pop-up menus. There were new printer drivers (except the ImageWriter LQ) that were faster than the older ones.

The Macintosh system had for some time used files that had two parts, called forks—a data fork and a resource fork. A resource fork was intended to store structured data (such as an icon picture associated with the file, or other information). Some of the 16-bit files included in System 5.0 on the IIGS now also included resource forks. IIGS users were urged not to try to copy these files with 8-bit utilities because the old utilities didn't know about resource forks, and would not copy them correctly.[10, 11]

Three updates to System 5 were released. System 5.0.2 came out in December 1989 (5.0.1 never appeared for end users), 5.0.3 came out a year later in December 1990 (primarily providing faster printer drivers), and 5.0.4 was released in February 1991 with further bug fixes.[12, 13, 14, 15, 16]

GS/OS SYSTEM 6

Before Apple programmers released System 5.0, they already had plans in store for further improvements to the system software. Apple representatives attending the A2-Central Summer Conference in July 1991 in Kansas City announced plans for a major update, System 6.0, which was expected for release in late 1991. It would take five 800K disks to hold the files for all of the planned enhancements that would make up the new system.

System 6.0.1 startup screen – Photo credit: personal

Also announced were plans for an Ethernet card (previously discussed) and a card to handle a SuperDrive, a high-density drive that could read 3.5-inch 800K and 400K disks, and could

---

10 Weishaar, Tom, "Apple Announces Faster IIgs". *A2-Central*, June 1989, Vol 5, No 5, pp 5.33-5.35.
11 Deatherage, Matt, "The Operating System", *The Apple II Guide*, (Cupertino, CA, Apple Computer, Inc., 1992), 111-113.
12 Doms, Dennis, "Miscellanea", *A2-Central* (December 1989), 5.83.
13 Doms, Dennis, "Miscellanea", *A2-Central* (December 1990), 6.84.
14 Doms, Dennis, "Miscellanea", *A2-Central*, (April 1991), 7.17-7.18.
15 Deatherage, Matt, "The Operating System", *The Apple II Guide*, (Cupertino, CA, Apple Computer, Inc., Fall 1990), 117-125.
16 Deatherage, Matt. "The Operating System", *The Apple II Guide*, (Cupertino, CA, Apple Computer, Inc., 1992), 111-113.

potentially read 720K and 1.44 MB MS-DOS disks, although no mention was made of support for those formats.

Apple IIGS power users were calling for the ability to use Macintosh HFS (Hierarchical Filing System) disks, as well as the older Apple II DOS 3.3 and Pascal formats. Although simple third-party translation programs existed that allowed transfer of files from Mac disks to ProDOS disks, these did not provide the same ease of use that would be offered by being able to simply mount the disks (as could be done with ProDOS and CD-ROM disks).

To these users, it sounded like a straightforward proposition, but the increased complexity of the Mac HFS directory structure made it a difficult task. Not only did the Mac disks contain more information about each file than did ProDOS disks, but the names of files on Mac disks (as on DOS 3.3 disks) could contain characters that were illegal for ProDOS file names.

To help with this problem, the new file system translators (FSTs) were designed to watch for potentially illegal filenames, and to make suggestions for alternate names that were legal. Apple software engineers had always made it clear to programmers clamoring for additional FSTs that such changes were more than just dropping the new FST into the SYSTEM/FST folder on a boot disk. Modifications were necessary throughout GS/OS to accommodate these new features, and the time needed to make these changes was becoming longer than originally planned.

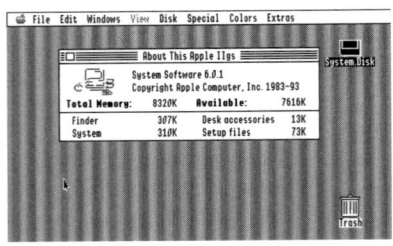

GS/OS 6.0.1 About this Apple IIGS – Photo credit: personal

To allow some improvements to be made available without waiting for them all, the system software engineers had divided tasks during 1990, putting the features that could be programmed most quickly onto a fast track that would allow them to be released as Version 5.0.3 later that year.

The other half of the team worked on the rest of the planned enhancements for what would become System 6.0. When 5.0.4 was completed, the entire team again came together to continue work on this upgrade. After fourteen months of hard work, they were finally ready to release GS/OS System 6.0 in March 1992.

New FSTs were released, providing full read and write access for Macintosh HFS disks, and read-only access for DOS 3.3 and Apple Pascal disks. Also provided were drivers to allow support of the Apple Scanner, the slot-based Apple II Memory Expansion card (which on the IIGS worked primarily as a RAM disk), and the Apple Tape Drive. The SCSI drivers were enhanced, and the Apple 5.25 disk driver was made faster. A new printer driver was included, to support the new Apple StyleWriter inkjet printer, and more large fonts were included.

Though the Apple IIGS Finder worked in System 5 and before, it needed some additional work to improve its performance and features. For this, Apple turned to a new person on the Apple II engineering team. Andy Nicholas had written the file compression and archive utilities *ShrinkIt* and *GS-ShrinkIt* while in college. After graduating he was hired to work on the Apple II Engineering team that was responsible for updating GS/OS.

Nicholas took the Finder from the earlier versions of GS/OS and completely redesigned it. He added a Windows menu, to make it easier to switch between windows that were buried under other windows. From this menu he also provided the option to arrange the windows into a staggered stack. For those using the IIGS with a hard drive, the new Finder also made it easier to tunnel down through various levels of folders, closing the higher-level folders to minimize desktop clutter.

There were several new applications that Apple included with System 6:

- *Archiver*, a hard-drive backup utility with a GUI interface. It could compress files, create an exact image of the drive, or just backup files.
- *synthLAB* was an application to demonstrate the capabilities of the MIDI Synth toolset. It allowed creation of new instruments, recording of custom MIDI sequences, or playback of music files.
- Apple also threw in a simple GS/OS text-editing program called Teach, which was capable of reading files in various formats, including plain ASCII, 8-bit *AppleWorks*, *AppleWorks GS*, and *MacWrite 5.0*. Teach did not save files in all of these formats, however—it saved files as styled text files (with fonts, margins, etc.), as plain ASCII files, or as Installer scripts.

System 6 added enhancements to media controls for devices such as videodisk players and CD drives. It included the Universal Access suite of controls for accommodation of computer users with disabilities. One feature, Sticky Keys, made it possible to hold down multiple keys (such as open-apple-P) one at a time. This feature was built into the ROM 03 Apple IIGS computer, but not on ROM 01; System 6 made it work on either model. It was activated by pressing the Shift key five times quickly.

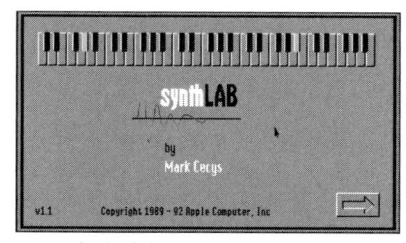

synthLAB splash screen – Photo credit: personal

MouseKeys allowed the keypad to move the mouse on the screen, while Video Keyboard displayed a keyboard on the screen which was clickable with the mouse pointer. CloseView zoomed in on areas of the screen on desktop GUI applications.

For System 6, the Control Panel New Desk Accessory (first introduced with System 5) was redesigned. Each Control Panel file was now its own NDA, and more than one could be open at a time.

Additional Control Panels added were Sounds (which allowed different pre-recorded sounds to be assigned to various system events), SetStart (to set the startup disk device), Media Control, Namer (to assign names to printers on an AppleTalk network), and one that allowed network booting directly into ProDOS 8 (particularly helpful in a school environment with a number of computers all linked together).[17]

ProDOS 8 was updated to v2.0 (followed shortly by v2.0.1), but was assembled using 65c02 opcodes, and so was usable only on the Apple IIGS, IIc and enhanced IIe. One of the changes in this version of ProDOS 8 allowed 8-bit programs access to as many as fourteen disk devices on a single slot. This made large, partitioned hard disks usable on older Apple II models.[18] ProDOS 8 v2.0.2 and 2.0.3 were the last revisions to be released by Apple, the latter accompanied by BASIC.SYSTEM 1.5.

The final version of GS/OS was 6.0.1, but its release was complicated by internal politics at Apple. Its story is connected with that of the final days of the Apple IIGS (which will be discussed later).

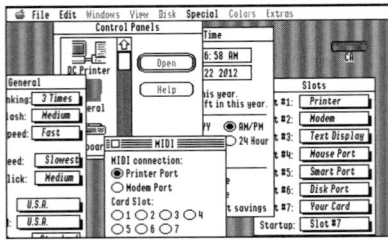

GS/OS 6.0.1 Control Panel NDA – Photo credit: personal

TIMELINE

The start dates for Apple DOS, ProDOS, and GS/OS:

Apple Pascal – *August 1979*

DOS 3.3 – *August 1980*

Apple CP/M – *March 1980*

Apple III SOS
– *September 1980 - April 1984*

ProDOS 1.0 – *October 1983*

ProDOS 8 v1.2 – *September 1986*

GS/OS 3.2 – *July 1988*

ProDOS 8 v1.7 – *August 1988*

GS/OS 4.0 – *September 1988*

ProDOS 8 v1.8 – *June 1989*

GS/OS 5.0 – *July 1989*

GS/OS 5.0.2 – *December 1989*

ProDOS 8 v1.9 – *August 1990*

---

17 Swihart, Tim, "What's New In System 6", *A2-Central* (February 1992), 8.1-8.5.
18 Deatherage, Matt. "The Operating System", *The Apple II Guide*, (Cupertino, CA, Apple Computer, Inc., 1992), 111-113.

ProDOS 16 v1.0
– *September 1986*

ProDOS 16 v1.1
– *December 1986*

ProDOS 8 v1.3 – *January 1987*

ProDOS 8 v1.4 – *April 1987*

GS/OS 2.0 – *May 1987*

GS/OS 3.1 – *December 1987*

ProDOS 8 v1.5 – *April 1988*

ProDOS 8 v1.6 – *June 1988*

GS/OS 5.0.3 – *December 1990*

GS/OS 5.0.4 – *February 1991*

ProDOS 8 v2.0 – *January 1992*

ProDOS 8 v2.0.1 – *March 1992*

GS/OS 6.0 – *March 1992*

ProDOS 8 v2.0.2
– *November 1992*

GS/OS 6.0.1 – *June 1993*

ProDOS 8 v2.0.3 – *June 1993*

CHAPTER 35

Hyperactivity

MACROS AND SCRIPTS

With the increase in sophistication of applications came a secondary level of programming. This extension was commonly called a macro, meaning that a single command accomplished several commands that ordinarily took more effort.

Early examples of macros were available in some DOS 3.3 utilities, where, for example, pressing Ctrl-C from the keyboard caused the word "CATALOG" to appear on the command line. In this example, a macro was used to save keystrokes and speed up repetitive activities. Similar macros were available for BASIC programmers, making a control-key sequence print out many of the common BASIC keywords, thus speeding code entry.

(This type of macro was different from macros used in some assemblers, such as Big Mac/Merlin and the Pascal assembler. In those assemblers, a macro was a new command that was defined to represent several standard assembly operation codes. This did not shorten the final resulting program, but made it possible to more easily enter repeated sequences of codes.)

Applications began to appear to take advantage of macro capability (either offered with the program or as a third-party add-on product). With time, some of these macro features became so complex that they evolved into programming languages in their own right. In fact, many of them were referred to as scripting languages, since they directed the function of a program, as a director uses a script to film a movie.

Scripts were most popular with telecommunications programs, where the process of logging onto a remote computer, downloading new messages, and uploading replies could be automated with a script that analyzed the responses from the other computer and took appropriate action. Scripts were also popular in programs like Apple Writer (with its WPL or Word Processing Language) and AppleWorks (via add-ons like KeyPlayer or UltraMacros)– each with its own method of automating repetitive tasks.

A LEAP IN COMPLEXITY

The environment for writing, compiling, and debugging programs evolved along with the applications created by those programs. Originally, the Apple II and other computers of the day were used in a command-line interface environment. This means that each command was typed one at a time, and sometimes batched together to simplify a repetitive process (as with EXEC files under Apple DOS).

Any program that was created with a command-line oriented language, such as BASIC, had to be started by typing the proper command from the keyboard. Misspell the word LOAD and it would stubbornly refuse to do what was intended, along with displaying an error message. The same command line was used for entering the lines of a BASIC program, or running the program. This method was used because it was what programmers of the day were accustomed to. Nearly every computer prior to the microcomputer revolution worked in the same way, even if it was entered using punched cards instead of a keyboard.

There were minor differences between computer languages, but none really changed the way in which people used computers (outside of research efforts at places like the Palo Alto Research Center) until the release of the Xerox Star in 1982, the Apple Lisa in 1983 and the Macintosh in 1984. These offered a radically different method of operating a computer.

Instead of typing each command, the user pointed to something on the screen and clicked on it using the mouse. Apple designers extended this concept to every application released with the Lisa and Macintosh. This new environment was called a graphic user interface (GUI), and used the concept of objects rather than typed commands.

To delete a file, it was not necessary to type DELETE PROGRAM. Instead, the user pointed to the picture (icon) representing the file and dragged it onto a picture of a trashcan. This desktop offered more complex commands chosen from menus. Those menus appeared in boxes called windows that pulled down like a window shade from command category names on a menu bar.

As the command line disappeared, so did traditional methods of handling program data. Words were still typed into a document on a word processor, but many of the features that set up margins, tabs, and page breaks were translated into graphic icons selected with the mouse. Eventually this progressed into the world of the programmer. The program code was entered much like a word processor, and the command to compile it into an executable program was now selected from the menu bar at the top of the screen.

HYPERTEXT

The term hypertext was created by *Computer Lib* author Ted Nelson, and referred to a method of allowing a user to move from one concept to another in a text document by linking the two concepts together.[1] The first type of program that used this concept was a simple text based one. Certain words were marked to indicate that other information about that word was available elsewhere. Moving a cursor to that word and pressing a key jumped to the additional facts.

For example, in an article about the history of music, the word "sonata" might be highlighted. Selecting this word jumped to another article that discussed sonatas in greater detail. When finished, the user could jump back over this link to the place where the original article left off.

In 1986 a remarkable program became available on the Macintosh that was, for a time, included with each Mac sold. *HyperCard* was a comprehensive system that used the idea of hypertext, plus it added a programming language that consisted of words and phrases as close to English as anything else previously available on a microcomputer. The HyperCard system took care of the details of how to draw boxes and buttons, and left it to the user to define where to put them and how to label them. And because of the language (which Apple called *HyperTalk*), user actions could do more than just move to a different screen (which the program called a card). It was possible to design simple databases, games, and much more using this system. Because it called a single part of an application a card, a collection of cards comprising an entire HyperCard application was called a stack.

Tutor-Tech, released in 1988 by Techware Corporation, was the first comprehensive hypertext system available for the Apple II series. It worked on 8-bit Apple II models, and was designed primarily for use in a classroom setting. Entirely graphics-based, it defined certain parts of the screen as buttons. Moving the pointer to a button area allowed the program to move to a different screen or caused something

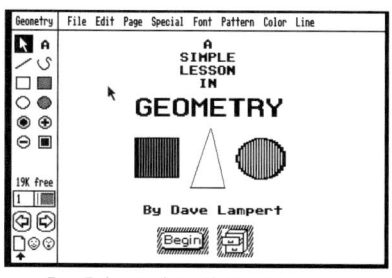

Tutor-Tech screenshot – Photo credit: personal

else to happen. As with any graphic interface, icons that represented certain functions were used to designate commands. For example, to exit the program, the user simply pointed to a picture of a door labeled EXIT.

With the release of the IIGS, the power was finally available in the Apple II world to create a similar product. But it didn't come first from Apple Computer; instead, Roger Wagner Publishing introduced a product called *HyperStudio* in May of 1989. This program used the super hi-res graphics modes accessi-

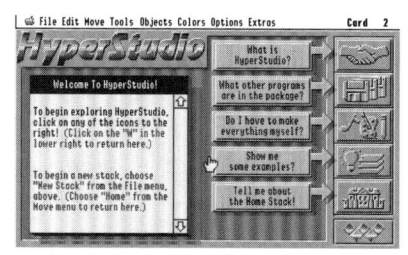

HyperStudio screen shot – Photo credit: personal

---

1 Doms, Dennis, "An Applesoft for the 1990's", *A2-Central* (March 1991), 7.09-7.13.

ble on the IIgs to create its own type of stacks. Like HyperCard on the Macintosh, HyperStudio used buttons and objects on the screen to direct movement through a stack application. It also included a plug-in peripheral card that made it possible to easily digitize sounds to use in stacks. Though more extensive than Tutor-Tech, it was not quite as flexible as HyperCard, since it lacked a true programming language.

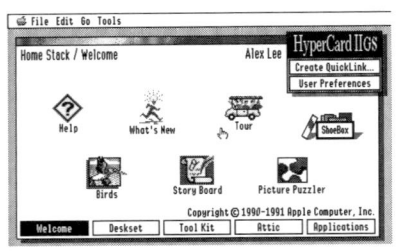

HyperCard IIgs screen shot – Photo credit: personal

In January 1991, Apple released *HyperCard IIgs*, a conversion of the Macintosh product. This finally allowed a fully programmable hypermedia environment on the IIgs. Later in the year Roger Wagner Publishing responded with an updated version of HyperStudio that also included a programming language similar to HyperTalk, which afforded more control over the stacks that were created.

Although neither of these products gave the user power over details of the computer system itself (as was possible with programs written in C or assembly language), it made it possible for a beginner to create programs that had outstanding graphics and sound without having to know exactly how the hardware produced these effects.

This, along with the flexibility of these products, led editor Dennis Doms in an *A2-Central* feature article to suggest that HyperCard IIgs (and now also possibly HyperStudio) would become the Applesoft of the 1990s; that is, an Apple IIgs user with HyperCard IIgs could create programs as easily as the Applesoft programmer of 1980 could do, but with far more attractive results. And had the Apple IIgs been allowed to survive with support and updates, that might have indeed been the end result.[2]

TIMELINE

HyperCard – *1986*

TutorTech – *1988*

HyperStudio – *May 1989*

HyperCard IIgs – *January 1991*

---

2 Doms, Dennis, "An Applesoft for the 1990's", *A2-Central* (March 1991), 7.09-7.13.

CHAPTER 36

Magazines on the Newsstand

A successful product often results in an entire subculture devoted to supporting and enhancing that product. The first publications serving the Apple II community were often created out of the efforts of a small number of individuals, working on their own. They had a specific focus and goal, and the reader base was compatible with that focus. And most limiting, the distribution of these homebrew magazines was handled by computer stores and subscriptions.

The continued popularity of the Apple II and the smaller magazines produced for it eventually caught the attention of national publishing houses. Seeing the monetary potential in producing similar magazines, and having the reach of national and international distribution, these publishers provided a service that the homebrew magazines could not—they could be purchased in places beyond a computer store, electronics shop, or subscription only. This broad availability brought computer information to the average person.

It was an advantage to the Apple II community, having additional sources of information on hand. It was, however, a great disadvantage to the pioneering publications that did not have the resources of a large company. The emergence of these newer magazines drew away advertising dollars that kept these earlier magazines alive, and likely hastened their demise.

A+ (Nov 1983 – May 1989)

Ziff-Davis had been involved in magazine publishing since its founding in 1927, often focusing on magazines that featured hobbies, including electronics. With the rise of the microcomputer in the late 1970s, magazines focused on this newest of hobbies were becoming more plentiful, and Ziff-Davis got involved. They purchased *Creative Computing* from founder David Ahl, and in November 1983 they entered the booming Apple II market with a new magazine, A+. Subtitled, "The Independent Guide For Apple Computing", its editor was Maggie Canon, who was formerly editor-in-chief of the weekly computer news magazine, *InfoWorld*.

In her initial editorial, Canon stated that the target reader was the "typical Apple user, whom marketing types like to refer to as an 'achiever'. An 'achiever' can be described as a man or woman in the age group of 18-45, who is using an

Apple computer for professional purposes... Professional users span the entire spectrum of the working world, from writing a manuscript to keeping the books to forecasting markets, from working at home to working in a large corporation." She went on to state that the focus of articles in A+ would be practical applications and how to use them, comparative reviews of products, departments focused on user groups, a place for questions and answers, news, and education.

Columns that regularly appeared in the magazine included "A+ Dispatches" (brief news stories), "Rescue Squad" (user help column), "That's Entertainment" (reviews of game software), "Apples at Work" (how businesses used computers), "Programming" (how to make use of programs, rather than teaching computer programming), "Telecommunications" (stories about ways to use a modem), "Product News" (information on new hardware and software products), and "A+ Directory" (classified ads). Later in its run, the magazine had a column called "Product All-Stars", a classified-style listing of popular software and hardware. By the early part of 1984, A+ had added a section in the magazine to focus on Macintosh news and products.

A+, November 1983, premier issue – Photo credit: personal

With the first issue of A+, the magazine also ran an advertisement for A+ *Disk Magazine*, a bimonthly collection of software for the Apple II. It was not directly related to the content of A+ magazine, but was considered another publication of Ziff-Davis. That disk magazine ran for a total of seven issues during 1984.[1]

Since competitor *inCider* had come to print earlier in the year, there was a rivalry of sorts between the two magazines while they were both being published—until they later merged into *inCider/A+*.

During the latter part of the A+ publishing run, Gary Little became its editor. He was responsible for the Binary II file archive format, and had written technical books about the Apple IIe and IIc. The editor that he replaced (who was the successor to Maggie Canon) had left to take a job with Apple Computer. Not long after he started, and just prior to the magazine's merger with *inCider*, Little was also hired away by Apple. It was felt by some subscribers that Little's short stint with A+ significantly improved the magazine, and they were saddened to see him go.

---

1   Effrron, Morris, editor of A+ Disk Magazine, in personal email to author, October 24, 2012.

When *Creative Computing* ceased publication in December 1985, subscribers found Ziff-Davis had transferred their remaining issues to A+. In 1989, the publisher chose to discontinue A+, and allowed it to merge with *inCider* magazine.

INCIDER (Jan 1983 – May 1989), INCIDER/A+ (Jun 1989 – Jul 1993)

Nearly a year before the appearance of A+, a new Apple II magazine had appeared on the newsstand. *inCider* was started by Wayne Green, who had published technical magazines for many years. One of the most well-known was the amateur radio magazine called 73, which he started in 1960. Becoming excited about the new microcomputer industry, Green started the influential *BYTE* magazine in September 1975. Because of the outcome of a divorce, he lost control of *BYTE* to his ex-wife, and responded by starting yet another new magazine, *Kilobaud* (later called *Kilobaud Microcomputing*, and then *Microcomputing*). He started a magazine for the TRS-80 computer (80-Micro) in 1980, and by 1983 decided to start a magazine that was focused on the Apple II.

inCider was not a programming magazine, but it did carry some type-in listings and had columns that answered reader's questions about programming. Columns carried in the magazine included "AppleWorks in Action" by Ruth Witkin; "Press Room" by Cynthia Field (which detailed ways to do desktop publishing with *Print Shop*, *Publish-It!*, *AppleWorks GS*, and *GraphicWriter*); "Bridging the Gap" by Gregg Keizer (discussing ways to help the Apple II and Macintosh work peaceably together); "Apple IIgs Basics" by Joe Abernathy (highlighting programming on the IIgs); and "Apple Clinic" (questions and answers about using Apple II computers).

inCider, Jan 1983, premier issue – Photo credit: personal

Transitions in the magazine began during its first year in print. In June 1983, Green sold his publishing company, Wayne Green, Inc., to CW Communications, Inc., which was itself a subsidiary of International Data Group (IDG), an international media organization. The change was not visible in the magazine until the February 1984 issue, when the masthead changed to indicate that it was now being published by Wayne Green Publishing Group, a member of CW Communications. The change in overall ownership provided a far wider distribution than was possible with Green's smaller company.

Starting in July 1984, the cover art was also changed. Instead of the stylized "inCider" that made the "C" look like an apple, and the subheading "Green's Apple Magazine", it was changed to read "inCider – The Apple II Journal." In subsequent years, the "Apple II Journal" subheading was dropped. Green also began to have less personal involvement in the magazine, with his editorial gradually changing over to a different editor-in-chief.

In 1989, IDG began its first move from traditional tools used to publish a magazine to desktop publishing with *QuarkXPress* on a Macintosh. The first magazine to receive this treatment was *inCider*, and it began with the December 1989 issue. The new art director for this project had been instructed to transition the art style in such a way as to be undetectable to the readership; the new layout was to look the same as the old layout, simply produced with newer tools.[2]

inCider/A+ July 1993, final issue – Photo credit: personal

As the Apple II market declined, so did available advertising dollars. This led Ziff-Davis to discontinue A+ and sell the subscriber list to *inCider* in 1989. Although the combination title "*inCider/A+*" was felt to be awkward, it was intended to retain the readers from both publications. According to former editor-in-chief Dan Muse, "Like any kind of merger, the A+ readers and the *inCider* readers were a little different—I think our readers tended to be more technical, and the A+ readers tended to be a little more trendy and into well-designed, slicker layouts than maybe we were doing as *inCider*. We tried to accommodate both by not losing our tech edge, but also tried to beef up some of our production values to make it a little more similar to what A+ was doing."[3]

In December 1990 the editors chose to broaden their audience by adding coverage of the Macintosh computer to the Apple II features. This was a highly unpopular move with Apple II loyalists, who already had quite enough of Apple Computer telling them to upgrade to a Mac. Polluting their Apple

---

2 Goode, Roger, as quoted by Lee, Alex, "Professional Desktop Publishing and the Apple II", *What Is The Apple IIGS?*, <www.whatisthe2gs.apple2.org.za/professional-desktop-publishing-and-the-apple-ii/>.

3 Muse, Dan, quoted in "An inCider's Perspective", *Juiced.GS* (June 2012), 4-8.

II publication with this younger sibling infuriated many, and they vowed to let their subscriptions expire. However, at this point in time there were few national Apple II publications remaining, and no others that appeared on the magazine racks at large newsstands (since *Nibble* had gone to subscription-only distribution). Apparently IDG as the publisher of *inCider/A+* felt that they couldn't survive without making some attempt to broaden their customer base by adding Mac content to combat a shrinking market. For several months afterward, the magazine shrunk in size, eventually going from a square-bound back to a stapled format. This shrinkage stabilized in early to mid 1992, and by late that year, *inCider/A+* was still in print.

However, rumors began to surface in October 1992 about plans by inCider/A+ to change to a format that would focus almost entirely on the Macintosh, with significantly less attention paid to the Apple II.[4] Initially, the plan called for inCider/A+ to cease under that name with the January 1993 issue, and it would reappear as just A+ in February 1993. Reasons cited for these changes were declining advertising revenue, and the hope that by changing focus to the Macintosh (particularly from the point of view of educators), they could continue.

Cameron Crotty, Associate Editor of *inCider/A+*, stated on the online service, GEnie, "*inCider/A+* is going primarily Macintosh. The shift will occur in February and will probably include a name change (not finalized). WE WILL CONTINUE TO COVER THE APPLE II FOR AS LONG AS IT REMAINS FEASIBLE. I cannot say (because I do not know) whether the coverage would be mixed in or in a separate section (input would be appreciated). With the shift in focus, we are also trying to enlarge the book..."

He further stated, "Right now, inCider/A+ has two choices: 1) stay with the Apple II and be dead in 6-8 months or 2) shift to the Mac and try to survive. We believe that there is a low-end Mac niche at least as large as our current circulation (perhaps larger), and that most of our readers (75% or more) will maintain their subscriptions (numbers from editorial surveys and such). We also believe that we can attract the advertising we need to survive by shifting to the Mac. We may be wrong. We may be dead in 6-8 months anyway. But a change has to be made. We cannot survive on our current course."

There was, of course, considerable discussion of this planned move via online services. Some advertisers, like Quality Computers, threatened to withdraw its advertising entirely if such a move took place. Perhaps it was because of statements like this, or perhaps Crotty spoke out without authority to do so. In any case, there was considerable back peddling on the announcements that began to appear. Joe Kohn (former chief sysop for the Apple II group on The Source) had been writing a column in *inCider/A+*. He stated

---

4   Weyhrich, Steven, "inCider Twists The Knife", *A2 News Digest* (October 1992).

that there had been no corporate decision to make any changes and previous statements should be disregarded.[5]

inCider/A+'s new editor-in-chief wrote an editorial for the February 1993 issue of the magazine. In his editorial, he took great pains to point out that the rumors were inaccurate from the beginning. Yes, with the March 1993 issue they had plans to redesign the layout of the magazine, and probably put the Mac content in a separate section, but he firmly stated that it would remain oriented to the Apple II.[6]

However, it was eventually clear that IDG would not continue producing a losing venture. *inCider*/A+ abruptly ceased publication with the July 1993 issue, with no announcement to subscribers until Quality Computers sent out a letter. Quality, which had decided by early 1993 to start its own Apple II magazine, arranged to take over *inCider*/A+'s remaining subscription base and fulfill it with their publication. IDG then planned to begin a new Macintosh publication called *Mac Computing*, utilizing most of the old *inCider*/A+ staff. However, after the first issue was produced and distributed, IDG changed its mind and terminated the project.[7]

With the disappearance of *inCider*/A+, so also ended the era of newsstand Apple II magazines.

THE APPLE IIGS BUYER'S GUIDE (Oct 1985 – Oct 1990)

Ted Leonsis, a venture capitalist, started Redgate Publishing in 1981. The company created a computer magazine called LIST, which printed hardware and software reviews for MS-DOS and CP/M computers (and a "list" of available software). When Steve Jobs was preparing to release the Macintosh, he was concerned that customers would have the impression that there were only a few applications available for it. Through the help of Macintosh marketing leader Guy Kawasaki at Apple, Leonsis met with Steve Jobs and agreed to make a version of his review magazine for the Mac. Jobs provided Leonsis with the names of all third-party companies who produced software for the Macintosh, and these companies were solicited for a list of their products to print for free in the magazine. Also included in that offer was the opportunity to run ads in this publication.

The first issue of *The Macintosh User's Guide* came out at about the same time as the Macintosh was released, shipping to all Apple retailers. Apple considered the publication so important to the company that it paid Redgate Publishing one dollar for every issue they printed, in essence subsidizing its launch.

---

5 Weyhrich, Steven, "More On The Changes At inCider...", *A2 News Digest* (November 1992).
6 Weyhrich, Steven, "inCider Removes The Knife", *A2 News Digest* (December 1992).
7 Weyhrich, Steven, "inCider: R.I.P.", *A2 News Digest* (June 1993).

The Macintosh Buyer's Guide was a great success for Redgate, and a year later the company began work on a similar magazine for Apple II users. Paul Pinella, who was Editor-in-chief at Redgate, was felt to be ideal to lead the project. He was an Apple II enthusiast who had owned an Apple II Plus long before he began to work at Redgate. He helped create *The Apple II Review* for Redgate, and stated in the first issue that the goal of the magazine was to look at the newest and best products available for the Apple II, and do hands-on reviews of them. Over fifty were reviewed for the first issue, including software, hardware, and accessories.

Though the goal was to run *The Apple II Review* as a quarterly publication, the second issue did not appear until the spring of 1986. Redgate had chosen a particularly difficult time in which to launch a new magazine, just after the 1984-85 era when several pioneering Apple II publications had gone out of business due to insufficient income from advertising (including *Softalk*, *Peelings II*, and *Apple Orchard*) and the onset of competition in 1983 from large publishers such as Ziff-Davis (A+) and CW Communications (*inCider*). One additional issue was released (Fall/Winter 1986) and then Redgate released a single issue of a magazine called *Apple IIGS Graphics & Sound* for Fall 1987.

Apple II Review, Fall 1985 cover
− Photo credit: Dr. Kenneth Buchholz <apple2online.com>

By this time, it was clear that Apple had positioned the Macintosh as its main focus, with the Apple II relegated mostly to the education market. Since the Apple IIGS was much more Mac-like, Pinella and the management at Redgate hoped there would be some co-development of similar products for the Mac and IIGS. This could potentially generate more advertising revenue to support an Apple IIGS magazine. They decided to name it *The Apple IIGS Buyer's Guide*, to connect with the existing *Macintosh Buyer's Guide*, and they planned to have a similar release schedule (quarterly), with the first issue appearing in Fall 1987 (along with the above-mentioned *Apple IIGS Graphics & Sound* magazine).

In his editorial in the first issue of this renamed magazine, Pinella was effusive over the potential of the year-old Apple IIGS. His goal, he said, was to focus on reviews of products that were unique to the IIGS. By the Spring 1989 issue, the magazine also included an extensive Apple IIGS Hardware and Software Directory. The editor changed starting with the Spring 1990 edition. The cover for most of its latter run boasted "More than 650 Product Listings and Descriptions". This sub-heading remained for the 14th and final issue, released in the Fall of 1990, which focused on educational software.

The demise of *The Apple* IIGS *Buyer's Guide* came about because the advertising market Redgate had hoped for never materialized. With some rare exceptions, makers of Macintosh products and Apple IIGS products usually did not come from the same company. Also, Apple was putting less and less of its company resources into the Apple IIGS, so Redgate had to withdraw and puts its efforts primarily on the Mac version of its guide.

In 1993, America Online acquired Redgate Publishing and took ownership of all of Redgate's magazines, whether in or out of print.[8]

Apple IIGS Buyer's Guide, Fall 1990 cover
– Photo credit: Dr. Kenneth Buchholz <apple2online.com>

TIMELINE

The start and end dates for major publisher magazines:

A+ – *November 1983 - May 1989*

inCider – *January 1983 - May 1989*

The Apple II Review – *September 1985 - September 1987*

The Apple IIGS Buyer's Guide – *September 1987 - October 1990*

inCider/A+ – *June 1989 - July 1993*

---

8   In 2010, Dr. Kenneth Buchholz, the administrator of the web site apple2online.com contacted America Online, and obtained permission to host high quality scans of The *Apple II Review* and *The Apple IIGS Buyer's Guide* on that site.

CHAPTER 37
Black Hat Contagions

As the computer revolution gained an ever-increased presence in the world, problems with computer viruses, worms, and Trojans frequently appeared in the news. Windows-based computers seemed to get the lion's share of these, and Mac OS X continued to have virtually no viruses or malware. Ongoing efforts were made to reduce the chances that computer users would unwittingly install these damaging pieces of software on their computers, and even web sites had to be designed with care.

In the first two decades after the microcomputer revolution was launched, the vector for viruses to attack a particular platform nearly always was through the disk operating system, and the same method was used to spread the virus. The disk system was a prime target, since it typically resided on the startup disk (a floppy disk or in later years a hard disk). It was an advantage to have a disk-based DOS, as it made it easy to deliver updates. The disadvantage was that it also smoothed the road for hiding malicious software in the DOS code. (For example, Commodore's PET, VIC-20, and Commodore 64 had the disk operating system in firmware, and so could not be updated—but for this reason they were almost completely immune to viruses.)

But outside of the major modern operating systems, it is generally not remembered that viruses have been around nearly as long as there have been microcomputers. In fact, the first record of a virus on a microcomputer was one that affected the Apple II.[1]

UNNAMED FIRST VIRUS

David Ferbrache in his book, *A Pathology Of Computer Viruses* (published in 1991 by Springer-Verlag), wrote that the first virus for a microcomputer appeared in 1980 on an Apple II. This happened shortly after Apple released DOS 3.3. According to Ferbrache, this virus was written for research purposes and never publicly released. The virus intercepted every executed

---

[1] The majority of the material presented in this chapter is excerpted (with permission) from an article written by Doug Cuff in the March/April 1994 issue of *II Alive* magazine, published by Quality Computers, with additional research done to clarify information that was not available when his article was originally written.

CATALOG command. It looked for a specific marker byte in the disk directory; if found, the virus then wrote the full DOS 3.3 code and the virus itself to the boot sectors of the disk while keeping track of how many times it had been copied. A second version, written by a friend of the original programmer, made the code more efficient and smaller in size. Neither virus was ever released into the wild.

ELK CLONER

In July 1981, the first named virus for an Apple II appeared. It was called *Elk Cloner*, and resided in the boot sectors of a DOS 3.3 floppy disk. This virus intercepted several DOS commands, including RUN, LOAD, BLOAD, and CATALOG. A counter byte was kept in the boot sectors, and depending on the count would execute various actions. It might infect a disk, reboot, print the version number of the virus, invert the screen, click the speaker, flash text, substitute letters on the text screen, crash the Monitor, or print out a quirky poem.

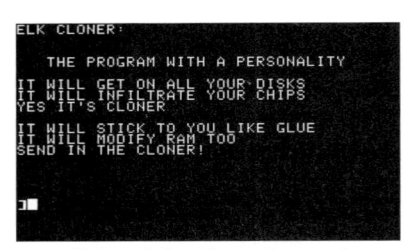

The Elk Cloner virus infected any disks that were not write-protected. It was written by Richard Skrenta, a ninth grade student in Pittsburgh, Pennsylvania, who wanted to play pranks on his Apple II-using classmates. The poem appeared if the user pressed the RESET key after the fiftieth use of an infected disk.[2, 3]

Elk Cloner display – Photo credit: personal

VIRUS 3 (DELLINGER VIRUS)

In December 1981, Joe Dellinger, an undergraduate at Texas A&M University, wrote the next documented virus for the Apple II. He was experimenting with DOS 3.3 to find out what was the minimum change necessary to make it copy itself, specifically to make DOS 3.3 itself act like a virus. He found that he only needed to change 16 bytes of code to make this happen. Unlike the Elk Cloner virus, Dellinger's virus code was written to do nothing more than copy itself. He wrote the virus code to execute when the CATALOG command was issued, much like the earliest unnamed virus previously mentioned.

Dellinger showed his work to some friends, and several of them began to work on improving the code. In early 1982, the group was done with "Virus

---

2 Paquette, Jeremy, "A History of Viruses", *Symantec*, <www.symantec.com/connect/articles/history-viruses>, accessed October 20, 2012.
3 Skrenta, Rich, "About", *Skrentablog*, <www.skrenta.com/about.html>, accessed May 29, 2013.

version 1". Although it infected disks as it was designed to do, it had some side effects. One of the unexpected side effects of the virus involved disks that had been modified in a way that was not directly supported by Apple. For example, the DOS 3.3 INIT command put the full version of DOS onto the first three tracks of a 5.25-inch floppy disk; third-party utilities made it possible to remove DOS from a disk (which made it unbootable), and thus gain back that space. Since Dellinger's virus specifically wrote DOS 3.3 and itself into that space on a disk, a disk modified to free those tracks would be unstable—files stored there would overwrite the image of DOS 3.3 (and the virus), and when the virus wrote DOS and itself to those tracks, files that were stored there became corrupted.

When the group completed "Virus version 2" several months later, it specifically checked for a disk modified to remove DOS, and if that was found, the virus disconnected itself from DOS and "committed suicide." This time no unwanted effects were found, and Dellinger tried it out on his own collection of DOS 3.3 disks (much like early medical researchers sometimes did their research on themselves). As he and his friends continued to experiment on it, their care at avoiding its spread to others became more lax, and Dellinger found that people at his graduate school were reporting that their pirated copies of the game Congo were not working properly; specifically, the hi-res graphics screen appeared smeared. On investigating, he found the virus had made its way onto those disks. In response, he wrote a program to clean the virus from infected disks.

When Dellinger took a closer look at the version 2 code, he found that it made DOS 3.3 one sector (256 bytes) larger than it should have been. Dellinger started working on version 3 of the virus, and planned that it should take up no extra space on a disk or in memory. Dellinger and his friends made use of small free areas in DOS 3.3, and created a version that behaved like version 1, but without the problems caused by version 2. By the time Dellinger graduated from Texas A&M in the fall of 1983, he checked out some disks belonging to friends. Some of those disks had version 3 of the virus on them, but since it was benign he made no effort to remove the virus. He moved on to Stanford University.

Dellinger later heard that some Apple II disks at the University of Illinois at Urbana/Champaign seemed to have a virus that was randomly formatting disks. Further investigation into this problem found that some disks seemed to have a form of partial immunity to the effects of the disk-formatting virus. Instead of being erased, these disks just crashed when booting, which prevented the disk initialization from happening. They found that these crashing disks had been previously infected with an undetected virus—Dellinger's Virus 3.[4]

---

4 Dellinger, Joe, "An early virus (Joe Dellinger)", *Yarchive.net*, <yarchive.net/risks/early_virus.html>, accessed October 20, 2012.

APPLE WORM

As part of research into the concept of self-modifying code, William R. Buckley and Dr. James Hauser of California Polytechnic State University at San Luis Obispo wrote a short 6502 assembly program in 1985. The BASIC program that loaded and executed this code was designed to work on an Apple II, but the machine code could run on any 6502-based computer.

Rather than a virus, which attaches itself to existing code to move from computer to computer, this program was considered to be an example of a worm—self-executing and able to change its address in order to execute at any location in memory. Unlike code that is written to be location independent (code that does not do any hard jumps to an address within itself), this worm would specifically modify hard addresses, in order to continue to run at whatever location to which it moved itself.

Buckley and Hauser wrote articles describing their work, published in both *Scientific American* and *Call-A.P.P.L.E.* in 1985. The Applesoft program printed in those articles loaded the 6502 instructions into the text screen memory, turned on graphics mode to allow the code to be visible as lo-res blocks, and executed one iteration of the code. Each subsequent keypress moved it forward in memory, which could be seen on the lo-res graphics screen, until it ran into the soft-switches past $C000, which would either cause a system crash or some other strange effect.

If the Apple Worm had been written to be destructive, it would have been necessary to find a way to execute it and keep it running through memory, replacing valid data with the worm itself, and defying efforts at removing it. Instead, the researchers wrote their sample code to simply illustrate what could be done with the concept.[5]

LEE'S DISKITIS

First appearing during 1984, *Lee's Diskitis* changed the text "DISK VOLUME" on a DOS 3.3 to read "LEE'S DISK" when a CATALOG was displayed. Every disk command caused the virus to check for its ID byte; if not found, it would write the entire infected operating system to the disk. Unlike Virus 3, this virus was less careful about non-standard DOS installations. If a disk with Diversi-DOS was in the disk drive, Lee's Diskitis damaged it so that it would crash when trying to boot that disk. Disks that had been modified to free up the first three tracks also became damaged, as described earlier.

To remove the virus, it was necessary to first power off the Apple II, boot a known clean disk, and then copy DOS from that disk to the infected disk.

---

5 Buckley, William R, and Hausesr, Dr. James, "Simple Worms", *Call-A.P.P.L.E.* (November 1986), 12-17.

Nibble magazine once published a program that copied DOS from one disk to another, which effectively disinfected a disk containing Lee's Diskitis,.

INIT VIRUS

Guy T. Rice was an Apple II utilities author and A2Pro sysop on GEnie. In 1988 he reported another virus that he had first encountered back in 1984. Unlike the viruses that existed before, this one, dubbed the *Init Virus*, was intentionally destructive. After a certain number of times that a disk had been booted, the DOS 3.3 INIT command was executed, erasing the disk and all its contents. The Init Virus differed from normal DOS 3.3 by only forty to fifty bytes. Online discussion of this virus when Rice brought it to light speculated that it might have been what was afflicting the computer lab at the University of Illinois at Urbana/Champaign when Joe Dellinger found his Virus 3 was providing a type of immunity to the problem. However, by that time no copies could be produced to examine and determine if this were true.

CYBERAIDS

With the proliferation of computer bulletin board systems across the country during the 1980s came a number of boards dedicated to hackers who were interested in cracking copy-protected software. This interest sometimes extended to breaking into secure computer systems, and even theft from those systems. Unlike many BBSes, which sought wide exposure, to attract greater and greater numbers of members, these underground hacker systems were intended to be quiet, private, and invitation-only. This was done to avoid attention, especially from authorities trying to track those who were breaking into secure systems.

The culture of these underground hacker groups was not unlike that of street gangs—the status of a hacker was based on the daring of his exploits. More sophisticated copy-protection systems required more skill to break. Therefore, the hacker who was successful in cracking a piece of software also wanted to call attention to his exploits. This was usually advertised by including a splash screen prominently featuring the codename of the hacker or hackers (such as "The Grand Vizier" or "Ma$ter Hackr$"), and possibly the name of a group or BBS. With time, some of these hackers turned their attention to ProDOS and looked at ways not to defeat copy protection (ProDOS was unprotected), but instead how to create a virus for it. And just like the vanity splash screens on cracked commercial software, the virus authors wanted to let the world know who had made this virus.

It took nearly five years after the introduction of ProDOS in 1983 for someone to attach a virus to it. The *CyberAIDS* virus burst upon the scene in 1988, and reproduced by attaching itself randomly to SYS files in the root directory of all mounted disks. The virus was sophisticated enough to bypass locked files by unlocking them first. However, write-protecting the disk kept the virus from altering those SYS files.

A2-Central's editor Dennis Doms disassembled an early version of CyberAIDS, and noted:

> *CyberAIDS attaches itself to the system files by moving 6 bytes from the start of the file to the end of the file, replacing these [6] bytes with a JMP [three bytes] and three consecutive $13 bytes used as an ID.*

These three $13 bytes near the beginning helped identify an infected file. The virus code itself was copied to the end of the file. When an infected file was executed, it jumped immediately to the CyberAIDS code, and then returned to normal execution of the SYS file.

Part of CyberAIDS worked at making copies of itself. Another part checked and updated a counter. Like other viruses that did not immediately make their presence known, CyberAIDS waited until that counter reached 16, at which point the virus deployed itself and displayed the vanity screen. The reason for the delay was likely to make it harder to pinpoint when the virus was acquired, which would delay its detection and eradication. In this sense, these viruses were not unlike biological viruses, which may be undetected for a while before they manifest symptoms.

The first version of the virus displayed a screen that indicated it was written by "The BOY!" and included a phone number with a New York State area code. The screen displayed the date only as a year, 1988. The second version was more completely dated April 13, 1988, and displayed a more detailed vanity screen.

Tom Weishaar of *A2-Central* posted this message on GEnie about the virus:

> *When a SYS file containing the CyberAIDS virus is executed, the disk drive will turn off and then back on again. While the drive spins the second time, CyberAids tries to replicate itself inside all of the online SYS files that are in root directories. It doesn't look in subdirectories, it doesn't (can't really) mess with write-protected disks, it doesn't attack locked SYS files, and it doesn't attack the PRODOS file. CyberAIDS also updates a counter stored in the last byte of the first block of the disk directory. When this counter reaches 16, CyberAIDS writes $FFs through the root directory of all online volumes and puts a message describing what's happening on the screen.*

He went on to say that Quality Software's *Bag Of Tricks 2* could recover the damaged directory. MR.FIXIT, a part of Glen Bredon's *ProSel* suite of utilities, could also recover subdirectories that were damaged. Weishaar's post also included an Applesoft program that could look at a file and determine whether or not it contained the virus.

One Apple II user who was hit by this virus found he was able to recover most of what he lost through the use of ProSel utilities. He found one of the infected SYS files and sent it to ProSel author Glen Bredon, who analyzed the file and created a program called *Apple Rx*, which could detect and remove the virus. The authors of the virus reportedly called Bredon on the phone and harassed him about his virus detection program.

CyberAIDS activation screen – Photo credit: personal

FESTERING HATE

Still hiding their identify, the same group who created CyberAIDS came back with a new version in June 1988. This one, called *Festering Hate*, worked in a similar fashion. It attached itself to SYS files on all available volumes. According to Glen Bredon, who disassembled the virus to see how it worked (and how to neutralize it), it only affected SYS files in the root directory. There was a random factor that determined whether the virus would replicate itself. Like CyberAIDS it could attack locked files, but still was unable to act on a disk that was write-protected. The virus spread from underground pirate BBSs through a telecommunication program called *ZLink*, which was a valid program but which had been infected with the virus.

The first reports on this virus found that the code for Festering Hate added about eight 512-byte blocks to the size of an infected SYS file. It would not attack the file PRODOS unless its name was changed to something else. The 4th through 6th bytes of a file with the virus were harder to identify than CyberAIDS. Instead of three bytes that were easy to see ("13 13 13") as had been the case with CyberAIDS, Festering Hate used different bytes that added up to $39.

The virus put a one-byte counter in block 0 of a disk that had infected files, and with each reboot of that disk it incremented the counter. This time the counter for this virus had to reach 25 before the virus started destroying the entire disk (not just the directory), which further delayed discovery. Presumably this allowed the virus to spread further before it deployed. Since it completely destroyed all the data, an infected disk could *not* be recovered.

While the disk destruction process was going on, a picture appeared on the hi-res screen. It displayed the words "Festering Hate", a picture of a needle injecting a diskette, and the Electronic Arts logo and company name. The picture then scrolled off the screen, and was replaced by this text screen:

```
[ANOP] -666-    FESTERING HATE    -666- [FUG]
==================================================
 The Good News: You now have a copy
    of one of the greatest programs
         that has ever been created!
 The Bad News: It's quite likely
    that it's the only program you now
         have in your possession.
==================================================
 Hey Glen! We sincerely hope our
    royalty checks are in the mail!
    Seeing how we're making you rich
    by providing a market for virus
         detection software!
==================================================
 Elect LORD DIGITAL as God committee!
==================================================
     >/> The Kool/Rad Alliance! <\<
     Rancid Grapefruit -- Cereal Killer
==================================================
 This program is made possible by a
    grant from Pig's Knuckle ELITE
    Research    Orderline 313/534-1466
======[(C) 1988 ELECTRONIC ARTS]========
```

The complaints in this screen that focused specifically on Bredon are ironic, as his updated Apple.Rx program was made available as a free download, as well as being available as part of his commercial ProSel utilities package. Similarly, ProLine BBS author Morgan Davis wrote and released the freeware *Virus.MD* to help diagnose and treat the problem. Most likely the complaints about Bredon were because he had been one of the first to find a solution for Festering Hate and make it widely available, which blunted the intended malicious effect of the virus. The sysops for the Apple II communities on CompuServe, GEnie, America Online, and Delphi began to use these and other programs to scan new uploads, to ensure they were virus-free before making them available for download. These viruses did not noticeably affect members of those online services.

The phone number listed was for private investigator John Maxfield, whose cases involved computer crime and hackers. Most likely, Maxfield's number was included simply to irritate him. What is unknown is whether Electronic Arts was mentioned because the virus authors liked or disliked the company.

Oddly enough, *2600 Magazine* (a hacker publication), published the source code for CyberAIDS and Festering Hate in the summer of 1988 in an article written by someone who called himself "The Plague of MOD." The article identified "Cereal Killer" as another name for Lord Digital (Patrick Karel Kroupa), who had a long history of involvement in underground hacking and phone phreaking groups, including The Apple Mafia, the Knights of Shadow, and the Legion of Doom. "Rancid Grapefruit" was also known as Dead Lord (Bruce Fancher), and was likewise a member of the Legion of Doom. With the publication of the *2600 Magazine* article, the virus authors' interest in writing further Apple II viruses appeared to have disappeared, and no further versions of these virus programs for the Apple II were released.[6]

LOAD RUNNER

The Apple IIGS *Load Runner* virus was first identified in July 1989. It was named after the famous Brøderbund game *Lode Runner* (though spelled differently), and was thought to have originated in France being spread through a IIGS fast disk copy program called *Speedy Smith*. This program used its own disk operating system, which made it hard to examine. Since the text screens displayed by the virus were in French, as were Speedy Smith's screens, it was thought to have originated in that country.

Load Runner affected the boot block only on 3.5-inch disks; it did not affect 5.25-inch disks or hard drives. The virus activated when an infected disk was booted on any odd-numbered day in October when the time in minutes was divisible by 8 (8, 16, 24, 32, 40, 48, and 56). It changed the screen color to an alarming red with white text, and printed a countdown message:

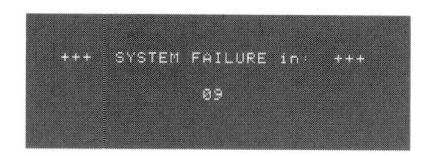

It took four seconds to count down from 9 to 0. The screen would then change to a green background, with the border color cycling through all colors, and the following text was displayed:

The computer then became unresponsive. Rebooting from another disk resulted in that disk also becoming infected.

On the displayed screen, the number in the upper left corner represented the number of copies the virus made of itself before it was triggered ($000F in this example would be a count of 15). The name "Lyon" was thought to refer to the city of Lyon, France. Translation of the text after the title read, "Artists

---

6   Sterling, Bruce, *The Hacker Crackdown: Law and Disorder on the Electronic Frontier* (Bantam Books, 1992).

Associates first non-destructive virus on IIGS, by Super Hacker & Shyrkan, of Masters Cracking Service, 1988, Lyon." It is not clear whether or not this was trying to call itself a non-destructive virus.

When an infected disk was booted, it copied itself to RAM on the IIGS, and then looked for 3.5-inch disks to which it could spread. If a 3.5-inch disk was inserted before the power was shut off, and the system was re-booted, that disk would also become infected. When the virus deployed and displayed its red countdown screen and green result screen, it had also wiped out the boot block of the disk in the 3.5-inch drive. It was significantly less destructive than CyberAIDS or Festering Hate, but it did cause damage nonetheless.

To remove the virus, it was necessary to completely power off the computer and restart with a clean disk. A simple reboot (by pressing Ctrl-open-apple-RESET) did not remove it from memory. Examining block 0 on a boot disk could help identify whether or not it was infected. If the first three bytes were "01 A9 50", the Load Runner virus was likely on that disk.

Besides Glen Bredon's Apple.Rx and Morgan Davis' Virus MD programs, Vitesse of La Puente, California sold a program called *Exorciser* that could be used to find and eliminate this and other known viruses. Neil Parker wrote a freeware program, *VIRUS.KILLER*, which checked the memory for the virus, and then examined disks to look for the infection and remove it if found.

BURP

In late 1989 a new virus for the Apple II appeared, though it seems to have not spread beyond the borders of Texas. Anti-virus software author Glen Bredon was notified of it, and added detection of this virus to his Apple.Rx program. *BURP* attached itself to all SYS files it could find on any disk volume that was currently mounted (CyberAIDS and Festering Hate limited their activity to a single SYS file). Also, BURP recursively examined subdirectories and attached itself to SYS files it found there.

When the BURP virus activated, it destroyed volume directories and then renamed the damaged disk to "BURP!"

BLACKOUT

The Apple IIGS virus known as Blackout also went by the names *Apocalypse I* and *Apocalypse II*. It was similar to Load Runner because the only types of disks affected were 3.5-inch disks.

When activated, Blackout made it look as if the IIGS was not working at all. There was no beep when starting, and the screen display remained blank. Even the disk drives did not make any noise. When these symptoms occurred, it meant Blackout had made changes to the Control Panel settings, changing the background and text color to black (which was ordinarily not allowed by the Control Panel), moving the sound volume to zero, and changing the startup disk to "ROM Disk", which usually had no bootable volume at all. Since these settings were stored in the Battery RAM, the changes lasted through a reboot, whether a cold boot (from power off) or a warm boot.

It was easy to return settings to normal, if a IIGS user realized that Blackout was the cause of the problem. To do this, it was necessary to power on while holding down the Control and Option key. Though not visible, a screen was displayed at this point that allowed three choices: pressing "1" jumped to the Control Panel, pressing "2" or to set the system standards to 60 hertz or 50 hertz, and pressing "3" continued starting the system. Pressing the number "2" at this point changed all of the Control Panel settings to their defaults (for 60 hertz operation), which restored the proper screen colors, sound volume, and "Scan" as the startup slot.[7]

CONCLUSION

When Steve Wozniak designed the Apple-1, the Apple II, and the Disk II, there was no concept of security issues for the personal computer platform. The computing world at that time was much like a small town, where everybody (for the most part) trusted each other, and nobody locked their doors. In fact, there was not much reason to lock the doors because there wasn't anything of value to steal. But like a town that grows, security became important as the number of Apple II owners increased, and the viruses mentioned in this chapter appeared. However, it was not something that Apple addressed (the problem was not widespread enough to warrant such action), but rather it was dealt with by applying a fix after an act of vandalism (much like fixing damage caused by a burglar, but not thinking of putting a lock on the door to prevent future burglaries).

Even on the Apple IIGS and its more sophisticated system software, security was still not a big enough problem to warrant security software beyond those previously mentioned programs. They could scan for known viruses, but were not sophisticated enough to detect suspicious activity by an unknown virus.

However, further virus detection turned out to be unnecessary. By the time CyberAIDS, Festering Hate, Load Runner, and Blackout had come and gone, the Apple II and IIGS platform appeared to have been abandoned as a target for authors of viruses and other malware, and nothing further appeared. Those interested in writing viruses had apparently moved on to the greener fields with larger numbers of potential victims (and greater glory for

---

7 Cuff, Douglas, "Infected: A Guide To The Early Diagnosis And Cure Of Apple II Viruses", *II Alive*, (March/April 1994), 28-33.

the hackers) found in the MS-DOS and Windows platforms, and to a lesser extent, the Macintosh. Interestingly, even the Amiga and Atari ST computers, which were released in 1985 (a year before the Apple IIGS) were a much greater target for viruses in their day. In many cases, virus authors were likely to be teenagers who had a lot of time on their hands, little concern for the effects of a virus on others, and owned a computer they could afford (something less expensive than an Apple II or IIGS).

TIMELINE

Unnamed First Virus – *1980*
Elk Cloner – *July 1981*
Virus 3 – *December 1981 - 1983*
Lee's Diskitis – *1984*
Init Virus – *1984*
Apple Worm – *1985*

CyberAIDS – *April 1988*
Festering Hate – *June 1988*
Load Runner – *July 1989*
BURP Virus – *October 1989*
Blackout – *c. 1990*

CHAPTER 38
BASIC Evolves

After Applesoft II was released in May 1978, no major changes were made to the language thereafter. Some slight adjustments were made to accommodate updates to the Apple II hardware with the introduction of the Apple IIe and later models, but actual updates or modifications to the language did not happen.

This does not mean, however, that Applesoft became of no consequence to the platform. Its true importance was so great that it became a negotiating point between Apple and Microsoft during the 1980s. And BASIC itself eventually appeared on the Apple II platform in more advanced forms from other companies.

APPLESOFT TWEAKS

Applesoft in the original IIe was unchanged from the II Plus version. When the compact Apple IIc was introduced in 1984, however, Apple's programmers had cautiously made a few improvements to the language:

- Input processing was changed to allow lowercase entry of Applesoft commands (they were translated into uppercase)

- Screen output commands (such as PRINT, TAB, and HTAB) were modified to properly handle the 80-column screen

- Program lines (when listed) were changed to begin in column 2, making screen editing easier

- All of the cassette tape routines (LOAD, SAVE, SHLOAD, STORE, and RECALL) were removed, since the hardware did not support cassette I/O. The keywords were still in the token table, but now pointed to the same memory vector as the ampersand ("&") command.

They also patched the lo-res graphics commands (GR, HLIN, VLIN, PLOT, and SCRN) to work with double lo-res graphics. However, a bug was introduced that allowed plotting vertically to areas outside of the double lo-res graphics screen, which would land right in the beginning of the $800 space where the Applesoft program text was located (similar to the PLOT bug in Applesoft I).

> When the Apple IIe Enhanced ROMs were made available, Applesoft in those ROMs had undergone some similar modifications. All the above IIc changes were added, with the exception that double lo-res graphics capability was not added (lack of ROM space), and the cassette I/O commands were not removed (since the cassette input and output port was still present).
>
> The version of Applesoft on the Apple IIgs closely resembled the Apple IIc variant, the only exception being a fix of the double lo-res PLOT bug. However, a bug in the SCRN function that applied to double lo-res mode was *not* fixed. No additional changes to Applesoft beyond those in the IIc version appeared in the Apple IIc Plus.
>
> The manuals written for Applesoft II were far more comprehensive than either the older "Blue Book" or Jef Raskin's Integer BASIC tutorial. It gave not only programming examples for each of the commands, but included information about the various ways in which each Applesoft statement could be used. It also mentioned some of the differences between Applesoft and Integer BASIC (for those who wanted to convert their older programs), and gave a little information about the internals of Applesoft to aid in creating machine language additions to the language.

APPLESOFT – THE LICENSING DEADLINE

A significant part of the Applesoft story occurred in March of 1985. At this time, Apple was still struggling to market the new Macintosh and Lisa computers to sell enough units to become profitable on their own. The company depended heavily on the continued strong sales of the Apple II line, specifically the Apple IIe and IIc computers. An ominous event was looming on the horizon, however, and it was one more way in which Apple and Microsoft were beginning to come into conflict with one another.

The eight-year license on Applesoft BASIC (which was actually Microsoft's old 6502 BASIC modified by Randy Wigginton) was due to expire in 1985. If Apple could not renew the license they could no longer include the same BASIC with the Apple II line, causing new Apple II computers to become incompatible with a large body of existing software.

By this time, an Apple II was practically defined by the existence of Applesoft in ROM; there would be no more Apple II without Applesoft. It would be unthinkable to revert back to the product that Apple *did* own (Integer BASIC) at that late date. And without the Apple II to provide a steady income while the Macintosh market slowly expanded, there just might be no more Apple Computer.

Back in 1977 when Apple was granted the eight-year license for Microsoft's 6502 BASIC, Microsoft was inexperienced and in a much tighter situation financially. By 1985, however, they knew Apple was dependent on Applesoft and they could expect much more in return. However, rather than proposing a financial deal, Microsoft offered to swap a second eight-year license for Applesoft BASIC in exchange for something that Bill Gates had his eye on: MacBASIC.

This product had been in development at Apple for years, and progress was slow. But Microsoft had built its original business on supplying BASIC for every computer, and to be denied a foothold on the Macintosh was unacceptable to Bill Gates. In exchange for a renewal of the Applesoft license, Steve Jobs had no choice but to sell the source code for MacBASIC to Microsoft (for only one dollar).

Applesoft survived, but Apple probably got the better end of the deal. Unlike the Apple II, which included the language on each computer sold, MacBASIC was sold as a separate product for the Mac. As a result, its penetration to the Mac market was far lower. Furthermore, BASIC on the Macintosh (and MS-DOS computers) never really turned out to be important in the same way that BASIC was in the 1970s and early 1980s.

Even Gates admitted that the deal for Applesoft's renewal was not the smartest decision he had ever made. Microsoft could have demanded a high price for Applesoft and Apple would have had no choice but to pay it to them.[1, 2]

APPLESOFT – THE LEGACY

Overall, the importance of Applesoft as the key to productivity on the Apple II cannot be overstated. Following the release of the Apple II Plus in 1979, every variety of Apple II contained Applesoft in virtually an unchanged form. This made it possible for anybody to write programs that all other Apple II users could use, since the language did not have to be purchased or added. If there were thousands of Integer BASIC programs written during the two years when the Integer BASIC Apple II was the only available choice, there were hundreds of thousands of Applesoft programs that appeared in the years following. Even in its later years, it was not uncommon for an application to include a configuration module written in Applesoft using the disk commands available with BASIC.SYSTEM in ProDOS. It was often faster to write such a program in BASIC, and the author knew without a doubt that his customer would be able to run it.

APPLESOFT 3?

In 1979 there were rumors at the third West Coast Computer Faire about an enhancement to Applesoft II that was in the works at Apple. Those circu-

---

1 Manes, Stephen, and Paul Andrews, *Gates* (New York: Doubleday 1993), 278-280.
2 Hertzfeld, Andy, "MacBasic", *Folklore.org*, <www.folklore.org/StoryView.py?project=Macintosh&story=MacBasic.txt>, retrieved Mar 2, 2013

lating the rumors named it Applesoft 3, and had heard that it would be as much of an enhancement over Applesoft II as that version was to Applesoft I. Supposedly it was intended to merge DOS and BASIC, and would include such powerful functions as IF-THEN-ELSE, PRINT USING, WINDOW, and VIEW PORT. It was predicted to be a RAM version only, occupying about 24K of disk space.

Inside Apple headquarters, there had indeed been a move to create a better Applesoft, starting in late 1978. Internally it was called Basic III (or Basic ///), and was indeed RAM-based, with the additional features mentioned above. This more powerful revision of Applesoft II was originally intended for the Apple II, although that would soon change.

When the Apple III project was getting far enough along to start planning a shipping date of March 1980, they found that Pascal for the Apple III would not be ready on time. It was decided to take Basic III, which was working well on the Apple II in a beta form, and modify it to work on the Apple III.

Donn Denman was hired for the Apple III team to do this conversion. He programmed the changes using a 6502 cross-assembler running on a PolyMorphic Poly-88 computer (an Altair clone). He collaborated with Taylor Pohlman, who had much experience with BASIC. They produced what became Business Basic on the Apple III, and the original code never became a product on the Apple II.[3, 4]

Coincidentally, the work done on Business Basic was later revived in the attempt to create *GS Basic* for the Apple IIGS.

A comparison of the source code for Business Basic and Applesoft shows that they share much of the same code. This confirms that Applesoft (or, really, Microsoft's 6502 BASIC) is at the core of this Apple III language. It even contains the same Microsoft Easter egg (the company's encoded name) as in Applesoft, at the same relative location (after the definitions of powers of pi).

BASIC EXTENDERS AND OTHER BASICS

On the 8-bit Apple II models, several utilities were created to extend the usability of Applesoft and overcome some of its limitations.

One of these limitations was Applesoft's slow execution speed. In response, the software company Beagle Bros sold a utility in 1986 called the *Beagle Compiler*. Written by Beagle programmer Alan Bird, it took an Applesoft program and created an executable binary program that ran just like the original.

---

3 Aldrich, Darrell. "The Computer Faire And The Apple", *PEEKing At Call-A.P.P.L.E.* (Seattle, Washington, Vol. 2, 1979), 158.
4 Pohlman, Taylor, "The Apple III and Business Basic", *Phase //// Conference*, Wheaton, IL, October 1987.

This binary ran much faster than the original, though some programs could not take advantage of it due to memory constraints. Also, it could not speed up floating-point calculations (trigonometry and logarithmic functions, division, and the rounding function). On the whole, however, it was fast. One reviewer claimed the compiler could speed up programs by five to fifteen times.[5]

MD-BASIC

Another method of optimizing Applesoft was MD-BASIC, sold for $89.95 by Morgan Davis Group. Davis wrote it to speed up his *Proline* bulletin board software. MD-BASIC took an Applesoft program and created a highly optimized version of it that ran on any Apple II. Written in C, the MD-BASIC optimizer ran only on the Apple IIGS, but the programs it created could run on any Apple II.

Due to the increased memory available on the IIGS development environment, more features were incorporated into the language. MD-BASIC allowed logical statements that did not come naturally in Applesoft, such as IF-THEN-ELSE and WHILE-WEND statements. It also allowed meaningful variable names (using more than two significant characters), did not require line numbers, and had named subroutines. The BASIC program could be written and designed in a standard word processor, with as much commentary as desired.[6]

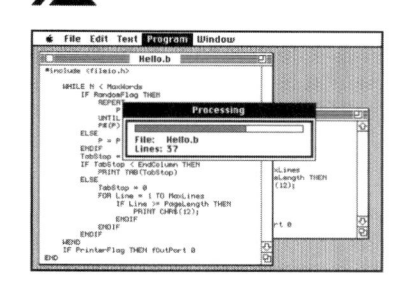

MD-BASIC manual cover - Photo credit: personal

AC/BASIC

Applesoft on the Apple IIGS was virtually the same ROM-based language that appeared on the Apple II Plus back in 1979, with all of the memory limitations of those early models. It utilized the lowest 48K of RAM and could not make use of the extended memory on the IIGS. For those who wanted to program in BASIC and surpass these limitations, other options became available within two years of the release of the IIGS.

In February 1988, Absoft released AC/BASIC, a 16-bit BASIC for the Apple IIGS, selling for $125. It was a compiled BASIC, and was almost completely compatible with versions of *Microsoft BASIC*, as well as Absoft's AC/BASIC for the Commodore Amiga. Like other modern BASIC languages, it did not require line numbers, and allowed access to IIGS graphics, sound,

---

5 Shapiro, Phil, "Ask Uncle DOS", *Open-Apple* (August 1988), 4.55-4.56.
6 Davis, Morgan, "MD-BASIC", *Morgan Davis*, <www.morgandavis.net/blog/2009/08/09/md-basic/>, accessed October 20, 2012.

and GUI interface elements. It worked under the APW (Apple Programmer's Workshop) editor.

GS BASIC

Developed at Apple by John Arkley, the ill-fated *GS BASIC* for the Apple IIGS was an interpreted BASIC capable of accessing the advanced features of the IIGS. It was derived from Apple III Business BASIC, though the original work on it was done through a contract with an outside company, Regent Systems. Arkley began to adapt it for the IIGS in June 1986, and by November he had a functioning version.

One of the challenges he had to overcome was making this interpreted language properly interact with the Apple IIGS toolbox. Since it was modeled off of Business BASIC, it offered more sophisticated data file read and write (all Applesoft could do was save and load text, and translate that text into numbers), and it had more advanced commands such as DO-WHILE and UNTIL options. It was actually much closer to newer versions of Microsoft BASIC than it was to the ten-year-old Applesoft language.[7]

During the time when GS BASIC was being developed, the Macintosh was finally beginning to gain some traction in the marketplace. Since management at Apple was putting most of its efforts into promoting the Mac, the resources designated for the Apple II continued to fall. One of the victims of this was GS BASIC. Although it was never officially released beyond beta copies sent out to developers, some of these have survived. A comment made by one user who tried it out years later mentioned how slow it was compared to Applesoft. A simple program that used a FOR/NEXT loop to count from 1 to 10,000 took four seconds to run under Applesoft, but took 43 seconds to run under GS BASIC. The explanation was that the language made heavy use of Apple's SANE routines (Standard Apple Numerics Environment) on the IIGS. Although the SANE package offered significantly higher precision floating-point math, in many side-by-side comparisons, Applesoft ran faster. (Certainly for a simple counting loop, high precision math was unnecessary and overkill.)[8]

Micol Advanced BASIC

Micol Systems released *Micol Advanced BASIC* for $145 in November 1988. It worked much like Applesoft, and did not have the steeper learning curve of other versions of BASIC. It was a compiled BASIC, meaning it ran faster, and as with other BASIC languages offered at this time, line numbers were optional.

---

7 Arkley, John, "Real Time Conference: GS BASIC", A2Pro Roundtable, *GEnie*, access date unknown.
8 Chan, Thye, "GS BASIC", *Newgroups.derkeller.com*, accessed September 10, 2007.

It offered named procedures and more structured loop commands, a CASE statement, a PRINT USING command, and could support strings as long as 1,023 characters. It worked on the Apple IIGS, and could use all of the available IIGS RAM. Enhancement and bug-fixing on the language continued until 1994.

GSoft BASIC

BASIC beyond Applesoft on the Apple IIGS was not a popular option with casual programmers. The ease of use and inclusion of Applesoft made it the first go-to language for quick and easy projects. If programmers wanted a powerful language, they turned to Pascal, and, increasingly, to C. As a result of this, by 1992 most of the IIGS-specific BASIC programming languages were no longer available or supported.

GS BASIC had died on the vine at Apple, having never moved beyond a beta release for developers. AC/BASIC and another product, *TML BASIC*, did not stay on the market for very long. Micol Advanced BASIC was still available in 1992, but it did not support access to the Apple IIGS toolbox, and did not have PEEK, POKE, or CALL commands or more modern equivalents.[9]

After Hayden Publishing decided to get out of the software business in 1984, Mike Westerfield was able to regain control of his ORCA/M assembler. He immediately formed his own company, The Byte Works, to continue to upgrade and improve his assembler. Ultimately, he produced several programming languages for the Apple IIGS during the late 1980s and into the 1990s. The last language that he added to his stable of products was *GSoft BASIC*.

Westerfield released his product in August 1998, six years after Apple stopped selling the IIGS. It was an interpreted BASIC, and was more like Applesoft than most other similar languages, with additional features that took if far beyond the capabilities of that twenty-year-old language. It could run with line numbers like classic BASIC, or it could run in the same program editor without line numbers as any other Byte Works language. It also offered access to the IIGS Toolbox (code built into the ROM of the computer), which the previous BASIC compilers did not.

GSoft BASIC initially sold for $60, and the company also marketed two separate reference books for the language. For those who didn't want to spend the money, The Byte Works also offered *FREE.GSOFT*, a scaled down version of the language. Westerfield released updates in November 1998 to version 1.1, and in February 1999 updated it again to version 1.2. The Byte Works also sold a course on programming in GSoft BASIC in 1999.[10]

---

9   Deatherage, Matt, "Amplifications and Corrections", Ask Uncle DOS, *A2-Central* (November 1992), 8.78.
10 Weishaar, Tom, "A Month of Firsts", *Open-Apple* (March 1988), 4.9.

In 2011, Westerfield released GSoft BASIC as freeware. At the same time he began to sell a product called *techBASIC* for iOS, designed to run on the iPhone, iPad, and iPod touch. The techBASIC language was derived from GSoft BASIC, and added matrix operations which most versions of BASIC had neglected, though it was part of the original BASIC language description when it was created in 1964.

TIMELINE

Integer BASIC – *June 1977*

Applesoft I – *January 1978*

Applesoft II – *May 1978*

Applesoft IIc – *April 1984*

Applesoft IIe Enhanced – *March 1985*

GS BASIC – *1987*

AC-BASIC – *February 1988*

Micol Advanced BASIC – *November 1988*

MD-BASIC – *1993*

GSoft BASIC – *August 1998*

CHAPTER 39

Hardware for the Next Generation

Advancements in hardware continued in the computer world after the Macintosh and Apple IIc were released in 1984, and all models of the Apple II that came out afterwards would benefit from this new technology. From video and sound to accelerators and printers, products became available to help keep up with the rest of the computing world. When the IIGS was released in 1986, hardware makers began work on a whole new batch of products.

VIDEO CARDS

When the Apple IIe was released, with its RAM-based method of displaying 80 columns of text, nearly all the older 80-column cards disappeared from the market. By the early 1990s, only Applied Engineering produced a card for those remaining II and II Plus users who wanted an 80-column display.

Apple II Video Overlay Card

In 1989, Apple Computer released the Apple II Video Overlay Card. This card made it possible to display screen images from an Apple IIe or IIGS onto video from other sources. The combined real-time video output could be displayed on a monitor and recorded onto a VCR. It included *VideoMix*, an application to manage the merged images. The result was advertised as being broadcast quality (for that era), although it was marketed primarily to schools for creating student video presentations.

Apple II Video Overlay Card demo – Photo credit: screen shot from Apple Computer video, "Welcome To The World of the Apple II Video Overlay Card"

Second Sight

Sequential Systems began work in 1994 on a new video card, which they called the Second Sight card. The world of Apple II developers had shrunk by that time, and it was not uncommon for people from different companies to help each other out. Andrew Vogan (of CV Technology) and Joe Yandrofski (of Sequential Systems) designed the card, with firmware written by two additional Sequential programmers. Though it was also compatible with the Apple IIe, the target audience for this card consisted of Apple IIGS owners, for whom Apple had stopped manufacturing the necessary RGB monitors. The Second Sight card was intended to interface with VGA or SVGA monitors, which were plentiful in the PC world. It was designed to handle all of the standard graphics modes of the IIGS, as well as some of the text and video modes supported by SVGA monitors (although existing Apple IIGS software would not work with these special SVGA modes). Furthermore, it could take video display on the IIGS that did not look very good on RGB and make it look much cleaner.

Released in June 1995, the card sold for $199.95, and over the next three years Sequential sold over 400 cards to dedicated Apple IIGS users who wanted to make use of SVGA monitors. A last run of the cards was planned in the late 1990s, and then it disappeared from the market.

SCANNERS

A common theme from the early days of microcomputing was finding a way to import things from the paper world into the digital world of the computer. One method to import digital images into a computer was to scan them. In 1990 an unnamed company in Japan released a hand-held scanner. It worked by illuminating the document to be scanned with an array of green LEDs (light-emitting diodes), and used an optical sensor to pick up the image and transmit it back to the computer, where the image was processed and displayed. The hardware was licensed to a number of companies in the US who released it under their own name. Logitech sold it as the ScanMan 32 for the Windows and Macintosh markets; Datel named it the GeniScan GS4500 Hand Scanner for the Amiga; and two Apple II companies licensed it for that platform under their own product name.

In February 1990, Vitesse released it as the Quickie hand scanner, selling it for $199. Thunderware sold the same device as the LightningScan for the Mac, and LightningScan GS for the Apple IIGS. To use this device, a document was placed in the included plastic tray, and then the scanner was pulled down first the left side and then the right side of the document. The software could then reassemble it into a single image.

Later, Vitesse sold *InWords* for $75—software that could perform OCR (optical character recognition), making it possible to change a scanned document into a text file.

The LightningScan GS offered the same scanning options as did the Quickie. The primary difference lay in the software used to process the scanned image. A comparison revealed that the LightningScan software favored photograph scans, while the Quickie was better at scanning line art.[1]

In 1994, Vitesse released Quickie-C, a $99 Apple IIGS NDA (New Desk Accessory) that allowed color scanning with the Quickie scanner. However, the software was reputedly unstable and did not work well. In fact, most users believed that the earlier version of the Quickie software worked better than later versions.[2, 3]

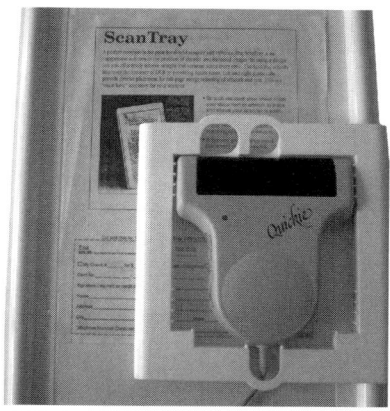

Quickie hand scanner with plastic tray used to secure the page being scanned – Photo credit: François Michaud

SOUND CARDS

Applied Engineering, which had a history of creating sound cards for the Apple II, released the Sonic Blaster card for the Apple IIGS in 1989 for $129. It was a stereo card for both output and input of audio. The Audio Animator released the same year offered all of Sonic Blaster's features as well as MIDI input/output, for $239.

In 1993, ECON Technologies created the SoundMeister card for the IIGS, which offered stereo sound, line and amplified outputs, and microphone and line level input (for recording and digitizing sound). The company had planned on a SoundMeister Pro version, but it turned out to be more expensive to develop and sell than ECON felt it could risk, and in December 1993 they made an official announcement that the project had been cancelled.

MEMORY EXPANSION

The release of the Apple IIGS provided yet another opportunity for larger RAM cards sold by third-party companies. Apple offered its own Apple IIGS Memory Expansion Card, but started at 256K and topped out at just 1 MB of storage. Although other companies produced memory cards, Applied Engi-

---

1 Kohn, Joe, "Which do YOU like better, Quickie or Lightning scan?" in comp.sys.apple2 posted September 1, 1997; Internet.
2 Gentry, W. Scott (moderator), "Vitesse, Inc. – Quickie Hand Scanner", Apple II Art & Graphics Forum, America Online, August 10, 1990, transcript, <mirrors.apple2.org.za/apple.cabi.net/FAQs.and.INFO/A2.AOL.Collectives/GRAPHICS/AGR081090.TXT>
3 Gentry, W. Scott (moderator), "Doug Penney and Brian Smith of Thunderware, Inc, – LightningScan GS", Apple II Art & Graphics Forum, America Online, April 20, 1990, transcript, <mirrors.apple2.org.za/apple.cabi.net/FAQs.and.INFO/A2.AOL.Collectives/GRAPHICS/AGRLOG.4.20.90.txt>

neering was again at the forefront in 1987 with two cards, the GS-RAM (up to 1.5 MB for $379) and GS-RAM Ultra (up to 4 MB for $1,959). By 1990 they began offering an additional card, the GS-RAM Plus, which raised the maximum capacity to 6 megabytes.

As the price of RAM dropped, other companies sold memory cards for the IIGS, including the Sirium RAM IIGS, CV Technology, and Sequential Systems RAM-GS, in 4 MB and 8 MB sizes. By the latter half of the 1990s, these cards could be purchased for under $300.

COPROCESSORS

After the original success of the Microsoft SoftCard, the most successful coprocessor sold for the Apple II was the PC Transporter, produced by Applied Engineering. It was originally designed by a company in the San Jose area called The Engineering Department (TED). That company's founder was Wendell Sander, the hardware engineer who formerly had worked at Apple and was involved in the design of the Apple III and parts of the SWIM chip (Sander-Wozniak Integrated Machine)[4] used in the IIc and IIGS.

Around 1986 Applied Engineering entered discussions with TED about acquiring the PC Transporter to sell and market. At that time, the board was about four times its final production size. AE's people were able to reduce the number of components down to just a few custom ASIC chips. The software that managed the board came from TED.[5]

It was finally released in November 1987 as a card that plugged into any of the motherboard slots (except slot 3). It also included one or more IBM-style disk drives. The PC Transporter used an 8086 processor and ran about three times as fast as the original IBM PC. It used its own RAM memory, up to a maximum of 768K, which could be used as a RAM disk by ProDOS (when not in PC-mode). It used some of the main Apple memory for the interface code that lets the PC Transporter communicate with the hardware.

PC Transporter 1988 – Photo credit: Applied Engineering 1988 catalog

---

4 Huston, Cliff, e-mail message to author, April 1, 2010; The SWIM chip has been incorrectly called the "Super Wozniak Integrated Machine" in many publications over the years. Cliff Huston states clearly that it was the "Sander-Wozniak Integrated Machine", recognizing the work done by Wendell Sander in creation of it.
5 Holcomb, Jeff, A2 Roundtable, Category 11, Topic 7, *GEnie*, accessed March 1992.

Chapter 39 | Hardware for the Next Generation

The PC Transporter underwent some minor hardware changes and several sets of software changes (mostly bug fixes and a few new features). The hardware revisions occurred primarily because of the availability of cheaper RAM (the original RAM was more expensive and difficult to obtain). Additionally, AE replaced the onboard ROM with software loaded from a disk, which made it easier to distribute system upgrades that enhanced hardware performance.[6, 7, 8] The major limitation for this product was reluctance on the part of Applied Engineering (or possibly the cost of creating upgrades) to match the changes that occurred in the MS-DOS world, to produce a version of the Transporter that used a more advanced microprocessor (80286, 386, or 486). By 1991, this had become more of a limitation for those who wished to use both MS-DOS and Apple II software on the same Apple II computer, since MS-DOS software by that time required more powerful processors.

ACCELERATORS

In 1986 Applied Engineering introduced the TransWarp accelerator board. This product lasted in the marketplace longer than any other accelerator, possibly because AE did far more advertising than the companies producing the older boards. The original TransWarp was available with a 65c02 processor and 256K of high-speed RAM for $249, or a 65802 for $338.

Also, although the TransWarp could not accelerate a CP/M card plugged into the Apple II, it was at least compatible with such cards. The earlier accelerator cards were often incompatible with a CP/M card installed.[9]

TransWarp – Photo credit: Applied Engineering 1986 catalog

The next step in accelerator technology was to put all the components of an accelerator board into a single chip. These accelerators on a chip made it possible to speed up even the Apple IIc, which did not have physical slots. This technology came to market when two rivals, the Zip Chip and the Rocket Chip, were released. The Zip Chip, sold by Zip Technology, was

---

6 Utter, Gary, A2 Roundtable, Category 14, Topic 12, *GEnie*, accessed December 1991.
7 McKay, Hugh, A2 Roundtable, Category 14, Topic ˉ 2, *GEnie*, accessed December 1991.
8 Jones, Jay, A2 Roundtable, Category 14, Topic 12, *GEnie*, accessed December 1991.
9 Sander-Cederlof, Bob, "Review of Applied Engineering Transwarp", *Apple Assembly Lines* (V6N6, March 1986).

introduced at the May 1988 AppleFest conference in Boston, and the Rocket Chip, sold by Bits & Pieces Technology soon after.

Running at 4 MHz, the Zip Chip was a direct replacement for the 6502 or 65c02 on the Apple II motherboard. It contained its caching RAM within the processor housing, the difference being mostly in height (or thickness) of the integrated circuit. Installing it was a bit trickier than simply putting a board into a slot; the 6502 had to be removed from the motherboard with a chip puller, and the Zip Chip installed (in the correct orientation) in its place. Software to control the speed of the chip was included, and allowed for ten different speeds, including the standard 1 MHz speed (some games were simply too fast to play at 4 MHz, and software that depended on timing loops to produce music had to be slowed down to sound right). The controlling software also let the user determine which (if any) of the peripheral cards should be accelerated. The Zip Chip even allowed the user to decide whether to run all sound at standard speed or at the fast speed.

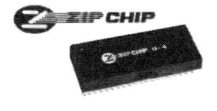

Zip Chip 4 MHz – Photo credit: Yuji Takahashi's Apple II World

Rocket Chip – Photo credit: unknown

The Rocket Chip, by Bits & Pieces Technologies, was almost exactly the same as the Zip Chip, with a few minor exceptions. It had the ability to run at up to 5 MHz, and could be slowed down below 1 MHz (down to 0.05 MHz). In 1990, when Zip released the Zip Chip 8000, an 8 MHz version of its accelerator, Bits & Pieces introduced a 10 MHz Rocket Chip.

From the start, there was animosity between Zip Technology and Bits & Pieces Technologies, with mutual accusations of intellectual property theft. The Bits & Pieces people alleged that they had performed the original work on a single chip accelerator with the Zip people, but Zip had taken the plans and specifications without their permission. Subsequently, they formed their own company and designed their own chip from scratch. Zip, on the other hand, insisted that Bits & Pieces had stolen the technology from them. The case eventually went to court, with the judge deciding that Zip Technology was the originator of the technology. Bits & Pieces was then forced to stop production on the Rocket Chip.

Applied Engineering's next version of their plugin-board accelerator, the TransWarp II, performed acceleration using technology licensed from Bits & Pieces. This made it unnecessary to use the high-speed RAM on the original TransWarp. Early TransWarp II boards ran at 2.5 MHz; later versions pushed this speed to 3.58 or 7.16 MHz. A control panel on the computer was used to change settings on the card, much as the Zip Chip and Rocket Chip used.

However, when Bits & Pieces lost its court case, Applied Engineering was also forced to cease sales of the TransWarp II.

By 1989, the market for accelerators for 8-bit Apple II computers was waning, but owners of the 16-bit Apple IIGS were clamoring for faster speed. This was made more important after the release of GS/OS System 5 in 1989. With its Mac-like desktop (but in color), the IIGS could do more — but it took a hit in performance. Applied Engineering met this demand with the release of the TransWarp GS in late 1988, which sold for $399. It offered a top speed of 7 MHz (compared to the native Apple IIGS speed of 2.8 MHz). It worked in slot 3 or 4 on the IIGS, and could be configured via GS/OS Control Panels or via the text-based Classic Desk Accessories.

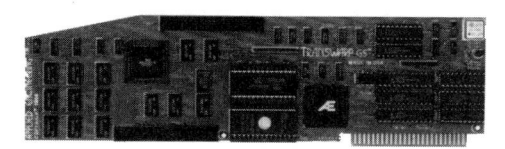

TransWarp GS 1989 – Photo credit: Applied Engineering 1989 catalog

The TransWarp GS was popular because it made the Apple IIGS more usable in its graphic desktop mode (and of course it also accelerated text-based software). It was also popular for those who dared to physically modify the card to run even faster than the 7 MHz speed at which it was rated. One method was to increase the amount of RAM used for caching from 8K to 32K. The other modification was to change the oscillator on the board from 28 MHz to 40 MHz. If successful, this resulted in speeds as high as 10 MHz, and with the cache RAM upgrade, it increased the performance of certain tasks as much as three times. Applied Engineering offered this modification, for about $109, for those who feared damaging their card by doing it themselves.[10, 11]

Zip Technology got into the Apple IIGS accelerator market in 1990 with the ZipGS card. The card used new technology that combined the functions of several individual chips onto a single chip. The 7 MHz card sold for $199, with faster speeds of 8 or 9 MHz, or larger RAM cache sizes costing more. The product also advertised a lower power draw, which was supposed to make it run cooler.

Originally, Zip Technology had promised three different versions of their accelerator: The Zip GS, Zip GS Plus, and Zip GSX. The first two were to be simple 65816 replacements, just as the older Zip Chip had been a replacement for the 6502 or 65c02 microprocessor on 8-bit Apple

---

10 Link, John, "Accelerate Your TransWarp GS Card - Part 1", *AppleWorks Forum* (March 1991).
11 Link, John, "Accelerate Your TransWarp GS Card - Part 2", *AppleWorks Forum* (April 1991).

II computers. However, these chip-based versions never appeared; adding the cache and other hardware to a 65816 made it too large to work well in a IIGS, because the height of the thicker chip blocked access to four slots. The product that eventually was released was the Zip GSX card, which had a ribbon cable that plugged into the 65816 socket on the motherboard after removing the original processor. As with the TransWarp, there were Classic Desk Accessory and Control Panel connections to change settings on the card.

Zip GSX card – Photo credit: personal

Zip Technology caused some frustration amongst users who wanted a IIGS accelerator. The product was announced, and then nothing appeared for quite a while. It appeared that they were funding the research and development of the Zip GSX with money from early orders; it was not until nearly a year had passed before the product began to ship. They further irritated customers by shipping new orders first, and filling the older orders later.

In comparing the two accelerators for the Apple IIGS that made it to market, they differed in some small ways. The TransWarp GS was more careful to accelerate the firmware and the IIGS user experience, whereas the Zip GSX was strictly a hardware accelerator. Because of the difference, the Zip GSX did its job and didn't always slow for certain tasks (some of the IIGS diagnostic tests would always fail when the Zip GSX was on), where the TransWarp handled some of those details.

INKJET PRINTERS

By the late 1980s, a new kind of print technology appeared. Inkjet printers worked somewhat like a dot-matrix printer, but the print head sprayed ink through as many as 64 holes in patterns to form characters as it moved across the paper. The advantage over dot-matrix impact printers was the ability to form more solid characters. In fact, the quality was almost as good as a laser printer. The advantage over laser printers was cost. In the early 1990s, the best price for a laser printer was over $1,500, but inkjet printers sold for as low as $300. The disadvantage for Apple II users was that although it was easy to print text, printing graphics was difficult due to insufficient interest in producing print drivers for the Apple II. At a bare minimum, it was possible to use some of the printers in a mode that emulated older dot-matrix printers. These ink-jet printers could even produce graphics, as long as the emulated dot-matrix mode supported graphics.

One of the earliest offerings of this technology for consumer sales was the Hewlett-Packard DeskJet 500. Introduced in late 1990, it originally sold for $729, and within a couple of years was down to $299. It offered both serial and parallel connections to the computer, and produced high quality print output from an Apple IIe, IIc, or IIGS. It was possible to use the printer from AppleWorks, and with proper drivers, from the Apple IIGS and its graphics-based software. Later revisions of the DeskJet series in 1994, the 520 and 560c, were also useable with these Apple II models. However, these newer HP printers did not come with serial connectors, and so a parallel interface card was necessary to connect them.

Apple entered the ink-jet printer market in May 1991 when it released the Apple StyleWriter. A modification of Canon's BubbleJet series, this printer performed excellent reproduction of text and graphics—on a Macintosh. It was not until the release of GS/OS System 6 that Apple provided drivers to make it possible to use this printer on the IIGS. Drivers for later versions of the StyleWriter were never released for the IIGS.

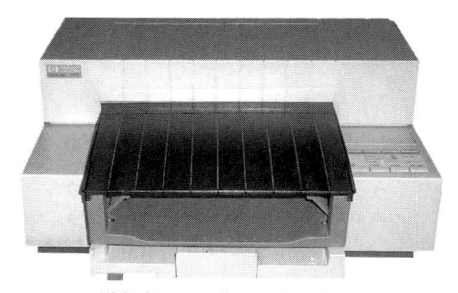

HP DeskJet 500 – Photo credit: unknown

Unlike the inkjet printers sold by Hewlett Packard, the StyleWriter did not have a built-in set of fonts. Instead, it was entirely graphics-driven, and required the computer to send all text as it appeared on the screen. This was appropriate for the Macintosh and for 16-bit software on the IIGS, but it was not practical on 8-bit models of the Apple II.

To provide maximum flexibility with software-based fonts, the StyleWriter received text in the form of dynamically created bitmapped fonts, using the new TrueType font technology released in March 1991 in a partnership between Apple (who developed the font system) and Microsoft (who created the print engine). With TrueType, a single font could be resized under software control. The older Macintosh (and GS/OS) fonts required a separate font for each size in a family (Courier 8 for 8-point type, Courier 10 for 10-point type, and so on); with TrueType there was just a single font file for each typeface. In early 1992, the ability to handle TrueType technology came to GS/OS through *Pointless*, an extension released by WestCode Software (a company formed by former Beagle Bros programmers Alan Bird and Rob Renstrom).

TIMELINE

AE TransWarp – *January 1986*

PC Transporter – *November 1987*

AE GS-RAM – *1987*

AE GS-RAM Ultra – *1987*

AE TransWarp II – *1988*

Zip Chip – *May 1988*

Rocket Chip – *June 1988*

AE TransWarp GS – *November 1988*

Apple II Video Overlay Card – *April 1989*

AE Sonic Blaster – *1989*

Zip GSX – *1990*

Quickie scanner – *February 1990*

LightningScan GS – *August 1990*

HP DeskJet 500 – *August 1990*

Zip Chip 8000 – *September 1990*

AE GS-RAM Plus – *1990*

Apple StyleWriter – *May 1991*

SoundMeister – *April 1993*

HP DeskJet 520, 560c – *March 1994*

Quickie-C – *March 1994*

Second Sight card – *June 1995*

CHAPTER 40

Ahead of their Time: Digital Magazines

Producing a computer magazine has typically required a significant investment by an established publishing company. On the other hand, magazine content was easy to come by because users in the early years of the microcomputer revolution enthusiastically shared what they learned. It was easy to print, photocopy and distribute this knowledge—that was what most early computer user groups did with their newsletters. But to assemble quality photos, commission artwork, layout and typeset the material, and make it look professional—that required an investment in money that many did not have.

An alternative means of distribution arose by making use of the very computers that aspiring publishers wanted to write about. Computers would do more than just help create the content—they were the media used to read the content. This was something that had never before been tried; in fact, it had never previously been possible to create and duplicate words and pictures in a form other than printing on paper. As mentioned earlier, science fiction writers in the 1960s envisioned a future where paper books did not exist, but instead books would be stored as book-films and viewed using a film player in the home. The idea of using the computer itself as a way to store and view printed material was beyond their conception.

The digital publisher in the era of the early microcomputer needed no more than his computer and a stack of floppy disks for duplication. The more sophisticated publisher might buy himself a disk duplicator to speed the process. And if the magazine was published as a specially formatted file uploaded to an online service, the process was even simpler than that. Later, in the Internet era, it would be necessary to own or pay for a server to deliver the content to web subscribers; in this earlier time, it was only necessary to store a master copy of the physical media after the initial duplication (or, in the case of online magazines, the source text file after it was uploaded).

This chapter looks at the best-known Apple II-focused disk and online publications, and one produced with more modern tools.

SOFTDISK (Sep 1981 – Aug 1995)

One of the longest-lived magazines in the Apple II world, *Softdisk*, entered the scene as one of the first magazines distributed solely in a machine-readable form, and continued in that form through its entire run.

Jim Mangham was a programmer at Louisiana State University Medical Center in Shreveport, Louisiana. In 1981, he and former LSU mathematician Al Vekovius felt that it was the right time for an Apple II disk-based magazine. They believed the media had an advantage over print magazines by providing ready-to-run programs that did not have to be typed in, yet could still be listed and modified by the subscriber if desired. The idea was not unique in the computer world as a whole; *CLOAD* for the TRS-80 began as a magazine on cassette as far back as 1978, and other paper publications offered companion disks containing programs from a specific issue. But no one had yet put a whole magazine on disk for the Apple II, and Vekovius and Mangham decided to fill that gap.

Mangham, his wife and Vekovius formed a company to carry out the plan. Vekovius worked on the business aspects while Mangham handled the programming. Originally, they planned to call it *The Harbinger Magazette*. After preparing the preliminary first issue, Mangham called Al Tommervik of *Softalk* magazine to discuss advertising. Tommervik thought it was a great idea, and not only wanted to advertise it, but also asked to be a partner in the venture. In exchange for part ownership in the disk magazine, *Softalk* would provide free advertising for the disk magazine, and space in the *Softalk* booth at computer shows. Tommervik also wanted to be able to include programs from the paper magazine on the disk.

Tommervik suggested that they change the name to *Softdisk* (since it would be, in essence, a *Softalk* publication). By the time they were ready to mail out the first issue, they had fifty subscribers, due to pre-advertising in *Softalk*. Since Mangham needed a minimum of two hundred pieces to qualify for a bulk postage rate, his father found one hundred and fifty disks in his mailbox that month.

To create this new "magazette", Mangham chose to use double-sided disks that were pre-notched on both edges, to make both sides useable. (Recall that the Disk II drive could only use one side of the disk at a time, and so it was a common practice to conserve money and use the other side by cutting a notch on the edge of the disk opposite the factory one and flipping the disk over.) These double-sided disks were expensive, costing him three dollars apiece, and so he set up the subscriptions to require return of the previous issue in order to get the next one (it was left up to the reader to make his own copies to keep). When the disk was returned with the five dollars for the next issue, the reader could also use a simple text editor on the disk to submit letters to the editor, comment on the previous issue's contents or ask other questions. This return disk could also be used for submitting programs, pictures, or articles for use in future issues of *Softdisk*. Some of the subscribers that became prolific contributors of material even ended up working at the magazine.[1]

Since *Softalk* magazine provided free advertising for *Softdisk*, it contributed to the success of the disk magazine. Some of the revenue for the magazine came from subscription payments, and some came through advertising in *Softdisk* itself. Ads were sold by the disk sector, and provided an advertiser a unique opportunity—to offer a potential customer a chance to see the program being sold. Some of the ads were made even more entertaining through animation (usually using the text screen to save disk space). This was most prominent in the ads the magazine created for its own products; by 1983 they had begun a line of software called "Rich and Famous" (which they said was what the authors wanted to become). Consisting of programs written by regular *Softdisk* contributors, these disks sold for $9.95 apiece, and a $4 royalty on each disk went to the author. The disks offered various types of games, including hi-res graphics adventures and card games, office-based utility software, general Apple II utilities, and disks of music (in Electric Duet format, the program written by Paul Lutus that could play two-voice music on Apple's one-bit speaker).

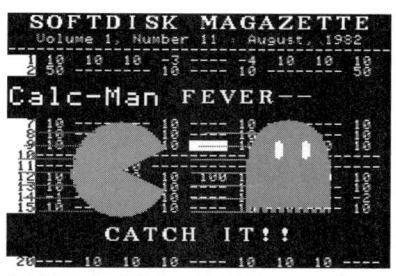

Softdisk #10, Aug 1982, featuring *Calc-Man*, a game that was a cross between *Pac-Man* and *VisiCalc* - Photo credit: personal

Softdisk 28 – Photo credit: personal

Each issue had a digital cover, which consisted of a hi-res picture and the issue number. These were eventually changed to look just like the *Softalk* logo, with an animated globe in the upper right corner. Starting in August 1983, *Softdisk* expanded to two double-sided disks, and the two-way subscriptions now requested that only one of the two had to be returned. One-way subscriptions were also offered to those who didn't want to bother returning the disks.

By December 1983 (issue #27), *Softdisk* became available through retail stores (primarily computer stores, but later also through bookstores) at the price of $12.95 per issue. Vekvious also began publishing a disk magazine called *Loadstar* for the Commodore 64 computer in June 1984, at a price of $9.95 (a lower cost since it was a single disk per issue).[2]

---

1 -----. "The History of Softdisk: Part 1." *Soft Talk* (Softdisk Publishing company newsletter) (October 1987).
2 -----. "The History of Softdisk: Part 2." *Soft Talk* (Softdisk Publishing company newsletter) (November 1987).

The print magazine *Softalk* disappeared after its August 1984 issue, leaving the future of *Softdisk* in doubt. Since the print magazine was now bankrupt, the possibility existed that the disk magazine could be liquidated along with other assets. To avoid this outcome and to ensure the future of the magazine, *Softdisk* purchased back its shares from the magazine's creditors (at an inflated price) and continued on its own. Although a few ads were placed in other Apple II magazines, they continued primarily on word-of-mouth referrals (which didn't increase circulation by much). Sales of side items (primarily blank disks) helped cover operating expenses during this difficult time.[3]

In May 1985, the two-way disk subscriptions were discontinued, and Al Tommervik started a brief tenure as editor-in-chief. He helped develop a more professional appearance for the magazine (as well as for Loadstar), through higher quality graphics and an improved cover design. When the new editor-in-chief began in late 1985, these changes continued. Instead of the older text-based interface that had been used from the beginning, nearly all of the screen displays were changed to graphics, with upper and lowercase characters displayed on the hi-res screen on any Apple II.

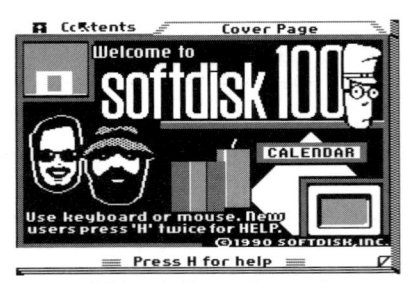

Softdisk 100 – Photo credit: personal

Softdisk, Inc. added a disk magazine in 1986 for the IBM PC, called *Big Blue Disk*.[4] At this time *Softdisk* magazine itself began including re-releases of older commercial software whose publishers were willing to inexpensively license publishing rights. It also began to publish newer shareware programs. The first series of software reruns were games previously released by Polarware (formerly known as Penguin Software).[5]

By 1987, *Softdisk* again began advertising itself in print magazines. This began a large expansion in circulation for the magazette and its sister publications. November of that year (issue #73) saw the changeover from the older DOS 3.3 operating system exclusively to ProDOS. This issue also introduced a more Mac-like graphic user interface that supported a mouse or joystick (as well as the keyboard), featuring pull-down menus and animated graphics. It also divided up the four disk sides into directories that allowed the entire issue to be installed into a folder on a hard drive. Within the next year or so, retail distribution of its publications was discontinued and distribution returned exclusively to subscriptions.[6] (This story continues later in the chapter.)

---

3 -----. "The History of Softdisk: Part 3." *Soft Talk* (Softdisk Publishing company newsletter) (December 1987).
4 -----. "The History of Softdisk: Part 4." *Soft Talk* (Softdisk Publishing company newsletter) (January 1988).
5 -----. "The History of Softdisk: Part V." *Soft Talk* (Softdisk Publishing company newsletter) (February 1988).
6 -----. "The History of Softdisk: Conclusion." *Soft Talk* (Softdisk Publishing company newsletter) (March 1988).

… CHAPTER 40 | Ahead of their Time: Digital Magazines

SCHOLASTIC MICROZINE (Mar 1983 – May 1992)

Scholastic Inc. was originally founded in 1920 to publish youth magazines. By the 1940s the company expanded into publication of paperback books for school children. Dick Robinson, son of the company founder, became president in 1974 and chairman in 1982. Aware of the developing software market in education, Robinson started a software publishing division at Scholastic the same year he became chairman.

One of the first two employees of that division was Deborah Kovacs, hired as Creative Director. Kovacs soon began work on a school edition of Brøderbund's word processor, *Bank Street Writer*. Later, a software developer named Dan Klassen, who headed ITDA (Information Design Technology Associates), came to Scholastic with an idea for a computer-based magazine on disk. Klassen had previously worked with MECC (Minnesota Educational Computing Consortium), which had been involved in putting Apple II computers into Minnesota schools in the late 1970s, as well as development of numerous educational programs. He had met with the editor-in-chief of *Family & Home Office Computing Magazine* to discuss this idea, and was connected with Deborah Kovacs.

Klassen had envisioned a monthly disk magazine that would include four programs, plus games, utilities, and interactive fiction. As he and Kovacs of Scholastic discussed the concept, it was determined that it was impractical to produce this type of product on a monthly basis, and it would be more realistic to put out four issues per year. They started creating the first issue of what they called *Microzine* in the summer of 1982. By the fall, they had two additional staff members. Klassen's group worked on the design and software development for the disk magazine, and the Scholastic team worked on the visual appearance and creative and editorial content. Their target audience was school children in grades 4 to 6.

The first issue of *Microzine* was unveiled at the January 1983 Consumer Electronics Show, then released to stores by March 1983. The box containing the first issue was in the unusual shape of a parallelogram, and contained a mystery adventure that involved exploring a haunted house, a computerized notebook for keeping secret information, a program for creating computer graphics, and an interactive interview with Robert McNaughton, who played Elliott's brother Michael in the 1982 movie, *E.T. - The Extra-Terrestrial*. After the second issue of *Micro-*

Scholastic Microzine #1 – Photo credit: personal

zine came out, the parallelogram box was replaced with packaging more typical of computer software being sold in stores.

Scholastic stayed with the original schedule of publishing four issues per school year. Each issue had an interactive text adventure, called a Twistaplot, a type of Choose Your Own Adventure story that Scholastic was also selling as a print book at the time. The magazine also had a program that demonstrated something that a computer could do (such as a word processing or database use), another miscellaneous program, and a final smaller program the emulated some of the content of a print magazine (letters to the editor, jokes submitted by readers, and a puzzle). The second editor of *Microzine*, Amy (McKinley) Kefauver, stated, "Our goal was to make the kids able to use the programs without *ever* having to ask for help. The programs were designed to have a help screen constantly available by pressing the '?' key."

Scholastic Microzine #26 – Photo credit: personal

Lorraine Hopping Egan wrote some of the scripts for stories on *Microzine*, and later with *Microzine, Jr.*, which was for grades K-4. That disk magazine was only distributed for a short time. Story adventures that Egan wrote include:[7, 8, 9]

- *Escape from Antcatraz* – explore a doomed underground ant nest as you search for an exit
- *Quest for the Pole* – an Arctic adventure based on the doomed Franklin expedition
- *The Balloonatics* – a language arts learning adventure for *Microzine Jr.*, which took kids around the globe
- *Safari!* – point-and-click adventure game for *Microzine Jr.*, to play as one of 6 animals, zebra, elephant, hyena, and so on; the correct choices depended on which animal one had chosen

---

7 Kefauver, Amy, e-mail message to author, April 2, 2012.
8 Kovacs, Deborah, e-mail message to author, April 20, 2012.
9 Egan, Lorraine Hopping, e-mail message to author, March 29, 2012.

UPTIME (Oct 1984 - Dec 1988)

UpTime was a magazine on disk started by Bill Kelly in 1984, initially operating out of his father's basement under the name *Softyme*. The first issue was only for the Apple II, and shipped seventy-two copies. Kelly charged $7.50 per issue, or $48 for a one-year subscription, which was less than the cost of a subscription to competitor *Softdisk*. Like *Softdisk*, *UpTime* was shipped on a two-sided disk (with content on both sides of the disk).

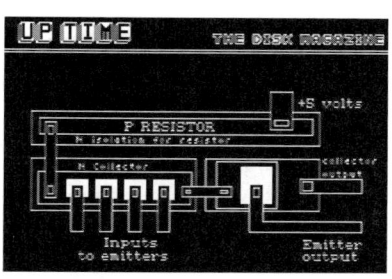

The first issue contained a number of software offerings, including ten games, plus a card game, two home productivity programs (a database and a check book), a program to create pie graphs, a horoscope program, and a disk map utility. There were reviews of word processor *Format IIe* (rated as very good) and *ALA Payroll One Step* (rated as not so good).

UpTime #1, Oct 1988 – Photo credit: personal

By 1986, Kelly claimed a subscriber base of 35,000, and a Macintosh version was in the works. The subscription rate had increased to $66 per year for the Apple II edition, and the Macintosh subscription was expected to have an annual subscription cost of $90. In an article published the following year, Kelly estimated that he had as many as 300 programmers submitting content to the magazine.

UpTime v13n12, Dec 1988 – Photo credit: personal

A year later, Kelly renamed his publishing company to Viking Technologies, and claimed a combined circulation of 50,000 for his disk magazines, with different versions covering the Apple II, Commodore, Macintosh, and IBM PC.[10]

Later issues of *UpTime* were distributed with Diversi-DOS (as the disk operating system) on 5.25-inch disks. Some issues of *UpTime* for the Apple II were distributed on 3.5-inch disks using a modified version of DOS 3.3 that could run on that type of disk. Lane Roathe (who later moved to *Softdisk*) designed a graphic user interface for the *UpTime* desktop program distributed during the last eighteen months of its run.

Also during the last eighteen months of *UpTime*, several different people served as editor, and its final year was notable for John Romero's contributions. He created a graphics system called *GraBASIC*, which was an exten-

---

10 Shannon, L.R., "PERIPHERALS: A Magazine On A Disk", *The New York Times*, June 10, 1987, <http://www.nytimes.com/1987/10/06/science/peripherals-a-magazine-on-a-disk.html>, accessed October 20, 2012.

sion to Applesoft. It was featured in the last three issues of *UpTime*, with programs that demonstrated its uses. And in the final issue of *UpTime*, Romero created a game that used his *GraBASIC* system. It was the first of what became a famous series of games by Romero, featuring a protagonist named Dangerous Dave. The game in this last issue was called *Dangerous Dave in the Deserted Pirate's Hideout*.

After the last issue in 1988, Softdisk, Inc. acquired *UpTime* (see below). Lane Roathe, John Romero, and *UpTime* editor Jay Wilbur moved to Shreveport to begin work for *Softdisk*.

The story of *UpTime* is a little difficult to piece together. For one, with the high subscriber numbers that Kelly gave in a magazine interview in 1987, it would suggest that the company was strong and flush with cash, with products for the PC and Macintosh on their way. And yet, by the end of 1988, the company is sold to its competitor, Softdisk, Inc., about the same time that future gaming software stars Romero, Wilbur, and Roathe left the company. It has disappeared so completely that there is virtually nothing about the company or its disk magazines that can be found in Internet searches.

Another problematic issue regarding the run of *UpTime* is its issue numbering system. The December 1988 issue is labeled as volume 13, number 12. However, *UpTime* did not start until 1984, and ran for four years. The volume number of its first issue was volume 10. These highly unorthodox naming methods, giving the impression that the disk magazine had been around for a much longer time, calls into question whether or not it was as successful in the marketplace as Kelly had claimed.

SOFTDISK G-S (Nov 1989 – Mar 1997)

The first issue of *Softdisk* G-S was released in November 1989, supporting the Apple IIGS desktop interface guidelines. Like the ProDOS version of *Softdisk*, the magazine could be read on the 3.5-inch disks on which they were shipped, or could be installed on a hard drive.

Softdisk G-S #82 – Photo credit: personal

Softdisk, Inc. for a short time became the home for several skilled Apple II programmers who wanted nothing more than to make great games. At a gaming convention in 1989, publisher Al Vekovius met and offered a job to Jay Wilbur, the editor at the competing disk magazine UpTime (see above). Wilbur was tiring of the cold winters at *UpTime*'s home in New Hampshire and decided to accept the position. He asked if he could bring along two Apple II game programmers who were also ready for a change. Vekovius, who believed the game market would be more profitable than magazines, agreed to take them also.

One of the programmers, John Romero, had been writing games for the Apple II for several years, having some published in *Nibble* and *A+*. Lane Roathe had written the graphic shell for *UpTime* disk magazine and was intensely interested in games. In May 1989, Wilbur started as managing editor for *Softdisk*, while Romero (who had added IBM PC programming to his Apple II skills) started working on games and utilities for *Big Blue Disk*. Roathe initially worked in the Apple II group, but Romero's desire to make big games soon changed that.

Romero convinced Vekovius to allow him to start a disk publication specifically for PC games. In 1990, *Gamer's Edge* was created, and Roathe became its editor. Jay Wilbur knew of an Apple II game programmer who would be able to help with translations of Apple II games to the PC for inclusion in issues of *Gamer's Edge*, and so he put Romero in touch with John Carmack. They also recruited Adrian Carmack (not related to John), who was working as an intern at Softdisk, Inc., and was talented at creating computer art for the company's Apple II projects.

Between the four, they created content for *Gamer's Edge* for over a year, and Vekovius looked at the disk magazine as a possible way to save the company. The downturn in the Apple II market had led him to the difficult decision of laying off a number of people from the *Softdisk* division during 1990. A quality games publication for the growing PC market could be a big help.

However, in the process of making games for the magazine, John Carmack had figured out a tricky technical issue involved with making games scroll left and right on the screen. Once he had this mastered, the *Gamer's Edge* group decided to start making their own games to sell under the shareware model. With Tom Hall also working on graphics, the group left in February 1991, just after issue #113 of *Softdisk* was released.

They ultimately went on to create the genre of what became known as first-person-shooter games, in which the player viewed the action from the eyes of the character on the screen, instead of from above or to the side as games had nearly always appeared up to that point. This "game engine" ultimately led to the creation of *Wolfenstein 3D* (a PC game based on the older Apple II game, *Castle Wolfenstein*), and ultimately to the multiplayer monster battling games *Doom* and *Quake*.[11]

Numerous other Apple II programmers worked on or contributed to *Softdisk* over the years. An important one was Peter Rokitski. He was an Apple II programmer who had co-created *Situation: Critical*, an arcade-style Apple II game back in 1984. He began submitting programs for publication in *Softdisk* in 1988, and was involved in the magazine's beta-testing program that same year. The same month that Romero and his friends left the company,

---

11 Kushner, David, *Masters of Doom* (New York, Random House, 2003).

Rokitski was hired as a full-time programmer for the magazine. Over the next several years, his programs appeared in nearly all of the monthly issues.

By the time of the release of the final issue of *Softdisk*, #166 in August 1995, Rokitski was running *Softdisk* virtually alone. Though his official title was that of technical director, he filled the role of programmer, editor, quality assurance and program scout—everything but duplicating and mailing the disks. Rokitski later became the editor for *Softdisk* G-S and continued in that position until its last issue, #82, released March 1997.[12]

The other monthly disk publications from Softdisk, Inc. were gradually discontinued, with Loadstar for the Commodore 64/128 lasting the longest:

- *Softdisk* (Apple II) – 1981 to 1995
- *Loadstar* (Commodore 64/128) – 1984 to 2008 (249 issues)
- *Big Blue Disk* (IBM PC) – 1986 to 1991
- *Diskworld* (Macintosh) – 1988 to 1993
- *Softdisk G-S* (Apple IIGS) – 1989 to 1997
- *Gamer's Edge* (IBM PC) – 1990 to 1993
- *On Disk Monthly* (IBM PC) – 1991 to 1993
- *Softdisk CGA* (IBM PC without graphics) – 1993 to 1996
- *Softdisk PC* (IBM PC with graphics) – 1993 to 1998
- *Softdisk for Mac* (Macintosh) – 1993 to 1998
- *Softdisk for Windows* – 1994 to 1999

Likely seeing that the market for disks on magazine would not last forever, Softdisk, Inc. began to offer web hosting services in Shreveport, Louisiana starting in 1995. By 2002 it also hosted an online store for downloadable Windows, Macintosh, and Palm OS software, continuing these operations until 2006. In 2002, a collection of all old issues of *Softdisk*, *Softdisk G-S*, and *UpTime* (which Softdisk bought out in 1988) were released as CD-ROM collections, sold by Syndicomm.

RESOURCE CENTRAL DISK PUBLICATIONS

Tom Weishaar began publication of a paper newsletter in 1985, following in the wake of the *Softalk* bankruptcy. After several years, he branched out to provide disk-based publications that were focused on specific Apple II groups—primarily programmers.

One of the first new disk magazines focused on the growing popularity of hypermedia programs. Bill Atkinson's *HyperCard* for the Macintosh, released in 1986, and Roger Wagner Publishing's *HyperStudio* for the Apple IIGS in

---

12 Rokitski, Peter, e-mail message to author, February 2001.

1989, were at the forefront of this new style of programming and presentation. To help enthusiasts who wanted to learn more about hypermedia and how to use it, Resource Central started a disk-based magazine in December 1989. *Stack-Central* (later renamed *Studio City*) was produced on a bimonthly basis, and consisted of HyperStudio stacks and resources.

Two years later, in June 1991, *Script-Central* started with a similar hypermedia focus, dealing with *HyperCard IIGS*, which had just been released by Apple. With both disk publications, the content on each issue's 3.5-inch disks consisted of stacks that could be used to read about the respective programs. Also included were sound files, graphics files, and other software tools that could be utilized by programmers for HyperStudio or HyperCard IIGS.

The content on *Studio City* and *Script-Central* disks was designed to work very much like the World Wide Web would when it appeared. Like web pages, these disk magazines displayed a color graphic background, had picture or text buttons that linked to other articles (stacks) or cause another action to happen (playing a sound or animation). *Script-Central* took navigation a step further, displaying a picture of the "Script-Central" building, with clicks on the front door allowing "entry" to the building.

Script-Central building, the first scene on this disk magazine – Photo credit: personal

Inside was a receptionist's desk, over which hung a picture of "our founder" (Tom Weishaar). Since there were two floors in the building, clicking in the appropriate areas allowed the reader to either go down the hall to offices (representing articles or columns) on the first floor, or take the elevator to the second floor offices (with more articles).

Script-Central interior, access to the rest of the disk magazine contents – Photo credit: personal

Moving into the literary frontier of hypermedia was the disk magazine *HyperBole*, which began in March 1991. It was created by Greg Roach of HyperBole Studios, and utilized HyperStudio. It consisted of poetry, art, and sounds, combined together in a way that surpassed the traditional printed form. In the "pages" of HyberBole were what became the world's first interactive multimedia novel, *The Madness of Roland*. The story had a medieval theme, with the story told from various points of view, depending on which picture was selected on the door that introduced the story. To read the entire story required going back to the main door and selecting a different picture. Sound and graphics were also integrated into articles that appeared in this disk-magazine.

Resource Central also produced two other disk publications, both aimed at a specific group. In August 1990, the company began distribution of another bimonthly disk magazine, *TimeOut-Central*. This was devoted to AppleWorks and the TimeOut series of enhancements created by Beagle Bros. A few months after its introduction, Randy Brandt (co-author of AppleWorks 3.0 and several of the TimeOut programs) took over as editor.

For programmers, *8/16-Central* began in December 1990. It specialized in articles and program code for both 8-bit Apple II models and the IIGS. It was a continuation of a short-lived print magazine called *8/16*, formerly produced by Ariel Publishing Co., and was itself preceded by several separate newsletters that specialized in Applesoft, assembly language, and other programming languages for the Apple II series. *8/16-Central* was a monthly disk, but it didn't generate enough subscribers to last very long. In October 1991 it was discontinued, and the remaining subscriptions were transferred to GS+ magazine.[13]

GENIELAMP A2 (Apr 1992 – Oct 1997) / GENIELAMP A2PRO (Feb 1993 – Jan 1996)

As previously described, the GEnie online service began in 1985 and had early representation of the Apple II platform. That led to a long-running digital magazine with editions for several different computer platforms, although the Apple II edition was the most long-lived. It began due to, of all things, an Atari computer.

John Peters was an Atari ST user who lived in Denver in 1990. He started a text-based magazine called *TeleTalk Online*, targeting members and sysops of BBSs. He started by uploading his newsletter locally, but soon it spread nationwide, migrating from BBS to BBS. After three issues, Peters found that he was receiving e-mail messages about *TeleTalk Online* from all over the country. He signed up with PC Pursuit, a GTE service started in 1985 that offered unlimited non-primetime connections to online databases, bulletin boards, regional networks, and personal computers in several large metropolitan areas. This allowed him to access BBSs located in different parts of the United States. Being able to personally deliver his digital magazine accelerated the rapid growth of his magazine.

With the experience gained from his foray into digital publishing, Peters wrote the Chief Sysop for GEnie's Atari Roundtables, asking him if there was any interest in a magazine in the style of *TeleTalk*. CompuServe already had a magazine called *ST Report*, and GEnie was interested in something to com-

---

13 Later, the contents of the entire run of *8/16-Central* were upload as individual file archives to GEnie's A2Pro library on the same exclusive basis as were the contents and disks for of *Apple Assembly Line*.

pete with it. As a result, *GEnieLamp ST*, the first GEnieLamp publication, started in June 1990. It became a popular download amongst the members of that Roundtable, and in a short time it caught the eye of Kent Fillmore, who was a product manager for GEnie. Fillmore asked Peters if he would be interested in expanding the GEnieLamp concept to other platforms. Peters accepted the challenge, sought and found assistants from selected Roundtables to act as co-editors, and on April 1, 1992 three additional GEnieLamp magazines appeared, for the Macintosh, IBM, and Apple II platforms.

Over the next several years, monthly editions of the GEnieLamp magazines appeared, some lasting as late as 1996. The Apple II edition consistently gained strength (in terms of numbers of downloads) over the length of its run, and was possibly the most active of the GEnieLamp editions. According to John Peters, the Apple II edition had the greatest readership, and the GEnie Apple II community was "the fun one." A many as ten different editions of GEnieLamp were eventually in circulation. The GEnieLamp magazines were formatted for an 80-column monospaced text screen, and made frequent use of ASCII art.

Peters acted as publisher and editor for each of the GEnieLamp editions, and a member of each of the targeted Roundtables was recruited as Co-Editor.

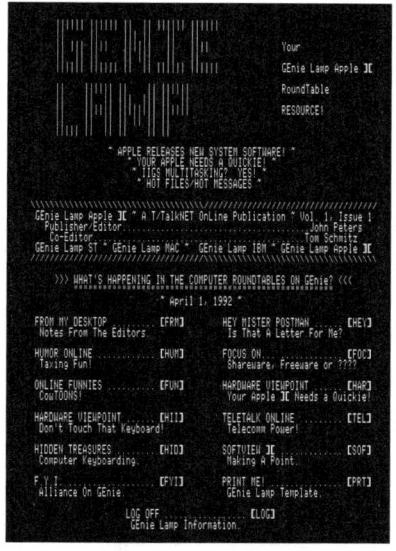

The starting pages of the first edition of GEnieLamp A2, April 1992 – Photo credit: personal

For the Apple II edition, A2 Roundtable member Tom Schmitz was selected. Schmitz, a resident of Hawaii, continued in that position for the first six issues, until the demands of his job made it necessary to relinquish that position to Darrel Raines. Raines had made several contributions to the newsletter, beginning with the August 1992 issue.

John Peters wanted his online magazines to present general articles that were interesting to any computer owner, along with platform-specific columns to fill out the remainder of the newsletter. Also, an important part of each issue was a distillation of postings from the Roundtable containing information, humor, and news. The template that he followed in most issues of *GEnieLamp A2* during its first year was to start with his editorial, include a note from Tom Schmitz or Darrel Raines, then move on to Apple II news, gleanings from postings on the A2 Roundtable, and finally a mixture of technical articles. Most of these articles were specific to the Apple II, but some were general enough to appeal to any computer user. He also arranged for the articles to all be identified with a three-character index code, surrounded by brackets, such as [HUM], [HEY], and so on (see image above).

By the third issue, Tom Schmitz's title was elevated to that of Editor for the A2 edition, and Phil Shapiro, who had contributed articles from the very beginning, was listed as a Co-Editor. With issue number 4 in July 1992, contributions from the Apple II Programmers Roundtable (A2Pro) were added, making the official title *GEnieLamp A2/A2Pro*. This combined A2 and A2Pro Roundtable coverage continued until February 1993, when the combined size of contributions from the two Roundtables made it prudent to split off *GEnieLamp A2Pro* as a separate publication.

To promote the new publications, Peters devised a "Computer Wars" contest to allow readers to send in reasons why they thought their computer was the best. Although the largest number of responses came from the Apple II readers, the winning computer was not an Apple II. In the September 1992 issue, the first place award went to a user whose essay described "the modem" as the best computer (because it made any computer extensible to a larger network). Second place was awarded to the HP-15C Advanced Programmable Scientific Calculator, and third place was the NeXT computer.

During this first year of publication, Peters also introduced the DiskTop Publishing Association (later called the Desktop Publishing Association), to promote digital publications. He and other DPA members later designated November as "Electronic Publishing Month".

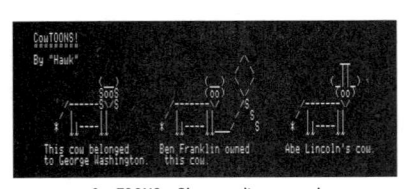

CowTOONS – Photo credit: personal

To round out the newsletter, ASCII art made its debut in the September 1992 issue, with CowTOONS—ASCII drawings of cows. (ASCII art—pictures created using monospaced screen fonts—had been popular even back in the days of mainframe computers.) Also introduced during that first year were word-find puzzles in the form of the "Search-Me!" column.

The HUMOR ONLINE column began in the first issue, and continued through most of the run of *GEnieLamp A2*. Titles of these stories included: Chocolate Layer Cake 1040; Shareware registration incentives that don't work; Political Viruses; Fifty Ways to Hose Your Code (song parody); The Oyster; IBM's "Timeless" processor chip; Monty Python humor in the Atari ST Roundtable; the B*st*rd Operator From Hell; Apple vs. IBM (pounding nails with your head); and The Art of Flaming.

Apple II-specific content that appeared during the first year of *GEnieLamp A2* included software and hardware announcements (including Apple IIGS System 6 and HyperCard IIGS), promotion of the A2-Central Summer Conference (the first of many years of plugs for KansasFest), as well as some of the earliest developer comments about an Apple IIGS emulator (for 386/486 computers).

A new editor was assigned to *GEnieLamp A2* in the summer of 1993. Doug Cuff had been a subscriber to GEnie a few years earlier, but had been absent for a while. After seeing *GEnieLamp A2* posted on a local BBS, he decided to get involved again. Cuff applied for the position of editor. John Peters felt he was the most qualified applicant and appointed him to the position. Cuff produced the August 1993 edition and continued until December 1996, a total of 41 issues.

Changes that occurred during Cuff's tenure as editor included taking over the "From My Desktop" editorial column. It soon became the responsibility of each GEnieLamp editor to assemble and distribute the monthly newsletter. By 1995 this job was made more difficult by the shrinking base of authors. In fact, when one of his contributors could no longer write the monthly "Treasure Hunt" article about great files in the A2 library, Cuff himself took over this task.

During 1995, it was the sad task of *GEnieLamp A2* to also report on news about the loss of Resource Central/ICON, the National AppleWorks User Group, GS+ magazine, and *Softdisk*. By this time, newcomer *II Alive* was also on the ropes. In his editorial in the January 1996 issue of *GEnieLamp A2*, Cuff made an effort to find positives in the Apple II world that had occurred during 1995:

> In fact, we made out like bandits in 1995. We got new hardware: the SecondSight card and, along with the rest of the micro world, IOmega ZIP drives. We got new software: Quick Click Morph, TimeOut Statistics, Convert 3200, Quick Click TIFF Reader, Deja II (AppleWorks 5.1 for the Mac), Opening Line, TouchTwo AppleWorks macros, Print 3200, and PMPFax, not to mention shareware/freeware efforts such as II Not Disturb, Blockade [a game from Brutal Deluxe], and Pix Whiz [a New Print Shop color picture editor].
>
> We also got significant updates and upgrades for some of our software: Spectrum v2.0, Balloon v2.0, AppleWorks v5.1, rSounder v3.0, AutoArk v1.1, TimeOut ShrinkIt v5, One Touch Commands 5, GEnie Master 5, CoPilot for GEnie v2.5.5, The Tinies (with a new construction set), an improved variable-time SHR screen saver, and a patch for the HFS FST.

Of course, being a publication that focused on the Apple II on GEnie, the newsletter reported about the changes to the service itself, and not in flattering terms. It was during 1996 that General Electric sold GEnie to a new company that seemed intent on running it into the ground (as previously described). The unpopular actions of the new owner reduced Genie's memberships (the new name no longer capitalized the first E), including those from the A2 Roundtable. Previously, management had made it possible for Doug Cuff and the other GEnieLamp editors to pay writers who contributed to the newsletter by giving them credit towards their online charges. The new owners took away this privilege.

In March of 1996, new forms of *GEnieLamp* A2 became available in addition to the text version. HyperCard IIGS and HyperStudio stacks of the A2 edition were available for download. The HyperCard stack (and conversion stack) was written by Joshua Calvin, and was not significantly different from the text edition. The HyperStudio edition included a comic strip called *Hog Heaven*.

By July 1996, *GEnieLamp* A2 was the single remaining GEnieLamp publication. Two other remaining editions, the IBM and Mac versions, had concluded their run as of the June 1996 issue. Part of the reason for their disappearance was likely due to the decision by the new Genie management that GEnieLamp editors could no longer have special paid accounts as had been offered in the past. It was only through intervention by John Peters as the head of GEnieLamp that any editor accounts were preserved—and only Cuff felt motivated to continue in his role as a GEnieLamp editor.

Not only did the new Genie management feel that continuing to have free editor accounts was not necessary, they decided to close the DigiPub roundtable where all of the various GenieLamp editing activity took place. In the August 1996 issue, Cuff announced this change, as well as notifying readers that *GEnieLamp* A2 was now the only publication in the GEnieLamp series released that month. Cuff also took pains to ensure that all of the *GEnieLamp* A2 issues from the very beginning up to the current issue were available in the A2 Roundtable library.[14]

By the end of 1996, Cuff finally decided to retire from his run as editor, after 41 consecutive months (nearly three and one-half years) in that position. Ryan Suenaga, a resident of Hawaii, had been active in the A2 Roundtable for several years. In 1995 he was the host of a late-night RTC (real time conference), as well as writing articles contributed to other publications. He took over the position of editor in January 1997. After his first issue, Suenaga decided to no longer include John Peters name in the masthead, as he was no longer involved. (In fact, by April of 1997, Peters had terminated his Genie account.) Doug Cuff was listed as "Editor Emeritus" in each issue of that year, and continued writing articles for the publication.

The last year that *GEnieLamp* A2 was published was also Suenaga's only year as editor. However, the conclusion of the online magazine had nothing

---

14 A few years later, David Kerwood started one of the very first web sites dedicated to the Apple II, A2-Web, at www.a2-web.com, and he made the full run of *GEnieLamp A2* and its successor available for download.

to do with any failings on his part. The A2 Roundtable continued to contract, and *GEnieLamp A2* contained postings from members (and some leaders) who posted goodbye messages as they announced their plans to migrate over to Delphi, which was viewed as more Apple II-friendly. In his last "From My Desktop" editorial, Suenaga stated that although the October 1997 issue was the last of the *GEnieLamp A2* series, he had plans to create a new newsletter—this time from Delphi. Cuff contributed another article for the last issue, lamenting the way in which the Genie management had abandoned the newsletters that had for so long been a valuable advertisement to attract members to the online service. And like Suenaga, he beckoned readers to come over to Delphi as a new home for the Apple II community:

> ... we – first me and then the final editor, Ryan – kept GenieLamp A2 arriving, month after month. We've been "all alone" out there for a while now. We didn't much care that we didn't have a home. We didn't let the fact that we didn't have a staff stop us. We kept bringing out the magazine every month.
> All the other editions stopped in June 1996, but not GenieLamp A2. It kept going, to the last man standing. We Apple II folk have had a lot of experience at this sort of thing. We know how to keep going while the fickle majority withdraw – editor Ryan Suenaga particularly so.
> The fact is, for almost a year, Ryan has been producing GenieLamp A2 all by himself, and Ryan isn't finished, not by a long way. He's simply moving to Delphi, and taking his one-man online magazine with him to Delphi. It'll have a different name there, and perhaps Ryan can scare up some semi-regular staff there. I'm hopeful that he will – people like to be in on a fresh start.
> That's why I'm not shedding any tears. This final issue of GenieLamp A2 may turn out to be one of the best things that ever happened to it. It's getting a rebirth over on Delphi. We all hope to see you over there.

In the final issue, the ending masthead still listed (in memoriam, so to speak) the staff of all of the now-defunct *GenieLamp* newsletters that had served for so many years, including the Atari ST, IBM, Macintosh, and PowerPC editors.

An article written in 1996 by Doug Cuff summarized the start and end dates of the GEnieLamp publications.

	FIRST ISSUE	LAST ISSUE
GEnieLamp ST	Jun 1990	Mar 1996
GEnieLamp TX2	Dec 1990	Mar 1996
GEnieLamp A2	Apr 1992	Oct 1997
GEnieLamp IBM	Apr 1992	Jun 1996
GEnieLamp Mac	Apr 1992	Jun 1996
GEnieLamp MacPro	Dec 1992	Feb 1993
GEnieLamp A2Pro	Feb 1993	Jan 1996
GEnieLamp IBM MM	Jun 1994	Dec 1995
GEnieLamp PPC	Nov 1994	Dec 1995
GEnieLamp Windows	Mar 1994	Sep 1995

THE LAMP! (Jan 1998 – Aug 2007)

The closing months of 1997 made it clear that Genie as an online home for Apple II users was becoming unsatisfactory. Ryan Suenaga, who had been editing *GEnieLamp A2*, chose to discontinue the newsletter following the October 1997 issue. However, he promised to return with a new publication, from a new base on Delphi. That return happened three months later, with the first issue released in January 1998.

Suenaga had considered several possible names, including *Delphi Oracle* (which was already in use), but with the help of several friends he finally settled on *The Lamp!* This maintained a connection to the older GEnieLamp name, but had the added advantage of not linking itself specifically to Delphi. This was ultimately a good thing, as events later turned out.

With a musical reference to Emerson, Lake & Palmer, editor Suenaga began his first editorial for *The Lamp!* by giving a brief story of the path from Genie to Delphi, and ending with the statements, "Apple][Forever. And forever on Delphi."

In creating the new newsletter, he did not take a radical departure from the format that had been established five years earlier by John Peters when he created the first series of GEnieLamp newsletters. He still had a venue for information gleaned from online postings, product reviews, an editorial, and extra articles as they became available. It was mostly a matter of finding new titles for these columns. Using a baseball motif, the editorial "From My Desktop" became "Opening Pitch," the "Log Off" credits sections became "Extra Innings," and just to be different, "Hey Mister Postman" became "A Funny Thing Happened." He also made small changes in the layout and appearance of the table of contents, but retained the bracketed three-letter indexing system that Peters had originated (but which had not yet been put to use).

With Apple II activity still occurring on Genie as well as on Delphi, the information reproduced in *The Lamp!* was an amalgam of both. It docu-

CHAPTER 40 | Ahead of their Time: Digital Magazines

mented the transition of library files from Genie to Delphi (and how much work that entailed), the impending loss of text-only access for CompuServe users, and (as in past years) the run-up to KansasFest and the post-analysis of events that happened there. Doug Cuff continued to be involved in the new online newsletter by writing an update to his KansasFest guide, initially titled "The Accidental Tourist at KansasFest".

The February issue included a "State of the II, 1999," and in which Suenaga lauded the possibilities of emulators like *Bernie][The Rescue* and *Sweet16*, and compared what he had predicted for 1998 and what 1999 offered:

> Since the time I wrote those words, we've had a large influx of new and exciting products (introductions were centered largely around KansasFest)--from freeware and shareware to commercial software to reclassifications of classic favorites. Yet almost a year later, the Apple II marketplace continues to struggle.
>
> Those Apple II developers and publishers who continue to produce software and hardware do so mostly as a labor of love, but without enough financial support to keep them in business, how long will that last?
>
> Will we learn from the lessons that the last year has taught us?
>
> There's still time to seize the day. Make 1999 the year that 1998 could have been–the year of the Apple II comeback.

The Lamp!, January 1998 first issue masthead
– Photo credit: personal

In the September 1999 editorial, Suenaga announced that due to work schedule changes, December would be his final issue. The new editor would be Lyle Syverson, who had an article appearing in that issue. Syverson began his run as editor with the January 2000 issue. He had started back in 1987 with a Laser 128, learned about the platform by subscribing to Apple II magazines, and by 1993 he had purchased a modem to join in the telecommunications revolution. He initially started on GEnie, using an offline reader to automate his online sessions, and closely followed and participated in the activity there. By 1993 he was ready to upgrade his computer to an Apple IIGS. When the prices on Genie became too expensive for his tastes in 1996, he moved to the APPUSER forum on CompuServe, and stayed until early

1999, when text-based access there was terminated. He then migrated to Delphi, saw Suenaga's request for a new editor and offered his services.

Although he used the same format as the previous editor, Syverson did make a few changes. The first editorial that he used had the same title, "Opening Pitch," but the following month he personalized it by changing the title to "High Above the Rock River," named after the river that ran past his apartment.

During 2000, Delphi began to show some of the same instability as had been seen on Genie, as Delphi tried to transition from a text-based service to a combination text- and web-based service, and changed from subscription to free access. *The Lamp!* also reported on the efforts of Eric Shepherd to provide a service that acted and worked like Genie of the past, and could work as a stable alternative to Delphi.

That year also, many of the discussions reproduced in *The Lamp!* involved education of new users about old hardware. There were also announcements about several CD-ROM collections of software, including *Opus][* from The Byte Works (a collection of everything ever sold by that company). Many other older software titles were being reclassified as freeware or public domain. Publisher Ryan Suenaga continued to make an appearance in *The Lamp!*, with his announcement of the *Time in a Bottle* project, a CD-ROM collection of files that had been rescued from Genie.

In 2001, the available information to print in *The Lamp!* began to include postings from Shepherd's Syndicomm.com bulletin board, since participation in the Delphi Apple II forum had significantly declined with the failure of the text side of the service. By 2002 there was virtually no further mention of Delphi in *The Lamp!*, and by 2005 it had been removed from the masthead.[15]

Editor Syverson continued regularly putting out an issue of *The Lamp!* on into 2007, but much of the content of this online magazine had traditionally depended on what was posted on the online service that Apple II users called home. In the process of migrating from GEnie to Delphi to Syndicomm/A2-Central, the number of available places that Apple II enthusiasts could go for sharing and finding information was multiplying with the number of available web sites on the growing Internet. Consequently, the volume of messages on the A2-Central BBS became more and more sparse, and there was progressively less content with which to create an online newsletter. Where the length of each issue averaged 98K during the first year *The Lamp!* ran in 1998, it was down to 55K in 2004, and by 2007 it was down to 27K. Syverson chose simply to not release an issue in September 2007. Within three years, the A2-Central BBS had gone offline.[16]

---

15 During 2003 my own series began, called "Illuminating The Lamp", giving the history of *GEnieLamp A2* and *The Lamp!* on a year-by-year basis, taking time out to discuss the history of the development and release of *Wolfenstein 3D* for the Apple IIGS. The series lasted into late 2004, with sometimes several months between installments.

16 Syverson held the record as the longest running editor in the entire run of *GEnieLamp A2* and *The Lamp!*, with a total of 92 issues that he created and released, over seven and one-half years in total. The next runner-up was Doug Cuff, who produced 41 issues of *GEnieLamp A2*, just under three and one-half years, and last of all Ryan Suenaga at 34 issues, just under three years. Thanks to the efforts of Syverson, he kept a record of the activities on the Apple II community in its last productive years on Delphi and during nearly its entire time on the A2-Central/Syndicomm BBS.

CALL-A.P.P.L.E. – ONLINE (May 2002-)

Bill Martens had joined the Apple Pugetsound Program Library Exchange beginning back in 1981, at the age of 17. At this time the club had been in existence for just four years, and Martens helped in the office with user surveys and production of their public domain software disks. Later, he created the Pascal Anthology Disk, which sold from 1981 through the late 1980s. After 1982 he stopped working regularly with A.P.P.L.E. and went on to other positions, from running the computer labs at Washington State Community Colleges, to eventually (in 1989) working in Japan to build office infrastructures for Tokyo financial institutions.

But throughout all of these changes, he continued to have a fondness for his Apple II roots, and beginning in 1999 Martens started to organize his collection of A.P.P.L.E. software and magazines. After retiring from his Tokyo consulting job in 2001 he continued his personal archiving project, completing his collection of the *Call-A.P.P.L.E.* magazine. About this time, Martens began to reestablish contact with those who had been associated with the company. He spoke with Val Golding, and then also with the former directors and those who had been involved in management of A.P.P.L.E, as well as many of the writers for the magazine.

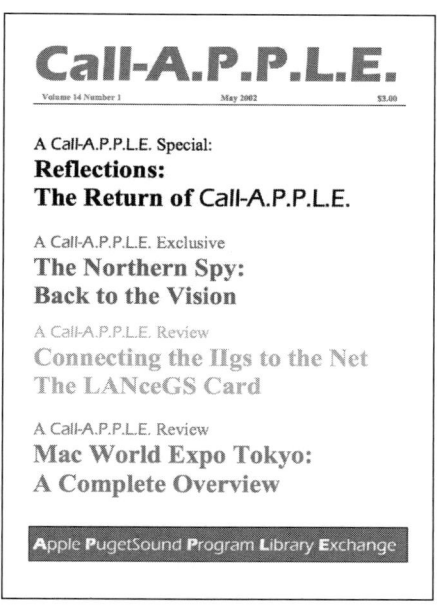

Call-A.P.P.L.E. May 2002 – Photo credit: Bill Martens

When he discussed his project with Rick Sutcliffe (who had written a column called "The Northern Spy" during the later years of *Call-A.P.P.L.E.*), he suggested that they get both the user group and the magazine going again. In further discussion with those he had previously contacted, Martens found their response to be quite positive. Together they decided that the time had come to bring the group back to life, and in February 2002 the new A.P.P.L.E. was born.

In the process of creating this new group, bringing back the *Call-A.P.P.L.E.* magazine was part of the vision. This time, rather than a printed version and the costs associated with distribution, the A.P.P.L.E. board decided to create and distribute the magazine via—what else?— the Internet. They distributed the magazine in the Adobe Portable Document Format (PDF), which gave greater control over the appearance of each page than would be possible with HTML code for web pages. Val Golding, now 71, agreed to participate as a director, and to write again with a column called, "The Editor *Still* Bytes Back," a reprise of his former editorial column. The first issue, Volume 14, No. 1, appeared online in May 2002. Its cover format was a return to the heyday of the print magazine (see the 1981-style cover that is reproduced above). Future issues were available via subscription, and it was planned that articles would cover the Macintosh as well as the original focus of the club, the Apple II. In fact, the June 2002 issue had a review of an IDE card for the Apple II, and even had a new Applesoft program for manipulating hi-res graphics screens. Again, as stated in Golding's final editorial in the previous incarnation of *Call-A.P.P.L.E.*, the group had come "full circle".[17]

TIMELINE

The start and end dates for digital magazines:

Softdisk
– *September 1981 - August 1995*

Softdisk G-S
– *November 1989 - March 1997*

Scholastic Microzine
– *March 1983 - May 1992*

Uptime – *October 1984 - December 1988*

Stack-Central / Studio City
– *December 1989*

Timeout-Central
– *August 1990*

8/16-Central – *December 1990 - October 1991*

Hyperbole – *March 1991*

Script-Central – *June 1991*

GEnieLamp A2
– *April 1992 - October 1997*

GEnieLamp A2Pro
– *February 1993 - January 1996*

The Lamp!
– *January 1998 - August 2007*

Call-A.P.P.L.E. (online)
– *May 2002 -*

---

17 Martens, Bill, e-mail message to author, May 2002.

CHAPTER 41
Latter Day Languages

In the early years of the Apple II (and most other microcomputers), BASIC was supreme, followed closely by various assemblers. BASIC was good for quick projects, while assembly language was necessary to create compact code that fit in the limited available memory.

By the time of the release of the newer generation Apple IIe and IIc, which used the 65c02 processor, and the IIgs with its 16-bit 65816 processor, some of the older languages gained new power, while new languages appeared that made it possible to create more complex software. This chapter will look at some of these new and enhanced programming packages.

ASSEMBLERS

LISA Assembler

Randall Hyde had originally published his LISA assembler in 1979 through Programma and later Sierra. After Sierra stopped publishing programming tools in 1983, Hyde reacquired the rights to the program and for a while published it himself.

When the Apple IIgs was released in 1986, Hyde turned maintenance of the LISA assembler over to Brian Fitzgerald. Back in 1982, Fitzgerald had started his own software company named H.A.L. Labs (not related to Japanese console gaming company HAL Laboratory) to publish a game he had written. Fitzgerald updated the LISA assembler to work with the IIgs and its 65816 processor and larger memory space. The new version he named *LISA816*, adding macro capability, an improved screen editor, and more. LISA816 continued to be a fast program, and could assemble code at the rate of 150,000 lines per minute.

With the decline in the Apple II market and the greater popularity of the ORCA/M assembler for the IIgs, H.A.L. Labs released LISA into the public domain in 1987.

MERLIN

Southwestern Data Systems commercially released Glen Bredon's Merlin assembler in 1982, making it available to a larger marketplace then when it had previously been available through the A.P.P.L.E. user group.

Bredon continued to work on enhancements to the product and in 1985 Roger Wagner Publishing (the new name for Southwestern Data Systems) released *Merlin Pro*. This update offered both DOS 3.3 and ProDOS versions, and it worked with the 80-column mode of the 128K Apple IIe and the Apple IIc. It offered pre-commented files that could be used with the Sourceror disassembler to create an annotated disassembly source file for Applesoft.

About the same time that Merlin Pro was released, Roger Wagner Publishing ported over a version that ran on the Commodore 64, calling it *Merlin 64*. Its feature set was very much like that offered by Merlin Pro. The following year the company released *Merlin 128*, for use on the Commodore 128.

With the introduction of the Apple IIGS in 1986, Bredon updated the many utilities he had written for the 8-bit Apple II series to function in the IIGS environment. In 1987 he also updated his assembler to work on the new computer, and it was released as *Merlin 8/16*. The package offered three versions of the assembler: Merlin 8 for DOS 3.3, Merlin 8 for ProDOS, and Merlin 16 for ProDOS 16. The latter version could create executable binary files for the 65816 and 65802 microprocessors, in addition to the earlier 6502 and 65c02. Merlin 8 could assemble code for the 6502, 65c02 or 65802. It also offered an enhanced *Sourceror/XL* disassembler, which could handle the 16-bit opcodes for the 65816.

The final version of Bredon's assembler was *Merlin 16+*, exclusively intended for use with GS/OS, the last versions of the Apple IIGS operating system.

Merlin 16+ manual cover – Photo credit: personal

ORCA/M

In 1982 Hayden Software published Mike Westerfield's ORCA/M assembler, modeled after the style of the IBM 360 mainframe assembler. Westerfield continued development on his assembler, and within two years he was making changes to adapt it to work under ProDOS. However, in 1984 Hayden Publishing decided to shut down its software publishing division. Westerfield was able to take back control of his assembler, and decided to start his own company, The Byte Works, to continue to sell and upgrade ORCA/M.

ORCA/M played an important role in the development of application software for the Apple IIGS. When Apple and Western Design Center (WDC) began to collaborate on a 16-bit version of the 6502, David Eyes from Hayden brought together Westerfield with Bill Mensch of WDC. Westerfield ultimately designed the opcode syntax for the 65816 and 65802 processors, and then used this knowledge to update ORCA/M to work with these processors earlier than any other company.

Apple took notice of the capabilities of this assembler, and elected to contract with The Byte Works to make ORCA/M the official development environment for the Apple IIGS, which was code-named Cortland in the latter days of its development. The *Cortland Programmer's Workshop* gave tools to the developers who wanted to create software for the new computer, to be ready when it was released in September 1986.

When Apple released the software package, they changed the name to *Apple Programmer's Workshop*, abbreviated APW. Apple allowed The Byte Works to continue to sell ORCA/M separately, which Westerfield continued to enhance, and under which he later released other languages, all of which could be used together in large projects.

PASCAL COMPILERS

TML Pascal / Complete Pascal

TML Systems first released its native code Pascal compiler, *TML Pascal*, for the Apple IIGS in 1987. Not only did it take advantage of the power of the Apple IIGS desktop, but it was also possible to use it as a learning environment to enter and run textbook Pascal programs.

It later became *TML Pascal II* in 1989 to run under GS/OS, with full access to the IIGS Toolbox.

Complete Technology, Inc., purchased *TML Pascal* and in 1990 released it as *Complete Pascal* 1.0 (which was *TML Pascal II* 1.1 with some minor changes). They advanced it to *Complete Pascal* 2.0 in 1991; however, soon after this happened, a fire destroyed the offices of Complete Technology in Denver, and the company did not recover from this loss. In 2009, the copyright holder and author for Complete Pascal released the product for free distribution.[1]

---

1 Zaleski, Paul, "Complete Pascal (Formerly TML Pascal II)",*PZ's Apple IIgs Programming Software Pages*, <www.snowcat.com/a2programming/index.htm>, accessed October 20, 2012.

ORCA/Pascal

Apple adopted the ORCA programming environment from The Byte Works for the new Apple IIGS in 1986 (as mentioned above), creating the *Apple Programmer's Workshop* (APW). The money earned from Apple in that deal made it possible for The Byte Works to work on other languages, including ORCA/Pascal.

Apple tried to hire other programmers to create a version of Pascal to run under APW, but this never worked out. This left ORCA/Pascal as the only version of Pascal that was compatible with APW, and able to share its libraries with other languages under that programming shell.[2]

LOGO

The Logo language had been designed for use in education, and was best known for its turtle-graphics that allowed easy creation of line art on the computer screen, or with a mechanical floor turtle. The Byte Works provided two versions of the Logo language specifically for the Apple IIGS. One was *3D Logo*, and the other was *HyperLogo*, a $60 scripting language that ran under Roger Wagner Publishing's *HyperStudio* development environment. HyperLogo worked as a replacement for SimpleScript, which was HyperStudio's built-in scripting language.

Both 3D Logo and HyperLogo were full implementations of Logo, with the added ability to create three-dimensional images. The 3D turtle could draw in either true 3D (which required special glasses to view) or in perspective mode (3D images mapped in 2D).

It also had support for Talking Tools, which allowed creation of programs that talked to the user. 3D Logo included additional commands to allow creation of desktop programs that could launch from the GS/OS Finder. Stacks (as the collections of display screens in HyperStudio were called) created with HyperLogo could be distributed to a HyperStudio user who didn't own the HyperLogo add-on language, as The Byte Works provided a run-time module to distribute with the stack.

C

The C language, developed in conjunction with Unix, offered some of the best of both worlds to programmers. It provided the power of assembly language when needed, while delivering the data handling and structured programming abilities of a high level language. Although it had limited use

---

2 Westerfield, Mike, telephone interview with author and e-mail addressed to author, March 15, 2012.

on the 8-bit Apple II models, the power of the 65816 and larger memory size of the IIgs made this a popular language for 16-bit programmers.

Apple released APW/C, made to run under the Apple Programmers Workshop on the Apple IIgs not long after the computer was released. However, ORCA/C from The Byte Works was a more full-featured version of the language, and was compliant with the ANSI (American National Standards Institute) C standards published in 1990.

Years after the Apple II platform had ceased production, another C compiler became available. CC65 was a cross-compiler written originally in the early 1990s by John R. Dunning for the Atari XL. He created it to compile a subset of the full C language. With time, other programmers expanded it beyond the Atari, eventually making it as much compliant with ANSI C standards as was possible. However, certain parts were not implemented (high-precision 64-bit integers, for example) because it was felt that they did not make sense for use on the 6502 processor.

Unlike the other C compilers mentioned previously, CC65 was made to run on a broad range of more modern systems (Windows, Macintosh, and Unix) to create code that would then be transferred to the target system. Computers on which the compiled code would run included several of the later Commodore series, the Nintendo Entertainment System, and the Atari Lynx. In October 2009 a version of CC65 was released that was able to create code that could run on the Apple II.[3]

TIMELINE

LISA816 – *1986*

Apple Programmers Workshop – *September 1986*

Merlin 8/16 – *1987*

TML Pascal – *1987*

ORCA/Pascal – *1987*

Merlin 16+ – *1988*

Complete Pascal – *1990*

HyperLogo GS – *November 1993*

3D Logo – *November 1993*

CC65 – *October 2009*

---

3 Olefsky, Jake, "The History and Popularity of the C Programming Language", *JAKE*, <www.jakeo.com/words/clanguage.php>, accessed March 14, 2013.

CHAPTER 42
Small Publisher Magazines

In the mid-1980s, the major publisher houses were making a foray into the world of Apple II magazines. While this brought knowledge about the Apple II to the newsstands and to the average consumer, the loss of the first generation magazines left a void for the technical Apple II user. To meet this need, new publications appeared, working on a similar small scale as did the first magazines that appeared in the early days of the Apple II. Because of their closer focus on a particular audience and lower publication expenses (usually working with a smaller staff), some of these lasted longer than the big-publisher offerings.

OPEN-APPLE / A2-CENTRAL (Jan 1985 – Feb 1995)

Many individuals have made a significant impact on the Apple II community. Some created the hardware and software that made the computer work; some publicized and educated others; some created users groups; and some tried to influence the path taken by Apple. There are few who played a role in *all* of these categories. Tom Weishaar was one of that select group.

After earning a degree in English, film, radio, and television from the University of Iowa, Tom Weishaar decided to join the Peace Corps. He served for two years in India, teaching modern agriculture techniques, and found it an enriching experience. When he completed his commitment, he returned to school and received his master's degree in journalism from the University of Kansas. Afterward he worked at the Commodities News Service, where he was editor for the *Cotton Trade News*.

When the Apple II came out in 1977, Weishaar decided that he wanted one. He purchased a 16K Apple II with Integer BASIC and a modem, but no disk drive, printer, or monitor (he used his television). For a long time, that was all he had. He taught himself BASIC and assembly language, and wrote a program called *Frame Up*, which presented hi-res graphics in a slideshow fashion (not unlike the later, more sophisticated Microsoft program, *PowerPoint*).

Looking for a publisher for his program, Weishaar saw a reflection of his own personality in Beagle Bros. He contacted the company to see if it would be interested in selling Frame Up. Not only was it willing to sell that program, but it also later marketed another of Weishaar's efforts, a DOS 3.3 speed-up and enhancement program called *ProntoDOS*.[1]

Because of his Beagle Bros fame, Bert Kersey became involved in *Softalk* magazine partway through its run. He wrote a column called "DOSTalk" from April 1982 through February 1983. The following month, in place of the DOSTalk column, Softalk published an article submitted by Weishaar, explaining how to speed disk access. As Kersey had decided he no longer wanted to write the DOSTalk column, Weishaar volunteered to take over, and from April 1983 until the magazine folded in August 1984 he continued writing about Apple DOS and later about the newer ProDOS.

Tom Weishaar
– Photo credit: *Softalk* October 1983, p. 69.

After the fall of *Softalk*, Weishaar realized there was still a need for a technical publication to serve beginning and intermediate Apple II users. Taking this experience and his past work as editor for the Commodity News Service, he decided to start a newsletter that would offer the type of information he had previously provided in DOSTalk, but as a monthly eight-page newsletter.

He called this newsletter *Open-Apple*, leveraging the name of the special open-apple key on the Apple IIe keyboard, with the additional meaning of openly sharing information about the Apple II. The first trial issue (Volume 1, No. 0) was mailed out to the old *Softalk* mailing list. That issue included information about Applesoft and Logo, along with reader's letters—some left over from DOSTalk, but some intentionally phony, with return addresses like the Okefenokee Swamp. At $24 for a one-year subscription, its cost was as much as full-sized magazines of the day. However, *Open-Apple* did not carry any advertising and was very information-dense.[2]

Open-Apple, January 1985 – Photo credit: personal

As the newsletter matured over the years, the coverage of Logo disappeared, and Applesoft dwindled as well, reflecting changes in reader interests. During the late 1980s, coverage of AppleWorks was heavy, and nearly ev-

---

1 Yuen, Matt, "Exec Beagle Bros", *Softalk* (October 1983), 66-74.
2 Weyhrich, Steven, "MACH Interview: Tom Weishaar", *M.A.C.H. News* (July 1991), 6-11.

ery issue contained some way to patch the program to add specific functions. Coverage of the IIGS was also prominent, and Weishaar struggled to find a balance without ignoring the sizeable number of readers who still owned the older 8-bit Apple II models.

In December 1988, the name of the newsletter was changed to *A2-Central*. Several reasons were given for the change. One was similar to the reason given by A.P.P.L.E. for changing its name to TechAlliance—Apple Computer was in the habit of threatening legal infringement against those who used its name without permission (or at least licensing it). Another was to indicate Weishaar's wider vision for the newsletter: to be the center of the Apple II universe.

Earlier in 1988, Weishaar had also taken on the task of serving as the manager of the Apple II roundtables on the online service GEnie. This increased the information available to him for his publication, as well as allowing a more prompt exchange of information with his readers. In fact, there was a great similarity between the conversations that took place on GEnie, in the reader questions section of *A2-Central*, and the old "Open Discussion" part of *Softalk* magazine. New users could ask, "How do I get a program to run with my printer?" and experienced users could quickly offer answers online.

A2-Central, June 1993 – Photo credit: personal

Because the newsletter included international readers, and these readers had difficulty obtaining certain Apple II-related products or books, a catalog was added to the *A2-Central* line-up in early 1989. This list initially consisted primarily of printed material, but quickly expanded to include software and hardware. February 1989 also saw the first of "A2 on Disk," which included a text file of the current month's newsletter, as well as an assortment of the latest shareware and freeware programs for the Apple II.

In July 1989, Weishaar promoted and organized the first of what became an annual user conference in Kansas City, bringing together professional developers, representatives from Apple, and enthusiasts of the platform. Though the event was a success, it added significantly to Weishaar's work load. He realized that he needed a break from the monthly deadline of five years of writing *A2-Central* (and DOSTalk for nearly eighteen months before that).

One of the first changes Weishaar made was a re-assignment of responsibilities within the company. Dennis Doms had for some time helped create each issue, and was familiar with the content and style. He was promoted to editor of *A2-Central*, and Weishaar moved himself to the position of publisher. It did not result in any significant change in the newsletter, but it allowed Weishaar to channel his energies into the management of the company.

Not long after this, the company released additional publications. To reduce confusion, Weishaar changed the name of the company to Resource Central, and left *A2-Central* as the name of its flagship publication. The new offerings were not additional paper newsletters, but were instead disk-based publications: *Stack-Central* (later *Studio City*), *Script-Central*, *Hyperbole*, *TimeOut-Central*, and *8/16-Central* (previously discussed).

A2-Central (the newsletter) underwent very few changes during these years. Its focus shifted slightly to keeping readers informed of the newest changes in the Apple II world (in terms of products and events), whereas previously it spent a lot of time talking about specific products (which were now covered by the spin-off disk publications). The newsletter's editorship changed a few more times as well, moving from Dennis Doms eventually to Ellen Rosenberg, who implemented a new policy of accepting feature articles from outside authors for the first time since *A2-Central* began publication.

With the shutdown of *Nibble* magazine in 1992, *A2-Central* agreed to take over its subscription list. It was hoped that many of the new subscribers would see enough value in *A2-Central* to renew when the time came, but unfortunately not enough readers did. Weishaar even tried a new paper newsletter called *Fishhead's Children*, intended to be a resource for those who had to bridge themselves between the Apple II, Macintosh, and MS-DOS computers.[3] However, the new publication did not have enough subscribers to maintain a positive cash flow, and in June 1993 a letter was sent out to subscribers of both *Fishhead's Children* and *A2-Central*:

> Dear Subscriber,
> Dominoes are falling at Resource Central and you've been hit.
> As the Apple II nears the end of its life cycle, renewals to our flagship publication, the paper version of *A2-Central*, have fallen to less than 20 per cent. That domino has been teetering ever since we took over *Nibble*'s subscribers a year ago.
> We had hoped to stabilize the situation with a new publication, *Fishhead's Children*, which would take us into new territory. Unfortunately, that publication hasn't been the success we had hoped it would be. For each $100 we've spent trying to obtain new subscribers, we've taken in less than $10. We can no longer carry this expense without putting our entire company in jeopardy, so that domino has ceased publication and fallen.
> Without a successful *Fishhead's Children*, there's nothing to pay the even-increasing bills the paper version of *A2-Central* is running

---

3   Its name was somewhat of an inside joke that was probably not widely known, that being the original name of the FID file utility on Apple DOS 3.3, FISHEAD.

up. *A2-Central-On-Disk* continues to have strong renewals, as do our other disk publications, but they're not big enough to continue supporting our paper publications. It all means that I have no choice but to cease publication of the paper version of *A2-Central* as well.

The letter went on to explain that the value of remaining subscriptions (not counting the old *Nibble* people) would be credited to the subscriber's account, and could be refunded or applied to another product sold by Resource Central. *A2-Central on Disk* would continue as it had before; it cost the company much less to duplicate and mail disks than it did to print and mail paper newsletters. The *A2-Central* newsletter continued to appear on *A2-Central on Disk* in a digital, rather than paper format.

Because of these changes, the January 1994 issue of *A2-Central on Disk* was renamed to simply *A2-Central*. Weishaar asked John Peters to come onboard to help organize and staff what was now a newsletter on disk. Peters had been overseeing the online GEnieLamp newsletters on GEnie for several years, and he formatted the text for the digital *A2-Central* in a similar manner. Peters gathered several veteran Apple II writers to assist in producing the text of the newsletter each month, as well as collecting the freeware and shareware files that were included with each issue.[4] Doug Cuff, who was editor of *GEnieLamp A2* and a contributing editor for *II Alive*, was also tapped to write articles for *A2-Central*, and eventually took over as editor.

A2-Central, Jan 1994 – Photo credit: personal

Still trying to keep his company going, Weishaar realized that the only solution for the loss of Apple II readers was to expand coverage to include other platforms. In the spring of 1994 he announced the formation of ICON, the International Computer Owners Network. It described itself as a multi-system worldwide user group, with the goal of educating the public about computers and related technologies. It was itself a transition from Resource Central and its Apple II-centric publications to be more inclusive of other computers (Macintosh and PC).

As part of this effort, Weishaar also asked Peters to create three new disk publications to address these non-Apple II groups: *Macrocosm* for the Macintosh, *Solid Windows* for Windows, and *Config.Sys* for MS-DOS. The existing disk magazines for the Apple II were also still promoted.

---

4 At this time my own independent monthly news compilation, the *A2 News Digest*, became exclusively a part of *A2-Central*. The Digest had previously been available on GEnie as source material for Apple user group newsletters.

To discuss ICON and its activities, Weishaar started a quarterly paper newsletter, *Ahs* (which rhymed with "Oz," a Kansas connections because of *The Wizard of Oz* stories). It was available to anyone who was a subscriber to an ICON publication. Three issues of *Ahs* were printed.

Despite all of these efforts, the declining interest for Apple II publications continued. The financial constraints this caused made it necessary for ICON to ultimately take the difficult step of shutting down all of its operations in February 1995, bringing to an end all of its existing disk publications.

Ahs:
Releasing the power of computers to everyone."
Masthead for *Ahs*, Spring 1994 – Photo credit: personal

Weishaar's interest in and dedication to the Apple II has been publicly recognized in several ways. He was chosen as a recipient of the Apple II Individual Achievement Award for 1991, and at KansasFest 2010 he and three other former leaders of Resource Central were also awarded one of the first "Apple II Forever" awards, in thanks for their many contributions to the community. His philosophy was summed up by his statement, "The significant thing about the Apple II has always been the community of people that has sprung up around the machine, teaching other people how to use it, designing hard and software for it, exposing its inner flesh to the light of day, and using it to manage businesses, run church groups, educate children, and turn out prosperous and happy human beings."[5]

APPLEWORKS FORUM / NATIONAL APPLEWORKS USERS GROUP (Aug 1986 – Dec 1995)

Warren Williams first learned about mainframe computers while he was earning his doctoral degree at the University of Rochester in 1965. He continued to pursue statistical and research work with similar computers at Eastern Michigan University. With the appearance of microcomputers in the late 1970s, Williams began to investigate how they could make an impact on education, first with a borrowed Apple II in 1979, and then the following year with his first purchased computer, a TRS-80 Model II. That same year Williams began to teach classes on the use of computers in education, but he had a problem finding software that was both powerful and easy to use. After an upgrade to the new Apple IIc in 1984 and the subsequent release of AppleWorks that same year, he finally found the software that met his requirements.

During the summer of 1984, Williams wrote a manual for his classes on how to use AppleWorks. It was well received by his students and administra-

---

5 Weishaar, Tom, *A2-Central Catalog* (Fall 1990), 2.

tors, and he began to give talks about the use of AppleWorks. Around this same time, Williams met up with Cathleen Merritt, who was working towards a second Master's degree, in Educational Technology. Williams hired her to help with these presentations at conferences and meetings. Merritt likewise was impressed with the power offered by AppleWorks, and began teaching it to other graduate students.

Williams and Merritt continued to give presentations about AppleWorks over the next two years. After a talk they gave in 1986 at the Michigan Association of Computer Users for Learning conference, an audience member suggested the formation of a national user group focused on AppleWorks. Over one hundred interested people stayed on after their talk to discuss how to make this happen. The National AppleWorks Users Group (NAUG) was first announced that year in April at the Educational Computer Conference in San Diego. In August they mailed out the first issue of NAUG's newsletter, *AppleWorks Forum*.

The pair continued to give introductory and advanced talks about AppleWorks across the country, and this provided publicity for NAUG. From 1987 to 1988, they gave more than 75 seminars in 60 cities across the country, with attendance typically from 80 to 150. This resulted in attendees applying for membership in the organization. Memberships surpassed 16,000 from 51 countries in November 1990, making NAUG the world's largest computer user group, and it did not drop below that number until late 1991. By 1993, it still had over 8,000 active members, and nearly eight times that many who had expressed interest in the group at one time or another. These members drew from every state in the United States, and from forty-two countries around the world.

AppleWorks Forum v10n1 front page – Photo credit: personal

Two NAUG members helped create a BBS for NAUG in June 1988 to help members communicate with each other. That BBS was started on an Apple II Plus, and eventually increased to three Apple II computers that were networked together, handling three phone lines. In 1993 it was handling 50 to 80 calls per day, and provided over 200 MB of downloadable files (primarily AppleWorks templates created by the members).

Volunteers played a large role in NAUG's success. There were 150 members who provided their contact information so that other members could call them with questions about AppleWorks. It ultimately offered a 24-hour service, provided the member was willing to pay long-distance charges (some of these volunteer members were as distant as Australia and China). During 1988, online help was also offered via email, primarily through CompuServe accounts.

The monthly newsletter featured editorial columns and additional articles contributed by members. Volunteers helped Cathleen Merritt make the selection of articles that appeared in each issue. The final copy was then delivered to a graphics designer and page layout specialist, who transferred the articles from disks in AppleWorks format to *Quark XPress* on a Macintosh, and then printed the final result on a LaserWriter. These pages were then reproduced in a high-density final format and printed by a local service bureau.

In an interview in 1993, Williams described some of the many ways in which AppleWorks was being used across the country. For several years, a member of NAUG who was the chief writer for the news broadcast *ABC Evening News with Peter Jennings* used AppleWorks to create the scripts for that television program. AppleWorks was also used in the production of the Broadway play, *Cats*. Another member used it to help manage a $4 million hog farming operation.

In early 1992, NAUG helped start a second group, the ClarisWorks Users Group, at the request of Claris, who was by then publishing AppleWorks for the Apple II and *ClarisWorks* for the Macintosh. The first issue of *ClarisWorks Journal* was published in February 1992, and continued until January 2008 (later changing its name to *AppleWorks Journal* after Apple changed the name of that Mac program from ClarisWorks to AppleWorks).

By 1992, as the Macintosh was finally reaching critical mass and popularity, NAUG's membership began to decrease. By 1995 it was no longer possible to continue the group, and it published the final issue of *AppleWorks Forum*—the last of a run of 113 issues—in December 1995. Existing subscribers were offered a refund of their remaining subscription, or a full-year subscription to major magazines, membership in the ClarisWorks Users Group, a complete set of back issues of *AppleWorks Forum*, or other AppleWorks products at discount prices. Williams and Merritt promised continued availability of the files from NAUG on America Online, CompuServe, GEnie, and the NAUG BBS.[6, 7, 8]

GS+ (Sep 1989 – Aug 1995)

In the late 1970s, Steven Disbrow entered the world of microcomputers with his purchase of a TRS-80 Model I, which came complete with cassette storage and 4K of memory. To learn more about his computer and what it could do, he picked up a newsstand magazine called *80-Micro* (published by Wayne Green, who had also started *BYTE* and *inCider* magazines). What he

---

6 Shapiro, Phil, unpublished interview, June 5, 1993.
7 Williams, Warren, e-mail message to author, May 22, 2012.
8 Williams, Warren, and Merritt, Cathleen, "AppleWorks Forum Ceases Publication", *GEnieLamp A2*, Dec 1995.

liked about these magazines was the lighthearted way in which they presented information about the TRS-80, which infused a sense of fun into the reading and computing experience. Active also in the local TRS-80 user group, Disbrow disdained the Apple II and those who used them.

Despite these opinions, Disbrow found it necessary to make a change in 1984. In order to do some schoolwork, he needed the ability to communicate with a mainframe computer via modem. He found that it was going to be expensive to upgrade his TRS-80 to allow use of a modem. He discovered that the newly released Apple IIc with a 300-baud modem, available together for about $1300, was actually less expensive than the upgrade path he was facing. He decided to cross enemy lines and entered the Apple camp.

Over the next two years, Disbrow became more familiar with his new Apple IIc, through the help of books and newsstand computer magazines. These magazines announced the new 16-bit Apple IIGS when it was released in 1986, and this piqued his interest. While browsing available computer magazines at the newsstand, he noticed that many of the publications for the Atari ST included a disk with each issue. Disbrow went so far as to contact several of the available Apple II magazines to see if they had any similar plans for inclusion of a companion disk, but none of them seemed interested. When he was finally able to purchase his own IIGS, and saw that there still was no combination magazine and disk for the computer, he decided that he would start one himself.

GS+ September-October 1992 – Photo credit: Andrew Molloy

Disbrow created a company that would be the publisher behind his new magazine. His girlfriend at the time told him that he had such a big ego, he should name it after himself. Though he didn't go that far, he decided to name his company EGO Systems.

The new magazine was ready for release in September 1989. Because Disbrow had chosen to exclusively cover the Apple IIGS, he named it GS+. It was published on a bi-monthly basis, and the byline on the cover of each issue reminded subscribers of what made his magazine unique: "The First Apple IIGS Magazine + Disk Publication!" Remembering the humor and fun of 80-Micro, Disbrow was determined to follow the same path. He felt this was especially important, considering the generally negative attitude that was prevalent among Apple II users at the time, as they saw less and less active support from Apple for their platform. GS+ concentrated on news, software and hardware reviews, published programs and utilities for the IIGS (along with source code for each program on the companion disk), and interviews with people who were involved with the IIGS.[9]

After the first issue had been printed, it was initially available only in Disbrow's home town, Chattanooga, Tennessee. Joe Wankerl, a college student in the same city, found the magazine and logged into a BBS that Disbrow was running. He offered Disbrow some ideas for programs, and after Wankerl graduated, he was made Technical Editor for the magazine.

Wankerl became responsible for reviewing content for the magazine, to ensure it was technically accurate. He also took on the responsibility of writing much of the software that was featured in the magazine, and was in charge of putting together the disk associated with each issue. The focus on programming that Disbrow put into each article extended to including source code for all of the software featured. In a sense, GS+ offered open source software before it came into common usage.

Because of its focus on programming, it was also a natural fit for GS+ to pick up the subscribers from *8/16-Central* when that publication closed in 1991.

During its run, Disbrow and Wankerl included several important utilities on the disk that accompanied the print copy of GS+, including *EGOed* (a word processor in a desk accessory), *Replicator* (a desktop-based disk duplicator), *Cool Cursor* (an animator cursor for the mouse pointer), *ICE* (an icon editor), *Ellifont* (allowed the user to double click a font to see a sample), *FinderBinder* (matched documents with their programs), *Rainbow* (offered color control of icons and windows on the IIGS desktop), and many others.

GS+ magazine had a loyal and enthusiastic subscriber base. Despite his lack of backing by a large publisher (as *A+* and *inCider* enjoyed) Disbrow's efforts were rewarded in 1992, when GS+ was awarded honorable mention as the best Apple II publication (beaten out by *A2-Central*). The magazine had its own category in the A2Pro Roundtable on GEnie to help with customer support and also to solicit authors.

Disbrow had to deal with legal challenges during the run of the magazine. Even though he did not use "Apple" in its name, lawyers from the company contacted him and told him that GS+ infringed on their product trademark for "Apple IIGS Plus" (the ROM 04 computer that was cancelled in 1989). Disbrow tried to run a contest with readers to select a different name, but he didn't feel that the entries were very good. As a last effort, he sent an overnight letter directly to Apple CEO John Sculley, explaining the situation, and asking for his clemency. Two days later, Disbrow received a

---

9 Disbrow, Steven, "Old Timers: Magazines", *1992 A2 Central Summer Conference* (tape) (July 1992).

phone call directly from Apple's chief legal counsel, and was told that Sculley had specifically stated that EGO Systems could use the name GS+ for as long as it wanted.

Even the American Red Cross had its attorney contact EGO Systems about its logo. It was the opinion of their lawyers that the plus sign after the "GS" could be confused with the logo for the Red Cross, even though it was displayed on the cover in italics. The logo on each cover was in a solid color, and sometimes the color was red. Disbrow promised the lawyer that they would not use red in the logo again, and EGO was left alone. (However, according to Disbrow, they forgot to avoid using red, and the red plus sign appeared again.)

As with other Apple II publications, the decline in Apple II users (and, therefore, subscribers) that accelerated in the mid-1990s made it increasingly difficult for Disbrow to keep the magazine going. He decided to cease publication after the August 1995 (volume 7, number 1) issue. In his "Writer's Block" editorial in that final issue, he explained his reasons for closing down the magazine. Other products that GS+ had been selling through EGO Systems would continue to be available, as would back issues of GS+. To help subscribers who still had issues coming to them, Disbrow offered back issues, disks of the text of out-of-print issues of the magazine, or credit towards anything in the EGO Systems catalog. On a personal level, Disbrow continued writing by contributing articles to Joe Kohn's *Shareware Solutions II* newsletter beginning in late 1995.

Two years later, on June 27, 1997, it was necessary for EGO Systems to close down operation of its Apple II mail order business. In May 2001, an agreement was announced that gave Syndicomm an exclusive license to distribute GS+ magazines and software.

II ALIVE (Mar 1993 – Winter 1996)

Joe Gleason was the president of Quality Computers, an Apple II mail order company based in St. Clair Shores, Michigan. He observed with considerable concern the gradual erosion of Apple II information in traditional magazines. When *inCider/A+* added Macintosh coverage, this signaled the decline in the fortunes of that magazine, which was Quality's major advertising outlet. Quality had begun a combination magazine and catalog called *Enhance*, with a focus towards educators (where the Apple II was still fairly strong). But Gleason wanted something more.

Jerry Kindall, who worked at Quality and was a frequent presence on the online services, made this announcement in October 1992: "When *inCider/A+* decided to switch over to a primarily Macintosh focus, we decided the time was right for us to start our own Apple II publication to fill the void. *II*

Alive will begin publication in 1993. Every single article will discuss the Apple II. Every single ad will promote Apple II products. The Mac will be mentioned only in connection with the Apple II (as will the IBM)—for example, in articles on networking or file exchange."[10]

They planned to initially offer the magazine on a bi-monthly basis, and for people who subscribed before December 31, 1992 they offered a free videotape that highlighted new Apple II products. A sample issue of the magazine was mailed out to everyone on Quality's mailing list in early 1993, and the first official issue appeared in March 1993. The logo on the cover had a circle with the words "Celebrating the Apple II" around the title, announcing the flavor of the magazine. Kindall was named as editor-in-chief, and eventually he hired other staff to help him, including Ellen Rosenberg as managing editor (formerly editor of *A2-Central*) and Doug Cuff as consulting editor (also editor of the online magazine *GEnieLamp* A2 and writing for *A2-Central*).

II Alive V2N6, Jan 1995 – Photo credit: personal

II Alive V3N1, July 1995 – Photo credit: personal

By the second official issue, July/August 1993, Kindall announced that IDG Communications, the publisher for *inCider/A+*, had decided to transfer remaining subscriptions for that magazine to *II Alive*.

Regular columns featured in *II Alive* included "Test Drives" (reviews of new products), "Ask Mr. Tech" (technical questions and answers), "Head Of The Class" (programs that were of particular interest to educators), "AppleWorks At Large" (tips on uses for that program), "Macro Exchange" (sample UltraMacros programs for AppleWorks), "Modem Nation" (information about telecommunications), "Shareware Spy" (discussion of freeware and shareware software), and more.

Compared to *inCider*, this magazine seemed to have fun with the articles it presented, and attempted to capture a little of the flavor of *Softalk* from the old days. Because of Quality's introduction of AppleWorks 4 in the fall of 1993, the

---

10 Weyhrich, Steven, "But New Apple II Magazines Are Coming!" *A2 News Digest* (November 1992).

November/December issue was not available until late in December (Kindall also was responsible for writing the manual for that program); however, after this misstep they worked hard at returning to their correct bi-monthly schedule.

The continued decline in the Apple II market also had an effect on this final attempt at a glossy magazine. After the January-February 1995 issue, the magazine had to reduce to a two-color magazine, with fewer pages. New managing editor Doug Cuff pointed out that just as the Apple II market was smaller than it was in the past, so also II Alive had to shrink in response. It continued in this smaller format for six issues, and in the final year was able to come out only on a quarterly basis. The magazine also suffered from a rotation of editors, due to the financial constraints associated with a shrinking readership. The last issue was Volume 4, Number 4, from winter 1996.

SHAREWARE SOLUTIONS II (July 1993 – July 1999)

Joe Kohn established his name in the Apple II world by administrating the Apple II forums on The Source. Later, he started a column entitled "Shareware Solutions" in *The Apple IIGS Buyer's Guide* about shareware software and how to obtain it. When that magazine went out of print in 1990, Kohn moved his column to *inCider/A+*, and continued to share his knowledge with readers until that magazine also disappeared. In his columns, he had taken efforts to make disks available to readers who didn't have modems, disks that contained some of the best available shareware and freeware programs he could find. He decided to continue in these efforts on his own, and in mid-1993 he began a self-published newsletter called *Shareware Solutions II*.

In his announcement on GEnie, Kohn stated:

> [This newsletter will] take Apple II users on an exciting journey into the future. Each month, I plan to write articles about freeware/shareware (of course) and will continue to provide low cost freeware/shareware disks to subscribers via the mail. There will also be Apple II oriented reviews and articles that focus on low cost solutions to common Apple II problems. There will be columns geared to novices and new modem owners; techies, hackers, teens, senior citizens and educators alike should find lots to interest them ... Subscribers will learn how to tame their Apple II computer, and will learn what it will take to make their Apple II a powerful computer solution well into the next century and beyond.
>
> I believed it when Apple proclaimed "Apple II Forever," and Shareware Solutions II will help to make that more than just an empty slogan!"[11]

---

11 Weyhrich, Steven, "Joe Kohn Plans Shareware Newsletter", *A2 News Digest* (May 1992).

Rather than to try to stick to a specific publishing schedule, Kohn decided to sell his subscriptions on the basis of the number of issues, rather than by the year. As his bi-monthly schedule fell behind at times this plan turned out to be wise. The content of his newsletter reflected the extra care that could be taken when a deadline didn't have to be rigidly adhered to; his 20-page newsletter was consistently excellent, with extended articles that reviewed software, hardware, and gave detailed accounts of KansasFest. He also often included special offers on commercial software for his readers.

Shareware Solutions II, Vol 3, No 4 – Photo credit: personal

Kohn released 22 issues of his newsletter, Volumes 1-3 with six issues each, and four issues in Volume 4. The declining Apple II market paralleled the slowing release of new issues of *Shareware Solutions II*. Although Kohn never officially announced he was discontinuing the newsletter, for all practical purposes its final issue was in July 1999. For several years after this, Kohn became more active in support of clean air and water and other environmental concerns.[12]

In early January 2010, Joe Kohn died at the age of 62 from complications of lung cancer.

THE APPLE BLOSSOM (Jan 1995 – Feb 1998)

Steve Cavanaugh was a computer teacher in an elementary school for three years before he moved on to work for Mosby-Year Book, a medical publisher. There, he created the layout for books, using *Quark Xpress* on a Macintosh. When he had been teaching, he had arranged meetings with other computer teachers in the area to discuss how to use computers to teach students. For those who had not been able to attend the meetings, he wrote up the information in a newsletter.

In late 1994, he conceived the idea of making the newsletter available as a download on Genie, and found others who were interested in what he had written. He called it *The Apple Blossom*, and in it Cavanaugh wrote about products for the Apple II, both hardware and software, as well as reviews, to help schools become aware of what was new when the teachers simply did not have time to do the research on their own. The popularity of this newsletter made him decide to change it to a print publication available by subscription. Part of this was due to problems people had with printing what he had tried to digitally distribute in AppleWorks GS format; that program was

---

12 Death Notice - Joseph Kohn, *San Francisco Chronicle*, January 8, 2010.

notoriously difficult to use properly with some printers. Also involved in the decision was his inability to continue to distribute it solely at his own expense.

The Apple Blossom, V3N4 – Photo credit: Ken Gagne

During 1995 he released four issues, and was able to increase his output to six issues in 1996, with a subscription fee of $12 per year. By that time he had subscribers in 30 states and in Canada. He worked during the second year to produce articles that explained how to use certain programs on the Apple II, as well as making other computer platforms work with the Apple II, particularly using of content that was not designed specifically for the Apple II (such as translating pictures for MS-DOS or the Mac to a format that Apple II could use).

By that time Cavanaugh was creating his publication not in AppleWorks GS but in a simple IIGS word processor called *ShadowWrite*, with page layout created in *GraphicWriter III*. He printed the final copy on a LaserWriter. His subscribers also received his Apple II Vendor Directory, which provided information for over 90 companies who serviced or sold Apple II hardware and software. He also began to accept articles by other authors, including a regular column of interviews with Apple II notables called "Talking II" written by Ryan Suenaga.

In 1997, Cavanaugh branched out to digital distribution with a different publication, *Hyper Quarterly*, a disk-based subscription specifically for the Apple IIGS and the software product HyperCard IIGS. Though he only produced three issues between 1997 and 1999, the two 800K disks included in each issue contained HyperCard stacks for presentation and education, as well as art and icons to use in stack creation. To produce these, he had the help of Gareth Jones (editor of *Apples BC News*, newsletter of the Apples BC user group in Vancouver, British Columbia) and Bruce Caplin

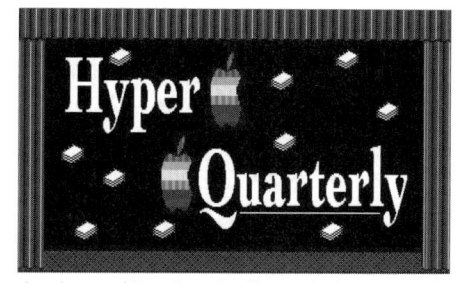

Sample cover of *Hyper Quarterly* – Photo credit: Steve Cavanaugh

(best known by his online handle, "Hangtime", who had edited *Script-Central* for Resource Central).

With the Internet becoming the primary source of information for computer users, the number of renewals was no longer sufficient to keep these publications going, and only three issues of *The Apple Blossom* were produced in 1997 and one final issue in February 1998. Cavanaugh moved his index and a sampling of his content to a web site by 1999.[13, 14]

JUICED.GS (Jan 1996 –)

In the closing months of 1995, things were looking grim in the Apple II world. Many of the companies that had supported the Apple II and IIGS were finding it harder to stay in business. GS+ magazine had closed down in August, and *II Alive* was not looking very healthy, which further hampered the abilities of those remaining vendors to get information about their products into the hands of potential customers.

When GS+ ceased publication, it motivated one Apple II owner who was an unknown to most of the online community. Max Jones, a newspaper editor from rural Indiana, decided to take action and apply his skills towards the Apple II. He created a new 20-page magazine using AppleWorks GS and its page-layout module. He uploaded his sample issue of what he named *Juiced.GS* to the GEnie A2 Roundtable library, as well as uploading it to libraries on other online services.

To his surprise, this trial issue met with an enthusiastic response. Jones had solicited articles from several experienced Apple II experts, including a review of *PMPFax* (a fax program in a New Desk Accessory for the Apple IIGS), and an opinion column by Ryan Suenaga (who would later become editor of *GEnieLamp A2* and *The Lamp!*). The first official issue published in February 1996 included an article about the Apple IIGS prototype codenamed "Mark Twain" that had been discovered.

Jones found it difficult to produce an issue of Juiced.GS with AppleWorks GS, due to persisting bugs in the program. He soon switched over to GraphicWriter III, and was sufficiently satisfied with the experience that he wrote a review of the program, *using* the program, and compared its features to those available in AppleWorks GS. The result was so positive that Seven Hills Software (the publisher of GraphicWriter III) asked to use the review to promote its product.

As for production of the magazine, *Juiced.GS* was a one-man operation. Jones printed his issues at "Just Copies" in Terre Haute, Indiana, and he collated and stapled the resulting pages himself.

---

13 Cuff, Doug, "Steve Cavanaugh, publisher of The Apple Blossom", *GEnieLamp A2*, (March 1996).
14 Cavanaugh's web site, www.appleblossom.net, was still working in 2013.

Promotion of the magazine was easy to do via GEnie, CompuServe and Delphi, but those Apple II users who did not get online were unaware of *Juiced.GS*. Jones' circulation significantly increased after an advertisement for Juiced.GS ran in a catalog Steve Disbrow (of GS+) distributed for his EGO Systems products. Jones also included a collection of shareware on two disks with each issue of the magazine in its early days, which made software available to those who were not part of the online world.

By 2000, Jones' own personal responsibilities became more demanding, as he became the editor of *The Tribune-Star* in Terra Haute. He connected with Eric Shepherd, who was at that time the owner of Syndicomm, and it was decided that Syndicomm would take over publication of the magazine at the beginning of 2002. Ryan Suenaga, who had been writing for *Juiced. GS* almost since the beginning, was made editor-in-chief, and Max Jones stayed on as Associate Editor.

With a new regime responsible for the magazine, it was decided to abandon the tradition of creating it on a genuine Apple IIGS, and instead final production occurred on a Macintosh, which allowed the inclusion of more photographs. The new publishers had fun with photos on the cover, such as a swimsuit issue, which featured an Apple IIGS as the model wearing the swimsuit.

In 2006, Suenaga stepped down and Ken Gagne became editor-in-chief, with frequent contributor Andy Molloy as associate editor. Gagne took the production completely over to a Macintosh, making use of *Pages*, Apple's consumer-level word processing and page layout program for the Macintosh. The following year, publishing

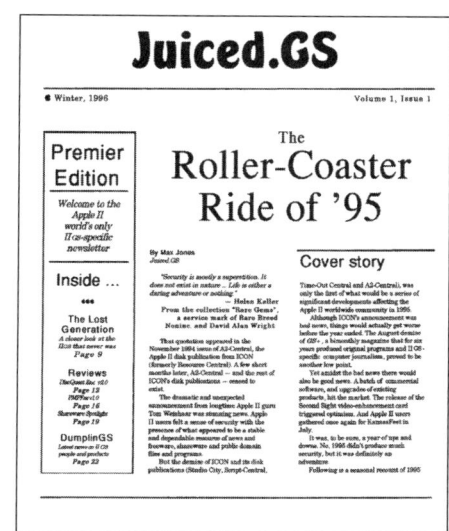

Juiced.GS, Winter 1996 – Photo credit: personal

Juiced.GS, June 2011 – Photo credit: Ken Gagne

was also transferred over from Syndicomm and Eric Shepherd to Gagne, putting the roles of publisher and editor to a single person again for the first time since Max Jones started *Juiced.GS*. However, Shepherd continued to write a column for each issue of the magazine.

During his run as editor, Gagne maintained the original layout and format of the magazine. Beginning in 2011, the magazine's covers began appearing in color, along with a more visually striking design. By that time, the costs of printing in color had decreased from those faced by Apple II magazines in the past. Where these previous magazines gradually became simpler and had to change to a less expensive printing process as their subscriber base shrunk, *Juiced.GS* improved with age. As the publication moved into the second decade of the new century, its subscriber base was actually showing a consistent increase, year to year. The magazine also celebrated its status as the longest running continually printed Apple II magazine of all time.[15]

TIMELINE

The start and end dates for small publisher magazines:

Open-Apple / A2-Central
– *January 1985 - February 1995*

AppleWorks Forum
– *August 1986 - December 1995*

GS+ – *September 1989 - August 1995*

II Alive – *March 1993 - Winter 1996*

Shareware Solutions II
– *July 1993 - July 1999*

The Apple Blossom
– *January 1995 - February 1998*

Juiced.GS – *January 1996 -*

---

15 Gagne also created the *Juiced.GS* web site, which showcased additional products. For 2010 and 2013 he produced a wall calendar with color photos previously seen only in gray scale in the pages of the magazine. Starting in 2011 he introduced *Juiced Concentrate*, bundled collections from past issues featuring articles dealing with a single subject, such as File Transfer, Copy Protection, Podcasting, TCP/IP, and BASIC.

CHAPTER 43
New Horizons for AppleWorks

GRAPHIC USER INTERFACES

To make computers easier for people to use, it was necessary to overcome both the fear problem and the frustration problem. Those who were inexperienced in the use of computers were often afraid that they would press a button that would cause something terrible to happen. If they overcame that fear, they still had to face the frustration of trying to decipher cryptic error messages ("*** TOO MANY PARENS" or "$27 Error").

Adding familiar images to the screen, like the file card menus in AppleWorks, diminished the fear factor. Making the keys that controlled certain features work consistently from the word processor to the database to the spreadsheet decreased the frustration factor even further. But there were still barriers to overcome in making computers easier to use.

The Lisa and Macintosh lacked the previous standard of typed command input to control programs. Instead, they used a bit-mapped graphics screen to represent a desktop, with pictures (called icons) that represented a program to run or a file to load. It took the point and shoot interface to the limit—users used the mouse to move a pointer on the screen onto an icon representing that program, and then clicked on it to start the program

For more complex control, the Mac used a variation on the magic menu system: A menu bar at the top of the screen gave a list of command words, arranged horizontally on the same line. Pointing to one of the words and holding down the mouse button caused a menu to descend like a window shade, displaying several further available options. A command could be executed by moving the mouse to that item on the drop-down menu (such as "Delete") and clicking on that highlighted selection. This approach made use of the Lisa and Macintosh considerably easier for the novice computer user, although some commands were also given keyboard equivalents similar to the old "Ctrl" key commands, so a more experienced user could execute them without having to take his hands off the keyboard.

If AppleWorks could be considered easy enough to use without opening the reference book, this graphic user interface (GUI) was even more so. It also provided a standard environment that all programs written for the Mac could use, making it easier to learn how to use a new program.

Although the 6502 processor did not have the power of the 68000 in the Mac, some programs became available for the Apple II that tried to make use of the same concept of overlapping windows, pull-down menus, and a mouse (or joystick) driven pointer. Quark released a program selector called *Catalyst* that used a similar graphics-based desktop, icons for files, and the point-and-click method of file execution. It was included with some of the early UniDisk 3.5 drives, and on Quark's hard drives.

Another company, VersionSoft (from France) had a program called *MouseDesk*, which was distributed in America by International Solutions. MouseDesk worked just a bit better than Catalyst, but did not do very well as a standalone product, especially with Catalyst being given away free with the new UniDisk. Eventually, International Solutions made MouseDesk available for only ten dollars via mail-order, hoping to get it into general use so that their other graphic and mouse-based products sold better. Although that did not happen, International Solutions eventually sold the distribution rights for MouseDesk to Apple Computer. Apple then modified the program and included it as a rudimentary desktop (modeled after the Macintosh Finder) for their first versions of the ProDOS 16 System software for the Apple IIGS.

With the release of the IIGS, it became possible for better GUI software to be produced for the Apple II. The 65816 processor had a bit more power, and the IIGS provided a better quality graphics environment (via its super hi-res mode) and more available memory than was possible on older 8-bit Apple II models.

APPLEWORKS GS

In its day, AppleWorks was probably one of the most powerful integrated programs ever written, in terms of speed (being text-based) and overall usability for a wide range of purposes. The one single problem it caused in the Apple II world was that being so comprehensive it literally killed the market for nearly every other text-based word processor, database, or spreadsheet program. There was little point in creating a new text-based program in either of these categories, since AppleWorks 3, 4 and 5 covered all those areas so comprehensively. For the majority of users on the Apple IIe, IIc, and even the IIGS, AppleWorks met all of their productivity software needs. And on the Apple IIGS with expanded memory, the 4 and 5 versions made it possible to process and manipulate tremendous amounts of data easily.

However, AppleWorks on an Apple IIGS could not take advantage of some of the features that GS/OS offered: easy access to foreign disk storage formats, use of outline font technology (via Westcode Software's *Pointless*), access to a graphic-based work environment, the ability to switch between multiple programs (via program switchers like Seven Hills Software's *The Manager* and Procyon's *Switch-It!*) and many other features that IIGS users wanted.

Outside of the Apple II, Macintosh and MS-DOS users wanted a simple integrated software package like AppleWorks, one that had sufficient capability in each of its modules that met the needs of average home computer users. In 1985, just one year after the release of AppleWorks, a small company in Santa Cruz, California began writing an integrated software program intended for the Macintosh. The package offered the same three modules as AppleWorks on the Apple II, plus communications and graphing. Robert Lissner, the creator of AppleWorks, was involved in the early stages, writing the database module.[1] Microsoft became aware of the project, and eventually took it over completely. In May 1986 Microsoft released *Microsoft Works* for the Macintosh, and by the following year it had a version for MS-DOS. It was common to find the program in the bundled software package found on new MS-DOS computers. Within two years, Microsoft had a version of Microsoft Works that ran under version 2 of the nascent Windows operating system.

With the immense popularity of Microsoft Works, the newly formed Claris wanted an integrated software product for the Macintosh to compete with it. And just like Microsoft, they looked to a startup company for the programming expertise to make it happen.

APPLEWORKS GS - ORIGINS

StyleWare, Inc. was a small Apple II software company based out of Houston, Texas. An engineering student at Rice University, Kevin Harvey, started the company in 1985 with two friends. The company released a graphic interface word processor for the Apple IIe and IIc in April 1986, calling it *MultiScribe*. Within a year the company added *MultiScribe GS*, which offered the same features for the more powerful Apple IIGS desktop environment.

Amongst several other products that enjoyed modest success in the Apple IIGS marker, StyleWare began work in 1986 on an integrated package for the IIGS. They wanted to create something that would offer the power of AppleWorks, but with the additional capabilities offered by the graphic interface of the IIGS. Its word processor module included the ability to handle different fonts, print styles, and included a spell checker and thesaurus. The spreadsheet could do color charting and improved recalculating. Also to be included was a module to allow the user to create and edit graphics, and a telecommunications module to allow connection to dial-up bulletin boards and online services. To tie it all together, there was a desktop publishing module, which would easily allow text and graphics to be combined together in the same document (some-

---

1   Maremaa, Tom, "Microsoft Prepares Jazz Sandwich", *InfoWorld* (May 27, 1985), 29.

thing which at the time was not commonly available in higher end products). They called it *GSWorks*, and StyleWare distributed a few pre-release copies of the program at AppleFest in May 1988, promising a final release late in the year. However, something happened to change those plans.

By this time, Claris was in its second year of existence, and still did not have any integrated software package for the Macintosh to compete with Microsoft Works. When the company became aware of GSWorks, they approached StyleWorks and asked to buy the program. They were told that while the program by itself was not for sale, the owners of StyleWorks might be interested in selling the entire company.

In the summer of 1988, just a few months after AppleFest, Claris announced that they had purchased StyleWorks, making StyleWorks president Kevin Harvey the Group Program Manager for the Apple II, and bringing over many of the other StyleWorks programmers. Early information about the deal stated that Claris would take over sales of MultiScribe and MultiScribe GS and the other programs StyleWare had been selling. The public announcement was that this purchase highlighted Claris' commitment to the Apple II. They announced that they would take GSWorks and re-package it as *AppleWorks GS*, potentially doing for the IIGS what AppleWorks had done for the Apple IIe and IIc. Claris also announced prices to allow customers to upgrade from Apple Writer and MultiScribe (either version) to AppleWorks 2.1 or AppleWorks GS.

What the company ultimately decided to do was to sell everything besides GSWorks to Beagle Bros (who ultimately revised MultiScribe and MultiScribe GS and re-released them as *BeagleWrite* and *BeagleWrite GS*). During the last few months of 1988, Harvey's team hurriedly finished up work on AppleWorks GS, and released version 1.0 before the end of the year.

One of the StyleWare programmers recalled the massive push that was required to get the program completed and released. At one time he and others on the team worked 140 hours per week to get it done. Hearn also recalled difficulties the team had in creating the program in the first place.

> *What we were doing with AppleWorks GS was really pushing the development platform way past what it was reasonably capable of. It was not possible to get it to assemble into a single application using the provided tools (which, for much of the development period, were in a state of flux, and frequently broken—we spent a lot of time debugging the OS and dev tools); it was too large. I was actually the one that wrote the multiple image loader that stitched the various pieces of the program together. Yes, it was pretty hacky, but it was necessary.*[2]

---

2 Hearn, Bob, e-mail message to author, September 30, 2013.

Another programmer on the team commented that the IIGS operating system itself was a major problem at the time.

> But the real problem was the OS itself. There were major bugs that made a decent product impossible at that date. [For example,] if a font was purged during printing the OS would crash, but it wasn't possible to prevent it.[3]

After the AppleWorks GS project was completed, Claris had intended to use their experience with that program to come up with a product to compete with Microsoft Works. It could not be done as a direct translation; AppleWorks GS was written in 65816 assembly language, and as such would require extensive reworking to be changed to 68000 assembly code for the Macintosh. However, Claris' direction changed once again soon after the StyleWorks purchase, and the company changed its mind about creating a "MacWorks" type of program.[4]

Some of the StyleWare programmers later left Claris to form their own company, and began their own work on an integrated software package for the Macintosh. By early 1990 they had a working program that they started to offer to software publishers. Claris eventually decided that they wanted this program, and in July of that year bought it, and brought the programmers back to Claris to complete it.

Thought it took over a year, in October 1991 *ClarisWorks* version 1.0 was released. Claris finally had the hit program they wanted; it soon surpassed Microsoft Works in sales on the Macintosh. The program underwent several revisions over the next ten years, and was commonly bundled with Macintosh computers sold during the 1990s, used in the home as well as in schools.[5]

After Apple reabsorbed Claris in 1998, ClarisWorks was re-branded as AppleWorks, and versions were sold for both the Macintosh and for Windows. The name made for some confusion, since Apple did not bother to distinguish it from the older Apple II version. By 2007, as Apple transitioned its hardware line from PowerPC to Intel processors, AppleWorks was formally retired, and a suite of programs that went by the name *iWork* replaced its functionality.

APPLEWORKS GS - THE PROGRAM

AppleWorks GS was a program that had many things it did well, and several that did not get fine-tuned sufficiently to make it a great product. It was possible to have as many as fourteen different document windows open at once.

---

3   Holdaway, Scott, e-mail message to author, September 30, 2013.
4   Jones, Gareth, "The Life And Times Of AppleWorks GS", Juiced.GS (Late Summer 1997).
5   Hearn, Bob, "A Brief History of ClarisWorks", <groups.csail.mit.edu/mac/users/bob/clarisworks.php>, accessed October 20, 2012.

One could use the Control key and drag a selected block of data between windows, something that even the Macintosh could not at that time do. Besides those features mentioned earlier, the word processor module was fast, and offered access to a thesaurus (though it did not have the ability to do footnotes). The database and spreadsheet modules were state-of-the-art for 1988, fast, and made it easy to export and import data as text (including formulas) for connection with other programs. The graphics module included both drawing and painting tools, something that at the time no other IIGS program offered. Best of all, it could directly import and use any of the file formats of classic AppleWorks.

Drawbacks of the program were the rudimentary nature of the telecommunications module, not at all up to contemporary capabilities. Furthermore, the program loaded from disk very slowly, taking several minutes to start up under the 4.0 version of GS/OS which was currently available. Printing a document could be exceedingly slow, with one writer to *A2-Central* in January 1989 complaining that it took him *fifteen minutes* to print one and a half pages of text.[6]

AppleWorks GS startup screen – Photo credit: personal

Selection screen for AppleWorks GS modules

To address some of the bugs in the first release, Claris came out with AppleWorks GS 1.0v2 early in 1989. When Apple released GS/OS 5 in July 1989, AppleWorks GS was updated to v1.1, as v1.0v2 would not function under the new operating system. The only other changes offered by Claris after that point was to make available a different set of installation scripts for the program to work with GS/OS 6 when it came out in 1992. Claris never again updated the program itself after they released version 1.1.

Other than bugs in the program, problems that began to affect users of this program had to do with advances in GS/OS and other software that left AppleWorks GS behind. Most other actively supported software would be updated to handle such new features. However, AppleWorks GS was left more or less frozen to the feature set it had when it was first released in 1988. It could not directly import the newer file formats that became available with the 1993 release of AppleWorks 4. It could not load or save to the Teach file format that was used in GS/OS 6. And the word processor module could size fonts no greater than 48 points, even after other similar programs could exceed that limitation.

---

6 Hesselman, Tom, "Ask (Or Tell) Uncle DOS", *A2-Central* (January 1989), 4.91.

After the initial excitement of this Claris product for the Apple IIGS, users soon developed the same frustrated attitude toward that company that they had toward Apple. It was focused on its Macintosh products, and seemed to want nothing more to do with the Apple II.

APPLEWORKS GS - RESURRECTION?

When Quality Computers licensed AppleWorks from Claris in 1994, they also were given access to the source code for AppleWorks GS. When this was announced, there was much rejoicing amongst the ranks of Apple IIGS users, who were hopeful that there would finally be a revision to that program as well, to correct the many known problems it had. Anticipating great things, Quality went so far as to announce a planned shipping date, and took pre-orders for it from excited customers.

To work on the update to AppleWorks GS, Quality hired the services of Jim Merritt, who had worked on GS/OS System 5 at Apple. The project was split into two parts. The first that was planned was an update from the five-year-old 1.1 version to 1.2. The purpose of the 1.2 revision would be primarily to address known bugs, and to make it smaller and faster. A more comprehensive update to AppleWorks GS 2.0 was planned for a later date, and would offer new features. These included:

- The ability to import AppleWorks 4 documents and Teach documents, handle larger font sizes, and support the system sounds offered in GS/OS System 6
- For the word processor they planned support for macros, style sheets (which would define the general layout of a document), the ability to import simple Macintosh word processing documents, and an option to show invisible formatting characters (spaces, tabs, and carriage returns)
- For the page layout module, automatic word wrap around graphics and a print preview mode was to be added
- The graphics module was to be enhanced to use handle Bezier curves and allow rotation of graphics in increments of one degree
- Support for the Zmodem file transfer protocol was to be added to the telecommunications module

Merritt put together a preliminary team of programmers to help with the project. To their dismay, they found that the source code for AppleWorks GS was poorly organized and lacked comments within the code to explain what different parts did. Furthermore, as mentioned earlier, the source code was so large that it could not create a single object code file that could be executed. Under the older version of MPW (the *Macintosh Programmer's Workshop*) on which it had been written, it was necessary to take the two separate object files it created and then manually patch the two pieces together in memory. (Apparently the multiple image loader that had been used to connect the various pieces was not included with the source files provided by Claris.)

Also, there were sections of the undocumented source code for which Claris programmers were unable to identify a purpose, and they were unwilling to remove that code for fear that it would cripple the program. Adding to the problem was the way in which Claris produced its two updates, done as quick patches, rather than recompiling the code.

Even when Merritt's team was finally able to get it to successfully compile, the resultant program files were not byte-for-byte identical to AppleWorks GS v1.1 as shipped by Claris. To get things to this point had taken them four months of their time.

Because of these significant roadblocks, Merritt had several other talented Apple IIGS programmers take a look at the source code, and in every situation he was told the same story: it was simply not possible to upgrade the program, and would be better to just rewrite the application from scratch. Quality Computers knew this to be an economic impossibility, considering the declining Apple IIGS market, and in July 1994 it was announced that the AppleWorks GS project had been cancelled.[7]

There were, however, other opinions about the state of the AppleWorks GS source code. One of the other programmers who was given a chance to look at the code was Bill Heinemann. He had a long history of creating code for video games for the Apple II, IIGS, and other computer platforms. He stated that he had been able to get AppleWorks GS v1.1 to compile without much effort, and had begun to work on the list of revisions. He had estimated that he could have finished v1.2 in four months of part time work, and v2.0 in an additional six months. However, the costs to Quality Computers for this programming apparently exceeded what they could budget for it, and he stopped work when he realized that he was not going to be paid.[8]

THE END OF APPLEWORKS

When Quality Computers licensed AppleWorks and AppleWorks GS in 1993, the contract specified royalties that would be owed to Claris for sales of these products. Additionally, a clause was included that specified potential penalties that Quality would owe to Claris if the products did not appear within a certain period of time. With AppleWorks it was no problem, since it was ready to go. For AppleWorks GS it was a different issue, since the code that was delivered was not in a usable condition. Potentially, Quality was liable for payments of hun-

---

7 Kindall, Jerry, "AppleWorks GS Not Arriving At All?" *GEnieLamp A2* (July 1994).
8 Jones, Gareth, "The Life And Times Of AppleWorks GS", *Juiced.GS* (Late Summer 1997)

dreds of thousands of dollars to Claris if it could not deliver a 2.0 version of the program. After some further negotiation with Claris, Quality was able to get the penalty clause for AppleWorks GS dropped. Ultimately, Quality had to announce that there would be no update for AppleWorks GS as they had originally planned.

The failure of the AppleWorks GS update effort was regrettable, but was not as great a loss as it was made out to be. By the time the project was started, there were stand-alone programs that could take the place of each of the modules in AppleWorks GS, and exceed their capabilities. Furthermore, the framework provided by GS/OS and Apple's user interface guidelines significantly simplified the old difficulties of sharing information between those different programs. This was significantly different than the environment that existed ten years earlier when Lissner first created AppleWorks for 8-bit Apple computers. The ease of copying and pasting between the Apple IIGS programs available by 1994 made the integrated features of AppleWorks GS less necessary.

A year later, Scantron Corporation acquired Quality Computers to get access to its educational customers. They changed the company name to Scantron Quality Computers. When the licensing contract with Claris expired, Scantron did not choose to renew it. Within four years, all of Quality Computers' software under their Q-Labs brand was released as freeware, and "Quality Computers" was dropped from the company name, returning it to the original name Scantron.

BEYOND THE APPLE II

Despite the failure of AppleWorks GS, the original AppleWorks continued to be a popular product, even on the Apple IIGS (which could offer a large desktop in which to create and edit files). In the early 1990s, Intel-based PCs and the Macintosh were becoming fast enough to reasonably emulate older computers, including the Apple II and IIGS. Randy Brandt and Mark Munz conceived of a way to run AppleWorks 5.1 on both 68000 series and PowerPC Macintosh computers. Code-named "Phoenix II", and released by JEM Software as *Deja][*, the program was not written to look like AppleWorks; it actually *was* AppleWorks, powered by a 65c02 emulator with appropriate patches to allow it to access files directly on the Macintosh HFS file system.

Deja][required the user to own the AppleWorks 5.1 installation files. When running under Mac OS 7 through 8.6, it was possible for the Mac to move files to and from ProDOS-formatted 3.5-inch disks inserted in the Mac's floppy drive. Because of this feature of the Mac OS, Deja][could directly load and save AppleWorks files to an actual Apple II 3.5-inch diskette, enhancing the simulation of a real Apple II. Furthermore, the program was designed to share clipboards between the Macintosh and the AppleWorks environment. Because TimeOut and Ultra 4 were built into AppleWorks 5.1, all of the capabilities offered by these add-on utilities were fully supported. Brandt and Munz also created some additional macro commands specific to Deja][which could directly interface with the Macintosh for functions such as speaking text, dialing the modem, and so on. Originally released through JEM Software as a commercial program in October 1995, it was reclassified as freeware in 1999.

With Apple's move in 2002 to Mac OS X as the primary operating system for the Macintosh platform, and the transition from the PowerPC to Intel processors in 2006, Deja][no longer functioned. Beginning that year, Mark Munz began a project of his own to update the emulator. He named the new version Deja IIx. It turned out to be a major project, requiring not only a new version of the underlying 65c02 emulator (to run on an Intel processor instead of the older PowerPC code), but also changes to how it loaded files into the emulated AppleWorks program. Rather than depending on ProDOS disk images, Deja][had loaded all of the files directly from folders on the Mac hard drive, using specific Mac OS system calls. With Mac OS X, these system calls no longer worked, and he had to revise the code that loaded the ProDOS files that made up the various parts of AppleWorks, as well as the word processing, database, and spreadsheet files it was to work on.[9]

Deja][program icon

Deja IIx program icon

TIMELINE

AppleWorks 1.3 – *February 1986*
MultiScribe – *April 1986*
AppleWorks 2.0 – *September 1986*
MultiScribe GS – *April 1987*
AppleWorks 2.1 – *September 1988*
AppleWorks GS 1.0 – *December 1988*
AppleWorks GS 1.0v2 – *February 1989*

AppleWorks GS 1.1v2 – *July 1989*
AppleWorks 3.0 – *June 1989*
ClarisWorks 1.0 – *October 1991*
AppleWorks 4.0 – *November 1993*
AppleWorks 5.0 – *November 1994*
AppleWorks 5.1 – *July 1995*
Deja][– *October 1995*
Deja IIx – *2002*

---

9 As of publication, Munz has continued to sporadically work on it; his progress can be viewed at his blog at dejaiix.blogspot.com

CHAPTER 44

Falling Out of Favor

After the release of the Macintosh in 1984, Apple executives had a schizophrenic relationship with the Apple II. This was likely driven by the charismatic Steve Jobs, who viewed old technology with disdain and only wanted to look forward. His immaturity (he turned 30 in 1985) and focus on the future often caused him to charge ahead without considering the political consequences of his actions.

Furthermore, the Mac had gotten off to a slow start during 1984, and the promised Macintosh Office of 1985 was not doing much better. Sales of the Mac and of the Apple IIc were not meeting predictions, and by spring of that year the company's stock price was at an all-time low.

None of these issues fazed Jobs. He had his eyes on a company he wanted Apple to buy, one which could make flat panel display technology. He was envisioning a "BookMac" (as he then called it) that would bring the power of the Macintosh to a handheld format. At the company's board meeting in April 1985 he laid out his plans for the creation of the product, the factory to build it, and projected sales.

The board listened, and then told him that with the way things had gone so far with the Mac, there was no way that they were going to invest additional money into another unproven technology. Furthermore, CEO John Sculley made it clear that he wanted Jobs to leave his position as manager of the Macintosh division. He could continue to function as chairman of the company, but either Sculley would be the one in charge, or the Apple board would have to find another president.

The aftermath of the meeting led to a showdown a month later, in which the board let Jobs know that they agreed with Sculley. They removed Jobs from the Macintosh division, and within a few months he left the company.[1]

A consequence of Jobs and his "losers versus winners" philosophy was that he passed it on to many within the company. The core differences between the Macintosh and the Apple II camps influenced the company focus (or lack thereof) in a way that would remain an issue for years to come. Although sales of the Apple II were carrying the company, the powerful voices

---

[1] Rose, Frank, *West of Eden* (New York, Penguin Books, 1989), 260-284.

that remained after Jobs' departure ensured that the voice of the Apple II would continue to grow fainter as time passed.

The Apple II products released by the company during the latter half of the 1980s reflected the need of the company to keep its cash cow strong, while buying time to allow the Macintosh prove itself in the marketplace.

APPLE IIE PLATINUM

A few months after the release of the Apple IIGS, the Apple IIe also received an update. In January 1987 the company announced the Platinum Apple IIe. It had the same product shape that had been present since the case was first designed ten years earlier, but the most striking difference was its color. No longer its classic beige, the new IIe was given the same platinum gray appearance of the nearly all of the rest of Apple's product line at the time. Beyond its new color, the Platinum IIe keyboard received the most obvious changes, bringing it to a near match with the Apple IIGS.

Like the IIGS keyboard, a numeric keypad was now included, and the RESET key was moved to the same location as it was on the Apple IIc and IIGS.

The motherboard had 64K RAM in only two chips (instead of the previous eight), and the onboard ROM had been condensed from two chips to just one. An "Extended 80-Column Card" with 64K extra memory was included in all units sold, and was physically smaller than previous versions of the memory card. The motherboard connector for an external numeric keypad connector was left in place, despite being included with the keyboard.

Platinum Apple IIe – Photo credit: Vectronics Apple World

No ROM changes were made. The old shift-key modification was installed by default, making it possible for older programs to determine if the shift key was being pressed. However, a hardware bug was discovered after the product shipped. If the rarely used third game controller was installed, one that actually used the third push-button input (which was where the shift-key mod was internally connected), the combination of pressing shift and the third push-button simultaneously caused a short circuit that shut down the power supply (requiring the power be turned off and then on again to get the computer to restart).[2]

---

2 Weishaar, Tom, "Apple Introduces An Updated IIe", *Open-Apple*, (January 1987), 3.1.

APPLE IIC PLUS

During 1987, someone at Apple decided that the IIc needed to be upgraded. Shortly before July, three years after its original 1984 introduction, it was felt that the Apple IIc would benefit from the larger capacity Apple 3.5 drive as its internal drive. The primary intent was to make only this change, while leaving the rest of the IIc as it was. As with most other Apple projects, this went by various internal code names during its development, including Pizza, Raisin, and Adam Ant.[3]

Trying to use the Apple 3.5 drive in the Apple IIc was certainly an engineering problem. The 1 MHz 65c02 was simply not fast enough to take raw data off the Apple 3.5 drive, decode it into usable data, and pass it to the operating system. The "intelligent" 3.5-inch drive was designed in the first place for that very reason. To solve the problem, Apple contracted with an outside firm to design a special digital gate array that made it possible for the 1 MHz 65c02 to just barely keep up with the data transfer rate from the Apple 3.5 drive. In accomplishing this, it needed an extra 2K of static RAM space to decode the raw data from the 3.5-inch drive. This extra memory had to be available outside the standard Apple IIe/IIc 128K RAM space, since there was simply not enough free memory to spare even that little bit of space. The code Apple engineers wrote to use the drive was so tight that there were exactly enough clock cycles to properly time things while controlling the drive. (Each assembly language instruction takes a certain number of clock cycles; these cycles have to be taken into account for timing-sensitive operations such as disk and serial port drivers.)

To support older Apple II software that came only on 5.25-inch disks, the disk port on the back was now changed to handle not only external 3.5-inch drives (either UniDisk 3.5 or Apple 3.5), but also up to two Apple 5.25 drives which could be chained together (the same drives used with the Apple IIGS). These could be chained together as could the 3.5-inch drives. The IIc Plus, then, could have three external 3.5-inch drives and two 5.25-inch drives attached, in any mixture of Apple 3.5, UniDisk 3.5, or Apple 5.25 drives.[4, 5]

Apple IIc Plus and external Disk 5.25 – Photo credit: personal

The IIc Plus design was not thought out completely from start to finish, however. After they did the work with the special gate array to make the

---

3   A+ Staff, "NewsPlus", *A+* (October 1989), 18.
4   Weishaar, Tom, "Apple rediscovers the Apple II", *Open-Apple*, (November 1988), 4.73.
5   Mutant_Pie, Forums, *Applefritter*, <www.applefritter.com/forum> accessed June 14, 2010.

original IIc architecture work properly, someone else decided that it was not a good idea to release a 1 MHz computer in 1987. They reasoned that customers want speed. In the world of the IBM PC and its clones, each year faster and faster models were being released. It was decided to retrofit the new IIc with a faster 4 MHz version of the 65c02. That change, had it been done from the start, would have made engineering the internal 3.5-inch drive simpler; they could have simply used the processor at 4 MHz for 3.5-inch drive access, and then used the true system speed (as selected by the user) for all other functions. The complicated gate array would not have been necessary. But, since the faster speed was added as an afterthought, and the project was under a tight schedule, the gate array design was not changed.

To accomplish the faster processor speed for the IIc Plus, Apple went to another outside firm, Zip Technology. This company had already marketed an accelerator, the Zip Chip, which was popular as an add-on product for existing Apple II computers. Users could remove the 6502 or 65c02 chip in their computer, replace it with the special Zip Chip, and suddenly they had a computer that ran up to four times as fast. Apple licensed this technology from Zip, but engineers balked at actually using the Zip Chip itself for the IIc Plus. Part of this was because of the size of the Zip Chip. The chip was shaped like a standard integrated circuit, but was thicker vertically than a basic 65c02. Inside the extra space was a fast 65c02 processor, plus some caching RAM, all squeezed into a space that would fit even into the original Apple IIc (where space was at a premium).[6]

Zip had wanted Apple to buy its Zip Chip and simply use that product in the IIc Plus. Obviously, this would have been to Zip's advantage financially. However, the thicker vertical size of the Chip made testing the completed computer more difficult, and it would be a problem to isolate product failures to the Zip Chip, instead of something else on the motherboard. By using a 4 MHz 65c02 and two 8K static RAM chips as separate components in the IIc Plus, Apple engineers could ensure that it would work and be available in a large enough volume for production. When they were designing the IIc Plus, Zip Technology could not guarantee they could provide reliable products in the volume Apple needed.

The IIc Plus did not have the 12 VDC input on the back panel, as did the earlier IIc computers; instead, the power supply was built-in. This was not because it was necessarily a better design, as an internal power supply was actually less reliable ultimately than the external power supply, since it exposed the internal components to higher levels of heat over the lifetime of the product. But because many people had criticized the IIc external power

---

6 The Zip Chip "cache" was a piece of RAM memory used to hold copies of system memory that the processor was frequently accessing. For instance, if a lot of graphics manipulation was occurring, the caching RAM would hold a copy of part of the graphics RAM, and could access it much faster than the standard RAM. This was part of what made an after-market accelerator work.

supply (called a "brick on a leash" at Apple), they had decided to make it internal on the IIc Plus as it was on all of its other products. This change apparently did not cause any significant problems, as few people were actually trying to use the IIc as a portable computer (with a battery pack).

The memory expansion slot on the IIc Plus was not compatible with the memory cards that Apple had produced for the older IIc. This was primarily a timing problem; it was not because the RAM chips in the memory card were not fast enough to keep up with the 4 MHz speed of the IIc Plus. The IIc Plus also had an additional connector at the opposite end of a memory card plugged into the expansion slot. Signals from port 2 were made available at that end, so third party companies could make a card that was a combination RAM card and internal modem. However, for reasons which will be discussed, this did not come about.

Other changes in the IIc Plus included a slightly redesigned keyboard and mini-DIN-8 connectors on the back panel for its serial ports (to be more compatible with Apple's new Macintosh and IIGS keyboards).

The IIc Plus ROM was called revision 5 (the previous Revised Memory Expansion IIc was labeled as revision 4). The main changes present were the ones that supported the internal Apple 3.5 drive. Firmware on the new IIc was not any larger than the 32K on the previous models, but it did use the entire space (the previous IIc didn't use the last 8K available in the ROM).[7, 8]

APPLE IIC PLUS: PRODUCT INTRODUCTION

In September 1988 the Apple IIc Plus was introduced to considerably less fanfare than the original IIc was in April 1984. There were no promises of "Apple II Forever" this time; instead, it warranted little more than a press release in various Apple II magazines of the time. Its selling price was $675 (or $1,099 with a color monitor). This was remarkable, considering that the original Apple IIc without a monitor sold for nearly double the price ($1,295) and it had far less capacity and power than this new version. Some models of the IIc Plus even shipped with 256K of extra memory already added. It was faster than any other Apple II (including the 2.8 MHz IIGS), and was probably the finest 8-bit computer Apple ever produced.

APPLE IIC PLUS: LESS THAN A SUCCESS

Early on, the Apple IIc Plus was a big seller, and by January 1989 it was above forecasted sales levels. However, this sales pace was not sustained, as customers seemed to want the IIe with its slots, or the greater power of the IIGS.

---

7 Weishaar, Tom, "Ask Uncle DOS", *Open-Apple* (January 1989), 4.91.
8 Weishaar, Tom, "Miscellanea", *Open-Apple* (May 1989), 5.27.

There were some products that were designed by third-party developers for both the IIc and IIc Plus that never made it to the market for various reasons. Applied Ingenuity (later known as Ingenuity, Inc.) had two products that would have markedly increased the portability of the IIc/IIc Plus. One was an internal hard disk they called CDrive, which would have replaced the Apple IIc or IIc Plus internal floppy disk drive (converting it into an external floppy drive). Even more unique was CKeeper, which was a multi-function card with many features. It could hold up to 1.25 MB of extra RAM; it had a clock/calendar chip that was ProDOS compatible; it had firmware routines to support dumping text or graphics screens to the printer; it could function as a built-in assembly language program debugger; and best of all, it had a feature called RAMSaver, which maintained power to the RAM chips during a power failure or if the power switch was turned off. Both of these products never saw the light of day, primarily because the company went out of business before they were released.[9, 10]

Chinook Technologies actually finished design on an internal modem for the IIc Plus, but never released it. This card, 1.5 by 6 inches in size, would have mounted inside the disk drive shield. It connected to a small box attached to the outside of the IIc case, where there were cutouts provided by Apple for connection of an anti-theft cable. This external box had phone jacks for the phone line and a telephone, just like most external modems. Undoubtedly it was never released because of Apple's indifference towards the IIc Plus.[11]

With inadequate support by Apple marketing, third-party hardware and software developers had little motivation to design new products for the IIc Plus. Therefore, no unique products emerged on the market to take advantage of its features. Finally, in September of 1990 Apple discontinued the IIc Plus, leaving the Platinum Apple IIe and the Apple IIGS as the remaining bearers of Wozniak's legacy.

APPLE IIE EMULATOR CARD

In early 1991, Apple introduced a hardware add-on card for the Macintosh LC computer (the first low cost Mac that could display color)[12], allowing it to emulate a 128K Apple IIe. This Apple IIe-on-a-card cost only $199, but the Mac LC needed to use the card sold for $2,495, which made the combination the most expensive Apple II ever made.

---

9 -----,"Ingenuity News", *II At Work* (Vol. 2, No. 1, Spring 1990), 30.
10 Mazur, Jeffrey, Forums, *Applefritter*, <www.applefritter.com/forum>, accessed June 14, 2010.
11 Hoover, Tom, e-mail message to author, November 1991.
12 The very first Macintosh to be able to display color was the Macintosh II, released in 1987 at the high base price of $3898. The Macintosh LC appeared in October 1990, at the slightly more reasonable cost of $2400, and was specifically targeted to the home user.

CHAPTER 44 | *Falling Out of Favor*

Apple engineers had managed to put the function of an entire IIe onto a card smaller than the old Disk II controller card. The Apple II interface software ran on the Mac and accessed the features of the card, and with version 2.0 it made more of the memory allocated to the Macintosh available for use on the emulated IIe. However, unlike all previous versions of the Apple IIe, there were no hardware-based slots on the IIe card; instead, it used software-based slots that were allocated by moving icons (that represented various peripherals) into "slots" on the Mac screen.

Macintosh LC running Apple IIe emulator
– Photo credit: Francois Michaud

To use 5.25-inch disks with this Apple IIe, there was a cable that attached to the card. The cable split into a game connector (for paddles or joystick operation) and a connector that accepted IIc- and IIGS-style 5.25 drives.

The IIe card ran at a "normal" (1 MHz) speed and a "fast" (2 MHz) speed.[13] It had limitations, however. For a 1991 Apple II, it was limited in being unable to be accelerated beyond 2 MHz (the Zip Chip could run a standard IIe at 8 MHz), and the screen response seemed slow, since it was using a software-based Mac text display instead of the hardware-based Apple II character ROM.

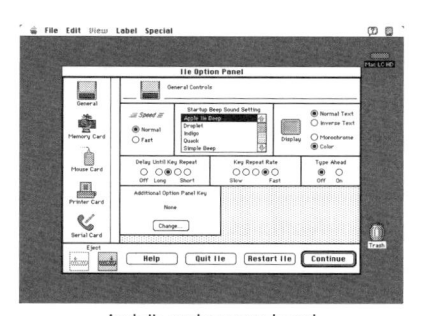

Apple IIe emulator control panel
– Photo credit: J Mayrand's Computer Museum

As a Macintosh it lacked the power and speed of the newer Macintosh II models (which also ran color displays). But if having an Apple II and a Mac in one machine was important (as it was at many schools that had a large investment in the Apple II), this was the best way to do it.

Apple IIe card for Mac LC, and cable for disk drive and joystick
– Photo credit: David Schmidt

---

13 Doms, Dennis, "The Apple II as Mac peripheral", *Open-Apple*, (July 1991), 7.43-7.44.

FADING LIGHT

As Apple's efforts to promote the Macintosh were finally translating into improved sales of the platform, it accelerated the company's de-emphasis of the Apple II line—both the older 8-bit models and the newer IIGS. It went so far as to have its developer technical support staff specifically recommend that new applications not be created for the Apple II or IIGS, but rather for the Macintosh. Apple authorized dealers tended to direct potential customers away from purchase of any new Apple II product, and towards the Macintosh platform, often making this advice because "the Apple II is about to be discontinued anyway."[14]

APPLE II ETHERNET CARD PROJECT

As Apple continued its efforts to find a way to emerge above the dominance of Intel and Microsoft, a few projects that were not directly to the benefit of the Macintosh were allowed to move forward. Because of the strong classroom presence of the Apple II series, connecting the computers together in a school computer lab was important to educators. In March 1988 Apple introduced several products to make it easier for administrators to create networks of Apple II, Macintosh, and MS-DOS computers.

The Apple II Workstation Card allowed an Enhanced Apple IIe or Apple IIGS to connect to Apple's proprietary network, which they had named Apple-Talk. File server software running on a Macintosh made that networked computer appear as if it were a hard drive on the Apple II, and programs made for network use could load and run from that file server. This made it unnecessary to load the program onto each individual computer on the network (and avoid the expense of a hard drive on each computer).

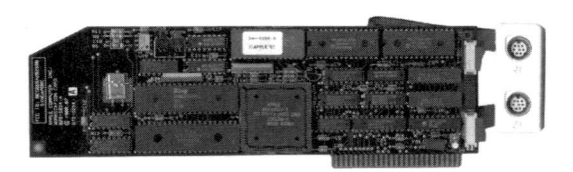

Apple II Workstation Card – Photo credit: Tony Diaz

To an Apple II computer with the Workstation Card, the network connection appeared both as a disk drive *and* as a printer, allowing the network to be used both for file storage and retrieval as well as a conduit to a central

---

[14] Ironically, a very similar scenario would reappear to plague Apple in the late 1990s, when buyers who came to a computer store to look for a new system were directed by the sales people away from a Macintosh model (despite the ease of setup and use that Apple constantly advertised) to various brands of Windows-based PC's, telling the customer as an aside remark that "Apple wasn't going to be around much longer anyway."

printer. Further enhancements for the IIGS came in July 1989 when GS/OS System 5.0 was released, improving the ability to allow an Apple IIGS to boot up and function completely over an AppleTalk network.

With the increase of networks based on the Ethernet protocol, the next obvious evolution of network hardware for the Apple II was a peripheral card that worked on Ethernet the same way that the Workstation Card worked with AppleTalk. By 1991, engineers in the Apple II group at Apple had completed a design for a card based on the Workstation Card, with the same ability to boot an Apple II or IIGS over an Ethernet connection, or to print to a central printer on that network. The original design for the card used a 2 MHz 65c02 processor, 32K of RAM for packet buffering and miscellaneous card use, as well as 128K of ROM (which was divided into four banks that were swapped in as needed, somewhat like the extra ROM code on the Apple IIe and IIc computers). This ROM code handled the AppleTalk protocols for network communication. The card was to use the AAUI (Apple Attachment Unit Interface, Apple's proprietary Ethernet connector) to plug the card into a network.[15]

For reasons that involved estimated costs of production versus sales, the first design for the Apple II Ethernet Card was scrapped, and a second card was designed during 1992-93. This card was not based on the earlier Apple II Workstation Card, and rather than using custom-designed Apple parts it used less-expensive "off-the-shelf" parts in its design. It still used the AAUI connector, but instead of the 65c02 processor used by the Workstation Card and the previous Ethernet card, this version utilized a 65816 running at 4 MHz to handle data processing functions for the card. Apple ordinarily tended to be secretive about products that were being designed; in this case, this revised Ethernet card was openly acknowledged by Apple representatives, and at the 1992 A2-Central Summer Conference they announced that the 6.0.1 revision of GS/OS would be released simultaneously with the new Ethernet card, with a predicted release date of late 1992.

RUMORS

Meanwhile, the developer community at large was anticipating another Apple II project—a new revision to the Apple IIGS line. At the September 1988 AppleFest conference in San Francisco, Apple CEO John Sculley had stated that there would be "a new Apple II CPU in 12-18 months." Even though the ROM 03 revision to the Apple IIGS was released a year later (August 1989), rumors were circulating that Apple was working on a yet more

---

15 Diaz, Tony, "The Apple][Ethernet Card:][be or Not][Be Was It's Question", *The Apple II Information And Pictoral Reference*, <www.apple2.org/AllEthernet.html>, accessed October 20, 2012.

powerful Apple IIGS, something that could be a redesign and not just an update. It spurred hope that the best was yet to come.

Beta units Apple had sent to developers resulted in some leaked details about this updated IIGS. In early 1990, they believed that this so-called "ROM 04" revision would provide an improved screen resolution of a more industry standard 640 by 480 (this had not been tried with the original IIGS design, for reasons of backward compatibility and to keep the cost down). The new computer was also expected to run at a faster speed, to as much as 7 MHz.[16] The Apple SuperDrive (an improved disk drive which allowed reading and writing 3.5-inch, 1.4 MB disks formatted for MS-DOS) was available for the Macintosh, and rumors indicated this was included in the new IIGS. Adding fuel to the fire, Western Design Center (the company that had designed the 65816 microprocessor) had expressed interest in creating a further enhancement to the processor line with a 32-bit version called the 65832.

The expected release date came and went without any further mention of a new Apple IIGS. Even the rumors quieted down, especially after Apple USA president Bob Puette was quoted by the San Francisco Chronicle in late October of 1988 stating that Apple was "phasing out the Apple II line." Apple public relations later stated that this comment had been taken out of context, and Puette made a later clarification:

> We remain committed to our millions of Apple II customers and we want to make sure that they understand the high level of support that Apple has behind the Apple II product line. We want Apple II owners to remain happy with their investment in Apple II technology and we continue to look for more ways to protect that investment and extend the life of Apple II products — both as standalone computers and as part of networks. We will continue to sell, support, and service the Apple II product line and provide product enhancements to that line as long as customer demand warrants it. We plan to continue to enhance the existing product line through updates to system software and peripheral add-ons. We fully expect Apple II computers to continue to serve education and other customers satisfactorily for many years to come
>
> On the other hand, we have no plans at this time to introduce new, standalone Apple II models. However, we will incorporate Apple II technology into current and future platforms, as we have with the Apple IIe card for the Macintosh LC. We believe that this compat-

---

16 Sewal, Murphy, "Vaporware", *Apple Pulp (H.U.G.E. Apple Club News Letter)*, (March 1990).

ibility strategy will preserve customers' investments in Apple II, while allowing them to move to new technology platforms if they wish.[17]

The network connectivity implied by his remarks referred undoubtedly to the as-yet-unfinished Ethernet card. And with this remark it would appear that the question about a further revision of the Apple IIGS was settled for good.

MARK TWAIN

And yet, there were still efforts within Apple to bring about a final revision to the Apple IIGS, one that would make it better and more capable. The IIGS still had people within the company who poured out their hearts in making changes to improve the computer, both in software and hardware. Some of these same people had created the advances in the GS/OS system software that made the computer faster without requiring any changes in hardware, and also made it possible to take advantage of new peripherals as they became available. With this same fervor, they had indeed been creating the rumored next generation Apple IIGS.

The IIGS they were creating was a logical extension of the capabilities of previous models of the computer, combined with features that were most needed to provide usability with the new IIGS software appearing on the market. The newest versions of GS/OS continued to require more memory to run properly, so this computer was built with 2 MB of RAM on the motherboard. For RAM upgrades beyond this minimum, the older memory expansion slot was eliminated, and replacing it were two slots for SIMM (single inline memory modules) RAM cards. These compact packages were at that time becoming the industry standard, and were being included in all newer Macintosh models.

The firmware code in the ROM 04 IIGS was to include the new tools that later appeared in GS/OS System 6 (tools that would be loaded into RAM at boot time with older IIGS models, just as the ROM 03 tools were loaded from disk in ROM 01 computers). With the increased size and complexity of System and application software, a hard drive was changing from a luxury to a necessity, and so a 40 Meg SCSI hard drive was included. And to make the SCSI experience complete, a high-speed DMA (direct memory access) SCSI port was to be included on the rear panel for attachment of additional SCSI devices. The SuperDrive (mentioned above) was also included as a built-in device, making it possible to have a very complete IIGS system without attaching additional hardware. As a finale to the new system, Apple planned to bundle HyperCard IIGS with the computer. The one predicted

---

17 Deatherage, Matt, A2 Roundtable, Category 5, Topic 14, *GEnie*, accessed October 1990.

enhancement that did not make the final cut was a speed increase beyond the original 2.8 MHz.

The code name assigned to this new Apple IIGS was "Mark Twain", because of the writer's oft-repeated quote, "The reports of my death have been greatly exaggerated." It was to be a triumph over the writers in the media who continued to insist that the end of the Apple II line of computers was just around the corner.

This wonderful new Apple IIGS had many things going for it, but the one thing that it did *not* have was someone in a position of power at the company who would champion the machine, and push for its full support and promotion. This had been the biggest problem with the IIGS beginning with its original release in 1986. After the product introduction, which involved a couple of television and magazine ads, Apple turned its attention to other concerns and left the Apple IIGS to sell itself. What promotion was done for the IIGS or products associated with it was done with all the fervor Apple had applied to the Apple II line since the Apple III had been designed (in other words, very little).

THE BEGINNING OF THE END

Knowing that local Apple computer user groups contained the most enthusiastic owners and users of Apple products, the company had been nurturing those groups from its early days. For years, it had supplied information through newsletters and directly to user groups. For the evening of September 25, 1991, Apple's User Group Connection planned a unique event. The company's first nationwide user group meeting was planned via a live video presentation. It was broadcast on UG-TV, a satellite channel available to anyone with a consumer satellite receiver. In some cities, the feed was picked up and broadcast on cable community access channels, and in other places larger groups rented the necessary equipment to view the event.

The broadcast showed a prerecorded tour of the Apple Campus (which some felt was too long and uninteresting), and then it proceeded with product introductions. These included the Apple II High Speed SCSI card and GS/OS System 6, the new Macintosh System 7, the Macintosh Classic, and the Apple IIe Card for the Macintosh LC. Conspicuously absent was the highly anticipated ROM 04 Apple IIGS. In reality, the Apple II engineering team members were ready to demonstrate it—but it was pulled from the program at the last minute, a decision that ultimately meant that it would never appear.

The cancellation of the ROM 04 project was not announced officially anywhere (since the product itself had never been formally acknowledged). It resulted, however, in an unexplained delay in the release of the Apple IIGS

System 6.0 until March 1992. That year passed from spring into summer, and despite its announcement by Apple at the 1992 A2-Central Summer Conference in July, the promised Apple II Ethernet Card also failed to materialize. The final blow to the Apple IIGS occurred in December 1992, when it failed to appear on the new product price lists released by Apple (although the Apple IIe still remained on the list).

In the aftermath of the discontinuation of the IIGS, Apple representatives met with the Bay Area Apple User Group in the San Francisco area to let them know of the decision to terminate production of the IIGS. During the meeting, the news was met with a quiet resignation, rather than the anger that had often greeted Apple's anti-Apple II decisions in the past. They were also told some of Apple's reasons for the decision. They were, as before, making the Macintosh the future of the company, and it was felt (rightly so) that further enhancements to the IIGS would take away sales of the Macintosh LC, the new consumer color computer that Apple was promoting. A IIGS plug-in card for the Macintosh had been considered, but it was determined that the cost to produce it would be as much as the cost of the entire Mac LC. Apple had also looked into creating a reengineered IIGS, to reduce production costs (which would make it possible to continue to build and sell the IIGS). This, however, never went beyond the initial research. Finally, the user group representatives were told that it had been hoped at Apple that GS/OS System 6 and HyperCard IIGS would give Apple II users a taste of the Macintosh experience, and encourage them to switch platforms.[18]

They were further told that there were no plans to license Apple II technology for other companies to build and sell, as it would compete with Apple's own products. No future hardware products would appear after the Ethernet card was released. They would, however, continue to work on printer and network software enhancements.

THE END

Unfortunately, early 1993 passed without any announcement of an impending release of the promised Apple II Ethernet card. Apple's previously stated intent was that the Ethernet card and GS/OS System 6.0.1 would be released at about the same time, since a major reason for this minor revision was to include the system code to support the card. But the System 6.0.1 update appeared quietly in March 1993, without any mention of the Ethernet card, and by the time the next A2-Central Summer Conference was held in July, it was clear that the card would never be released. The exact reason for the termination of this project turned out to be financial. It was predicted at

---

18 E'Sex, Lunatic, A2 Roundtable, Category 5, Topic 4, *GEnie*, accessed December 1992.

Apple that the card would sell no more than 5,000 units, and although this would be a success for most small Apple II businesses, for Apple it was just not worth it. Apple was not, of course, interested in licensing the technology to anyone else to produce and sell, though it had briefly considered allowing Apple Australia to do it.[19]

The Platinum Apple IIe remained in production until November 1993. During that month, the new dealer price lists from Apple excluded any mention of the Apple IIe, effectively discontinuing the last remaining self-contained Apple II computer. The Apple IIe Emulator Card continued to be sold until May 1995.

DISCOVERY

An archeologist becomes excited when a find is made that illuminates his understanding of the past. In the same way, an Apple II enthusiast loves to discover something that he's never seen before. In the mid 1990s, discoveries were made in two separate parts of the country that provided further insight to the story of the aborted "ROM 04" Apple IIGS.

In 1993, Jim Pittman was at the University of New Mexico Computing Center, and there he came across a previous Apple employee. Pittman was a member of the AppleQuerque Computer Club, and on that particular day he was using his old Apple II Plus as a terminal to access the University's Unix system. The former Apple employee, who had worked in the Apple II group, commented favorably on seeing an Apple II still in use. As their conversation continued she mentioned to Pittman that she had in her possession an Apple IIGS prototype that had never been released. Pittman was not too interested in it at that time; but in the fall of 1995, nearly two years later, when he later mentioned this chance conversation to two of his club members, they were *very* interested. Jim was able to contact her again, and his club got permission to examine the computer in detail. Assisting Pittman in the evaluation were two other members of the AppleQuerque user group: Joe Walters, who was also one of the sysops in CompuServe's Apple II Forum; and Mike Westerfield of The Byte Works, author of most of the high level professional grade programming languages (*ORCA/M*, *ORCA/Pascal*, and others) available for the Apple IIGS. Together, they brought a considerable amount of end-user Apple II and IIGS experience to the evaluation.[20, 21]

In Petaluma, California, Joe Kohn came across a similar discovery in late 1995. Kohn had a long history with the Apple II, as head sysop for the Apple

---

19 Diaz, Tony, "The Apple][Ethernet Card:][be or Not][Be Was It's Question", *The Apple II Information And Pictoral Reference*, <www.apple2.org/AllEthernet.html>, accessed October 20, 2012.
20 Jones, Max, "The Lost Generation Of The IIGs", *Juiced.GS* (Volume 1, Issue 1: Winter 1996).
21 Pittman, Jim, "The Apple IIGs 'Mark Twain' Prototype or 'Super Apple II'", *AppleTalk* (AppleQuerque Computer Club), (February 1996).

CHAPTER 44 | Falling Out of Favor

II area on the online service The Source, and later in writing his own newsletter. At a meeting of the Gravenstein Apple User Group, a woman brought a computer that she claimed was an Apple IIGS to a meeting. When she entered the room with the computer, Kohn had to stop his presentation to look at it, as he immediately noticed that it was different from a standard IIGS— there was a cutout in the front that was not supposed to be there. The owner said she had received two of them, plus a spare motherboard, from a friend of a friend, originally passed down from someone who used to work at Apple. On the bottom of the computer, it read "Prototype: Mark Twain". Kohn knew this was something very special. With some effort, he was able to make a trade to obtain these prototypes.

Mark Twain, front view – Photo credit: Tony Diaz

Joe Kohn enlisted the help of Tony Diaz, who sold Apple II peripheral cards, hardware, and software, and repaired and collected Apple II computers. Together, they worked to analyze the Mark Twains he had obtained, and published the results of their efforts in the Gravenstein group newsletter. Similarly, Pittman and Westerfield told their own story in the AppleQuerque Computer Club newsletter.

There were some minor differences between the prototypes, but they had much in common. On startup, the screen did not display "ROM 04", but still read "ROM 03". The computer booted, not from a floppy disk, as had every IIGS ever sold by Apple, but from an internal hard drive, which no Apple II ever had as standard equipment. It booted directly to the Apple IIGS Finder desktop, and in checking "About the Finder" from the Apple menu, it showed the presence of 2 MB of RAM on the motherboard; the ROM 0 and ROM 01 models came with 256K of RAM, and the ROM 03 was sold with no more than 1 MB of RAM. The 65816 processor was still at the standard 2.8 MHz "fast" speed that every IIGS offered since its release in 1986.

Inside the computer, the layout was generally the same as a standard Apple IIGS, but with several important exceptions. On the front left panel of the computer a slot had been expertly cut for access to an internal 3.5-inch disk drive. The floppy disk drive may have been a SuperDrive, but it did not have the circuitry or driver support to allow access to the larger capacity 1.4 MB 3.5-inch disks that a SuperDrive was capable of handling. The floppy drive sat in front of a differently shaped power supply, and on top of a half-height Quantum LPS 40 MB SCSI hard drive. The hard drive was plugged into a built-in high-speed SCSI card, and included a connector on the back to allow attachment of additional SCSI drives. Because of the SCSI circuitry included on the motherboard, slot 7 was absent.

Further examination of the internals of the computer revealed that the motherboard was 1.5 inches wider than older models. Not only was slot 7 missing, but slot 5 was also gone because of the internal 3.5-inch drive. The traditional IIGS memory expansion slot was missing, and in its place was a pair of empty 64-pin SIMM slots to expand on the 2 MB of RAM that was on the motherboard.

The sound circuitry had been improved to produce stereo, and also included was an audio input jack that allowed recording digitized sound.

There were some hand wiring changes that had been done to the motherboard, though the exact nature of these was unclear. The back panel opening for slot 1 was blocked by the position of the power supply, and the power plug and power switch had been moved a short distance from their usual location.[22, 23]

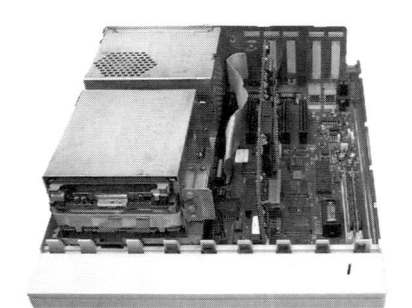

Mark Twain, interior view – notice on the left the 3.5-inch drive above, the 5.25-inch hard drive below, the SCSI connector to the back, the differently sized power supply, and SIMM cards on the front right – Photo credit: Tony Diaz

Clearly, these prototypes were works-in-progress for the improved IIGS that was supposed to have been introduced to the world at that September 1991 Apple User Group satellite broadcast. To these Apple IIGS veterans, this Mark Twain IIGS did not really offer anything to them that they did not already have. If fact, the enhancements that they had by this time added to their own Apple IIGS computers (additional memory, a 65816 accelerator card, and a large hard drive with a very fast interface card) made this 1991 prototype *less* capable than the machine they were used to running. However, they were all favorably impressed with the potential that the Mark Twain had offered (for 1991), and most who saw it felt that had it been released in 1991, they would have been interested in purchasing one. Certainly, it was a more significant enhancement to the Apple IIGS than was the ROM 01 to ROM 03 upgrade in 1989 (which only offered increased RAM and improved firmware). The Mark Twain offered not only a further increase in the standard amount of RAM supplied with the computer, but also the benefits of a built-in floppy disk and hard drive storage. In the same way that the Apple IIc provided an "all-in-one" solution to Apple II Plus and IIe users, with the added benefit of five empty slots for even further expandability, this truly had the potential to be the pinnacle of the IIGS series. Joe Kohn, in his comments about the Mark Twain, speculated that it was designed to be an under $1000 computer for the classroom, focused on compatibility with

---

22 Jones, Max, "The Lost Generation Of The IIGs", *Juiced.GS* (Volume 1, Issue 1: Winter 1996).
23 Pittman, Jim, "The Apple IIGs 'Mark Twain' Prototype or 'Super Apple II'", *AppleTalk* (AppleQuerque Computer Club), (February 1996).

existing software, and to compete against the inroads made there by IBM PC clones. What Apple released instead was the Macintosh LC and the Apple II Emulator Card, and made it unnecessary to bother to complete the Mark Twain project.[24]

Because of comments made by Apple's legal department to the publisher of GS+ magazine (recall that Apple's lawyer had said that "GS+" infringed on one of Apple's trademarks), it was quite likely that the computer, had it been released, would have been called the Apple IIGS Plus.

TIMELINE

The start and end dates for the Apple IIGS, Apple IIe, and Apple IIc:

Apple IIe (all versions) – *January 1983 - November 1993*

Apple IIc (all versions) – *April 1984 - September 1990*

Apple IIGS – *September 1986 - August 1987*

Apple IIe Platinum – *January 1987 - November 1993*

Apple IIGS ROM 01 – *September 1987 - July 1989*

Apple IIc Plus – *September 1988 - September 1990*

Apple IIGS ROM 03 – *August 1989 - December 1992*

Apple IIe Emulator Card – *March 1991 - May 1995*

Apple IIGS Plus "Mark Twain" – *September 1991 (cancelled before release)*

Apple II Ethernet Card version 1 – *1991 (not released)*

Apple II Ethernet Card version 2 – *1992 (not released)*

Mark Twain prototype first discovered (Pittman) – *1993*

Mark Twain prototype analyzed (Pittman, Kohn) – *October 1995*

---

24 Kohn, Joe, "The Computer That Could Have Changed The World", *GravenStein Apple User Group* newsletter, (1996).

CHAPTER 45
Online Assimilation

The late 1990s were difficult times both for Apple II users and for text-based online services. The oldest of those services had been started as a way to make money from time-sharing computers when they were not busy. Being successful was a double-edged sword—if the after-hours use as an online service was successful, it put extra load on the mainframe computers. The other cut was that as the World Wide Web continued to gain ascendency, it was lessening demand for text-based services. The increasing availability of Internet access and web browser improvements were drawing customers away from a boring text-only interface to the colorful point-and-click world offered by Netscape and Internet Explorer.

The latter part of that decade was also notable for wild speculation by the stock market in tech companies that were staking out territory in the new world of the Web. It resulted in what was called the dot-com bubble, where huge amounts of investment dollars and venture capital went into nearly any company that claimed to have a web presence. This happened regardless of whether or not that company had a valid or workable business plan. The bubble of speculation ultimately resulted in a crash as many of the companies that were not making money went out of business.

This same financial lure caused each online service to try to find a way to transform itself into a web presence. In this environment, those who used a computer that could not easily handle HTML or web pages with pictures were finding it more difficult to continue to have a nationally available home base for their online activities. For Apple II users, as text access for CompuServe and Genie began to fall apart in the last half of the decade, the next safe harbor that appeared on the horizon was Delphi. And although it was not nearly as large as those other services, Delphi was one that managed to transition itself to the World Wide Web, something the others could not accomplish.

DELPHI (1983 – 2001)

Delphi had its origins as the world's first online encyclopedia back in 1981. Wes Kussmaul had gone with his 14-year-old daughter to the public library to help her research information on eight world leaders. He was frustrated to see how much of the available information was out of date by several years. Kussmaul felt that an encyclopedia needed to be more current than was possible with printed books, and so formed the General Videotex Corporation (GVC) to create a computerized encyclopedia that would provide more timely information.

As the foundation of his knowledge base, Kussmaul purchased rights to the *Cadillac Modern Encyclopedia*, which had been published in 1973 by Random House. The book was a high-school reference, and likely its smaller scale made it less costly to license for the purposes of a dial-up computer reference. GVC transcribed the 1,954 pages of the encyclopedia into ASCII text files and then created a database program to allow access to the files. Many of these files included rudimentary hyperlinks between the various entries. He hosted this database and the encyclopedia files on a time-sharing system in Texas.

To meet Kussmaul's requirements for up-to-date information, he hired fourteen editors to regularly review the 24,000 entries in his encyclopedia. An editor from United Press International provided additional information for current events with stories from the UPI wire service.

The Kussmaul Encyclopedia was available by late 1981, and was initially marketed as a bundle complete with a personal computer and modem to access the encyclopedia. It was felt that schools and libraries would be the primary customers for the product.

Two versions of the Kussmaul Encyclopedia were initially marketed. The basic package, for $895, included a Tandy Color Computer, a modem, a cassette recorder for storage, and an online account for the encyclopedia database. Included with the package was access to CompuServe and the Dow Jones information service, as well as Comp*U*Star, an online shopping service.

For $2,750, the deluxe version of the encyclopedia provided a 48K Apple II Plus, a Hayes Micromodem II, and a disk drive. In addition to the services in the Color Computer edition, it included a copy of *Apple Computer's Dow Jones Portfolio Evaluator*, a $50 standalone program that could retrieve securities values from Dow Jones, then calculate and display the current value of an investor's portfolio.[1]

In 1982, General Videotex expanded the services offered, including home banking, email, simple chat functionality, and simple bulletin board areas. To provide greater accessibility, the company added dial-up connections through Telenet, Tymnet, and Sprintnet.

The new expanded service launched itself officially under the name Delphi in March 1983, taking after the Oracle of Delphi in ancient Greece, a

---

1 Needle, David, "Videotex encyclopedia service is always up-to-date", *InfoWorld* (November 23, 1981), 29.

place where prophecies and wisdom were passed down to worshippers of the Greek god, Apollo.[2]

Delphi added features in 1984, including improved chat (called Conference) and bulletin board areas called SIGs (Special Interest Groups). These had the same function as CompuServe's Forums and GEnie's Roundtables. The members who were recruited to run a SIG were compensated a percentage of the revenue generated by traffic on his or her SIG.

Also offered were weather forecasts from Accu-Weather, Associated Press news, classified ads, and a member directory. General Videotex also arranged for connections to outside services, including the Online Airline Guide, the North American Investment Corp., Dialog (a commercial online search service), and Dialcom (an early commercial email service).[3]

Over the next decade, Delphi enjoyed growth, but it lagged well behind that of CompuServe, Prodigy, America Online and GEnie. By 1993 it had around 100,000 subscribers, but did not have the finances to expand its offerings to compete with the larger services. Delphi's directors began to look at outside funding.

One of the companies they approached was Rupert Murdoch's News Corporation. Murdoch's company had significant offerings in media that none of the other online services had available to them, including newspapers, book publishers, and television. News Corporation did not have an online service, and larger companies already owned the other four services. The deal made between Delphi and Murdoch became more than just funding, with the outright purchase of Delphi in February 1993, including every share of stock, for a bargain price of about $3 million.[4]

Photo credit: *Delphi - The Official Guide*, 1993

In 1985, as Delphi users formed SIGS for various topics and home computer platforms, the Apple II SIG came into existence. SIG posts on Delphi were organized into a threaded message base. Posts could be read in numerical order, or in the threaded order by using a "Follow" command that grouped related messages. There were fifteen main topics in the Apple II forum.

The Apple II Database was a library of files available for download, and also offered quick access outside of Delphi to Internet files via FTP (file transfer protocol). As early as 1992 it was possible to send or receive email outside

---

2 Kussmaul, Wes, "How I Learned These Things", *Own Your Privacy*, (PKI Press, Waltham, MA, 2007), 55.
3 Banks, Michael, "The Second Wave", *On the Way to the Web: The Secret History of the Internet and Its Founders*, (Apress), 80-82.
4 Garfinkel, Simpson, "The Delphi Deal", *Wired 2.01 Electrosphere* (1994), <simson.net/clips/1994/94.Wired.TheDelphiDeal.txt>, accessed October 20, 2012.

of the Delphi system to the Internet at large, well before it was possible on the other national online services. Additionally, Delphi made it easy to access Usenet newsgroups.[5]

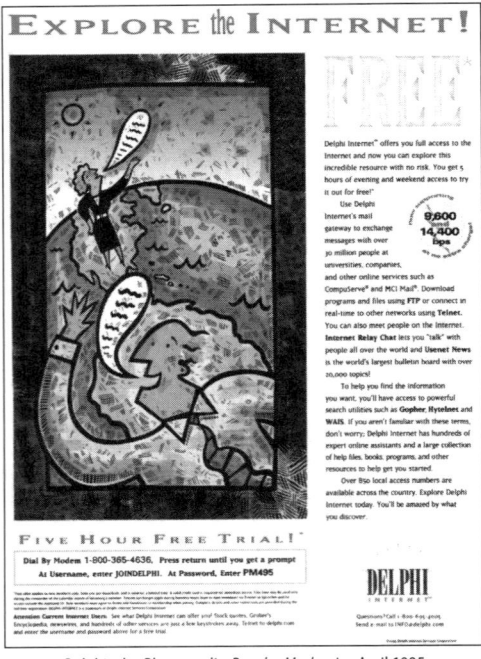

Delphi ad – Photo credit: *Popular Mechanics*, April 1995

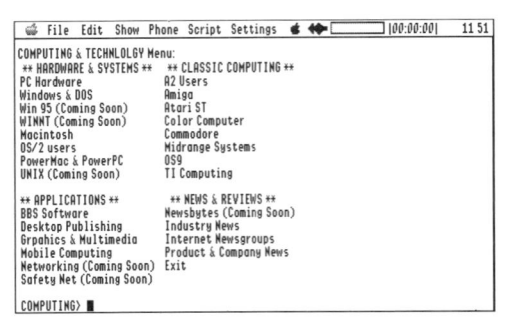

Delphi screenshot, Nov 1996
– Photo credit: adapted from photo in *Juiced.GS*, Fall 1996

By 1996, traffic and revenue was down, and News Corporation sold Delphi to a group of investors that included Bill Louden, who had started GEnie back in 1985. They began to work on migrating the content and function of Delphi to the Web. They also changed the service to free access, supported by web-based advertising (at the height of the dot-com bubble).

As mentioned in the GEnie story, chief sysop Gary Utter gave hints that changes were in the wind in his keynote address at KansasFest 1996. He announced it was necessary for the Apple II online community to spread outside of Genie, due to its uncertain future. A formal announcement was made in November of that year that Syndicomm had created its own Apple II forums on Delphi for A2 and A2Pro, with a similar structure as found on their Genie counterparts. As on Genie, Delphi had online conference areas which were open nightly to help Apple II users and hold special conference events. The new A2 forums went live on November 18, 1996.

The advantage of using Delphi was that it could be accessed via telnet from any Internet connection, and did not have to depend on Delphi-specific local dial-up phone numbers. The cost for telnet access to Delphi could be as low as $3 per month, if paid a year in advance. Furthermore, users had

---

5 Kellers, Tim and Hartley, Charles, "Checking Out Delphi and GEnie", *II Alive* (January/February 1995), 6-9.

a choice of text-based or Web-based access. The message base that was displayed was drawn from the same database, and so was identical whether read through telnet as text, or using a web browser. At that time, Delphi management stated that they were committed to maintaining text-based access for their users.

Utter's frustrations with Genie came to a head, and on January 1, 1997 he regretfully announced that he was abandoning the A2 Roundtable for the new forums that had been created on Delphi. He urged other Apple II users to join him there, as he strongly felt that it was Delphi that held the future for Apple II online access and community. Some others who chose to stay on Genie criticized this move, as they felt that it would certainly kill off Genie if everyone left.

By August 1997 there were a few hundred new Delphi members in the A2 Forum and activity was increasing. The primary factor limiting the migration of new users was the sparse numbers of files in the A2 library on Delphi. However, for months before starting on Delphi, Syndicomm had been systematically downloading files for archival purposes from the A2 Roundtable on Genie, and efforts were being made to upload them to the Delphi library. It was a large collection of as many as 14,000 files, and the process of uploading them was slowed by the need to create descriptions and keywords for each file, and also to make sure that the original uploader had not specified that the file could only be uploaded to Genie.

A unique event for Apple II users was held from 1998 through 2000, originating from Delphi. Joe Kohn, former Chief Sysop of the Apple II group on The Source and publisher of the *Shareware Solutions II* newsletter began weekly online chats each Monday night. Having a chat or online conference was not so unusual, but what was unusual was the way in which they were conducted. Through the technical efforts of two Apple II and Mac programmers, these chats managed to connect Apple II users in the CompuServe, Genie, and Delphi chat areas, and did so in such a way as to make it look as if all of the connected users were in a single large online conference. This had never been tried before.

It was accomplished through the use of special scripts on the Macintosh telecom program *ProTERM Mac*. A message center core directed traffic between various script modules, one for each online service to which it was connected, and kept track of the last fifty lines of text submitted to it. Each script would send out to its respective online service any messages that had not yet appeared on that service. With *ProTERM Mac* in control, a message typed by someone on Genie appeared on Delphi and CompuServe, and responses on one of those other systems were likewise mirrored to the other two. These weekly tri-system chats continued until March 1999, when CompuServe closed down its text access.

Kohn tried to keep it going as a dual-system chat, but was hampered in his efforts in April 1999 when Genie's A2 Roundtable became unavailable for three weeks (as mentioned previously). When Genie A2 RT was functioning again, the Delphi/Genie chats were resumed for a while. Kohn continued these weekly Monday night chats into 2000, but they were less well attended than they had been when there were three systems.

During 1999, Delphi programmers continued building up the service's web access, mirroring content posted on the text side so it was also available to anyone visiting with a standard web browser, and vice versa. Synchronization between the two was still a problem at times, and became visibly apparent when daylight savings time began in April of that year. A bug in the software resulted in a large number of duplicated messages in the A2 Forum (and in many of Delphi's other forums). By late in the year the company was focusing almost entirely on web access, and paying less and less attention to the text part of the service. In fact, it was late in the year that Delphi discontinued its dial-up access, and made text access available only via telnet. *The Lamp!* online newsletter took time in November 1999 to explain to those who had previously only used dial-up about the process needed to connect to Delphi via telnet.

To try to keep the system going, Delphi joined forces with another Internet service. The WELL (Whole Earth 'Lectronic Link) had been formed back in 1985 by one of the founders of the early 1970s *Whole Earth Catalog*. The WELL was originally a dial-up BBS, but in the early 1990s it became one of the first dial-up ISPs (Internet Service Providers). Its focus was creation of online virtual communities where people with similar interests could message each other and share information. The company whose software ran The WELL called itself Well Engaged, and in January 2000 Delphi joined with that company to form Prospero Technologies. Prospero's task was to manage Delphi's message boards and chat services. As a result of this merger, Delphi reduced its own technical staff, which added to the dysfunction of the A2 Forum.

Those remaining staff experienced more and more problems keeping the text and web sides synchronized with each other. In August 2000, Delphi announced that as of November 1st of that year they would no longer bill users for the service. For those who were using Delphi's "legacy services" (text-based access), they would keep it running but would do no technical support. This made direct access of Delphi by an Apple II very tenuous, as it could disappear at any time.

By late 2000, Delphi announced its plans to move entirely to web-based access. It could not promise that the text side would continue. Technical support was further decreased and it was clear that it was only a matter of time before the text side would fail. It took only until mid-January 2001 before the synchronization between the text and web sides of Delphi failed for good.

On February 22nd, they announced that no further attempts at synchronization between the text and web side would be attempted. Within a month, Delphi told its customers that as of May 1, 2001 all text-based services would be discontinued. This included email accounts, text posted to forums, and text-based chat. Syndicomm quickly took archives of bulletin board messages from Delphi and made them available on A2Central.com.

Since the several hundred Apple II users on Delphi depended on their offline readers to automate their sessions, it was felt likely that activity in the A2 Forum was going to drop quickly as users continued their move to A2Central.com. Despite Delphi's official cancellation of the text-based access, some users were still able to connect via telnet as late as the start of 2002, though it quickly disappeared after that.

During the first decade of the 21st century there was a lot of shuttling back and forth of what was left of Delphi. Prospero sold the Delphi Forums in 2001 to Rob Brazell (who owned a number of other Internet properties), and sold the delphi.com domain name to the Delphi Corporation, manufacturer of automotive parts. Brazell had high goals and plans for the Forums, but within a year Prospero had reacquired Delphi Forums from him. By 2008, Mzinga, Inc., bought out Prospero. Finally in September 2011, Dan Bruns (who had been involved with Delphi back in the General Videotex days, and was in the group of investors who had purchased Delphi back from News Corporation back in 1996) bought Delphi Forums back from Mazinga. These forums still existed in 2013, with free access for posting in forums, and two paid levels of premium access that provided a type of web hosting.

After the failure of telnet access in 2002, activity continued in a much-reduced extent in the A2 and A2Pro Forums on Delphi. Gary Utter continued to act as host, until his untimely passing in March 2004. Bruce Caplin, best known by his handle "Hangtime," was a Syndicomm and A2-Central staff member from the early 1990s, and was asked to take over as host. In 2013 his name was still listed; however, by that time the forum was infrequently visited, and sometimes weeks passed with no new posts. With effort, it was at that time still possible to find and read old posts from as far back as 1998.

APPLELINK PERSONAL EDITION / AMERICA ONLINE (1988 – 1994)

William von Meister, who had started The Source back in 1979 and was then pushed out in a power struggle, bounced right back and found other computer-related ventures to pursue. He tried a concept called the Home Music Store, in which music was beamed to a satellite, then sent to a cable television system and piped to a customer's home, where it could be recorded. Initially Warner Bros had agreed to license its music to von Meister's venture, but later decided to back out of the deal, stating that the retailers who sold its records across the country would not allow this threat to their business. The executive from Warner suggested that von Meister consider using his idea for something different, like computer video games.

After this little setback, von Meister turned his attention to doing just that. He started a company called Control Video Corporation, and a dial-up connection service called Gameline. It worked with the Atari 2600 game system, and was actually an Atari VCS cartridge with a phone connector on it. It used a 1200-baud modem, and allowed the customer to connect to a data center in Virginia and pay one dollar to download a VCS game. This game would expire after eight plays, and then the customer had to pay to download it again. Planned enhancements included email, news, banking, and searchable information.

Control Video Corporation hired Steve Case as a marketing executive in January 1983. Unfortunately, the crash in the video game market put considerable stress on Control Video's finances, and by May 1983 the company was near bankruptcy. The CEO and other remaining employees worked on ideas to try to keep the company going, but by 1985 von Meister had left. In May of that same year the company was reorganized under a new name, Quantum Computer Services. It made use of the company's dial-up capacity by launching Quantum Link, a service focused on the Commodore 64 and 128 computer platforms. The software had its own take on point and click, using the cursor keys to select options from a colorful screen. It was a popular way for Commodore users to connect to a national service and the options available beyond a dial-up BBS.

Meanwhile, Apple Computer had created its own online network that went live in July 1985. Called AppleLink, its target audience was not the general public, but was exclusively for Apple employees and certified dealers, and later for software developers. It made use of a graphic user interface different from that of the Macintosh but utilizing the same concept of files and folders, with the addition of bulletin boards and email (within the system).

To operate this on the server end, Apple contracted with GEIS (General Electric Information Services), the same entity that ran the text-only GEnie service discussed previously, using its Mark III timesharing computers. Under contract, a programmer with Central Coast Software wrote the Pascal-based software that ran on the local computer to connect to the system. GEIS charged Apple a high price for using its system, about $30 million per year. This required Apple to pass on the cost to AppleLink's subscribers, which translated to $15 per hour during business hours. The economics of this deal provided no income to Apple.

Steve Case of Quantum wanted to expand his Quantum Link service beyond the Commodore market, and Apple wanted something like AppleLink to connect with its customers. It took months of meetings with Apple before Case could get the company to agree to let Quantum handle the project, but by 1987, they were ready to start what was known internally as Project Samuel. Quantum would create and operate the online system, and Apple would help with development of the client software. This software had to meet Apple's requirements that it look like an Apple product, have screens designed the way Apple wanted them, and Quantum was required to make available adequate customer service. Apple promised to help promote the product, and would receive a royalty of ten percent on all subscribers. It was designed initially to be used with the Apple II, but its ultimate target was the Macintosh market (typical of the internal company focus at the time).

The final product, AppleLink Personal Edition (or ALPE) was announced at AppleFest in Boston on May 20, 1988. (The old AppleLink was renamed to "AppleLink Industrial Edition" to differentiate it from this new consumer system.) To use the ALPE software cost $15 per hour during prime time, and $6 per hour evenings and weekends. It was planned to offer Apple reference materials, downloadable software, and an online store. The system would also offer access to other general services, similar to what Quantum offered with Q-Link. In October 1987, to prepare for the launch, Quantum hired Kent Fillmore away from the A2 Roundtable on GEnie to help recruit sysops for the various areas that would be hosted on ALPE.

AppleLink IIgs start screen – Photo credit: personal

AppleLink Personal Edition, IIe screenshot – Photo credit: personal

While the development process was finishing on the Apple client, Quantum had been working on a product for the IBM PC market. In August 1988, Quantum started their PC-Link service, developed in conjunction with Tandy. This gave the company three similar services, with three target markets, all with similar names—AppleLink Personal Edition, Quantum Link (by this time known as Q-Link), and PC-Link.

Quantum and Apple had conflicts regarding distribution of the ALPE software. Quantum wanted to see it given away, bundled with new computers and other products sold by Apple, in order to gain as wide a distribution as possible. Although Apple did give away a lot of system software to its customers in this era, the company decided that this was one product they would not give away. Though announced in May, it did not officially launch until October of 1988.

AppleLink Personal Edition (and likely PC-Link and Q-Link) was unique for an online computer service in its use of a custom terminal program. Rather than requiring the user, possibly a novice, to spend a lot of time learning how to use a terminal program, a modem, *and* ALPE, Quantum and Apple had designed a special program that handled all the communication details, including the sign-on password (in the early days of its use). Each time that the user signed-off from ALPE, a new, randomly selected password was selected and saved on the ALPE disk for the next time. ALPE was aware of this password, and so the chances of someone breaking in on another user's account was nearly eliminated.

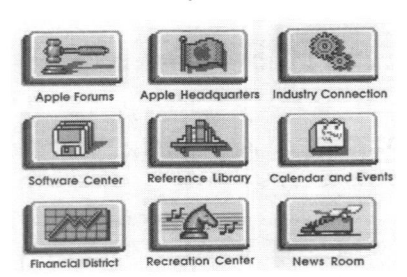

AppleLink icons – Photo credit: *AppleLink Users guide*, 1988

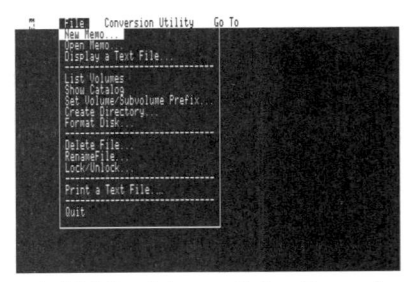

AppleLink MouseText screen – Photo credit: personal

The ALPE client was easy to use. It was not a full GUI on the Apple II or IIGS, though there were graphic icons that could be selected with a mouse (if present) or keyboard cursor keys. Once initially configured for the modem card in the Apple II, the ALPE client transparently handled the call and login.

When the connection was made, icons allowed a choice between Apple-specific or general services.

Although the icons gave it a graphic interface appearance, when actually interacting with the system the screens displayed were 80-column text dressed up with MouseText to draw boxes, scrollbars and other graphic-like elements.

The general section was directed to entertainment, business services, online shopping, and general education. There was also a place for playing online games, alone or with other users. An "auditorium" (chat room) could be used for members to attend conferences with special guests, allowing direct questions and answers with the guests.

The Apple Community section was important to the dedicated Apple II (or Macintosh) user. Here, direct contact with Apple Computer, Inc. was available through the "Headquarters" icon, as well as other hardware and software vendors. Apple product announcements and information about products in testing could be found here, as well as direct access to Apple engineers and developers. There were forums for discussing various aspects of Apple computing, an "Apple University" that offered courses on productivity, programming, and specialized software applications, and a library of downloadable programs.

Considering the rocky relationship between Quantum and Apple, it is not surprising that by 1989 a divorce was in the works. However, like any divorce, it turned out to be messy and expensive. The original contract allowed Quantum exclusive use of the Apple logo in association with an online product. This amazingly poor decision on the part of Apple could hamper the ability of Apple to create its own online service with its own logo! To resolve the situation, in June 1989 Apple paid $2.5 million to Quantum to recover the rights to use the Apple logo in the context of an online service. By October of that year, Quantum gave AppleLink Personal Edition a new name: America Online (AOL), still at that time exclusive to the Apple II and Macintosh. It continued to be slightly less expensive than the other major online services, and because of the ALPE software still the easiest to use for the beginner.[6]

Quantum Computer Services went through some changes as the business grew. In 1991, Steve Case became CEO of the company, and the America Online service was expanded from its Apple II and Mac base to add an MS-DOS client. By 1993 it added a client for Windows 3.1. As the Macintosh and Windows clientele increased, the company decided on November 1, 1994 that it was time to discontinue its legacy services (Q-Link and PC-Link). Unfortunately, the company also decided to cancel the Apple II and IIGS editions of its AOL software.

America Online logo during the 1990s – Photo credit: unknown

The original AppleLink Industrial Edition network remained in use by Apple employees, dealers, and software developers. However, it cost Apple to continue to participate in that system (even though an internal study found it saved far more money than it cost, when compared with the previous system of telephone support). Efforts were made to reduce employee use of AppleLink, and by 1992 it actually generated a small profit (though it still cost a high price to pay GEIS to maintain and support the service). Apple tried again to enter the world of online services, contracting again with America Online to create what they called eWorld, a Macintosh-only service that began in June 1994. It never grew sufficiently to make it worthwhile, and Apple pulled the plug in March 1996.[7, 8, 9]

In its post-Apple II era in the mid-to-late 1990s, AOL became a significant player in introducing online activities to the casual computer user. Not only did the service offer a wide variety of services within its borders, America

---

6   Cooper, Vince, "AppleLink-Personal Edition", *Call-A.P.P.L.E.* (July-August 1988), 8-13.
7   Linzmayer, Owen, "Telecom Troubles", *Apple Confidential 2.0* (No Starch Press, 2nd edition, January 2004), 147-151.
8   "AppleLink Personal Edition", <iml.jou.ufl.edu/projects/fall2000/mcatee/main2.html>, accessed October 20, 2012.
9   Lambert, Laura, "Steve Case (1958-), Founder, America Online", *The Internet: A Historical Encyclopedia, Volume 1* (MTM Publishing, Inc., Santa Barbara, California, 2005), 53-57.

Online also developed a portal to the World Wide Web in general, so much so that in the eyes of some people, AOL was the Internet.

America Online became such a powerful company that with the dot-com bubble of the last half of the 1990s, it had amassed a high enough stock valuation to purchase media giant Time Warner in 2000, putting the online service first in the new corporate name, AOL Time Warner.

The company was constantly sending out introductory disks to lure new users to the service, first with 3.5-inch floppy disks, and then CD-ROMs. After the collapse of the bubble and the recession of 2001, all tech stocks saw a significant decline in value, and the value of AOL dropped as well. The expected synergy between the two companies did not happen, and with the corporate struggle that developed, ultimately AOL was dropped from the name, and it again became Time Warner. By 2005, Steve Case had also resigned from the Time Warner board.

By 2009, AOL was sold off, and the company attempted to find a new identity. As the public understanding and acceptance of the Internet and the World Wide Web increased, fewer people found it necessary to use AOL as their gateway to the rest of the Internet, and instead connected via a local service provider and a standard web browser. By the second decade of the new millennium, many people still had America Online accounts, and used it as the home page on their web browser, but the content unique to AOL had significantly declined in importance.

The success of America Online had much to do with the simplicity they brought to the user online experience, giving customers a graphic interface that sidestepped the need for the command line. Just as the Macintosh and Windows interface helped bring a whole new group of customers to computers, the AOL visual and sound interface dovetailed nicely with the up and coming Internet web browser experience, and made nearly everyone familiar with its "You've got mail!" sound.

Additionally, the company's aggressive marketing methods of sending out disks and later CD-ROMs with trial subscriptions was another factor that made the public aware of the service. Neither the marketing nor the user interface was something that the older services could hope to match.

Unfortunately, the learning curve through which AOL carried its customers also made it possible for those customers to abandon AOL's "walled garden" and transition to an Internet service in which AOL did not play any role.

A2CENTRAL.COM / SYNDICOMM (2001 – 2010)

After the failure of Genie and subsequent loss of direct Delphi access, those Apple II users who still wanted to gather online directly were in need of a new home. Certainly, the community was smaller than it had been during the Wild West days of the major online services that began in the late 1970s. But there was simply nothing available via a web browser that offered what they previously had in CompuServe, GEnie, and Delphi—a single access point where a large number of Apple II fans could meet to discuss any facet of their favorite platform.

Eric Shepherd was a prolific programmer for the Apple IIGS who had been involved in the online community of Apple II users for many years. In 2000, he started a web site, www.a2central.com, dedicated to posting articles, reviews, and news for Apple II users. He began to envision a wider role for it, something that would be accessible to an Apple II directly through a dial-up Internet account. He wanted to add a message board, a place to download files, and a chat area. It would be, in a sense, much like a BBS from the single-user dial-up days, but accessible to more than one user at a time, just as the older national online services had been.

Through the help of another programmer they were able to use the PERL programming language and MySQL databases to emulate the appearance of GEnie during its glory days, creating multiple "roundtables" for different topics. He negotiated the purchase of Syndicomm from owners Dean Esmay and Gary Utter, and by January 2001 he was ready to offer a new online home for the Apple II community that was still on Delphi. Membership was priced at $15 per month, which included 10 megabytes of personal disk space on the Syndicomm server.

The new service offered both telnet and web access, as had Delphi. It had a more robust library than had been present on Delphi, offering Xmodem, Ymodem, and Zmodem access for downloads. The library was better organized than had been possible on the older systems, with customized sorting available to make it easier to find files for download.[10]

Ewen Wannop had created an offline reader for Delphi, named Crock O' Gold. He modified that set of Spectrum scripts to be compatible with the new Syndicomm online, and called it SOAR (*Spectrum Offline Automated Reader*). It was used by members for several years.

Shepherd was able to get his site officially licensed by Apple as a user group for the purpose of the distribution of Apple II system software, and was also authorized to make the software available in archive formats useful to Apple II users (not just the Macintosh Disk Copy format as was then found on Apple Computer's FTP site). By November 2001, the web site offered Apple II system and starter kit disks, and had an online store.

In August 2006, Shepherd decided to refocus Syndicomm on its sales of existing software and hardware products. He transferred management of the forums and A2Central.com (now identified without the original "www"

---

10 Ward, Tony, "A New A2 Library Close To Home", *Juiced.GS* (April 2001), 14-15.

prefix) to Sean Fahey of Kansas City. Fahey chose to use a different system for the forums, something simpler to operate and maintain. He chose an open-source BBS software program, which went live in November 2006.

This new system continued online for about four years, until Fahey took it down in 2010. By that time, there was little remaining activity on the forums, although email and newsgroup access were still both busy. For regular contact, many preferred to use an IRC (Internet Relay Chat) chat room.

After 2010, A2Central.com continued as a web site featuring news and information about the Apple II.

TIMELINE

The Source – *July 1979 - August 1989*

CompuServe – *July 1979 - December 1998 (end of Apple II service)*

Kussmaul Encyclopedia – *November 1981 - February 1983*

Delphi – *March 1983 - May 2001 (end of Apple II service)*

AppleLink Personal Edition – *October 1988 - September 1989*

America Online – *October 1989 - November 1994 (end of Apple II service)*

A2Central.com / Syndicomm – *January 2001 - June 2010*

GEnie – *October 1985 - December 1999*

CHAPTER 46

Reunions

Apple II fans first met and shared their passion at computer stores, then in user groups, and later through publications and online communities. And when convention-style events began, both regional and national, this community took on yet another facet. These events provided interactions between hardware and software developers and their customers that went far beyond anything previously available. During the peak years of the Apple II, large shows like these were the dominant venues for product announcements and news, including those from Apple.

But this was not to last. In the era of falling popularity of the Apple II, it was necessary to find new ways for the remaining developers and dedicated Apple II owners to keep in touch with each other. Some of these relationships persisted through the platform's transition from active use to nostalgia and collectability.

Elsewhere in this book, there have been repeated mentions of this annual trek to Kansas City, Missouri in the heat of the summer to learn about, share, and preserve the Apple II. The story of KansasFest is an important part of the account of what came after Apple abandoned and later forgot about the computer that set the course of its success. The narration does not start, however, with the first meeting in 1989. Instead, we will examine something called AppleFest.

APPLEFEST

Vendor fairs were a significant part of the beginnings of the microcomputer revolution. One of the earliest such shows was PC '76, held in Atlantic City, New Jersey, in August 1976. Wozniak and Jobs attended, and showed off the Apple-1.

The success of the show inspired Jim Warren, Homebrew Club member and editor of *Dr. Dobb's Journal*, to have a bigger event in California. Eight months later, Warren organized the first West Coast Computer Faire, which was also held for two days in April 1977. Apple used this event as the debut for the newly completed Apple II. The show was

Personal Computing
76 Consumer Trade Fair
Atlantic City, N.J.
August 28th-29th
from PC '76 flyer – Photo credit: B. Degnan, VintageComputer.net

wildly popular and became an annual occurrence for several years afterwards, but it also spawned similar meetings elsewhere in the country. As with the West Coast Computer Faire, most of the early shows were general in focus and covered multiple platforms. As a particular computer became sufficiently popular, it was possible to hold an event specifically for that platform.

Back on the east coast, it was the Boston Computer Society that finally created an Apple-only show. Originally formed in 1977, the BCS had members representing many different brands of computers, and in 1980 a separate Apple user group merged with them. Through the leadership of member Jonathan Rottenberg, this Apple division ultimately created the first exclusive event, Applefest '81, held June 6-7 at the Boston Plaza Castle. Apple Computer itself was in attendance, and both Steve Jobs and Steve Wozniak gave talks. With 10,000 attendees over the two-day event, it was an unqualified success.

The popularity of the first event demanded it be held again, but first some organizational changes were required. The Applefest event had taken on a life of its own, becoming much larger than the entire Boston Computer Society. To avoid a conflict of interest, the BCS board decided to separate themselves from the event and licensed it to an outside company, Northeast Expositions (later called National Computer Shows). This company held annual shows for the next several years, with Rottenberg as a consultant.

Applefest '83 ad – Photo credit: *Softalk*, October 1983

Applefest '82 again was held in Boston in June, but it was also expanded to cover three additional cities across the country: Minneapolis, Houston, and San Francisco (in September, October, and November, respectively). Applefest '83 was held in Boston (May), Anaheim, and San Francisco (October).

In 1984, National Computer Shows hosted an event for both Apple and the IBM PC in a single show, but it was less successful, possibly as an economic consequence of the tech industry downturn that year, and the company did not repeat the effort again.[1,2] This crippled the momentum that had been built up over the previous years.

Though there were a couple of smaller events that used the Applefest name in 1985 and 1986, it was not until AppleFest '87 (now using camel-case capitalization) that a major show was again held. The show was now hosted by Cambridge Marketing, and two cities were selected: Boston in May and San Francisco in September. Keynote speakers at the west coast event included Steve Wozniak and Del Yocam, Apple's Chief Operating Officer. For the San

---

1 McCann, Mary, "Boston's Fest For Apple," *Boston Computer Update* (July/August 1981), 41-42.
2 Rottenberg, Jonathan, e-mail message to author, July 30, 2012.

Francisco AppleFest, Apple distributed buttons that read "Ten Years Strong" (referring to the tenth anniversary of the Apple II). In his speech, Yocam had many positive things to say about the Apple II and its future in the company.

The Apple Programmers and Developers Association (APDA) distributed beta copies of the BASIC for the Apple IIGS that was in development, as well as the first non-beta version of the Apple Programmers Workshop and System Software 3.1 for the IIGS. A few months later at the Boston AppleFest '88 in May, AppleLink Personal Edition was introduced, and at the San Francisco AppleFest in September of that year, CEO John Sculley told the world about the new Apple IIc Plus.

However, politics within Apple were changing the face of AppleFest. The company was pushing for more of a business focus on the Macintosh, but restricting the Apple II to education and home. This corporate attitude was reducing the Apple II emphasis at AppleFest, and Exposition Management (the new name for Cambridge Marketing) found it necessary to add Macintosh space in order to make the event profitable. For Apple II enthusiasts, the addition of the Mac caused reactions ranging from annoyance to outrage.

Tom Weishaar used the platform of his newsletter (*Open-Apple* and later *A2-Central*) to write articles expressing his concern about Apple's treatment of the Apple II. In 1987 he discussed Del Yocam's speech at the September AppleFest, how the speech and the company's actions in supporting the Apple II were not in sync with each other.[3] He later had a chance to interview Yocam[4] and discuss these concerns. Although Yocam reiterated the company's commitment to the Apple II, Weishaar pointed out that Apple's allocations of resources was still not consistent with that statement. Similarly, *Apple Direct*, a new publication by Apple Developer Services begun in November 1988, touched on the Apple II, but most heavily dealt with issues involving the Mac.[5]

RESOURCE CENTRAL EVENTS – 1989 TO 1994

Tom Weishaar, through Resource Central, was a powerful voice for the Apple II, between his flagship newsletter, *Open-Apple*, his disk magazines, the company's involvement with the A2 and A2Pro Roundtables on GEnie, and the software, hardware, and developer materials that it sold. He kept in contact with companies that supported the Apple II, and they could see that the actions taken by Apple did not bode well for the future of the platform. For these reasons, Weishaar decided to hold his own national conference, free of the Macintosh. He first made mention of it in the February 1989 issue of *A2-Central*.

---

3   Weishaar, Tom, "Reality And Apple's Vision," *Open-Apple* (November 1987), 3.74-3.74.
4   Weishaar, Tom, "Del Yocam, Education and the Apple II," *Open-Apple* (July 1988), 4.40-4.44.
5   Weishaar, Tom, "An Apple II For The Student," *A2-Central* (January 1989), 4.88-4.89.

We're taking over Kansas City's Avila College campus on the weekend of July 21-22-23 for an A2-Central Developer Conference. For one slightly extravagant fee you'll get a conference teeming with Apple II hardware and software developers, all your meals, and – if you're at the head of the line – free dormitory accommodations. Apple has already committed to send us some engineers, evangelists, and support types and to throw a party, so plan now on coming to KC this summer.[6]

Designed as more of a developer education meeting than a vendor fair, the first event was planned to host as many as 400 attendees, the maximum number that Avila could handle. Airfare discounts were negotiated with a local travel agency, space was made available at the college for as many as 210 to stay on campus in the dorms at no additional cost, and arrangements were made with several local hotels to have free shuttle bus service to the campus for those who didn't care for the college dormitory experience.

In the promotional material for the conference, it was billed as a chance to "meet the people who will make the Apple II's future." Kicked off with a Real Programmer's Party hosted by Apple Computer on the evening before the conference, it was followed by two full days of sessions, including some given by members of the Apple II division. Over 100 developers attended, a sobering result for Weishaar, but those who came were the most dedicated and prolific developers for the platform.

A2-Central Developer Conference
The only conference in the world just for **Apple II** developers.
Kansas City—Friday and Saturday—July 21-22, 1989

Photo credit: Resource Central catalog, May 1989

After the event, Bill Kennedy, the technical editor of *inCider*, said, "For most attendees, including myself, the Developers Conference hosted by A2-Central in July was an experience bordering on the religious."

The event would continue for decades to come in one form or another, though not with the same name. At the second conference, held July 20-21, 1990, the title was changed to "A2-Central Summer Conference", de-emphasizing the need to be a developer in order to attend.

Apple officially attended a number of the early conferences in order to communicate with resellers and dealers to discuss marketing strategy for its products. In 1990, Apple representatives gave an unusual demonstration of the speed of the new Apple II SCSI card when coupled with a hard drive. Playing actual video was not something most home computers could do in 1990 (the first versions of QuickTime for the Macintosh and Microsoft's

---

6 Weishaar, Tom, "Miscellanea," *A2-Central* (February 1989), 5.5.

Media Player for Windows did not appear until 1991). However, the Apple II team showed how the SCSI card with direct memory access (data being moved directly to the video screen memory) was capable of sequentially loading and displaying several hundred gray scale frames from the movie *The Empire Strikes Back* on an Apple IIGS.

In 1991, Apple was again present to announce System Software 6.0, with a release expected before the end of the year. They also announced *HyperCard IIGS* version 1.1, the aforementioned Ethernet peripheral card, and a SuperDrive card.[7] The company had also formed an Apple II Business Unit, but Apple USA had not provided any funding to do much with it.[8] Notably there were fewer Apple engineers in attendance, and more products announced by third-party vendors.

In 1992, the keynote speech was given by Tim Swihart, manager of the Apple II Continuation Engineering Group, who spoke about the changing position of the Apple II within the company. The Apple II Business unit, introduced the previous year, had been disbanded, though the Ethernet card was still being completed and was to be released along with System Software 6.0.1.[9]

From 1989 to 1994, the A2-Central Summer Conference educated developers and helped encourage the Apple II community in the face of declining support and resources from Apple Computer, Inc. By the 1991 conference, attendees were beginning to refer to it as "KansasFest", the name a derivative of the AppleFest event of the past. (By this time, AppleFest itself was fading away, with MacWorld becoming the premier event.) Attendance was still respectable in 1992 with just over 130 attendees—this for the 15th anniversary of the release of the Apple II, which included a videotaped interview with Steve Wozniak by Tom Weishaar just for the event.

In the advertising for the fifth KansasFest in 1993, *A2-Central* stated that although the 1992 event had been successful, it was a *lot* of work. It was decided to scale it back to something more like the early days of the conference, with two days of meetings and a third unstructured day on Saturday. They made it clear in the brochure that this might be the last time the event would be held.

Those changes resulted in a much smaller attendance of just over ninety in 1993, but it paid for itself and Weishaar decided to try it one more time. By the time of the sixth summer meeting in 1994, Resource Central had changed its name to ICON (International Computer Owner's Network), in an attempt to broaden its subscriber base, allowing the inclusion of Macintosh and MS-DOS or Windows topics. For the annual summer event, it was decided to not use "A2-Central Summer Conference", but instead use the shorter name, "ICONference." Weishaar explained these changes in a March 1994 post on GEnie.

---

7   Doms, Dennis, "KansasFest 1991," *A2-Central* (September 1991), 7.57-7.58.
8   Doms, Dennis, "Apple's Developer Message," *A2-Central* (September 1991), 7.58-7.59.
9   Rosenberg, Ellen, "KansasFest Is...," *A2-Central* (September 1992), 8.60-8.62.

The final makeup of the event will depend entirely on who comes. Yes, as an ICON event, it opens the possibility of having info on other platforms. Even last year, as an Apple II event, there were an awful lot of Macintoshes around. On the other hand, as an event with a long history as the premier gathering of Apple II folks, I'm sure the Apple II presence will continue to be strong. Users have made up the majority of the attendees for some time. While there are seminars that are of interest only to developers, there are others that are of a more general interest. There is no reason not to come because you're "just a user." There is nothing about this event that's outside the control of any of you. Let us know what you want and we'll either get it or delegate getting it to you <g>. Seriously, Sally, Jeff, and I can't put this whole thing together ourselves. We need those of you who want to come to participate in the planning and organization, which means you can make it whatever you want it to be.[10]

At the revised conference in 1994, Apple Computer gave a preview of Macintosh System 7.5. Even Microsoft was invited, and its representative gave two sessions, one a preview of Windows 4 (eventually released as Windows 95), and the other a demo of *Microsoft Office* for Windows. Even the Newton MessagePad was featured, with Joe Wankerl of GS+ magazine explaining how to program on it.

KANSASFEST – 1995 ONWARD

After the 1994 conference in Kansas City, its continued existence was in doubt. Weishaar's publishing organization had closed down in February, and so would not be running any such meeting in 1995. As soon as the announcement of the demise of ICON was posted online, informal discussions began on GEnie and elsewhere amongst interested members of the community who wanted to see KansasFest continue.[11]

Cindy Adams was a GEnie member who had begun working in the A2 Roundtable in May 1994 hosting online user group meetings and other chat sessions. She had attended ICONference in 1994, and had run events for the Boy Scouts. Adams offered to head a committee to make it happen, thinking, "How hard could this be?"[12]

The committee contacted Avila College, and were able (on relatively short notice) to schedule three days, July 27th to 29th. By May 1995, the event had received enough registrations to pull it off. Joe Kohn and editor

---

10 Weishaar, Tom, "KansasFest Plans," *GEnieLamp A2* (March 1993).
11 Shepherd, Eric, e-mail message to author, August 6, 2012.
12 Adams, Cindy, e-mail message to author, May 26, 2012.

Doug Cuff writing in *GEnieLamp A2* promoted the event during June and July of that year. The annual reunion—now officially known as KansasFest—would go on.

The final year of Apple's official involvement with the conference was in 1996. Apple employees Andy Nicholas and Dave Lyons demonstrated *Gus*, an Apple IIGS emulator for PowerPC-based Macs that was being developed on their own time. It did not yet emulate the Ensoniq audio chip, nor could it replicate the IIGS serial ports, but it showed promise. Plans were to have it ready for beta testing by later in the year, and Nicholas and Lyons had envisioned it as another way for schools to transition to the Macintosh, by making it possible to continue to use old Apple II software.[13] Sadly, by 1997 Gus had disappeared due to a corporate decision at Apple to cease work on it.

Although Apple had cancelled its Apple II emulator, the dream remained alive. The first Mac-based IIGS emulator was unveiled a year later at KansasFest 1997, named *Bernie][The Rescue*. (This was later updated in 2006 for the latest Macintosh operating system and unveiled at KansasFest as *Sweet16*.)

Ostensibly, one of the most important aspects of a computer show is the release of new products, and KansasFest has helped launch a number of Apple II products over the years—even well past the end of Apple's support for the computer.

One of the primary challenges of the 1990s was allowing Internet access for the IIGS. First came the *Spectrum Internet Suite*—scripts that provided web browsing, email, Telnet, and file management under Spectrum. Then came *Marinetti*, a GS/OS control panel that added a TCP/IP stack to the system, making it possible for an Apple IIGS to connect directly to the Internet via a modem. This was taken to a new level a few years later with the release of the *LANceGS* card, an Ethernet card for the Apple IIe or IIGS.

Internet access was even possible on older 8-bit Apple II computers with the Uther Apple II Ethernet card, and the Cayman GatorBox, which could bridge an Ethernet connection with LocalTalk on an older Macintosh, making it possible to get an old Apple II online.[14]

Other advancements for the Apple II were often announced or discussed at KansasFest. In 2005 a session was held discussing the Apple II port of *Contiki*, an open-source, multi-tasking operating system designed to provide modern Internet connectivity on 8-bit computers with small amounts of available memory.

Even mundane problems encountered by Apple II collectors were conquered by product demonstrations at KansasFest. Hardware expert Tony Diaz addressed the effect of age on the color of computer cases. He demonstrated

---

13 Kohn, Joe, "KansasFest 1996," *Shareware Solutions II* (v3n2, 1996).
14 Gagne, Ken, "KansasFest 2005, *Juiced.GS*, Sept 2005, pp. 2-6.

the use of "Retr0Bright", a chemical mix based on hydrogen peroxide, which could be used to remove the yellowing on old plastic computer cases.[15]

Just for fun, KFest hosted a number of extracurricular activities at each year's event. These included Hackfest (with the goal of creating a fully functioning program before the event was completed), celebrity roasts, a contest to wear the wackiest necktie, swap meets, video game competitions (featuring Apple II games of course), banquets, trivia game shows in the same vein as Jeopardy, video showings (such as watching old recordings of TV shows like the *Computer Chronicles*) and more.

Each year of the conference included a keynote speaker—someone from the industry who had a notable impact on the Apple II world. These included Bill Mensch (designer of the 65816 processor), Steve Wozniak, David Szetela (the former editor-in-chief for *Nibble* magazine who later worked at Apple Computer starting in 1987 as head of Apple's Evangelism department), Gary Utter (GEnie A2 Roundtable Chief Sysop), Lane Roathe (who worked at *Up-Time* and *Softdisk*, which helped spawn Id Software), Jason Scott (the documentary filmmaker of *BBS: The Documentary* and *Get Lamp*), Mark Simonsen (who owned and operated Beagle Bros during its TimeOut days), Bob Bishop (an early Apple employee who was probably best known for his clever Integer BASIC program, APPLEVISION), John Romero (famous for creating Wolfenstein 3D, Doom and Quake with John Carmack), and Randy Wiggington (Apple employee #6, who had been responsible for creating Applesoft, and the RWTS routines for Apple DOS).

Logo for KansasFest 2012 (featuring graphics from some of John Romero's Apple II games)
– Photo credit: KansasFest Committee

The 1996 edition of KansasFest was notable for the previously mentioned keynote address given by Gary Utter. Part of the purpose of his talk was to prepare people for the inevitable need to leave GEnie. But he primarily wanted to point out to the seventy plus attendees that it was the community of Apple II users who were actually more important than the computer itself:

> It is not the Apple II, but the COMMUNITY that we need to strive to preserve. We had no control over what Apple would do with the II. But even though they tried to kill it, it lives still, through our efforts, and the efforts of other like us, across the country and across the world. It lives because the community that grew up around the II, OUR community, MADE it live, and continues to do so.

---

15 Gagne, Ken and Drucker, Ivan, "KansasFest 2009," *Juiced.GS Sampler 10, Best of Juiced.GS*, 8-12.

> *I can tell you, with complete confidence, that it is possible for the A2 community to grow and thrive. What we CANNOT afford to do ... is to wait for someone else to do it for us, to wait for some turn of events to fall in our favor. We have to make our own future; we have to build what we want to see.*[16]

The survival years, 1995 to 2000, involved double efforts. It became a challenge to keep the annual event going without a parent company behind it, and to help maintain the Apple II when Apple had completely abandoned it. During these years, several companies that had products for the Apple II fell by the wayside as their customer base shrank to unsustainable levels.

The primary outlet to advertise KansasFest was the online world. The collapse over at GEnie had a deleterious effect on 1997, with a drop to only forty-seven attendees. This decline continued until the event reached a new low of 34 in 2002.

The Apple II itself was also undergoing a transition. It had already passed through a time when the computer was showing its age, when its value had dropped considerably, and many were abandoning it for newer hardware. It had been passing through an era when it truly was obsolete, where only the devoted continued to do things with it. By 2001, it was beginning to reach the point where it was becoming valued for its oldness and nostalgia more than for its power as a daily workhorse. The KansasFest events similarly were in the process of changing to match this new era.

The committee was able to reverse these numbers for 2003 by inviting Apple co-founder Steve Wozniak as the keynote speaker. This news resulted in a jump to sixty attendees, the highest since the years just after Resource Central stopped sponsoring the event.

By the middle of the first decade of the new millennium, KansasFest had completed its transition from a developer and programming-focused conference to a gathering of computer enthusiasts who were simply interested in doing interesting or unusual things with the Apple II platform. They now relished its limitations of only 48K or 64K of memory, instead of feeling constricted by it, as they would have in the late 1980s. And some enterprising hardware and software hackers were finding things that could be done with an Apple II that had never been envisioned by Wozniak when he designed it back in 1977. Though there were still sessions that dealt with the Apple IIGS and its Macintosh-like Toolbox programming environment, the 8-bit Apple II environment began to get more attention than it had for quite a while.

---

16 Utter, Gary, transcript of KansasFest 1996 keynote.

Steve Wozniak at KansasFest 2013 wearing the official T-shirt for the event – Photo credit: Daniel McLaughlin

There was something about direct interaction with other like-minded fans of the Apple II that happened in the college dormitory environment of KFest that could not happen anywhere else. Whether it was a presentation by hacker-extraordinaire Jeri Ellsworth or a surprise drop-in by the Woz himself, each KFest delivered a unique experience. And as the event moved into its third decade of existence, it continued to see new attendees. For the years 2009 to 2013, over ten percent of attendees were there for the first time, and during this period total attendance increased each year.

Ivan Drucker stated it this way in his review of the 2011 event in *Juiced.GS*:

> *I view this spirit as being embodied in the computer itself. The first Apple II was born of the imagination and passion of just two men. When you turned it on, you got a blinking cursor; if you popped off the lid, eight empty slots stared back at you. What was in the box were, effectively, programming manuals. It almost demanded: "Make me do something!" The last Apple II to roll off the assembly line in 1993 was largely unchanged from the first in 1977. It made the same demand, offered the same challenge. KansasFest is where Apple II users come to answer it ... Anyone who has something new or interesting to share has the opportunity to present before his or her fellow conference-goers.*[17]

---

17 Drucker, Ivan, "The Year After We Make Contact," *Juiced.GS* (September 2011), 10.

EPILOGUE
The History of this History

This book is the product of my own personal experience, and years of collecting information from books, magazines, and personal interviews to fill in the gaps that were beyond my own knowledge. My goal was not to document the story of Apple Computer, but deal specifically with anything that involved the Apple II series. The formal education I received, however, was neither as a writer nor as a programmer. Science was my passion in high school and college, and my goal was to become a physician.

Despite this, my path through college to attain my degree in chemistry and move on to medical school took me into the world of computers, at least as an aside. Through my subscription to *Popular Electronics*, I read in 1975 about these amazing little computer kits put out by MITS, the Altair 8800 and later the Altair 680. Although these greatly interested me, the money needed to order one of these kits was far beyond what I could scrape together. However, my college offered computer classes, and so in my sophomore year I decided to take a class in FORTRAN. The hardware at the college was a small mainframe, the IBM 1130. It was the size of a large desk, had a similar-sized punched card reader, a large and noisy line printer, and a two-foot diameter removable hard disk that held one megabyte of storage. The console had a keyboard and Selectric-style typewriter (not typically used by the FORTRAN students), some awesome green, yellow and red lights, lots of switches and a couple of dials—and I was fascinated with it. I had always found math classes enjoyable, and with that background I took to FORTRAN as if it were my native language. By mid-semester I had completed the textbook and was working on my own programs.

I eventually was allowed to do work-study in the computer center during my junior and senior years, helping other students use the computer, but still leaving time for my own projects. I learned how to directly enter my programs on the console/typewriter, bypassing the extra step of having to create and load punched cards. I got to experiment with a BASIC interpreter for the 1130, and even wrote a very simple game based on *Star Trek* (resulting in a short write-up in the college newspaper).

Author at IBM 1130 console – Photo credit: *The Midland*, March 15, 1976

I also created a database program for my music tapes, allowing me to print listings of the songs in any order. (Years later, I used this database to tag my music as I imported it into iTunes.) And when I found card images on a disk pack for a 16K FORTRAN version of the classic mainframe *Star Trek* game (which was later ported to nearly every microcomputer that was made during the 1970s), I made it my personal project to find a way to break it up into pieces that would allow it to fit into the 8K memory of our IBM 1130.

After starting medical school in 1978, I no longer had access to that small mainframe computer, but was no less enthusiastic about computers. I visited a local Radio Shack to play with the TRS-80, and saw an Apple II (color!) at a local Team Electronics store. At the med center, I discovered a North Star Horizon (an S-100 computer running CP/M) at the pharmacy college, and was allowed to try it out. There was another North Star in the hospital pharmacy administration office, which was more convenient for me. I learned a little about the Z-80 processor and programs that could run under CP/M, but soon afterwards they also purchased a couple of Apple II Plus computers.

At first I was a little skeptical. It offered only 40-column text display, compared to the wider display on the North Star. However, the Apple II had graphics, and was better suited for games. I was also permitted to make use of these computers when no one else was busy with them (which was most of the time). With a computer offering nearly eight times the memory of the one I'd used in college, the ability to store its programs on a small flexible disk, and programs I could type in from magazines, the fascination of this computer was a significant distraction. Nevertheless, I was able to discipline myself to focus on my medical training, and completed it successfully in the spring of 1982. Since I was offered a residency in the same hospital where I'd done my medical schoolwork, the Apple II was still available in my off hours.

My self-education on that computer gave me an outlet to adapt my FORTRAN experience to Applesoft BASIC. My experience in squeezing a 16K program into an 8K computer paved the way for me to rewrite and enhance a program for printing labels for IV drugs that the pharmacy was using. What I was paid for that work, combined with my own savings, allowed me to finally obtain my own computer. I proudly brought home a brand new Apple IIc in 1984, and regularly updated it with every free hardware enhancement that Apple released.

The addition of a modem brought me to the online world of microcomputers in the 1980s, and a membership to GEnie gave me access to many experienced Apple II users who knew much of the story from before the Apple II Plus. Their knowledge, combined with information I gleaned from the magazines to which I subscribed, helped me better understand the story of the Apple II.

Let me also point out that during my high school and college years, I enjoyed the history classes that I took. I liked to understand how things progressed from start to finish, and how they changed along the way. Furthermore, part of my medical training involved learning how to get a medical history from a patient, and how to write it out in a clear and orderly fashion. Add to that my enthusiasm in explaining medical problems and procedures to patients, and the result was a desire to convey the story of the Apple II and its idiosyncrasies to others.

My opportunity for this came when I was allowed to be a contributing writer to the newsletter of our local Apple user group. I conceived the idea of a continuing series that told about the Apple II from its start to the present. With "a little help from my friends," I started this story in 1991 and completed it in early 1992, ending up with a fairly comprehensive history. Compared to a typical book on the market, my history only suffered from a lack of direct interviews with the primary players who had worked on the Apple II from the beginning. This was not necessarily bad, as I had not written these stories with the idea that I would ever be printing it as a book.

Parts of it had become outdated even as early as the end of 1993. It was necessary to create revisions that documented the removal of the IIGS from Apple's price lists in late 1992, and of the same loss of the IIe at the end of 1993. My original final chapter (from 1991) included some conclusions about where I felt the platform was going, based on my experience with the ever-helpful community on GEnie in the A2 Roundtable. In that chapter, I predicted that with used systems becoming available at lower prices, there would be an influx of new owners who could be helped by experienced owners, and there would be a revival (or at least a healthy maintenance) of the platform.

Obviously, that was an overly optimistic view of the future, and it did not happen.

What my predictions failed to take into account was the fact that the tech world did not stand still, and newer, faster, more capable (and more interesting computers) were being released every year. The abandonment of the Apple II did not result in its widespread adoption by new users. Schools held onto their Apple II computers for many years, but when they were reaching the end of their lifespan, they were not replaced with more secondhand Apple II units, but with inexpensive PC clones.

We continued to hold the opinion that it was "us against the world," that we had the best and most useable computer of them all, regardless of what other people believed. Those who discarded the Apple II and moved on were at worst traitors, and at best misguided and misinformed. This attitude carried us through the 1990s, as the Apple II world continued contracting around us, with the failure of the online services we relied on for community, and the loss of those companies who faithfully provided products until they could no longer stay in business.

Yet, with time even the most hardened Apple II proponent was finding it attractive to add a second computer to make use of the up-and-coming Internet, and the Apple II became more of a secondary platform.

Whereas I ended the original history of the Apple II with a guarded optimism, I feel that I can offer a more realistic optimism than was possible in 1992. Like a beloved classic car, the Apple II continues to live on, either as an original device that is maintained in working condition, or as a digital recreation that can even exceed the capabilities of the actual hardware.

Apple II Forever. It looks like that statement has a few more years of life in it.

APPENDIX A
Software Hits

The magazine *Softalk* tracked sales of Apple II software during it years of publication from 1980 to 1984. This information was tabulated in a monthly column, "Softalk Presents The Best Sellers", which included a "Top Thirty" list, as well as top selling programs in several specific categories. Further, in April of each year (1981 through 1984) it presented a list of the top new programs for the previous year, as voted by *Softalk* readers.

For the monthly compilations, editor Al Tommervik contacted a sample of Apple-authorized retails stores throughout the country, and asked the store managers what programs were doing well and how many copies they were selling. This gave somewhat more useful information than what could be learned from contacting the software companies themselves; they would only be likely to know how many copies of a program were shipped, and not necessarily be relied upon to tell how many were returned unsold. *Softalk* used a formula that created an index number for each program, determining its position on the Top Thirty list. The index number also gave an indication of the relative strength of each program's sales.

Another service provided by *Softalk* each month, beginning in the May 1982 issue, was a column called "Fastalk". Here were listed new program releases, as well as other older Apple II programs that continued to enjoy popularity. The introduction for the column stated, "Fastalk is a quick guide to popular, specialized, new, and classic software. When you need a particular kind of program or just want to see what's new, Fastalk is the place to look for fast answers." They listed new programs with a check mark, and if it failed to gain popularity, it was dropped after three months. A "bullet" marked titles that *Softalk* magazine designated as classic, "based on its ability to stand up over time, its significance for its time (breaking new ground, or introducing a new genre), or its archetypical qualities." They went on to mention that some programs listed in "Fastalk" were included simply because they met a need that no other software package could, even if they were not high volume sellers.

In trying to create a compendium of the best Apple II software over the years, I have relied heavily on the *Softalk* best seller list and the "Fastalk" column for the years 1980 through 1983—years for which the annual Top Thirty lists are available. I have reproduced the annual lists for 1978-80, 1981, 1982, and 1983, both the Top Thirty and the specific lists for each category. When a program was also listed in "Fastalk" as a classic, or if I felt it was a unique program, I have included *Softalk's* capsule description with the program entry. If I have comments of my own, they are included in parentheses.

For the years after *Softalk* ceased publication, I have had to simply list popular programs I've found advertised or reviewed in other magazines from that point onward. Sources for these additional lists include A+, *inCider*, *inCider/A+*, *II Alive*, *GEnieLamp A2*, *The Lamp!*, and *Juiced.GS*.

MOST POPULAR OF 1978-80

The Top Ten

- *Super Invader*, M. Hata, Creative Computing; arcade. "Progenitor of home-arcades. Still good hi-res, still a challenge." (This was an Apple version of *Space Invaders*)
- *Adventure*, Crowther & Woods; adventure. "The original text adventure, created on mainframes, contributed to by so many over a long time. Very logical within fantasy framework, excellent puzzles, maps; complex, convoluted, and great. Solving problems takes precedence over life/death peril. Several publishers including Microsoft, Apple Computer, and Frontier Computing."
- *VisiCalc*, Bricklin & Frankston, Personal Software; spreadsheet. "Electronic worksheet for any problem involving numbers, rows, and columns. No programming necessary."
- *Sargon II*, Spracklen, Hayden; strategy game. "Computer chess game with seven levels of play."
- *Asteroids In Space*, Wallace, Quality Software; arcade. "Make little asteroids out of big ones, plus occasional hostile alien ships. Hyperspace, autobrake, autofire." (Later called *Meteoroids In Space*, this was a clone of the popular arcade game, *Asteroids*, which itself was similar to a very early computer game called *Spacewar*, written to run on the CRT screen of a PDP-1 by hackers at MIT in the 1960s.)
- *Flight Simulator*, Artwick, SubLogic; strategy. "Uses aerodynamic equations, airfoil characteristics for realistic takeoff, flight, and landing. Two years on the Top Thirty." (Later updated to give animated 3-D color graphics, transcontinental flight, and a World War I aerial battle.)
- *Hi-Res Adventure #2: The Wizard and The Princess*, Williams, On-Line Systems; adventure. "The king has offered half his kingdom to the one who will bring back the kidnapped princess. Cross mountains, deserts; battle the wizard to claim your reward."
- *Odyssey: The Compleat Apventure* [sic], Clardy, Synergistic Software; fantasy. "Fantasy adventure far beyond one place and one setting. Castles, catacombs, an ocean voyage, and the orb of power."
- *DOS 3.3*, Apple Computer; operating system.
- *Apple Writer*, Lutus, Apple Computer; word processor. "The most popular word processing program in town. Type, erase, move words around, save and insert segments from disk, and print out. Easy to use."

Runners Up

- (tie) *Bill Budge's Space Album*, Budge, California Pacific; arcade.
- (tie) *Temple Of Apshai*, Epyx/Automated Simulations; fantasy. "Lead title in Dunjonquest series, winner 1981 Academy of Adventure Gaming Arts and Design 'Computer Game of the Year' award."
- *Hi-Res Adventure #1: Mystery House*, Williams, On-Line Systems; adventure. "Whodunit in a Victorian mansion. First adventure with pictures. Two-word parser with logical comprehension."
- *Cyber Strike*, Nasir, Sirius Software; arcade.
- (tie) *EasyWriter*, Draper, Information Unlimited; word processor. (The author, John Draper, was the "Captain Crunch" of blue box fame, friend of Jobs and Wozniak, and an early Apple employee.)
- (tie) *Dogfight*, Basham, Micro Lab; arcade. (This was later included as a free bonus with Bill Basham's *DIversi-DOS* speedup for DOS 3.3. It would allow as many as eight players to play at once, assuming all those hands could get to their respective controlling keys on the keyboard without too much local conflict.)

MOST POPULAR OF 1981

The Top Thirty:

- *Raster Blaster*, Budge, BudgeCo; arcade. "First realistic pinball game."
- *Castle Wolfenstein*, Warner, Muse; strategy game. "First game to fuse successfully strategy, home-arcade, fantasy. Escape from Nazi stronghold with secret plans. Room layout changes with each new game. Enemy speaks (in German)."
- *Apple Panic*, Serki, Brøderbund; arcade. "Rid a five story building of crawling apples and butterflies by running up and down connecting ladders, digging traps, then covering critters before they devour you. Extremely addictive, excellent hi-res play." (This was my first Apple game, and I can agree with the description.)
- *Olympic Decathlon*, Smith, Microsoft; arcade. "Ten standard decathlon events. Hi-res animated athletes, muscle-stirring music; you provide the sweat."

APPENDIX A | Software Hits

- *Gorgon*, Nasir, Sirius Software; arcade. "Fly over planet shooting and dodging invaders and saving kidnapped inhabitants. Outstanding hi-res graphics, challenging refueling sequence." (Clone of arcade game, Defender.)
- *Alien Rain*, Suzuki, Brøderbund; arcade. "Monsters in this home-arcade classic seem to take it personally when you gun down one of their kind." (The original name of this game was actually *Apple Galaxian*, but both the company that produced the arcade game *Galaxian* and Apple Computer objected to their name being used in the title of this game, so Brøderbund was obligated to change it to something else. This became quite typical for computer translations of arcade games; even if it looked and acted much like a particular arcade game, it was unlikely that the game's arcade name would appear on the personal computer version, unless it was an authorized version.)
- *Wizardry*, Greenberg & Woodhead, Sir-Tech; fantasy. "Ultimate role-playing fantasy; ten-level maze in hi-res. Generate 20 characters, 6 at a time on expeditions. Gripping game; superbly reproduced."
- *DOS 3.3*, Apple Computer; operating system.
- *Space Eggs*, Nasir, Sirius Software; arcade. (Unofficial port of arcade game *Moon Cresta*.)
- *Sneakers*, Turmell, Sirius Software; arcade. "Many-layered shooting game; one of the best. Stomping sneakers and other creatures requires varying techniques. Fun."
- *Ultima*, British, California Pacific; fantasy. "Hi-res color adventure, progressing from Middle Ages to beyond the space age. A masterpiece."
- *Snoggle*, Wada, Brøderbund; arcade. (maze game similar to *Pac-Man*.)
- *DOS Tool Kit*, Apple Computer; utility.
- *DB Master*, Stone, Stoneware; database. "Comprehensive database-management system with password protection, extensive report creation options. 1,000 characters per record." (The most comprehensive database program ever released for the Apple II, it survived through various versions up until 1991, when it was finally discontinued. It was eventually available in a shareware form, *DB Master Version 5*, and a commercial version, *DB Master Pro*.)
- Personal Filing System (PFS), Page, Software Publishing Corporation; database. "User controls data in totally unstructured database. Up to thirty-two pages (screens) of information in each record." (Later renamed *PFS: File*, the IIe version supported 80-columns, upper/lowercase. Written in Pascal.)
- *Pool 1.5*, Hoffman, Germain & Morock; Innovative Design Software (IDSI); arcade. "Makes most shots you could on a real pool table, with advantages of instant replay and slow motion. Four different games, also offers a higher or lower friction mode." (This game was great; with the low friction mode you could almost clear the table on the first shot, as the balls would continue to rebound until they finally slowed to a stop and fell into the pockets.)
- *Sabotage*, Allen, On-Line Systems; arcade. (Use a cannon to shoot at helicopters dropping paratroopers.)

- *Zork*, Blank & Liebling, Infocom; adventure. "Part one of mainframe adventure; understands complete compound sentences and questions. Simultaneous manipulation of objects. Text." (These games accepted far more complex commands than most adventure games of the time. Instead of just "Get knife," *Zork* understood commands like "Get gold knife from stone table," and later Infocom games could even handle sentences such as, "Say to elf, 'Don't crush that dwarf'".)
- *Magic Window*, Shannon & Depew, Artsci; word processor.
- *Robot War*, Warner, Muse; strategy. "Strategy game with battling robots is great teaching device for programming." (This game allowed the user to create a robot using its simple programming language to determine how it fought. The two robots fought on a hi-res arena, displaying score and stats as the battle automatically played. In some parts of the country, *Robot War* aficionados had tournaments pitting one person's robot-program against another. It gave experience in simple artificial intelligence programming.)
- *Locksmith*, Omega Microware; utility. (Used for duplicating copy-protected software.)
- *Gobbler*, Lubeck, On-Line Systems; arcade. (Another Pac-Man clone.)
- *Falcons*, Varsanyi & Ball, Piccadilly Software; arcade. (Battle the aliens.)
- *ABM*, Warner, Muse; arcade. (Clone of arcade game *Missile Command*.)
- *Epoch*, Miller, Sirius Software; arcade.
- *Asteroid Field*, Nitchals, Cavalier Software; arcade.
- *Threshold*, Schwader & Williams, On-Line Systems; arcade.
- *WordStar*, MicroPro; word processor.
- *Hi-Res Adventure #3: Cranston Manor*, DeWitz & Williams, On-Line Systems; adventure.
- *SuperScribe II*, Kidwell, On-Line Systems; word processor.

MOST SOFTWARE OF 1982

The Top Thirty:

- *Choplifter*, Gorlin, Brøderbund; arcade. "Fly your chopper to rescue 64 hostages, avoiding interceptor jets, homing mines, and tanks. Challenging, realistic, and playful. Stunning graphics." (One of the few games that appeared first on a personal computer and later was translated for play on a coin-operated arcade game. You really wanted to rescue these little people running out of their barracks, waving to your helicopter for help, while ignoring the enemy aircraft and tanks that were shelling them and your 'copter.)
- *Wizardry*, Greenberg & Woodhead, Sir-Tech; fantasy.
- *Cannonball Blitz*, Lubeck, Sierra On-Line; arcade. (Clone of arcade game *Donkey Kong*.)
- *Knight Of Diamonds*, Greenberg & Woodhead, Sir-Tech; fantasy. Second scenario in Wizardry series.
- *Night Mission Pinball*, Artwick, SubLogic; arcade.
- *Star Blazer*, Suzuki, Brøderbund; arcade.

- *Snack Attack*, Illowsky, DataMost; arcade. (Pac-Man style game.)
- *Taxman*, Fitzgerald, H.A.L. Labs; arcade. "Very smooth, fast-moving eat-the-dots—all you expect from fruit to nuts. Keyboard control returns excellent expert-pleasing response; turn on a Sheila-sized dime." (A very accurate reproduction of *Pac-Man*, complete with "cartoons" every few levels. So accurately did it imitate the game that Atari sued H.A.L. Labs, took the *Taxman* source code, changed the names back to the original *Pac-Man* names, and released it as Atari's official port of the game ot the Apple II.)
- *Ultima II*, British, Sierra On-Line; adventure.
- *Graphics Magician*, Jochumson, Lubar, & Pelczarski, Penguin Software; graphics utility. "Outstanding animation package consisting of a picture editor and shape table extender designed to allow programmers to design and store graphics files. Comes with utility program to transfer binary files."
- *Swashbuckler*, Stephenson, DataMost; arcade. (Side-view game involving sword fighting.)
- *Home Accountant*, Schoenburg, Grodin, & Pollack, Continental Software; home finance.
- *Serpentine*, Snider, Brøderbund; arcade.
- *The Arcade Machine*, Jochumson & Carlston, Brøderbund Software; arcade. (Promised the ability for the non-programmer to create an arcade game. Results were inconsistent.)
- *Bandits*, Ngo & Ngo, Sirius Software; arcade.
- *Frogger*, Lubeck, Sierra On-Line; arcade. "Not even close." (That is all the comment *Softalk* gave it in the "Fastalk" column. This official version of the arcade game for the Apple II got poor reviews when it was released, as the graphics were not as good as the Apple II was capable of doing. Nevertheless, *Softalk* readers rated it as the 16th best program of 1982!)
- *Crossfire*, Sullivan, Sierra On-Line; arcade. "Critters come at you from four directions on a grid laid out like city blocks. Strategy and intense concentration required. Superb, smooth animation of a dozen pieces simultaneously. One of the great ones."
- *Threshold*, Schwader & Williams, Sierra On-Line; arcade.
- *Microwave*, Zimmerman & Nitchals, Cavalier Computer; arcade.
- *Time Zone*, Williams & Williams, Sierra On-Line; adventure. "'Microepic' hi-res adventure featuring ten periods from past and future history all over world and universe on eight double-sided disks. Good puzzles, many dangers."
- *Bag Of Tricks*, Worth & Lechner, Quality Software; utility.
- *Deadline*, Infocom; adventure. "Episode one in a projected series of murder mysteries by the authors of *Zork*. Interrogate, accuse, make transcripts. Includes inspector's casebook, lab report."
- *Zork II*, Blank & Liebling, Infocom; adventure.
- *David's Midnight Magic*, Snider, Brøderbund Software; arcade. (Pinball game.)
- *Bug Attack*, Nitchals, Cavalier Computer; arcade. (Clone of arcade game *Centipede*.)
- *Aztec*, Stephenson, DataMost; arcade.
- *Snake Byte*, Summerville, Sirius Software; arcade.
- *Apple Mechanic*, Kersey, Beagle Bros; utility.

- *Sensible Speller*, Sensible Software; word processor utility. "Spell-checking program sports listable 85,000 words, extensible up to 110,000 words. Recognizes contractions, gives word counts, word incidence, number of unique words. Clear documentation and simplicity of operation. Works with many word processors' files. Best of breed." (Originally called *The Apple Speller*.)
- *The Mask Of The Sun*, Anson, Clark, Franks, & Anson, Ultrasoft; adventure.

MOST POPULAR OF 1983

The Top Thirty:

- *Lode Runner*, Smith, Brøderbund; arcade. "Ascend 150 unique levels in super run-climb-dig-jump game—or design your own puzzles, scenes, and setups—in quest to retrieve stolen gold from the Bungeling Empire." (Another one that I once saw on an stand-up arcade game, though executed there more poorly than on the Apple version.)
- *Pinball Construction Set*, Budge, Electronic Arts; arcade.
- *Exodus: Ultima III*, British, Origin Systems; fantasy.
- *Zaxxon*, Garcia, Datamost; arcade. (Port of arcade game.)
- *Legacy Of Llylgamyn*, Woodhead & Greenberg, Sir-Tech; fantasy. Third *Wizardry* scenario.
- *Miner 2049er*, Livesay & Hogue, Micro Lab; arcade. "Run jump, climb, and slide through the mines, reinforcing the groundwork along the way. Elevators, cannons, chutes, and ladders help as you avoid or stomp mutants on the way. Hot stuff, best of the genre."
- *Apple Writer IIe*, Lutus, Apple Computer; word processor. "Includes WPL (word processing language). Additional functions menu; continuing features and functions menu; continuous readout of characters and length. IIe has shift, shift-lock, and tab, four-arrow cursor control, and delete key; data files compatible with [Apple Writer] II."
- *Hard Hat Mack*, Abbot & Alexander, Electronic Arts; arcade. "Poor Mack. He must avoid vandals, inspectors, falling rivets, and hungry cement mixers to complete his building."
- *Bank Street Writer*, Kuzmiak & The Bank Street College Of Education, Brøderbund; word processor.
- *Ultima II*, British, Sierra On-Line; fantasy.
- *Music Construction Set*, Harvey, Electronic Arts; music utility. "Interactive music composition and learning tool allows user to create music or experiment with included music library."
- *Multiplan*, Microsoft; spreadsheet.
- *Stellar 7*, Slye, Software Entertainment; arcade.
- *Double-Take*, Simonsen, Beagle Bros; utility.
- *QuickFile IIe*, Lissner, Apple Computer; database. (Predecessor to database module of *AppleWorks*; written in Pascal.)
- *Zork III*, Blank & Liebling, Infocom; adventure.
- *Drol*, Ngo, Brøderbund; arcade.
- *Beagle Basic*, Simonsen, Beagle Bros; language.
- *Mask Of The Sun*, Anson, Clark, Franks, & Anson, Ultrasoft; adventure.

- *A.E.*, Wada, Brøderbund; arcade.
- *ProntoDOS*, Weishaar, Beagle Bros; operating system.
- *Julius Erving and Larry Bird Go One-on-One*, Hammond, Bird, & Erving, Electronic Arts; arcade. "Graphically and intrinsically captures the moves, grace, and bearing of basketball forwards Dr. J and Larry Bird as they play one on one. The best video basketball imaginable, for one or two players."
- *Sargon III*, Spracklin, Hayden; strategy. "Plays good chess fast. Much improved from Sargon II, contains 107 classic games from the past for instruction or entertainment."
- *Beagle Bag*, Kersey, Beagle Bros; utility.
- *Rocky's Boots*, Robinett & Grimm, The Learning Company; education.
- *The Quest*, Snell, Toler, & Rea, Penguin Software; adventure.
- *Sammy Lightfoot*, Schwader, Sierra On-Line; arcade.
- *Planetfall*, Meretzky, Infocom; adventure.
- *Fontrix*, Boker & Houston, Data Transforms; graphics. "Character generator creates unlimited number of typefaces, uses them to write on a screen extended 16 times. Extremely significant development in graphics." (The "extended screen" meant that the work space was zoomed in on one sixteenth of the full size of the image, allowing creation of complex and detailed graphics.)
- *Enchanter*, Blank & Liebling, Infocom; adventure. "First of trilogy sequel to *Zork* expands interaction with other characters, goes above ground, increases use of logical magic. No big breakthroughs, but simply delightful."

RELEASED IN 1984

- NOTE: Software listings from this point onward represent programs that I could find information about, or ones with which I personally had experience. These certainly do not represent a comprehensive listing of all Apple II software ever released. For example, there was a large body of educational software produced for the Apple II, some of it possibly amazing; I just don't know much about most of it.

Adventure:

- *Crypt Of Medea*, Sir-Tech.
- *Sourceror*, Infocom; adventure. "Sequel to Enchanter. Navigate a 3-D maze, part the Red Sea, wax floors, avoid traps, and cast spells to rescue the guild master from a demon. Delightful."

Business/Productivity:

- *Bank Street Speller*, Brøderbund.
- *IACcalc*, International Apple Core; spreadsheet.
- *Sideways*, Funk Software; prints spreadsheets sideways.

Communications:

- *Data Capture //e*, Southeastern Software.

Education/Hypermedia:

- *Wiztype*, Sierra OnLine; educational, typing tutor. (Features characters from *The Wizard Of Id* comic strip.)

Graphics:

- *Beagle Graphics*, Simonsen, Beagle Bros.
- *Pixit, Baudville*; graphics utility.
- *Print Shop*, Brøderbund; graphics printing utility. (This was a significant program, making it possible for the first time for a novice user to easily create greeting cards, signs, and banners using graphics pictures and different fonts. It not only spawned many imitators, but a third-party industry that specializes in supplying graphics, borders, and more fonts.)

Home:

- *A+ Disk Magazine* (disk magazine)
- *UpTime* (disk magazine)

Home-Arcade:

- *Arcade Boot Camp*, Besnard, Penguin Software.
- *Fat City*, Weekly Reader Family Software.
- (The following were released by Atarisoft as "official" conversions of popular coin-operated games).
- *Battlezone*
- *Defender*
- *Dig Dug*
- *Donkey Kong*
- *Galaxian*
- *Joust*
- *Ms. Pac-Man*
- *Robitron 2084*

Programming/Utilities:

- *Apple Mechanic*, Beagle Bros; graphics.
- *Aztec C*, Manx; language.
- *Catalyst IIe*, Quark; program selector.
- *David-DOS II*, David Data; operating system.
- *DiskQuik*, Beagle Bros; DOS 3.3 utility.
- *DOS Boss*, Beagle Bros; DOS 3.3 utility.
- *DoubleTake*, Simonsen, Beagle Bros; DOS 3.3 utility.
- *Essential Data Duplicator III*, Utilities Microware; utility.
- *Fat Cat*, Bird, Beagle Bros; DOS 3.3 catalog utility.
- *Frame-Up*, Weishaar, Beagle Bros; early hypermedia presenter.
- *Master Diagnostic +*, Romano, Nikrom; hard disk diagnostics.
- *ProDOS User's Kit*, Apple Computer.
- *Silicon Salad*, Kersey & Simonsen, Beagle Bros; DOS 3.3 utilities.

Strategy:

- *Baltic 1985: Corridor To Berlin*, Strategic Simulations.
- *Beyond Castle Wolfenstein*, Warner, Muse.
- *RDF 1985*, Strategic Simulations.

Word Processing / Desktop Publishing:

- *AppleWorks*, Lissner, Apple Computer. "Word processor, database, and spreadsheet—each full-size, full-featured. Holds several files on 'desktop'. Proportionally spaced type. A winner, for IIe, IIc.
- *Cut & Paste*, Electronic Arts.

- *Jack2*, Business Solutions, Inc.; integrated software.
- *Practicalc II*, Practicorp; integrated software.
- *Simply Perfect*, LJK; integrated software.

RELEASED IN 1985

Adventure:

- *A Mind Forever Voyaging*, Infocom.

Business/Productivity:

- *ProFiler 2.1*, Pinpoint; database program.
- *SuperCalc 3A*, Sorcim/IUS Micro Software; spreadsheet.

Education/Hypermedia:

- *Stickybear Math*, Weekly Reader Family Software.
- *Stickybear Typing*, Weekly Reader Family Software; typing tutor.

Graphics:

- *Dazzle Draw*, Brøderbund; double hi-res graphics paint program.
- *Take 1*, Baudville; animation, graphics.

Home:

- *Managing Your Money*, MECA; home finance.

Home-Arcade:

- *Gato*, Spectrum Holobyte.
- *I.O. Silver*, Brandt, Beagle Bros.

Programming/Utilities:

- *Blankenship BASIC*, Blankenship & Assoc.; Applesoft pre-processor.
- *D-Code*, Beagle Bros; Applesoft debugging utility.
- *Diversi-Copy*, Diversified Software Research; fast disk copy program.
- *Extra K*, Beagle Bros; Applesoft utility to use 128K RAM.
- *ProByter*, Beagle Bros; ProDOS utilities.
- *ProSel*, Bredon; ProDOS program selector, later renamed *ProSel 8* after a 16-bit version was released in 1989.

Word Processing / Desktop Publishing:

- *Magic Office System*, Artsci; Integrated software, with word processor, spreadsheet, graphics, and spell checker.
- *Newsroom*, Springboard; First WYSIWYG desktop publishing program for Apple II, including clip art graphics, limited page layout, several font sizes, and capability of sending files, modem to other platforms running the Newsroom program, even if they weren't Apple II computers.
- *Pinpoint Desk Accessories*, Pinpoint; AppleWorks utility.
- *Sensible Grammar*, Sensible Software; grammar checker.
- *MouseWrite*, Roger Wagner Publishing; Word processor with a Mac-like desktop using MouseText characters.

RELEASED IN 1986

Adventure:

- *Bard's Tale*, Electronic Arts.
- *Hacker*, Activision; Unique in that there were virtually no instructions on how to play; you had to figure it out as you went, trying to "hack" into a fictional mainframe computer.
- *Hitchhiker's Guide To The Galaxy*, Infocom; Adventure based on the book of the same name.
- *Ultima IV*, Origin Systems.

Business/Productivity:

- *Bank Street Filer*, Sunburst Communications; database.
- *VIP Professional*, VIP Technologies; spreadsheet.

Communications:

- *Point-To-Point*, Little, Pinpoint Publishing; terminal program.

Education/Hypermedia:

- *Stickybear Printer*, Optimum Resources; graphics printing program with some features similar to Print Shop.
- *Reader Rabbit*, The Learning Company.
- *Writer Rabbit*, The Learning Company.

Graphics:

- *Fantavision*, Brøderbund; animation program.

Home:

- *Clan Perfect Accountant*, Sir-Tech; finance.
- *On Balance*, Brøderbund; finance.
- *Smart Money*, Sierra OnLine; finance.

Home-Arcade:

- *Autoduel*, Origin Systems.
- *F-15 Strike Eagle*, MicroProse.

Programming/Utilities:

- *Beagle Compiler*, Beagle Bros; Applesoft compiler.
- *Font Mechanic*, Beagle Bros; font editor for graphics.
- *Shape Mechanic*, Beagle Bros; graphics shape editor.
- *Micol BASIC*, Micol Systems; alternative to Applesoft.
- *MouseDesk*, International Solutions; double hi-res graphics program launcher, modeled after the Macintosh Finder. Eventually purchased by Apple and modified for their first version of the IIgs Finder.
- *Program Writer*, Beagle Bros; Applesoft program editor with an AppleWorks-like interface.
- *Triple Dump*, Beagle Bros; graphics printing utility, supporting every printer in the known universe.

Word Processing / Desktop Publishing:

- *AutoWorks*, Bird, Software Touch; AppleWorks macro program.
- *Fontworks*, Software Touch; AppleWorks WP utility.
- *KeyPlayer*, Pinpoint Publishing; AppleWorks macro program.

- *MacroWorks*, Brandt, Beagle Bros; AppleWorks utility, first macro program for AppleWorks.
- *MouseWord*, International Solutions; graphics-based word processor.
- *Multiscribe*, Styleware; graphics-based word processor, with multiple fonts and graphics capability.
- *Word Perfect*, Satellite Software; word processing.
- *SuperMacroWorks*, Brandt, Beagle Bros; AppleWorks utility, upgrade to MacroWorks, worked only with AppleWorks v2.0 or v2.1.

RELEASED IN 1987

Adventure:

- *Maniac Mansion*, Lucasfilm; Unique game allowing control of three characters at a time (out of six possible choices), each with varying abilities, which allowed slightly different outcomes.
- *Tass Times In Tone Town*, Electronic Arts; GS.
- *Tower Of Myraglen*, PBI Software; GS.

Business/Productivity:

- *Back To Basics Accounting*, Peachtree Software; GS.
- *BusinessWorks*, Manzanita Software Systems.

Communications:

- *AE MouseTalk*, United Software Industries; telecommunications program.
- *ProTERM*, Checkmate; telecommunications program.

Education/Hypermedia:

- *Where in The USA is Carmen Sandiego?*, Brøderbund; educational.

Graphics:

- *Certificate Maker*, Springboard; graphics printing utility.
- *Clipcapture*, Clipcapture; graphics conversion utility.
- *Deluxe Paint II*, Electronic Arts; GS; paint program.
- *Design Your Own Home*, Abracadata; graphics & design.
- *Design Your Own Train*, Abracadata; model train layout design.
- *Graphic Edge*, Pinpoint; graphics & design.
- *Paintworks Plus*, Activision; GS; paint program.
- *Walt Disney Comic Strip Maker*, Bantam Electronic Publishing; graphics utility.

Home:

- *The Music Studio*, Activision; GS; music utility.

Home-Arcade:

- *Flobynoid*, FTA.
- *Marble Madness*, Electronic Arts.
- *Mean 18*, Accolade; GS.

Strategy:

- *Balance Of Power*, Mindscape.
- *Strategic Conquest II*, PBI Software; GS.

Word Processing / Desktop Publishing:

- *GraphWriter*, DataPak Software; GS; desktop publishing.
- *Multiscribe GS*, Styleware; GS; desktop publishing.
- *Printrix*, Data Transforms; typesetting program.
- *Springboard Publisher*, Springboard Software; desktop publishing.
- *TimeOut DeskTools*, Beagle Bros; AppleWorks utilities.
- *TimeOut FileMaster*, Brandt, Beagle Bros; AppleWorks file management utilities.
- *TimeOut Graph*, Renstrom, Beagle Bros; AppleWorks SS utility.
- *TimeOut QuickSpell*, Bird, Beagle Bros; AppleWorks WP spelling checker.
- *TimeOut SideSpread*, Beagle Bros; AppleWorks SS utility.
- *TimeOut SuperFonts*, Beagle Bros; AppleWorks WP utility.
- *TimeOut UltraMacros*, Brandt, Beagle Bros; AppleWorks utility, successor to *SuperMacroWorks*.

RELEASED IN 1988

Adventure:

- *Beyond Zork*, Infocom.
- *DreamZone*, Electronic Arts.
- *Nord And Bert Couldn't Make Heads Or Tails Of It*, Infocom.
- *Questron II*, Strategic Simulations, Inc.
- *Ultima V*, Origin Systems.
- *Wizardry IV — The Return Of Werdna*, Sir-Tech.

Education/Hypermedia:

- *Designasaurus For The IIgs*, Britannica Software; GS.
- *HyperStudio*, O'Keefe, Mueller, & Kashmarek, Roger Wagner Publishing; GS; hypermedia.
- *Mavis Beacon Teaches Typing*, Software Toolworks.
- *Talking Stickybear Alphabet*, Weekly Reader Software; GS.
- *Where in Europe is Carmen Sandiego?*, Brøderbund.

Graphics:

- *Labels, Labels, Labels*, Big Red Computer Club; graphics printing utility.
- *PaintWorks Gold*, Activision; GS; paint program.
- *Print Magic*, Epyx; graphics printing utility.
- *Print Master Plus*, Unison World; graphics printing utility.
- *Print Shop GS*, Brøderbund; GS.
- *Super Print*, Scholastic Software; graphics printing utility.
- *VCR Companion*, Brøderbund; graphics utility, processor for VCR taping.

Home:

- *Diversi-Tune*, Diversified Software Research; GS; music program.

Home-Arcade:

- *Alien Mind*, PBI Software; GS.
- *Chuck Yeager's Advanced Flight Trainer*, Electronic Arts.
- *Test Drive*, Accolade; GS.
- *Tetris*, Spectrum Holobyte.
- *Wings of Fury*, Brøderbund.
- *Zany Golf*, Harvey, Electronic Arts; GS.

Programming/Utilities:

- *AC/BASIC*, Absoft;GS; BASIC language.
- *GEOS*, Berkeley Softworks; 8-bit graphic user interface.
- *Softswitch*, Roger Wagner Publishing; GS; Program switcher for 8-bit software.

Word Processing / Desktop Publishing:

- *AppleWorks GS*, Claris; GS; Integrated software, modification of GS-Works.
- *Medley*, Milliken; GS; Integrated software.
- *Publish-It!*, TimeWorks; desktop publishing.
- *TimeOut DeskTools II*, Beagle Bros; AppleWorks utility.
- *TimeOut MacroTools*, Beagle Bros; AppleWorks macros.
- *TimeOut Paint*, Beagle Bros; AppleWorks graphics utility.
- *TimeOut PowerPack*, Brandt, Beagle Bros; AppleWorks utility.
- *TimeOut Thesaurus*, Beagle Bros; AppleWorks WP utility.
- *WordBench*, Addison-Wesley; GS; word processing.

RELEASED IN 1989

Adventure:

- *2088: The Cryllan Mission*, Victory Software; GS.
- *Neuromancer*, Interplay; GS.
- *Times of Lore*, Origin.
- *Warlock*, Three Sixty Pacific; GS.
- *Wizardry V: The Heart of the Maelstrom*, Sir-Tech.

Graphics:

- *Graph-It!*, TimeWorks.
- *Nucleus demo*, FTA; GS.

Home:

- *Smart Money GS*, Brøderbund; GS; home finance.

Home-Arcade:

- *Arkanoid II: Revenge of Doh*, Taito; GS.
- *Bad Dudes*, DataEast; GS.
- *Crystal Quest*, Casady & Greene; GS.
- *Gnarly Golf*, Britannica Software; GS.
- *John Madden Football*, Antonick, Electronic Arts.
- *Qix*, Taito.
- *Space Harrier*, FTA; GS.
- *The Hunt for Red October*, Software Toolworks; GS.
- *The Last Ninja*, Activision.

Programming/Utilities:

- *GS Font Editor*, Beagle Bros; GS.
- *Photonix*, FTA; fast disk copy utility; GS.
- *ProSel 16*, Bredon; GS; Program selector and utilities package, updated for GS/OS.

Strategy:

- *Battlechess*, Camasta, Interplay; GS.
- *Dive Bomber*, Epyx.
- *War in Middle Earth*, Melbourne House; GS.
- *The King of Chicago*, Cinemaware Corp.; GS.

Word Processing / Desktop Publishing:

- *II Write*, Random House Media.
- *TimeOut Report Writer*, Verkade, Beagle Bros; AppleWorks DB utility.
- *TimeOut Telecomm*, de Jong & Munz, Beagle Bros; AppleWorks telecomm program.
- *WordPerfect IIgs*, Word Perfect Corp.; GS.

RELEASED IN 1990

Adventure:

- *Dragon Wars GS*, Heineman, Interplay; GS.
- *Keef the Thief*, Electronic Arts; GS.
- *Knights of Legend*, Origin.
- *Mines of Titan*, Infocom.
- *Prince of Persia*, Brøderbund.
- *Shogun*, Infocom/Mediagenic.
- *The Third Courier*, Accolade; GS.
- *Windwalker*, Origin.
- *Wraith: Devil's Demise*, Carmack, Nite Owl Productions.

Business/Productivity:

- *DoubleData*, Brandt, JEM Software; AppleWorks DB enhancement.
- *GeoCalc*, Berkeley Softworks; spreadsheet.
- *GeoFile*, Berkeley Softworks; database.

Communications:

- *GS-ShrinkIt*, Nicholas; GS; file archive utility.

Education/Hypermedia:

- *Katie's Farm*, Lawrence Productions; GS.
- *GS Numerics*, Spring Branch Software; GS.
- *McGee*, Lawrence Productions.
- *New Talking Stickybear Opposites*, Weekly Reader Software; GS.
- *Modulae demo*, FTA; GS.
- *New Talking Stickybear Shapes*, Weekly Reader Software; GS.
- *Nexus*, Golem Computers; hypermedia.
- *Playroom*, Brøderbund; educational.
- *StoryWorks*, Teacher's Idea & Information Exchange.

- *Symbolix*, Bright Software; algebraic math calculation and graphing package, GS.
- *Talking Dinosaurs*, Orange Cherry Software; GS.
- *Where in Time is Carmen Sandiego?*, Brøderbund.

Graphics:

- *Bannermania*, Brøderbund; graphics printing utility.
- *Delta Demo*, FTA; GS.
- *Delta Drawing Today*, Power Industries; graphics utility.
- *Platinum Paint*, Beagle Bros; GS; graphics drawing utility.
- *Super Print II: The Next Generation*, Scholastic; graphics utility.
- *The New Print Shop*, Brøderbund; update to graphics printing utility.

Home:

- *Jam Session*, Brøderbund; GS; music program.
- *Softdisk G-S*, Softdisk Publishing; GS; disk magazine.

Home-Arcade:

- *Airball*, Micro Deal; GS.
- *Bouncing Bluster*, Vallat & Dove; GS.
- *Dark Castle*, Three Sixty Pacific; GS.
- *Oil Landers*, FTA; GS.
- *Orbizone*, Pangea Software; GS.
- *Qix GS*, Taito.
- *Senseless Violence II*, Pangea Software; GS.
- *Slipheed*, Sierra On-Line; GS.
- *Task Force*, Brittanica; GS.
- *Tunnels of Armageddon*, California Dreams; GS.

Programming/Utilities:

- *Font Factory GS*, Seven Hills Software; GS; font editor.
- *Genesys 1.2*, Doty, SSSi, Inc.; GS; resource editor and developer utility.
- *GSBug 1.5*, Apple Computer; GS; debugger.
- *Logowriter GS*, Logo Computer Systems; GS.
- *MD-Basic*, Morgan Davis Group; GS; allows writing of structured source code, which is translated into tightly organized Applesoft code executable on any Apple II.
- *ORCA/C*, ByteWorks; GS; C language.
- *Photonix II*, FTA; commercial version of their fast disk copy program; GS.
- *Salvation – Deliverance*, Vitesse; GS; disk recovery.
- *Salvation – Exorciser*, Vitesse; GS; virus detector/eliminator.
- *Salvation – Guardian*, Vitesse; GS; disk backup utility, later renamed Salvation – Bakkup.
- *Salvation – Renaissance*, Vitesse; GS; disk optimizer.
- *Salvation – Wings*, Vitesse; GS; program launcher.

Strategy:

- *Chessmaster 2100*, Software Toolworks.
- *Halls of Montezuma*, Strategic Simulations; GS.
- *Omega*, Origin.
- *Revolution '76*, Britannia Software; GS.
- *Solitaire Royale*, Spectrum Holobyte; GS.

Word Processing / Desktop Publishing:

- *AW 3.0 Companion*, Beagle Bros; AppleWorks patching utility.
- *Outliner*, Brandt, Beagle Bros; AppleWorks WP utility.
- *TimeOut MacroEase*, Brandt & Munz, Beagle Bros; AppleWorks macro collection.
- *TimeOut SuperForms*, Verkade, Beagle Bros; AppleWorks WP utility.
- *TimeOut TextTools*, Munz, Brandt, & Bangerter, Beagle Bros; AppleWorks WP utilities.
- *Ultimate Fonts*, Cadieux, Kingwood Micro Software; AppleWorks macros that modify WP text to add the codes allowing inclusion of appropriate characters from other languages for printing with *TimeOut SuperFonts*.

RELEASED IN 1991

Adventure:

- *2088: The Cryllan Mission, The Second Scenerio*, Victory Software; GS.
- *Gate*, Bright Software; GS; Escape from a castle, battling monsters and solving puzzles. Includes animation, stereo music, and many sound effects.
- *The Immortal*, Electronic Arts; GS.

Education/Hypermedia:

- *GeoQuiz*, PC Globe.
- *HyperBole*, Resource Central; GS.
- *HyperCard IIgs*, Apple Computer; GS.
- *McGee At The Fun Fair*, Lawrence Productions; GS.

Graphics:

- *Mickey's Crossword Puzzle Maker*, Walt Disney Computer Software.
- *SuperConvert*, Harper, Seven Hills Software; GS; graphics utility.

Home:

- *NoiseTracker*, FTA; MOD music player; GS.
- *ShoeBox*, Seven Hills Software; GS; HyperCard IIgs application for keeping track of household information that is usually hard to find when you want it. Includes HyperCard IIgs (minus the manuals).

Home-Arcade:

- *Bouncin' Ferno*, FTA; GS; Game with some similarities to Marble Madness but completely different play, in which a ball moved on a surface with the mouse must be bounced up to get power pellets that lengthen its life. Freeware.
- *Pipe Dreams*, Lucasfilm.

Word Processing / Desktop Publishing:

- *Children's Newspaper Maker*, Orange Cherry Software; GS; desktop publishing.

- *Companion Plus*, Munz & Brandt, Beagle Bros; AppleWorks patch utility, major upgrade from AW 3.0 Companion.
- *Edlt-16*, Doty, SSSi, Inc.; GS; text editor.
- *InWords*, Westcode; translates scanned text into a file that can be used with any word processor.
- *Mercury*, MECC; GS; desktop publishing.
- *TotalControl*, Brandt & Verkade, JEM Software; AppleWorks DB utility.
- *Ultimate Words*, Cadieux, Kingwood Micro Software; AppleWorks macros that check text for capitalization, punctuation, and grammar errors.

RELEASED IN 1992

Business/Productivity:

- *Formulate*, Seven Hills Software; GS; A "word processor for math"; helps in creation of math related documents that involve specialized formulas and symbols.

Education/Hypermedia:

- *First Aid With Reddy*, Quality Computers; Medical emergency education program for children ages 6 and older,
- *Storybook Weaver GS*, MECC; GS.
- *The Treehouse*, Brøderbund; Seven educational games for ages five and above in the environment of a treehouse. Click on various objects with the mouse and learn in areas including music, animals, math, money, and more.

Graphics:

- *DreamGrafix*, DreamWorld Software; GS; Edit and display GS graphics in super hi-res 320 and 640 modes, as well as 3200 mode.
- *Imagemaster: Basic Paint*, Jada Graphics; GS; Paint program for 320 mode super hi-res GS graphics, utilizing up to 136 colors simultaneously. Has 64 built-in palettes and an unlimited number of custom palettes.

Home:

- *ANSITerm*, Parkhurst Micro Products; GS terminal program that displays ANSI graphics, compatible with ANSI BBS software.
- *MODZap*, Ian Schmidt; MOD music player; GS.
- *soniqTracker*, Tim Meekins; MOD music player; GS.
- *Your Money Matters*, Peterson, Software Solutions; GS; Full-featured financial program that runs specifically under the GS/OS desktop environment. Manage, budget, and reconcile any account, print checks, more.

Home-Arcade:

- *DuelTris*, David Seah; Inca-themed Tetris, against another player or against the computer; GS.
- *Milestones 2000*, Ken Franklin, ReliefWare;

- *Out of this World*, Heineman, Interplay; GS; Travel through a science-fiction world where hostile creatures lurk at every turn. Excellent graphics, and capability of modifying the video display to allow the game to run well on a non-accelerated GS. Sold as *Another World* outside of the US.
- *Pick'n'Pile*, Procyon; GS; Game with some elements similar to Tetris.
- *Space Fox*, Bright Software; GS; Guide spaceship through nine levels of hostile aliens. Over 1 MB of sound files enhance this game.

Programming/Utilities:

- *AutoArk*, Econ Technologies; GS; Data compression and decompression software, to conserve on disk storage.
- *Desktop Manager*, TMS Peripherals; GS; Add-on utilities (CDAs?) that work with both ProDOS 8 and GS/OS applications. Includes mini-word-processor, appointment calendar, calculator, print manager, disk manager, screen saver, more.
- *Disk Tools*, Gum, Office Productivity Software; AppleWorks TimeOut application that provides volume and file backup capabilities, with compression (if desired).
- *Express*, Seven Hills Software; GS; Print spooler for GS/OS software, using available memory as a buffer. Requires hard drive.
- *FlashBoot*, Quality Computers, GS; Loads RAM disk on bootup with any software program wanted, then can boot from that RAM disk for speed. Most useful for those with slow hard drives or no hard drives.
- *Foundation*, Lunar Productions; GS resource editor.
- *GNO/ME*, Procyon, Inc; GS; Multi-tasking environment for GS/OS programs.
- *HardPressed*, Westcode; GS; Data compression and decompression utility to conserve on disk storage.
- *ORCA/Debugger*, Byte Works; GS; source-level debugger for C and Pascal programmers. Especially helpful in identifying and fixing problems with CDevs, XCmds, and Finder Extensions. Compatible with Apple's GS-Bug.
- *Pointless*, Westcode; GS; GS/OS Init that makes possible the use of TrueType scalable fonts on the IIGs, allowing display and printout of characters in many point sizes without jagged edges on the characters.
- *Signature GS*, Proni, Quality Computers; GS; Collection of CDevs to enhance the GS/OS environment, including Phantasm [screen saver], Graffiti [desktop pattern editor], Sonics [customize sounds for system events], and BootMaster [modifies active/inactive status of GS/OS drivers, CDAs, and NDAs.
- *Six Pack*, Tudor, Quality Computers; GS; Utilities to add more functions to GS/OS Finder.
- *Switch It*, Econ Technologies; GS; GS/OS program switcher that can suspend one program and jump to another, leaving the first program in memory.
- *System Software 6.0*, Apple Computer; GS; New version of GS/OS system software with many enhancements over the previous version 5.0.4. Available free from dealers, online services, and user groups as a copy, but the disks and manual together for a reasonable cost. A winner!

APPENDIX A | *Software Hits*

- *Universe Master*, Proni, Econ Technologies; GS; Disk management program, including volume repair and file recovery utilities, multi-level catalog listings, block editing, and more, in a smoothly integrated desktop environment.

Word Processing / Desktop Publishing:

- *DB Pix, Brandt*, JEM Software; AppleWorks DB utility that allows your to display graphics pictures while in the database. Supports single and double hi-res, as well as Print Shop graphics, and displays the picture on the screen next to the database record.
- *TimeOut Grammar*, Beagle Bros/Quality Computers; AppleWorks grammar checker for the WP. Re-write of the older Sensible Grammar, improved, making it available from within AppleWorks.
- *Ultra 4.0, Brandt*, JEM Software; AppleWorks utility that enhances UltraMacros 3.x to give more macro commands and easier-to-read macro programs.
- *Ultra Extras*, Brandt, JEM Software; Add-on commands for Ultra 4.0.

RELEASED IN 1993

Adventure:

- *The Lost Treasures of Infocom*, Activision; nineteen classic Infocom adventure games in one package for the IIGS.
- *The Secrets of Bharas*, Victory Software; Ultima-style RPG, GS.

Education/Hypermedia:

- *Gold Rush*, Sierra; simulation of the California gold rush.
- *The Lost Tribe*, Lawrence Productions; lead your prehistoric tribe to safety.

Home:

- *BottomLine*, Quality Computers; home finance manager.

Home-Arcade:

- *Ant Wars*, Karl Bunker; use your army of red ants to destroy the black ants
- *FloorTiles*, Karl Bunker; place colored tiles on a grid
- *Mazer II*, Farfetch Software; navigate a maze to destroy monsters; GS.
- *Spy Hunter GS*, Shane Richards; clone of classic arcade game, GS.

Programming/Utilities:

- *Kangaroo*, Brainstorm Software; utility to simplify loading and saving files, GS.
- *ProBoot*, Sheppyware; boots other drives without having to go to the Control Panel; GS.
- *Switch-It!*, Procyon; multi-application for System 6.0, acting as a Mult-Finder for the IIGS.

- *The Manager*, Seven Hills Software; also offered Multi-Finder capability under System 6.0 on the IIGS.
- *Super Menu Pack*, Seven Hills Software; enhances GS/OS menus, GS.
- *Twilight II*, DigiSoft Innovations; screen saver, GS.
- *Virus MD*, Morgan Davis Group; detect and remove several Apple II viruses.

Word Processing / Desktop Publishing:

- *Addressed For Success*, Econ; IIGS program that handles large mailing lists and creates labels and other lists in the GS/OS environment.
- *AppleWorks 4*, Quality Computers.
- *ShadowWrite*, Horstman, Bright Software; full-featured word processor in a new desk accessory, GS.
- *TypeSet*, Disbrow & Wankerl, Westcode Software; IIGS utility designed to work with Pointless as an aid to organizing fonts and printing samples.

RELEASED IN 1994

Adventure:

- *Ultima GS*, Vitesse; re-creation of Ultima as a GS game, though without any updates to graphics.

Home:

- *Spectrum*, Seven Hills Software; GS-specific telecommunications software

Home-Arcade:

- *Ancient Glory*, Logical Design Works; adventure and combat-oriented game, GS.

Programming/Utilities:

- *System II*, Kitchen Sink Software; graphic desktop for Apple IIe or IIc

Word Processing / Desktop Publishing:

- *AppleWorks 5*, Quality Computers; the final and most full-featured update to this powerhouse.
- *Quick Click Calc*, The Byte Works; GS-specific spreadsheet.

RELEASED 1995 – 2013

- NOTE: New software released after 1994 was usually distributed as shareware, and later more frequently as freeware or public domain. From 2008 onward, many of the offerings are designed to work on the older 8-bit Apple II series, and not just on the IIGS.
- *ADT*, Guertin, utility; transfer disk images to an Apple II from a Mac or Windows computer (1999).
- *ADTPro*, Schmidt, utility; transfers files and disk images between an Apple II and a Mac or Windows computer (2007).

- *Animasia 3-D*, Animasia, graphics; create, rotate, 3D objects, multiple layers, GS (1995)
- *Arachnid*, Howe, telecom; graphic web browser for GS (2000).
- *BabelFish*, Seven Hills Software, utility; data translation between applications, GS (1998).
- *Convert 3200*, Brutal Deluxe, graphics; graphic conversion utility for the GS (1996).
- *Contiki OS*, Schmidt (port based on original work, Dunkels), utility; multi-tasking operating system, allowing TCP/IP connections for 8-bit Apple II from II Plus upward (2004).
- *Deathbounce*, Mechner, game; Asteroids-like game for any Apple II, written in 1982 but not released until 2012.
- *Deskplay*, Ninja Force, music; NDA that allows playing MOD files while using other software on the GS.
- *DiskMaker*, Sheppyware, utility; GS program to transfer disk images back to physical media.
- *DiskMaker 8*, Percival, utility; 8-bit version of DiskMaker, (2006).
- *DMS Drummer*, Mahon & 8-Bit Weapon, music; drum sequencer software for Apple IIe and later (2011).
- *Escape from the Homebrew Computer Club*, Schmenk, game; lo-res graphics first-person navigation game (2007).
- *Fishhead*, Brutal Deluxe, utility; GS utility to copy files from a disk, even if the disk media is damaged (2012).
- *GShisen*, Sherlock, game; GS tile matching game based on Shisen Sho (1998)
- *GSoft BASIC*, The Byte Works, programming; robust BASIC language for the IIGS (1998)
- *Hammurabi*, Compter, game; empire-building game (2001)
- *ImageMaker*, Sheppyware, utility; GS program to create disk images from physical media.
- *LemmingsGS*, Brutal Deluxe, game; port of Lemmings to the GS (1996).
- *Marinetti*, Bennett, utility; TCP/IP stack for GS/OS (1997)
- *Megacycles*, Bock, game; for GS (2010).
- *MountIt*, Brutal Deluxe, utility; Init to allow mounting of Apple II disk images to the GS/OS desktop (2009).
- *NadaNet*, Mahon, utility; simple networking for the Apple IIe (2007).
- *NakedOS*, Haye, programming; a barebones disk operating system for the Disk II (2010).

- *NiftySpell*, Vavruska, productivity; spell-checker for the IIGS in an NDA (1998).
- *NuInput*, Drucker, programming; improved Applesoft INPUT statement (2010).
- *Quick Click Morph*, Westerfield, The Byte Works, graphics; change one picture to another, GS (1995).
- *SAFE*, Wannop, telecom; FTP client for GS (2001).
- *SAFE2*, Wannop, telecom; FTP client for GS (2006).
- *SAM*, Wannop, telecom; email client for GS (2004).
- *SAM2*, Wannop, telecom; update to SAM, GS (2010).
- *Samurai*, Ninja Force, telecom; IRC client for a Marinetti-equipped GS.
- *Shipwrecked*, Howe, game; graphic adventure, requires Hypercard IIGS (2000).
- *Silvern Castle*, Fink, game; RPG game written in Applesoft, with graphics and an extensive game play (1999).
- *Slammer*, Drucker, programming; simple way of adding assembly language code to an Applesoft program (2010).
- *SNAP*, Wannop, telecom; NNTP client for GS (2007).
- *Spectrum Internet Suite (SIS)*, Weiss, telecom; using Spectrum, provides simple web page browsing, email access, Telnet, and file management for the IIGS (1997)
- *Super-Mon*, Haye, programming; add-on tools for Apple II Monitor (2010).
- *T40*, Brutal Deluxe, graphics; create and save 40-column text screens, primarily for the purpose of creating ASCII art (2011).
- *Taifun Boot*, Ninja Force, utility; allows installation of multiple operating systems on a single GS/OS volume.
- *Telnet NDA*, Howe, telecom; desk accessory to run a Telnet session while running another GS program (2012).
- *Trasher*, Sheppyware, utility; GS extension to simplify deletion of files from desktop (2011).
- *WebWorks GS*, Sheppyware, telecom; HTML editor for web page creation on the IIGS (1998).
- *Wolfenstein 3D*, Sheppyware with help of many others, game; port of the classic first person shooter to the IIGS; requires an accelerator card (1998).
- *Zephyr*, Soberka & Froggy Software, monochrome double hi-res graphics shooting game, written in 1987, but not released until 2013; sent out as floppy disk in zip-lock bags, much like software in the early years (2013).

APPENDIX B
Apple II Timeline

1968

September
- Steve Wozniak starts college at the University of Colorado; later that year he is put on probation for "computer abuse"

1970
- Steve Wozniak and Bill Fernandez build the "Cream Soda Computer"

1971
- Bill Fernandez introduces Steve Jobs to Steve Wozniak

November
- Intel 4004 processor advertised in the fall 1971 issue of *Electronic News*; Regis McKenna, whose agency would later be hired to advertise the Apple II computer, designs the promotion

1972
- Wozniak and Steve Jobs start their first joint business venture, selling "blue boxes" at Berkeley dorms.

April
- Intel 8008 microprocessor, which runs at a speed of 200 kHz (or 0.2 MHz) ($120)

September
- Steve Jobs starts at Reed College

October
- ARPANET earliest demonstration at First International Conference on Computer Communication

November
- Atari Pong

1973

January
- Steve Wozniak joins Bill Fernandez working at Hewlett-Packard in their calculator division
- Jobs drops out of Reed College, but continues to take classes there

February
- Micral N (Réalisation d'Études Électroniques; based on Intel 8008)

1974

April
- Intel 8080 microprocessor ($360)
- Steve Jobs begins work at Atari

March
- Scelbi-8H (Scelbi Computer Consulting; based on Intel 8008)

July
- Mark-8 (Jonathan Titus; based on Intel 8008)
- Jobs and his friend Daniel Kottke take a trip to India

October
- *Creative Computing* starts publication

November
- Motorola 6800 microprocessor ($175)

1975
- Wozniak and Jobs create Breakout in hardware for Atari

January
- Altair 8800 (MITS; based on Intel 8080) appears on the cover of the January issue of *Popular Electronics*

March
- First meeting of Homebrew Computer Club
- Wozniak begins designing his own home computer

July
- Sphere-1 (Sphere Corporation; based on Motorola 6800)

September
- *BYTE* begins publication
- MOS Technology 6501 ($20) and MOS Technology 6502 ($25) microprocessors; available at Wescon 75, the annual West Coast electronics show

November
- Jobs suggests to Wozniak that they sell his single-board computer circuit board

December
- Paul Terrell opens the first Byte Shop in Mountain View, California, and begins selling the Altair 8800
- Jobs and Wozniak decide on the name "Apple" for their company
- IMSAI 8080 (IMS Associates; based on Intel 8080 and the S-100 bus)

1976

- Poly-88 (Polymorphic Systems; based on Intel 8080 and the S-100 bus)
- Shugart SA400 minifloppy disk drive (Shugart Associates)
- Datanetics keyboard (Datanetics, Inc.)
- Adversary Video Games system (National Semiconductor), eventually a source of some of the first Apple II game paddles

January
- First batch of bare Apple-1 printed circuit boards are delivered to Wozniak

March
- Wozniak's Apple Computer (the Apple-1) is demonstrated to the Homebrew Computer Club
- Steve Jobs and Paul Terrell meet, and Apple gets its order for 50 completed Apple-1 boards for the Byte Shop
- Apple-1 computers begin to be delivered for sale at the Byte Shop at the list price of $666.66

April
- Wozniak, Jobs, and Ron Wayne form the Apple Computer Company on April Fool's Day; twelve days later, Wayne decides to withdraw from the company; the company uses a small office on Welch Road in Palo Alto, California as a mail drop and phone answering location.
- Atari Breakout (their own redesign of Wozniak's hardware)

May
- Wozniak envisions improvements to the Apple-1, and begins design on what will become the Apple II

June
- Texas Instruments TMS9900, the first 16-bit microprocessor

July
- *Interface Age* begins publication; features an article about Apple and the Apple-1
- Apple II prototype demonstrated to Chuck Peddle of Commodore
- Intel veteran Mike Markkula agrees to invest in the company, making it possible to complete development of the Apple II and buy the parts to build it
- Zilog Z-80 microprocessor ($25), compatible with Intel 8080, plus added instructions

August
- PC'76 show in Atlantic City, New Jersey; Jobs and Wozniak attend and demonstrate the Apple-1 and its cassette interface and BASIC
- Wozniak completes Apple II prototype; Chris Espinosa begins working on games and demonstration software for it

September
- Wozniak gets Breakout working in software on the Apple II

October
- Wozniak is persuaded to leave Hewlett-Packard and work at Apple full-time
- Commodore International buys MOS Technology

December
- Apple II demonstrated at the Homebrew Computer Club

1977

- Sol-20 (Processor Technology; based on Intel 8080 and the S-100 bus)

January
- Apple incorporates, with Mike Markkula as one third owner
- Apple moves from the garage owned by Steve Jobs' parents to a building on Stevens Creek Boulevard in Cupertino, California
- Commodore PET 2001 (Commodore International; based on MOS 6502) announced at Winter Consumer Electronics show

February
- Markkula hires Mike Scott as the first president and CEO of Apple

April
- Apple II introduced at the first West Coast Computer Faire on April 16

May
- First Apple II boards (computer without case, keyboard or power supply) ship on May 10
- *BYTE* publishes an article entitled "The Apple II" by Steve Wozniak, giving a hardware and firmware description of the computer

June
- First Apple II systems (with case, keyboard, and power supply) ship on June 10

August
- Apple pays $10,500 to Microsoft for first half of the license fee for 6502 floating point BASIC; Randy Wigginton begins to work on adapting it to the Apple II
- Radio Shack announces the TRS-80 (based on Zilog Z-80) with 4K RAM, 4K ROM, display monitor and cassette tape storage for $599

September
- Wozniak, Espinosa, and Wigginton have to discontinue their attendance at the Homebrew Computer Club; work at Apple is now taking up all of their time
- Apple Hand Controllers (paddles)

October
- *BYTE* publishes an article entitled "SWEET 16: The 6502 Dream Machine" by Steve Wozniak, describing the 16-bit computer emulator he included in the Apple II Integer BASIC ROM
- Apple II Parallel Printer Interface Card
- *Micro* begins publication
- Commodore PET 2001 available for purchase, featuring 8K RAM, 14K ROM, and 8K Microsoft BASIC for $795

November
- TRS-80 available for purchase
- Wigginton completes work on Applesoft I

December
- Wozniak begins work on a floppy disk drive and controller

1978
- Apple II Euromod
- Apple Centronics Printer Card

January
- Applesoft I (cassette) and manual
- Centronics 779 printer

February
- Apple II Reference Manual (the "Red Book")
- *Call-A.P.P.L.E.* begins publication

March
- Centronics µicroprinter P1 thermal printer
- IP-125 and IP-225 printers (Integral Data Systems)

April
- Apple II Communications Interface Card
- Novation CAT modem

May
- Applesoft II (cassette) adding hi-res graphics commands and other features ($20); revised manual ("Blue Book") not out until August
- *Contact*, Apple's first user newsletter, begins publication

June
- Disk II floppy disk drive with DOS 3.0 ($495)
- Applesoft Firmware Card ($200)
- Apple Modem IIA / IIB bundle (with re-branded Novation CAT modem) ($495)

July
- Apple DOS 3.1 (July 20)
- After release of the Disk II, sales of the Apple II quickly jump from 1,000 per month to 10,000 per month
- Motorola 6809 microprocessor ($26), successor to the 6800

August
- Apple II Serial Interface Card ($195)

October
- *Softside* begins publication

1979
- Usenet Internet discussion system started
- Apple Forth 1.6 (Cap'n Software) and AppleFORTH 1.2 (Programma) languages

January
- ITT 2020 (ITT Consumer Products), authorized clone of the Apple II

February
- Programmer's Aid #1 ROM

May
- Apple Clock (Mountain Hardware, Inc.)
- Trendcom 100 thermal printer

June

- Apple II Plus
- Corvus hard drive and Corvus Systems interface card for Apple II
- ALF Music Card MC16 (ALF Products, Inc.)
- Terrapin Turtle robot
- DOS 3.2

July

- DOS 3.2.1 (July 31)
- The Source online service begins (Source Telecomputing Corp.)
- MicroNET online service begins (CompuServe)
- MAUG (MicroNET Apple User Group) is one of the early forums on MicroNET
- Intel 8088 microprocessor ($125)

August

- Apple Pascal, Apple Language Card
- Apple Writer 1.0
- Apple II Europlus
- Tasman Turtle robot

September

- Jef Raskin's Macintosh project formally begins, although some preliminary work was done as early as late 1978
- Paper Tiger 440 and 460 printers (Integral Data Systems)
- Trendcom 200 thermal printer

October

- Integer BASIC Firmware card for the Apple II Plus ($200)
- VisiCalc (Personal Software, Inc.)
- International Apple Core formed in San Francisco
- *Contact*, Apple's first user group newsletter, ceases publication
- *Compute!* begins publication
- Micromodem II (Hayes Microcomputer Products)
- ALF Music Card MC1 (ALF Products, Inc.)

November

- Burrell Smith modifies Apple Language Card to use 32K for Lisa team
- TI 99/4 (Texas Instruments; based on TMS9900)
- Atari's 400, Atari 800 computers (based on MOS 6502)
- Introl/X-10 card and controller (Mountain Hardware, Inc.)

December

- Steve Jobs accompanies Lisa engineers on the second visit to Xerox PARC
- Centronics 730 printer
- Micronet Modem

1980

- TRS-80 Color Computer (Radio Shack; based on Motorola 6809), with capability of using ROM program cartridges
- Apple Pascal 1.1, Apple PILOT, Microsoft COBOL (languages)
- Zork (Personal Software), an advanced version of the old game Adventure
- Unnamed First Virus written (for Apple II)
- H&R Block purchases CompuServe, and renames MicroNET to CompuServe Information Service
- QuickFIle (for Apple III)
- Apple Hand Controllers (paddles)
- Seagate ST-506 hard drive
- Time II card (Applied Engineering)

January

- *Nibble* begins publication
- Apple Graphics Tablet

March

- *Apple Orchard* begins publication
- Apple Silentype printer
- Microsoft Z-80 SoftCard (later called just "Microsoft SoftCard") demonstrated at the fifth West Coast Computer Faire (fifth because there were two Faires held in 1979)
- Apple CP/M
- Videoterm 80-column card (Videx, Inc.)

May

- *Peelings II* begins publication
- Sup'R'Terminal card

June

- Thunderclock Plus card (Thunderware, Inc.)

July

- Apple II j-Plus in Japan
- Apple FORTRAN (language)

August

- Apple DOS 3.3 (Aug 25)
- Apple Writer 1.1
- Centronics 737 printer
- Epson MX-80 printer

September

- Apple III (based on MOS 6502B), with built-in disk drive and four peripheral slots ($3495)
- Jobs is excluded from the Lisa project
- *Softalk* begins publication
- Mountain Music System (Mountain Hardware, Inc.)

October

- *Apple Assembly Line* begins publication

November

- Motorola 68000 microprocessor

December

- Jobs increasingly becomes involved in Jef Raskin's Macintosh project
- Apple's initial public stock offering; 4.6 million shares were purchased

1981

- Atari VCS (later called Atari 2600) and Mattel Intellivision home video games systems
- Bill Mensch and his company, Western Design Center, creates the 65c02, a low-powered CMOS version of the 6502
- Apple II Parallel Interface Card
- Apple Joystick
- Apple Writer][
- Krell Logo and Terrapin Logo (languages)
- Sound I, Sound II, and Speech I cards (Street Electronics)
- Supertalker (Mountain Hardware, Inc.)

January

- Apple Super Serial Card
- The problems causing Apple III computers to mysteriously fail are identified, and steps are taken to correct them
- Commodore VIC-20 (based on MOS 6502A), with 5K RAM, BASIC in ROM, serial, cassette, and modem interfaces, and color, capable of using program cartridges ($299)
- *hard core: The Journal of the British Apple Systems User Group* begins publication

February

- Steve Wozniak and his fiancee, Candy Clark, are injured in a plane crash; he begins a leave of absence from Apple
- Apple announces that it will no longer offer a built-in clock/calendar in the Apple III, due to unavailability of reliable parts; the price is dropped $50 in compensation for this missing component
- Jobs completely takes over the Macintosh
- February 25th, "Black Wednesday" at Apple, as CEO Mike Scott fires over forty people, including half of the Apple II team, in an effort to shake the company out of its complacency; Scott is soon moved from the position of CEO to Vice-Chairman, and many of the fired engineers are later rehired

March

- Shipments of the Apple III resume after correction of reliability problems
- Enhancer][(Videx, Inc.)

April

- Mike Markkula becomes CEO and Steve Jobs becomes chairman of Apple
- Smartmodem (Hayes Microcomputer Products), first product to use what became known as the Hayes command set
- Osborne 1 (based on Zilog Z-80), first successful portable computer

May

- Apple IIe project begins with work on custom chips

June

- Apple begins airing commercials featuring Dick Cavett as a spokesman for their products
- Applefest '81 held June 6-7, sponsored by Boston Computer Society; the first Apple-only trade show
- Walt Broedner delivers his custom chip designs for the Apple IIe to Synertek
- Apple-CAT II modem (Novation, Inc.)

July

- Former CEO Mike Scott resigns from Apple
- *Hardcore Computist* begins publication
- *Windfall* begins publication (United Kingdom)
- Elk Cloner virus first appears
- LPS II Light Pen System (Gibson Laboratories)

August

- IBM PC (based on Intel 8088)

September

- ProFile 5 MB hard disk for the Apple III ($3,499)
- *Softdisk* begins publication; one of the first disk-based magazines
- *pom's* begins publication (France)

October

- Apple introduces the Family System, which includes an Apple II Plus computer, Disk II drive, RF modulator, tutorial, software, manuals, and software directory ($2,495)

November

- Apple announces that it will no longer allow its products to be sold to consumers via mail or telephone orders; as a result, six retailers file suit against Apple
- Kussmaul Encyclopedia online service begins

December

- Synertek delivers the first samples of the MMU and IOU for the Apple IIe
- Virus 3 (Dellinger Virus) written

1982

- Kaypro II portable (based on Zilog Z-80), with 9-inch screen and software included, to compete with the Osborne
- Epson MX-100 printer
- MPC BubDisk bubble memory card (Intel Corporation)
- Legend 128KDE memory card (Legend Industries, Ltd.)
- Number Nine Apple Booster accelerator (Number Nine Computer Corporation)
- Echo II sound card (Street Electronics)

- HERO-1 robot (Heathkit)
- GraFORTH and TransFORTH II (languages)
- Apple SuperPILOT (language)
- MOS Technology 6510 microprocessor (modified version of 6502)

January

- Basis 108 (German clone of the Apple II Plus)
- TRS-80 Model 16 (based on Motorola 68000 and Zilog Z-80), with 128K RAM, and 8-inch disk drive ($4,999)
- Intel 80286 microprocessor ($360)

February

- Steve Jobs appears on cover of *Time*
- RAMDisk 320 (Axlon Company)

March

- Apple announces it will take legal action against Asian makers of Apple II clones
- Epson's MX-80 and MX-100 printers are becoming popular as inexpensive dot-matrix printers
- Franklin Ace 100 (Franklin Computer Corporation), Apple II Plus clone

April

- Xebec S1410 controller and 5 MB hard drive

May

- Apple sues Franklin Computer Corporation for patent and copyright infringement in the creation of its Franklin Ace line of computers; ruling from this trial is initially found in favor of Franklin

June

- Apple Computer makes the "Fortune Double 500" list at number 598
- Applefest '82 is again held in Boston
- The Incredible Jack (Business Solutions), the first integrated software program for the Apple II
- Franklin Ace 1000 (Franklin Computer Corporation)
- Smartmodem 1200 (Hayes Microcomputer Products)

July

- Apple Logo (language)

August

- Commodore 64 (based on MOS 6510), with 64K RAM, 20K ROM with Microsoft BASIC, color and custom sound chips, and serial interface ($595)
- Franklin Ace 1000 Plus (Franklin Computer Corporation)
- Synetix 2202 SSD solid state disk drive (memory card)

September

- Steve Wozniak holds the first "US Festival"

October

- Apple Dot Matrix Printer ($699)

November

- Applefest/San Francisco '82
- Bank Street Writer (Brøderbund Software)
- Franklin Ace 1100 and 1200 (Franklin Computer Corporation)

December

- Apple IIc project begins
- Apple throws a "Billion Dollar Party" for its employees to celebrate the milestone of being the first personal computer company to reach a $1 billion annual sales rate

1983

- WDC 65816 microprocessor (Western Design Center), 16-bit update to the 65c02 compatible with most 6502 software
- Apple II ProFile interface card
- Apple Pascal 1.2 (language)
- Aztec C65 (Manx Software System, Inc.; language)
- M-c-T SpeedDemon accelerator (Microcomputer Technologies)
- Accelerator II (Saturn Systems)
- TOPO I robot (Androbot, Inc.)
- Tandy Model 100 (based on Intel 80C85A) ($799)

January

- Apple IIe ($1,395) and Lisa ($9,995) announced at the January 19th stockholders meeting, with Apple IIe 80-Column Card and Extended 80-Column Card
- Apple Letter Quality Printer ($2,195)
- QuickFile IIe and Apple Writer IIe
- *inCider* begins publication
- ORCA/M (Hayden Software), DOS 3.3 assembler
- Franklin Ace 1200 (based on MOS 6502, with a Zilog Z-80A coprocessor) with 128K RAM, an 80-column text card, and a Disk II-compatible drive ($2,200)
- The January issue of *Time* magazine names the computer as its "Man Of The Year" for 1982
- Compaq Portable (based on Intel 8088), one of the first IBM PC compatible computers ($3,590)
- Lotus 1-2-3 (Lotus Development Corporation)

February

- Apple UniFile and DuoFile disk drives (also called the Apple 871 drive) announced for the Apple III

March

- *Scholastic Microzine* begins publication
- IBM PC-XT (based on Intel 8088)
- Lotus 1-2-3 replaces VisiCalc as the best-selling computer program in America
- Delphi online service begins (General Videotex Corporation), replacing the Kussmaul Encyclopedia

April

- John Sculley leaves PepsiCo and becomes CEO of Apple; Mike Markkula becomes Vice-Chairman

May

- Apple makes the "Fortune 500" list at position 411
- "Kids Can't Wait" program begins, in which Apple donates 9000 computers to California public schools
- Steve Wozniak holds second (and final) "US Festival"

June

- Millionth Apple II produced
- Wozniak returns to Apple
- First 16-bit Apple II project ("Apple IIx") begins

August

- Third Circuit of the U.S. Court of Appeals reverses the ruling by a lower court in the copyright and patent infringement case brought by Apple against Franklin Computer; ruling in favor of Apple set the legal basis for declaring computer software covered by copyright law

September

- Sprite I, Sprite II, and SuperSprite cards (Synetix Systems)

October

- ProDOS v1.0
- Texas Instruments discontinues its TI-99/4A home computer due to decreasing sales (and significant price pressure from Commodore)
- *The Australian Apple Review* begins publication (Australia) Applefest/San Francisco '83
- MemoryMaster IIe card (Applied Engineering)
- KoalaPad (Koala Technologies)

November

- *A+* begins publication
- Due to the immense popularity of the IBM PC and others like it, pioneering computer companies North Star, Vector Graphic, and Cromemco begin to suffer significant decreases in sales, resulting in layoffs
- Microsoft Word (distributed with the November 1983 issue of *PC World*)

December

- Apple III Plus, with interlaced video mode that doubles the screen resolution, a clock/calendar function, repositioned cursor-control keys and a "delete" key, and operating system revisions ($2,995)
- Apple ImageWriter printer ($675)
- /// E-Z Pieces (for Apple ///)
- Apple IIe sells quite well during the holiday season

1984

- Apple Logo II (language)
- Apple Hand Controller IIe, Apple Joystick IIe and IIc
- Lee's Diskitis virus and Init Virus appears
- PHD-10 hard drive (Percom)
- Accelerator IIe (Saturn Systems)
- Rana Systems 8086/2
- ALF 8088 coprocessor (ALF Products, Inc.)
- TOPO II robot (Androbot, Inc.)

January

- ProDOS v1.0.1
- Macintosh (based on Motorola 68000) ($2,495).
- *1984* commercial promoting the Macintosh aired during the Super Bowl
- Lisa 2 ($3,495, $5,495), offered as a free upgrade to owners of the original Lisa; replaced the faulty Twiggy floppy drives with the 3.5-inch floppy drive used in the Macintosh
- *Windfall* changes its name to *Apple User*.

February

- ProDOS v1.0.2
- *Peelings II* ceases publication

March

- Apple IIx project cancelled
- Apple Modem 300, Apple Modem 1200
- Rana 8086/2 (Rana Systems)
- Commodore's VIC-20 discontinued
- Laser 3000 (Video Technology), Apple II Plus clone

April

- Apple IIc ($1,295), Apple Scribe color printer ($299), and Disk IIc; launched at "Apple II Forever" event
- Apple III and III Plus discontinued
- AppleWorks 1.0
- Timemaster II (Applied Engineering)

May

- The Print Shop (Brøderbund Software)
- Apple Duodisk floppy disk drive unit for the Apple II ($795); older Disk II discontinued
- AppleMouse II
- Cricket sound device (Street Electronics) for the Apple IIc
- LaserJet laser printer (Hewlett-Packard)

June

- BASIC.SYSTEM v1.1
- Apple Color Plotter ($779)
- Apple ImageWriter Wide Carriage version introduced ($749)
- Apple Scribe printer available to purchase

July

- ComputerEyes video image capture card (Digital Vision, Inc.)
- Gibson Light Pen System (Gibson Laboratories)

August

- ProDOS v1.1
- Basic design work on Mega II chip completed
- *Softalk* ceases publication, succumbing to bankruptcy
- *Softside* ceases publication
- PVI Drum-Key drum synthesizer (Ensoniq Corp)
- Commodore buys Amiga Corp
- IBM PC AT (based on Intel 80286) introduced, with 256K RAM, and a high-density disk drive ($5,469)

September

- ProDOS v1.1.1
- Apple Writer II v2.0, first version to run under ProDOS
- *Apple Orchard* ceases publication
- *Peeker* begins publication (Germany)
- Ultraterm 132-column card (Videx, Inc.)
- Macintosh 512K ("Fat Mac")

October

- *Micro* ceases publication
- *UpTime* disk magazine begins publication
- FreeWriter (Paul Lutus), word processor derived from Apple Writer
- Digital Paintbrush System (Computer Colorworks)
- Discussions about 16-bit Apple II are revived

November

- Two millionth Apple II sold
- Apple buys every page of advertising in the election year issue of *Newsweek* magazine, promoting the Macintosh and its "Test Drive A Mac" campaign
- Muppet Learning Keys (Koala Technologies)
- Sider 10 MB hard drive (First Class Peripherals), the first low-cost hard drive for the Apple II ($695)

December

- AppleColor 100 Monitor, Apple's first RGB monitor, with a switch that changes to a monochrome display mode, and a motorized screen tilt feature.
- ThunderScan scanner (Thunderware, Inc.), works by replacing the ink cartridge in an ImageWriter printer
- Timemaster H.O. clock card (Applied Engineering)

1985

- Apple SuperPILOT Special Edition (language)
- Apple Pascal 1.3 and Instant Pascal (language)
- RamWorks memory card, IIc System Clock (Applied Engineering)
- FrEdWriter (Al Rogers), enhancement of FreeWriter word processor
- Ohio Kache Card (Ohio Kache Systems)
- Apple Worm written
- PageMaker (Aldus Corporation; for Macintosh)

January

- Apple's annual stockholder meeting almost totally ignores the Apple II, despite having its best sales quarter ever, while concentrating on the Macintosh; leaves the Apple II division demoralized.
- Apple LaserWriter laser printer and AppleTalk introduced as part of the Macintosh Office System
- Macintosh XL, a refitted Lisa 2 with an internal hard drive and a program called MacWorks XL, which emulated a 64K Macintosh; required a change in built-in monitor to display square pixels like on the Mac
- *Open-Apple* begins publication
- Atari 520ST (based on Motorola 68000)

February

- Wozniak takes leave of absence from Apple to start a new company, CL9
- Wozniak and Jobs receive National Technology Medal from President Reagan
- Tandy Model 200 laptop (based on Intel 80C85A)

March

- Enhanced Apple IIe
- Apple CEO John Sculley asks employees to take a week of vacation and announces that Apple's manufacturing plants will close for one week, to work off excess inventory
- *Tremplin Micro* begins publication (France)

April

- Addison-Wesley Publishing takes over printing of Apple manuals
- Macintosh XL discontinued
- IBM PCjr discontinued
- Lotus Development Corporation buys Software Arts from Bricklin and Frankston, and stops sales of VisiCalc

May

- Apple's eight-year license of Applesoft BASIC from Microsoft is up for renewal; in exchange for another eight-year license and the right to continue to sell the Apple II computer with Applesoft in ROM, Steve Jobs is forced to give the code for MacBASIC to Microsoft
- Apple reorganizes again, bringing the Apple II and Macintosh product groups together
- Steve Jobs is ousted from the Macintosh team, and made a chairman with no responsibilities
- Quantum Link online service begins (Quantum Computer Services), for Commodore 64 and Commodore 128 users
- Smartmodem 2400 (Hayes Microcomputer Products)

June

- Apple lays off 1200 employees and records a loss of $40 million, at that time its first and only quarterly loss as a public company
- Apple UniDisk 5.25

July

- AppleLink online service begins (for use by Apple Computer and registered developers only)
- AppleWorks 1.1
- Pinpoint Desk Accessories (Pinpoint Publishing, Inc.)
- Amiga 1000 (Commodore International; based on Motorola 68000), OS can do multitasking ($1,295)

August

- Mockingboard sound card (Sweet Micro Systems)

September

- Apple UniDisk 3.5, Apple II Memory Expansion Card, Quark Catalyst (program selector)
- Apple ImageWriter II ($595), offering color and ability to print MouseText
- Apple ColorMonitor IIe and IIc ($399), able to display composite color (not RGB) but can still produce readable 80-column text
- Apple Personal Modem 300/1200
- Steve Jobs resigns as chairman of Apple to start a new company, NeXT, Inc; several Apple employees resign from Apple to join him.
- Apple sues Jobs, alleging that he breached his duties as chairman and misappropriated proprietary information
- *The Apple II Review* begins publication

October

- GEnie online service begins (General Electric Information Services); the American Apple Roundtable (AART) for the Apple II begins at the same time
- Franklin ACE 2000 and ACE 500
- AppleWorks 1.2

November

- Apple IIc UniDisk 3.5 upgrade
- Apple Writer 2.1
- Microsoft Windows 1.0
- Sider II (First Class Peripherals), external hard drive ($895).

December

- *Creative Computing* ceases publication.
- *Interface Age* ceases publication.

1986

- RAMWorks II, RAMFactor, Z-RAM (for Apple IIc), and Phasor sound card (Applied Engineering)
- No-Slot Clock (SMT Peripherals)
- MultiKache card (Ohio Kache Systems)
- HyperCard (for Macintosh)
- LISA816 assembler (Randall Hyde and Brian Fitzgerald)

January

- Macintosh Plus and LaserWriter Plus
- Apple and Steve Jobs reach out-of-court settlement
- Transwarp accelerator (Applied Engineering)

February

- Steve Jobs sells all but one share of his Apple stock, leaving Mike Markkula as the largest shareholder
- AppleWorks 1.3
- B-Sider (First Class Peripherals)

March

- Laser 128 (VTech)

April

- MultiScribe (StyleWorks)

June

- MacroWorks (Beagle Bros)

July

- Cortland Programmer's Workshop (programming environment for Apple IIGS)

August

- *AppleWorks Forum* begins publication
- *hard core* changes its name to *Apple2000*.
- AutoWorks (Software Touch)

September

- Apple IIGS ($999), Apple 3.5 drive, Apple 5.25 drive
- Apple IIc Memory Expansion upgrade
- Apple IIe 128K price reduced
- Apple II SCSI controller card, Apple Hard Disk 20S.
- Apple RGB Monitor ($499), Apple Monochrome Monitor ($129), and AppleColor Composite Monitor ($379
- ProDOS 16 v1.0; original ProDOS becomes ProDOS 8 v1.2
- AppleWorks 2.0
- Apple Programmer's and Developer's Association (APDA) created

November

- Penguin Software, a pioneer in removal of copy protection, is forced by Penguin Books to change its name; the company chooses "Polarware"
- SuperMacroWorks (Beagle Bros)

December

- ProDOS 16 v1.1

1987

- CMS SCSI card and hard drive (CMS Enhancements, Inc.)
- RAMCharger, RAMWorks III, GS-RAM, GS-RAM Ultra, and Z-RAM Ultra 1, Ultra 2, and Ultra 3 (Applied Engineering)
- TimeOut and UltraMacroWorks (Beagle Bros)
- GS BASIC under development at Apple
- Merlin 8/16 assembler (Roger Wagner Publishing)
- TML Pascal (TML Systems), ORCA/Pascal (The Byte Works) (languages)

January
- ProDOS 8 v1.3
- Platinum Apple IIe with built-in keypad ($829)
- Amiga 500 (Commodore International; based on Motorola 68000)

February
- Apple II SCSI Card revision B (fixes problems encountered when trying to use the card on the IIGS)

March
- Macintosh SE and Macintosh II
- Amiga 2000 (Commodore International; based on Motorola 68000)
- *Peeker* ceases publication

April
- ProDOS 8 v1.4
- MultiScribe GS (StyleWare)
- IBM PS/2 line introduced, with the first version of the OS/2 operating system
- Microsoft Windows 2.0

May
- Apple IIGS System Software v2.0
- AppleFest '87 held in Boston
- Zip Chip 4 MHz accelerator chip announced (Zip Technology)

July
- Claris, a software company spun-off from Apple, is created; it will handle AppleWorks and Macintosh software previously sold by Apple

August
- *The Australian Apple Review* ceases publication

September
- Apple IIGS ROM 01 upgrade
- *The Apple II Review* changes its name to *The Apple IIGS Buyer's Guide*
- AppleFest '87 held in San Francisco

October
- TimeOut (Beagle Bros), enhancements for AppleWorks

November
- PC Transporter (Applied Engineering)
- Datalink 1200, Datalink 2400 modems (Applied Engineering)

December
- Apple IIGS System Software v3.1; first version with the Finder
- BASIC.SYSTEM v1.2

1988
- TransWarp II (Applied Engineering)
- TutorTech (Techware Corporation)
- Merlin 16+ assembler (Roger Wagner Publishing)

January
- Apple IIc Revised Memory Expansion version
- Apple LaserWriter II
- Publish-It! (Timeworks); first serious desktop publishing program for the Apple II
- Laser 128EX (VTech)

February
- AC-BASIC (Absoft Corporation)

March
- AppleCD SC (CD-ROM drive, $1,199) for both the Macintosh and Apple II
- Apple II SCSI Card Rev C, supporting partitioning on large capacity disk drives
- Apple II Workstation Card ($249) to allow the Apple IIe to connect to an AppleTalk network
- Tom Weishaar (of *Open-Apple*) begins as manager of the Apple II Roundtables on the GEnie online service.

April
- ProDOS 8 v1.5
- CyberAIDS virus written

May
- AppleLink-Personal Edition online service (Quantum Computer Services) announced at AppleFest '88 in Boston
- *Apple Assembly Line* ceases publication
- Zip Chip (Zip Technology) finally available for sale
- *Apple User* ceases publication

June
- ProDOS 8 v1.6
- Festering Hate virus written
- Rocket Chip (Bits & Pieces Technology)

July
- Apple IIGS System Software v3.2; it is the first version that can boot over an AppleTalk network
- Laser 128EX/2 (VTech)

August
- ProDOS 8 v1.7
- PC-Link online service begins (Quantum Computer Services) for PC users

September
- Apple IIGS System Software v4.0; first version to be called GS/OS, and is written entirely in 16-bit code

- Apple IIc Plus ($675, or $1,099 with color monitor), announced at AppleFest '88 in San Francisco
- AppleWorks 2.1
- Macintosh IIx with SuperDrive (high density floppy disk)
- Zip Chip finally available for shipment

October

- Claris purchases StyleWare
- AppleLink Personal Edition online service begins (Quantum Computer Services)
- SyQuest 44 and 100 MB cartridge hard drives (SyQuest Technology, Inc.)
- Chinook CT-20c hard drive (Chinook Technology, Inc.) for Apple IIc

November

- Transwarp GS accelerator (Applied Engineering)
- Micol Advanced BASIC (Micol Systems, Inc.; language)

December

- A.P.P.L.E. (Apple Pugetsound Program Library Exchange) changes it official name to TechAlliance; Apple's lawyers don't like other companies using the company's name
- *Open-Apple* changes its name to *A2-Central* (for similar reasons)
- *UpTime* disk magazine ceases publication, purchased by *Softdisk*
- Apple Computer purchases the Apple Programmers and Developers Association (APDA) from TechAlliance
- AppleWorks GS 1.0 (Claris Corporation); it is a somewhat modified version of StyleWare's GS-Works
- Steve Jobs announces the NeXT computer

1989

- Sonic Blaster sound card (Applied Engineering)
- ComputerEyes GS (Digital Vision, Inc.), video image capture card

January

- *Tremplin Micro* ceases publication

February

- AppleWorks GS 1.0v2

April

- Apple II Video Overlay Card

May

- HyperStudio (Roger Wagner Publishing), the first Apple IIGS hypermedia product.
- *A+* and *inCider* merge to become *inCider/A+*

June

- ProDOS 8 v1.8
- BASIC.SYSTEM v1.3

- AppleWorks 3.0
- The Source is sold to CompuServe
- Apple Computer pays $2.5 million to Quantum Computer Services to recover the rights to use of the Apple logo for an online service

July

- First A2-Central Developer's Conference (KansasFest)
- Apple IIGS System Software v5.0
- Load Runner virus appears
- Vulcan internal hard drive (Applied Engineering)
- AppleWorks GS 1.1v2

August

- Apple IIGS ROM 03 introduced
- BASIC.SYSTEM v1.4
- The Source is shut down, and customers are offered a credit to join CompuServe

September

- GS+ begins publication
- Macintosh Portable and Macintosh IIci

October

- AppleLink Personal Edition is renamed America Online
- Burp virus appears

November

- *Softdisk G-S* begins publication

December

- Apple IIGS System Software v5.0.2
- *Stack-Central* begins publication

1990

- GS-RAM Plus (Applied Engineering)
- Blackout virus appears
- Complete Pascal (Complete Technology, Inc.; language)

January

- *Call-A.P.P.L.E.* ceases publication

February

- Last ARPANET computer decommissioned
- Quickie hand scanner (Vitesse) for the Apple IIe and IIGS

March

- Apple II High Speed SCSI card
- Macintosh IIfx

May

- Microsoft Windows 3.0
- RamFAST SCSI card (CV Technology)

June
- BASIC.SYSTEM v1.4.1

July
- Second A2-Central Summer Conference (KansasFest)

August
- ProDOS 8 v1.9
- Apple buys back Claris Corporation as a wholly owned subsidiary
- DeskJet 500 (Hewlett-Packard) ink-jet printer
- LightningScan GS hand scanner (Thunderware, Inc.)
- *TimeOut-Central* begins publication

September
- Zip Chip 8000 (Zip Technology)

October
- Macintosh Classic, Macintosh LC, and Macintosh IIsi
- *The Apple IIGS Buyer's Guide* ceases publication
- *pom's* ceases publication

December
- Apple IIGS System Software v5.0.3; there were problems with the ImageWriter driver under low memory situations, so it was not widely distributed
- Apple IIc Plus and ImageWriter LQ discontinued
- Zip GSX (Zip Technology)
- *8/16-Central* begins publication
- 1990 Apple II Achievement Awards held at AppleFest in Long Beach, California

1991
- Floptical drive (Insite Peripherals)

January
- HyperCard IIGS

February
- Apple IIGS System Software v5.0.4
- America Online adds a client for MS-DOS users, in addition to its existing Apple II and Macintosh customers

March
- Apple IIe card (for Macintosh LC) ($199)
- InWords (Westcode); optical character recognition software for the Quickie hand-scanner
- *Hyperbole* begins publication (hypermedia disk magazine)

May
- Apple StyleWriter ($599) and Apple Personal LaserWriter LS ($1,299); at the time of the announcement, neither can work on the Apple II or IIGS

June
- AppleCD SC Plus, faster than the original CD-ROM drive ($799)
- *Script-Central* begins publication

July
- Third A2-Central Summer Conference (KansasFest)
- Apple IIGS System Software v6.0 pre-announced
- *Computist* ceases publication

September
- Apple's first User Group Television live satellite broadcast; the Apple IIGS Plus is almost announced, but the project is killed by Apple management at the last minute

October
- ClarisWorks 1.0 (Claris) for Macintosh
- *8/16-Central* ceases publication

November
- Apple II SuperDrive Card for Apple II

December
- Pegasus internal SCSI hard drive (Econ Technologies)

1992
- Apple CD 150

January
- ProDOS 8 v2.0

March
- Apple IIGS System Software v6.0; includes a driver to allow the Apple StyleWriter printer to be used on the IIGS
- ProDOS 8 v2.0.1

April
- 1991 Apple II Achievement Awards presented
- *GEnieLamp A2* begins publication
- Microsoft Windows 3.1

May
- Express (Seven Hills Software), a software-based print spooler for the Apple IIGS
- The A2 Roundtable on GEnie announces the Lost Classics project, coordinated by sysop Tim Tobin, which has the object of locating and re-releasing older Apple II software that has disappeared from the marketplace

APPENDIX B | *Apple II Timeline*   545

- Ultra 4.0 (JEM Software), an upgrade to the UltraMacros macro language for AppleWorks 3.0
- *Scholastic Microzine* ceases publication
- MODZap 0.6 and soniqTracker 0.3 MOD music players for IIGS, starting a friendly rivalry between the two programmers, each trying to top each other

July

- Fourth A2Central Summer Conference (KansasFest); it celebrates the 15th anniversary of the release of the Apple II
- Apple IIGS System Software v6.0.1 announced
- Foundation (Lunar Productions), resource editor for the Apple IIGS
- *Nibble* ceases publication

August

- Paul Lutus agrees to allow Apple Writer v2.1 and GraFORTH to be reclassified as freeware
- Earliest mention of an Apple IIe emulator in the GEnie A2 Roundtables, designed to run on 386 or 486 PCs

November

- *Apple2000* ceases publication
- ProDOS 8 v2.0.2

December

- Apple IIGS discontinued

1993

- MD-BASIC (Morgan Davis Group; language)

January

- America Online adds a client for Windows users

February

- *GEnieLamp A2Pro* begins publication

March

- Randy Brant begins working on TheWorks 4.0, code-named "Quadriga," designed to be an add-on patcher program for AppleWorks 3.0 for Quality Computers (this later becomes AppleWorks 4)
- *II Alive* begins publication

April

- Twilight II (Digisoft Innovations) an updated and enhanced version of their original shareware GS/OS screen saver
- SoundMeister stereo card and sound digitizer (Econ Technologies) for the IIGS

June

- *A2-Central* discontinues its paper edition, switching to a disk-only newsletter

- System 6.0.1 for the IIGS, and System 4.0.2 for 8-bit Apple II computers
- John Sculley steps down as CEO of Apple, later leaving the company altogether
- Randy Brandt publically announces his Quadriga project
- *Apple Assembly Line* now available in a digital form, exclusively on GEnie
- HardPressed (Westcode), disk compression software

July

- Fifth A2-Central Developer's Conference (KansasFest)
- *inCider/A+* ceases publication
- *Shareware Solutions II* begins publication

August

- Quality Computers announces that it has obtained the rights from Claris to publish updates to AppleWorks and AppleWorks GS
- Newton MessagePad (original)

October

- Delphi sold to News Corporation

November

- Apple IIe discontinued; only remaining Apple II sold is the Apple IIe card for the Macintosh LC
- DiskQuest (Sequential Systems), makes several commercial CD-ROM products readable by Apple II computers
- AppleWorks 4
- 3D Logo and HyperLogo GS (The Byte Works; languages)

1994

- Iomega Zip Drive
- ZipDrive GS (Zip Technology), hard drive on a peripheral card

February

- Apple changes the status of HyperCard IIGS to be the same as System Software, in that it is available from qualified sources for the cost of a download or the cost of the disk media

March

- Applied Engineering goes out of business
- DeskJet 520, 560c (Hewlett-Packard) ink-jet printers
- Quickie-C color hand scanner (Vitesse)

May

- Bluedisk controller card (///SHH Systeme), allows connection of MS-DOS disk drives to an Apple II, allowing simple transfer of files between a PC and an Apple II with the bundled with MS-DOS Utilities (Peter Watson)
- Commodore International announces that it is voluntarily going out of business and into liquidation
- SyQuest 270 MB cartridge drive (SyQuest Technology, Inc.)

June
- Apple II SuperDrive interface card and SuperDrive are discontinued

July
- Sixth A2-Central Summer Conference; now named ICONference, and open to platforms other than the Apple II
- AppleWorks 5, code-named "Narnia", is announced by Randy Brandt
- Quality Computers announces it has to cancel plans to update AppleWorks GS, due to multiple problems with the source code and the significant cost required to fix it
- STM - Stop The Madness (Jim Nitchals), Apple II Plus emulator for any Mac running System 7

August
- AppleWin (Michael O'Brien), Apple IIe emulator for Windows 3.1 and Windows 95, first beta version

November
- America Online discontinues its Apple II service, effectively locking these users out (since it required proprietary software to access the service)
- AppleWorks 5

December
- Vitesse announces they expected to ship Wolfenstein 3D for the IIgs by late in the month, selling it for $39.95; however, it does not actually appear for over three years

1995
- Focus Hard Card (Parsons Engineering), hard drive on a peripheral card

January
- *The Apple Blossom* begins publication

February
- *A2-Central* and all other ICON disk magazines ceases publication, and ICON and Resource Central closes its doors

March
- Apple releases its new price list, no longer carrying any remaining Apple II products

May
- Apple IIe Card for the Macintosh LC is discontinued

June
- Second Sight card (Sequential Systems), which allows a IIgs to display video on a standard VGA monitor

July
- KansasFest 1995 is held, the first event organized and run by volunteers
- AppleWorks 5.1
- Quality Computers sold to Scantron Corporation, becoming Scantron Quality Computers

August
- *Softdisk* ceases publication
- *GS+* ceases publication
- Microsoft Windows 95
- SyQuest EZ135 cartridge drive (SyQuest Technology, Inc.)

September
- *Compute!* ceases publication

October
- Deja][(Mark Munz and Randy Brandt), a focused AppleWorks 5.1 emulator for the Macintosh
- "Mark Twain" Apple IIgs prototype analyzed by Jim Pittman and Joe Kohn in separate published reports

December
- *AppleWorks Forum* ceases publication
- PMPFax (Parkhurst Micro Products), fax management software for IIgs
- Convert 3200 (Brutal Deluxe), distributed in the U.S. by Joe Kohn of *Shareware Solutions II*

1996

January
- *GEnieLamp A2Pro* ceases publication
- *II Alive* ceases publication
- *Juiced.GS* begins publication

March
- General Electric sells the GEnie online service to Yovelle Renaissance Corp., which changes the name to "Genie," and promptly makes significant hikes in the monthly fees

April
- Yovelle announces a "Genie Lite" lower-cost pricing package, with limited access to Roundtables
- A group of investors purchase Delphi back from News Corporation, begin to transform it into an ad-supported online service

May
- Yovelle decides it cannot afford the large number of customers moving to the "Genie Lite" plan, and cancels it

- Bright Software changes its name to Fast Eddie Labs, and announces the release of a beta version of its Apple IIGS emulation software, code-named Fast Eddie, and written by Henrik Gudat and Andre Horstmann
- XGS (Joshua Thompson), earliest version of an Apple IIGS emulator for Linux and X-Windows

July

- KansasFest keynote speaker Gary Utter points out the coming need for a new online home, as Genie was beginning to fail
- Gus (Andy Nicholas), Apple IIGS emulator for the Macintosh, demonstrated at KansasFest; ultimately, Apple management prevents this from being even as an unofficial product
- GEnieLamp A2 is the only digital newsletter in the GEnieLamp series still being produced and distributed each month
- Many Genie members are migrating to CompuServe or Delphi, due to the changes made in the costs of the service

November

- Syndicomm starts A2 and A2Pro forums on Delphi, patterned after the same-named Roundtables from Genie

1997

January

- First beta versions of F.E. Systems Apple II emulator

March

- *Softdisk G-S* ceases publication
- Spectrum Internet Suite (Seven Hills Software, Geoff Weiss and Ewen Wannop), makes it possible to access graphic Internet web pages directly with a IIGS using a dial-up shell account
- A2-Web (David Kerwood), first Apple II-focused web site, calls itself "The Mother Of All Apple II Websites"

April

- Tiger Learning Computer (Tiger Electronics) authorized Apple IIe clone, test marketed

May

- Steve Jobs, having returned to Apple, cancels what he feels are unessential projects, including the license to Tiger Electronics for the Tiger Learning Computer

June

- Genie management decides to close lower traffic Roundtables, resulting in the closure of A2Pro, merging its contents into the A2 Roundtable

July

- Marinetti (Richard Bennett), a significant enhancement for the Apple IIGS that makes it possible to connect to the Internet through a direct dial-up connection

September

- KEGS (Kent's Emulated GS, Kent Dickey), Apple IIGS emulator for HP series 9000/700 workstations

October

- *GEnieLamp A2* ceases publication

1998

January

- *The Lamp!* begins publication
- Joe Kohn and *Shareware Solutions II* begin to host Monday multi-system chats that combine Genie and Delphi into a single chat room, later adding CompuServe users
- Genie is no longer able to sign up new users, as its software cannot handle a credit card with an expiration date past 12/99

February

- Wolfenstein 3D (Eric Shepherd and others), IIGS port of the popular first-person shooter, available on February 14th as a freeware product
- *The Apple Blossom* ceases publication
- America Online purchases CompuServe Information Services

May

- *BYTE* ceases publication
- KEGS emulator ported to Linux on x86 computers

July

- 10th annual KansasFest; web site specifically for KFest is created for the first time
- GSoft BASIC (The Byte Works) for the IIGS announced
- KEGS emulator ported to Linux on PowerPC

September

- Marinetti 2.0

December

- CompuServe (now owned by America Online) discontinues its text access, requiring a proprietary front-end program

1999

January

- Delphi begins to mirror its text-only content to web-accessible pages
- Patches are needed to update ProDOS to handle dates for 1999 and beyond

February

- CompuServe closes APPUSER, the Apple II user forum

March
- Joe Kohn's multi-system chats are reduced to only Delphi and Genie, as CompuServe drops its text access and excludes direct Apple II computer connections

April
- Genie begins to experience hardware and software failures. For three weeks, the A2 Roundtable is completely inaccessible, even to the sysops
- Scantron Quality Computers releases all former Q Labs branded software for the Apple II as freeware; within a year, all traces of Quality Computers were gone, and the name reverted back to the original, Scantron Corporation

May
- The Genie A2 Roundtable is again working, but continues to experience sporadic failures during the rest of the year
- Seven Hills Software, long-time Apple II software publisher, changes its name to My eSource

July
- *Shareware Solutions II* (unofficially) ceases publication
- Sweet16 (Eric Shepherd), BeOS port of F.E. Systems' Bernie][The Rescue Apple IIGS emulator

August
- GSoft BASIC (The Byte Works; language) now available

September
- Sequential Systems announces it will be making one final run of 200 RamFAST SCSI controller cards; by late in the year, the company has changed into an Internet service provider

October
- Delphi drops support for direct dialup, requiring text-based access via a Telnet connection; this move makes it necessary for Apple II using members of Delphi to get some other dialup account that offers Telnet, in order to continue to access the Delphi A2 and A2Pro forums
- Several important Apple II programs have user-contributed patches to deal with Y2K-related date issues

December
- Members of Genie's SFRT (Science Fiction Roundtable) begin to hold a wake to watch the last hours of Genie, starting December 27. The final end of the Genie legacy text service is on December 30 at 2:15 pm PST

2000

July
- KansasFest, dubbed "Y][KFest," webcasts its sessions

August
- Marinetti Open Source Project announced on Delphi A2 Pro forum

November
- Delphi makes its services free, but also drops maintenance for its Telnet and text-based access; though still available via a web browser, traffic on the A2 and A2Pro forums drops dramatically
- KEGS is ported to Windows, as KEGS32

December
- Syndicomm open its own Telnet-accessible home for Apple II users, modeled after the format of GEnie in the mid-1990s
- Delphi and Well Engaged combine to form Prospero Technologies, which is supposed to keep Delphi running

2001

January
- My eSource (formerly Seven Hills Software) is no longer in business
- Syndicomm Online begins service

February
- Delphi announces that the text and web access to its forums will no longer be synchronized

May
- Delphi completely discontinues text-based access to its forums, while continuing web-based access

2002

May
- CFFA (Compact Flash for Apple) card (Rich Dreher), allows a CF card to work as a solid-state disk drive for the Apple II
- *Call-A.P.P.L.E.* (digital) begins publication

June
- Vince Briel releases his Replica I, an Apple-1 compatible computer, pre-assembled or in kit form.

July
- At KansasFest 2002, Eric Shepherd announces Project Barney, an agreement with Softdisk Publishing to allow Syndicomm to distribute the Apple II publications *Softdisk* and *Softdisk G-S* on CD-ROM
- KEGS is ported to Mac OS X, as KEGS-OSX.

October

- ActiveGS (Free Tools Association), a web browser plugin that makes it possible to run Apple IIGS software in a web browser; it is derived from the KEGS emulator v0.60

November

- Ken Dickey releases his own update to KEGS that runs under Mac OS X, Windows, and Linux

2003

April

- Virtual II (Gerard Putter), Apple II Plus emulator, including speaker sounds and emulation of the Apple II cassette interface; later version included sounds of the Disk II drive while in operation and added emulation of the Apple IIe

July

- 15th annual KansasFest; Apple co-founder Steve Wozniak gives the keynote
- Marinetti 3.0 beta (Richard Bennett)
- CD-ROM releases of *Softdisk* and *UpTime* (Syndicomm)

2004

March

- KEGS-X, a port of KEGS for the Xbox game console

July

- Sweet16 (F.E. Systems), first experimental release of a Mac OS X version

2005

February

- Silver Platter (Kelvin Sherlock), a web server, running on a IIGS as a New Desk Accessory

June

- Uther Apple II Ethernet card (A2Retrosystems)

July

- KansasFest is held at a new venue, Rockhurst University, still in Kansas City, Missouri

August

- Mockingboard v1 (Henry Courbis), a clone of Sweet Micro Systems version C of the Mockingboard sound card

2006

May

- *1 MHz* (hosted by Carrington Vanston), the first Apple II podcast

July

- Sweet16 (Eric Shepherd) IIGS emulator for Mac OS X
- Mark Munz begins work on Deja IIx, an update to the Deja] [emulator for AppleWorks 5, designed to run under Mac OS X.
- *A2Unplugged* (hosted by Ryan Suenaga), podcast about the Apple II

December

- AppleIIGo emulator, written in Java, as a Mac OS X widget

2007

August

- *The Lamp!* ceases publication

November

- LittlePower Adapter (Littlejohn Systems), Apple II replacement power supply; company eventually has available power supplies for the Apple II, IIe, and IIGS

2008

January

- Dan Budiac is the winning bidder on eBay for a new-in-box, never opened Apple IIc from 1988; for his winning bid of $2600, he joyfully opens the box to use the Apple IIc

July

- 20th annual KansasFest

2009

July

- AOL shuts down CompuServe Classic (what was left of the old CompuServe)

October

- CC65 (C language for Apple II)

2010

June

- Syndicomm Online closes down

July

- First presentation of "Apple II Forever" awards at KansasFest
- Mockingboard v1a (Tom Arnold), an authorized clone of ReactiveMicro's Mockingboard v1 card

October

- A2Central BBS closes down

2011

February

- Best of FTA app for iOS (Free Tools Association), based on the ActiveGS emulator; bundles many of the famous FTA demos for the Apple IIGs; enterprising hackers find ways to put other disk images into the archive to run Apple II software on iOS devices
- Open Apple (hosted by Ken Gagne and Mike Maginnis), Apple II podcast

July

- A2MP3 card (Vince Briel), allows an Apple II to act as a host and power supply for a USB memory stick containing a collection of MP3 songs
- CFFA 3000 (Rich Dreher), an update to his earlier CFFA compact flash adapter for the Apple II, now supporting USB memory sticks

October

- Apple co-founder Steve Jobs passes away on October 5 after a long battle with cancer

2012

June

- 35th anniversary of the release of the Apple II
- *The New Apple II User Guide* (written by David Finnigan), the first book about the Apple II printed in over a decade

August

- *What's Where In The Apple* (written by William F. Luebbert), re-released as an ebook, updated and enhanced

2013

July

- 25th annual KansasFest, with keynote by Randy Wigginton; Steve Wozniak make a surprise appearance, and both he and Wigginton stayed to listen to over half of the sessions presented; also present was a genuine Apple-1, brought to KFest by its owner after he heard Woz was there

INDEX

///SHH Systeme, 362
& command (Applesoft II), 53
110 baud, 95
1200 baud, 95
128KDE Soft Disk, 267
18SRC, 267
1977 Trinity, 40, 55, 61, 151, 196
1984 commercial, 246
2020 Reference Manual, 148
2600 Magazine, 396
300 baud, 95
3D Logo, 444
4004 microprocessor, 7-8, 133
45-RPM record, 79
5 1/4 inch floppy disk, 56, 353
555 timer (chip), 59
556 timer (chip), 59
6501 microprocessor, 16
6502 microprocessor, 164
6502 assembley language, 116
6502 microprocessor, 11, 16, 48, 80
6522 VIA chip, 312
65802 microprocessor, 164
65816 microprocessor, 164, 340, 441
65c02 microprocessor, 142, 143, 164, 340
6800 microprocessor, 11, 163
68000 microprocessor, 163, 339
6801 microprocessor, 163
6802 microprocessor, 163
6809 microprocessor, 80, 163
73 magazine, 383
8-inch floppy disks, 353
8/16 Central, 430, 450, 456
80-column cards, 92-94
80-columns, 136, 193, 197-198
80-Micro magazine, 383, 454
8008 microprocessor, 7-8, 133
8031 microprocessor, 333
8048 microprocessor, 164
8051 microprocessor, 164
8080 microprocessor, 8, 133
A.P.P.L.E., 44, 47, 82, 90,
    143, 217, 340, 439

A/D converter cards, 334
A+ Disk Magazine, 382
A+ magazine, 274, 290,
    349, 381-383, 427
A2 on Disk, 449
A2-Central, 175, 380, 449
A2-Central Developer Conference, 510
A2-Central Summer Conference, 159,
    371, 483, 487, 510-511
A2Central.com, 499, 505
A2Pro, 393
AAUI, 483
ABC Evening News with
    Peter Jennings, 454
Absoft, 405
AC/BASIC, 405
Accelerator II, 143
Accelerator IIe, 143
accelerators, 142-144, 413-416
Accessory Parts Division, 305
Accidental Empires, 222
accoustic coupler, 96
Accu-Weather, 495
ACE, 367
ACE 100, 318
ACE 1000, 318-319
ACE 1000 Plus, 319
ACE 1100, 319
ACE 1200, 319
ACE 2000 series, 320
ACE 500, 320
acoustic modems, 106
Adams, Cindy, 512
Adams, Tony, 332
ADB, 346
ADB connector, 305-306
Advanced Disk Utility, 369
Advanced Research Projects
    Agency (see "ARPA")
Adversary Video Games system, 306
advertising (Apple II), 216
advertising (AppleWorks), 274, 276
Ahl, David, 381

Ahs newsletter, 452
AIM-65, 80
Air Force Academy, 166
ALA Payroll One Step, 425
Albuquerque, New Mexico, 10
Alcorn, Al, 6
ALF 8088 co-processor, 142
ALF Music Card MC16, 169
ALF Products, Inc., 142, 169
ALF's Apple Music II, 169
All One Farm, 18
Allen, Paul Gardener, 8, 134
Alltech Electronics, 361
ALOHANet, 103
alphaSyntauri, 169
Alps Electric Company, 60
Altair 680 (microcomputer), 11
Altair 8800, 9-13, 105, 133, 185
Alto (computer), 240
America Online (see "AOL")
American National Standards
    Institute (see "ANSI")
American Red Cross, 457
Amiga, 108, 399, 410
Anadex, 233
analog/digital converter cards, 334
Androbot, Inc., 333
ANIMALS, 71
ANSI, 253, 356
ANSI C standards, 445
ANSI character set, 108
AOL, 112, 294, 388, 503-504
AOL Time Warner, 504
APDA, 82-83
Apocalypse I, 398
Apocalypse II, 398
Apple (naming the company), 18
Apple 1 (design by Wozniak), 13-17
Apple 3.5 drive, 355-356, 477
Apple 5.25 drive, 355
Apple Assembly Line (newsletter), 185
Apple Assembly Lines (assembler), 163

Apple Attachment Unit
  Interface (see "AAUI")
Apple BASIC (see "Integer BASIC")
Apple Blossom, The, 460
Apple Box (primitive modem), 90
Apple Campus, 486
Apple CD, 362
Apple Centronics Printer Card, 91
Apple Clock, 335
Apple Color Plotter, 236-237
Apple Communications Card, 98
Apple Computer Company
  (inception), 17-21
Apple Computer Company
  (incorporation), 20
Apple Computer UK, 148, 156
Apple Computer's Dow Jones
  Portfolio Evaluator, 494
Apple Desktop Bus (see "ADB")
Apple Direct, 509
Apple DMP (see "Apple Dot
  Matrix Printer")
Apple DOS, 109, 205
Apple Dot Matrix Printer, 235
Apple File Exchange, 368
Apple Forth, 256
Apple FORTRAN, 253-254
Apple Graphics Tablet, 308-309
Apple Hand Controllers, 306-307
Apple II (product introduction), 36
Apple II (units sold), 122
Apple II Business Unit, 511
Apple II Communications
  Interface Card, 91
Apple II Continuation
  Engineering Group, 511
Apple II design, 27-35
Apple II Ethernet Card, 483, 487
Apple II Euromod, 149
Apple II Europlus, 149
Apple II Forever, 246
Apple II High Speed SCSI card, 360, 486
Apple II Individual
  Achievement Award, 452
Apple II j-Plus, 150
Apple II Museum, 248
Apple II Parallel Interface Card, 91
Apple II Parallel Printer Interface Card, 90
Apple II Plus, 115-123, 322
Apple II prototype, 24
Apple II Reference Manual, 90, 117, 317
Apple II Review, The, 387
Apple II SCSI card, 359
Apple II Serial Interface Card, 91
Apple II Super Serial Card, 93, 346
Apple II System Utilities, 367

Apple II Vendor Directory, 461
Apple II Video Overlay Card, 409
Apple II Workstation Card, 482
Apple IIA, 193
Apple IIB, 193
Apple IIc, 320-321
Apple IIc Plus, 477-480
Apple IIe, 320-321
Apple IIe 80-Column Text Card, 267
Apple IIe Emulator Card, 480-481
Apple IIe Enhanced, 202
Apple IIGS, 108, 339-351
Apple IIGS Buyer's Guide, The,
  290, 386-388, 459
Apple IIGS Graphics & Sound, 387
Apple IIGS Memory Expansion Card, 412
Apple IIGS Plus, 491
Apple III, 127, 272, 404
Apple III (development), 193-197
Apple III operating system (see "SOS")
Apple IIx, 341-342
Apple ImageWriter, 235
Apple ImageWriter II, 235-236
Apple IPO, 240
Apple Language System, 128
Apple LaserWriter, 236
Apple Learning Strategy, 327
Apple Letter Quality Printer, 235
Apple Logo (language), 259
Apple logo (wood-cut), 22
Apple Logo II (language), 259
Apple Mafia, The, 396
Apple Modem 1200, 98
Apple Modem 300, 98
Apple Mouse II, 313
apple orchard (farm), 18
Apple Orchard magazine, 153, 175-176
Apple Pascal, 198
Apple Pascal 1.2, 261-262
Apple Pascal System (see "Pascal System")
Apple Personal Modem, 99
Apple Pie (software), 272
Apple PILOT, 208, 257
Apple Plot, 208, 218
Apple Post, 208
Apple Programmer's
  Workshop (see "APW")
Apple Programmers and Developers
  Association, 82-83, 509
Apple Pugetsound Program Library
  Exchange (see "A.P.P.L.E.")
Apple Scribe printer, 236, 243
Apple SCSI Manager, 370
Apple Silentype, 233
Apple Slices, 154
Apple Software Bank, 218

Apple Star Trek, 79
Apple StyleWriter, 417
Apple Super Serial Card, 92
Apple SuperDrive, 484
Apple SuperPILOT, 258
Apple User, 155-156
Apple Worm, 392
Apple Writer, 178, 208,
  218, 225, 271, 377
Apple Writer][, 228
Apple Writer 2.0, 228
Apple Writer 2.1, 228
Apple Writer IIe, 228
Apple-1, 58, 507
Apple-1 club, 26
Apple-1 early user experiences, 25
Apple-1 magazine advertisement, 23
Apple-1 Owner's Club, 26
Apple-Cat II, 96
APPLE-TREK, 74, 75
Apple.Rx, 395
Apple's User Group Connection, 486
Apple2000 magazine, 154
AppleBug, 162
AppleFest, 414, 468, 483, 501, 508-509
AppleFORTH 1.2, 256
AppleLink, 500
AppleLink Industrial Edition, 501
AppleLink Personal Edition, 297, 501
AppleNet, 107
AppleQuerque Computer Club, 488
Apples BC News, 461
Apples British Columbia
  Computer Society, 110
AppleSeed, 86
APPLESIG, 290
Applesoft, 327, 333, 401-403, 448
APPLESOFT (program), 71
Applesoft 3, 404
Applesoft Firmware Card,
  71, 115, 127, 265
Applesoft I, 48-51
Applesoft I manual, 51
Applesoft II, 52
Applesoft Tool Kit, 164
AppleTalk, 345-346, 367, 482
APPLEVISION, 159
AppleWorks, 152, 185, 210, 221, 229,
  337, 377, 430, 452, 454
AppleWorks 1.x (development), 271-275
AppleWorks 2.0, 275-276
AppleWorks 3.0, 280-283
AppleWorks 4, 284-286, 458
AppleWorks 4.3, 328
AppleWorks 5, 286
AppleWorks 5.1, 473

INDEX

AppleWorks Forum, 453-454
AppleWorks GS, 370, 460, 462, 466-474
AppleWorks Journal, 454
Applied Engineering, 98, 164, 172,
    188, 267-268, 336, 361, 409,
    411, 412-413, 415
Applied Ingenuity, 480
APW, 406, 443
APW/C, 445
Archiver, 373
Ariel Publishing Co., 430
Arkley, John, 116, 165, 406
ARPA, 101-105
ARPA Information Processing
    Techniques Office, 101
ARPANET, 13, 101-105
Artscene (BBS), 108
Artsci, 80
ASCII art, 107
ASCII characters, 231, 258
Ashton-Tate, 135
ASIC chips, 412
Asimov, Isaac, 289
ASR-33 Teletype (see "Teletype
    model ASR-33")
assemblers, 441-443
Assembley Lines: The Book, 183
assembly language, 159-167
Associated Press news, 495
Association for Computing Machinery, 23
AT&T, 91, 102, 105
ATA, 357
Atari, 16, 215
Atari 2600, 500
Atari 400, 86
Atari 800, 80, 86, 201, 215-216
Atari Corporation, 311
Atari Logo, 259
Atari Lynx, 445
Atari ST, 399, 430, 455
Atari VCS cartridge, 500
Atari XL, 445
Atari, Inc., 5-6
Atkinson, Bill, 126, 347
Atlanta, Georgia, 295
Atlantic City, New Jersey, 24, 507
Audio Animator, 411
audio record, 79
Auricchio, Rick, 67, 199
Australia, 322, 326
Australian Apple Review, 156-157
Australian Business PC Report, 156
Australian Commodore Review, 156
automated dress pattern program, 79
Autostart ROM, 117, 265
AutoWorks, 279

Avante-Garde, 94
Avila College, 510, 512
Axlon, Inc., 266
Aztec C65, 261
B-Sider, The, 358
Babylon 5, 299
Back-It-Up!, 186
backpack (Bell & Howell), 118-119
Bag of Tricks 2, 395
Bank Street Music Writer, 171
Bank Street Writer, 423
bank-switching memory, 199
BASIC, 11, 185
    (Apple II), 32
    (on the Apple 1), 21-22
    III, 404
    Input/Output
        System (see "BIOS")
Basis 108, 325-326
Basis Microcomputer, GmbH, 325
BASUG, 153
Battery RAM, 398
baud, 95
Baum, Allen, 2, 4, 13, 30, 78
BBS, 105-111, 287, 393, 430, 500
BBS uses, 106
BBS: the Documentary, 514
BDS C, 261
Beagle Bros, 182, 276, 278-280, 404, 447
Beagle Buddies, 283
Beagle Compiler, 404
Beagle Works, 271
BeagleWrite, 468
Because It's Time Network (see "BITNET")
Bell & Howell, 118
Bell & Howell Apple II, 317
Bell 101 dataset, 95
Bell 103 dataset, 95
Bell 103A dataset standard, 91
Bell 202 standard, 95
Bell 212 standard, 95
Bell Laboratories, 104, 260
Bell Telephone, 95, 105
Benatar, Pat, 246
Beneath Apple DOS (1981), 65, 67
Bennett, Richard, 301-302
Berkley, California, 335
Bernie][The Rescue, 437, 513
Best of Contact '78, 86
best selling software, 221, 225, 521-532
Betamax, 314
Big Blue Disk, 422, 423
Big Mac, 163, 165-166
Binary II, 110
binary numbers, 24
BIOS, 127, 134

Bird, Alan, 279, 281, 404, 417
Birmingham Sound Reproducers, 334
Bishop, Bob, 79, 514
Bit Pad, 308
BITNET, 104
Bits & Pieces Technology, 414
Blackjack (computer game), 26
Blackout virus, 398-399
block lists, 206
Blue Book, 51, 402
blue boxes, 4
BlueDisk card, 362
Bolt, Beranek and Newmann, 259
bomb (practical joke), 3
Book of Macintosh, The, 240
BookMac, 475
bootleg tapes, 4
Boston Computer Society, 188, 508
Boston Plaza Castle, 508
Boston, Massachusetts, 279, 332
Boy Scouts, 512
Brandt, Randy, 278-283, 430, 473
Brazell, Rob, 499
Brazilian import restrictions, 317
Breakout, 6, 24, 27, 169, 306
Bredon, Glen, 165, 395, 396
BRIAN'S THEME, 38, 75, 120
brick (see "power supply")
BRICK OUT, 74, 75
Bricklin, Dan, 222
British Apple Systems User
    Group (see "BASUG")
Broderbund, 182, 310, 397, 423
Broedner, Walt, 197
Bruns, Dan, 499
Brutal Deluxe, 108
BSR X-10, 97
BSR, Ltd., 334
BubbleJet, 417
Buckley, William R., 392
Budge, Bill, 312
Bugbyter, 165
bulletin board (GEnie), 296
bulletin board system (see "BBS")
bundles (Apple II), 45
burn-in (Apple 1 testing), 19
BURP virus, 398
Burroughs (electronics manufacturer), 3
bus (Altair), 11
Bushnell, Nolan, 5, 6, 266, 333
Busicom, 7
Busicom 141-PF desktop calculator, 7
Business Basic, 404, 406
Business Solutions, 271
BYTE magazine, 38, 40, 173, 177, 200-
    201, 332, 349-350, 383

Byte Shop, The, 18-24, 27
Byte Works, The, 212, 407, 438, 443
C language, 261, 444
C-Vue LCD, 250
C. Itoh, 235
C1P, 80
C64 (see "Commodore 64")
CACHE (see "Chicago Area Computer Hobbyist Exchange")
Cadillac Modern Encyclopedia, 494
Cal-400, 326
calculator crash, 9, 15
calculators, 4
California Polytechnic State University at San Luis Obispo, 392
Call Computer, 50, 117
Call-A.P.P.L.E., 47, 82-84, 120, 348, 392, 439
Cambridge Marketing, 508
Cambridge, Massachusetts, 259
Canon, 417
Canon, Maggie, 381
Cap'n Crunch, 256
Cap'n Software, 256
Caplin, Bruce, 462, 499
Carlston, Doug, 182
Carmack, Adrian, 427
Carmack, John, 427, 514
Carrolton, Texas, 267
Carson City, Nevada, 357
case design, 243
case design (Apple II), 33-34, 40
Case, Steve, 500-504
Cassette Applesoft, 85
cassette interface (Apple-1), 22
cassette recorder, 494
cassette tape, 11
cassettes (Apple II), 42-43
CAT, The (computer), 322
catalog listing (DOS 3.1), 71
Catalyst, 466
Cats (Broadway play), 454
Cavanaugh, Steve, 460
Cayman GatorBox, 513
CB radio market, 78
CB Simulator, 292
CBBS (see "Computer Bulletin Board System")
CC65, 445
CDrive, 480
censorship, 186-187
Central Coast Software, 500
Central Point Software, 186, 323
Central Processing Unit, 7
Centronics 730 printer, 232
Centronics Data Computer Corporation, 90

Centronics Model 101, 90
Centronics printer, 50
Centronics printer interface, 322
Cereal Killer, 396
Cerf, Christopher, 310
CES, 58-59, 63, 193, 309, 424
CFFA, 363
CFFA 3000, 363
Chalkboard company, 249
character display (Apple 1), 17
Chatsworth, California, 141
Chattanooga, Tennesse, 456
checkbook program, 56
Chicago Area Computer Hobbyist Exchange, 106
Chinook Technology, 358, 480
Chlebek, Terry, 360
Choose Your Own Adventure, 424
Christensen, Ward, 106, 109
Chuck E. Cheese, 333
Chula Vista, California, 230
Citizen's Band radio system, 292
Civil War, 289
CKeeper, 480
Claris, 275, 467
ClarisWorks, 271
ClarisWorks Journal, 454
ClarisWorks Users Group, 454
Classic Desk Accessories, 370
clipboard, 273
CLOAD magazine, 420
clock, 345
clocks, 335-337
clones, 317-328
CloseView, 373
CMS Enhancements, 359
co-processors, 141-142
COBOL, 255
code names (Apple IIc), 242
color (Apple II), 27-28
COLOR DEMO, 220
COLOR DEMOS, 71
Colucci, Jill, 246
command line interface, 218-220
Commodities News Service, 447
Commodore 128, 500
Commodore 64, 86, 201, 344, 389, 421, 500
Commodore Amiga (see "Amiga")
Commodore Electronics, Inc., 28, 39, 48, 145
Commodore PET (see "PET")
comp.sys, 111
comp.sys.apple2, 111
comp.sys.mac, 111
Comp*U*Star, 494

company logo, 37
Compaq, 357
compiled language, 160-161
Complete Graphics System, 182
Complete Pascal 1.0, 443
Complete Technology, Inc., 443
composite video, 322
CompuCom, 288
CompuServe, 112, 154, 291-295, 437, 453, 494, 497
CompuServe Information Service, 291
CompuServe Network Services, 294
Computer Bulletin Board System, 106, 109
Computer Chronicles, 514
Computer Colorworks, 311
Computer Lib, 378-379
Computer Mart, The, 23, 27
Computer Science Research Network (see "CSNET")
Computer Shopper, 229, 236
ComputerEyes, 314
Computist, 185-191
concussion, 340
Config.sys (disk magazine), 451
Congo (game), 391
Consumer Electronics Show (see "CES")
Consumer Reports, 178
Contact magazine, 85-86, 176
Contiki, 513
Control Data Systems, 116, 357
control panel, 347-348
Control Panel, 398
Control Panel New Desk Accessory, 374
Control Program for Microcomputers (see "CP/M")
Control Video Corporation, 500
Controller, The (program), 207
cooling fan (Apple II), 34
coordinates, 311
coprocessors, 412-413
Copy II Plus, 186, 323
copy protection, 185
copyright laws, 317, 318
Core, 188
Cortland Programmer's Workshop, 443
Corvus Systems, 207, 357
Cotton Trade News, 447
Couch, John, 241
counter byte, 390
Courbis, Henry, 171
CowTOONS, 432
CP/M, 110, 133-136, 217, 319, 322, 326
CPU (see "Central Processing Unit")
crackers (copy protection), 108
Cragmont cream soda, 2

INDEX

Cream Soda Computer, 2
Creative Computing, 173, 278, 381, 383
Cricket, 170
Cringely, Robert X., 222
Crock O'Gold, 505
Cromemco Dazzler, 24
cross-assembler, 117, 161
Crossley, John, 176
Crotty, Cameron, 385
CSNET, 104
CT-20, 358
CT-30, 358
Cuff, Doug, 434, 437, 451, 458, 513
Cupertino, California, 2, 357
customer registration cards, 282
CV Technology, 360, 410, 412
CW Communications, Inc., 383
CyberAIDS, 393-395
dacron, 311
daisy wheel printer, 231
Dali, Paul, 242
Dallas Apple Corps, 163
Dallas Semiconductor, 336
Dangerous Dave, 426
DARPA (see "ARPA")
Darth Vader, 179-180
Dartmouth University, 81
data compression, 110
data packets, 102
Data Reporter, 189
database management, 271
Database Publications, 155
DataLink 1200, 98
DataLink 2400, 98
Datanetics, 30-31, 305
Datel, 410
David-DOS, 207
Davis, Morgan, 396
Dazzle Draw, 310
DB Master, 207, 271
DB Pix, 283
DB-9 connector, 309
dBase, 135
DCA (see "Defence Communications Agency")
De Anza Community College, 2
Dead Lord, 396
Defence Communications Agency, 103
Deja][, 473
Deja][x, 474
Dellinger, Joe, 390-391
Delphi, 301, 436, 493-499
Delphi Corporation, 499
delphi.com, 499
Democrat, 107
Demon Internet, 112

Demoscene (BBS), 108
Denman, Don, 404
Denver, Colorado, 142, 430
Depew, William, 180
Desk Accessories, 370
DeskJet 500, 285, 417
DeskJet 520, 417
DeskJet 560c, 417
DeskTools (TimeOut module), 280
desktop, 273
Desktop Publishing Association, 432
Detroit, Michigan, 3
device drivers, 205
Devner, Colorado, 443
Dialcom, 495
Dialog, 495
Diana (see "Low Cost Apple")
Diaz, Tony, 489, 513
Dick Smith Electronics, 322
Digital Equipment Corporation, 2, 7
digital magazines, 419-440
Digital Paintbrush System, 311-312
Digital Research, 133
Digital Vision, Inc., 314
DIN sockets, 119
DisAssembler (program), 26
Disbrow, Steven, 454
Disk Applesoft bugs, 71
Disk Cache, 370
disk capacity, 59
disk controller (driver), 65
disk drive mechanism, 57
disk drives (see "floppy drives")
Disk II (costs), 60
Disk II (design), 56-60
Disk IIc, 248
Disk IIc, 354
disk interface card, 57
disk magazines (see "digital magazines")
disk maps, 206
disk operating system (see "DOS"), 63
disk sectors, 59
disk storage density, 127
disk track, 59
distributed network, 102
Diversi-DOS, 207, 392, 425
DMA, 485
DNS, 105
domain name server (see "DNS")
Doms, Dennis, 380, 394, 449
Doom, 427
DOS 3.1
 (development of), 63-68
 bugs, 72
 error messages, 71-72
 features, 69

 manual, 68
 startup screen, 70
 user experiences, 72
 version naming, 67-68
DOS 3.2, 73
DOS 3.2 manual, 73
DOS 3.2 System Master disks, 74
DOS 3.3 development, 136-139
DOS File Buffers, 65
DOS File Manager, 207
DOS hooks, 53
DOS INIT command, 70
dot matrix printer, 90, 231
dot-com bubble, 493, 496
double density floppy disks, 353
double sided floppy disks, 353
DoubleData, 283
Dow Jones, 288
Dow Jones information service, 494
downloading files (BBS), 109
Dr. Dobb's Journal, 507
DRAM, 16, 58, 143
Draper, John, 256
Dreher, Rich, 363
Drucker, Ivan, 516
drug use, 3
Drum-Key, 170
Duke University, 111
Dunning, John R., 445
DuoDisk, 354
Dvorak keyboard, 203, 245
Dylan, Bob, 4
Dynamic RAM (DRAM), 16
earthquake, 248
Easter egg, 350-351
Easter egg (Applesoft II), 53
Eastern Michigan University, 452
Eastern religion/philosophy, 5, 6
EasyWriter, 256
Echo II card, 170
ECON Technologies, 361, 411
EDASM, 165, 207
Editor/Assembler II (see "EDASM")
Educational Computer Conference, 453
Egan, Lorraine Hopping, 424
EGO Systems, 455-457, 463
Eisenhower, Dwight, 101
Electric Duet, 108, 169, 421
Electronic Arts, 396
Elizabeth Computer Center, 331
Elk Cloner, 390
Ellsworth, Jeri, 516
email, 102, 104-105, 495-496
Emerson, Keith, 170
Emerson, Lake & Palmer, 170
Empire Strikes Back, The, 511

encyclopedia, 493-494
Engineering Department, The, 412
Enhance magazine, 457
enhancements (Apple II), 44
Enhancer][, 305
Ensoniq Corporation, 170, 344
Ensonique, 513
Epson, 233
Epson FX, 328
error messages (DOS 3.1), 71-72
Esmay, Dean, 300, 302, 505
Espinosa, Chris, 36, 41
Esslinger, Harmut, 243
Eternal September, 112
Ethernet, 482-483, 513
Ethernet card, 371
etiquette on Usenet, 112
Euroapple, Inc., 145
European magazines, 151-157
European voltage standards, 6
Europress, 155
eWorld, 503
Exorciser, 398
expansion slots (Apple II), 29-30
Exposition Management, 509
Expressload, 369-370
Extended 80-Column Card, 476
external modems, 95-96
Exxon Enterprises, 174
Eyes, David, 166, 443
Fahey, Sean, 506
Fairchild Research & Development, 58
Fairchild Semiconductor, 1, 28
Family & Home
    Computing Magazine, 423
Fancher, Bruce, 396
FAQ, 113
FCC (see US Federal
    Communications Commission)
FDOS, 320
feedthroughs (PCB), 59
Ferbrache, David, 389
Fernandez, Bill, 2-3
Festering Hate, 395-396
FID, 207
file downloading (BBS), 109
File Manager, 65, 67
file naming (SOS), 205
File System Translator (see "FST")
file transfer protocol (see "FTP")
file types (DOS 3.1), 69
file types (Pascal System), 128
FileMaster (TimeOut module), 280
Fillmore, Kent, 297, 431, 501
Finder, 367, 369, 373
    Finkenstadt, Andy, 303

Fire in the Valley (book), 59
firmware, 389
firmware (Apple II Plus), 116
firmware (IIGS), 346
First Class Peripherals, 357
First International Conference on
    Computer Communication, 102
first person shooters, 427
first virus, 389
Fishhead's Children, 450
fishing line, 311
Fitzgerald, 441
flat panel display, 475
floating point operations, 47
floppy drives, 55-58
floppy ROM, 79
floptical drive, 362
flow charts, 1
Flying Colors, 311
FM (see "frequency modulation")
FM broadcasting, 288
Focal language (Apple-1), 25
Focus Hard Card, 361
Fontrix fonts, 312
FontWorks, 279
FORMAT (DOS command), 65
Format IIe, 425
formatting of a floppy disk, 64
FORTH, 255-257
FORTRAN, 2, 125, 253-255
FORTRAN II, 163
FORTRAN IV, 163
forums, 292
Fountain Valley, California, 30
FP (DOS 3.1 command), 71
Frame Up, 447-448
Franklin Computer Corporation, 318-321
Franklin CX, 320
Franklin Office Manager, 320
Frankston, Bob, 223
FrEdWriter, 230
Free Tools Association, 108, 152
FreeWriter, 230
French, Gordon, 13
frequency counter, 4
frequency modulation, 59
Frequently Asked Questions (see "FAQ")
friction feed, 234
Frieberger and Swain (authors), 59
Frogdesign, 243
Frogger, 216
FST, 368, 372
FTA (see "Free Tools Association")
FTP, 287, 495
full-duplex, 91, 95
Fylstra, Dan, 223

Gagne, Ken, 463
Game BASIC (see "Integer BASIC")
game design (Atari), 5
Game of Life, 23
game paddles (see "paddles")
Gameline, 500
GamePaks, 218
Gamer's Edge, 427
Garamond Condensed Italic, 243
Gates, William Henry III, 8, 22, 185, 403
GCOS, 295
GCR (see "group code recording")
GE CoPilot, 298
GEIS, 295, 500
Gemmell, Rob, 243
General Comprehensive Operating
    System (see "GCOS")
General Electric, 433
General Electric Information
    Services (see "GEIS")
General Videotex Corporation, 494
GEnie, 154, 229, 292, 295-304,
    385, 393, 430, 449
GEnie A2 Roundtable, 462
Genie Lite, 300
GEnie Master, 298
GEnieLamp, 451
GEnieLamp A2/A2Pro, 432
GEnieLamp ST, 431
GeniScan GS4500 Hand Scanner, 410
Georgia Online, 295
German version of Apple IIe, 203
Gernelle, Francois, 7
Get Lamp, 514
Gibson Laboratories, 310
Gibson Light Pen, 310
Gibson Light Pen System, 311
Gibson, Steve, 310-311
Gleason, Joe, 284-285, 457
GNO/ME, 112
Golden United Life Insurance Co., 291
Golding, Val J., 47, 82, 166, 175, 439
Goltz, John, 291
Gopher, 287
GraBASIC, 425
GraFORTH, 256-257
Grammar Gobble, 328
Granger, Indiana, 85
Graph (TimeOut module), 280
Graphical User Interface (see "GUI")
Graphically Speaking (book), 183
Graphics Exhibitor, 310
GraphicWriter III, 461, 462
Graphtrax ROM, 233
Grappler, 228
Gravenstein Apple User Group, 290, 489

INDEX

Green, Wayne, 383-384
group code recording, 59, 141, 322
GS BASIC, 404, 406
GS-RAM, 412
GS-RAM Plus, 412
GS-RAM Ultra, 412
GS-ShrinkIt, 110, 373
GS/OS, 368-369, 466, 513
    Finder, 444
    System 5, 369-371, 483
    System 6, 371-374, 470, 485, 486
    System 6.0.1, 483
GS+ magazine, 455-457, 430, 462
GSoft BASIC, 407
GSWorks, 468
GTE, 321
GUI, 378, 465, 502
Gumby, 342
guru, 6
Gus emulator, 513
H.A.L. Labs, 441
H&R Block, 291, 294
Haba Systems, 272
Hackensack, New Jersey, 299
hackers, 108-109
Haight, Charles, 186-187
half-duplex, 95
Hall, Tom, 427
Hamurabi (computer game), 26
Hancock, Herbie, 170
hand-held scanner, 410
hard core (magazine), 153
hard drive, 356-358, 485
hard reset, 117
Hardcore Computing, 186
Hardcore Computist, 188
Hare Krishna, 5
Harris, John, 215
Harvard Associates, 331
Harvard Business School, 222-223
Harvey, Kevin, 467
Harvey, Mike, 173
Harvey's Space Ship Repair, 177
Hauser, James, 392
Hawaii, 431
Hawkins, Trip, 224
Hayden Publishing, 407
Hayden Software, 162, 165, 167, 178, 442
Hayes command set, 98
Hayes Micromodem 100, 96
Hayes Micromodem II, 96
Hayes, Dennis C., 96
head load solenoid (disk drive), 57
heat generation, 245
Heath, 332
Heath Hero, 332

Heathkits, 3
Heinemann, Bill, 472
HERO-1, 332
Hertzfeld, Andy, 233, 312
Hewlett-Packard, 2, 4-5, 13, 28-29, 236
Hewlett-Packard Explorers Club, 3
Hewlett, Bill, 3
hexidecimal numbers, 24
hi-res graphics commands, 52
high-level language, 161
Hillman, Dan, 342
Hobart, Tasmania, 331
Holt, Rod, 34, 49, 57
Home Music Store, 499
Homebrew Computer
    Club, 13-18, 22, 507
Homebrew magazines, 77-87
Honeywell, 295
Hong Kong, 321
Hoover, Tom, 298
HOPALONG CASSIDY, 121
House of Representatives (US), 288
Houston, Texas, 177, 467, 508
HP (see "Hewlett-Packard")
HP 65 calculator, 18
HP-15C calculator, 432
HUFFIN, 164
Huston, Cliff, 49-51, 57-58
Huston, Dick, 49, 63, 65, 207, 209
Huthig-Verlag Publishing, 157
Hyde, Randall, 164, 175, 441
hydrogen peroxide, 514
Hyper Quarterly, 461
Hyper-C, 261
HyperBole, 429, 450
HyperCard, 379, 428
HyperCard IIGS, 380, 461, 485
HyperLogo, 444
hypermedia, 429
HyperStudio, 379, 428, 444
HyperText, 378-380
I/O connector, 306
IBM, 56
IBM 1130, 255
IBM 360 mainframe, 133, 166, 442
IBM 370 mainframe, 116
IBM Logo, 259
IBM PC (units sold), 122
IBM PC/AT, 357
IBM PCjr, 249
IBM Selectric typewriter, 31, 231
IBM-PC, 86, 190, 217, 412, 422
ICON, 451, 511
ICONference, 511
icons (GUI), 242
IDE, 357

IDG Communications, 383, 458
IDT Corporation, 299
II Alive, 457-459, 462
IIc System Clock, 337
III E-Z Pieces, 209, 272
ImageWriter, 314
ImageWriter LQ, 367
IMI-7710 hard drive, 357
IMSAI, 134
IMSAI 8080, 11, 49-50
inCider magazine, 184, 348,
    382, 383-386, 510
inCider/A+ magazine, 284, 382-
    383, 384-386, 457
Incredible Jack, The, 271
index hole sensor (disk drive), 57
India, 6, 447
Indiana, 462
INFINITE NO. OF MONKEYS, THE, 75
Infocast, 288
Information Age, 289
InfoWorld, 184, 381
Ingenuity, Inc., 480
Init Virus, 393
inkjet printers, 416-417
input devices, 305-315
Input/Output Unit, 199
Insite Peripherals, 362
Insoft, 256
Instant Pascal, 262
Institute for Information Systems, 125
Integer BASIC, 43, 47, 58, 120
Integer Firmware Card, 265
Integral Data Systems, 234
integrated circuit, 1
Intel, 1, 7-8, 28, 133
Interface Age, 30, 77-80, 173
interface cards, 90, 359
internal modems, 95
International Apple Core, 153, 175-176
International Computer Owners
    Network (see "ICON")
International Data Group (see "IDG"), 383
International Memories, Inc., 357
International Solutions, 366, 466
International Telephone &
    Telegraph (see "ITT")
International Timesharing, 163-164
international versions (Apple IIc), 244
Internet, 293-294, 462
Internet (development), 104
Internet Explorer, 493
Internet Protocol (see "IP")
Internet Service Provider (see "ISP")
interpreted language, 160-161
Introl/X-10 controller, 335

InWords, 411
Iomega Corporation, 362
IP, 104
IP-125 printer, 234
IP-225 printer, 234
iPad, 408
iPhone, 408
IPO (Apple), 240
iPod touch, 408
IRC, 506
ISP, 498
ITDA, 423
ITT 2020, 146, 317
ITT Consumer Products, 146
IWM chio, 355
Janoff, Rob, 37
Japanese Apple II computer, 150
Jawbreaker, 216
JEM Software, 283, 473
Jennings, Peter J., 223
Jet Propulsion Laboratory, 225
Jobs, Paul Reinhold (father), 3
Jobs, Steven Paul
    (Macintosh development), 239-242
    (Apple Computer Inc.
        formation), 17-21
    (leaving Apple), 347, 475-476
    (pre-Apple biography), 3-6
Jones, Bob, 77-78
Jones, Gareth, 461
Jones, Max, 462
joysticks, 307-308
Juiced.GS, 462, 516
Jupiter II (microcomputer), 11
Just Copies, 462
Kache Card, 360
Kane, Mike, 218
Kansas City Cassette interface standard, 79
Kansas City, Missouri, 371, 506, 507
KansasFest, 300, 302, 437,
    460, 496, 512-516
Kapor, Mitch, 225
katakana characters, 150
Kawasaki, Guy, 386
Kefauver, Amy (McKinley), 424
Kelly, Bill, 425-426
Kennedy, Bill, 510
Kersey, Bert, 182, 278, 448
keyboard, 11
keyboard (Apple II), 30-32
Keyboard Company, The, 305, 308
keyboard revisions (Apple II Plus), 121
keyboard synthesizer, 170
keypad, 305
KeyPlayer, 377
Kildall, Gary, 133-134

killer app, 159
Kilobaud magazine, 383
Kilobaud Microcomputing, 173, 383
KIM-1, 26, 80, 223
Kindall, Jerry, 457
Kinder Logo, 332
Klassen, Dan, 423
Knights of Shadow, 396
Koala Pad, 249, 309-310
Koala Technologies, 249, 311
Koffler, Gary, 180
Kohn, Joseph, 290, 295, 385-386, 457,
    459-460, 488, 490, 497, 512
Kottke, Dan, 6, 19, 312
Kovacs, Deborah, 423
Krell Logo, 259
Krell Software Corporation, 259
Kroupa, Patrick Karel, 396
Kussmaul Encyclopedia, 494
Kussmaul, Wes, 493
La Puente, California, 398
Lafayette, Colorado, 361
Lamp!, The, 436-438, 462, 498
Lancaster, Don, 229, 236
LANceGS card, 513
Lange, Joachim, 362
Language Card, 82, 198, 265
Language System, 257
Las Cruces Computer Club, 178
Las Vegas, Nevada, 58
Laser 100, 321
Laser 128, 323-324, 437
Laser 128EX, 324-325
Laser 128EX/2, 325
Laser 3000, 322
Laser Universal Disk Controller, 324
LaserJet printer, 236
LaserWriter, 367, 454, 461
Laughton, Paul (DOS programmer), 66
lawn sprinkler system, 335
Lazerware Microsystems, 164
LCD screen, 475
Lechner, Pieter (author), 65
Lee's Diskitis, 392
Legend Industries, Ltd., 267
Legion of Doom, 396
Lehtman, Harvey, 343
Leonis, Ted, 386
license (Applesoft), 402
LightningScan, 410
LightningScan GS, 411
Lingo, 326
link, 379
LISA Assembler, 164, 441
Lisa computer, 122, 127,
    194, 200, 378, 465

Lisa computer (development), 240
LISA816, 441
LISP, 259
Lissner, Rupert J. (AKA Robert),
    209, 272, 276, 467
LIST magazine, 386
List Processing (see "LISP")
lithium batteries, 336
LITTLE BRICKOUT, 120
Little, Gary, 110, 382
Liverpool UK Bulletin Board, 154
lo-res graphics commands, 52
Load Runner (virus), 397
Loadstar, 421
LocalTalk, 513
Locksmith, 186
Lode Runner (game), 397
Logitech, 410
Logo Computer Systems, Inc., 259
Logo language, 259-260, 331, 448
Lomond, California, 335
Longmont, Colorada, 357, 358
Lord Digital, 396
Lost Classics Project, The, 229
Lotus 1-2-3, 271, 274, 285
Lotus Development Corporation, 225
Louden, Bill, 295, 496
Louisiana Purchase, 103
Louisiana State University
    Medical Center, 420
Low Cost Apple, 197
low-level language, 161
LPS II Light Pen System, 310
LSD, 3
Lubbert, William F., 81
Lunar Lander (game), 26
Lutus, Paul, 169, 225, 256, 421
Lyons, Dave, 513
M*A*S*H, 178
M&R Electronics, 35, 44
M&R Enterprises, 92
M6800 (microcomputer), 11
Mac Computing, 386
Mac User, 156
Mac-envy, 339
MacBASIC, 403
MacBinary, 110
Macintosh, 122, 190, 239-242, 465
Macintosh Buyer's Guide, 388
Macintosh Classic, 486
Macintosh HFS, 372
Macintosh LC, 480
Macintosh Office, 475
Macintosh Programmer's Workshop, 281
Macintosh System 7, 486
Macintosh System 7.5, 512

INDEX

Macintosh User's Guide, The, 386-387
MacPaint, 275, 347
MacPascal, 263
Macrocosm (disk magazine), 451
macros, 279, 377
MacroWorks, 278
MacTech Quarterly, 83
MacWorks, 469
MacWrite, 275
Madison Avenue, New York City, 23
magazines, 447-464
Magic Memory, 322
magic menu, 221, 273
Magic Window II, 322
MagiCalc, 322
Main DOS Routines, 65, 67
mainframe computer, 7,
   95, 101, 161, 288
Manchester University, 155
Mangham, Jim, 420
Manhattan, New York City, 23
Manock, Jerry, 34, 243
manual
   (Apple II), 41, 215
   (Apple-1), 36
   (DOS 3.1), 68
   (DOS 3.2), 73
   (Applesoft I), 51
Manx Software Systems, 261
marijuana, 3
Marinetti, 513
Mark III timesharing system, 500
Mark Twain prototype, 485-
Mark-8 microcomputer, 8, 9
marketing (Apple II), 45
Markkula, Mike, 28, 36, 56,
   188, 207, 224, 239
Martens, Bill, 439
Massachusetts Institute of
   Technology (see "MIT")
MASTER CREATE program, 70
master disk, 70
Mastermind (game), 26
MAUG, 293
Maxfield, John, 396
MBA, 218
McCall's Dress Pattern Company, 80
McCarthy, John, 259
McDonald, Marc, 48
MCI WorldCom, 294
McIntosh Laboratory, 239
McKenna, Regis, 28
McNaughton, Robert, 424
McPheters, Wolfe, and Jones, 77-78
MD-BASIC, 405
Meakin, Derek, 155

MECC, 328, 423
Medfly, The (computer), 326
Mega II chip, 342
Melbourne, Australia, 332
memory expansion cards, 265-268
Memory Management Unit (see "MMU")
Memory Manager Toolbox, 366
MemoryMaster IIe, 267-268
Menlo Park, California, 13
Mensch, Bill, 340, 514
menus, 220-221, 465
Merlin, 165-166, 442
Merlin 128, 442
Merlin 16+, 442
Merlin 64, 442
Merlin 8/16, 442
Merlin Pro, 442
Merritt, Cathleen, 453-545
Merritt, Jim, 182, 471
message board, 106
MFM, 322
Michigan Association of Computer Users
   for Learning, 453
Micol Advanced BASIC, 406-407
Micol Systems, 406
Micral N, 7
Micro Cookbook, 276
Micro magazine, 80-81, 163
Micro Peripherals MPI model 99G, 119
MICRO-INK, Inc., 80
Micro-Peripherals, Inc., 362
Microchess, 26, 223
Microcomputer Associates, 11
Microcomputer Technologies, 143
Microcomputing magazine, 177, 383
Micromate Electronics, 97
Micromodem II, 97
MicroNET, 291
Micronet Modem, 97
Micropro, 135
Microproducts, 162
Microproducts/Apple II Assembler, 162
Microsense Computers Limited, 148
Microsoft, 48, 134, 402-403, 417
   BASIC, 321, 405
   Consumer Products, 134
   easter egg, 53
   FORTRAN, 254
   Office, 512
   SoftCard (see "SoftCard")
   Works, 271, 467, 469
Microsoft's first employee (see
   "McDonald, Marc")
Microtek, 233
MicroTimes, 290
Microzine, 423-424

Microzine, Jr., 424
MIDI, 170, 325, 369, 411
Midwest Affiliation of
   Computer Clubs, 291
military, 101
Mindscape, 171
Mini-Assembler, 120, 161
MiniScribe, 357
Ministry of Education (France), 148
Minitel, 152
Minneapolis, Minnesota, 508
Minnesota schools, 423
Mirage music synthesizer, 344
MIT, 223, 259
MITS (company), 9
MMU, 199
Mockingboard, 171
MOD (music file), 108
modems, 95, 455, 494
modem (110-baud), 50
Modem IIA, 98
Modem IIB, 98
Modem Magician, 110
Modem MGR, 110
Modified Frequency
   Modulation (see "MFM")
modulator-demodulator, 95
MODZap, 108
Molloy, Andy, 463
"monitor" (Apple 1 firmware), 14
Monitor IIc, 243, 248
Monitor III, 115
Monitor ROM, 30, 116-117, 147
Montellaro, John, 176-177
Moore, Rob, 344
Morgan Davis Group, 405
MOS Technology, Inc., 11, 15, 28, 80, 340
Mosby-Year Book, 460
Moscone Center, 246
Mossberg, Sandy, 174
motherboard revisions (Apple II Plus), 116
Motorola, 57
Motorola 6800 processor, 11
Mountain Computing, Inc., 169
Mountain Hardware, 335
Mountain Music System, 169-170
Mountain View, California, 3
mouse, 241, 244, 312, 465
Mouse IIc, 249
MouseDesk, 366, 466
MouseKeys, 373
MousePaint, 313
MouseText, 202-203, 228, 277, 313, 323
MouseWrite, 366
MPC BubDisk, 266
MPC Peripherals, 266

MPI, 233
MPW, 471
MR. FIXIT, 395
Mr. Invoice, 283
MRM recording system, 141
MS-DOS, 110, 399, 467, 503
MUFFIN, 164
Multi-Kache card, 360
Multiplan, 189
MultiScribe, 467-468
Munster, Germany, 325
Munz, Mark, 283, 473
Muppet Learning Keys, 310
Muppets, 310
Murdoch, Rupert, 495
Muse, Dan, 384
Music Card MC1, 169
music files, 108
Music Synthesizer card, 172
MX-100 printer, 233
MX-80 printer, 233
MySQL, 505
Mystery House, 180, 217
Mzinga, Inc., 499
NASA, 176, 225
National AppleWorks Users
    Group (see "NAUG")
National Computer Conference, 39
National Computer Shows, 508
National Educational Computing
    Conference, 279
National Science
    Foundation, 104, 105, 259
National Semiconductor, 306
National Television System
    Committee (see "NTSC")
NAUG, 453
NCR, 356
NDA, 411
Nelson, Larry, 26
Nelson, Ted, 378-379
Nero (Emperor of Rome), 183
NES, 445
netiquette, 112
Netscape, 493
Network News Transfer
    Protocol (see "NNTP")
New Desk Accessories, 370
New Mexico State University in
    Las Cruces, 176
New York City, 289, 394
New York State, 394
New York Times, 288
New Zealand, 322
newbies, 112
News Corporation, 495

Newton (touch tablet), 512
Newton, Isaac, 22
NeXT computer, 432
Nibble magazine, 86, 150, 157, 173-
    175, 385, 392, 450
Nibble Mac, 175
Nicholas, Andy, 110, 373, 513
Nintendo Entertainment
    System (see "NES")
NNTP, 111
No-Slot Clock, 336
nodes, 102, 289
NoiseTracker, 108
North American Investment Corp., 495
North Star Horizon
    microcomputer, 52, 117
North Star manual, 56
Northeast Expositions, 508
Note Sequencer, 367
Note Synthesizer, 367
Novation, 96
Novation CAT 300-baud
    accoustic modem, 98
NSFNET, 105
NTSC video, 145, 314, 326
nuclear attack, 102
NuFile eXchange (see "NuFX")
NuFX, 110
Number Nine Apple Booster card, 143
Number Nine Computer Corporation, 143
OCR, 411
Office System (Lisa), 272
offline reader, 298, 505
Ohio Kache Systems, 360
Ohio Scientific, 80
Olympia ES-100 typewriter/printer, 156
Omega Microware, 186
On-Line Systems (see "Sierra OnLine")
Online Airline Guide, 495
online games (BBS), 106
online shopping, 288, 494
online surveys, 106
open-apple (key), 198
Open-Apple newsletter, 273,
    297, 448-449, 509
Optical Character Recognition (see "OCR")
Opus][, 438
Oracle of Delphi, 494
ORCA/C, 445
ORCA/M, 166, 407, 441, 442-443
ORCA/Pascal, 444
Oregon, 225
Osborn, John, 311
Osborne-1, 78, 320
Osborne, Adam, 78
oscillator, 415

P-100 printer, 119
p-code, 125
P8 Serial Card, 92
P8A Serial Card, 92
Pac-Man, 216
paddles, 28, 42, 119, 306-307
Pages program, 463
PAL, 44, 145
Palo Alto, California, 22, 116
Palsoft, 147
paper tape reader, 11, 50, 66, 133
Paper Tiger 440 printer, 234
Paper Tiger 460 printer, 234
Papert, Seymour, 259
Parker, Neil, 398
Parsons Engineering, 361
Pascal, 125-131
Pascal 1.1 Firmware Protocol, 91
Pascal Anthology Disk, 439
Pascal disk system, 128-130
Pascal operating system, 110
Pascal System, 128, 205,
    254, 257, 258, 260
Pascal, Blaise, 125
Passport Designs, Inc., 170
password, 502
Password (game show), 180
patching software, 279-280
patent laws, 317
patents (Apple II), 37
Paterson, Tim, 134
PathFinder, 283
Pathology of Computer Viruses, A, 389
PC '76 (national computer show), 24, 507
PC Pursuit, 430
PC Transporter, 412-413
PC-Link, 501
PDP series of computers, 7, 22
PDP-10, 291
PDP-11, 125, 164
Peace Corps, 447
Pecan Software Systems, Inc., 254
Peddle, Charles Ingerham "Chuck", 15-16,
    28, 48, 145, 340
Peeker magazine, 157
Peelings II, 176-179
Pegasus 100i, 361
Pelczarski, Mark, 86, 182, 183
Pentagon, 101
Percom Data, 357
percussion synthesizer, 170
Peripherals, 89
PERL language, 505
Personal Software, 223-224
PERT schedules, 224

INDEX

PET 2001 microcomputer, 29, 39, 48, 55, 80, 224, 389
Petaluma, California, 290, 488
Peters, John, 430, 451
Petters, Kristi, 327
Phase Alteration by Line (see "PAL")
Phasor card, 172
PHD-10 hard drive, 357
Phoenix (code name), 342
Photo Shop GS, 283
Picture Chompers, 328
PIE Writer, 178
PILOT, 257
Pinball Construction Set, 312
Pinella, Paul, 387
Pinpoint Desk Accessories, 276
Pinpoint InfoMerge, 277
Pinpoint KeyPlayer, 277
Pinpoint Publishing, 110, 276-277, 280
Pinpoint Spell Checker, 277
Pittman, Jim, 488
Pittsburgh, Pennsylvania, 390
Pizza Time Theater, 333
PL/M, 133
Plague of MOD, The, 396
Plan 80, 218
plane crash, 340
Platinum Apple IIe, 476, 488
Plaza Hotel, 289
plotter, 236-237
PMPFax, 462
Pohlman, Taylor, 182, 404
Point-to-Point, 110, 298
Pointless, 417, 466
Polk's Hobby Department Store, 23
Poly-88 computer, 11, 404
Polymorphic Systems, 11, 404
pom's magazine, 151-152
Pong, 5, 6, 16
Pontiac, Michigan, 267
Popular Electronics (magazine), 9, 10
Porsche, 276
Portland, Oregon, 18
PostScript language, 236
Powell, Gareth, 156
Power Pad, 249
power supply, 478-479
PowerPC, 473, 513
PowerPoint, 447
PR-40 printer, 79
practical jokes, 2, 4
Precision Echo Phase II, 326
pressure feed (see "friction feed")
prime time hours, 288
Print Shop, 283
printed circuit boards (PCB), 19

PRINTER (program), 227
Printer IIA, 232
printers, 11, 231-237
Prism printer, 234
private investigator, 396
Processor Technology, 11
ProDOS, 109, 210-213, 336-337, 393
ProDOS 16, 365-367, 466
ProDOS 8, 365
ProFile hard drive, 357
Programma International, 164, 256
Programming Language for Microcomputers (see "PL/M")
programming logic, 1
ProLine, 107, 112
Proline BBS, 405
ProntoDOS, 207, 448
ProSel, 395
Prospero Technologies, 498
ProTERM 3.0, 298
ProTERM Mac, 497
pseudo-code (see "p-code")
Publish-It!, 236
Puette, Bob, 484
PUFFIN, 164
punched cards, 7
PVI, 170
Q-Labs, 473
Q-Link, 500, 501
QC10 hard drive, 249
QST (microcomputer magazine), 7
Quake (game), 427
Quality Computers, 284, 385, 457, 471
Quality Software, 395
Quantum Computer Services, 500
Quantum Link (see "Q-Link")
Quantum LPS 40 MB SCSI hard drive, 490
Quark Engineering, 249, 466
Quark XPress, 384, 454, 460
QUERTY, 245
Quick-Draw, 239
QuickDraw II, 347
QuickFile, 218, 272
QuickFile IIe, 272
Quickie C, 411
Quickie hand scanner, 410
QuickSpell (TimeOut module), 280
Quinn, Peter, 199
Qume, 235
R2E (French company), 7
Radio Shack, 291
Radio Shack TRS-80 (see "TRS-80")
radio signal interference, 35
Radio-Electronics (magazine), 8, 9
Raines, Darrel, 431
RAM (Apple II), 29

RAM chips, 14
RAM-GS, 412
Rambo, 342
RAMCharger, 268
RAMdisk 320, 266
RAMFactor card, 268
RamFAST SCSI card, 360
RAMWorks card, 268
RAMWorks II card, 268
RAMWorks III card, 268
Rana 8086/2 co-processor, 141
Rana Systems, 141
Rancid Grapefruit, 396
Random House, 494
Randy's Weekend Assembler, 162
Raskin, Jef, 41, 126, 239-242, 307, 312, 347
Raster Blaster, 312
RAWDOS, 73
RC, 333
READ (DOS command), 65
Read/Write Track/Sector (see "RWTS")
Reader's Digest Association, 289
Real Time Conferences, 296
recording disc, 79
recording head (floppy disk drive), 64
Red Book, 41, 116, 117, 317
Redgate Publishing, 386
Redmond, Washington, 266
Redondo Beach, California, 162
Regent Systems, 406
Regis McKenna, Inc., 28
Regis McKenna Agency, 37
registration cards, 282
removable storage, 362
Renstrom, Rob, 281, 417
Republican, 107
research virus, 389
RESET key, 121-122
Resource Central, 450, 511
Resource Central disk publications, 428-430
Resource Central/ICON, 433
resource forks, 371
RetroBright, 514
Revision 7 motherboard (Apple II Plus), 121
RF modulator, 250
RF television interface (Apple II), 34
RGB adapter, 250
Rice University, 467
Rice, Guy T., 393
Rickard, Jay, 342
Roach, Greg, 429
Roathe, Lane, 425, 427, 514
Roberts, Henry Edward "Ed", 9

561

Robinson, Dick, 423
Robitaille, Roger, 86
robots, 331-334
Rocket Chip, 414
Rocky Clark, 340
Roger Wagner Publishing, 379, 442
Rogers, Al, 230
Rokitski, Peter, 427-428
ROM, 14
Romero, John, 425-426, 427, 514
Rose, Frank (author), 60
Rosenberg, Ellen, 450, 458
Rottenberg, Jonathan, 508
Roundtables, 298-299, 430
RS-232, 97, 322
Rutgers University, 165
RWTS, 65, 211
S-100 bus (Altair), 11, 96
S-100 computers, 335
S-100 disk interface card (Shugart), 57
S-C Assembler II, 162-163, 185
S-C Macro Assembler, 163, 185
SA390, 57
SA400 controller, 59
SA400 minifloppy, 56
San Antonio, Texas, 216
San Diego, California, 230, 453
San Francisco Apple Core, 297
San Francisco Bay, 1
San Francisco Chronicle, 484
San Francisco, California, 116, 246, 508
San Jose, California, 357, 412
San Marcos, California, 336
Sander-Cederlof, Bob, 163-164, 185
Sander, Sara, 205
Sander, Wendell, 58, 205, 412
SanDisk, 363
Sandy's Word Processor, 156
SANE routines, 406
Santa Clara Valley, 1
Santa Cruz, California, 467
Sara's Operating System (see "SOS")
Sargon chess, 162, 177
SASI, 356
SATNet, 103
Saturn Systems, 143, 322
ScanMan 32, 410
scanners, 314, 410-411
Scantron Corporation, 473
Scantron Quality Computers, 473
SCELBI Computer Consulting, 7
SCELBI-8H microcomputer, 7
Schmitz, Tom, 431-432
Scholastic, Inc., 423
school adoption of computers, 118
science fair, 1

Science Fiction Roundtable, 303
Scientific American, 225, 392
Scott, Jason, 514
Scott, Mike, 28, 50, 82
Scribe printer, 310
script, 377
Script II, 218
Script-Central, 429, 450, 462
SCSI, 357, 485
Sculley, John, 247, 274,
     456, 475, 483, 509
Seagate Technology, 356
Seattle Computer Products, 134
Seattle, Washington, 82
SECAM, 44, 145
Second Sight card, 409-410
secretary of defence (US), 101
sector on disk (see "disk sector")
SEEK (DOS command), 65
semiconductor chips (history), 1
Sensible Software, 186
Sequential Systems, 361, 409, 412
serial port, 244
Sesame Street, 310
Seuss, Randy, 106
Seven Hills Software, 462
Seymour, Connecticut, 308
ShadowWrite, 461
Shannon, Gary, 162
Shapardson Microsystems, 66
Shapiro, Neil, 293
Shareware Solutions II, 457, 459
Shepherd, Eric, 463, 505
shift registers, 17
Shockley Semiconductor Laboratory, 1
Sholes keyboard (see "QUERTY")
shortcut commands, 273
Shreveport, Louisiana, 420
Shrewsbury, New Jersey, 261
ShrinkIt, 110, 373
Shugart Associates, 56, 356
Shugart floppy disk drive, 133
Shugart, Alan, 55
Shuttle Mission Simulator, 177
SID sound chip, 344
Sidekick, 277
Sider II, The, 358
Sider, The, 357
SideSpread (TimeOut module), 279
Sierra OnLine, 164, 180, 217, 441
SIGs, 495
Silicon Valley, 1
Silicon Valley Software, 253
Simonsen, Mark, 279, 514
simple mail transfer
     protocol (see "SMTP")

SimpleScript, 444
simulators (aeronautics), 177
Sirium RAM IIGS, 412
Situation: Critical, 427
Skrenta, Richard, 390
slave disk, 70
slot machine, 5
Smartmodem, 98
Smartmodem 1200, 98
Smartmodem 2400, 98
Smartport controller, 345
SmartWatch DS1216 chip, 336
Smith, Burrell, 241, 266, 312
Smith, William V. R. III, 80, 180
SMT Peripherals, 336
SMTP, 105
Snow White (style), 243
SOAR, 505
Sofsearch International, 216
soft sectoring, 57
Softalk magazine, 156, 179-184, 221,
     225, 246, 274, 428, 448
Softape, 80, 180
SoftCard, 135, 198, 254, 261, 412
Softdisk, 420
Softdisk G-S, 426-428
Softdisk, Inc., 426
SofTech Microsystems, 254
Softkey Publishing, 188
softkeys, 188
Softline, 183
SoftSide magazine, 86-87
Software Arts, 224
software charts, 521-532
Software Touch, 279, 280
Softyme, 425
Sol-20 (microcomputer), 11
solenoids, 232
Solid Windows (disk magazine), 451
Solomon, Les, 9
Sonic Blaster, 411
soniqTracker, 108
Sonotec, 148
Sony, 243, 355
Sophisticated Operating
     System (see "SOS")
SOS (Apple III), 205
sound cards, 411
sound chip (IIGS), 344
Sound I card, 171
Sound II card, 171
Sound/Speech I card, 171
Soundchaser System, 170
SoundMeister, 411
SoundMeister Pro, 411

INDEX

source code (6502 BASIC and Applesoft), 117
Source, The, 288-291, 459, 499
Sourcerer, 166, 442
Sourcerer/XL, 442
Sousan, Andre, 145
Southern California Computer Society, 77-78
Southwest Technical Products Corporation, 11
Southwest Technical Products PR-40 printer, 79
Southwestern Data Systems, 166
Soviet Union, 101
Space Shuttle Landing program, 177
SPACE WAR, 307
spaghetti code, 255
Special Delivery Software, 218, 226
Special Interest Groups (see "SIGs")
Spectrum (program), 154, 513
Spectrum Internet Suite, 513
speech synthesizer, 332
SpeedDemon, 143
Speedy Smith, 397
Spellbinder, 156
Spergel, Marty, 35
Sphere-1 (microcomputer), 11
spreadsheet, 271
Springboro, Ohio, 360
Springer-Verlag, 389
Sprintnet, 494
sprites, 259
Sputnik, 101
SRAM, 14, 143
ST Report, 430
ST-506 hard drive, 356
St. Albans, UK, 153
St. Clair Shores, Michigan, 457
St.Game, 183
Stack-Central, 429, 450
Standard Apple Numerics Environment (see "SANE")
Stanford University, 391
Star Trek (game), 26, 58, 289
Starkweather, John, 257
StarSprite I, 94
StarSprite II, 94
StarSprite III, 94
Static RAM (SRAM), 14
Sticky Keys, 373
Stickybear, 328
Stockdorf, Germany, 362
storage density (floppy disk), 59
Straczynski, J. Michael, 299
Street Electronics, 170
Studio City, 429, 450

StyleWare, Inc., 467
StyleWriter inkjet printer, 372
stylus, 308
Suenaga, Ryan, 434-438, 461, 462-464
Summagraphics Corp., 308
Sunnyvale, California, 1
Sup-R-Term, 228
Sup'R'Mod, 35, 44
Sup'R'Mod RF modulator, 92
Sup'R'Terminal card, 92
Super Bowl, 246
Super Serial Card, 334
SuperDrive, 485
SuperMacroWorks, 279
Supertalker, 170
Sutcliffe, Rick, 439
Suther, Kathryn Halgrimson, 82
SVGA monitors, 410
SVI, 250
Sweet Micro Systems, 170
SWEET16 (interpreter), 120, 162
Sweet16 (emulator), 437, 513
Swihart, Tim, 511
SWIM chip, 412
SWTPC PR-40 (printer), 26
Syndicomm, 300, 438, 463, 496
Synertek Systems, 197, 199
Synetix SuperSprite, 93
Synetix Systems Sprite I, 93
Synetix Systems Sprite II, 93
Synetix, Inc., 93
synthLAB, 108, 373
Syntix 2202 SSD, 266
Syntix Industries, 266
SyQuest Technology, Inc., 362
sysop (BBS), 106, 287, 296
System 2.0, 366
system operator (see "sysop")
System Software 1.0, 365
System Software 3.1, 367
System Software 3.2, 367
Syverson, Lyle, 437
Szetela, David, 514
TABBS, 154
tablets, 308
Talk Is Cheap, 298
Talking Tools, 444
Tandy, 501
Tandy Color Computer, 494
Tandy Radio Shack, 39
Tasman Turtle, 331-332
Tax Planner, 218
TCP, 104
TCP/IP, 104, 513
Teach (program), 373, 470

Teacher Education and Computer Center, 230
TechAlliance, 83, 449
techBASIC, 408
Techware Corporation, 379
TED TWO, 165
TED/ASM assembler, 162
TEDITOR, 227
Telecomputing Corporation of America, 288
TELENET (service), 104, 289, 494
telephone hacking (see "blue boxes")
TeleTalk Online, 430
Teletype, 11, 13, 44, 50, 218-219
Teletype model ASR-33, 31, 44
telnet, 496
Terrapin Inc., 332
Terrapin Logo, 259, 332
Terrapin Software, 259
Terrapin Turtle robot, 259, 332
Terre Haute, Indiana, 462
Terrell, Paul, 18
Texas A&M University, 390
Texas Instruments, 9, 15-16, 163, 169, 201, 215, 259
thermal printers, 233
thesaurus, 470
THINK Technologies, 262
Thiriez, Herve, 151
Thornburg, David, 309, 310
Thunderclock Plus, 335
ThunderScan, 314
Thunderware, Inc., 314, 335, 410
TI-960 minicomputer, 163
TI-980 minicomputer, 163
TI-99/4A, 201, 215, 259
TI-990 minicomputer, 163
Tibbets, Greg, 182
Tiger Electronics, 327
Tiger Learning Computer, 327
Time II, 336-337
Time in a Bottle, 438
time sharing system, 222
Time Warner, 504
timeline, 533-550
Timemaster H.O., 337
TimeOut, 276, 279-280, 430, 473
TimeOut-Central, 430, 450
timing hole, 57, 64
Titan Technologies, 143
TKC (see "Keyboard Company, The")
TML BASIC, 407
TML Pascal, 443
TML Pascal II, 443
TML Systems, 443
Tobin, Tim, 229

564 Sophistication & Simplicity

Tokyo, Japan, 439
Tommervik, Al, 184, 200, 420, 422
Tommervik, Margot, 180
tone generators, 4
TOPO I, 333
TOPO II, 333
TopoBasic, 333
TopoForth, 333
TopoLogo, 333
Torzewski, Joe, 25-26, 85
Toshiba portable computer, 242
TotalControl, 283
trace (PCB), 59
track on disk (see "disk track")
track zero sensor (disk drive), 57
tractor feed, 234
Traf-O-Data, 8
TransFORTH II, 257
transistor circuit, 1
transistors, 1
transmission control protocol (see "TCP")
TransWarp, 413
TransWarp GS, 415
TransWarp II, 415
Tremplin Micro magazine, 153
Trendcom 100 printer, 232
Trendcom 200 printer, 232
Tribble, Bud, 241
Tribune Star, The, 463
Triple Desktop, 285
Tripp, Robert M., 80
TRS-80, 26, 29, 39, 55, 224, 357, 420
TRS-80 Model I, 86, 321, 454
TRS-80 Model II, 452
TrueType, 417
Tulin Technology, 362
Turing, Alan, 38
Turkey in the Straw, 159
turntable, 64
turtle, 331
Turtle graphics, 257
Tustin, California, 359
Tutor-Tech, 379
TV Typewriter, 11
TX-80 printer, 233
Tymnet, 289, 494
UCSD, 239
UCSD p-System, 125-126, 254
UCSD Pascal Assembler, 164
UG-TV, 486
Ultima V, 172
Ultra 4.0, 283, 473
UltraMacros (TimeOut
    module), 152, 280, 377
Ultraterm card, 92
UniDisk 3.5, 250, 477

UniDisk 3.5 drive, 355, 466
UniDisk 5.25 drive, 354
United Press International, 289, 494
Univers Condensed, 243
University of California, 41, 125-126, 257
University of Colorado, 2, 3
University of Illinois at
    Urbana/Champaign, 391
University of Iowa, 447
University of Kansas, 447
University of New Mexico
    Computing Center, 488
University of Rochester, 452
Unix, 110, 112, 261, 299, 341, 488
Unix to Unix Copy Protocol (see "UUCP")
unnamed virus, 389
UNUSON, 340
upgrades (Apple-1), 45
UpTime, 425-426
US Federal Communications
    Commission, 35, 324
US Festival, 340
Usenet, 104, 111-113, 496
user experiences (Apple II), 40
user group (Apple-1), 25
Uther Apple II Ethernet card, 513
Utter, Gary, 300, 301, 496, 499, 505, 514
UUCP, 104, 111, 112
Valentine, Don, 28
Vancouver, British Columbia, 462
Vector 1 (computer), 106
Veit, Stan, 23-24
Vekovius, Al, 420, 426
vellum-thin paper, 80
vents, 245
Verizon Communications, 294
Verkade, Dan, 283, 285
VersionSoft, 466
VHS, 314
VIC-20, 389
video acquisition system, 314
video camera, 314
video cards, 92-94, 409-410
video display (Apple 1), 17
video games, 500
Video Graphics Controller, 344
Video Keyboard, 373
Video Technology, Inc. (see "VTech")
video terminals, 13
videodisc players, 314
VideoMix, 409
Videoterm card, 92
Videx, 92, 305
Viking Mars missions, 225
Viking Technologies, 425
Virtual Combinatics, 276

Virus 3, 390
Virus version 1, 390-391
Virus version 2, 391
viruses, 389
VisiCalc, 193, 207, 222-225, 271, 340
VisiCalc Business Forecasting Model, 224
VisiCorp, 224-225, 340
Vision-128 RAM card, 156
VisiTrend/VisiPlot, 224
Vitesse, 398, 410
Vogan, Andrew, 410
Vogan, Drew, 360
voice synthesis, 170
Volkswagen bus, 18
volume number (DOS 3.1), 69
volumes (Pascal System), 129
von Meister, William, 288, 499
VTech, 321
Vulcan, 361
Wagner, Roger, 159-160, 166, 181, 183
Walters, Joe, 488
Wang Laboratories, 90
Wankerl, Joe, 456, 512
Wannop, Ewan, 154, 505
Warner Bros, 499
Warp Six, 107
Warren, Jim, 36, 38, 507
Washington State
    Community Colleges, 439
Washington, DC, 102
Wayne Green Publishing Group, 383
Wayne Green, Inc., 383
Wayne, Ron, 5, 20, 34
WDC, 340
We Are Apple (lyrics), 246
Weishaar, Tom, 84, 182, 209, 273, 297,
    394, 428, 447-452, 509
WELL, The, 498
Welsh, Carson, Anderson & Stower, 290
WESCON, 16
West Coast Computer Faire, 36, 38, 49,
    134, 175, 357, 404, 507
West of Eden (book), 60
WestCode Software, 417
Westerfield, Mike, 166, 407, 442, 488
Western Design Center, 443, 484
Western Digital, 357
What's Where in the Apple (book), 81
Whole Earth 'Lectronic Link
    (see "WELL, The")
Whole Earth Catalog, 498
Wigginton, Randy, 36, 49-52, 58, 65, 82,
    117, 162, 340, 514
Wikipedia, 113
Wilbur, Jay, 426
Wilkins, Jeffrey, 291

INDEX

Williams, Ken, 217
Williams, Roberta, 217
Williams, Warren, 452
Winchester hard drive, 249, 356-357
Windfall, 155
windows (GUI), 242
Windows 3.1, 299, 503
Windows 95, 299, 512
Windows platforms, 399
Wirth, Niklaus, 125
Wolfenstein 3D, 427
wood-cut logo, 22
Word Perfect, 276
word processing, 271
Word Processing Language (see "WPL")
WordStar, 135, 156
Workbench Series, 165
World Wide Web, 493, 504
WorldCom, 294
worms, 389

Worth, Don (author), 65
Woz Wonderbook, 40
Wozniak, Stephen Gary
 (pre-Apple biography), 1-5
 (biography 1981-1984), 340-342
WPL, 228, 229
WRITE (DOS command), 65
WSM Group, 261
X-10, 334-335, 336
XDOS, 206-
Xebec Corporation, 357
Xerox Alto (see "Alto")
Xerox Palo Alto Research Center
 (see "Xerox PARC")
Xerox PARC, 239, 309, 378
Xerox Star, 378
XModem protocol, 109, 505
Y2K, 299, 302
Yandrofski, Joe, 410
Ymodem protocol, 302, 505

Yocam, Del, 274, 508
Yovelle Renaissance Corporation, 299-300
Z-80 coprocessor, 319
Z-80 microprocessor, 52, 164, 360
Z-RAM card, 268
Z-RAM Ultra 1, 2, and 3, 268
Zardax, 156
Zen Buddhism, 5
Ziff-Davis, 381
Zip Chip, 414, 478
Zip Drive, 362
Zip GSX, 416
Zip Technology, 361, 414, 478
ZipDrive GS, 361
ZipGS card, 415
ZLink, 395
Zmodem protocol, 302, 505
Zork, 107, 189, 223